From materials earlier published under the auspices of the
Committee on Chinese Thought of the Association for Asian Studies
by Stanford University Press

CONFUCIANISM AND CHINESE CIVILIZATION

Edited, with an Introduction, by

ARTHUR F. WRIGHT

Atheneum New York 1964

Arthur F. Wright

INTRODUCTION

The essays in this volume are a selection from studies of the Confucian tradition published over the last several years by the Committee on Chinese Thought of the Association for Asian Studies. The Committee was formed in 1951 and completed its work in 1962. It was supported until 1957 by the Committee for Comparative Studies of Cultures and Civilizations of the University of Chicago, and thereafter by the Rockefeller Foundation.

The scholars who formed the Committee sought a deeper understanding of key Chinese ideas and of the influence of those ideas, on patterns of behavior, on the formation of institutions, and on the many men who, by their cumulative efforts, built the great and distinctive civilization of China. As the Committee's work proceeded, we moved into areas of Chinese history and culture that had been little explored, and we found some striking new relationships between historical data and ideas. But after five research conferences and the publication of five symposium volumes, we know we have only made a start. Vast reaches of time and phenomena remain to be explored.

The tables of contents of our successive volumes reproduced at the end of the book provide a synopsis of the Committee's work from our early tentative efforts to our more intensive studies of the Confucian tradition. At each stage we sought out scholars whose interests were tending to converge on common problems; each conference provided an opportunity for them to subject their ideas to discussion and criticism from those at work on related subjects. In recent years we were able to invite scholars from abroad, so that our last three volumes contain articles by scholars of eight nations.

The selection of twelve essays from the thirty-five that make up our three volumes on Confucianism was made on the basis of recommendations from all the authors who contributed to the three volumes. Some superlative essays have necessarily been omitted. Hopefully, readers of this volume will be stimulated to turn to the original volumes for the essays we could not reprint.

The historic civilization of China developed over more than three millennia. Sometime before 1500 B.C. scattered settlements of Neolithic tillers came to be organized into larger political and territorial units centered on walled towns. These towns with their surrounding farmlands were eventually knit together in the political and cultural order of Shang. In the eleventh century B.C., the Shang gave way to the Chou, which set up a more elaborate system of regional hegemonies subordinate to the Chou king and his clan. The rapid advance in technology, arts, and communication under the Chou rent its political fabric asunder and ushered in the period of the Warring States (481-221 B.C.), China's classical age. This period saw the first great flowering of Chinese speculative thought. Among its seminal thinkers were Confucius and the two great developers of his ideas, Mencius and Hsün-tzu; Mo-tzu, who propounded a new ethic for a new society; the classical Taoists, who found in Nature the model for a better human order; and the Realists or Legalists, who foreshadowed the modern totalitarians in their exaltation of state power. The Realists were the architects of the first unified empire of China, in 221 B.C. But it was the Confucians who developed from that beginning the social and political order of imperial China, an order that was to endure for more than two thousand years.

The Confucian social order consisted of two main classes: the peasant masses, who produced food and cloth and provided soldiers and corvée laborers as the state needed them; and a numerically small elite, which had a monopoly of literacy, statecraft, and administrative skills. The elite was intensely jealous of its prerogatives and sought always to prevent new classes or groups from attaining power in society. Small intermediate groups were grudgingly allowed: merchants, artisans, the military. But the elite repeatedly insisted on the economic primacy of agriculture (they enjoyed landed income as well as official salaries), and on the subversive and parasitic character of other occupations.

The literate elite, early in the development of the imperial order, had entered into an alliance with monarchy. The monarch provided the symbols and the sinews of power: throne, police, army, the organs of social control. The literati provided the knowledge of precedent and statecraft that could legitimize power and make the state work. Both the monarch and the literati were committed to a two-class society based on agriculture. This alliance was often uneasy and sometimes broke apart, but since each party was indispensable to the other's welfare, it was always renewed.

The division of labor and the division of power just described were norms to which society and state perennially returned. But this order was subject not only to the tensions between monarch and elite but also to challenge from other social groups. Time and again, ambitious men—great landlords, religious leaders, warlords, eunuchs, merchants great and small—fought their way to power and wealth. Even the normally docile peasantry could be goaded into explosive rebellions that cost millions of lives and decades of chaos. The literati were supposed to have a monopoly on writing of all kinds, but with the invention of printing and the growth of cities from the eleventh century onward, plebeian writers of popular literature began to find an audience. In short, the imperial Confucian order was more an ideal than a reality. The bland and static picture of Chinese society so often served up to Western readers is a myth. Such periods of tranquility as we do encounter in Chinese history represent no more than a momentary equilibrium among all the forces at work in the society.

The Confucians, to whom we now turn, were never the passive beneficiaries of a changeless social order. As members of the elite, they had notable privileges and immunities, but they had to fight hard to keep them. Each generation had to deal with disruptive forces: a willful emperor who defied the established elite and relied on eunuchs or upstarts to execute his policies; regional magnates whose power, if unchecked, would pull the empire apart and restore the chaos of feudalism; waves of religious enthusiasm among the peasant masses, spurred on by demagogues bent on rebellion; moral flabbiness and corruption in the elite itself.

How did the Confucian literatus view the world? What principles did he invoke in dealing with the problems of his own time?

Confucians of all ages viewed the natural and human worlds as an organism made up of multitudinous interconnected parts. When any one of the parts fell from its place or was disrupted in its functioning, the harmony of the whole was impaired. Heaven, which was neither deity nor blind fate, presided over this organic whole and was a force for harmony and balance. But man was the principal agent of both harmony and disharmony. Out of ignorance or perversity, men could cause serious disruptions; by the application of knowledge, wisdom, and discipline, men could restore harmony. Either man in the mass or an irresponsible elite might destroy harmony, but only the learned and the wise could restore it. The wise and the learned were to be found among the Confucian elite. Their wisdom—the keys to harmony—came from two sources: from the Confucian classics, and, secondarily, from the histories and other writings that contained the past experience of the Chinese.

Learning alone, it was early recognized, did not make a sage. A man became a sage only through long study and self-discipline. Proper self-cultivation developed humaneness or love (*jen*); it gave a man an almost

viii

mystical empathy for his fellow men, and an acute sensitivity to all the delicately balanced forces at work in the universe. Such a man, or one approaching him in attainments, might then "govern the state and pacify the world." Indeed, all his self-cultivation was directed precisely toward the exercise of power.

Thus there devolved upon the sage, and, when a sage did not appear, upon men of lesser wisdom, the awesome duty of assuring harmony in the world. Such men had to persuade and coerce their fellow men into behavior conducive to harmony; they had to devise institutions that would promote such harmony. And they were obliged to do so in the face of appalling obstacles: capricious rulers, self-interested or heterodox men of power, upheavals of nature, alien invasions, the pressing needs of the state, the incubus of past events.

What values did the Confucian sage or worthy assert, and what institutions did he favor, as he persisted, generation after generation, in his Sisyphean labors?

Harmony, universal and unalloyed, was perhaps the highest good, but in a less abstract sense harmony meant the good society. And the good society was seen as a past utopia, a golden age, the ideally friction-less holistic order that had existed in remote antiquity. That order was a hierarchy: state and society were fused into a seamless whole, and every man knew his place and was content. A monarch presided over the whole, next in rank came the elite, and at the base of the pyramid came the peasantry. The order was not static: Confucians insisted that the elite be open to those of moral worth. Even the monarch, in the utopia of remote antiquity, had been chosen for his merit, and the introduction of the hereditary principle in imperial times led to endless tension and discord.

The basic social unit of the Confucian system was the well-ordered family. The family was seen as a microcosm of the socio-political order; the wise father was a model for the wise ruler or minister, and dutiful children were the models for properly submissive subjects who knew their place, their role, and their obligations to others. Both the family and the state were governed by the *li*, the norms of proper social behavior. The ancient sage-kings, it was believed, had prescribed observances, taboos, and rituals that ensured the well-being and happiness of their subjects. Later men had codified these prescriptions, creating a body of norms that provided for all social contingencies. It was the duty of the father to teach the *li* in the household. It was the duty of the monarch and officials to make them known to the populace so that one and all might live according to the same time-tested norms.

The *li*, spread by fathers, village elders, and government officials, and supplemented by the discipline of ordered family life, would in turn foster social virtues: filial submission, brotherliness, righteousness, good faith, and loyalty. Moral instruction took many forms. Conspicuously virtuous men were singled out for public recognition, exhortations to virtue were read in the villages, the *Classic of Filial Piety* was drummed into the young, stories of sages and other models of virtue were read by the literate and purveyed to the masses by storytellers and dramatic troupes. The power of example, of models of conduct, had been extolled by Confucius and was a basic principle of child-rearing and education in imperial China.

The prime living exemplars for any age, as the Confucians saw it, were the best of the scholar-officials. Steeped in the classics and in history, shaped by stern family discipline, tempered by introspection, and sobered by their vast responsibilities, these men were thought to have the power to transform their environment, to turn ordinary folk into the path of virtue. When opportunity offered, they were expected to nurture the same virtues in their official colleagues, and even in the emperor, whom they had the obligation to admonish whenever he did violence to the *li* or the cardinal virtues. They were also to serve as interpreters and transmitters of the heritage, and as artists and thinkers who would adorn and enrich it. If such men prevailed, they would preside over a balanced and homogeneous order. Friction and power struggles could not occur, subversion would wither in the sunshine of the people's content, and a benign nature would smile upon a smoothly running world.

The essays selected for this volume are meant to illustrate the effects of this world view and its associated patterns of behavior on the development of Chinese civilization. They also suggest the Confucian tradition's capacity for adaptation, as well as something of its inner variety. Mr. Schwartz's essay alone deals exclusively with problems of Confucian thinking. It defines some of the continuing tensions in Confucian thought, tensions that deeply affected men's view of the world and the choices they made. Every Confucian of every generation had to choose between self-cultivation and the pursuit of power. Yet in theory the two were reconcilable: the inner cultivation of the self was seen not as an end in itself, but as a means toward ultimate self-fulfillment in the world of action. In troubled times Confucian statesmanship was impossible, but the perfected man could still serve as a living example to his community and, more important, as teacher of a generation that might ultimately use what they learned from him to "put the world in order." The moral imperative to effective action is one of the basic elements in the Confucian tradition.

One realm of action was the building of institutions consonant with the ideal Confucian order. This was not easily done, since the built-in anomalies of the imperial system and the forces of secular change caused problems the sages had not foreseen. Mrs. Liu's essay describes one type of idealistic institution building and what came of it. Sweeping social changes from the ninth century onward had disrupted the family structure that Confucians regarded as essential for the good society. To counteract this disruption, a movement arose to create new clan organizations with carefully worked out arrangements for educating the young, caring for the aged, and maintaining moral standards. Yet it was not long before the new clans had departed decisively from the ideals of their founders. They became interest groups with tendencies to coercion and corruption; their codified rules quoted copiously from the classics, but much of what they prescribed was simply shrewd practical advice distilled from experience on the farm or in the market place. The clan system continued down to modern times to play a role in society, but hardly the role of moral leadership that the Confucian idealists had envisioned.

Mr. Hucker deals with the evolution of a key institution of the Chinese state, the censorate. Confucius had laid on the loyal minister the moral obligation of remonstrance. But he could not have foreseen the growth of the imperial bureaucracy, much less the evolution of an office that combined remonstrance with the ruler and the policing of officialdom (a legacy of the Realists). The tragedy Mr. Hucker unfolds is that of the later imperial bureaucracy. Remonstrance all but disappeared. The emperor, however degenerate, was exalted into a demi-god; the literati lost much of their independence and self-respct; the whole fabric of state and society was weakened by corruption. Yet Confucian officials continued for four more centuries to summon up from their heritage the courage and enterprise to make their alliance with the monarchy work.

The Confucians from the beginning used literature and the arts in the service of an ideal moral order. They were never unchallenged in either realm, for Taoist ideas periodically infiltrated both literature and painting, and Buddhism for several centuries had a pervasive influence on the whole of Chinese culture. Mr. Cahill shows us two phases of Confucian influence on the theory of painting. The first, lasting for the first millennium of the imperial order, was characterized by a naïve didacticism: events and men were to be painted in such a way as to encourage virtue and discourage vice. The second phase was determined by a succession of new forces in Chinese thought: the revived Taoism of the third to the fifth centuries A.D., the spread of Buddhism, and then the revival of Confucianism from the eleventh century onward. Briefly, this second Confucian theory of painting held that the quality of a painting lay in the character of the artist. One sees in a painting—whether landscape or still-life—the artist's perfection of character. In a new context and with a new, highly sophisticated vocabulary, the centrality of moral perfection was reasserted. Painting was seen as a means of expressing the attributes of the Confucian perfected man and of inspiring emulation.

Confucian literati were both the guardians and the developers of the art of letters. They wrote the state papers, the histories, the encyclopedias, the poetry, the commentaries. More than this, they were the arbiters of form, content, and taste: this poet's work is tainted with Taoism; that author's prose is over-ornamented, decadent, unable to communicate the perfection of the sages' teachings. Yet, as Mr. Frankel's essay shows, there was an ambivalence in the Confucian attitude toward the literary art. Virtuosity was greatly esteemed; so was an eloquent and forceful style. But literary talent as such did not put a man in the Confucian pantheon, for literary men were often failures in the world of action. They lacked the practical ability and the moral stamina that led to the highest form of self-fulfillment.

Another dimension of Confucian concern with literature is illustrated in Mr. Ruhlmann's essay. This was the effort to shape and use popular literature for Confucian social ends. Popular songs, dramas, and folktales were filled with good and evil figures; the Confucians were concerned to emphasize the Confucian virtues of the good and the anti-Confucian vices of the evil. This meant a tension between didactic demands and the demands of versimilitude. The Confucians never fully achieved the control they sought, but the corpus of popular literature shows the tenacity and resourcefulness of their efforts.

As we have seen, it was in politics that the Confucian literatus typically sought fulfillment, fame, immortality. And since the Confucians wrote the histories, statesmen and noted officials crowd their pages, providing what must be the world's longest and most detailed account of political action. Here again moral judgments are paramount: quotations are selected from documents to highlight a moral point; biographies are grouped by moral categories; explicit moral judgment is passed on a sequence of events or on a person. Confucian historians did not set out to tamper with evidence to teach a moral lesson. Rather they were convinced that there *was* a moral dynamic in human affairs, and that particulars in accord with this assumption were inherently more credible than other particulars.

Two of the three men introduced under the heading "Men and Power" have suffered from the moral preoccupations of the historians; the third has benefited from them. Sui Yang-ti (ruled 604-616) seems to us now a brilliant and creative ruler, with some not uncommon human failings. But the Confucian historians, influenced by his costly military campaigns and building projects and the fact that he ultimately lost his throne, saw him as evil through and through. And so they made of him a minatory figure and placed him in the sequence of "bad last" rulers, a category dating from the distant past. Thus stereotyped, Sui Yang-ti found his way into popular story and drama as an arch-villain whose appearance sent thrills of horror through the audience.

Feng Tao, studied by Mr. Wang, is a far different type. He was a very ordinary man, a run-of-the-mine Confucian who lived in a time of political upheaval (882-954) and served as a high official under five successive dynasties. Near-contemporary accounts do not make him out a villain, and Feng himself deemed his record spotless. (In an autobiographical statement, he pictured himself as a Confucian paragon: filial, kind, loyal, and all the rest.) The villainous Feng Tao of Confucian tradition was the work of the Neo-Confucian moralists and historians who became increasingly influential from the twelfth century onward. Passionately devoted to reforming and strengthening the Confucian moral code, these men were outraged by Feng's easy accommodation to successive rulers. They singled him out as the very embodiment of deceit, opportunism and disloyalty.

Yüeh Fei (1103-41) was perhaps the first of China's "national patriotic" heroes. Having spent the whole of his active life as a military leader against the barbarian enemies to the north of the Sung empire, he was disgraced and murdered by the Chief Minister Ch'in Kuei. Because he died in this way, the usual obituaries and eulogies were not written, and thus the record of his life is scanty. Perhaps for this very reason, there is no ambiguity about the image of Yüeh Fei in history and popular literature. He is the stalwart, single-minded, and dedicated general, as sternly kind to his troops as he was loyal to his ungrateful prince. Sui Yang-ti and Feng Tao became minatory figures, while Yüeh Fei became an exemplar of the heroic virtues. All lost, in the process, some of their traits as believable human beings.

The Confucian tradition permitted and indeed encouraged certain varieties of protest. Two of these varieties are illustrated in the papers by Mr. Nivison and Mr. Mote. Mr. Nivison's study of the tradition of protest against the examination system illustrates again the continual tension between Confucian ideals and reality. Some critics urged a return to a simpler society, to the moral order envisioned by the sages, in which men of virtue were recognized, recommended, and employed without benefit of examination. Others felt that the ancient moral order was gone beyond recall and that the examination system should be reformed to turn out more men of intellectual and moral stature, and fewer memorizers, parroters, and the products of cram schools. No extreme positions were taken: neither the Taoist position that the organized social order might be dispensed with, nor the Realist position that men should be chosen simply for their ability to operate the machinery of the state. The Confucians of imperial China, though heir to many of the institutions of the Realist state, clung to an intermediate morality, the perfected man in the state's service.

Mr. Mote deals with the reactions of Confucians in an age of cataclysm—the period of Mongol rule, 1279-1368. The Confucian classics provided ample sanction for withdrawal from active life: indeed, withdrawal was the only course open to a man of integrity who failed to find an upright prince to serve. The Neo-Confucianists of the twelfth century had gone even further: by their lights it was immoral for a man to serve more than one ruler in any circumstances (hence their harsh treatment of Feng Tao). Both these sanctions were employed by Confucians to avoid service under the hated Mongols. But a Confucian in retreat still felt an obligation to society and to his heritage. So these men studied, taught, and wrote, in the hope that the teachings of the sages would survive and a body of men versed in them would be available when a new regime appeared.

In a tradition's end, as in its origins and growth, there may be clues to its basic character. Mr. Levenson's study of the "love-death" of Confucianism and monarchy reviews the long and uneasy alliance between the monarchy and the Confucian literati. In Yüan Shih-k'ai's belated effort to revive the monarchy in 1916, Mr. Levenson sees the dissolution of both parties to the alliance. The creed of the Confucian literati dissolved with the collapse of the social order for which that creed was meaningful. The monarchy was destroyed by its century of ineptitude, its freight of anachronisms, and its final capitulation in 1911.

Imperial Confucianism was a strong and supple creed, strong enough to impose its values, supple enough to adjust to changing circumstances for over two thousand years. If it broke some worthy men and condemned others to frustrating lives, it also provided the normative ideas that brought Chinese society back, again and again, to long periods of stability and creative achievement. As the central tradition of the massive human achievement that we call Chinese civilization, it deserves our attention and our respect.

Introduction

CONFUCIANISM AND
CHINESE CIVILIZATION

1   Ideas and Values

Benjamin Schwartz

SOME POLARITIES IN CONFUCIAN THOUGHT

One of the striking insights that have emerged from the comparative study of thought is the realization that what might be called the problem of founders and followers is both universal and perennial. Whether we deal with Confucianism or Buddhism, Christianity or Marxism, we are soon confronted with certain characteristic questions. How do the interpretations of the followers relate themselves to the original or "primitive" teachings of the founders? Or, conversely, can the original teachings of the founders be extricated from the interpretations of the followers? Questions of this nature come up even in an intellectual tradition as close to our own time as Marxism, where all the utterances of the founder are extant and available. Everywhere we find claims that certain interpretations represent the true tradition while others are partial or total distortions. Everywhere we find generations which revolt against what they regard as the formalized, unauthentic perversions of the original vision and which attempt to recapture that vision in its pristine freshness—only to be accused of one-sidedness and distortion by their successors within the tradition.

Often, when confronted with the incubus of interpretations, schools, and sects which has accumulated over the ages, one is tempted to give up the search for any underlying unity. The social historian may be quite content to study later interpretations in terms of the interests and preoccupations of given times and places without attempting to relate these interpretations to the original doctrine or to the tradition as a whole. In China, for example, one might treat the Neo-Confucian developments of the Sung period simply as a manifestation of the social and cultural situation of that period.

Important as it is to place a given mode of thought in its historical setting, an exclusively historical approach eliminates a whole living dimension of the intellectual situation. The Neo-Confucianists were not interested in creating "Neo-Confucianism"; they were deadly serious in their effort to recapture the original Confucian vision. It would be unsafe to assume that in carrying out their attempt to relate their own preoccupation to the Confucian tradition as a whole they were necessarily greater fools or knaves than we. Their thought must be understood *both* in the context of the times *and* in terms of the *Problematik* inherent in the tradition as a whole. There are, of course, tendencies that bear no relationship—or only a tenuous relationship—to the tradition and that nevertheless insist on appropriating the name. The outer limits of any stream of thought are seldom obvious, and certain tendencies may hover on the edge between the stream in question and other streams. Within the Chinese world of ideas Confucianism seems to blend at one of its edges with Taoism and at the other with Legalism. In order to discern the limits, however, we must have some grasp of the *Problematik* of the tradition as a whole; and to achieve such a grasp, we must have the courage to be ahistorical—at least provisionally. We must be willing to confront ideas with each other across the centuries, suspending for a moment our concern with specific historical contexts. We must be willing to confront Confucius with Wang Yang-ming and Wang An-shih with Ku Yen-wu.

The founder himself is seldom an academic philosopher bent on building a rigidly coherent system. More often than not, he is simply a man seized with an overwhelming vision which he must proclaim. He is not necessarily concerned with the mutual consistency of all his utterances, and on many problems his thought may be fruitfully ambiguous. Therein may lie one of the secrets of his greatness. Nor is he generally concerned with aspects of reality which do not impinge on his vision. It is generally the followers who assume the burden of defending the vision against hostile challenge and who must attempt to relate the vision to those aspects of experience which the founder has left out of account. If the vision is accepted by a whole society and becomes an "official" philosophy, the problem of relating it to new realities becomes particularly acute. Such a problem arose when Confucianism became the official philosophy of a centralized bureaucratic state—a state which hardly embodied the Master's own vision of the ideal polity. In the course of defending and applying the vision, many of the problems implicit in it become explicit and many of its inner polarities come to the surface.

Confucianism was such a vision and such a philosophy. In the following pages I shall use the metaphor of polarity to deal with certain themes within Confucianism which seem to me to be of some importance. We cannot use words such as antithesis, contradiction, and dichotomy because the alternatives in question were regarded by the Master and by most orthodox Confucianists not as antithetical but as inseparably complementary. And yet, over the course of the centuries it became obvious that tensions existed between the poles in question; that some men gravitated to or toward one pole rather than the other in spite of their nominal commitment to both.

A central polarity in such works as the *Analects* is the polarity of self-cultivation (*hsiu-shen, hsiu-chi*) leading to personal self-realization (the attainment of the highest virtues of *jen* or *cheng,* and the ordering and harmonizing of the world (*chih-kuo p'ing t'ien-hsia*). This polarity could fully concern only those with a vocation for political and cultural leadership—the superior men, or *chün-tzu.* It is, of course, true that Confucius speaks of "teaching" the people (e.g., in *Analects,* Book XIII, chap. ix); what they are to be taught, however, is presumably no more than the rudiments of proper family relationships. They are hardly in a position to achieve the extensive cultivation required for the achievement of full self-realization, and it is obvious that only those in public office can do anything substantial to order human society.

In the *Analects* and in the *Great Learning* the two aims form two parts of an indivisible whole. In the latter work we find a logical progression from one to another; and Confucius himself states that "he (the superior man) cultivates himself in order to give rest to the people" (*Analects,* Book XIV, chap. xlv). The superior man can achieve complete self-realization only in his public vocation. It might indeed be stated that a commitment to public service—even when such service is unattainable—forms one of the basic criteria distinguishing the Confucian ideal of self-cultivation from some competing ideals in the Chinese world. Conversely, society can be harmonized and set in order only when men who have approached the ideal of self-realization are in public office. Here we find what may seem to many the extravagantly "idealistic" view of government so peculiar to Confucianism— a view which sees in government primarily an agency for bringing to bear on society as a whole the moral influence of superior men through the power of moral example and of education.

Theory was one thing, practice another. The central tragedy of the Master's own life was his failure to find any opportunity to fulfill his public vocation in a manner in keeping with his superior attainments in the realm of self-cultivation. The superior man is not always blessed with "times" (*shih*) propitious for the public employment of his talents. The times will remain out of joint so long as superior men are not in positions of responsibility, but such positions are not to be attained when the times are out of joint. There is here an element of fate which lies beyond human control. Confucius himself, however, offers a concrete model of how the superior man behaves in such periods. He does not give up his attempts to fulfill his vocation. Beyond that, he contents himself with achieving as high a degree of self-cultivation as possible, while fulfilling his role as teacher and preserver of the Way.

This tragic motif in the life of Confucius was to be repeated in the lives of innumerable idealistic Confucian gentlemen down through the centuries. Within the centralized bureaucratic state of the post-Ch'in period, the times were frequently unfavorable in the eyes of truly dedicated *chün-tzu*. We do not assume that such "idealists" were more numerous in China than elsewhere. In China as elsewhere, however, it was usually the idealist who worried himself about the yawning abyss between the ideal and the actual. Men soon came to wonder whether it was in fact possible to pursue the goals of self-cultivation and of setting the world in order with equal hopes of success. Furthermore, as the bureaucratic machinery of the imperial state became more articulated and complex, there soon emerged, on the level of practice, the problem of whether the self-cultivation of the superior man, which was based primarily on his conscientious adherence to the prescriptions of proper behavior (*li*), was qualification enough for an official post which seemed to call for training in professional statecraft and various specialized skills. Did not the "ordering of society" require some sort of professional science of government? Self-cultivation in private life was all very well, but how could its influence be brought to bear within this type of state?

A debate involving this issue came to a head in the controversies of Wang An-shih and his enemies during the Northern Sung dynasty. While this debate was undoubtedly strongly enmeshed with social and economic interests, in this paper we are concerned with its ideological aspects. Again, it must be stressed that neither side in the debate ever explicitly renounced either pole of our polarity. If Wang An-shih was convinced that society could be improved only by reforming its wayward institutions and enacting new laws, if he was convinced that professional statecraft was essential, he never on that account renounced the aim of self-realization. His opponents, while attacking his emphasis on professional specialization and his reliance on institutional machinery, for the most part maintained their dedication to the perfection of society. There were, to be sure, borderline cases—men like the mystical Chou Tun-i (1017–73), who renounced all public office to devote himself exclusively to a life of philosophic meditation and self-cultivation—but the typical statesman had a foot in both camps. Wang An-shih's more prominent enemies, for example, for all their emphasis on the virtues of self-cultivation and moral excellence as a means of ordering society, had definite notions in the realm of what might be called state policy (*chih-shu*). These notions will be discussed in greater detail below. At this point it need simply be noted that those who stressed self-cultivation were not all indifferent to the institutional setting of society or the proper policies of state. One even finds among them "feudal utopians"—men like Liu Chih (eleventh century) and many Sung Neo-Confucians—who look back to the idealized social order of the Chou period as the only order in which the self-cultivation of the *chün-tzu* can be made a force for the salvation of society.

While both sides claim commitment to both poles, however, they tend to accuse each other (often quite rightly) of glaring one-sidedness. In the eyes of his opponents Wang An-shih was a man indifferent to his own moral cultivation and the moral cultivation of his subordinates, a man who relied on machinery to achieve the goals of society. His goal, furthermore, was not the Confucian "ordering of society" but the Legalist goal of "wealth and power." To Wang An-shih, his opponents were selfishly absorbed in their own self-cultivation at best, or in their own interests at worst, and unwilling to support the institutional reforms that were indispensable to social order and harmony.

THE INNER AND OUTER REALMS

The polarity of self-cultivation and the ordering of society concerns the ideals of the superior man—his life aims. The polarity of the "inner" (*nei*) and "outer" (*wai*) concerns the two realms of reality which bear most immediately on the achievement of these ideals. The two polarities are intimately related, but their relationship is complex. One cannot assume that even those overwhelmingly concerned with self-cultivation will be exclusively concerned with the "inner" realm, or their adversaries with the "outer."

The first elucidation of this polarity can be found in the famous debate of Mencius and Kao-tzu which appears in Book VI of *Mencius*. The key problem is the relation of the "inner" realm to the "outer" in accounting for the bases of human culture. Both realms are touched on in the sayings of Confucius, but nothing is said of the relation between them. Living in a later century, when the vision of the Master had already come under serious challenge, men like Mencius and Kao-tzu were forced to deal explicitly with problems which remain implicit in the *Analects*. The polarity which first emerged in this debate was then carried forward in the discussions of Hsün-tzu.

The outer realm is the objective social and cultural order, and in the first instance, the *li*, the binding tissue of objective prescriptions, rules, rites, and mores which holds that order together. The social order in question is specifically the ideal social order which in Confucius' judgment had been realized in actuality during the early Chou period. Interestingly enough, Mencius, Kao-tzu and Hsün-tzu all accepted the nature of this objective order as an unquestioned datum. The point on which they differed was the relation of this outer realm to the inner, the innate spiritual and moral capacities of the individual human being considered in isolation from the objective, normative cultural order. Was the outer realm an outgrowth of capacities and potentialities present in the inner realm, or was the moral content of the inner realm largely a product of culture? The question was by no means an academic one. Men had strayed from the Way; how was one to go about leading them back?

To Mencius, the good social order was the outer manifestation of spiritual and moral capacities innate in the individual human being. In Western terminology we might say that the natural law is imprinted on the human heart. To Kao-tzu the individual human being considered in isolation was nothing but a collection of rudimentary biological appetites. The objective cultural order could not be explained in terms of the capacities of the individual; on the contrary, the social and cultural order had an autonomous life of its own (as many modern schools of sociology believe it has), and human capacities were a result of the "internalization" of the values inherent in the order. Hsün-tzu goes still further: not only can one not explain human culture in terms of the innate capacities of the individual, but the individual's propensities actually run counter to the aims of higher culture (it is in this sense that human nature is bad), and it is only with considerable difficulty that he is transformed into a child of culture.

It is interesting to note that in dealing with the outer realm all three men concerned themselves primarily with the *li*. Although the *li*, to be sure, are part of the outer realm, they are only a part. Even in the *Analects* we have some discussion of *hsing*, penal law, and of *cheng*, government in the sense of state policy and concern for proper institutions. Yet Confucius himself, like Mencius and Kao-tzu, was overwhelmingly concerned with the *li*, for although the *li* are part of the outer realm they represent an essentially moral force. To the extent that the *li* can be successfully implemented, penal law and institutional devices can be de-emphasized. Hsün-tzu had essentially the same attitude; where he differed with Mencius was over the type of "educational" philosophy required in order to realize the moral order. Whereas Mencius felt that a gentle regimen was all that was required in order to get men to behave properly, Hsün-tzu called for draconian educational methods emphasizing discipline and a detailed and explicit working out of the rules of behavior. To both, however, education in the *li* was a central factor.

Hsün-tzu, however, was by no means willing to rely wholly on the *li*. His conception of the outer realm embraces the four categories *li, yüeh, hsing,* and *cheng*—"rites," music, penal law, and government. He tends in particular to place a high valuation on the coercive force of penal law as a supplement to *li* in achieving social order and harmony.

In the generation immediately following Hsün-tzu we find a decided shift of commitment from rites and music to laws and government. This shift was the work of the so-called Legalists, two of whom—Han Fei-tzu and Li Ssu—were reputedly disciples of Hsün-tzu. The Legalists departed altogether from Confucianism: not only were they completely indifferent to the inner realm and committed to the outer realm to the extent of championing brute force and institutional conditioning, but their very ends were no longer Confucian ends. Their goal was a wealthy and powerful state, not the Confucian vision of an ordered world of peace, harmony, and simple contentment. In a world where the great powers of the Warring States period were girding themselves for the final battle, they offered themselves as experts in the arts of enriching and strengthening the state. They strove to create a "rationalized" military and state machine, and to bring the masses into line by a severe system of penal law on the one hand and incentive awards for good performance on the other. From their point of view the whole fabric of the *li* was entirely irrational and irrelevant.

The distinction between means and ends which we have just made must be underlined if we are to understand the controversies stirred up by such figures as Wang An-shih. To the more orthodox line of Sung Confucianists any heavy reliance on laws and institutions was evidence of the desire to achieve Legalist ends. The Legalist philosophers and the Ch'in dynasty had established a close association between the two. In their view, Wang was clearly a Legalist; his insistence on new laws and institutions put him on the outer side of the outer realm. However, he and the other Sung "utilitarians" argued in effect that they were not Legalists since their end was to "order society" in terms of the Confucian image of the good order. Confucius himself, after all, had not entirely neglected laws and institutions.

Wang's case was somewhat weakened by the fact that many of his proposed reforms were in fact aimed at "wealth and power." He argued, however, that his emphasis on wealth was tied to the legitimate Confucian goal of assuring the people's livelihood, and that the defense of the realm was necessary to the achievement of peace and harmony. His opponents argued that he had committed himself to both Legalist means and Legalist ends.

It must be emphasized again that just as Wang An-shih's opponents by no means renounced the goal of "ordering the world," neither did they reject all concern for the outer realm. They were, of course, deeply committed to the objective prescriptions of the *li*, which they regarded as the sine qua non of self-cultivation. Beyond this, many of them had very positive ideas about how the state should be governed. One must here draw a distinction between a concern for the general institutional setting of human behavior and the belief that human behavior can be completely conditioned by institutional devices and laws. Confucius' own judgments take for granted an acceptance of the institutional framework of the early Chou period, but he does not assume that the presence of the framework guarantees the presence of the Way. What is desired is an institutional framework which will facilitate the influence of men of superior cultivation on society as a whole.

The "feudal utopians" found the solution in an idealized Chou feudalism: a state in which decision-making power is dispersed among many local rulers, each of whom confronts his Confucian ministers on a face-to-face basis and can thus be brought under their moral influence. The whole notion of the ruling class as an agency of moral example becomes more plausible within this context. On the other hand, the more realistic opponents of Wang An-shih—men like Chu Hsi—while regretfully conceding that the idealized Chou order could not be revived, opposed further tendencies toward bureaucratization in the form of new laws, institutional reform, and further intervention of the state in the economy. Positively, they did their utmost to increase the influence of self-cultivation as a force in government. In their view of self-cultivation, they tended to emphasize the resources of the inner realm.

Their economic policy followed the teachings of Confucius and Mencius: i.e., they accepted the notion that the uncultivated masses could be led to good social and ethical behavior only by the guarantee of a minimal level of economic security. In their opinion, this economic security could best be brought about by a "light government" policy. If government would refrain from heavy taxes, excessive corvée demands, ambitious military ventures, and displays of pomp and luxury, the people would be able to create its own economic welfare, and it might then be led by a virtuous ruling class to conform to the Way.

In spite of this type of concern with objective considerations, most of Wang An-shih's opponents (Ssu-ma Kuang is an exception) sided with Mencius in his view of the inner and outer realms. They were presumably concerned only with those factors in the outer realm which they saw as inhibiting the outflow of the spiritual forces latent in the inner realm. Only the more extreme among them turned away from all concern with the outer.

A third polarity that can be discerned within the Confucian tradition is the well-known polarity of knowledge and action. Here again we have no neat antithesis; here again the Master saw the two poles as complementary. Over the course of time, however, we find not only differences of emphasis, but also widely divergent notions of the nature and content of knowledge and the nature and content of action.

In the *Analects* knowledge (*chih*) and learning (*hsüeh*), are basic values. In attempting to revive the ideal order of the early Chou, Confucius necessarily stressed the knowledge of its elements: the order could be restored only to the extent that its culture, its institutions, and its *li* were known. The nature of this knowledge was not theoretical and abstract but concrete and factual. Confucius' good society was not like Plato's Republic—an ideal construct built up step by step by a systematic process of deductive reasoning and then contrasted to all merely "conventional" social orders. His good society had been realized in the flux of history. To know this order one had to know the facts about it. The type of knowledge required was empirical and "scholarly."

Nevertheless, the knowledge in question was by no means a chaotic heaping up of miscellaneous facts. There was the constant assertion that embedded in these facts was a coherent, underlying unity which could be apprehended by the perceptive disciple. "My Way," states Confucius, "is that of an all-pervading unity" (*Analects*, Book IV, chap. xv). Confucius himself did not extract any system from his separate reflections on the Way; he shied away from what might be considered ontological questions, and it was left to his followers to deal with these questions. Even such early works as the *Great Learning* and *The Doctrine of the Mean* attempt to furnish an abstract and reasonably logical account of the broad underlying principles of the Way. Presumably this effort to elucidate general principles was made at a time when the Master's thought required some sort of defense against hostile challenge. When Mencius and Hsün-tzu devoted a great deal of attention to the question of "human nature" in spite of the Master's silence on this subject, they were not simply repudiating the Master's soberly "positivistic" approach. Those who were challenging Confucius' dicta were also challenging what they regarded as his unstated assumptions. By the same token, the Master's defenders felt obliged to clarify and defend these unstated assumptions.

When we turn to the Neo-Confucian philosophers of the Sung dynasty, we find that they confronted the challenge of Buddhist metaphysics in addition to the challenge of native anti-Confucian philosophies. They simply assumed that if there was an "all-pervading unity" underlying the Master's teachings, the philosophic principles involved could be abstracted from the knowledge of the facts for purposes of philosophic reflection. On the other hand, to Tai Chen (1724–77) and other "radical empiricists" of the Ch'ing period this effort to deal with general philosophic principles without regard to concrete facts implied a belief in a sort of self-contained realm of ideal essences. Tai Chen believed that only by clinging compulsively to the facts could one be in contact with the Way, which was inextricably imbedded in them. The discussion of abstractions apart from concrete facts was merely "empty talk."

The issue of the content of knowledge also becomes deeply enmeshed with the attitudes toward the inner and outer realms. The Neo-Confucian philosophers of the Chu Hsi school were deeply committed to the importance of self-cultivation. Since the inner realm was the realm of human nature (hsing), they were naturally very concerned with the attributes of the hsing. It was precisely the inner realm of the hsing, however, which bound man to the cosmos as a whole. "What heaven confers," states the Doctrine of the Mean, "is the hsing." Even writers like Hsün-tzu who denigrated the hsing conceived of it as part of the "heavenly" or cosmic order. Mahayana Buddhist philosophy probably reinforced this association. Thus to achieve a true comprehension of the hsing one must understand the ultimate nature of reality. Here we find a possible source of the Neo-Confucian concern with metaphysical knowledge.

This knowledge of the principles underlying the cosmos and the hsing was of course by no means knowledge for the sake of knowledge. Like Spinoza, the Sung Neo-Confucianists sought the kind of intellectual enlightenment that would free the spirit from the bonds of the affects. Chu Hsi himself conceived this knowledge still more broadly. He saw it, in fact, as being encyclopedic: the ultimate organizing principles of reality could be found not only in the inner realm which attaches man to the cosmos but also behind the outer realm of rites, music, law, and government with which man must be concerned. Among the late Neo-Confucianists, however, the Neo-Confucian emphasis on the inner realm became decidedly more pronounced and "knowledge" tended to become overwhelmingly a concern with metaphysical problems.

On the other hand, those who were concerned primarily with the outer realm—men otherwise as different in their outlooks as Wang

An-shih in the Northern Sung and Ku Yen-wu of the early Ch'ing—regarded knowledge of history, of the development of institutions, of the "li," and even of law as the central focus of real knowledge. To Wang An-shih such knowledge was the knowledge most relevant to his goal of ordering society. Ku Yen-wu's position was more complex. Although, like Wang, he stressed "practical statesmanship" (*ching-shih*) and the bulk of his scholarly investigations involved the outer realm, his conception of good statesmanship was substantially that of Wang's opponents. He favored an institutional setting which would make the self-cultivation of the *chün-tzu* a dominant force in human society. He did not feel, however, that individual self-cultivation required a deep concern for ultimate metaphysical problems. Self-cultivation was primarily a matter of moral training: "In your action be guided by a sense of shame; in your learning be comprehensive." The relationship between knowledge and the goal of self-cultivation has here become somewhat tenuous.

In the century following Ku Yen-wu the acquisition of knowledge came to be exalted in some quarters almost as an end in itself, without reference to the goals of either self-cultivation or the ordering of society. The school of empirical research (*k'ao-cheng*) conceived of knowledge essentially as precise factual knowledge of the cultural heritage. Its members refused to discuss abstract principles apart from the facts, and in this regard considered themselves closer to the Master than their metaphysically inclined predecessors. In their divorce of knowledge from all the larger concerns of Confucianism, however, they certainly drifted far from the Master's original intent.

The Sung controversies also disclose divergent views of the nature and content of action. The enemies of Chu Hsi and Wang Yang-ming saw them as primarily engrossed in their own self-cultivation even when they were deeply immersed in public activities—and with some justice, since both viewed the arena of public action primarily as a field for exercising their own moral musculatures, as it were. To Wang An-shih and his school, by contrast, action was primarily "social action" —the framing and administration of new laws which would affect society as a whole and not merely a given official's own arena of action. Chu Hsi and Wang Yang-ming were both capable and vigorous officials who performed most spectacularly in the positions they occupied, and both were very much concerned with their own performance as officials. Chu Hsi would indeed have argued that the example of a noble and capable official who does his job well is more important to the ordering of society than elaborate blueprints of institutional change.

It is important to emphasize that an orientation toward the pole of action in the Confucian tradition was not necessarily an orientation toward the general type of social and political action which modern men tend to regard as "practical." The Tung-lin party of the late Ming period, which was deeply concerned with the social and political situation of its own times and firmly dedicated to moral action, conceived of such action largely in terms of exhorting the ruling class to honor the prescriptions of the *li*; it was markedly indifferent to laws and institutions.

Divergent conceptions of the nature and content of knowledge and action necessarily lead to divergent conceptions of the relations between the two. To Wang Yang-ming, Chu Hsi's notion that only a knowledge of all the principles underlying the myriad phenomena of reality could lead to self-realization was a snare and a delusion: clearly the intellectual baggage of Chu Hsi's latter-day disciples bore little relationship to their day-to-day behavior. (One is reminded of Kierkegaard's disgust with the Hegelian university docents who could devise philosophies of universal history but were unable to introduce any elevation into their own squalid lives.) According to Wang, man manifests his spirit by acting in the concrete situations which confront him. It is ridiculous to suppose that a whole system of universal knowledge must intervene between man and his action.

This belief did not lead Wang Yang-ming to a repudiation of knowledge, but it did lead him to a radical redefinition of its content. There was nothing to be gained in seeking knowledge of the sum total of discrete general principles underlying all the phenomena of nature and human society; men should rather seek to know the mystic One Reality which is latent in the human spirit and which makes itself manifest whenever a man of superior spiritual insight faces up to the moral requirements of the concrete situation which confronts him. Ostensibly, to adopt this view is to reject the whole outer realm (except in so far as the situation which the Sage confronts may be considered outer), and to espouse a form of transcendental individualism which might easily break out of the bounds of Confucian objective morality altogether. Wang himself was not so radical. He continued to accept the "five relationships" and their outward manifestation, the prescriptions of the *li*. He assumed a happy coincidence between the intuitive impulses of the individual conscience and Confucian objective morality. The outer realm of the *li*, as he saw it, emerged directly from the inner realm of the human heart. Actually, among some of Wang's later followers—particularly the heterodox Li Chih (1527–1602)—the tendency to break out of the bounds of Confucian objective morality does indeed emerge.

I have here dealt in a very tentative and topical manner with three polarities within Confucian thought which seem to have an enduring importance within the tradition as a whole. The judgments expressed are preliminary judgments and are certainly open to further scrutiny. There are undoubtedly many other themes of equal importance. The aim of this paper has been to communicate some sense of the turbulent inner life to be found within a tradition which has often been portrayed in the West as a collection of trite copybook maxims blandly accepted in toto by innumerable generations of "scholar-officials." Confucianism has its own *Problematik* which we have only begun to explore.

In line with my purpose I have stressed the variety of alternatives available within the tradition. This does not mean that there is no common core of assumptions shared by almost all who call themselves Confucianists nor that there are no bounds (indistinct as these bounds may be) between Confucianism and other streams of thought.

Finally, it must again be stressed that no attempt has been made in this paper to link ideas to interest factors. However much the intellectual issues discussed may have become enmeshed with individual and group interests, no apology is required for an attempt to achieve an understanding of the ideas *qua* ideas.

2 Institutions

Hui-chen Wang Liu

AN ANALYSIS OF
CHINESE CLAN RULES:
CONFUCIAN THEORIES IN ACTION

The purpose of this paper is to examine the clan rules in Chinese genealogies from the viewpoint of Confucian theories in action—in other words, to examine how and with what effect the clan rules transmitted and applied the Confucian teachings to successive generations in the various clans. The data are found in the collection of genealogies in the East Asiatic Library, Columbia University. My earlier study of the clan rules[1] dealt chiefly with social control, and to a lesser extent with value schemes and group organization; the present paper is concerned above all with value schemes and their complex ramifications. For my earlier study I used only genealogies printed during the Republican years 1912–36, in order to include some account of modern changes within the surviving tradition; the present paper draws upon the entire collection, including the genealogies printed during the Ch'ing period.

The term clan rule designates any formal instruction, injunction, regulation, stipulation, or similar passage found in a genealogy which explicitly prescribes the conduct of clan members.

The forms of the clan rules vary. Some are merely collections of famous quotations, imperial injunctions, excerpts from the penal code, or mottoes stated by ancestral members of the clan. Others address themselves to such concrete matters as management of the ancestral hall, regulation of common property, and common clan activities. However, the majority of them follow a standard arrangement of articles or short paragraphs, each on a given topic indicated by a caption, an itemized heading, or the first sentence.

In general, these articles extol virtuous and desirable conduct on the one hand, and condemn deviations and offenses on the other. Some lay down more concrete specifications for the conduct of family, clan, individual, and social life. A number of clan rules, though not the majority, stipulate measures of punishment. The predominant emphases of all the clan rules are two: first, upon the ideal of orderly and harmonious life in kinship groups; and second, upon the observance of proper status relationships among kinsmen.

The clan rules are basically instructions. They depend on moral persuasion, and they derive their sanction from authority, that is, from such impersonal authorities as Confucianism and the law of the state as well as such personal authorities as the clan's ancestors, its formal and informal leaders, and its family heads. The punitive provisions in some of the clan rules—oral censure, ritual discipline, cash fines, corporal punishment, denial of clan privileges, expulsion from the clan group, and legal indictment—are paradoxically less punitive than protective. They are designed to warn the offender, to see to it that there will be no need for the law to punish him except as a last resort.

The clan rules, as guidance toward ideal conduct, could not be very effective beyond a certain point, depending upon how well a given clan was organized and operated. It seems that even the clans which were sufficiently well organized and wealthy enough to have their genealogies printed did not have the necessary organizational strength and appeal to make the clan rules rigidly binding upon their members. The clan rules nonetheless had an impressive normative influence, even upon members with little education.[2]

After the earlier aristocratic clans declined toward the end of the T'ang period, the importance of the primary group was rediscovered by the Sung Confucianists, who reinstituted the clan system as a means of promoting self-cultivation, rectifying social customs, and stabilizing society. The purposes stated by these pioneers are worth quoting. Chang Tsai of the Northern Sung period said:

To control the heart of the people needs the gathering of clan members and the promotion of good customs so that the people will not forget their origins. To achieve this purpose requires genealogy, clan organization, and the ancient system of *tsung-tzu* [head of the leading lineage by primogeniture as the clan head]. Without *tsung-tzu*, people do not know where their own lines of descent come from. Though this system has lapsed, genealogies have kept its spirit alive. If there is no genealogy, the families do not know their origins and cannot be kept together very long. Without a control among the kin, even the sentiment between parents and children tends to be weak.[3]

Chu Hsi, one of the great masters of Neo-Confucianism in the Southern Sung, has cited Ch'eng I, the Northern Sung philosopher, as saying:

Without the *tsung-tzu* as the clan head, the imperial court has no hereditary officials to depend on. If the system of *tsung-tzu* is revived, people will learn to respect their ancestors and value their origins, and then the court will naturally command more respect. In ancient times, young people looked up to their fathers and elder brothers. Now the reverse is true, because people no longer respect their origins. . . . Only recognition of the relationship between superior and subordinate, between high and low, can ensure order and obedience without confusion. How can people live properly without some means of control?

Furthermore, the system of *tsung-tzu* follows the principle of nature. For example, a tree has its trunk, coming up straight from its root, as well as its side branches. A waterway, however long, has its main stream among other divergent streams. This is natural. What is needed now is for a few families of leading officials to try to revive the *tsung-tzu* system, that is, the system of keeping families together. One way of achieving this objective is to follow the precedent of the T'ang period by establishing ancestral halls and clan estates, so that the ancestral inheritance remains intact and can be managed by one chosen person. The clan members should always assemble at a monthly meeting.[4]

At the time of the Northern Sung, pioneer efforts were made to improve upon genealogies and to strengthen clan organizations. Ou-yang Hsiu and Su Hsün were responsible for laying down the standards by which genealogies should be compiled. Fan Chung-yen set an example by establishing *i-t'ien* or charitable lands and *i-chuang* or charitable estates to aid poor clan members. Ssu-ma Kuang in his writings drew attention to family upbringing, manners, and training. These pioneer efforts gained an increasing following during the Southern Sung period.

However, the Sung genealogies, being a new growth, were relatively few in number. Mostly, they limited themselves to genealogical tables and did not incorporate clan rules as such. The full development of genealogies took place during the Ming period, owing to a number of factors: the state's interest in stabilizing the social order; the emphasis of the law upon the privileges and responsibilities of clans; the interest of scholar-officials in clan matters; the spread of learning among the common people; and the growing financial strength of the clans particularly in the provinces of Anhwei, Kiangsu, Kiangsi, Chekiang, Fukien, and Kwangtung, where revenue was derived from commercial as well as agricultural sources.[5] The development of printing was probably another factor. Underlying many of these factors was the widening and deepening influence of Neo-Confucianism with its emphasis on family discipline and individual self-cultivation. It was perhaps in the later part of the Ming period that clan rules became a standard feature in the fully developed genealogies.

This trend continued without basic change into the Ch'ing period. Several Ch'ing genealogies among the present data contain clan rules of Ming date.[6] Many other Ch'ing genealogies added new items to the old clan rules: new compositions, new compilations of old quotations, imperial injunctions, excerpts from the laws, borrowed passages from the rules of other clans.[7] These Ch'ing genealogies, on the whole, suggest that the elaboration and revision of clan rules reached a saturation point around 1880. The clan rules of subsequent date show no significant change in substance. It may be of interest to mention in passing that the rules of a Moslem clan named Chu in Chen-chiang, Kiangsu province, save for an introductory mention of the five pillars of Islam, is not distinguishable in the least from numerous other clan rules compiled after 1800.[8] Even after 1912, the overwhelming majority of the clan rules still abide by the old models. A few of them responded to modernization by limited adjustments deleting obsolete provisions and adding some modern features, but these adjustments were little more than futile efforts to keep an old heritage alive.[9]

The principal function of the clan rules is to exercise social control upon the clan's individual members, and especially to provide normative orientation, with concrete specifications for proper conduct and detailed description of desirable and undesirable behavior. The rules derived mainly from the Confucian teachings; but to these they added a second layer of more specific teachings, amounting to a sort of value scheme that was more directly applicable to behavior in and beyond the kinship groups than the broader tenets of Confucianism. It is this value scheme that interests us here.

THE VALUE SCHEME IN THE CLAN RULES

The generalization that the clan rules merely follow and pass on the Confucian teachings and adhere to the Confucian value scheme is an inadequate one, for it tends to obscure the flexibility of the rules, and their tendency toward making adjustments and modifications within the broad limits of Confucianism. One clan rule concedes that "there is more than one way to achieve the essence of good family life."[10] Another recognizes that "rituals are originally based upon human feelings and hence their observance should not be compulsory" regardless of circumstances.[11] Several clan rules adopt the principle that both "consultation of the old, set ways and consideration of their present applicability" are desirable.[12] Another, the work of an old lady and probably based upon her life experience rather than upon the Confucian theories, says that "studying books should not make one follow the books in a deadly rigid manner; and in managing a family one should not adhere to deadly fixed rules."[13]

The above quotations, a few examples among many, show that the clan rules were prepared to select, restate, and reinterpret the Confucian teachings to adjust them to the realities of life. Sometimes no adjustment was necessary; sometimes only a slight adjustment would do; sometimes traditional Confucianism had to give way altogether. In short, the value scheme in the clan rules resulted from a complicated process of two-way adjustment between doctrine and practical experience.

In the following pages, we shall consider four aspects of this complicated process. The first is the ideological make-up of the clan rules. The Confucian teachings are by no means the only component in the rules. Actually the ancient classics of Confucianism, though basic, are less in evidence than the later Confucianist teachings, especially those of the Neo-Confucianists from the Sung to the early Ch'ing period, with their admixture of Buddhism, Taoism, and folk religion.

The second aspect is the influence of the state. The law of the state, which incorporated some Confucian principles, is the legal basis of the clan rules. Many of the imperial injunctions on moral conduct, by which the state transmitted and applied such Confucian teachings as it deemed especially important, were embodied in clan rules. At the same time a suspicious attitude toward the state, the fruit of the people's practical experience in their relationship with the government, also found expression in the clan rules.

The third aspect is the influence of scholar-officials. Men of this class generally gave their clan organizations strong support and moral leadership, and usually were among the actual compilers of the clan rules. These scholar-officials combined the scholar's idealistic interests with the realistic interests of members of the ruling class. On the one hand, they were devoted to Confucian teachings; on the other, they had their responsibilities as family heads and community leaders. On the one hand, they knew that the clan rules could be made effective only by a strong clan organization, requiring the active participation of many more scholar-officials and members of their families; on the other, they realized painfully that the conduct of many upper-class members left much to be desired. On the one hand, they were loyal to the state; on the other hand, they were responsible to the clan and inclined to avoid government interference. These mixed motives are evident in the clan rules.

The fourth and last essential aspect in the value scheme of the clan rules is their response to prevailing social customs. The clan rules deal with what is as well as with what should be; and they necessarily pass judgment on at least some of the social customs with which they are concerned. This judgment is not a simple matter of approval or disapproval; it may be a persistent resistance, a permissive tolerance, an ambivalent acceptance, or a tacit approval. It must also be emphasized that the rules were directed above all to the clan's less educated and uneducated members. One clan rule, for example, states that it renounces the difficult classical language used in the famous rules of the past in favor of the simple, plain language that most people can understand.[14] Furthermore, the clan rules necessarily drew upon the kind of practical experience that was largely shared by the scholar-officials and the common people alike, so that in this sense, too, they may be said to have responded to the customs of the common people.

CONFUCIAN TEACHINGS IN THE CLAN RULES

Among the numerous ancient classics cited by the clan rules, the most important one is the *Li-chi* ("Book of Rituals"), especially the section entitled "Nei-tse" ("Domestic Rules"). Next in importance are the other classics on *li*, notably the *I-li*, the *Chou-li*, and the *Erh-ya*. Other passages come from the *Hsiao-ching* ("Classic of Filial Piety") and the *Analects* of Confucius. It is evident that the clan rules place their strongest emphasis upon *li*. In the words of the "Nei-tse," quoted by some clan rules, "*li* serves to determine the closeness or distance of relations, to settle what is the proper conduct in doubtful circumstances, to distinguish kin from non-kin, and to clarify what is right and wrong."[15] The term *li*, sometimes translated as "propriety," refers not merely to rituals, ceremonies, and manners, but more important than that, to proper conduct and its ethical basis. It signifies both the conventions and the principles which regulate all group life, and particularly the life of kinship groups. Take the ancestral hall and the activities there, for example; one clan rule explains, "The ancestral hall is established, first for the remembrance of the ancestors; second, for the purpose of uniting the sentiment of clan members; and third, for the sake of teaching those to come the virtues of filial piety and sincerity."[16]

When the clan rules cite other classics such as the Book of Changes, the Book of Poetry, and the Spring and Autumn Annals, they are concerned mainly with bringing metaphysical interpretations, aesthetic sanction, and historical precedents to the support of the approved conventions and principles called *li*.

The clan rules quote several other pre-Han works, among them the *Hsün-tzu* and the *Kuan-tzu*. The Confucianist philosopher Hsün-tzu stressed the restraining aspects of *li* and pointed to the need for punitive regulations. His work paved the way for the clan rules to cite the *Kuan-tzu* on the desirability of supporting *li* with institutional and legal controls. Many Han writings are also quoted, especially the following: Chia I, *Hsin-shu*; Liu Hsi, *Shih-ming*; Pan Ku, *Po-hu-t'ung*; Wang Ch'ung, *Lun-heng*; Yang Hsiung, *Fa-yen*; and Ying Shao, *Feng-su*

T'ung-i. These books have two characteristics in common: (1) they develop the Confucian doctrines on *li* to include an emphasis upon *ming-chieh* (integrity); and (2) they advance the concept of *kang-chi* (governing principles and discipline) as being necessary for all organized groups. In short, in Han Confucian teachings, the basic emphasis on *li* took two forms: voluntary control by self-respect and disciplinary restraint by institutions.

Besides the above, the clan rules often quote some writings of the period between Han and T'ang which deal with the family. Among these are Pan Chao's *Nü Chieh* ("Instructions for Women"), a classic on the proper conduct of ladies, and Yen Chih-t'ui's *Yen-shih Chia-hsün* ("Family Instructions") probably the earliest systematically compiled work of the kind. While Yen's book in the main follows Confucianism, it also provides in detail more practical ways of behaving and treating people. Liu P'ien's work, also on family instructions, reflects the aristocratic mode of living during the T'ang period.

The Sung Neo-Confucianists in reviving Confucianism developed it to a new height. They amplified the significance of self-respect and stressed self-cultivation in accordance with the metaphysical concepts of *li* (principles) and *hsing* (nature). They implemented the principle of disciplinary restraint by strengthening institutional control, particularly in the family and by extension in the clan, to a greater degree than before. As we have seen, it is the Neo-Confucianist teachings that occupy the foremost place in the clan rules.

Many clan rules quote with reverence the *Chia-li* ("Family Rituals") by Chu Hsi and *Chia-i* ("Family Manners") by Ssu-ma Kuang. Fan Chung-yen is highly praised for originating the system of the charitable estate, which provides regular relief and aid to poor clan members; and the "Rules of the Charitable Estate of the Fan Clan" is cited in many of the clan rules. Almost equal in fame was the "Chih Chia Ke-yen" ("Motto on Family Discipline") composed by Chu Yung-ch'un (better known by his courtesy name, Po-lu), an early Ch'ing scholar who remained loyal to the Ming and adhered consistently to Chu Hsi. (A number of clan rules mistakenly attribute the "Chih Chia Ke-yen" to Chu Hsi himself.)

Some clan rules include all or part of the *hsiang-yüeh* (community pact), a system devised during the Northern Sung period by Lü Ta-lin and his brothers, who formulated it in four principles: mutual encouragement of virtue, mutual rectification of faults, mutual friendship through observing proper etiquette, and mutual aid in case of trouble. It was widely adopted during the Southern Sung period. Especially popular was *Chu-tzu Tseng-sun Lü-shih Hsiang-yüeh* ("A Revision of the Lü Community Pact by Chu Hsi"). In the Ming period, Wang Yang-ming officially issued his remodeled community pact known as "Nan Kan Hsiang-yüeh" and put it into effect in southern Kiangsi in combination with a system of community surveillance of crime. From then on, the community pact system was followed in many areas.[17]

A fairly large number of clan rules include elaborate collections of quotations from famous scholars and scholar-officials, mainly from the Sung period to the early Ch'ing. Of the sixty frequently cited, more than forty are named in the *Ssu Ch'ao Hsüeh-an*, a kind of cyclopedia listing the various Confucian schools of learning and their notable scholars during the Sung, Yüan, Ming, and Ch'ing dynasties.[18] The quotations generally follow the Sung emphasis on *li*, self-respect, self-cultivation, and disciplinary restraint both self-imposed and institutional. These were the paramount Confucian (or rather, Neo-Confucian) values during the Ch'ing period when these clan rules were compiled.

This brief survey has shown the selective accumulation of the Confucianist teachings in the clan rules. One clan rule that illustrates this selective accumulation very nicely requires the clan in its meetings to hear lectures on the following: (1) the community pact; (2) imperial injunctions on moral conduct; (3) factual instances of filial piety, other merits, and demerits; (4) Chu Hsi's *Chia-li* ("Family Rituals"); (5) other writings on family discipline and self-cultivation by famous authors; and (6) the clan rule itself. After the lecture, the clan meeting should proceed to reward meritorious conduct and punish offenses among the members.[19] This example, which is one among many, demonstrates that the classics and the early writings, though upheld as the basic sources of the clan rules, are not as useful as the Neo-Confucianist teachings which deal specifically and directly with the family, the clan, and proper behavior beyond the kinship group.

The Confucian teachings in the clan rules became more or less conventionally fixed during the course of the eighteenth century. In this regard, it is pertinent to mention the encyclopedia, *Ku Chin T'u-shu Chi-ch'eng*, completed in 1725, which covers numerous kinship and social relations in its various sections, notably in its section on family norms ("Chia-fan-tien"). We find that the clan rules deal with a number of topics covered by this section of the encyclopedia: parents, father and son, mother and son, discipline of children, sons of the wife and sons of concubines, adoption, adopted heirs, womanhood, grandchildren, brotherhood, man and wife, clan relations, and domestic servants. In other topics, however, the clan rules fail to take much interest: among these are grandfather and grandson, wet nurse, sisterhood, sister-in-law and brother, uncle and nephew, aunt and nephew. Significantly, the clan rules are almost unanimously silent on the relationship between mother and daughter-in-law, which has a special heading in this section of the encyclopedia, and in general they express far less interest than the encyclopedia in relationships between various maternal relatives.[20]

This comparison definitely underscores the family-centered, patriarchal nature and the hierarchical emphasis of the clan rules. However, there is another point of comparison which is even more important. The encyclopedia quotes the ancient classics and writings on Confucian theory extensively; but the clan rules prefer to quote from more recent writings of a more practical kind. The availablity of the encyclopedia probably enriched the contents of the clan rules; but the Confucian materials selected from it were primarily those that seemed most relevant to family and clan activities in daily life.

There is further evidence that clan rules took their ultimate form in the course of the eighteenth century. Ch'en Hung-mou, a leading scholar-official active in the government during the early years of the Ch'ien-lung reign (1736–96), edited several compilations of Confucian writings of a utilitarian nature. His compilations, collectively known as the *Wu Chung I-kuei* ("The Five Collections of Rules"), consist of the *Yang Cheng I-kuei* ("Rules on Proper Upbringing"), the *Hsün Su I-kuei* ("Rules on Social Customs"), the *Chiao Nü I-kuei* ("Rules on Teaching Girls"), and two other sets of rules on the conduct of government officials.[21] One clan rule says that the *Wu Chung I-kuei* should be kept handy for constant reference.[22] The reason is not hard to find. Both this compilation and many clan rules share the same purpose, namely, to transmit and apply the Confucian teachings in practical matters. The appearance of this compilation probably contributed to the growth of the clan rules into generally accepted and even fixed models.

As might be expected, the Neo-Confucianist teachings found in the clan rules contain some minor admixtures of Buddhism and Taoism. One clan rule goes to the extreme of quoting many Buddhist and Taoist sayings and equating them with comparable Confucian teachings.[23] Several others admit the value of borrowing some good teachings from Buddhism. One says:

Han-shan said to his fellow Buddhist Shih-te: "People slander me, trespass against me, envy me, laugh at me, cause me harm, cheat me, and humiliate me. What should I do?" Shih-te replied, "I would just yield to them, tolerate them, suffer from them, be patient with them, avoid them, let them do what they wish, pay no attention to them, and wait to see what will happen to them several years later." Though this is a Buddhist saying, there is useful knowledge in it and it can be used as a principle in dealing with people.[24]

Other clan rules accept some Buddhist concepts but give them a Confucian interpretation. One of these rules reads as follows:

The Buddhists say that if you want to know about previous lives, look at the sufferings of this life. If you want to know about the next life, look at what is being done in this life. This is an excellent statement. However, what Buddhists refer to as previous lives and the lives to come stems from their theory of rebirth and transmigration of souls. I think what has happened before yesterday—the father, and the ancestors—are really the previous lives, and that what will happen after today—the sons and the grandsons—are really the lives to come.

A friend spoke to me of rebirth and emancipation. I answered that a family which has accumulated goodness will have lasting fortunes, while a family which has accumulated demerits will have misfortunes in the future. Is this not what we Confucianists believe in and an equivalent to the Buddhist theory of rebirth? A gentleman neither worries nor fears. He lives at peace and leaves the rest to destiny. Is this not what we Confucianists believe to be emancipation?[25]

A few clan rules advise their members to read *T'ai-shang Kan-ying P'ien* and follow *Kung Kuo Ke*; both are known to be colored by Taoism. However, these admixtures of Buddhism, and to a lesser extent of Taoism, caused no significant change in the value scheme of the clan rules. As will be shown later, the clan rules are generally opposed to the prevailing practices of organized religions. Adhering to the Confucian teachings in the main, they accept or reject certain religious influences largely on grounds of whether such influences strengthen or weaken the Confucian values they uphold.

STATE INFLUENCE IN THE CLAN RULES

The traditional Chinese state was interested in maintaining order through both the law and moral education. It relied to a certain extent upon the clan rules, which incorporate excerpts from the penal code in their texts, to transmit the law to clan members, as well as to uphold law-abiding conduct in general. Above all, however, the clan rules served as an instrument for passing along the *sheng-yü*, imperial injunctions on moral conduct. The *sheng-yü* are often termed "imperial instructions" or "educational edicts" on the grounds that they lie in the area of moral education; it seems more accurate to describe them as injunctions, for they were proclaimed by the Emperor and had the force of law.

These imperial injunctions had a complicated background. Mixing the Neo-Confucianist emphasis upon moral education and the state interest in controlling the social order, the Ming government instituted the *li-chia* neighborhood unit system to impose collective responsibility, the appointment of *lao-jen* (elders) to supervise village communities, and community meetings at the *shen-ming t'ing* (pavilion of moral education) and *ching-shan t'ing* (pavilion in honor of moral conduct) to encourage good conduct. Essential in all these institutions were the Six Injunctions proclaimed by the Emperor T'ai-tsu, the founder of the dynasty. This elaborate system of local control was disrupted around 1430 but revived briefly under the Wan-li reign (1573–1619).[26]

While in the beginning the Ch'ing government did not institute a system of local control as elaborate as that of the Ming, it did authorize the revival of the Six Injunctions in 1652, not long after its conquest of China proper. The Six Injunctions, together with commentaries on them, also spread to the Liu-ch'iu Islands and from there to Tokugawa Japan, where they were honored with many editions.[27] However, the Ch'ing government did not find the Ming document entirely satisfactory. The K'ang-hsi Emperor proclaimed his own Sixteen Injunctions in 1670 and his son, the Yung-cheng Emperor, issued in 1724 the 10,000-word *Sheng-yü Kuang Hsün* as the official commentary on the Sixteen Injunctions. From time to time, enthusiastic local government officials circulated their own editions of these texts. Other interested officials compiled and printed additional explanations (some of them in the colloquial language), illustrations,[28] and historical examples.

The Ch'ing government required local magistrates to give lectures on the imperial injunctions, but most magistrates did so only occasionally and in a very perfunctory manner.[29] The clan rules seem to have provided a much more effective channel of communicating the imperial injunctions to the clan groups.

The Six Injunctions read as follows:

1. Render filial piety to your parents.
2. Respect your seniors by generation and age.
3. Remain in harmony with clan and community members.
4. Teach and discipline your sons and grandsons.
5. Attend to your proper vocation.
6. Do not do what the law forbids.

It may be seen that the Six Injunctions emphasize family responsibilities more than clan activities; family security more than clan welfare; conformity to conventions more than self-cultivation; and obedience to law more than other Confucian virtues.

The Sixteen Injunctions read as follows:

1. Be steadfast in filial piety and brotherhood.
2. Be close to fellow clan members.

3. Be kind to community people.
4. Take care of farming productivity.
5. Be industrious and thrifty.
6. Support schools.
7. Abjure heretical religions.
8. Learn the law and statutes.
9. Follow the rituals in showing deference to others.
10. Attend to your proper vocation.
11. Instruct sons and younger ones.
12. Forbid false accusation.
13. Do not harbor outlaws.
14. Pay taxes.
15. Organize *pao-chia* neighborhood units to maintain local order.
16. Resolve enmities.

The Sixteen Injunctions are more comprehensive and more specific than the Six Injunctions. There are several close parallels between the Sixteen Injunctions and the clan rules. First, both follow the same sequence of arrangement in putting the general principles of desirable behavior at the beginning and the specific provisions on concrete matters—either desirable or, in most cases, undesirable conduct—toward the end. Second, while both the Sixteen Injunctions and many clan rules deal with intra-clan and community relations, their strongest emphasis is upon family order and family security. Third, those of the Sixteen Injunctions (7, 8, 12, 13, 14, 15) that stress obedience to the law and other required obligations to the state are reflected faithfully in many clan rules, sometimes in the identical wording.

Government efforts in moral education were by no means limited to the imperial injunctions. The K'ang-hsi, Yung-cheng, and Ch'ienlung Emperors each issued a number of supplementary edicts giving further specifications and direct applications of the injunctions to particular cases. These edicts were largely of two kinds. The first kind censured certain influential, wealthy, and aggressive elements for engaging in various undesirable practices. Some edicts denounced those gentry who imposed their will upon the community;[30] others decried indulgence in luxury, especially in the matter of expensive funerals and weddings.[31] Clan organizations also had their faults; well-organized clans, as several edicts pointed out, were apt to start litigation against other people and even to engage in feuds with other clans.[32] The second category of edicts appealed to important elements in the community and the clan groups to assume leadership in upholding Confucian principles against undesirable religious influences. One edict after another called upon local leaders to combat belief in geomancy and witchcraft.[33]

Several edicts deplored the joining of religious orders, the holding of religious services in mixed company, and the practice of permitting women to visit temples.[34] The government took a particularly serious view of large pilgrimages across provincial boundaries, which might endanger state security.[35] Though the clan rules rarely cite these edicts specifically, they reflect an acceptance of the government's wishes by expressing the same views.

These edicts raise the question: What was the Ch'ing government's attitude toward organized clans on the whole? The government realized that it could not depend upon local government officials alone to propagate the imperial injunctions or to enforce moral education in general.[36] The suggestion that the *pao-chia* neighborhood units assume this responsibility did not seem feasible.[37] The alternative was to call upon the clan groups, especially the scholar-official leaders among them.

A memorial in 1736 pointed out significantly that the improvement of social customs and the spread of moral education must begin with the officials and their families. Unfortunately, it went on, many officials and their families were so selfish that they did not look after their clan members. Though the government sometimes commended a few officials who had donated land to their clans for the relief of clan members, this was hardly enough. This memorial suggested that a clan with more than 1,000 members should have a clan head with power to instruct and guide the members; that a clan with a record of several years without litigation should receive government commendation; and that individuals who made outstanding contributions to their clan, especially in relief during famine years, should be similarly rewarded and even given official titles. On the other hand, the government should punish both officials and scholars who mistreated their clan members. Only through such measures would it be possible to have the clan groups promote moral behavior.[38]

Though the government did wish to have the clan groups move in the direction suggested by this memorial, it did not want to regulate clan activities in such a formal manner. Furthermore, there was another consideration: from the viewpoint of the state, it might not be entirely desirable to have really strong clan organizations. Some clans in Kiangsi and Kwangtung provinces had already built up in the mid-eighteenth century unusually large memberships by including groups of the same surname who were not necessarily related by blood. Such clan organizations had not only extensive common properties but also great social influence. Looking upon such clans with political suspicion, the government compelled them to limit their membership to nearby kin and to limit their property holdings.[39] In fact, when a memorial

presented in 1768 again suggested the system of assigning official powers to the heads of large clan groups, the Ch'ien-lung Emperor rejected
it with a reprimand, pointing out that large clans often caused trouble
by fighting with other clans or by dominating the community, and that
to give clan heads official power would be tantamount to a revival of
feudalism.[40] In short, the Ch'ing government wanted the clans to promote moral education within their existing structure but did not want
them to become too influential. This limitation was also tacitly accepted by the clan rules.

So far, our discussion has separated the state from the scholar-officials. In reality, these two elements were closely related. The wishes
of the state, as expressed by the imperial injunctions and the numerous
edicts on moral education, were often the result of advice given by a
few scholar-officials who were particularly interested in these matters.
As we have seen, however, these scholar-officials served two masters.
On the one hand, as officials working for the government, they saw the
desirability of having clan organizations promote moral education and
take care of their members without troubling the government. On the
other hand, as clan leaders and thinking in terms of the clan's security,
they wished to avoid involvement with the government, whether in the
form of litigation, or in the form of government supervision of clan
activities. For this reason, the compilers of clan rules gladly went
along with the government in keeping the clan organization as it was.

The attitude of avoiding the government is clearly seen in three
injunctions which the clan rules generally give to their members. These
three injunctions stem not so much from the imperial injunctions or
from Confucian teachings as from the practical experience of the people in general. In other words, they reflect the effects of government
operations upon the people. The first injunction is not to discuss political matters. An early Ch'ing genealogy contains a Ming clan rule
which warns that political gossip is unbecoming to a cultivated man,
that criticism of local government officials is neither loyal nor kind, and
that ignoring this advice may bring disaster.[41] Though such specific
formulations are not numerous, practically all clan rules refrain from
mentioning politics.

The second injunction is to pay taxes promptly, primarily in order
to keep clear of the government. Prompt payment of taxes is both necessary and desirable—necessary because paying taxes is the duty of
subjects who should be loyal to the government and grateful for its
protection, desirable (and here the language of the rule is far more
emphatic) because of the hardship which comes with the collection of
tax arrears.[42]

The third injunction is to avoid litigation. The Confucian precept that clan groups should settle disputes among themselves is naturally a point, but by no means the only point here. Many clan rules base their advice on experience rather than on theory. They point out that the clerks in the local government are like "tigers and wolves," that many magistrates are unreliable and unpredictable and some of them are corrupt and cruel, and that litigation is invariably time-consuming and, as a result, financially ruinous. It is for these practical reasons that one should avoid litigation as much as possible and use clan arbitration to settle disputes.[43]

Confucian theory assumed that one who cultivated himself and disciplined his family should be able to influence society at large and contribute his share of leadership to government administration. While this assumption applied to a significant extent to the scholar-officials in government service, it was by no means applicable to the common people or private citizens, as can be seen from the clans' eagerness to avoid government interference. Despite the Confucian theory, the state definitely exerted a negative influence upon the clan rules; that is, the rules reflect a distinct conflict of interest between the clan and the state. As might be expected, the clan rules do not admit this discrepancy. At most, they try to justify a certain degree of dissociation from the government by stretching the meanings of such virtues as loyalty and honesty and by emphasizing the desirability of law-abiding conduct according to the imperial injunctions, regardless of how the law and the government happen to be operating. In any case, what the clan rules value are principally order and security for the family and for the clan.

SCHOLAR-OFFICIAL INTERESTS IN THE CLAN RULES

Idealistic Interests

The idealism of the scholar-officials in the clan organizations should not be underestimated. In the first place, they assumed the responsibility of moral leadership. Through the clan organizations they supported, the clan rules they compiled, and other clan activities in which they played a prominent part, they helped to instill Confucian values in the people under their influence.[44] Their function has been stated in many ways in the clan rules. One such statement is often cited:

Once a scholar has earned his degree, Heaven places the destiny of the common people in his hands. If Heaven does not want to save the people, why should Heaven bring up scholar-officials? If scholar-officials do not save the people, what is the use of their being officials?[45]

A true Confucian scholar-official has important roles, even when he does not happen to be in office. Another common quotation explains what the scholar-officials' interests should be and should not be:

The local gentry [*hsiang-shen*, principally former officials and close relatives of officials] is the hope of the country. By living at home and promoting good, a gentleman can move and influence the district and the neighborhood. He can also help train the coming generation. His substantial and moral contributions are a hundred times greater than those of a mere scholar. The best thing for a gentleman to do is to uphold the worthy, to make known what is good, and to exercise his leadership in improving social customs. Short of this ideal, he should at least keep himself upright, discipline those close to him, and maintain his integrity in peace and quiet. There is less to be said for those who look around for land and houses to buy. Even worse are those who trample upon weak and helpless people.[46]

Some scholar-officials went beyond this requirement of moral leadership and made concrete contributions to their clan organizations. They selected responsible clan officers, built ancestral halls and acquired ritual lands to support them, compiled genealogies and clan rules, promoted cordial relations within the clan and the community, established charitable granaries for relief purposes, set up charitable schools to educate the poor youths of the clan, rewarded members for exemplary conduct, and restrained those who had misbehaved—all with the aim of creating a morally uplifting and practically gratifying way of life.[47]

One clan rule records a donation of charitable land in the following words:

My father, Hsün-ch'in, had always admired the way Fan Chung-yen helped the clan [with charitable estates]. During his twenty years of government service, he saved money from his salary, after providing for his parents, and used the money to help poor clan members. After his retirement, he studied the rituals at home, contributed ritual lands, provided graveyards for those without descendants, aided orphans, and helped widows. He did not finish these tasks before he died. On his deathbed, he expressed regret that no charitable estate had yet been established and no charitable school had yet been set up for the clan. This was more than thirty years ago. I am now about fifty years of age, old, sick, and unable to do much. Deeply sorrowful that the wishes of my late father have not been realized, I now donate five *mou* of the land he left me to the clan as charitable land.[48]

Such efforts from father to son and even through several generations sometimes led to the building up of large charitable estates, as another clan rule shows:

Hsün Shu of the Han period and Ying Chan of the Chin period, in dividing their properties to provide for their clan members, earned unanimous praise. The term "charitable estate," however, originated much later with Fan

Chung-yen of the Sung period. . . . We, the Chao clan, moved from Chiang-yin to Ch'ang-shu in the time of our ancestor Sung-yün. We have remained together for ten generations and behaved toward each other with loyalty and kindness. Now, clan members have multiplied, and many are in need. My late father, Wen-piao, donated more than 400 *mou* of land to the clan, but this has been sufficient only for the purpose of helping to pay for weddings and funerals. A charitable estate in order to be registered with the government as such must have 1,000 *mou*. I tried to save money for thirty years but could not reach the objective. Unfortunately, my eldest son had studied hard and died early, leaving no one to assist me in this task. Nevertheless, this wish has never left my mind for a single day. I now put down the tentative regulations of our charitable estate in the hope that coming generations will join in this common effort.[49]

For clans that did not have charitable estates, the donation of ritual land served many useful purposes. Sometimes the donation was made by a single scholar-official, as in the following case:

Thanks to the benefits bestowed by our ancestors, I was fortunate enough to get government degrees. I felt that I should not keep my salary from many years of government service to myself. Originally, in proposing the building of the ancestral hall, the buying of ritual land, and aid for the aged and the orphans in the clan, I intended to contribute some 3,000 taels of silver. I did not anticipate that a severe famine, together with deficits in the treasury, would lead to my contributing more than 5,000 taels for relief in the area in which I served as an official. Consequently, my properties were sold, my family was reduced to poverty, and my intention to help the clan was no longer matched by my ability to do so. In spite of the difficulty, I have decided to give up the 250 *mou* of land on which the living of my family normally depends. This property is worth approximately 1,000 taels. I have turned in the registration of the land and the names of the tenants, so that the land shall be recorded [as clan property] for the use of the ancestral hall in accordance with common decision of the clan members. The use of the rental income shall of course depend upon the amount of the two harvests each year. However, it shall be generally as follows: one-third to defray the expenses of the spring and autumn rituals; one-third as savings to earn interest in order to build the ancestral hall; and the remaining one-third for the relief of the poor and the aged, for helping pay for weddings and funerals, and for clan rewards. All these outlays shall be made twice a year. It is hoped that the whole clan will understand my humble wishes, give more attention to education, and distinguish themselves in filial piety and brotherly love.[50]

It was not easy for many clans to own common property in land. Even building and maintaining an ancestral hall took great efforts. One clan rule testifies to this fact:

We, the Shen clan, had an ancestral hall which was donated by our ancestors I-chai and Fu-chai. I-chai, after his first government degree, became secretary in the Secretariat-Chancellery. After many years of service, he was a circuit intendant of defense in Shantung province. Fu-chai, after the same degree, took the examination at the Directorate of Education and became a government school administrator. When they came home, they planned for the ancestral hall. Without much savings from their salaries, they could do no more than buy a house outside the West Gate, which was then used as our ancestral hall. Owing to subsequent difficulties, only its main hall could be reserved for the tablets of our ancestors; the other rooms were leased or rented to meet the annual expenses of the rituals. Later on, during the reign of Tao-kuang, as no one managed it, the tenants simply took it over. After repeated negotiations by Chiu-fu, the former clan head, the clan's property rights were restored but not without costing a great deal of money. This expense was met by the former clan head and my late father, who each contributed 100,000 coins, and by small contributions from other members. It was by no means easy. From then on, the ancestral hall was registered with the local government. In 1851, the tablet of our foremost ancestor was placed in it, and the spring and autumn rituals were performed. The ancestral hall was finally in good order. Yet it was soon destroyed during the Taiping Rebellion. Now, after the government has recaptured the area, our clan members have to plan for its restoration.[51]

The pattern of group life promoted and the values advocated by the scholar-officials had a pervading effect among the general populace and made many features of the clan organization lasting. This has been confirmed by contemporary field surveys. Even in such areas as Manchuria, where, owing to relatively recent settlement, formal clan organization was generally lacking, a meeting of clan members sometimes adopted certain regulations in the absence of a written clan rule. Where there was no clan head, influential leaders were called upon to mediate in disputes between fellow members and to promote clan welfare.[52]

In conclusion, it should be emphasized that the idealism of even the most idealistic scholar-officials was not morally doctrinaire; it took into consideration many realistic aspects of life. An essential task in the compilation of clan rules is to narrow the gap between theories and reality by adjusting the theories within permissible limits and applying them as far as may be practicable. The clan rules, collectively speaking, represent efforts to specify the Confucian virtues in the light of actual conditions.

Realistic Interests

Compiled as they were by scholar-officials, the clan rules naturally devote more space to the interests of upper-class families than to the interests of ordinary members. Most rules, for example, include sections on training in proper manners, the importance of dignity, strict segregation of the sexes, and how to deal with domestic servants. Above all, the rules are concerned with the achievement and perpetuation of scholar-official status. Many quote Chu Hsi to the effect that a family's first duty is to educate its members for official careers, with a view to raising the family's social position.[53] Though the vocation of scholar is unanimously upheld as the best, a few clan rules express some reservations about it. They point out that not all scholars succeed in getting higher degrees and becoming government officials. In fact, many scholars after having earned their first degree find it necessary to earn a living by teaching, a vocation which is not only financially unsatisfactory but sometimes demeaning.[54] Other frustrated scholars who turn to such irregular activities as contacting and negotiating with government offices on behalf of other people are in effect tampering with justice and should be prohibited from doing so.[55] Nevertheless, the majority of clan rules insist that a scholar, though frustrated, has many advantages. He is addressed as "sir," he has the privilege of calling on gentry families, he may have the opportunity of becoming a private staff member under an official, and he can apply his knowledge to such vocations or pursuits as bookkeeping, letter-writing, fortune-telling, astronomy, geomancy, medicine, and the arts. Moreover, scholarship has intrinsic moral value in self-cultivation.[56]

The scholar-official status, comprising both power and wealth, is as important to the clan as it is to the family. Many clan rules urge the use of the clan's common fund for the promotion of education. The rules of wealthy clans provide for assistance to promising young members who are financially in need of help, either through a charitable school or otherwise. Individual rules set aside funds for essay contests, permit students to use rooms in the ancestral hall as studies, provide assistance to candidates in the government examinations, and specify rewards for the successful candidates.[57] One clan rule is especially remarkable. It stipulates that any poor scholar in the clan who keeps on studying, whether he is working as a tutor or not, shall receive an annual stipend of 16,000 coins if he is preparing to take an examination, and half this amount if he is not.[58] This stipulation is noteworthy for both its encouragement of hopeful scholars and its comfort to frustrated ones.

The active promotion of education in the clan group is variously motivated. The altruism of Confucian scholars is one motive, but not a strong one. The immediate motivation is the prestige of the clan, which will be greatly enhanced by an increase in the number of its scholars, and especially its scholar-officials.[59] There is also a long-range motivation: the wish to have more educated members to take the lead in clan activities, to spread Confucian moral education, and to strengthen the clan organization.

This long-range motivation can be best understood in the context of ancestral rites, the most important clan activity in terms of holding the group together. According to the clan rules, only a small number of select members are entitled on ritual occasions to such privileges as toasting with sacrificial wine and attending the commensal banquet afterwards. These select members are those who have made some contribution to either the clan's welfare or its prestige. They include the clan officers, members whose conduct has been highly exemplary, and venerable elders, but they consist mainly of scholar-officials and those who have donated money and land to the clan. The special honor accorded them at the ancestral rites serves more purposes than one—to induce them to engage in additional clan activities, to show appreciation of their contributions so far, to encourage them to give more, and to inspire other members to become scholar-officials and active leaders in clan functions.[60]

If there had been no clan organization, the transmission and application of Confucian theories would perhaps have been limited to the individual families of scholar-officials. On the other hand, to keep the clan organization going, the active interest and financial support of scholar-official members were indispensable. Ideally a clan had certain properties in addition to its essential properties. The essential properties were those dedicated to the ancestral cult such as the ancestral hall, the ancestral graveyard, and ritual land to provide the expenses required by the rites. The additional properties were those devoted to welfare functions such as charitable land, school land, educational land, and charitable granaries for emergency relief. The main source of all these common properties was the generous endowment of a few scholar-official members, while the rest came from surplus income of previously donated land under good management and miscellaneous donations from the membership at large.[61]

A number of clan rules stipulate various measures for raising support from scholar-official members—for example, a voluntary or required contribution upon receiving a civil service appointment, earning a degree, acquiring land, or inheriting an estate.[62] Such measures were especially helpful in rehabilitating clans that had suffered from disruptions, notably those caused by the Taiping Rebellion.[63] Yet the formal existence of these regulations did not necessarily secure the support they aimed at. Of the 151 clans that were well enough organized to have genealogies printed from 1912 to 1936, only about one-third had some kind of common land, and few of these had more than 100 *mou*.[64] Only twelve clans had large charitable estates. One clan rule laments the fact that in a very wealthy area such as Soochow only a dozen or so clans had charitable estates larger than 1,000 *mou*.[65] As we have seen, the most generous endowment of common land often came from an individual family, with the father's example inspiring the son to follow suit.[66] This indicates that the appeals the clan rules made to their scholar-official members were not always answered.

During the Yung-cheng period, the Ch'ing government tried to encourage scholar-officials to donate their property to their clans for the benefit of poor clan members in return for public commendation and merit rating in the civil service. However, this encouragement did not produce the desired results. As a memorial of 1736 pointed out,

It has always been true that the improvement of social customs depends upon the initiative of leading families and large clans and that the implementation of moral education should begin with the officials. Among the scholar-officials in recent times, some have done well for their clans and communities. However, many have been selfish. Some of these selfish scholar-officials provide their own families with many comforts but leave their brothers and cousins in poverty and in need. Some of them have many servants, expensive carriages, and horses, while they pay no attention to their clan members who have neither enough clothing nor sufficient food. . . . When scholar-official families so comport themselves, how can the common people be blamed for trespassing against and disputing with one another?[67]

The records of a few charitable estates show notable success in overcoming many difficulties of management and in maintaining the system of relief over a long period of time.[68] These few, however, are outstanding exceptions. Much more often the failure of scholar-officials to respond adequately to the welfare needs of their clan left the clan organization with no alternative but to limit the scope of its activities, to the disadvantage of poor members. For example, numerous clan rules fail to mention any concrete measure to assist poor widows except a vague appeal to their close kin for voluntary help as a moral obligation. A number of clan rules require a fee for participation in ancestral rites. Some clan rules even insist on a donation before permitting memorial tablets of deceased members to be placed in the ancestral hall.[69] Under these circumstances, poor members could not help losing interest in the clan organization. To borrow the words of the anthropologist Redfield, there was a class barrier "preventing the cultural influence of the ceremonial centers from filtering down to the rural masses."[70] The transmission and application of the Confucian heritage became limited largely to the privileged and relatively well-to-do.

Even more detrimental to clan cohesion than the scholar-officials' inadequate support were the deviations in the conduct of their family members.[71] The clan rules reflect a painful awareness of certain common deviations; there are numerous prohibitions, for example, against concubinage not for the justifiable purpose of begetting an heir, against indulgence in luxuries, and against conspicuous consumption in funerals and weddings.[72] The clan rules condemn the young members of wealthy families for not being industrious and thrifty, for wasteful hobbies, and for forming gangs with bad company.[73] Gambling, drinking, and visiting prostitutes are regarded as ruinous.[74] Opium smoking is banned in the relatively recent clan rules.[75] The use of power and prestige to take advantage of fellow clan members is another kind of misconduct generally forbidden.[76]

The very fact that these deviations are so often mentioned is probably an indication of their frequency. The corrupting influence of a comfortable life seems to be stronger than the influence of the Confucian teachings and mores. Against socially undesirable tendencies, the moral appeals of the clan rules fought a losing battle. One clan rule goes so far as to observe that a family would do well to reside forty *li* away from the city, so that its members could not often go to the market place and expose themselves to corrupting influences.[77] This suggests the existence of a conflict between the Confucian value scheme and the city mode of living; the Confucian value scheme seems to be primarily the projection of primary group life in rural communities, while the city mode of living, at least from the Confucianist viewpoint, usually leads people astray.

Basically the clan rules, in transmitting and applying Confucian theories, suffered from an insoluble dilemma: the necessity of depending on scholar-official leadership, and the fact that this leadership was exercised by only a very few idealistic scholar-officials while their many colleagues contented themselves with a less demanding interpretation of proper Confucian conduct.

The Interpretation of Confucian Values

The scholar-officials had an active interest in interpreting Confucian values for the benefit of clan members. Their interpretations as seen in the clan rules tend to combine theoretical teachings and practical experience, ideals and realities. By way of illustration we shall consider the five leading areas of interpretation: parent-children relationships, relationships between brothers, marriage relationships, clan relationships, and finally community relationships and friendship.

In parent-children relationships, a number of clan rules extol the value of filial piety on lofty philosophical grounds. For example, one rule says: "Filial piety is a matter of intuitive knowledge and ability, and in fact exists in man's nature itself. Failure to render filial piety to parents is a crime against Heaven."[78] However, the leading justification for filial piety in the majority of clan rules is reasonable, humane, and practical. It holds that since the parents have done so much in rearing their children, it is only fair for children to express their gratitude in return by respecting, pleasing, and taking care of their parents.[79]

What, then, constitutes filial piety in behavioral terms? The clan rules do not approve of going to such extremes as the famous historical example of cutting out a piece of one's own flesh as medicine to cure the illness of a parent.[80] They confine themselves generally to an ideal on the one hand and a minimum requirement on the other. The ideal is to give the parents, in addition to their daily sustenance, a psychological satisfaction by understanding, anticipating, and meeting their wishes. Even when the parents happen to be senile, harsh, mistaken, or hard to please, a good son defers to them without showing displeasure, meanwhile trying tactfully to dissuade them from making serious mistakes or at least to shield them from their mistakes. The minimum requirement is to show due respect and to provide for the parents. Failure to exert efforts toward the ideal is not regarded as an offense, but failure to meet the minimum requirement is condemned as filial impiety.[81] According to field surveys, this minimum requirement has been the norm of conduct among the common people.[82]

To the value of filial piety, the clan rules add a realistic qualification. It is necessary for the parents to recognize the growing importance of their sons when they come of age and are ready to take over the family affairs. It is also desirable for the parents to exercise their authority without partiality or abuse, but for the well-being of all family members. In other words, parental authority, though supreme in the family, is not absolute. It is qualified by the value of mutual kindness and understanding. In fact, a number of clan rules maintain that it would be advisable for the parents to be patient and tolerant in overlooking minor faults.[83] Field surveys indicate that this advice agrees with the norm of conduct among the common people. The common people usually consult their grown-up sons.[84] They also consider it justifiable to disobey parental orders which are improper.[85]

Filial piety has a value greater than itself; the clan rules regard it as the basic element in all subordinate-superior relationships. Many rules project the spirit of filial piety into respect for elder brothers, for senior clan members, and for superiors in general.[86] One rule, for example, follows the *Hsiao-ching* in suggesting that sobriety in life, self-respect in official conduct, and honesty to friends are all necessary attributes of a pious son. In short, a pious son is an ideal gentleman.[87]

Actually, however, the value of brotherly love is not on the same basis as filial piety. An elder brother is only a leader among equals, with no authority to regard his younger brothers as subordinates. Hence, the clan rules uphold brotherly love mainly by appealing to the extension of filial piety, to sentimental affinity, and to the practical advantages of brothers' co-operating with one another. The behavioral content of brotherly love as given by the clan rules clearly underscores its co-operative nature: affection and kindness on the part of elder brothers, respect and deference on the part of younger brothers. Essentially this means that brothers should compromise and not quarrel.[88] One clan rule puts it plainly: "There will be no insoluble difficulty among brothers if one of them suppresses his anger and makes up with a few kind words."[89] Another rule warns that "one who tries to correct his brother's mistake should never be so overanxious as to hurt his brother's feelings, since this would not help the situation at all."[90]

Brotherly love is essential to the realization of the ideal of the large joint family in which several generations live together. Not only did the clan rules extol this ideal, but the state gave such families official commendations. On the other hand, many clan rules recognize the almost inevitable frictions in large joint families. These frictions stem from many factors: the varying earning powers of brothers, the sharing of goods and services in the household, disputes over inheritance, favoritism of parents, and especially jealousy and resentment between sisters-in-law. The root of all these frictions is the fact that each component conjugal unit has an equal share in the common family property and resources.[91]

The provisions of the clan rules vary on how to deal with these frictions. Some idealistic rules advocate the elimination or suppression of disharmony by moral persuasion and ethical control. On the other hand, a few realistic rules frankly admit the desirability of breaking up a large joint family when disharmony prevails, a course of action suggested long before by the famous *Yüan Shih Shih-fan* ("Social Code of the Yüan Family") of the Sung period. One exceptional rule has a modern ring: it criticizes the large joint family for discouraging the talent and initiative of its individual members.[92] However, the majority of clan rules are in favor of a compromise between the ideal and the reality. They suggest that each conjugal unit may cook and dine separately while continuing to live with the others in the same household. In this manner, brotherly love can still be maintained.[93] By implication, each unit may generally manage its own expenditures from whatever sources it has. This majority opinion is again in accord with the prevailing practice among the common people as revealed by recent field surveys. Apart from the common property of the joint family, each brother or his wife has usually held a "small property" of his or her own. Ordinarily, brothers have refrained from breaking up the joint family as long as their parents lived.[94] The Confucian values of filial piety and brotherly love have probably helped a great many families to live together within three generations in a tolerably harmonious atmosphere.

As for marriage relationships, the clan rules invariably stress the wife's virtuous qualities as being essential to the family welfare. Both for moralistic reasons and for reasons of social prestige, the clan rules insist that marriage should be arranged with a family of spotless background and matching social status. Some clan rules based upon experience have added two qualifications to this general proposition. First, they quote Hu Yüan of the Sung period in saying that "a wife should come from a family of slightly lower position and a daughter should be married off to a family of slightly better circumstances," so that married women will be satisfied. Second, they warn that social status should not be mistakenly equated with wealth and influence. Marriages motivated by considerations of wealth and influence frequently result in disputes and unhappy relations between the two families. Furthermore, wealthy and influential families often produce conceited and quarrelsome girls. The clan rules urge their members to look for girls with virtuous qualities, adding that such girls are likely to be found in families of high moral standing.[95]

After marriage, according to the clan rules, a woman should follow the spirit of the "Domestic Rules" in the *Li-chi.* Ideally she should observe female seclusion and sex segregation, take her place next to her husband in the family hierarchy, identify her interest with the entire family rather than with her conjugal unit only, and fulfill her duties toward all other family members. In case her husband is over forty years of age and she has not had an heir for him, she should agree to his taking a concubine. In return, a wife is entitled to the respect befitting her status and to protection by the family and clan against mistreatment by her husband.[96] On the mistreatment of a wife by her mother-in-law, however, the clan rules are silent.[97]

The rules generally forbid a wife to assume power over her husband, although a wife will be highly praised for assuming family responsibility, taking care of the family's needs, and raising her sons from childhood when her husband happens to be stupid, ill-behaved, or dead. The stipulation against a wife's assuming power under normal circumstances is dictated by the very nature of family organization. She must be made to subordinate herself to her parents-in-law and to get along well with her sisters-in-law for the sake of family order and harmony.[98] If she should assume power over her husband, she would tend to favor her own conjugal unit over other component units in the family, and she might even disregard the interest of the whole family in favor of her own family by birth. This general proposition does not really preclude a wife's assuming control of domestic matters so long as what she does is not in conflict with family order, family harmony, and family interest. As a recent study points out, traditionally and also nowadays, in many families it is the wife who keeps the keys of the chest and controls the domestic economy.[99]

With regard to clan relationships, one value which all clan rules highly cherish is that of clan leadership. According to the ancient classics, the leader should be chosen in accordance with the feudal principal of primogeniture—the heir of the eldest line of descent, called the *tsung-tzu*. The clan rules, however, have realistically departed from this principle. Some rules keep the *tsung-tzu* as a titular head mainly for ceremonial occasions,[100] but others never even mention the title. The formal leadership of the clan is generally invested by the rules in the *tsu-chang* or clan head. A man chosen for this position, according to the rules, should have a fairly high generation-age status and a respectable enough record in the way of fairness, honesty, integrity, capability, and experience to command the respect of most clan members. He need not be wealthy or a scholar-official,[101] but if he is, so much the better.[102] The system of clan heads functioned with considerable effectiveness in rural areas until quite recently. A clan head, even when he was old, weak, and poor, still enjoyed respect and mediated between clan members.[103] For such a person often embodied the kind of practical Confucian virtues which both the clan rules and the common people valued.

Another important value in clan relationships was cordiality and mutual respect among members. The main difficulty was class differentiation. Theoretically, the relationship between members was governed by their respective generation-age status; in reality, however, members of lower generation-age status might have higher social positions. The clan rules had to find a realistic solution to this problem. As one clan rule explains,

Close and remote kin all belong to one indivisible body. Good and bad members are of the same descent. The clan relationship forbids deviation and wrong conduct; the sentiment of oneness requires mutual respect and kindness. However, social customs have deteriorated and good feelings have become less and less apparent than before. Most people base their claims on the prestige of their families.

They remain friendly to one another only in consideration of individual fortunes. If their wealth is about equal, they call each other brothers. If not, they do not see each other. Because of some disagreement, they would humiliate senior clan members or trample upon helpless members or minority members, without regarding this conduct as wrong. Because of some trivial irritating words, a junior member offends a senior member and considers himself to be the stronger of the two. Some clan members live close to one another, yet do not offer to one another congratulations or condolences on appropriate occasions. Though some clan members live in the same neighborhood, they do not help each other in emergencies.[104]

Such attitudes are detrimental to clan cohesion; at the same time, they are understandable and frequently encountered. The best solution the clan rules can offer is for those with better social positions to respect those with a higher generation-age status, and also for the latter to make due allowance for the former.[105] The value of cordiality and mutual respect is thus redefined by the clan rules in terms of social reality.

Finally, with regard to community relationships, the clan rules betray a discrepancy between their moral ideals and their practical advice. They uphold the value of mutual help among community people and neighbors but fail to specify when and how such help is to be given. In emphasizing community harmony, the clan rules generally give the advice that one should defer to community people, tolerate one's neighbors, and be tactful toward all. This amounts to recommending a desirable minimum of involvement in community affairs.[106] One clan rule frankly states: "Avoid being a witness or a guarantor and you will have no worry in your life," and "As an old saying goes, 'Many good deeds are not as good as none.' "[107] Though this statement is exceptionally outspoken, many other clan rules in less obvious words express the same lukewarm attitude toward community life.

The clan rules look upon community relationships essentially from the family and the clan standpoint. The following is a typical example:

When someone in the clan suffers humiliation and mistreatment from outsiders, the clan members shall use reason to obtain justice. . . . However, when a clan member disobeys the clan rules, indulges himself in misconduct, arbitrarily dominates the community, infringes upon property of other people, or violates the law, the whole clan shall spare no effort to correct his mistakes. If he reforms, he deserves respect; if he disregards advice three times in succession and his misconduct might implicate other clan members, he should be brought to the ancestral hall to be reprimanded by the clan head or sent to the government for due punishment. The name of such an offender shall not be entered in the genealogy and upon his death he shall not be buried in the clan cemetery.[108]

The clan rules contribute to good community relations mainly by their negative restraining influence upon the aggressive misconduct of their members.[109]

On the question of friendship, the clan rules are emphatically against keeping bad company, and especially against having friends who fritter away their time in entertainment, amusement, and unbecoming activities. They advise that one should not have too many friends, since this would entail too much expense and not enough benefits. Instead, one should keep a few well-chosen friends who are reliable and have good moral qualities. But even with such desirable friends, caution is still the watchword. One clan rule after another explains that though friendship is one of the five cardinal relationships honored by Confucian ethics, the members should be careful about it. The way to treat good friends is to be neither too intimate nor too stern, but to be sincere and respectful.[110] Several clan rules offer the frank suggestion, however, that in dealing with friends one should be "squarely" upright but at the same time "roundly" circumspect, emphasizing one quality or the other as the situation may require.[111]

According to Confucian theory, as mentioned earlier, one should extend one's moral influence beyond the family and the clan to the community and society at large. By contrast, the value scheme of the clan rules is rather strictly family- and clan-oriented.[112] The cohesion and consolidation of the clan group, while desirable, undeniably led to tension in the community between the clan and other groups, notably the poor tenants on the clan property and especially the members of competing clans. At worst, the strong we-group feeling of the clans must have made for community disharmony, lasting resentment, and even inter-clan feuds.

Furthermore, in overemphasizing family and clan control over individuals, the clan rules point toward a kind of personality characterized by modesty, caution, and restraint. This type of personality was well suited to the stable social order in traditional China, which was rigid in structure and conventional in mores, but it was scarcely active, resolute, and energetic enough to fulfill the original Confucian ideal of leadership in the service of the community and the state.[113]

In the preceding pages, we have seen how the scholar-officials' idealistic interests mingled with realistic considerations in their interpretation of Confucian values. In some cases, the clan rules strengthened the Confucian theories by making them more specific and applicable; in others, they modified the Confucian teachings just enough to make them reasonably workable in the face of admitted difficulties. In a few instances, the clan rules in effect abandoned the Confucian teachings altogether. They no doubt made significant contributions in spreading this adapted version of Confucian doctrine, but they did so at the price of weakening the vitality and narrowing the outlook of traditional Confucianism.

THE CLAN RULES' RESPONSE TO PREVAILING SOCIAL CUSTOMS

The clan rules are interested more in promoting ideal social customs than in discussing prevailing social customs; nevertheless, they cannot ignore the existence of the latter, many of which clearly do not quite agree with the Confucian teachings. In this connection we shall here consider the clan rules' pronouncements on two issues: first, the religious customs which prevailed among both the scholar-official class and the common people; and second, the remarriage of widows, which during the Ch'ing period was condoned only among the poor.

Neo-Confucianism took a somewhat ambivalent position with regard to Buddhism and Taoism. It was opposed to such of their practices and customs as conflicted or tended to compete with Confucianism; but at the same time it absorbed certain of their religious concepts on the philosophical level which were acceptable from the Confucian viewpoint. The clan rules in following the Neo-Confucianist teachings generally maintained the same attitude. They raise four major objections to religious practices.[114] First, they make a distinction between acceptable religion and improper heretical beliefs. The acceptable religions are Buddhism and Taoism. Some clan rules admit that these religions are law-abiding and not without beneficial teachings, but it is generally argued that they are overly profound and abstract, and hence beyond the comprehension of the common people.[115] The improper and heretical beliefs are those which lead people to believe mistakenly in gods, demons, promised good fortunes, and threatened misfortunes. Especially dangerous are the subversive secret sects, which the law explicitly forbids.[116]

Second, the clan rules theoretically permit no religion to subvert the family and the clan institutions. Many of the rules forbid their members to join religious orders on the ground that parents do not rear their children for such a purpose.[117] Other rules advise their members not to employ Buddhist or Taoist priests to pray for one's deceased parents because this would impiously suggest that the parents have sinned.[118] The presence of priests at funerals is also viewed as contaminating the Confucian rites.[119]

Third, the rules are most severe in condemning the practice of holding religious services in mixed company, which violates the principle of sex segregation. It is regarded as revoltingly vulgar for females to brush shoulders with strangers, and especially for them to make pilgrimages to temples.[120]

Finally, the clan rules express mild skepticism about the magic powers claimed by various religions. Some rules raise the question whether prayers and offerings are not a form of bribery in the hope of buying good fortune, pointing out that if they are, the deities are hardly worthy of their names. Other rules give the rational advice that for illness one should spend one's money on medicines instead of on prayers and superstitious offerings.[121]

The attitude on religious practices in the clan rules largely parallels that of the state. A memorial of 1655, soon after the Manchu conquest of China proper, criticized the spread of religions, especially Buddhism, during the Ming period at the expense of the Confucian rites. It condemned the wasteful practice of burning offerings at funeral services, the error of asking priests to pray for good fortune in the alleged afterlife, the use of precious resources to build temples and pagodas, and noisy religious gatherings. The memorial also recalled that the first emperor of the Ming had forbidden sending children into religious orders.[122] The Sixteen Injunctions proclaimed by the Emperor K'anghsi explicitly prohibited heretical beliefs. By government order many heretical shrines and images were destroyed. One edict after another was issued during the reign of Ch'ien-lung against sorcery, prayers for the cure of illness, pilgrimage across provincial boundaries, secret sects, the use of Buddhist priests in funeral services, and women's visits to temples.[123] While the government made some allowance for the common people in the matter of following prevailing social customs, it adopted a stern attitude toward scholar-officials who actively spread unorthodox beliefs.[124] The prohibition of secret sects with rebellious tendencies was of course strictly enforced for reasons of state security.

There is nonetheless an appreciable distance between the attitude of the clan rules and that of the government. The clan rules express their objections to religious practices in relatively mild language, and rarely stipulate any punishment for disregarding these objections. In a few cases, they actually sanction placing Buddhist images next to the ancestral tablets and inviting Buddhist or Taoist monks to be the caretakers of ancestral halls.[125] It is well known that the common people remained largely syncretic and polytheistic in their beliefs and customs.[126]

The clan rules are ambivalent on the popular belief in geomancy—the belief in "wind and water," which holds that the burial site of an ancestor, because of its topographical location and geological composition, will have mysterious latent effects upon the good fortune or misfortune of the descendants. In many instances this belief had become inseparable from the prevailing customs of the ancestral cult and closely identified with the family interest. A few clan rules express disbelief in it; a few others openly affirm it. A large number of them, however, sidestep the main issue of belief or disbelief and concentrate on lesser issues. They suggest that one should not spend too much time or money in looking for good geomantic sites, since such sites are often found accidentally; that burials should not be postponed for a long period while a good site is being sought; and that buried bodies should not be shifted to another site which is believed by a geomantic practitioner to be better.[127] This last point was also emphasized by an imperial edict in 1735.[128]

The clan rules on the whole tolerate many religious practices. Their disapproval of religions in general is broad and vague; their objections to some religious practices are mild or ambivalent; and even more significantly, on many other religious customs they are altogether silent. Although the Confucian teachings on religion were occasionally reasserted in their original purity, in general they gave ground to prevailing social customs.

The remarriage of widows offers another interesting illustration of the relationship between the clan rules and social customs. It was a few of the leading Sung Confucianists who first insisted that "losing chastity is a serious matter, while death by starvation is by comparison a small matter." At the beginning of the Ming period, the government adopted the policy of rewarding chaste widows with official commendation. The Yung-cheng Emperor of the Ch'ing period encouraged the building of memorial halls in honor of chastity and filial piety. With such government encouragement, and with the spread of Neo-Confucian teachings, the scholar-official class came to regard the remarriage of widows as infamous.[129]

Many poor families however did permit the remarriage of widows and in some cases even collected money from the prospective husband. A large number of clan rules do not discuss the remarriage of widows (except to forbid the remarriage of a widow to a clan member, or particularly to a brother of her deceased husband, in accordance with the state law)[130]—probably because the practice was considered beyond hope of correction. A few rules give a realistic appraisal of the problem.[131] They admit that "although the principle of chastity requires a woman to be faithful to her husband forever, even after his death, such conduct cannot be expected of, or imposed upon, every widow." These clan rules argue that though it is disgraceful for widows to remarry, adultery without remarriage would be far more shameful.[132] In approving remarriage reluctantly, several clan rules add the condition that widows who remarry must leave their family property and children behind to be taken care of by kind members in the clan.[133]

Confucian morality permeated society. Though the poor permitted the remarriage of widows, they did so only on practical grounds and for lack of alternatives.[134] In most cases the clan organization was unable to take care of widows whose families could not provide for them. Though a number of clan rules prohibit mistreatment, pressure, and other aggressive acts against helpless widows, and some provide mild punishment for such acts, many rules stipulate no punishment at all. The few clans which were able to give relief to poor widows from their charitable estates are the exceptions. Ironically, many clan rules show an eagerness to reap prestige for the clan from a widow of distinguished chastity by authorizing the use of common funds to solicit a government commendation for her and to build her a commemorative arch.[135] Indeed, a chaste widow apparently got more consideration from the clan after her death than during her lifetime. It is reasonable to suggest, though, that if the clan organizations had been better able to protect and provide for poor widows, the clan rules might have been readier to prohibit remarriage in accordance with Neo-Confucianist doctrine.

Once again we find the clan rules, while adhering to Confucian theories in the main, making a concession to prevailing social customs. Such concessions were not made lightly. They were permissible only when clan rule compilers considered them to be matters of minor importance and when neither the Confucian theories, nor the existing circumstances, nor the clan institutions, were capable of furnishing a better solution.

CONCLUSION: THE GREAT TRADITION AND THE LITTLE TRADITIONS

The foregoing analysis has shown that the clan rules represent a second-layer value scheme in operation, beneath the idealistic value scheme of Confucian theory and above the *ad hoc* expediency of everyday family, clan, and social life. They form a sort of subdivision within Confucianism, mixed with the influence exerted by the state, upheld by the inspiration of certain model scholar-officials, compromised to a certain extent by practical considerations, and mainly dependent upon the amount of support they can derive from other scholar-officials and their families.

The clan rules appear to have been effective in helping people to live in accordance with Confucian ideals and to place a high value upon the Confucian virtues. However, the tremendous emphasis upon conformity also helped to produce a type of personality more introspective and circumspect, and less energetic and active, than what the Confucian theories originally visualized. The clan rules necessarily modified Confucian teachings in the light of practical experience. Their efforts to arrive at a really satisfactory synthesis, however, were limited—not only by the uncompromising nature of many of the Confucian theories, but also by certain weaknesses in the clan organization. These limitations unquestionably made the clan rules less effective in influencing the common people than they might otherwise have been. Nevertheless, not a few values upheld by the clan rules were generally accepted.

Taking the clan rules as a point of departure and looking in both directions—their modifications of the Confucian theories on the one hand, and their effects upon the common people on the other—we find a state of affairs that fits very well into the conceptual scheme of great tradition and little traditions proposed by Redfield. The great tradition and the little traditions are dependent on each other in a given civilization. The great tradition belongs to a reflective minority; it is consciously cultivated and handed down through schools and temples, by philosophers, theologians, teachers, and literary men. The little tradition develops and keeps itself going in the lives of the majority of unlettered people, especially those in village communities, who take it for granted for the most part and make no conscious effort to analyze it or refine it. Within the great tradition are several subdivisions. The two traditions act upon and bring about modifications in each other.[136]

In terms of this conceptual scheme, we may identify Confucianism as the great tradition, and the clan rules collectively as both one of the subdivisions of the great tradition and a channel of communication between it and the little traditions. Precisely because it is a channel of communication, the instrument of a deliberate effort to spread the great tradition in the hope of modifying the little traditions, it has produced modifications within the great tradition itself by drawing upon, accepting, and tolerating some aspects of the little traditions; and it has also produced effects upon the little traditions in getting some aspects of the great tradition more firmly established.

One question should be raised: Under what conditions does this communication and modification process take place? Redfield has discussed one such condition; we shall add two others. First, the great tradition and the little traditions must have a fairly large common basis. Redfield makes this point by describing the general characteristics of the peasant attitude: the state of mind at once practical and reverent, the inseparable mixture of prudence and piety, the chosen mode of sobriety, the values of decorum and decency, and the restraint placed upon the showing of emotion.[137] Obviously the Confucian virtues— morality, rituals, self-cultivation, and self-restraint—are elaborations of the same characteristics.

Second, if the great tradition is to adopt some modifications from or draw closer to the little traditions, there must already be some elements in the great tradition which point in the same direction. This is a condition which this paper has repeatedly emphasized. We may illustrate it by yet another example. It is well known that the common people in China have always tried to avoid the government as much as they could. We have seen the clan rules adopt the same attitude, a negative disinterestedness in social and political activities outside the clan except on the part of those few who succeed in becoming prominent scholar-officials, a modification which is at variance with a cardinal assumption of Confucian political theory. But this modification is not due to the influence of the little traditions or the practical experience of the common people alone. Perhaps even more important was the influence of the state, through the law, the imperial injunctions, and other edicts, which, though formally associated with the great tradition, tended to discourage social and political activities. Also influential in this respect was the narrow familism developed by the scholar-officials, again a natural outgrowth of the great tradition, with its emphasis on the family and the clan.

Third, for the great tradition to have any effect upon the little traditions, there must already exist a functional basis for that effect within the little traditions. This is a contribution of Professor Niida's analysis of field survey data. The best example is parental authority in the family hierarchy. The Confucian ethics emphasize it, and this emphasis has definitely had effects upon the common people. However, it is not the only explanation for the universal acceptance of parental authority. Functionally, the necessity of regulating the use of labor within the family has the same result.[138] The effect of the great tradition is to reinforce and deepen, rather than to create, the value of honoring parental authority.

Because these three conditions were fulfilled, the clan rules were able to serve as a channel of communication between the Confucian theories and the common people, and hence as an instrument for modifying both the Confucian heritage and the ways of the unlettered.

Charles O. Hucker

CONFUCIANISM AND THE CHINESE CENSORIAL SYSTEM

Students of China have long been in the habit of labeling as Confucian all the traits, attitudes, practices, and institutions that have given to the Chinese people their distinctive Chineseness. We do this despite recognizing that each of these things is associated with its own separate ideological complex and that each of these ideological complexes—separate "Confucianisms," so to speak—is in turn derived only in part from the teachings of Confucius and his immediate disciples. The problem of developing a system of terms that will clearly differentiate these Confucianisms from one another and from the Confucianism of Confucius himself has long perplexed us, as is indicated by several contributions to the present volume.

We are perhaps especially inclined to speak of the Confucian state, referring by this term to the centralized, non-feudal, bureaucratic, imperial governmental system that appeared under the Ch'in dynasty in 221 B.C. and persisted thereafter without many basic changes until it disappeared with the Ch'ing dynasty in 1912. We call this system a Confucian state because, through much of its history, the imperial government supported the ethical teachings of the classical Confucian thinkers and their later interpreters as an official orthodoxy and because the scholar-bureaucrats who staffed the government mostly considered themselves to be Confucians. We nevertheless recognize that the Confucianism that is manifested in the so-called Confucian state is necessarily a distorted reflection of the views on government that were held by Confucius, who lived in pre-imperial antiquity. It has become a truism that this "Imperial Confucianism" is, as a matter of fact, a mixture of elements from many philosophical traditions.

Other papers in this volume demonstrate in different ways the eclectic character of Imperial Confucianism. The present paper attempts to do so by examining the ideological implications of one of the Confucian state's most characteristic institutions, the censorial system, with special reference to its workings during the Ming dynasty (1368–1644).

IDEOLOGICAL FOUNDATIONS OF THE CONFUCIAN STATE

The two major philosophical systems that contributed significantly to the formation of the so-called Confucian state both developed in the latter part of the feudalistic Chou dynasty (1122?–256 B.C.), in a chaotic period of multi-state competition that preceded unification under a Ch'in emperor. These were classical Confucianism, as founded by Confucius (551–479 B.C.) and expounded by Mencius (373–288 B.C.) and Hsün-tzu (fl. third century B.C.), and Legalism, as developed principally by Kung-sun Yang ("Lord Shang," fl. fourth century B.C.) and Han Fei (d. 233 B.C.). Both were products of their time to such an extent that each in its own fashion is primarily a theory of government, offering the promise of social stability. Legalism is almost exclusively so, and Confucianism is concerned with human problems of a more general sort only because its conception of government is a moralistic and hence a broadly inclusive one. Neither system of thought in its early form emphasizes metaphysics or other abstract concerns.

As they are applicable to state administration, the Legalist and classical Confucian doctrines differ markedly. The Legalists maintain, on the one hand, that:

1. Man is amorally self-seeking.

2. The people exist for the sake of the state and its ruler.

3. The people must therefore be coerced into obedience by rewards and harsh punishments.

4. Law is a supreme, state-determined, amoral standard of conduct and must be enforced inflexibly.

5. Officials must be obedient instruments of the ruler's will, accountable to him alone.

6. Expediency must be the basis for all state policy and all state service.

7. The state can prosper only if it is organized for prompt and efficient implementation of the ruler's will.

Conversely, in direct contrast, the classical Confucians maintain that:

1. Man is morally perfectible.

2. The state and its ruler exist for the sake of the people.

3. The people must therefore be encouraged toward goodness by education and virtuous example.

4. Law is a necessary but necessarily fallible handmaiden of the natural moral order and must be enforced flexibly.

5. Officials must be morally superior men, loyal to the ruler but accountable primarily and in the last resort to Heaven.

6. Morality—specifically, the doctrines of good government expounded in the classics and manifested in the acts of worthy men of the past—must be the basis for all state policy and all state service.

7. The state can prosper only if its people possess the morale that comes from confidence in the ruler's virtue.

In even more generalized terms, it might be said simply that classical Confucianism stands for the claim of the people against the state, for the supremacy of morality. At the other pole, Legalism stands for the supremacy of the state and its inflexible law.

In 221 B.C. the state of Ch'in was able to unify all China into the imperial pattern that predominated thereafter by utilizing Legalist ideas. But the regime's harsh and totalitarian policies provoked great resentment, and popular rebellions overthrew the Ch'in in 207 B.C. Subsequent Chinese rulers, while perpetuating the Ch'in imperial structure of government and many Legalist-like attitudes that were inseparably associated with that structure, dared not openly espouse Legalist doctrines. Under the Former Han dynasty (202 B.C.–A.D. 9) it was specifically ruled that no adherent of Legalism could even be employed as an official, and Confucianism was accepted as the orthodox philosophical justification of the state. From that time on, Chinese dynasties practiced Confucian-approved ceremonies and entrusted administration to scholar-officials versed in the literature of classical Confucianism.

The Confucianism that was thus adopted as the state ideology was not, however, identical with classical Confucianism. It was an interpretation by the Han-dynasty scholar Tung Chung-shu (179–104 B.C.). His Imperial Confucianism, for one thing, is more strongly theistic and metaphysical than the original. Moreover, it glorifies the ruler almost to the point of negating the anti-statism of the classical doctrine. That is to say, it compromises with the inescapable fact that the Chinese had to live with and under an autocratic, centralized government on the Ch'in pattern. It is consequently an amalgam of classical Confucian and Legalist ideas.

This official state ideology, furthermore, was by no means a static thing. It was modified anew from time to time. Some Taoist and even Buddhist ideas eventually came to be added to the mixture, though Confucian and Legalist elements remained at all times predominant. So great a change was wrought in the ideological alignment during the Sung dynasty (960–1279) that Western writers habitually label the new mixture Neo-Confucianism, to differentiate it clearly from classical Confucianism. We make further refinements by speaking freely of Han Confucianism, Sung Confucianism, or Ming Confucianism, for example, as identifiable subcategories within the broadly inclusive category of Imperial Confucianism.

Imperial Confucianism in all its varieties represents a compromising of certain basic principles in classical Confucianism. The process of change is particularly evident in the case of law. The early Confucian distrust of law simply could not persist once all of China was united under a centralized, bureaucratically administered government. The very vastness of the empire and the ever-increasing complexity of governmental responsibilities, coupled with an inevitable desire for uniformity and consistency in relations between state and subject, required some degree of compromise with the Legalist insistence on codification. Before long imperial Confucianists were compiling voluminous law codes and commentaries. But this was not a complete Confucian surrender to Legalist principles; rather, it has been called the Confucianization of Chinese law. The Legalist form of law was retained, but the laws were infused with a Confucian spirit. Confucian ideas were consistently brought into battle to "temper the rigor of the law" by injecting into juristic considerations the classical Confucian emphases on ethics and *li*, propriety.[1] Thus law, though elaborately codified, remained the instrument of morality. A differentiation between Legalist and classical Confucian influences in Imperial Confucianism consequently cannot be based on whether or not legal sanctions are relied upon. It must rather be based on the purposes for which legal sanctions are sought. Reliance on law to promote the state at the expense of the people might represent the persistence of a Legalist spirit, and excessive punishment in any case can be attributed only to Legalist influences. But reliance on law to promote equity and popular well-being clearly suggests the persistence of a Confucian spirit within a Legalist-like apparatus.[2]

In imperial times there was no opportunity for classical Confucian ideals to persist unmodified. State subsidization of Confucianism forced would-be bureaucrats of all persuasions, whether or not they were Confucian by personal conviction, to become at least nominal Confucians in order to pass the civil-service examinations that qualified one for office. It was inevitable that the bureaucratic ranks would include some men whose personal convictions resembled Legalist principles more than classical Confucian ones. But no one labeled himself a Legalist, and Legalism was not perpetuated as a philosophic tradition. Since everyone was Confucian, Confucianism necessarily assimilated certain Legalist elements. On the other hand, those bureaucrats whose personal convictions genuinely resembled classical Confucian principles had no choice but to adapt themselves to prevailing conditions of government service. This required that they manifest in practice certain attitudes consonant with Legalist principles and not consonant with classical Confucian ones, since the structure and much of the rationale of the state they served was Legalistic. They did so unwittingly, no doubt. Thus the seventeenth-century scholar Ku Yen-wu could justifiably lament that self-styled Confucians of his time righteously denounced Ch'in Legalism while being unaware that they still served it.[3]

Inasmuch as these bureaucrats owed their official status to demonstrated competence in the classical Confucian literature, sincerely considered themselves to be latter-day protagonists of classical Confucianism, and would have rejected in alarm any intimation that they were un-Confucian, it would be presumptuous indeed to suggest that some of them were little more than Legalists in Confucian dress. The bureaucratic ideology did include a spectrum of ideas ranging from Legalist-like realism at one extreme to unchallengeably Confucian idealism at the other, it is true; but they were all within the expanded mainstream of Imperial Confucianism. It has been proposed, consequently, that in referring to the ideas and motivations of bureaucrats in imperial times we should replace the words Legalism and Confucianism with such terms as "rigorist Confucianism" and "humanist Confucianism." In the following account of how these poles of thought manifested themselves in the organization and functioning of the imperial censorial system, I shall continue to refer to them as Legalism and Confucianism, but only for the sake of convenience and without meaning to imply that the early doctrines persisted as separate and competing traditions.

CHINA'S CENSORIAL SYSTEM

The traditional Chinese censorship that concerns us here has nothing to do, characteristically, with governmental control of private publications and entertainments. It is not a normal police activity. Rather, it represents an organized and systematic effort by the government to police itself. The scope of this effort was very broad, encompassing all levels of administration, all governmental personnel, and both policy-formulating and policy-implementing processes. Against the formulators of policy, its weapon was remonstrance; against the implementers, impeachment.

As in most other governmental systems, control powers in traditional China were widely exercised. Officials of every status, and non-officials also, did commonly impeach (or at least denounce) governmental personnel and remonstrate with their governmental superiors. In China, as we shall subsequently see, there were special sanctions for the general exercise of the right or obligation to criticize; and we shall take note of this general diffusion of the right to criticize to the extent that

Legalist or Confucian principles are related to it. But criticism of this sort—unorganized and unsystematized—is not the type of censorship that primarily concerns us. Our concern is rather with specialized censorship: highly organized, highly systematized, and highly institutionalized, concentrated in particular governmental agencies and officials whose prescribed function was to impeach or remonstrate or both, vested with high prestige and special sanctions, providing a routine surveillance over all governmental activities. It is this censorship that is distinctively Chinese and that has specially important ideological implications.

By Ming times the system had attained a high degree of complexity, both in its organization and in its functioning. It included hundreds of censorial officials grouped in three categories of agencies: (1) a Chief Surveillance Office or Censorate at the capital, (2) six Offices of Scrutiny also at the capital, and (3) thirteen Provincial Surveillance Offices, one located at each provincial capital. Within these three types of agencies were concentrated the powers and obligations of what the Chinese traditionally called surveillance officials (*ch'a-kuan*) and remonstrance officials (*yen-kuan*). Censors, supervising secretaries, and surveillance commissioners all had specified surveillance and impeachment functions of general scope. The supervising secretaries also exercised specially prescribed controls over the flow of documents to and from the respective ministries; virtually all state documents passed through their hands, whether memorials to the throne or decrees from the throne, and were subject to a kind of editorial veto by the supervising secretaries. Specialized remonstrance functions were not so widely diffused, however, being the prescribed additional duty of the censors and supervising secretaries only—in Chinese terms, "the avenues of criticism" (*yen-lu*).[4]

The roots of this censorial system go deep into Chinese history, and the manner of its evolution reveals something of the conception that underlay it. What is particularly apparent is that the amalgamation of surveillance and remonstrance functions into one agency, whether the Censorate or the combined Offices of Scrutiny, was a relatively late development. In origin and early evolution, the two functions were quite distinct.[5]

The term by which Chinese censors have always been known, *yü-shih*, probably has had longer continuous use as an official title than any other in any language; for it appears as a title in oracle bone inscriptions of the Shang dynasty (traditional dates 1766–1122 B.C.) and was used thereafter until A.D. 1912. Until Ch'in times, the title seems principally to have been associated with men who were court recorders and chroniclers.[6] Then it was adopted for use in the imperial Censorate, which was a creation of the Ch'in and Han rulers. The *yü-shih* of early imperial times may indeed have engaged occasionally in remonstrance, as was every official's wont, but their prescribed and characteristic function as *yü-shih* was to provide disciplinary surveillance over the bureaucrats, as instruments of monarchical—or at least of central administrative—control.[7]

Specialized remonstrance functions developed separately, being associated with the titles Supervising Secretary (*chi-shih-chung*, literally "palace attendant") and Grand Remonstrant (*chien-i ta-fu*), which seem to have been originated by the Ch'in dynasty. For many centuries both these titles, or near equivalents, were reserved for eminent dignitaries considered suitable companions and mentors for the emperors. The early supervising secretaries, therefore, did not exercise the clerkly control over documents that occupied their successors in Ming times. But by the T'ang era (618–907) both titles had come to designate normal bureaucratic positions. The supervising secretaries then did control documents as later, and the grand remonstrants bore the heavy assigned responsibility of criticizing the emperor himself.[8]

The first tendencies toward amalgamation of the surveillance and remonstrance functions appeared early in the Sung period, when special policy censors (*yen-shih yü-shih*) were established in the Censorate to "speak out about affairs." For a time newly appointed censors were even punished if, within a short time following appointment, they failed to submit criticisms of important matters. But this first Censorate invasion of the remonstrators' preserve was short-lived, and the traditional distinctions were quickly restored.[9]

Full-scale amalgamation of the surveillance and remonstrance functions came about under the "barbarian" Yüan dynasty (1260–1368), which succeeded the Sung and directly preceded the Ming. The Mongol rulers promptly abolished the title and office of remonstrator. They also converted the supervising secretaries from document inspectors to court annalists. The Censorate—the supreme instrument of monarchical control—was, on the other hand, greatly expanded in staff and scope. Its net of disciplinary surveillance was now thrown more efficiently over the bureaucracy than ever before, through the creation of branch Censorates and the establishment of Provincial Surveillance Offices ancestral to those of the Ming period but directly subordinate administratively to the metropolitan Censorate. This was probably the most highly centralized and most widely pervasive control system of Chinese history. Apparently as a sop to the native tradition, the Mongol rulers assigned to censors the additional duty of remonstrance. Kubilai Khan (reigned 1260–94), for instance, once announced: "The duties of the Censorate's officials lie in speaking out straightforwardly. If We should by chance commit improprieties, let them speak out vigorously, without conceal-ment and without fearing others."[10] Hence the absorption of the re-monstrance function into the surveillance organization was complete, undoubtedly to the detriment of its effective exercise. With the excep-tion of a few years early in the Ming period, the office of remonstrator was not again reconstituted. But supervising secretaries were restored to their old document-control functions by the founder of the Ming dynasty, and thenceforth they and the censors, equally, shared both remonstrance and surveillance functions.

When we consider the censorial system and its history in the light of the Legalist-Confucian tension within Imperial Confucianism, a few significant correlations suggest themselves. For one thing, I am inclined to believe that the very existence of the censorial establishment mani-fests Legalist concepts of state organization; it appears to me that only Legalist-inclined minds, with a bureaucratic passion for impersonality, organizational clarity, and efficiency, could have produced such an elaborate mechanism. On the other hand, the presence within the sys-tem of specialized remonstrance agencies, agencies whose very exist-ence calls into question the inviolability of the ruler's will, clearly sug-gests a genuinely Confucian influence. Further, it would seem that the evolution of the system—the progressive extension and systematization of censorship and the progressive curtailment of its remonstrance func-tions—indicates an increasing stress on Legalist principles at the expense of classical Confucian ones. This accords well with the prevailing interpretation of Chinese institutional history, which emphasizes the steady growth of despotic absolutism.

THE FUNCTION OF SURVEILLANCE

There can be no reasonable doubt, I think, that the censorial func-tions of disciplinary surveillance and impeachment must be viewed as manifestations of Legalist rather than classical Confucian ideas.

The classical Confucian thinkers and the early Legalists equally emphasized the need to obtain proper men for government office. But, whereas the Legalists were also very concerned with the problem of controlling men once in office, the Confucian thinkers had no worries on this score. They seemed to feel that once a morally superior man had been placed in authority, he could be trusted to do what was right. As a matter of fact, the whole spirit of classical Confucian political thinking clearly implies that he should not be interfered with. In at-tempting to place superior men in office to restrain the rapacious rulers of their time, Confucius and his followers could not concede, for strategic reasons, that the officials themselves might require restraints. And there was a principle involved, too. Confucius said, "If the ruler himself is upright, all will go well even though he does not give orders. But if he himself is not upright, even though he gives orders, they will not be obeyed."[11] Thus officials should be restrained, not by coercive surveillance, but by the virtuous example of their superiors. This principle was clearly cited in a great policy debate between Confucian-minded scholars and Legalist-minded ministers at the Han court in 81 B.C. The scholars indignantly rebuked the ministers for having put to death two magistrates, saying: ". . . when members of the reigning clan are not upright, then laws and regulations are not enforced; when the ruler's right hand men are not upright, then treachery and evil flourish. . . . Thus, when a ruler commits a mistake, the minister should rectify it; when superiors err, inferiors should criticize them. When high ministers are upright, can magistrates be anything else? It is indeed highly remiss of you who are in actual control of administration to find fault with others instead of turning to examine your own persons."[12] Criticism should be directed by inferiors at superiors, not vice versa.

Especially, classical Confucian thought does not condone informers. Confucius said that a superior man "hates those who point out what is hateful in others," and one of his immediate disciples said, "I hate those who mistake tale-bearing for honesty." "The gentleman," in Confucius' definition, "calls attention to the good points in others; he does not call attention to their defects. The small man does just the reverse of this." And Mencius' contempt for informers is plain: "What future misery have they and ought they to endure," he exclaimed, "who talk of what is not good in others!"[13]

The attitude of the Legalists was quite the reverse. They not only condoned informers; they would have the ruler encourage them and rely on them. Disciplinary surveillance was in fact a foundation stone in the Legalist-conceived state, and it was under the Legalist-dominated Ch'in dynasty that censorship of this sort was first institutionalized. The Legalists specifically maintained that criticism should be directed by superiors at inferiors: "In case of transgression of the law," Kung-sun Yang said, "then those of higher rank criticize those of lower rank and degree."[14]

Kubilai Khan once said of his three top-level governmental organs that "the Secretariat is my left hand, the Bureau of Military Affairs is my right hand, and the Censorate is the means for my keeping both hands healthy."[15] This was the Legalist conception manifested also in the censorial system of Ming China: both the Censorate and the Offices of Scrutiny were intended primarily to check on the performance of duties by officials and to denounce those who were remiss. The functions of all governmental agencies were carefully prescribed, in great detail, in such codifications as the voluminous 228-chapter "Collected Institutes of the Ming" (*Ta Ming Hui-tien*). The number and nature of impeachment entries in the day-by-day chronicles called "The True Records of the Ming" (*Ming Shih-lu*) make it quite clear that the censorial officials ordinarily devoted most of their time and energy to seeing that these functions were in fact performed, and performed as prescribed. The censorial officials were numerous and ubiquitous, and their surveillance processes were themselves voluminously prescribed and carefully routinized. The censors, supervising secretaries, and provincial surveillance commissioners—one or another—routinely examined all state documents; they routinely inspected all state files and accounts; they routinely received and checked activity reports from other agencies; they routinely visited and interrogated every official in the emperor's employ; they accepted and investigated complaints from the people. In consequence of their investigations, they impeached officials high and low for violations of the law: for being indolent and inefficient, for delaying or otherwise hindering the execution of state business, for keeping improper records, for being ignorant of state regulations, for failing to observe prescribed administrative routine, for failing to enforce state policies or regulations, for unprescribed expenditures, for freeing the guilty or punishing the innocent, for exceeding their authority, etc.[16] A very large proportion of all their recorded activities reflects a striking, and strikingly Legalist, concern for legality and efficiency not only in the thinking of those who prescribed the censorial rules but in the thinking of those who wielded censorial powers.

Empowered and expected to find fault with their bureaucratic colleagues, the censorial officials must necessarily have gained great satisfaction from the exercise of their surveillance and impeachment functions, especially since they were ordinarily young and new to the civil service. It was established Ming policy to appoint neophytes, apparently in the expectation that, being merely on the threshold of government careers, they would have little to lose and much to gain by the zealous prosecution of their assigned duties. And it was certainly true that a censor or supervising secretary who made a name for himself as a zealous investigator and impeacher could expect to rise rapidly into high civil-service ranks. The dedicated impeacher was a kind of ideal. Probably the most renowned censor-in-chief of the whole Ming period, Ku Tso, who conducted a great purge of the Censorate itself in 1428, was known awesomely as "Sit-alone Ku" because of the detached, unfriendly scrutiny that he daily inflicted on his fellow participants in court assemblies.[17]

Considering the circumstances, it is not surprising that these officials at times had to be dissuaded from excesses of Legalist zeal. In 1434, for example, a censor impeached a provincial official for punishing a criminal too lightly, only to be rebuked mildly by the Hsüan-te Emperor (1425–35) on the decidedly non-Legalist premise that "punishing too lightly and punishing too severely are not the same."[18] And even the tyrannical Yung-lo Emperor (1402–24) lost patience at his supervising secretaries' penchant for denouncing petty clerical errors in documents: "You have all recently made an endless fuss," he complained to a group of them, "about trifling errors in memorials, and rejected the memorials for this reason. This is really too much! Paperwork annoyances accumulate in bureaucratic work, and one's energy is sometimes exhausted by them, so that it is difficult to avoid errors. Hereafter, whenever memorials include erroneous characters in numbers, dates, and so forth, just block them out and rectify them in marginal notations. There's no need to inform me!"[19]

Thus the very existence—and certainly the elaborateness—of the censorial surveillance processes would seem justifiable only on Legalist and not on classical Confucian premises; and censorial officials, in carrying out their duties, consistently acted in accordance with Legalist ideas. They were called upon to uphold the law and tried to do so, being literal about it at times to the point of pettiness.

But Confucian ideas did make some inroads into this sphere of Legalist influence. This is largely because in imperial times Chinese law, as we have seen above, was no longer the amoral law conceived by the early Legalists, but had become Confucianized and hence moralistic. While upholding the law, therefore, censorial officials at the same time upheld morality, which was prescribed by law. Their impeachments clearly reveal this dual concern, and to that extent they manifest a Confucian influence. Officials were denounced not only for their illegalities in a narrow sense, but for personal immorality as well: for licentiousness, for venality, for improprieties of all kinds. The great authoritarian grand secretary of the sixteenth century, Chang Chü-cheng, for example, was denounced by censors and other officials for failing to observe the mourning rituals prescribed by Confucian tradition after his father's death in 1577.[20]

Confucian influence is similarly observable at times in what the censorial officials did not do. A good example is another instance of a censorial denunciation of Chang Chü-cheng, this one in 1576. A scathing broadside denunciation of Chang was submitted by a censor named Liu T'ai. Liu had originally won entry into the civil service at examinations presided over by Chang, and it had been on Chang's recommendation that he had subsequently been appointed to the Censorate.

In the view of Ming Confucians, these circumstances created a master-disciple bond between the two men. Liu's denunciation of Chang consequently provoked counteraccusations that Liu's act was one of gross impropriety. Chang himself seems to have been shocked most by this un-Confucian aspect of the attack, reflecting that no such "disciple" had attacked his patron throughout the two centuries of the Ming dynasty's prior existence. And Liu himself, in his denunciation, felt it necessary to apologize for and justify his breach of Confucian propriety, for which he was ultimately dismissed from the civil service.[21]

This incident suggests how classical Confucian ideas—emphasizing morality and the importance of personal relationships—consistently intruded into censorial operations. But it is particularly instructive in demonstrating that these Confucian ideas remained entangled with Legalist ones. For Liu's justification of his impropriety is stated as follows:

When I attained my doctoral degree Chang Chü-cheng was chief examiner, and when I was serving in a ministry it was Chang Chü-cheng who recommended my selection as a censor. I have therefore been abundantly favored by Chang Chü-cheng. The reason why I now attack him so presumptuously is that *the ruler-minister relationship is so important a one that it excludes consideration of personal favors.* I hope that Your Majesty, taking note of my unenlightened earnestness, will curb the minister's power so as to prevent him from disrupting the proper course of events and *impeding the state.* Then, though I should die, I shall not have died in vain.[22]

Here Liu appealed to the Legalist doctrine that loyalty to one's ruler overrides the obligations inherent in other relationships. Moreover, though Liu had in passing accused Chang of personal immorality, the argument on which he relied most heavily in denouncing Chang is not a Confucian, moralistic one but a strictly Legalist one: that Chang's growing authority endangered the state. In an earlier section of his impeachment he had pointedly called the Emperor's attention to the fact, as he saw it, that people were coming to stand more in awe of Chang than of the throne. There could hardly be a more naked appeal to the Legalist inclinations of an emperor.

THE FUNCTION OF REMONSTRANCE

On the conceptual level, the censorial function of remonstrance is even more clearly linked to classical Confucian doctrines than those of surveillance and impeachment are linked to Legalist doctrines. And it is because censorial officials were at their dramatic best in remonstrating that the whole censorial system can easily be misinterpreted as an essentially Confucian institution.

The recorded history of the feudal Chou period abounds in examples of ministers—recorders among others—who doggedly remonstrated with rulers, often at great cost to themselves. The early Confucian thinkers, always interested in imposing their own notions of good government on the rulers of their time, patterned themselves after these models. Confucius often rebuked the powerful to their faces, as when he told a grandee who had complained that his people were committing burglary, "If only you were free from desire, they would not steal even if you paid them to."[23] And Mencius, in his wide travels, repeatedly said such bold things to rulers that they "changed countenance" or hastily changed the subject.[24] The early Confucian thinkers, therefore, became through their own conduct examples to be emulated by later remonstrators.

Some classical Confucian doctrines seem at first glance to contradict the notion that morally superior men must remonstrate with their superiors. The great Confucian emphasis on loyalty and filial piety, for example, would seem to discourage remonstrance. And some of Confucius' own statements add to the apparent confusion. He once said, "A ruler in employing his ministers should be guided solely by the prescriptions of ritual. Ministers in serving their ruler, solely by devotion to his cause." When a disciple asked how one's friends should be dealt with, Confucius said, "Inform them loyally and guide them discreetly. If that fails, then desist. Do not court humiliation."[25]

These are by no means the only statements attributed to Confucius that are difficult to reconcile with the general tenor of his doctrines. Whether or not it can be considered that Confucius actually said such things does not concern us here. The statements, genuine or spurious, exist in the Confucian lore that was part of every Ming minister's intellectual baggage. Taken in isolation, they could be understood to sanction certain kinds of ministerial subservience and opportunism as being Confucian, despite their being clearly out of harmony with general Confucian principles and in essential accord with the Legalist view of ministership. It must also be admitted that the authoritarian Chu Hsi form of Neo-Confucianism, which was the officially orthodox Imperial Confucianism of Ming times, might have dissuaded remonstrators by emphasizing loyalty to the ruler even more strongly as a cardinal virtue.

Subservience and opportunism, however, are quite clearly not ministerial qualities that the early Confucians admired and advocated. Their own conduct and an overwhelming proportion of their comments on what ministers ought to be make this clear. When asked by a disciple how a prince should be served, Confucius said, "Do not deceive him, but when necessary withstand him to his face." Confucius also told a grandee that "if a ruler's policies are bad and yet none of those about him oppose them, such spinelessness is enough to ruin a state."[26] The great early compendium "Record of Ceremonial" (*Li-chi*) quotes Confucius in the same vein repeatedly. For example, "for one whose place is near the throne, not to remonstrate is to hold his office idly for the sake of gain."[27] And Mencius mourned, "Now-a-days, the remonstrances of a minister are not followed, and his advice is not listened to, so that no blessings descend on the people."[28]

The Confucian precepts about being loyal and those about remonstrating were easily reconciled; for loyalty was defined as being more than subservience. "How can he be said to be truly loyal," Confucius asked, "who refrains from admonishing the object of his loyalty?"[29] And Mencius said, "He who restrains his prince loves his prince." Mencius expanded on this concept often, notably in the following passage:

Among the people of Ch'i there is no one who speaks to the king about benevolence and righteousness. Are they thus silent because they do not think that benevolence and righteousness are admirable? [No, but] in their hearts they say, "This man is not fit to be spoken with about benevolence and righteousness." Thus they manifest a disrespect than which there can be none greater. I do not dare to set forth before the king any but the ways of [the idealized legendary emperors] Yao and Shun. There is therefore no man of Ch'i who respects the king as much as I do.

Mencius also explained that "to urge one's sovereign to difficult achievements may be called showing respect for him. To set before him what is good and repress his perversities may be called showing reverence for him."[30]

Even parents, to whom in classical Confucianism one owes primary loyalty, cannot be immune from remonstrance: "to remonstrate with them gently without being weary . . . may be pronounced filial piety"; "when they have faults, to remonstrate with them, and yet not withstand them . . . —this is what is called the completion [by a son] of his proper services."[31] The Confucian primer, "The Classic of Filial Piety" (*Hsiao-ching*), stipulates that one should serve a superior by assenting to his good inclinations but rescuing him from his evil inclinations. It also reports that when a disciple asked if filial piety meant for the son to obey the father's orders, Confucius said, "How can you say this! How can you say this! . . . When confronted with unrighteousness, the son cannot but remonstrate with his father and the minister cannot but remonstrate with his ruler. Therefore, when confronted with unrighteousness, remonstrate against it! How could merely obeying the father's orders be considered filial piety?"[32]

The Confucian-minded scholars who in 81 B.C. debated state policy with Han ministers put this problem of remonstrance, as so many others, in clear perspective. When rebuked by one of the ministers for their trenchant criticisms, they replied:

Benighted provincials that we are, who have seldom crossed the precincts of this great court, we realize that our wild and uncouth speeches may indeed find no favor here even unto offending the authorities. Yet, so it seems to us, as a medicinal tonic, though bitter to the palate, still is of great benefit to the patient, so words of loyalty, though offensive to the ear, may also be found beneficial to mend one's morals. A great blessing is to be able to hear straight-forward denial; it cheapens one to hear nothing but adulatory praise. As swift winds are raging through the forest, so flattering words encompass the rich and powerful. After hearing daily at this court controlling myriads of *li* [Chinese miles] of territory nothing but servile aye-aye's, you hear now the straightforward nay-nay's of honest scholars. 'Tis indeed a great opportunity for you, Lord High Minister, to receive a well-needed physic. . . .[33]

So strong was the classical Confucian insistence on this aspect of the loyal minister's service that remonstrance became not only the right but the duty of all officials in the Confucian state. "Such criticism not only served the people—it prolonged the life of the dynasty."[34] Emperors consistently, therefore, actually called upon their officials to remonstrate. And, as we have seen, remonstrance was institutionalized by the establishment of special remonstrance officials.

This theoretical concept of remonstrance, as I have already suggested, draws little support from Legalist ideas. The Legalist view of kingship has no place for the moralistic criticisms of the rulers that classical Confucianism advocates, and it would seem to imply a distaste for the very fact of remonstrance. Nevertheless, remonstrators in practice could gain considerable inspiration from the Legalist teachings; for the Legalists did advocate remonstrance of certain sorts.

Legalist writings, as a matter of fact, often sanction the remonstrance principle in general terms. Han Fei listed paying no heed to remonstrance among ten common faults of rulers and praised at great length some of the remonstrators of ancient times.[35] He warned rulers against ignoring advice and alienating "frank and straightforward speakers." He particularly warned that "if the ruler takes advice only from ministers of high rank, refrains from comparing different opinions and testifying to the truth, and uses only one man as a channel of information, then ruin is possible."[36]

This last-mentioned warning, especially, could well have been used by later censorial officials against any attempt to curtail the censorial "avenues of criticism." As a matter of fact, the very concept of an institutionalized system of remonstrance, like that of an institutionalized system of surveillance and impeachment, is apparently more Legalist than Confucian in its implications. When one concedes an advantage in the ruler's having an abundance and variety of opinions available, one implies that no one adviser can be trusted to have opinions that are consistently right or to express them sincerely. Original Confucianism, by contrast, would seem to imply that it is perfectly proper for the ruler to be guided by only one adviser, if this adviser is the best man available by Confucian standards. It is in this sense that classical Confucianism is authoritarian and Legalism egalitarian. What is right, in Confucianism, has no necessary correlation at all with majority opinion—except, of course, in the very vague premise that the mass of the people somehow manifests the will of Heaven.

It is precisely in regard to this basic premise, however, that Legalism's special bias regarding remonstrance appears. Han Fei reported, "They say that, of old, Pien Ch'iao [a legendary physician], when treating serious diseases, pierced through bones with knives. So does the sage *on rescuing the state out of danger* offend the ruler's ear with loyal words."[37] This makes explicit a basic difference in the Legalist and classical Confucian views of ministerial remonstrance. The Legalist-minded remonstrator rebukes the ruler for neglecting his own selfish interest, whereas the Confucian-minded remonstrator rebukes the ruler for deviating from the natural moral order and the interests of the people. The difference lies in the content of remonstrance, not in the fact of remonstrance.

An even more notable difference lies in the contrasting manners of remonstrance advocated by the two schools. Confucius urged his disciples to be ready, if attacked, "to die for the good Way," and warned that "to see what is right and not to do it is cowardice."[38] The Confucian-minded remonstrator must therefore stand firm for his principles, remonstrating bluntly, unflinchingly, and without compromise, whatever the cost to himself. This view of remonstrance is ridiculous in Legalist eyes. According to Han Fei, the Legalist remonstrator, being thoroughly opportunistic, "must carefully observe the sovereign's feelings of love and hate before he starts persuading him."[39] Whatever end the minister may wish to attain, he amorally phrases his remonstrance as an appeal to the ruler's self-interest and self-esteem, allowing no possibility of a reaction injurious to himself. "In general," Han Fei said, "the business of the persuader is to embellish the pride and obliterate the shame of the persuaded." Han Fei devoted a long essay to a detailed discussion, in an utterly Machiavellian spirit, of the techniques that a minister must employ if he hopes to impose his will on a ruler. "The dragon is a creature which is docile and can be tamed and ridden," he concluded. "But under its neck are reversed scales which stick out a full foot, and anyone who comes in contact with them loses his life. A ruler of men is much like the dragon; he too has reversed scales, and an adviser who knows how to keep clear of them will not go far wrong."[40] This opportunism contrasts sharply with the Confucian ideal. The Confucian must not only remonstrate about morality; he must do so in a moral manner.

Officials of necessity had to compromise this classical Confucian ideal once a centralized empire had been established. The early thinkers had served and taught in a social context that permitted them more freedom of movement than bureaucrats were later to enjoy. When their remonstrances went unheeded—or when they felt that, in general, the moral Way did not prevail—Confucius and Mencius merely left the court in question and wandered to another in search of more congenial surroundings. Both repeatedly urged that this was the only course open to a moral minister.[41] Especially in late Chou times, the competition between states was so keen that a renowned adviser could get a hearing and a substantial emolument almost anywhere, and this circumstance naturally emboldened such men as Mencius to speak very frankly to their temporary patrons, in a spirit of independence and detachment. But after all China had been brought under one rule by the Ch'in and Han regimes, the bureaucrat found himself in a much less enviable position. He might remonstrate, and if his remonstrances went unheeded or if his principles were consistently violated he might indeed withdraw from service. But where could he go? There was no escaping the state; there was only one ruler and only one governmental structure. The bureaucrat had the choice of giving loyal service to a ruler whom he might consider evil or of abandoning entirely the sense of political responsibility that is imbedded in the whole Confucian ideology.

Faced by this choice, some frustrated Confucians abandoned bureaucratic careers in favor of the anchorite self-cultivation that had always been advocated by China's anti-government Taoist thinkers.[42] Other Confucians resolutely upheld the traditional ideal of political service by remonstrating fearlessly, at the risk of disgrace and perhaps death for themselves and their families. The typical Confucian of imperial times, however, was neither a die-hard moralist nor a resigned hermit, but a practicing bureaucrat in circumstances which frustrated attempts to embody all the classical Confucian virtues. He kept himself alive and prospering, and hence able to provide the filial service to his parents that classical Confucianism demanded, by being prudently subservient to his ruler in much the way Legalism had prescribed. On the other hand, his subservience was so modified by moralistic considerations as to make him much less than an ideal Legalist minister and at times to bring disgrace and hardship upon his family, in contravention of a basic Confucian principle.

The practice of remonstrance in Ming times illustrates both the dangers that forthright remonstrators encountered in China's imperial history and the extent to which Legalist influence had affected this Confucian-hallowed institution.

At the outset it must be noted that the Ming government was especially ill-suited to forthright remonstrance. Its tightly centralized structure was unusually conducive to autocracy, and its emperors as individuals tended to be unusually despotic and tyrannical. The tradition was created by the founder of the dynasty, the Hung-wu Emperor (1368–98), who had risen from the status of an illiterate commoner. Almost fanatically jealous of his imperial power, he tried to secure and preserve it by ruthless Legalist means. He eventually exterminated many of the powerful men who had helped him gain the throne, together with thousands of their relatives and friends, and reorganized the government so as to centralize all control in his own hands.

The Hung-wu Emperor had a particular aversion to some aspects of the classical Confucian heritage. He honored Confucius himself, apparently because Confucius seemed to favor loyalty, stability, and order. The "True Records," as a matter of fact, show the Hung-wu Emperor to have been an unwearying lecturer on the subject of Confucian-style ministerial responsibilities. But Mencius infuriated him. He thought Mencius was disrespectful to rulers (this was undoubtedly true), and he said that if Mencius were still alive he would have to be punished severely. In 1394 he created a special board of scholars to edit the text of Mencius' writings, purging those passages that spoke disparagingly of the position of rulers and those that urged ministers to remonstrate against rulers' errors. In all, eighty-five passages were struck out. The emasculated edition that resulted was printed and circulated for official use in all schools.[43]

The Hung-wu Emperor's successors were, for the most part, of the same breed. Occasionally a Confucian-minded ruler such as the Hsüan-te Emperor (1425–35) emerged, and all Ming emperors, in accordance with the now long-established custom, recurringly mouthed the phrases that enjoined officials to speak their minds freely. The acknowledged dogma was that "since antiquity sage emperors and enlightened kings have established remonstrance officials in the desire to hear of their own shortcomings."[44] Nevertheless, the Ming emperors were characteristically intolerant of criticism; and the codified regulations as well as the successive imperial exhortations of the Ming period, while showing the greatest care for systematic and effective censorial surveillance over the bureaucracy, give little evidence that censorial officials were seriously encouraged to engage in remonstrance at all.

The Ming emperors specifically deprived censorial officials of at least one of their traditional privileges, that of submitting statements based on hearsay evidence. This seems to have been a valuable privilege in prior periods, in regard to both remonstrating and impeaching. The Hung-wu Emperor once demoted a censor for criticizing an official on the basis of what he had "heard in the streets."[45] Later emperors repeatedly rebuked censorial officials for "making vexatious demands based on rumor."[46] In a nostalgic manner, Ming officials sometimes reminded emperors of this lost privilege of protecting their sources of information, but in vain.[47]

That many censorial—and other—officials of the Ming dynasty nevertheless withstood emperors to their faces in the best Confucian manner testifies to the vitality of the tradition. The Ming dynasty, as a matter of fact, had a disproportionately large number of China's most famous remonstrators, perhaps because Ming remonstrators were so likely to be martyred. Censorial duty was very hazardous duty. "Of all the inner and outer offices," one Ming source testifies, "none is more difficult than that of the censorial personnel; moreover, none is more dangerous than that of the censorial personnel."[48] The fifteenth-century censor Li Shih-mien may have survived (barely) after rebuking the Hung-hsi Emperor (1424–25) for consorting with concubines during the prescribed period of mourning for his father.[49] And the early-sixteenth-century censor Chang Ch'in may have gone unpunished when, by bolting a frontier gate and guarding it with a sword brandished before the Emperor's astonished outriders, he prevented the Cheng-te Emperor (1505–21) and all his entourage from touring beyond the Great Wall.[50] But the historical record generally is a sad one for Ming remonstrators.

The tide of remonstrance advanced and receded in accordance with the personalities of the emperors—or of those who dominated the emperors. During the decade 1424–35, when the liberal and tolerant Hung-hsi and Hsüan-te Emperors reigned, there was very little remonstrance, apparently because there seemed little need for it. The sixteenth century saw a notable increase, and by the 1620's the "True Records" give the impression that censorial officials did little else but remonstrate. This rising tide was a censorial response to challenges posed by particular emperors: the Cheng-te Emperor (1505–21), the Chia-ching Emperor (1521–67), the Wan-li Emperor (1572–1620), and especially the T'ien-ch'i Emperor (1620–27).

The Cheng-te Emperor was a frustrated bravo. He loved gaiety and adventure, and he often wandered about the capital in disguise, seeking thrills. Military adventures pleased him especially; he staged special campaigns for no purpose other than to give himself the thrill of field leadership. In consequence of fancied victories, he then conferred upon himself ever more distinguished military titles: for example, the Chen-kuo Duke, Grand Defender, Controller of the Troops, August Martial Generalissimo, Supreme Commander of All Military Affairs (all one title). Court ministers often protested against his inanities, which were both wasteful and undignified. In 1519, on the eve of a grand "campaign" in South China, censorial officials led a host of ministers in vigorous remonstrance. As a result at least 33 officials were imprisoned, 107 were forced to prostrate themselves in ranks outside the palace gate for five days, and 146 men (with some duplications) were subjected to floggings in open court, of which eleven men died.[51]

The Cheng-te Emperor had no son, and a cousin succeeded him as the Chia-ching Emperor in 1521. A great ceremonial dispute immediately arose. It originated in the new emperor's wish to honor his natural father in sacrificial worship with the title "imperial father." Censorial officials and others objected, insisting that the Emperor recognize his actual uncle, the Hung-chih Emperor (1487–1505), as "imperial father" and relegate his own father to the status of uncle for the purpose of imperial sacrifices. The controversy lasted for several years, becoming almost impossibly confusing in a welter of proposals, counterproposals, and compromises. Court ministers, with censorial officials consistently in the vanguard, submitted remonstrances wholesale: 31 men at a time, 64 at a time, more than 100 at a time, 32 at a time, etc. At one point 220 officials went en masse to chant remonstrances outside the palace, pound noisily on its gates, and prostrate themselves weeping and wailing at the entrance, all in protest against a new proposal by the Emperor. The record shows that 134 of the remonstrators were promptly imprisoned, that a large number of others were flogged in open court, that some were dismissed from service, and that others were exiled to frontier guard duty as common soldiers. At least nineteen men are reported to have died of their punishments.[52]

The long reign of the Wan-li Emperor was marked by numerous controversies in which groups of officials for the most part attacked other officials rather than the Emperor himself. But the Emperor's intolerance of remonstrance provoked one great court storm comparable to those just described. This was a controversy over what was called "the root of the state." The Emperor did not have a son by his empress but had several sons by concubines. When the two eldest sons were still children, censorial and other officials began insisting that the

Emperor nominate the elder as heir apparent so as to make secure "the root of the state"—that is, the imperial succession. The Emperor refused. The resulting battle of wills between the Emperor and the officialdom lasted from 1586 until 1601, when the Emperor at last gave in. In the meantime dozens of officials had been degraded or banished for their temerity in remonstrating, and foundations had been laid for the bitter court factionalism that was to disrupt the Emperor's remaining years.[53]

The T'ien-ch'i era was characterized by almost incessant remonstrance. The T'ien-ch'i Emperor was indecisive and indolent and came increasingly to be dominated in all things by flattering, self-seeking palace intimates—especially an ambitious wet-nurse named Madame K'o and the most powerful eunuch of all Chinese history, Wei Chung-hsien. Palace intrigues were viewed with special alarm because China was just then being threatened seriously by the Manchus and because popular rebellions were becoming a serious domestic problem. Censors and supervising secretaries submitted remonstrances almost daily warning the Emperor against eunuch influence, and finally Wei Chung-hsien in 1624–26 conducted a great purge of the administration designed to quell all such opposition. Hundreds of officials lost their posts or were otherwise punished; fourteen ringleaders of the remonstrators lost their lives.[54] Eight of these were censors, and two were supervising secretaries. One list of 319 men who were punished one way or another for opposing Wei Chung-hsien includes a total of 76 censorial officials (censors and supervising secretaries combined)—more men than were listed in any of seven other categories.[55]

Such "remonstrance disasters" as these reveal that Ming censorial officials unquestionably did remonstrate forthrightly at great cost to themselves. Innumerable examples of individual remonstrators could be added. As regards the fact of upright remonstrance, consequently, there can be no doubt about the influence of the classical Confucian ideal. But it is equally clear that, in some of these cases and in others not yet discussed, Confucian-style remonstrance served ends that were consonant only with Legalist principles and, furthermore, was carried out in a distinctively Legalist manner.

It is particularly noteworthy that two of the great remonstrance controversies had to do with problems of imperial succession. I cannot pretend to understand all the subtle nuances of the "Great Ceremonial Debate" provoked by the Chia-ching Emperor. Shorn of its less important ramifications, however, the controversy pitted the Emperor and a few advisers (denounced as sycophants by Confucian-minded historians) against the mass of the officialdom over a problem in the peculiarly Confucian sphere of filial piety. The remarkable thing is that the officials gave precedence to the imperial succession over natural succession—that is, they insisted that the Emperor owed greater honor to his imperial predecessor than to his own father. That the debate took place at all reflects a Confucian penchant among the officials for moralistic problems which old-time Legalists would have considered trivial. But what the officials argued for seems to reflect Legalist conceptions of kingship and the state and is not consonant with classical Confucianism's conception of filial duty.

The case of the "root of the state" reflects the Ming entanglement of Legalist and classical Confucian ideas even more markedly. The Wan-li Emperor, whatever his actual motivations, took the seemingly Confucian stand that he would not designate an heir apparent until his sons had matured sufficiently to enable him to evaluate their potentialities. Against this, the officials consistently advocated compliance with "the laws of the dynastic founders," which they understood to require early recognition of the eldest imperial son as heir apparent. I have not observed any appeal in the officials' arguments to what is right or wise in moral terms; they merely invoked, in Legalist-sounding fashion, the sanction of law. The fact that the law involved here was the household law or precedents of the Ming emperors permits the rationalization that the officials were being Confucian in outlook after all, by urging the Emperor to show filial respect for the wishes of his ancestors. However, the officials' insistence that the imperial succession was the "root of the state" clearly violates a cardinal Confucian maxim, that the root of the state is the people.

The censorial attack on the eunuch Wei Chung-hsien during the 1620's culminated Ming officials' many warnings against eunuch influence. Eunuchs had contributed to the ruin of earlier dynasties, notably the Han and the T'ang; and the tyrannical Hung-wu Emperor had been clear-sighted enough to insist that palace eunuchs be limited in numbers and restrained from administrative activities. But his successors did not comply with these particular "laws of the dynastic founders," and authority repeatedly fell into eunuch hands. Historians agree that eunuch influence was significantly facilitated by the establishment in 1429 of a palace school for eunuchs. This violated the Hung-wu Emperor's doctrine that eunuchs should be kept illiterate, and it made possible the extensive eunuch interference in administration that marked the whole last half of the Ming era. So far as I can ascertain, no official protested against the establishment of the school. Perhaps officials at this time put their trust in the Confucian doctrine that education brings moral improvement. But as the eunuchs' influence on government increased, the officials did increasingly protest against it. They accused individual eunuchs of personal immorality, and they objected on moral grounds to many of the things eunuchs did. In general remonstrances against eunuch influence, however, they seldom relied on Confucian arguments—for example, that eunuchs, being by their nature the most unprincipled, subservient, and self-seeking of state employees, could be expected to exploit the people mercilessly rather than provide moral examples for them. Instead, they relied on the Legalist arguments that had been so well understood by the Hung-wu Emperor. They argued that eunuchs by their nature tended to usurp imperial authority and hence endangered the dynasty (as distinct from the people).[56] "They ought altogether to be kept at a distance, not being permitted to get control of affairs," one early official warned. "The events of Han and T'ang provide clear warnings."[57] The seventeenth-century denunciations of Wei Chung-hsien were in the same vein. His immorality was denounced, true; but the argument relied on most heavily was that he had usurped imperial authority.[58]

Similar Legalist-sounding arguments can be found, intermixed with Confucian-sounding ones, in the proposals for new policies and for more effective implementing of existing policies with which censorial officials deluged the throne throughout the Ming period.

Many censorial proposals, as well as direct remonstrances, reveal a genuinely Confucian concern for the popular well-being. Censorial officials, for one thing, often urged tax remissions for the people in areas where there had been natural disasters.[59] In the 1620's, when defense needs brought about general tax increases, censorial pressure for reductions and remissions became intense. The T'ien-ch'i Emperor responded that the censors and supervising secretaries—like the Confucian-minded scholars of 81 B.C. in the view of the Han ministers—were unrealistic and refused to recognize the practical problems of national defense. And the Emperor was similarly unimpressed by censorial suggestions that new financial needs be met, not by new taxes imposed on the people, but by palace economies.[60]

The treatment of prisoners was another subject that consistently aroused censorial officials to plead for humaneness in accordance with the Confucian tradition. They objected to the use of such torture instruments as the infamous cangue, and they repeatedly asked for medical assistance to sick prisoners.[61]

But Legalist attitudes were also regularly manifested in censorial proposals. They consistently appeared, for example, in proposals about national defense. The T'ien-ch'i Emperor may have thought his officials were impractical in this regard, but the "True Records" show that censors and supervising secretaries were in fact staunch champions of military preparedness—not only preparedness against outside invasion but preparedness against domestic rebellions. The old Confucian doctrine that moral virtue triumphs over force had apparently been completely discarded; not a single censorial proposal that I have encountered is based even indirectly on this doctrine. Instead, the censorial officials repeatedly urged that public order be forcibly maintained and the dynasty preserved. Though they generally seemed to believe that these ends could be achieved without increasing the people's burdens, as we have just seen, they adamantly demanded more defense funds, more effective recruitment and training, more effective checks against troop desertions, and so on. One censor in 1622 even proposed that taxes be specially increased to provide for an empire-wide local militia system, a proposal that is reported to have delighted the Emperor.[62]

Even as early as the 1420's and 1430's, when there was no significant outside threat to China and there was a notably high level of domestic contentment, censorial officials nevertheless were constantly harping on military preparedness and the possibility of domestic rebellion. Though much "banditry" could be attributed to popular distress and hence, according to Han Confucianism, interpreted as manifestations of Heaven's displeasure with the government, the censors and supervising secretaries generally advocated severely repressive policies. In 1428, for example, a censor-in-chief submitted the following proposal:

For the capture of fierce bandits there already are rules about promotions and rewards, but the law for catching bandits should emphasize severity. If it is severe, then men will not dare to become bandits and the catchers on their part will entirely exhaust their strength. Henceforth, whenever fierce bandits plunder and pillage an area, officials and lesser functionaries of the guards and civil offices and also the village and neighborhood chiefs should all be sent out to serve as soldiers so that captures might be effected. If they make captures within two months they will escape punishment, but if they have failed to do so when the time limit has expired, then, in accordance with the rules, they should be turned over for punishment. Moreover, when fierce bandits have been captured they should be asked during trial to identify the guards or battalions or subprefectures or counties in which they were formerly registered. If they had been soldiers, then those in charge of the appropriate troops should be punished. If they had been civilians, then the appropriate civil officials, lesser functionaries, village elders, and neighborhood chiefs should be punished. If this is done then men will know what to dread.[63]

The proposal shows an obvious correlation with the Legalist doctrine of handling men by rewards and, especially, punishments; and of meting out punishments rigorously according to fixed principles of group responsibility.

Another sphere in which Ming censorial officials showed a Legalist bias is that of administrative procedures. In general, the extreme systematization of procedures and the inflexible, objective standards of performance that characterize the Legalist doctrines were consistently advocated by Ming censors and supervising secretaries. Again and again we find them proposing elaborate procedural rules to be imposed on the officialdom[64]—understandably enough, since such rules (together with the objective evaluation techniques they would give rise to) would immensely simplify their own job of denouncing wrongdoing. This is perhaps one of the most obvious instances of the prevalence of Legalist-like attitudes in the bureaucracy.

The result of the Confucian-Legalist mixture that thus dominated censorial thinking was often a proposal to obtain ends sanctified by classical Confucianism by means advocated in Legalism. In 1624, for example, the censor-in-chief Kao P'an-lung proposed detailed regulations about local government that were prefaced with these remarks:

. . . If the subprefectures and counties are worthily administered, then the people are contented. If not, then the people are not contented. However, the empire includes 221 subprefectures and 1,166 counties. How is it possible in all cases to obtain those who are worthy of employment? Those who are worthy regard the ruler as Heaven, which cannot be deceived, and regard the people as their sons, who cannot be injured. Their observance of the law and performance of duty proceed from the fact that what the mind cannot endure is not done. Lesser men, being given something to admire, are stimulated to do good; being given something to dread, they *do not dare do what is not good.* But totally inferior men do not know what their duties are or what the regulations are; they merely give rein to their desires. This is preying on the people. Therefore, in governing, one should select those who are worthy and talented, get rid of those who prey on the people, and restrain mediocre men. *Mediocre men are the most numerous in the empire. They should be restrained by laws,* which do no harm to the worthy. Thus the prefect restrains the subprefectures and counties; the circuit intendants restrain the prefectures; and the governor and regional inspector restrain all without exception. These restraints cause everyone to observe the law, as in the case of farmlands having dividing lines which no one thinks to overstep. Then the empire is well governed![65]

Kao's emphasis on the contentment of the people, and a large proportion of the terminology he employs, reflect classical Confucian ideals. But his assumption that the masses of people are amoral and must be restrained by laws so that they "do not dare do what is not good" is altogether Legalist.

The same Legalist cynicism was dominant, in a different context, in a suggestion by the early-sixteenth-century supervising secretary Liu Ch'ih. When sweeping staff changes were being considered, Liu advised the Cheng-te Emperor to retain old hands in top-level administrative posts rather than bring in new blood. He did not argue that the existing executives were virtuous or that their experience was valuable. He merely suggested, curtly and cynically, that "it is better to keep a sated tiger than a hungry one"[66]—an apt maxim for any Legalist-minded employer of men, but hardly the voice of Confucian idealism.

CONCLUSION

China's traditional censorial institution has been extravagantly praised and extravagantly criticized. Some authorities have considered it an instrument of monarchical control over the bureaucracy, whereas others have considered it an instrument of bureaucratic control over the monarch. These conflicting evaluations naturally derive from the fact that the censorial system—like Imperial Confucianism as a whole—was based on discordant ideological premises. It was not the idealized creation of either Confucius or Kung-sun Yang; it was a complex of inherited practices that were influenced by both. From one point of view it was a Confucian institution, and from another it was a Legalist institution.

The individual censorial official was representative of the whole body of traditional Chinese bureaucrats in that, as an Imperial Confucianist, he was neither a genuine classical Confucian nor a genuine Legalist in outlook. His was not an either-or situation. His impeachment function stemmed from Legalist roots, but his manner of exercising it drew heavily on classical Confucianism. Conversely, his remonstrance function was primarily Confucian in origin, but his manner of remonstrating was often consonant with pure Legalism. We can do no more than speculate about his actual motivations.

Students of Ming documents are easily tempted to conclude that Ming censorial officials—and Ming bureaucrats in general—were in fact principally Legalist-minded in their motivations. The abject servility that characterized ministerial statements to the throne in this period is very striking. Not only were they filled with excessively humble terminology; they consistently attributed to the emperor—the "ruler-father" in their words—wisdom, goodness, and all other admirable qualities. However pointed the criticism, it was always sheathed in implications that the emperor, though wise and good, had been misled and deceived by unscrupulous attendants or advisers. However degenerate the emperor, he was always pictured in official documents as a paragon of virtue whose gracious benefits no minister could ever wholly requite. Thus, in practice, Ming ministers perfectly exemplified Han Fei's Legalist maxim that "the business of the persuader is to embellish the pride and obliterate the shame of the persuaded," and their servile expressions implied complete acceptance of the Legalist concept of ruler-subject relations.

Given the circumstances, these expressions of Legalist import could perhaps be dismissed as insincere conventions—as tactical devices employed by ministers with tongue in cheek because they could not be avoided. The evidence strongly suggests, however, that most of these protestations of abject devotion were perfectly sincere. Consider, for example, the case of the censor Tso Kuang-tou, who saw service under three emperors and was finally tortured to death in prison in 1625 at the instigation of the eunuch Wei Chung-hsien and by order of the T'ien-ch'i Emperor. After weeks of almost daily torture, on the point of death and apparently without any hope for his own survival or for his family's escape from ruin, he scribbled a series of private notes to his sons that include these statements:

At this moment my pain and distress are extreme; I can no longer even walk a step. In the middle of the night the pain gets still worse. If I want water to drink, none is at hand. Death! Death! *Only thus can I make recompense to the Emperor and to the two imperial ancestors.* . . . The bones of my whole body are broken, and my flesh is bloodlogged. . . . This loyal heart came to be at odds with powerful villains and brought about this sore calamity. All sorts of punishments I have willingly endured. Since I have already argued at the risk of my life, why need I shrink from running against the spear and dying? *My body belongs to my ruler-father.* I am lucky I shall not die in the arms of my wife and children; for I have found the proper place to die! *I only regret that this blood-filled heart has not been able to make recompense to my ruler,* and that my aged parents cannot once again see my face. This will be my remorse in Hades! . . . My misery is extreme; my pain is extreme. Why do I live on? Why do I cling to life? Death! Only thus can I make recompense to the Emperor and to the two imperial ancestors in Heaven.[67]

In the circumstances, hypocrisy is almost inconceivable.

The ruler-minister relationship envisioned by Confucius and Mencius had clearly succumbed; Tso's abject protestations of devotion to the throne are the badge of the Legalist sycophant. Paradoxically enough, however, any early Legalist would have repudiated Tso instantly, whereas Confucius would undoubtedly have acknowledged kinship with him. For Tso—and Ming ministers generally—did not mouth these phrases opportunistically. They *believed* them. And the capacity for selfless commitment that this implies is peculiarly Confucian and utterly foreign to the ideal minister in the Legalist conception.

Perhaps it is primarily in this sense that Imperial Confucianists remained Confucians at heart after all.

3 Arts and Letters

James F. Cahill

CONFUCIAN ELEMENTS
IN THE THEORY OF PAINTING

In most modern studies of Chinese painting, there has been a curious lack of reference to Confucian thought as a force in the creation of art and in the formulation of art theory. Such infrequent mentions of it as one encounters tend to be brief and unsympathetic. For Confucianism is reserved the doctrine that painting, by depicting exemplary themes, can serve as a didactic tool or a moralizing influence; all those views which involve the communication of intuitive knowledge, the operation of an aesthetic sense, or the embodiment of individual feeling are attributed to the working of Taoist and Buddhist ideas and attitudes. Similarly in matters of style: it is sometimes suggested that the Confucian temperament, when it found graphic expression, produced a dry academicism, while Taoism and Ch'an Buddhism fostered the more spontaneous, "untrammeled" styles.

The neglect and distortion of the role of Confucianism in the arts probably results in part from an extension into aesthetics of the unfortunately widespread view of the Confucian tradition as "inherently reactionary and sterile . . . in the political and social sphere,"[1] or from a supposition that its rationalist bent denied it any place in what are essentially non-rational processes, the production and appreciation of works of art. In addition, the more immediate appeal of Taoism and Buddhism—especially Ch'an Buddhism—to the modern Western mind has led to a concentration of attention upon Taoist and Buddhist elements in art as in other areas of Chinese culture. Added to these causes is the profound and protracted impact of one school of Japanese art-historical scholarship, itself strongly influenced by Zen Buddhist attitudes and tea-cult aesthetic, upon pioneer Western studies of Chinese art. Fenollosa, seeing the Chinese through Japanese eyes, announced that "a very large part of the finest thought and standards of living that have gone into Chinese life, and the finest part of what has issued therefrom in literature and art, have been strongly tinged with Buddhism."[2] Arthur Waley, at an early and still somewhat incautious stage in his distinguished career as an Orientalist, revealed a similar dependence on Japanese attitudes when he wrote: "it is in the language of Zen that, after the twelfth century, art is usually discussed in China and Japan."[3] We must assume that Waley had not yet acquainted himself with Sung and later Chinese art literature when he made this statement; because to have made it after having done so would be quite impossible.

The lack of any sound basis in Chinese art theory for such pronouncements has not diminished their effect on Occidental thinking. The fact that the great majority of painters who were philosophically committed at all (at least of those whose broader beliefs can be ascertained), and the majority of poets and calligraphers as well, were Confucian scholars, is unnoticed or ignored; or else it is supposed that when these scholars wrote and painted, they were somehow transformed into Taoists and Buddhists, and that when they thought and theorized about art, they renounced their basic beliefs and turned to the rival systems for guidance.

Joseph Levenson, for example, considering the Ming dynasty development of *wen-jen hua,* "literati painting" or painting done by scholar-amateurs, asks: "How could Ming Confucian intellectuals . . . reject the theory of painting which they associated with learning, and prize instead an anti-intellectual theory of mystical abstraction from civilized concerns? One might expect that Confucian traditionalists . . . would feel an affinity with an academic northern aesthetic and oppose the southern Ch'an . . . "[4] Levenson's association of *wen-jen hua* theory with Ch'an ideals seems to be based chiefly on the famous analogy drawn by Tung Ch'i-ch'ang (1555–1636), a leading late Ming spokesman for the literati painting movement, between the "northern and southern schools" of painting and the two branches of Ch'an. But the main outlines of *wen-jen hua* theory had been established some five centuries before Tung's time; and his analogy does not, in any event, require any close connection between literati painting and Ch'an.[5]

A characterization of literati painting by Alexander Soper may serve to represent another class of statements about painting of this school, which suppose it to have affinities with Taoism: "The 'literary man's style' of painting became the implacable enemy of the Academy and all its ways, the enemy of all organization, training, and planning; almost the exponent in art of a free, untrammeled Taoism, protesting against Confucian punctiliousness and formality."[6]

Among the relatively few contributions toward a more correct assessment of the influence of Confucian thought on art is the writing of Victoria Contag, who has sought to relate the Chinese artists' modes of representing a "second reality," especially within the literati painting school, to Neo-Confucian theories of knowledge.[7] Stimulating and convincing as I find her arguments, I do not intend here to follow her example and move between philosophy and painting proper. I shall instead confine myself to the exploration of possible instances of dependence upon Confucian ideas, not in the practice of painting but in the theory of it. I shall be concerned especially with the Sung dynasty *wen-jen hua* theorists' treatment of two problems: the function of painting, and the nature of expression in painting. But we must give some preliminary consideration to the ways in which these same problems were dealt with before the emergence of *wen-jen hua* theory, and to some Chinese notions about the other arts. In doing so, we shall begin to work toward a definition of what is specifically Confucian in Chinese art theory and criticism.

It is not easy to determine what views of painting prevailed during the Han and Six Dynasties periods, since so little writing on the subject has survived from these periods, and so little of that is pertinent to the broad questions proposed above. The earliest references to painting in extant literature seem to assign to it three main functions: the illustrative, the magical, and the moral. The first two, which are not of much concern to us here, since they play no important part in the later theorizing, may be illustrated with quotations from the *Lun Heng* by Wang Ch'ung (second century A.D.):

Popular legends, though not true, are impressively portrayed, and by these artistic representations, even wise and intelligent men are taken in.

By making pictures of dragons the duke of She succeeded in bringing down a real dragon.

The district magistrates of our time are in the habit of having peach-trees cut down and carved into human statues, which they place by the gate, and they paint the shapes of tigers on the door screens . . . These carvings and paintings of images are intended to ward off evil influences.[8]

Chang Yen-yüan, ninth-century author of *Li-tai Ming-hua Chi* ("Record of Famous Painters of Successive Dynasties"), draws upon Han dynasty and later sources in presenting the third, the moralistic view of painting. He cites the portraits of eminent and virtuous men which were painted on the walls of the Cloud Terrace and Unicorn Pavilion in the Han dynasty, and comments: "For to see the good serves to warn against evil, and the sight of evil serves to make men long for wisdom." He quotes the words of Ts'ao Chih (192–232) describing how people seeing pictures of noble rulers "look up in reverence," while those who see paintings of degenerate rulers are "moved to sadness."

Chang concludes: "From this we may know that paintings are the means by which events are preserved in a state in which they serve as models [for the virtuous] and warnings [to the evil]."[9]

The narrowness of these views of painting, and the probable reason for their early abandonment, lies in their failure to make any allowance for aesthetic value; a picture was successful to the degree that its subject was well chosen and convincingly portrayed. The often quoted remark of Han Fei-tzu, that "dogs and horses are difficult [to paint] and demons and divinities easy . . . because dogs and horses are things generally and commonly seen," whereas no one can reasonably dispute the painter's portrayal of demons,[10] implies such an absence of aesthetic criteria: exempt from criticism based on the verisimilitude of his picture, the painter of imaginary subjects should find his task "easy," since no other standard of judgment is to be applied to his work.

But there was no denying the wide variations in both style and artistic quality between one picture and another, variations for which these concepts of painting were helpless to account. One can imagine the perplexity of the Han dynasty Confucian scholar who happened to be endowed with an aesthetic sense, and found himself preferring a good picture of an unelevating subject to a bad one with a noble theme. Morality and art: what is the relationship between the two, and how are they to be reconciled? A problem which could not but concern the ethically-minded Confucianists, and which, in various later periods, was to trouble them in its relation to literature. Han Yü (768–824), who was "far more concerned with content than with elegance of language,"[11] was nonetheless suspected by the severe Chou Tun-i, an eleventh century Neo-Confucianist, of being too interested in style, not enough in doctrine. "Literary style is a matter of *art*," writes Chou, "whereas morals and virtue [*tao-te*] are the matters of real substance. If one is sincere about these substantial matters and uses art, then the beauty of one's writing will be loved; loved, it will be transmitted." Style for Chou Tun-i was only an ornament to ethical and moral content which made this content easier to assimilate; for him, "literature is the vehicle of Tao."[12] Some such means of justifying the elements of style and beauty in painting may have occurred to the Han dynasty scholars; the literature of the time gives us no clue.

Whether or not because of this inherent weakness, the notion that painting derives moral value from moral subject matter was fairly short-lived. By the time of Chang Yen-yüan, as we shall see when we come to consider Chang's own ideas (as distinct from those which he quotes or alludes to), it was invoked from the past in a somewhat ceremonious manner, but practically ignored in actual judgments of painters and paintings. Therefore, to offer this view of painting as if it were the sole contribution of Confucianism to painting theory, as some writers have done, is quite misleading. We can only say that it appears to have been the dominant Confucian view in the Han dynasty; what later Confucians thought about painting is what we shall try to determine later in this paper.

It is in the succeeding Six Dynasties period that serious discussions of painting are first composed, and new theories put forth which seek to enlarge the function of painting beyond that of simple representation. In the small corpus of critical and theoretical writing on the subject which survives from this period, we may distinguish two more or less distinct (although overlapping and not contradictory) notions about the nature and purpose of the art.

The first conceived of painting as the creation of *images*, symbolic abstractions of natural form and phenomena, analogous to the hexagrams of the *I-ching* ("Book of Changes") or to the graphs of the written language. A fifth century artist, Wang Wei, begins his essay on landscape painting by quoting a letter from his contemporary, Yen Yen-chih, who states that painting "is not to be practiced and accomplished merely as a craft; it should be regarded as of the same order as the images of the *Changes*."[18] Seen in this way, painting becomes a means of understanding and interpreting natural phenomena.

The other, historically more important view of painting in the Six Dynasties regarded it as the embodiment of the artist's feeling toward the thing depicted; the painter imbues his pictures of natural objects or scenes with some expression of his emotional responses to what he sees. If he is successful, the person who sees his picture will respond to it in a like way. The essay on landscape painting by Tsung Ping, a contemporary of the fifth-century Wang Wei quoted above, opens with a statement, typical for the period, of the ideal man's response to nature: "The sage, harboring the Tao, responds to external objects; the wise man, purifying his emotions, savors the images of things." Further on in his essay, Tsung explains the application of this response to painting: "Now, if one who considers the right principle to be *response to his eyes and accord with his heart* perfects his skill in keeping with this principle, then all eyes will respond to, and all hearts be in accord with [his paintings]."[14]

Although these two concepts are here treated as separate, they need not be. The one operation could, of course, serve as a means of accomplishing the other; the artist might embody his personal vision of the world and his understanding of it in his mode of transforming visual impressions into "images." But there was an element of Taoist mysticism as well, and perhaps of even older Chinese beliefs, involved in this notion of "response." The objects of nature, whether or not animate in the usual sense, were considered to be animated by spirit, or "souls" (*shen*). The human soul responds to these in a spiritual accord (*shen-hui*), which is the source of the sensitive man's profound feeling toward nature—or, if these "souls" have been captured by an equally sensitive artist, toward a picture of nature.

The closest philosophical affinities of both the above-mentioned theories seem to be with the school of Neo-Taoism, the strongest current of thought in this period. The view of paintings as abstractions of visual impressions into "images," symbolizing the configurations of the physical world, has its roots in the cosmological speculations of the Neo-Taoist school, and especially in its theory of the creation and significance of images.[15] The other view, that which sees painting as the embodiment of the artist's feeling toward his subject, is based upon what Fung Yu-lan terms the "sentimentalist" branch of the school,[16] wherein a deliberate savoring of physical sensations, and an intensification and refinement of one's emotional responses to them, overcame for a time the old warnings against attachment to sensible objects. That romantic movement whose adherents figure in the anecdotes of the *Shih-shuo Hsin-yü* seems also to have given rise to the earliest painting of natural scenery for its own sake in China, and to the belief that painting can serve as a substitute for that scenery by evoking the same feelings which the actual scene would evoke.

Something which corresponds to this latter view appears in literary theory of the time. The early-sixth-century *Wen-hsin Tiao-lung*, for example, describes how the poet is deeply moved by the changing aspects of the world, and continues: "And so the poet's response to things starts up an endless chain of associations; he lingers among myriad images, immerses himself in sights and sounds. He captures in words the spirit of things, depicts their appearance," calling forth a corresponding response in the reader of his poem.[17]

It is interesting to see how these ideas fared, and what others arose, in the T'ang dynasty, when Confucianism regained its dominance in government and society and the leading writers were Confucian scholars. The most important T'ang treatise on painting, Chang Yen-yüan's *Li-tai Ming-hua chi* opens with a fanfare of high-sounding generalities, meant to impress upon the reader the metaphysical and moral value of the art of painting:

Now painting is a thing which accomplishes the purpose of civilizing teaching and helps to maintain the social relationships. It penetrates completely the divine permutations of Nature and fathoms recondite and subtle things. Its merit is equal to that of any of the Six Arts of antiquity and it moves side by side with the Four Seasons. It proceeds from Nature itself and not from human invention.[18]

This introduction includes, as we have seen, a formal exposition of the moralistic, "elevated subject-matter" view of painting, with quotations from early writings. One might be tempted to concentrate upon this introduction, with all its echoes of Confucian ethical doctrine, in seeking to characterize the Confucian tone of Chang's book. But to do so would be a mistake, I think; for there is little indication in the rest of the book that Chang himself took very seriously the ideas he presents in his introduction. William Acker, who translated the first portion of the book, along with two earlier critical texts, says of such conventional references as Chang's: "Painting must be fitted into the Confucian scheme of the universe, and its uses demonstrated in terms of traditional Chinese thought.[19] Having discharged their responsibilities as Confucians in their prefatory remarks, he suggests, the critics go on to discuss individual painters and their works in quite different terms. They express admiration for vigorous or elegant brushwork, for noble conceptions, for brilliant stylistic innovations.

What is significantly absent from Chang Yen-yüan's own opinions, as they are stated or reflected in the main body of his book, is any reflection of that Six Dynasties view described above according to which a painting conveys the emotional response of the artist to the depicted object. In his treatment of the Sui dynasty painter Chan Tzu-ch'ien, Chang quotes the opinion of an early T'ang Buddhist monk, which includes the phrase *ch'u-wu liu-ch'ing*, "Aroused by things of the world he consigned his emotions to them"—that is, embodied his feelings about them in pictures of them.[20] But nowhere does Chang himself adopt this theory of expression. A possible reason for Chang's rejection of it, I think, is that its implications of *attachment to material objects* made it unacceptable to the Confucian literatus. This possibility will be further considered below.

There are scattered indications in *Li-tai Ming-hua Chi* that Chang, dissatisfied both with the Six Dynasties view of painting (with its overtones of Taoist mysticism) and with the older Confucian view which attached moral value to paintings by virtue of the subjects they portrayed, was working toward a new concept by which a Confucian humanist approach could be applied to his judgments of artistic quality, a concept which would also be in harmony with traditional Confucian attitudes toward the other arts. He begins to touch on the relationship between the artist and his work. "From ancient times," he writes, "those who have excelled in painting have all been men robed and capped and of noble descent, retired scholars and lofty-minded men . . ."[21] Two centuries later, this same observation was to be made to support one of the basic tenets of *wen-jen hua* theory. Nobility in a painting, the literati theorists were to insist, can only be a reflection of nobility in the man; the man is revealed in his works. Chang Yen-yüan's comments on the landscapist Yang Yen (late eighth century) contain the earliest statement I know in the painting literature of this notion of "seeing the man in his works":

He was polished and elegant in his bearing, vigorous and energetic in his spirit and feeling. He was good at landscapes; his works were lofty and unusual, refined and strong . . . When I look at the late Mr. Yang's landscape pictures, I see in imagination what he was as a man—his imposing stature and unconventionality.[22]

But Chang fails to develop the idea further. In another passage he takes up the fundamental Confucian problem of aesthetic quality vs. moral significance, making the same distinction between *te* (virtue) and *i* (art) as Chou Tun-i, quoted above, was to make for literature. He writes:

I, Yen-yüan, consider that the classical statement, "the perfection of virtue is primary, and the perfection of art follows afterward"[23] is a doctrine which disdains the man who has art but lacks virtue. But the princely man "follows the dictates of loving-kindness and seeks delight in the arts."[24] . . . Here, the Master esteems virtue and art equally. So, if someone lacks virtue but at least attains art, then even though he labor as hard as a menial servant, what cause is there for regret in this?[25]

From Chang's remarks, we see that the problem of the relative importance of "virtue" and "art," in the artist, in the creative process, and in the finished work, was a persisting one. In fact, Chang drew this distinction from the Classics, where it was made for music and ceremonial; Chou Tun-i later drew upon the same source. But Chang, as a critic of painting, is faced with (and ignores) a problem with which Chou was not troubled: what *is* moral significance, "virtue," in painting? Literature can state moral truths directly; painting cannot, except perhaps by its choice of subject; and as Acker remarks of the critics who make much of virtue, "there is no suggestion anywhere that they would have placed a bad portrait of Confucius above a good painting of an Imperial Concubine, merely because of the former's power to inspire emotions of reverence."[26]

The *wen-jen hua* theorists of the Northern Sung period were to arrive at a solution of this problem by finding for painting a means other than descriptive by which it might communicate the ineffable thoughts, the transient feeling, the very nature, of an admirable man, and so contribute to the moral betterment of those who see it. Before going on to this development, however, I should like to consider the occurrence of related ideas in the theory of the other arts: music, literature, and calligraphy.

The notion of art as communication, or as a revelation of the nature of the artist, appears earlier in other arts than it does in painting. Literature, as an extension of the basic verbal mode of expressing thought and feeling, is understandably the first to be treated in this way. In the *Lun Heng* we find the following observations:

The *I-ching* says that the feelings of a sage appear from his utterances . . . When he has expressed himself in writing, his true feeling shines forth in all its splendour.

The greater a man's virtue, the more refined is his literary work.[27]

The sixth-century *Shih P'in* says of the works of T'ao Ch'ien (365–427): "Whenever we look at his writings we see, in imagination, the virtue of the man."[28] And in the *Wen-hsin Tiao-lung*, about the same period, we are told that "although the period of a writer may be far removed in time, so that no one can see his face, yet if we look into his literary works, we seem immediately to see his mind."[29]

In speaking of literature as a revelation of thought and feeling, the writers of the above passages were probably not referring only—or even primarily—to straightforward statement or description of particular ideas and emotions. What is implicitly contained in a piece of writing, they felt, is likely to be more profound and meaningful than what is explicitly stated. In critical discussions of poetry and other literary forms, one finds frequent references to conceptions which "go beyond the literal meaning of the words." From early times, it was recognized that direct prose discourse is not always adequate to convey all that the writer might conceive and experience. The "Great Commentary" (*Ta-chuan*) to the *I-ching* says: "Writing cannot express words completely, and words cannot express thought completely."[30] It goes on to advance the notion that images and symbols can be used to embody ideas too abstruse for verbal statement. One of the Neo-Confucian philosophers, the eleventh-century Hsieh Liang-tso, writes:

The words of the sage are near and familiar, but his meaning is nonetheless far-reaching; for words have a limited capacity, while his meaning is inexhaustible. The words, being limited, can be investigated through commentaries; but the meaning, being inexhaustible, must be grasped with the spirit. It is like becoming acquainted with a man: yesterday you knew only his face, today you know his mind.[31]

The expression of what is either too subtle or too strong for direct verbal statement is one of the functions of art within the Confucian system. Both poetry (considered as a spontaneous outburst of song) and music are said to come forth when emotion becomes too intense and language, used in the ordinary way, will no longer suffice for its expression. The "Great Preface" ("Ta-hsü") to the *Shih-ching* says: "The feelings stir within one, and are embodied in speech. When speech is insufficient, one sighs and exclaims them. When sighs and exclamations are insufficient, one makes songs of them."[32]

An almost identical statement is applied to music at the end of the "Record of Music" ("Yüeh-chi") section of the *Li-chi*.[33] Chu Hsi (1130–1200), the leading figure in Neo-Confucianism, echoes this theory of poetry when he writes:

Someone asked me, "Why is poetry composed?" I answered, "Man is born in a state of tranquillity; that is his innate nature. He responds to things and is moved; that is the desire of his nature. Now, when he has such desire, he cannot be without thought, nor can he, when he thinks, be without speech. When he speaks, then what he cannot completely express in words comes out in sighing and singing; and this overflow always has a spontaneous music and rhythm, which the poet cannot restrain. This is why poems are made."[34]

The only function of the ordinary man's expressions of emotion, presumably, is the one suggested by the passages above: catharsis, the discharging of feelings which, if pent up, might becloud the mind. When the superior man sets forth his feelings, however, another purpose is served, and one which gives art a moral value in the Confucian system. If the manifold facets of the mind, the character, the exemplary qualities, of the superior man can be communicated in a work of art, then those qualities may be perceived by others and implanted in them. The "Record of Music" presents this view at length, making such statements as "Music displays the virtue [of the composer]" and "When notes that are correct affect men, a corresponding correct spirit responds to them [from within]." The superior man, it says, "makes extensive use of music in order to perfect his instructions."[35] The continuation of the conversation quoted above from the writing of Chu Hsi contains a clear statement of this idea of art serving as "instruction" by embodying the superior man's responses:

He then asked, "If this is so, what is the value of poetry as instruction?" I answered, "Poetry is the product of man's response to external things, embodied in words. Now, what the mind responds to may be either corrupt or correct; therefore, what is embodied in words may be either good or bad. But the sages above us respond only to what is correct, so that their words are all worthy of serving as instruction."[36]

Besides serving as "instruction," the artistic creations of superior men also fulfill another Confucian desideratum, that of fostering a community of spirit and a continuity of basic values within the literati tradition. The scholar who comes to understand his predecessors by reading their literary works or savoring their calligraphy and painting comes also to feel a kinship with them; another dimension, an extension into the past, is added to his sense of communion with men of like mind. Mencius saw literature as a means of nourishing such feelings of affinity:

The scholar whose virtue is most distinguished in the kingdom will make friends of all the other virtuous scholars of the kingdom. When the scholar feels that his friendship with all the virtuous scholars of the kingdom does not suffice, he proceeds to consider the men of antiquity. Reciting their poems, reading their writings, how can he help but come to know what they were as men?[37]

With the recognition of the long-established importance of these beliefs about the function of art, we begin to see why a new concept of painting was required in order that painting might attain a respectable status in the Confucian system. The weakness of the early moralist view which depended upon nobility of subject matter ("to see the good serves to warn against evil") was discerned already in the Han dynasty by Wang Ch'ung:

People like to see paintings. The subjects reproduced in these pictures are usually men of ancient times. But would it not be better to be informed of the doings and sayings of these men than to contemplate their faces? Painted upon a bare wall, their shapes and figures are there; the reason why they do not act as incentives, is that people do not perceive their words or deeds. The sentiments left by the old sages shine forth from the bamboos and silks, where they are written, which means more than mere paintings on walls.[38]

Elsewhere he writes that "the doings and sayings of worthies and sages, handed down on bamboo and silk, transform the heart and enlighten the mind . . . " His low opinion of painting was based on the failure of that art, as he saw it, to "transform" and "enlighten." *Wen-jen hua* theory overcomes this objection, as we shall see, with a new concept of the source of expression in painting, according to which the import of the picture is primarily dependent not upon its subject, but upon the mind of its maker.

To understand how it was possible to regard painting as capable of conveying human thought and feeling without depending upon the outward associations of its subject matter, we may look a bit further into theories of the other arts. Although poetry and music are treated as intimately related in the early Chinese literature, the modes of expression they depend upon differ in one fundamental way: in poetry, thought or emotion *can* be stated explicitly, although with an inevitable loss of nuance and often to the detriment of the poem as a work of art; whereas music can only symbolize it, suggest it, evoke it, always by non-descriptive, "abstract" means. However, a recognition of the inadequacy of direct verbal expression led the theorists to the view that purely formal means, dependence upon those artistic devices which distinguish the poem from the prose statement, were in some cases preferable in literature as well, having an immediacy denied to intellectualized discourse and allowing the communication of intuitive truths which cannot be presented in rational terms.

The theory of calligraphy is especially revealing in this connection, since the forms of calligraphy, like those of music, do not represent anything (the text written being more or less irrelevant to the work as calligraphy) and must rely on their inherent qualities without referring directly to anything in everday sensory experience. The earliest extant essay on calligraphy, the "Fei Ts'ao-shu" ("Polemic against the 'Grass' [cursive] Script") by Chao I of the late Han dynasty, already recognizes calligraphy as revealing not only the skill but also the nature and character of the writer—a recognition which was not to be accorded to painting until much later:

Now, of all men, each one has his particular humours and blood, and different sinews and bones. The mind may be coarse or fine, the hand may be skilled or clumsy. Hence when the beauty or ugliness of a piece of writing must depend both upon the mind and the hand, can there be any question of making [a beautiful writing] by sheer force of effort?[39]

By the Six Dynasties period, calligraphy was seen as a means of communicating the ineffable, functioning (as Wang Wei, in the same period, considered painting to function) in a symbolic way, as an abstraction of natural form, analogous to the hexagrams of the *I-ching*. Wei Heng, a Chin dynasty calligrapher, writes: "[The calligrapher] observes [and utilizes] the images of things to convey his thoughts; these are such as cannot be expressed in words."[40]

T'ang dynasty developments in the application of these ideas to calligraphy may be illustrated with quotations from two Confucian scholars of the period: Chang Huai-kuan, an eighth-century appointee to the Han-lin Academy; and the great littérateur and precursor of Neo-Confucianism Han Yü. Chang's essay entitled "I Shu" ("Discourse on Calligraphy") contains the following:

Cliffs and canyons compete for breath-taking effect, mountains and rivers strive respectively for height and depth. One gathers, as in a bag, these myriad phenomena, brings them into order as a single image. This one lodges in calligraphy in order to give rein to one's varied thought, or commits to calligraphy to release one's pent-up emotions.

Calligraphy and written documents, if they are of the highest order, all have a profound import through which the intent of the writer is revealed. Looking at them makes one understand him fully, as if meeting him face to face . . . Reading the words of the sages of the past is not the same as hearing them speak in person, but in appreciating the calligraphy of former masters, one can never exhaust their profound conceptions.

Of the Chin dynasty calligrapher Wang Hsi-chih:

When we look at his complete calligraphy, we lucidly perceive the aim and spirit of his whole life, as if we were meeting him face to face.[41]

In the first paragraph quoted above, we encounter for the first time the notion of "lodging," which was later to occur frequently in literati discussions of painting. To speak of "lodging," or embodying, one's thoughts and emotions in the work of art was a common way of describing the process of artistic expression. The final lines of *Wen-hsin Tiao-lung*, for example, are: "If my writing indeed conveys my mind, then my mind finds lodging." We shall encounter other uses of the term as we proceed, and its meaning will become more clear.

Han Yü, believing with Chang Huai-kuan in the capacity of calligraphy to manifest human feelings, applies to this art the concept of catharsis, mentioned above as one of the Confucian justifications for artistic creation: by allowing the writer to release his pent-up emotions, it forestalls the unseemly operation of those emotions in other directions, and so enables him to preserve his composure. For, as Hsün-tzu had said about music, "Man cannot be without joy, and when there is joy, it must have a physical embodiment. When this embodiment does not conform to right principles, there will be disorder."[42] Calligraphy, as well as good music, was evidently thought to "conform to right principles." Han Yü writes:

If a man can give lodging to his skill and knowledge, so that they respond sensitively to his mind but without damming up his energy, then his spirit will be whole and his character will be firm. Although external things come [into his cognizance], they will not adhere to his mind.

He then cites examples of people who have been fond of particular things or activities—food, wine, chess—and goes on:

These things they enjoyed to the end of their days, insatiably. How could they have leisure for other desires? The late Chang Hsü was good at the grass script; he did not develop other talents. Joy and anger, distress and poverty, sorrow, contentment and ease, resentment, longing, intoxication, dejection and unrest—anything which moved his mind he inevitably expressed in his grass script. He looked at things, saw mountains and rivers, cliffs and valleys . . . all the transmutations of events and objects in the world. The enjoyable, the awesome, all were given lodging in his calligraphy.[43]

The idea of embodying individual response and emotion in music or calligraphy was acceptable to these Confucians; the embodiment of it in painting, through representation of the stimulus of that emotion, evidently was not. Other T'ang dynasty Confucian writers, like Chang Yen-yüan, avoid presenting painting in such terms. I should like to suggest—and some quotations will be introduced below to support the suggestion—that the problem of *non-attachment* is involved here. Expressing emotion through the portrayal of whatever had inspired that emotion implied a dwelling on that thing, and on the state of mind it had evoked. Confucian writings cautioned, on the contrary, that one should allow one's mind to rest only lightly upon the things it comes into contact with, never to become captivated by them; the mind must always preserve a degree of aloofness. Expression in music and calligraphy entailed no description or representation of the original stimulus of feeling; it was not a matter of being moved by something one encountered and externalizing one's response in a picture of, or a poem about, that thing. The images of a representational art remained bound to the object of representation. The forms of a non-representational art were not so bound, could be invested with a more general import, and so could serve to reveal the nature and thought of the person who composed them.

The case of painting was complicated by the ambivalence of its very substance, its lines, forms, colors, textures: they might portray material things, but might also serve as somewhat independent expressive means, undergoing quasi-arbitrary mutations which had little or nothing to do with their descriptive function. Literary evidence indicates that as early as the T'ang dynasty, unorthodox kinds of brushwork which had previously been employed only in calligraphy were introduced into painting, not so much because they served better to reproduce the visible features of anything as for their inherent interest and their efficacy in displaying the temperament of the artist. This development in painting style evidently preceded, and perhaps to some extent stimulated, the emergence of the *wen-jen hua* concept. Technical innovations in art are not, ordinarily, the work of its critics; the expressive potentialities of brush and ink had to be expanded in fact before they could be expanded in theory.

A shifting of emphasis from the subject of the picture to its formal elements was thus facilitated; and as this shift went on, painting and calligraphy drew closer to becoming, in principle, a single art.[44] The way was opened for the evolution of *wen-jen hua,* and the recognition of painting, within the Confucian order, as a means by which the individual man could communicate to others the workings of his mind.

Although anticipations of some features of *wen-jen hua* theory can be discovered in pre-Sung writings (e.g., in Chang Yen-yüan's remarks about Yang Yen, quoted above), the formulation of this theory as a coherent body of doctrine did not take place until the late eleventh and early twelfth centuries. It was accomplished chiefly by members of a coterie of artists and critics, of which Su Shih, or Su Tung-p'o (1036–1101), was the central figure. Some of these men reveal in their writings an interest in Taoism and Ch'an Buddhism, but it generally goes no further than was normal for the somewhat eclectic Neo-Confucians They were, like most major figures of the *wen-jen hua* movement in later times, Confucian literati. Su Tung-p'o was fascinated, during various periods of his life, with Buddhist mysticism and Taoist alchemy, and objected to the stern morality of some Neo-Confucian philosophers;[45] but he also wrote commentaries on the Confucian Classics, expressed a deep admiration for Chou Tun-i,[46] and always preserved a thoroughly Confucian concern for human society.

The fundamental contention of the *wen-jen hua* theorists was that a painting is (or at least should be) a revelation of the nature of the man who painted it, and of his mood and feelings at the moment he painted it. Its expressive content therefore depends more upon his personal qualities and his transient feeling than upon the qualities of the subject represented. A man of wide learning, refinement, and noble character will, if he adds to these attributes a moderate degree of acquired technical ability, produce paintings of a superior kind.

To support this belief, it was necessary to suppose—sometimes in spite of the evidence, one feels—that the great painters of the past had all been what Chang Yen-yüan claims they were, "retired scholars and lofty-minded men." Chang himself stopped short of basing his critical judgments consistently upon this somewhat questionable criterion; the painter whom he praises above all others, Wu Tao-tzu, was a professional artist of no notable scholarly status. Su Tung-p'o, however, professed to prefer the works of the T'ang poet-painter Wang Wei (699–759) to those of Wu Tao-tzu; the latter, "for all his surpassing excellence, must still be discussed in terms of painting skill, while Wang Mo-chieh [i.e., Wang Wei] achieved his effects beyond the visual image."[47]

Kuo Jo-hsü, the late eleventh-century author of *T'u-hua Chien-wen Chih* and a leading spokesman for the *wen-jen hua* viewpoint, elaborates on Chang Yen-yüan's observation:

I have . . . observed that the majority of the rare paintings of the past are the work of high officials, talented worthies, superior scholars, or recluses living in cliffs and caves; of persons, that is, who "followed the dictates of loving-kindness and sought delight in the arts."[48] . . . Their elevated and refined feelings were all lodged in their paintings. Since their personal quality was lofty, the "spirit consonance" [of their paintings] could not but be lofty.[49]

Mi Yu-jen, son of another member of the Su Tung-p'o coterie, the painter and connoisseur Mi Fu (1051–1107), borrows the words of the Han dynasty Confucian Yang Hsiung in setting forth the view of painting as communication:

Yang Hsiung considered writing to be the "delineation of the mind." Unless a person has a firm grasp of *li* [principle], his words cannot attain [a high level of wisdom]. In this regard, painting, as a form of discourse,[50] is also a "delineation of the mind." In these terms it is understandable that all [outstanding artists] in the past should have been the glories of their respective ages. How could this be anything that the artisans for hire in the market place could know about?[51]

What Yang Hsiung had written is this: "Speech is the voice of mind; writing is the delineation of the mind. When this voice and delineation take form, the princely man and the ignoble man are revealed."[52] Kuo Jo-hsü also quotes these lines, prefacing them with the flat statement: "Painting is the equivalent of writing." Both calligraphy and painting he regards as "prints of the heart [mind]"; the painter's conception, he says, "arises in feeling and thought, and is transferred to silk and paper."[53]

It will be clear from these examples, which are typical of Sung dynasty *wen-jen* statements about painting, that literati painting theory is based upon, and completely in harmony with, the Confucian ideals of the arts which we have outlined above. As a worthy activity for the literatus who wishes to "seek delight in the arts" and to manifest his mind, painting is now a means of self-cultivation; and the products of this activity, as embodiments of the admirable qualities of cultivated individuals, serve a Confucian end in conveying those qualities to others. Along with literature and calligraphy, painting helps to maintain a desirable continuity within the great humanist tradition of the Confucian scholars, perpetuating feelings and awarenesses which would otherwise perish with the men who felt them.

A few qualifications should be made here. Obviously, not all good painters were sages or paragons of virtue; nor were all men of noble character good painters. No critic of any consequence ever judged a picture according to what he knew about the moral worth of the artist. A literati critic was likely, on the other hand, to consider the admirable qualities which he perceived in the picture to be reflections of admirable qualities in the man who produced it. The notion of "the man revealed in the painting" was used, that is, to account for excellence in art, not to determine it.

Also, one finds fewer explicit references to morality in the Sung dynasty discussions of painting than in some of the earlier writings on art quoted above. In Sung and later times, the men most admired were not those who merely exemplified the simple virtues. Such men were accorded their eulogies in the appropriate sections of the biographical compilations (Filial Piety, Unswerving Loyalty, etc.), but scarcely noticed otherwise. The Ideal Man, for the later periods in China, was a more complex figure, a richer personality; and the desire of later ages was to understand him, see him in all his richness and complexity. Treasured and transmitted were anecdotes reporting his behavior and sayings in various circumstances; his surviving literary productions; and, as revelations of even subtler facets of his mind than these could preserve, his calligraphy and paintings.

The transition from the romantic theory of expression, in which the artist's response to his subject determines the emotional content of the work, to the *wen-jen hua* theory in which the expression was less dependent upon subject matter, may be further illustrated with two short and syntactically parallel phrases which were applied to artists of the sixth and eleventh centuries. The first, used by an early T'ang writer in speaking of Chan Tzu-ch'ien, has already been quoted: "Aroused by things of the world, he consigned his emotions to them" (*ch'u-wu liu-ch'ing*). The second occurs in the comments on Wen T'ung, a painter of bamboo and a close friend of Su Tung-p'o, which appear in the early-twelfth-century catalog *Hsüan-ho Hua-p'u*: "Wen T'ung availed himself of natural objects in order to lodge his exhilaration" (*t'o-wu yü-hsing*).[54]

The ways in which these phrases differ reveal the change in attitude toward subject matter in painting. Response to particular objects or scenes in nature is no longer the stimulus of that emotion which impels one to artistic creation; instead, the painter "avails himself of things" (*t'o-wu*), or as other writers have it, "borrows things" (*chia-wu*), as vehicles for conveying feelings having no necessary connection with those things. *Ch'ing*, "emotion," has given way to *hsing*, "exhilaration." *Hsing*, in art theory, denoted an undefined intensity of feeling which, embodied in a work of art, could instill in that work a quality of subtle excitement without suggesting an unseemly display of strong and particularized emotion.

Even more interesting is the replacement of *liu* (rendered as "consigned" but more properly "to deposit, leave behind") by *yü*, "to lodge." Both *yü* and the closely related, often interchangeable *chi* are favored by the *wen-jen hua* writers for describing the embodiment of personal feeling in art; the combination *chi-hsing*, "lodging exhilaration," is especially common. Teng Ch'un, for example, writing of an early Sung landscapist in his *Hua Chi* (1167), speaks of works in which the painter has "lodged his exhilaration, pure and remote—true gentleman's brushwork!"[55] These terms do not appear in T'ang or pre-T'ang texts on painting; they are, I think, bound up with the *wen-jen hua* concept of artistic expression.

Su Tung-p'o seems to have considered the "lodging of one's mind" as a means of dispersing emotion, somewhat as did Han Yü. He writes the following of calligraphy, but might as well have written it of painting:

The traces of brush and ink are committed to that which has form [i.e., the writing itself]; and what has form must then be subject to corruption. But if, even though it does not achieve non-being, one can enjoy oneself with it for the moment, in order to give lodging to one's mind, forget the sorrows of one's declining years, then it is a wiser pastime than gambling at chess.

Nevertheless, to be able to maintain one's inner equilibrium without making use of external diversions is the highest achievement of the sages and worthies. But only Yen-tzu [Yen Hui, the favorite disciple of Confucius] could achieve that.[56]

Behind some part of *wen-jen hua* theory, I believe, lie Neo-Confucian attitudes toward the emotions and toward the proper modes of response to material things. Fung Yu-lan contrasts the Taoist insistence on non-attachment to the view of the Neo-Confucians, who "argue that there is nothing wrong with the emotions *per se*; what is important is simply that they should not be a permanent part of the person who sometimes expresses them." One's essential composure must not be disturbed; unbalance is to be avoided. The *Chung-yung*, a text highly esteemed and often quoted by the Neo-Confucians, says:

While there are no stirrings of pleasure, anger, sorrow, or joy, the mind may be said to be in a state of equilibrium. When these feelings have been stirred, and they act in their due degree, there ensues what may be called a state of harmony.[57]

Fung, quoting this passage, comments: "All such feelings are natural, and so must be allowed expression. But at the same time we must keep them ordered by means of 'instruction,' and must regulate their expression so that it will be neither too extreme nor too restrained."[58] A good part of *wen-jen hua* aesthetic is, in fact, a "regulation of expression" in terms of painting, aimed at ensuring that the artist does not commit the artistic equivalents of those excesses in human conduct against which the Confucians warn. The literati painters' theory of expression, by divorcing the import of the picture from that of whatever it represents, lessened the danger of "over-attachment." The same attitude operated, I believe, in both philosophy and art: the perfect man responds to natural stimuli, but is not permanently affected by them, because they do not alter his essential self; the scholar-painter makes use of natural objects only to "lodge his mind," not allowing them, or his feelings toward them, to dictate the import of his pictures.

Tung Yu, the early-twelfth-century author of *Kuang-ch'uan Hua-pa*, a series of colophons written for paintings, points out that the painter should rely primarily upon what is within himself, rather than upon what he sees outside. Tung tells the familiar story of how Wu Tao-tzu painted a landscape of a place he had visited without depending upon sketches, and comments: "The theorists say that hills and valleys are formed within the painter's breast; when he wakes, he issues them forth in painting. Thus the things leave no traces in him, whereas involvement would arise out of actual perception."[59]

The term *yü-i*, which in *wen-jen hua* writings has the sense of "lodging one's conceptions," is also used for "resting one's thoughts lightly upon" something, giving it one's passing attention. The two senses are not, I think, totally unrelated. Neither "lodging one's conceptions" in pictures or things nor "resting one's thoughts" on them implies any abiding concern with those things. Su Tung-p'o, composing a dedicatory inscription for his friend Wang Shen's "Precious Painting Hall" (Paohui T'ang), employs the same antithesis of the verbs *yü* and *liu* as we saw in the parallel phrases quoted above, to contrast a "lodging" or "resting" of attention with a more permanent "depositing" or "fixing." His argument adheres completely to the Neo-Confucian position, even making the standard distinction between that and the Taoist view. He writes:

The princely man may rest (*yü*) his thoughts on objects, but may not fix (*liu*) his thoughts on objects. If he rests his thoughts on them, then even subtle things will suffice to give him pleasure, and even extraordinary things cannot become afflictions [obsessions] to him. If, however, he fixes his thoughts on them, even subtle things will be afflictions, and not even extraordinary ones a pleasure. Lao-tzu says: "The five colors confuse the eye, the five sounds dull the ear, the five tastes spoil the palate . . ."; but the sage never really renounces these [sensual objects], for he merely rests his thoughts on them.

Now, of all enjoyable things, painting and calligraphy are best suited to giving men pleasure without at the same time influencing them. But if one's thoughts become fixed inextricably in things, this will lead to unspeakable disaster.

Su Tung-p'o tells how he himself has owned many notable examples of painting and calligraphy, but has allowed them to leave his hands without begrudging them. He comments:

It is like clouds and mists passing before my eyes, or the songs of birds striking my ears. How could I help but derive joy from my contact with these things? But when they are gone, I think no more about them. In this way, these two things [painting and calligraphy] are a constant pleasure to me, but not an affliction to me.[60]

The painter, by deriving the forms of his paintings from his own mind, can escape being "involved" with material things; the collector, avoiding over-attachment to the objects he owns, can prevent them from becoming "afflictions" to him. Tung Yu was once accused by a Ch'an Buddhist monk of encouraging such over-attachment to paintings by writing in praise of them. The two were discussing a " Grove of Pines" picture owned by the Ch'an master, whose name was Hui-yüan. Hui-yüan said:

The enjoyment of things weakens one's will; for one cannot forget one's love for them. This is another kind of corruption. You, moreover, write about these [paintings]; how can you escape increasing people's emotional attachments, multiplying their involvements?

Long ago, the master Hsüan-lan attained a "beyond-mind method" [*hsin-wai fa*]; he forgot himself and also forgot external things. He retained [*liu*] no resentment or desire. Chang Tsao once painted [the walls of Hsüan-lan's] house, doing old pines, thinking that these would be beautiful to look upon. Fu-tsai heard of this, and composed an encomium; Wei Hsiang made a poem to be attached to it. In a later age, these were called the "Three Nonpareils." Next day, Hsüan-lan saw them and plastered them over, saying, "They had no business scabbing up my walls!"

This is to say, why should such things be retained in the breast even though they be good? It's all the worse when one is stuck to a single thing and can't break loose from it!

Tung Yu replied:

If a person is sincere (*ch'eng*) within, he is released from such attachments, and although things be ever so numerous, revealing their images and baring their forms, they cannot become involvements to him. He who is cultivated within his mind is fixed and quiet, like still, deep water; since he does not offer a target for things, they cannot leave their barbs in him.[61]

However unsatisfying, or even irritating, this answer may have been to Hui-yüan, it is exactly the reply which a good Confucian should have returned to such a Buddhist outburst.[62] If you are so "uncultivated" that you must be afraid of your responses, it suggests, go and live in a monastery, or a cave; we Confucianists cultivate our minds and remain in the world. The key word in Tung's answer is *ch'eng*, "sincerity"—in the Sung period, a kind of summation of the Confucian virtues. "Sagehood is simply a matter of sincerity," writes Chou Tun-i. "Sincerity is the foundation of the five virtues, and the source of all virtuous conduct."[63]

It was the Confucian virtues, in *wen-jen hua* theory, which regulated the creation of paintings as well as the enjoyment of them. A painting done by a cultivated man was a reflection of his sincerity. To understand how it was so, we may consider a few more of the tenets of *wen-jen hua*.

Non-purposefulness; spontaneity. In the ideal creative act the painter creates as Heaven does, spontaneously, without willfulness. Su Tung-p'o reports a conversation between his friend Wen T'ung and a guest who argued that painting was not "in accord with the Tao," since the painter, through human activity, usurps the creative powers of Heaven. Wen answered:

But the Tao is what I love! I am quite unattached to bamboo . . . At the beginning, I saw the bamboo and delighted in it; now I delight in it and lose consciousness of myself. Suddenly I forget that the brush is my hand, the paper in front of me; all at once I am exhilarated, and the tall bamboo appears, thick and luxuriant. How is this in any way different from the impersonality of creation in nature?[64]

According to Mi Fu, the T'ang calligrapher Yen Chen-ch'ing criticized the writing of some of his famous predecessors as having "too much of purposeful activity, lacking the air of blandness, of something accomplished by Heaven."[65] This desirable quality of "blandness" will be considered later. While there are undoubtedly traces here of the Taoist concept of *wu-wei*, "non-activity," and perhaps of the Ch'an practice of empty-mindedness in meditation as well, such ideas were by this time so thoroughly assimilated into Confucian thought that the Sung scholars had no need to turn to other sources for them. Chou Tun-i begins the third section of his *T'ung Shu* with the words "Sincerity is non-acting" (*ch'eng wu-wei*). Ch'eng Hao, another Neo-Confucian philosopher who was contemporary with Su Tung-p'o, stresses the importance of emptying the mind:

Denying outer things and affirming inner ones is not as good as forgetting both outer and inner. When both are forgotten, one's mind is cleansed and uncluttered; uncluttered, it will be concentrated; concentrated, it will be clear. Once one's mind is clear, how can any further response to external things become an involvement?[66]

For the notion of non-purposefulness, the *Chung-yung* again supplies classical authority: "He who possesses sincerity is he who, without any effort, hits what is right, and apprehends, without the exercise of thought; he is the sage who naturally and easily embodies the right way."[67]

Creation as transformation; li (principle). Huang T'ing-chien (1045–1105), a friend and disciple of Su Tung-p'o, writes that if the artist has the conception of bamboo (for example) already formed before he begins to paint, then the brush and ink "transform" it (cause it to grow into full existence) just as natural objects are "transformed," matured by the forces of nature. "When one takes up the brush and ink, one's achievement is the same as that of natural creation."[68] Tung Yu writes in a colophon on a painting, "The sage transforms [or creates, *hua*] through movement of his spirit; his skill is identical with that of Heaven and Earth."[69]

Once more, the ideas underlying such statements are to be found in Confucian thought. The person who is possessed of "complete sincerity," says the *Chung yung*, "can assist the transforming and nourishing operations of Heaven and Earth . . . he can form a trinity with Heaven and Earth." And also: "It is only he who is possessed of the most complete sincerity under heaven, who can transform."[70] The leap from transformation as the moral betterment of the world (as the *Chung yung* intends it) to transformation as the creation of artistic form is a broad one, but not too broad for the agile-minded *wen-jen hua* theorists. Both kinds were seen as analogous to creation-transformation in nature, and so to each other.

An important element in the analogy between cosmological and artistic creation is the regulation of both by *li*, that "principle" or "natural order" which, in the words of Fung Yu-lan, "prevents the creative process from proceeding haphazardly."[71] Su Tung-p'o, in an often quoted colophon dealing with *li* in painting, distinguishes some things which have constant forms (people, animals, buildings) from others which have only constant *principle* (rocks, trees, water, clouds). Any deviation from "truth" in the former is easy to spot, he says, whereas only the most perceptive will detect a lack of *li* in the latter. The bamboo paintings of Wen T'ung, he goes on, "are in accord with natural creation, and also satisfying to human conceptions. Truly, they are embodiments [lodgings] of [the mind of] a man of complete wisdom."[72]

Tung Yu, in a colophon on a "Playing Dogs" painting, claims that a painter who catches the outer form and likeness of such things as dogs and horses is not necessarily skillful; to be called skillful, he must also capture their *li*.[73] Huang Kung-wang, in the Yüan dynasty, goes so far as to speak of *li* as "the most urgent necessity in painting."[74]

We need not expend any space here in establishing the importance of *li* in later Confucianism. *Li-hsüeh*, the "study of *li*," is in fact one of the Chinese terms for Neo-Confucianism. *Li*, for the Sung philosophers, was "that which is above form"; for the Sung *wen-jen hua* theorists, as well as for the philosophers, it was what guided the creation of form; for the artists, one may suppose, it was that sense of "rightness" which preserved the forms they produced from seeming "perverse and willful."

The virtue of concealment. Nothing was more vociferously abhorred by the literati critics than showiness—the deliberate display of brilliance, beauty, or skill. However admirable it may appear to the person capable of penetrating its seeming plainness, the painting must be unassuming always. We need not, when we observe this quality of plainness in the works of literati artists, attribute it directly to their Confucian background; it is more likely to be simply a manifestation of the more reserved and subtle taste of the cultivated man. But the statements applied to these works by the critics, especially their words of praise for "blandness" (p'ing-tan), certainly call to mind the Confucian disapproval of ostentation. The virtues sought in a painting corresponded closely to those which the Chung-yung assigns to the chün-tzu, the princely or superior man:

It is said in the Shih-ching, "Over her embroidered robe she puts on a plain, single garment," intimating a disinclination to display the elegance of the former. Just so, it is the way of the superior man to prefer the concealment [of his virtue] . . . It is characteristic of the superior man, though he appears bland, never to produce satiety . . .[75]

P'ing-tan, "blandness," came to be the quality most highly prized in human personality. Liu Shao, Wei dynasty author of the Jen-wu Chih ("Notices of Personalities"), writes:

In the character of a man, it is balance and harmony which is most prized; and for a character to have this balance and harmony, it must have blandness [p'ing-tan] and flavorlessness [wu-wei]. . . . Therefore, when one observes a man in order to inquire into his character, one must first see if he has blandness and only later seek for his cleverness and brilliance.[76]

One must hasten to add, as the Chinese writers frequently do, that the "blandness" was only apparent; a semblance of impoverishment in a painting should conceal an inner richness, serve as the plain garment which covers the embroidered robe. "Blandness" is not to be equated with dullness, either in the art work or in the man it reflects.

The preference for "awkwardness." Another attribute admired by the literati critics was cho, "awkwardness," the opposite of ch'iao, "skill." An admirable kind of "clumsiness" was held to be more difficult to achieve than technical competence, and to be the natural outcome of a truly spontaneous act of creation. That an element of Confucian morality is involved in this preference is suggested by Chou Tun-i's pronouncement on skill and awkwardness, which begins in a Taoist vein but ends in a Confucian one:

Someone said to me, "People call you awkward." I responded: "Skillfulness is what I detest. Moreover, it grieves me to see so much skill in the world." I was then pleased to make a poem:

"The skillful talk much,
The awkward keep silent.
The skillful exert themselves,
The awkward are more retiring.
The skillful are the thieves,
The awkward are the virtuous.
The skillful bring misfortunes upon the people,
The awkward bring them happiness."

Ah! if only all people in the world were awkward! Harsh government would be discontinued; there would be tranquillity above and obedience below; customs would be purified, and abuses ended.[77]

Skillfulness in painting carried the additional stigma of professionalism, and was always suspect of indicating a desire to please. Tung Yu writes:

The artisan-painter makes his work salable by his skillful craftsmanship; by giving pleasure to the vulgar ones of his time, he hopes to make his pictures easier to take. He is afraid only that the world will not want his pictures because they are different.[78]

Like all actions of the proper Confucian, painting must be motivated by a worthy aim—or, ideally, by no rationalized aim at all. In any event, desire to win the favor and patronage of others was decidedly *not* a worthy aim. The literatus could paint for either (or both) of two reasons: as a pastime in the intervals between scholarly pursuits, an outlet for excess energy; or as a means of presenting to the understanding of others something of his own nature, feeling, and thought.

The scholar who was equipped with only a moderate technical facility in painting, but who had practiced the self-cultivation and acquired the classical education of the ideal literatus, was thus considered to be better prepared to produce worth-while paintings than the professional who had concentrated upon learning the technique of the art. Feng Shan, an eleventh-century scholar and author of a commentary on the *Spring and Autumn Annals*, writes these lines in a poem about landscape painting:

> Creation by means of brush and ink is not an
>   achievement in itself;
> In essence it is the overflow of literary activity.
> Thus, true [painting] skill, in our time, is
>   the property of us Confucians.[79]

"Set your heart upon the Tao, support yourself by its power, follow the dictates of loving-kindness, and seek delight in the arts." With this quotation from the *Analects* of Confucius,[80] the anonymous author of *Hsüan-ho Hua-p'u*, writing in the early twelfth century, opens his first chapter. "Art," he goes on, "is a thing which the gentleman whose heart is set on the Tao cannot neglect; but he should only 'seek delight' in it, and no more"—that is, it must not be his chief concern in life, but only an avocation. "Painting is also an art," the passage concludes. "When it attains the highest point, then one does not know whether art is Tao, or Tao art."[81]

Such a statement—even more, the occurrence of it at the beginning of the imperial catalog of an emperor, Hui-tsung, who was not especially sympathetic to the *wen-jen hua* ideal—indicates the standing which painting had by this time attained within the Confucian community. Painting had joined literature, calligraphy, and music as an activity suitable for the literatus; and a responsiveness to the subtler qualities of painting, as well as to those of the other arts, was expected of the cultivated man. It was the formulation of *wen-jen hua* theory as a Confucian doctrine for the creation and evaluation of paintings, and the practice of painting by an increasing number of scholars, which had brought about this adoption of painting into the group of "polite arts," those with potential moral value to the individual and to society. The statement in the last quotation about painting and Tao is quite similar to what Chu Hsi writes of literary art: "The Tao is the root of literary art, and literary art the branches and leaves of the Tao . . . literary art *is*, in fact, Tao. Su Tung-p'o, in our time, has put it thus: 'What I call literary art has to be at one with *Tao*.' "[82]

We may conclude by observing how completely this same philosopher adheres to what was, by this time, the orthodox viewpoint for one of his class, when he comes to write about painting and calligraphy. Chu Hsi had no very profound interest in either art, and was no connoisseur; on one occasion, writing on a painting of oxen, he was guilty of echoing the eternal axiom of the philistine: "I don't know anything about painting, but I know that this is a *real ox* in this picture!"[83] Elsewhere, with no greater originality of thought but in better accord with prevailing views, he writes the following:

On a letter from Tu K'an (978–1057) to Ou-yang Hsiu (1007–72): "When I scrutinize and enjoy these 'delineations of his mind,' it is as if I could see the man."

On a landscape by Mi Fu: "These must be the most beautiful scenes from the hills and valleys within the breast of this old man, which at that moment he all at once spewed forth, to give lodging to his genuine enjoyment."

On the calligraphy of Huang T'ing-chien: "It cannot be judged in terms of skill and awkwardness. Rather, when I look at it I think back to all the loyal and worthy men of that age, and reflect how sad it is that they should have met with failure."

On an "Old Tree and Strange Stone" painting by Su Tung-p'o: "This piece of paper by the late master Su is the product of a moment's sport, the overflow of a playful spirit. He did not set out to do it with any special deliberation; and yet his proud bearing, revealed in it, reverberates through ancient and modern times. It serves to let us see in imagination the man himself."[84]

It would have distressed Chu Hsi deeply to be told that the paintings he admired, and the attitudes toward them which he accepted, were really expressions of Taoist or Buddhist mysticism. Fortunately for him, no one of his time was likely to tell him anything of the sort; for, so far as we can ascertain from surviving writings, nobody thought so. The assignment of a large part of what is vital and interesting in Chinese art to the opponents of Confucianism did not take place until very recent times. It rests, I think, on the flimsiest of foundations or on none at all; and it demands a strict reexamination. It may well prove in other cases, as in that of *wen-jen hua,* to have been an obstacle rather than an aid to our understanding.

Hans H. Frankel

T'ANG LITERATI:
A COMPOSITE BIOGRAPHY

The T'ang period, 618–907, was one of the great ages of Chinese literature. The volume of writing, both poetry and prose, was unprecedented in a culture where the elite had long prided themselves on their literary accomplishments. Poetry was written, chanted, and appreciated by all literate classes of T'ang society, down to the lowliest monks and courtesans, and an elegant prose style was deemed essential for all serious communications, public or private. Emperors, princes, and high officials surrounded themselves with distinguished men of letters, and even hard-bitten generals employed literati to write their proclamations, reports to the throne, and other documents. Great writers emerged who remain among the giants of Chinese literary history. They wrought significant changes in the form and content of prose and poetry. Literary skills were required for passing the examinations which fed personnel into the vastly expanded bureaucracy. For all these reasons, the man of letters looms large in T'ang society and culture. Hence it is only natural that a long section in the official history of the period is devoted to the lives of one hundred and one selected writers.

It is with these biographies that my paper deals. In deviating from the pattern of the other essays in this volume, each of which takes up a single life, I conform to the conception of my Chinese sources, where the literati are viewed not as individuals but as a group. I propose to examine first of all the scope of this section of the official history, to discuss the historians' criteria of inclusion and exclusion, their scale of values, and related questions. Second, I shall take up the content of these biographies under three headings, corresponding to the three aspects of the lives in which the historiographers are interested: official careers, literary achievements, and character. In trying to discern how the literary man lived and worked in T'ang times, we shall have to slice through many layers of historiographical conventions. The resulting composite biography is bound to be fragmentary and distorted, but it may nevertheless shed some light on the attitudes and behavior patterns of the T'ang man of letters, and his role in the society of his time.

The section of the *Old History of the T'ang Dynasty* (completed in 945) that comprises the biographies of one hundred and one literati is entitled "Garden of Letters."[1] This "Garden of Letters" is one of the special biographical categories (sometimes called "classified biographies") that appear, in varying numbers, in all the Chinese dynastic histories. These special categories seem to be reserved for those who fall short of the Confucian ideal of a well-rounded gentleman—the biographies of the greatest men of the dynasty are always unclassified. Furthermore, the classifications follow each other on a descending scale which roughly reflects the value system of the historiographers. On this scale, the literati rank rather low in the *Old History of the T'ang Dynasty*: the only categories below them are technicians, recluses, exemplary women, barbarians, and rebels.

Thus the selection of writers included in the "Garden of Letters" is not based on literary criteria alone. To be sure, some of the best-known poets and prose writers are included—men like Ch'en Tzu-ang, Li Hua, Wang Wei, Li Po, Tu Fu, Li Shang-yin, Wen T'ing-yün, and Ssu-k'ung T'u. But one misses others of equal stature, such as Chang Yüeh, Han Yü, Po Chü-i, and Li Te-yü. The explanation has already been suggested above: the latter were prominent statesmen, whereas the "Garden of Letters" is reserved for those who were famous *only* as literati, and this, in the view of the Confucian historiographer, is a shortcoming. Though brilliant and successful as writers, they all failed to win top positions in government service. Nearly all of them, however, did serve in the bureaucracy.

With this restriction in mind, it might be supposed that the one hundred and one biographies give us a fairly representative sampling of bureaucrats who were active in literature from all parts of China throughout the three hundred years of T'ang rule. But this is not the case. The selection is uneven in both time and space. If we divide the T'ang epoch into six periods of approximately fifty years each, and assign each of the one hundred and one literati to the period in which all or most of his political and literary activities occurred, we get the following distribution:

Period I	(618–649):	13	Period IV	(756–805):	6
Period II	(649–705):	38	Period V	(805–859):	6
Period III	(705–756):	33	Period VI	(859–907):	5

That is to say, seventy-one of the one hundred and one literati were active between the mid-seventh and the mid-eighth century, during the reigns of Kao-tsung, the Empress Wu, Hsüan-tsung, and some brief interregna; only thirteen belong to the first two reigns (Kao-tsu and T'ai-tsung); and a mere seventeen are registered for the entire second half of T'ang, beginning with the An Lu-shan insurrection, which marks indeed a turning point in many respects. The irregular distribution in time is partly due to the fact that many literati are assigned by the historiographers to categories other than the "Garden of Letters."

The distribution in space is also uneven. If we list the home regions of the literati in terms of modern provinces and arrange them in the order of frequency, the regional picture looks like this:

Honan:	23	Shantung:	5
Hopei:	14	Hupeh:	5
Kiangsu:	12	Szechwan:	5
Chekiang:	12	Kansu:	2
Shensi:	11	Anhwei:	1
Shansi:	10	Home unknown:	1

Many parts of China are not represented at all—regions in which the cultural level was still low in T'ang times.

By rearranging the above table to form larger regional units, we obtain the following:

Northeast (Honan-Hopei-Shantung):	42
Southeast (Kiangsu-Chekiang-Anhwei):	25
Northwest (Shansi-Shensi-Kansu):	23
West-central (Hupeh-Szechwan):	10

I have found no correlation between temporal and spatial distribution, that is, the regional distribution does not change significantly in the course of the T'ang dynasty.

I will now consider the official careers of the literati. The first point of interest in a man's career is how it started. This is usually but not always indicated in our biographies. The most-traveled route to office was the examination system, especially after the system was revamped and strengthened in the reigns of Kao-tsung and the Empress Wu. (For the two preceding reigns, 618–49, our record contains not a single instance of an examination leading to a career.) Of the eighty-eight literati who flourished from the mid-seventh century to the end of T'ang, all except three had official careers. One half of these eighty-five men—namely, forty-three—entered their career through an examination, usually the *chin-shih* examination (thirty-two instances).

Another important aid in getting an appointment was recommendation by an influential patron. This is reported in twenty-one of the ninety-six biographies that register an official T'ang career. Eight of these twenty-one record both an examination (the *chin-shih* in seven cases) and a patron. There were numerous other possible starts for a career. Some of these are of sufficient interest to be cited here.

K'ung Shao-an, the first of the one hundred and one literati, had the good fortune and foresight to befriend Li Yüan, the future founder of T'ang, when the latter was a military commander under the preceding dynasty, Sui, "punishing rebels" for the last Sui emperor. K'ung was then a Provincial Censor (*chien-ch'a yü-shih*), and his assignment was to check on the activities of Li Yüan. As soon as Li Yüan openly rebelled against the Sui and set up his own dynasty, K'ung hastened to the newly established T'ang court to demonstrate his loyalty to the new regime. He was rewarded with the job of Director of Decrees in the Imperial Secretariat (*nei-shih she-jen*) and with gifts of a house, two fine horses, money, rice, silk, and cotton. (We may note in passing that K'ung Shao-an was following a family tradition: his ancestors were nearly always on the winning side in one power struggle after another through four hundred of the most turbulent years in China's history.[2]) However, K'ung was surpassed by another man, Hsia-hou Tuan, who had also formerly been a Provincial Censor "supervising" Li Yüan's army. This man got to the T'ang court ahead of K'ung, and therefore received a better job, Director of the Imperial Library (*mi-shu chien*). K'ung expressed his chagrin in a manner befitting a man of letters: he improvised a poem at an imperial banquet, when the emperor called for poems on the theme "pomegranate." K'ung's contribution contained the couplet:

> A late comer am I,
> My blossoms don't open in time for spring.[3]

(The pomegranate blooms later than other flowering trees in China.)

Not every man of letters had the opportunity to cultivate the friendship of a future emperor, but obviously many successful careers depended on knowing the right people. Recommendation and patronage have already been mentioned. An interesting case of recommendation which did not come off is that of Hsiao Ying-shih (717–68). When he received the *chin-shih* degree in 735, he was familiar with the leading literati of his time. That was why, according to his biography, Chief Minister Li Lin-fu wanted to appoint him to a government office, and summoned him to his official residence. At the interview Hsiao appeared dressed in coarse hempen clothing (he was mourning his mother). Li was offended, and severely reprimanded him. Result: no recommendation, no appointment, and enmity between the two men. Hsiao then wrote a *fu* ridiculing Li, entitled "Fa ying-t'ao fu," parts of which are quoted in the biography.[4]

Just as French intellectuals gravitate to Paris, so the T'ang literati were for the most part anxious to be stationed at or near the imperial court. But it was usual for them to begin their official careers with a humble position in a provincial administration. As many as forty-five of our biographies mention a provincial post in the early part of the career. This seems to have been an established procedure. When Hsüeh Feng was recommended for the office of Director of Decrees in the second half of the ninth century, his enemy Liu Chuan objected, stating in a memorial that according to the system established in previous T'ang reigns, no one could become Director of Decrees in the Imperial Secretariat or the Imperial Chancellery who had not previously served in a provincial post. Hsüeh was consequently given a provincial appointment.[5]

But the initial provincial appointment did not necessarily cut the young writer off from the mainstream of cultural life. He often managed to be placed in a district near one of the imperial capitals or other metropolitan centers. In fact, our record does not contain a single case of the apprenticeship being served in a really remote province. Assignment to outlying areas does occur, as we shall see, as a punishment.

Some literati commenced their careers by serving in the court of an imperial prince as tutors, clerks, readers, librarians, or drafters of official documents. Fifteen such initial assignments are recorded in our biographies. They are a holdover from pre-T'ang times. Hence they are most common in the early period of T'ang rule, then gradually decrease, and cease altogether in the middle of the dynasty. Here are the details: In Period I (618–49), out of eleven literati who became T'ang officials, six started in a princely court; in Period II (649–705), seven out of thirty-seven; in Period III (707–56), two out of thirty-one; but none of the seventeen literati who lived in Periods IV–VI (756–907) began their careers that way.

An instructive example of a man of letters who got started on his career through princely patronage is Yüan Ch'eng-hsü. I quote from his biography:

During the Wu-te era (618–27), his reputation came to the notice of Li Yüan-chi, Prince of Ch'i, who summoned him to become a scholar in his court. Later the Prince's court was abolished. . . . When Kao-tsung was a prince and Emperor T'ai-tsung was selecting men of learning and character to be in his entourage, the emperor asked the Vice-President of the Imperial Secretariat, Ts'en Wen-pen: "Who among the renowned ministers of Liang and Ch'en may be cited as outstanding? And furthermore, are there any junior members of their families who may be summoned?" Wen-pen replied:

"When the Sui army invaded Ch'en, all the officials fled and scattered; none remained except Yüan Hsien, who stayed at his lord's side. When Wang Shih-ch'ung attempted to usurp the throne from the Sui, the regional officials petitioned him to proclaim himself emperor. But Yüan Hsien's son, the Director of Decrees of the Imperial Chancellery, Yüan Ch'eng-chia, pleaded illness and was the only one not to sign. These men, father and son, may well be called loyal and upright, and Yüan Ch'eng-chia's younger brother, Yüan Ch'eng-hsü, is a man of integrity and refinement. He is truly carrying on the family tradition." Consequently the emperor summoned him to become a Companion to the Prince of Chin and to be his Tutor, and also appointed him Scholar in the Academy for the Advancement of Letters.[6]

In the second half of the T'ang dynasty, and to a lesser extent before, the princes were replaced as patrons of the literati by powerful officials, civil and military. These officials surrounded themselves with scholars and writers for practical reasons as well as for prestige. For a talented young man, association with an influential person was often the only way to get ahead. But it always involved the risk of a sudden downfall if the patron should die or lose his position of power. "Guilt by association," an uncomfortably familiar concept in present-day America, was a common offense in T'ang China. It was the most frequent reason for inflicting demotion, exile, imprisonment, death, or some other form of punishment on the literati. Out of forty-two literati for whom punishment is recorded, twenty-six were charged with "having formerly befriended" some powerful personage who had suddenly become a criminal. Six of them fell when Chang I-chih and his brother Chang Ch'ang-tsung, former favorites of the Empress Wu, were executed in 705; the two brothers had brought many literati into the government. Fourteen were found guilty of some personal crime other than association (including two who were charged with association in addition to a crime of their own), and four were punished for unspecified crimes.

Wang Wu-ching was one of those who were disgraced and exiled (in his case to Ling-piao, in the extreme south) when Chang I-chih and his clique were executed, "because of his former association" with that group.[7] But in this and many other instances, it is difficult to determine whether the former association was the real reason for the man's downfall or merely a welcome excuse. Wang had been in trouble before. Once, when serving as Palace Censor, he had pointed out in open court that two Chief Ministers were violating court etiquette by leaving their places and chatting. The two Ministers did not take kindly to this criticism, and arranged for his speedy transfer from the Imperial Palace to the Palace of the Heir Apparent.[8]

"Association" is a cardinal feature in the biographies—not only as a criminal offense. We read much about who was associated with whom, and in what pursuit. Patronage, friendship, collaboration, and political cliques were very real phenomena in the lives of the literati. To seek out these associations was also an important concern of the historiographers. One of their tasks, as they saw it, was to fit each man into the proper groups, affiliations, classifications, and categories. They did this on a large scale when they made their selections for the "Garden of Letters." This category is in turn broken down into a number of special groups, some of which overlap. The subtle process of grouping within the chapter becomes partly visible in the peculiar phenomenon of the "attached" biographies. To be sure, in many cases this means simply grouping together various members of one family, a well-established practice in the dynastic histories. (An example of this use of the device is the first biography in the "Garden of Letters," the biography of K'ung Shao-an: attached to his life are brief notices of his father Huan, his elder brother Shao-hsin, his son Chen, Chen's son Chi-hsü, and another grandson of Shao-an, named Jo-ssu; only one of these—brother Shao-hsin—is presented as a man of letters in his own right.) But "attachment" was also used traditionally for grouping together men who were felt to belong together for reasons other than family ties.

Thus to the biography of Yüan Wan-ch'ing are attached those of four of his colleagues. The five were brought together by the Empress Wu in the late seventh century, and became known in their own time as "The Scholars of the Northern Gate" (*Pei-men hsüeh-shih*).[9] This appellation shows that the grouping was already an accomplished fact when the biographers went to work. Another group with a fixed name were "The Three Eminent Men of the Northern Capital" (*Pei-ching san chieh*). Two of these, Fu Chia-mo and Wu Shao-wei, were friends and colleagues. The third one, Ku I, is linked to them simply because he served in the same region (T'ai-yüan, the Northern Capital) at the same time (around 700), and because he was equally famous as a writer.[10]

The same lack of homogeneity is evident in the group of six contemporary writers attached to Ho Chih-chang (659–744). Five of them were, like Ho, from the area of modern Chekiang, but the sixth one, Li Ch'eng-chih, was from what is now Honan, and I have discovered no reason for his inclusion in the group.[11]

Another rather incongruous series of lives is appended to the biography of Li Hua: first, there is his friend and classmate Hsiao Ying-shih (both took the *chin-shih* degree in 735); then comes Li Hua's nephew Li Han, who was himself a writer of some note; next, there is Li Hua's friend Lu Chü; next, there are three other writers of the same period— Ts'ui Hao, Wang Ch'ang-ling, and Meng Hao-jan—who "acquired fame but no high official rank." The last biography in the group is that of Yüan Te-hsiu, another friend of Li Hua's.[12]

Association, then, is a cardinal but loosely used concept in the structuring of the biographies. Another key concept is "precedent." The biographer takes pains to record actions and events that started new procedures or served as models for later generations. He is interested in such precedents regardless of whether they affect the life of the individual. For example, the highest state examinations were held only in one place, the Western Capital (Ch'ang-an), down to 764. In that year, one of our literati, Chia Chih, proposed that they be held in the Eastern Capital (Lo-yang) as well, and his proposal was adopted. "This practice," says the biographer, "was initiated at that time."[13] He does not comment on this institutional change, which strengthened and expanded the examination system and made possible a greater influx of literati, particularly from northeastern China, into the bureaucracy. It is significant that Chia Chih, who proposed this innovation, was himself one of the northeastern literati; his family home was in Lo-yang.

In the biography of Kuo Cheng-i it is stated that when he was appointed Honorary Vice-President of the Imperial Secretariat in 681, he thereby became Minister Ranking with the Chief Officers of the Imperial Secretariat and the Imperial Chancellery (*t'ung chung-shu men-hsia p'ing-chang-shih*, often abbreviated *p'ing-chang-shih*), and that "the title *p'ing-chang-shih* as an appellation for Chief Ministers [*tsai-hsiang*] was first applied to Cheng-i and his colleagues."[14] Here it is clear that the historiographer is more interested in the change in bureaucratic nomenclature than in the man who was graced with a new title.

In the case of Chang Yün-ku, the manner of the subject's death leads to the establishment of a precedent. Chang was one of Emperor T'ai-tsung's favorites, but he was accused of mishandling a judicial case and executed by T'ai-tsung's order in 631. Then the emperor regretted his hasty decision and instituted a new procedure, providing that every death sentence was to be reviewed five times before it could be carried out. "This procedure," states the historian, "originated with the case of Chang Yün-ku."[15]

We turn now from the official careers of the literati to their literary activities. The biographies reveal a stereotyped image which the tenth-century historiographers had formed of the art of letters and of those who practiced it. The man of letters, as seen by them, was likely to be precocious, profoundly learned, endowed with a prodigious memory, and able to write at incredible speed. He tended to be haughty, and hence to offend his colleagues and superiors.

Precociousness will be discussed below in a different context. The association of book learning with literary excellence is entirely in keeping with the Confucian tradition. The stereotyped feature of a photographic memory—a natural corollary of the erudition prerequisite to literary composition—is repeatedly illustrated by graphic detail, which arouses our suspicions.[16]

Of Chang Yün-ku, for example, it is said that "he was able to recite stone inscriptions from memory, and to reconstitute the arrangement of a chessboard."[17] The same *topos* of memorizing stone inscriptions occurs also in the biography of Hsiao Ying-shih (717–68): "Once he went on an excursion to the Dragon Gate, south of Lo-yang, together with Li Hua and Lu Chü. The three of them read old stone inscriptions by the roadside. Hsiao Ying-shih could recite each one after reading it once; Li Hua had to read them twice before he could remember them; and Lu Chü thrice. Critics ranked the three men's intellectual stature in the same order."[18] This ranking of literati according to their intellectual and artistic abilities is one of the biographers' preoccupations.

Speed of literary composition is another *topos*. It crops up in eleven of the biographies, and also in the Introduction to the "Garden of Letters." It reflects, on the one hand, an actual phenomenon of literary craftsmanship in T'ang times. There were many occasions in the lives of the literati that called for improvisation and swiftness in writing: literary games and contests, public and private parties and celebrations, imperial commands and state examinations. The stock phrase *hsia pi ch'eng chang* ("as soon as the brush touches the paper, a composition is finished"), already common in earlier dynastic histories, occurs frequently in our biographies. It even became institutionalized in T'ang times as the name of a state examination.

On the other hand, the *topos* of speedy composition reflects a blurred concept of the art of writing in the layman's mind. The work of a creative genius appears to the outsider to be accomplished effortlessly and instantaneously.

The historiographer reveals himself to be an outsider when faced with the phenomenon of purely literary composition. One may even detect a trace of hostility in his attitude toward the man of letters. This is reflected in the frequent references to literary pride—another *topos*.

A typical anecdote brings together two poets of the early seventh century, Cheng Shih-i and Ts'ui Hsin-ming. I quote from the biography of Cheng Shih-i (whom the historian labels "frivolous"):

At that time, Ts'ui Hsin-ming considered his own writings to be nonpareil. . . . Cheng Shih-i once met him traveling on a river and said to him: "I have heard of your line, 'Maple leaves fall on the Wu River, cold.'" Ts'ui Hsin-ming, delighted, showed him more than a hundred of his poems. Cheng Shih-i looked at them, and without finishing his perusal, he said: "What I have seen is not as good as what I had heard." With these words he tossed them into the river. Ts'ui Hsin-ming was speechless, and rowed away.[19]

The haughtiness of the T'ang poets may have been exaggerated by their unsympathetic biographers, but it was certainly a real phenomenon, and not restricted to T'ang China. One of our contemporary English poets has said:

It is evident that a faith in their vocation, mystical in intensity, sustains poets. . . . Although it is true that poets are vain and ambitious, their vanity and ambition is of the purest kind attainable in this world, for the saint renounces ambition. They are ambitious to be accepted for what they ultimately are as revealed by their inmost experiences, their finest perceptions, their deepest feelings, their uttermost sense of truth, in their poetry.[20]

Hart Crane used to hand a sheet or two fresh off the typewriter to his friends at Sunday afternoon parties, and he would say: "Read that! Isn't that the grrreatest poem ever written!"[21]

The biographies are concerned not only with literary men's attitudes toward creativity but also with the sources of their inspiration. Hu Ch'u-pin (fl. second half of seventh century, died before 689) is stated to have needed alcohol in order to write,[22] and the drinking of wine is also mentioned in four other biographies.[23] The association of wine with literary creation was a well-established tradition in the T'ang period. It can be traced back to the time when the literati as a class achieved their prominent position in Chinese society, namely, the end of Later Han.[24] But the compilers of the *Old History of the T'ang Dynasty* were actually less interested in wine as inspiration for writers than in its effect on a man's official career. In the biography of Hu Ch'u-pin, they note that his intoxication never caused him to betray state secrets. And leaking official secrets, as we shall see, is an offense charged to several other literati. Of Ts'ui Hsien (*chin-shih* of 807, d. 834), they report that as a provincial administrator, he drank with his friends all day, then did excellent work on official documents all night, which caused his subordinates to admire him as a "divine being" (*shen jen*).[25]

Another source of inspiration for writing—music—is mentioned in the biography óf Li Han: "During the T'ien-pao era [742–56] he lived in Yang-ti. He perfected his writings with the utmost care, and his ideas formed slowly. He often requested musicians from the magistrate of Yang-ti district, Huang-fu Tseng. Whenever the flow of his ideas dried up, he had music played until his mind was at ease; then he proceeded to write."[26]

Finally, the specific occasion that led to the writing of a work of poetry or prose is frequently told, and in some cases, the work itself is quoted wholly or in part—a well-established feature in the biographies of the dynastic histories. But the compilers of the *Old History of the T'ang Dynasty* depart from earlier tradition by quoting only works they consider "useful," never those that are merely "beautiful." They thus carry out a policy credited to Emperor T'ai-tsung, under whose personal direction historiography was thoroughly reorganized and systematized as a state institution. The *Chen-kuan cheng-yao* by Wu Ching (670–749) sets forth T'ai-tsung's viewpoint as follows:

In the early part of the Chen-kuan era [627–50], T'ai-tsung said to Fang Hsüan-ling, who was in charge of compiling the history of the reigning dynasty: "Reading the Histories of Former and Later Han, We find that they quote Yang Hsiung's '*Fu* on the Sacrifice to Heaven at the Palace of the Sweet Springs' and his '*Fu* on the Emperor's Hunt with the Yü-lin Guards'; Ssu-ma Hsiang-ju's '*Fu* of Tzu-hsü' and his '*Fu* on the Imperial Hunting Park'; and Pan Ku's '*Fu* on the Two Capitals.' Since these works are written in frothy and flowery style, they are of no use as exhortations and admonitions; why should they be incorporated in books of history? But memorials to the throne and discussions of affairs with trenchant and straight wording and ideas, capable of benefiting the art of government—all such works should be included in the history of this dynasty, regardless of whether We have followed them or not."[27]

In accordance with this policy, we find a total of twenty-four works quoted in whole or in part in twenty-two of the one hundred and one biographies. The reasons for quoting these works are in some cases quite obvious, in others less so. As I see it, every quotation meets one or more of three qualifications: (1) it develops a concept dear to the historiographer's heart; (2) it criticizes a person or group disliked by the historiographer; (3) it illustrates the talent or character of the subject of the biography.

The first qualification is met by most of the quoted memorials and other communications addressed to emperors and heirs apparent. Though they are usually concerned with a specific problem which was acute at the moment, the historiographer must have felt that they all possessed a "timeless" value which warranted their inclusion in the dynastic history, for the indoctrination and edification of future generations.

Four of these quoted documents follow an established Confucian tradition in setting before incoming and future emperors the image of a perfect ruler. In one of these, Liu Hsien (d. 711 or 712) urges the Heir Apparent—later the Emperor Hsüan-tsung—to cultivate Confucian virtues rather than gratify sensual desires; he emphasizes the value of the Confucian Classics as models of style, and warns against flowery elegance. The biographer adds that Hsüan-tsung was pleased with the memorial and rewarded its author.[28]

Another memorial to the same Hsüan-tsung as Heir Apparent deals with a more specific situation: Chia Tseng (d. 727) opposes the employment of singing girls in the Heir Apparent's palace. (Hsüan-tsung's interest in music and musicians is a historic fact.) The Prince's reply, acceding to Chia Tseng's request, is also quoted.[29] It is noteworthy that, T'ai-tsung's opinion notwithstanding, the requests embodied in the quoted memorials were in most cases granted. In other words, the historiographer preferably cites documents that positively affected decisions and thus made history.

Some of the memorials in the "Garden of Letters" deal with state ceremonies and Confucian ritual. Ho Chih-chang outlines the procedure to be followed in the imperial sacrifice at Mount T'ai in 725.[30] Yang Chiung during the I-feng era (676–79) argued at length—and successfully—against a proposed change in the official robe patterns.[31] When Emperor Kao-tsung died in Lo-yang, the Eastern Capital, in 683, Ch'en Tzu-ang presented convincing arguments for proceeding with his burial right there, rather than at the Western Capital.[32] This is historically important in connection with the Empress Wu's shift of the capital from Ch'ang-an to Lo-yang, and the concomitant loss of power of the northwestern aristocracy centered around Ch'ang-an. In the early part of the K'ai-yüan era (713–42), a memorial by Hsü Ching-hsien succeeded in reducing the lavish awards to officials who did well in archery contests.[33]

The three last-mentioned memorials all stress the Confucian idea of economy in government expenditures. Others concern filial piety and ancestor worship: Sun T'i complained in 736 that his father was merely a District Magistrate (*hsien ling*), while he himself was already a Director of Decrees in the Imperial Secretariat (*chung-shu she-jen*). This demonstration of filiality got his father a promotion.[34] Hsü Ch'i-tan (630–72) pointed out in a memorial that it was unfair to degrade a man's ancestral shrine to atone for crimes committed by his descendants. He, too, carried his point.[35]

In the category of criticism of persons and groups disliked by the historiographers, there is Hsiao Ying-shih's *fu* satirizing Li Lin-fu (see above), and a long diatribe against the eunuchs, written by Liu Fen in 828 in response to an examination question set by the emperor himself.[36]

The third criterion for quoting from a man's works is mentioned specifically in several instances, and is perhaps applicable to other quotations as well: the passages are stated to represent the man's "special talent" (*ts'ai*), or some trait of his character, good or bad. For example, a statement presented to the throne by Kuo Cheng-i in 678, during a Tibetan invasion, advocating a more defensive military policy vis-à-vis Tibet, is quoted with evident approval and asserted to be typical of Kuo Cheng-i's "talent" (*ts'ai*).[37] On the other hand, Ssu-k'ung

T'u's (837–908) "Essay on the Hsiu-hsiu Pavilion" is quoted as "typical of his perverseness and swaggering pride."[38]

As far as references to literary style in the biographies are concerned, the historiographers show interest in matters of priority, imitation, innovation, and precedents. (We noted above a similar interest in precedents in connection with official careers.) The just-mentioned essay by Ssu-k'ung T'u is stated to be an imitation of Po Chü-i's "Tsui-yin chuan." Stylistic innovations are credited to Fu Chia-mo and his friend and colleague Wu Shao-wei (both fl. around 700). They created a new style, says their biographer, for stele inscriptions and eulogies. Based on the Confucian Classics, it became known as the "Fu-Wu style."[39] (A modern literary historian agrees that Fu's and Wu's prose writings mark a significant step in the development of the *ku-wen* movement.[40]) Li Shang-yin (812?–58?) began to write in "modern style" under the influence of his patron Ling-hu Ch'u.[41]

While the historiographers make occasional references of this sort to literary styles, they pay more attention to the *practical* aspects of literature. They tell us how the literati made use of their literary abilities in their workaday lives. Many of them found employment as tutors, secretaries, clerks, editors, librarians, propagandists, and the like, in government bureaus and private establishments. Some became ghost writers for highly placed officials: under the reign of the Empress Wu, Yen Chao-yin and Sung Chih-wen "secretly" wrote many of the pieces published under the names of the empress's favorite Chang I-chih and his associates.[42]

Li Shang-yin was in charge of composing documents at the headquarters of General Wang Mao-yüan. The General "admired his talent and married off his daughter to him." "Wang Mao-yüan," the biography goes on to explain, "though literate and trained in Confucian learning, came from a family of military men."[43]

Li Yung (678?–747) managed to amass a fortune by writing on commission. He ground out hundreds of obituaries, eulogies, and other prose pieces for private individuals, and for Buddhist and Taoist temples. The historiographer does not approve of such commercialism. He cites the opinion of "critics at the time" who held that "from antiquity down, no one had ever gone as far as Li Yung in selling his writings to acquire wealth."[44] In the style of these biographies, the historian often bestows praise and condemnation indirectly, through unnamed "critics at the time," and occasionally by citing the opinion of a prominent individual.

An understanding of the subtleties of literature was frequently a practical asset. For instance, during the campaign against Koguryö in

667, the commander of the Chinese garrison at Pyongyang wished to inform his commander in chief, Li Chi, that he was short of men and supplies. To keep this information from the enemy, he coded the message in the form of a *li-ho shih*—a poem in which one has to split the characters and recombine the elements in order to get the hidden meaning. When General Li Chi received the poem, he exclaimed: "What's the use of writing poetry in a military emergency like this? That man should be beheaded!" The situation was saved by one of our literati, Yüan Wan-ch'ing, who was on Li Chi's staff. He deciphered the code message, and reinforcements and supplies were dispatched at once to the Chinese garrison.[45] Though the historiographer does not say so explicitly, he is obviously delighted to expose the dullness of the military mind. (Compare the remark about General Wang Mao-yüan above.)

But during the same Korean campaign, Yüan Wan-ch'ing got into trouble through an indiscretion in the application of his literary skills. Li Chi ordered him to write the official proclamation of war. In the proclamation, Yüan included the phrase: "Koguryö does not know how to defend the strategic Yalu." This tipped off the enemy commander: he promptly stationed troops at the Yalu River fords, and the Chinese forces were unable to cross. For this mistake, Yüan was exiled to the extreme south—but he was amnestied soon thereafter.[46]

A critical situation which arose at a solemn court function in the last decade of the seventh century was retrieved through the literary skill of Wang Chü. Five imperial princes were being installed in their fiefs, and when the ceremony was already under way it was discovered, to everyone's dismay, that the documents of investiture had not been brought along. Then Wang Chü improvised the five complicated documents on the spot, dictating them to five scribes simultaneously, and the ceremony went on as planned.[47] (Again the *topos* of instantaneous composition.)

Another writer whose literary skills impressed the historiographers was Li Chü-ch'uan (d. 898). "Since the empire was then very unsettled, with people wandering hither and thither, eager for salary and position, he served various highly placed men as a writer in different parts of the country. . . . Li Chü-ch'uan's style and ideas were clever and swift, his brush sped as if it were flying, it spread to the far borders and left nothing unmoved." When he served on the staff of the warlord Wang Ch'ung-jung, "it was due to Li Chü-ch'uan's assistance that Wang Ch'ung-jung repeatedly acquired merit." Later Wang Ch'ung-jung was killed by his subordinates, and Li "was found guilty by the court councillors of having served" Wang. Consequently he was sent to an obscure provincial post. There he met another warlord and former acquaintance,

Yang Shou-liang, who exclaimed: "'Heaven has bequeathed Secretary Li to me!'" In Yang's service, Li together with his master was captured by an opposing military commander, Han Chien. But while Yang was killed by his captor, Li wrote a poem which so moved Han Chien that he released him and later put him on his own staff. On another occasion, when the emperor took up his temporary abode in the region governed by Han Chien, the latter found the local resources insufficient to support this added burden.

He therefore commissioned Li Chü-ch'uan to write an urgent appeal which was sent to all parts of the empire, asking for help in supplying provisions for the royal household and setting up the imperial residence. The appeal went out in all four directions, and in response supplies poured in. When Li Chü-ch'uan put ink on paper and set forth his arguments, both form and reasoning were perfect. Emperor Chao-tsung esteemed him profoundly. At that time Li Chü-ch'uan's fame spread all over the empire. When Chao-tsung returned to the capital, he gave him a special appointment as Imperial Adviser. He concurrently continued in his post as assistant to Han Chien.

As Li Chü-ch'uan had lived by the power of his brush, so he died by it, according to the biography. When the mighty warlord Chu Ch'üan-chung was preparing to make himself independent (he did overthrow the T'ang dynasty nine years later), he consulted Li about his plans. Li presented him with a statement, setting forth both the advantages and the disadvantages of Chu's plan. Chu Ch'üan-chung was displeased. On top of this, another man of letters in Chu's service was jealous of Li and pointed out to Chu: "'Imperial Adviser Li's statement is sincerely and beautifully written, but it does not redound to my master's advantage.' On that day," concludes the biography, "Li Chü-ch'uan was killed by order of Chu Ch'üan-chung."[48]

As we turn now to the third aspect of the biographies—character and personality—we find several key concepts emerging. One of these is the orthodox Confucian association of intellectual and moral qualities. For example, we saw above that Yüan Ch'eng-hsü was selected by Emperor T'ai-tsung as one of several "men of learning and character" to serve in the entourage of the Heir Apparent, and that he was said to have inherited these sterling qualities from his ancestors. The theory of inherited qualities accounts in part for the habit of listing ancestors, with official titles, near the beginning of many biographies. Another reason is the need to establish a man's family background and his aristocratic lineage, if any. An interesting case of inherited characteristics is described in the biography of Sung Ling-wen (fl. second half of seventh century): he was a strong man, a fine calligrapher, and a good writer; and each of his three sons inherited one of his three distinctions.[49]

Another key phenomenon is the biographers' failure to conceive a human life in dynamic terms of growth and development. Rather, they think of personality, career, and the capacity to achieve (in literature or any other field) as more or less fixed from the very beginning. This view is evident, for example, in the biography of Ts'ui Hsin-ming (b. in 580's, d. after 632):

Ts'ui Hsin-ming was born exactly at noon on the fifth day of the fifth month. At that time, several unusual birds with extremely small, five-colored bodies gathered on a tree in the courtyard, drummed their wings in unison, and chirped beautifully. The Director of the Imperial Observatory of Sui, Shih Liang-shih, had just come to Ch'ing Prefecture and happened to be present. He interpreted the omens as follows: "The fifth month is fire; fire is brightness; brightness is literary splendor. The exact hour of noon means the acme of literary perfection. Then there are birds of five colors, beating their wings and chirping. This boy will surely become a brilliant writer whose fame will spread over the entire world. Since the birds are small, his salary and rank will probably not be high." As he grew up, his learning was broad, and his memory keen. As soon as his brush touched paper, a composition was finished [hsia pi ch'eng chang]. Kao Hsiao-chi, who lived in the same rural area, had a knack for appraising character. He often told people: "Ts'ui Hsin-ming's talent and learning are rich and vigorous. Though his fame will be unsurpassed in his time, his rank will unfortunately not be exalted."[50]

A brilliant writer with low official rank—this formula fits practically all the literati in this chapter. We note in this passage four of the topoi encountered previously: spreading fame, broad learning, keen memory, and instantaneous creation.

This is the only reference to birth in the biographies. And it is mentioned here, not because the historian is interested in the event itself (he does not even state the year of birth) but because it reveals the pattern for the whole life. The pattern is not visible to ordinary mortals, but open to interpretation by experts. There are altogether nine predictions that were later fulfilled in the "Garden of Letters."

The concept of the fixed pattern also accounts, I believe, for the frequent references to youth. A man's early life is viewed not as a stage in his development but as the period when his personality type first becomes apparent. Thirty-three of the biographies mention traits manifested in youth, often in stereotyped terms. The statement that a man early in his life "was good at writing" (shan shu wen) occurs eight times in these same words, and ten more times in different words. In three biographies we are told that the boy could write well at a specified young age (six, eight, and nine sui respectively). The phrase "broadly learned" (*po hsüeh*) is applied to four young literati, and of three others it is said in different words that they studied hard in their youth. Five men of letters are asserted to have won early fame through writing, and five others through unspecified achievements (which are also likely to be literary in the context of the "Garden of Letters").

Should some of these allegations of precocious literary ability be discounted as exaggerations? This is hard to determine. We should note the historic fact that two of our literati, Yang Chiung (b. 650, d. between 692 and 705) and Wu T'ung-hsüan (fl. 779–94), actually passed the state examination for "divine youths" (*shen-t'ung*).[51]

Besides literary skill and book learning, there are other traits—good and bad—which may be manifested in a man's early life. Of Yüan Te-hsiu (696–754) it is said that "in his youth he was renowned for his filial piety,"[52] and the same formula is applied to Wang Chung-shu (762–823).[53] The biography of Wang Han (fl. first half of eighth century) states that "in his youth he was unconventional and unrestrained." In the course of the same biography, we learn that he was fond of horses, singing girls, hunting, drinking, and wild parties.[54] All these are vices charged to many other literati. It is apparent that the historiographer is not interested in a man's early life as such but in bringing to light early manifestations of his innate character.

The concept of the fixed pattern does not rule out the possibility of changes of character. In the biography of T'ang Fu (*chin-shih* of 810, d. 839 or 840) it is pointed out that in the first part of his life he was a good official and an upright man, but in the last years of his life, when he held powerful and lucrative positions on the southeastern coast (modern Fukien), he became greedy and corrupt. This came to light, notes the biographer, after his death, when his servants and concubines fought over his property, which was found to amount to 100,000 strings of cash.[55]

Ch'i Huan (d. between 746 and 756) is portrayed as a strange mixture of good and bad qualities. As Provincial Censor (*chien-ch'a yü-shih*) "he prosecuted those who had committed wrongs, but first tried to sway them from their evil ways. His contemporaries considered this to be a praiseworthy way of discharging the duties of that office." (Indirect praise, attributed to "contemporaries," as noted above.) Again, as prefect of Pien prefecture, "he governed with integrity and strictness; the people and his subordinates sang his praises." In another of his many provincial assignments, he improved transportation and increased revenue by altering river courses. In further attempts to repair waterways he failed. Once he was demoted for a mistake committed by many literati: he indiscreetly reported a private conversation with the emperor to another official. Later he was found guilty of embezzling goods, in collusion with eunuchs. He also maltreated one of his concubines. Yet such affairs are never mentioned unless it be to demonstrate a trait in the man's character, or to furnish the clue to an event in his career.

So far, Ch'i Huan looks like T'ang Fu: an inconstant type who changed from good to bad. But the end of the biography presents him in a different light: in the 740's Ch'i Huan was punished repeatedly, having incurred the enmity of Li Lin-fu, the dictatorial Chief Minister who got a bad press in the official histories. After Ch'i Huan died, "when Su-tsung ascended the throne, he was rehabilitated as one of those who had been entrapped by Li Lin-fu, and posthumously honored."[56] This concludes the biography. The historiographer apparently concurs in the final and official rehabilitation, which may or may not be intended to cancel the previously noted defects in the man's character.

Several other biographies are less ambiguous. They clearly depict their subjects as mixtures of good and evil. Ts'ui Hao (d. 754), for instance, "had superior talents but lacked the behavior of a gentleman. He was addicted to gambling and drinking. When he was in the capital, he would marry a girl for her beauty, and then abandon her as soon as he was even slightly displeased with her. Altogether he was married four times."[57]

Li Yung (678?–747) is praised repeatedly in his biography as a literary genius of early and steadily increasing fame. Some of his writings, says the biographer, "are highly esteemed by men of letters." He got his first (?) official appointment—as Imperial Adviser of the Left —through the recommendation of two high functionaries, Li Ch'iao and Chang T'ing-kuei. Their recommendation stated that "his writings are lofty and his behavior straight: he is fit to become an admonishing and warning official." One of his memorials, successfully opposing the appointment of a heterodox wizard, Cheng P'u-ssu, as Director of the Imperial Library, is quoted at length—a sign of approval. The same biography characterizes him as "boastful" and "gay and extravagant," and notes that "he freely engaged in wild hunting." He is furthermore criticized, as already mentioned, for amassing wealth by writing on commission.[58]

The rationale behind the mixture of good and evil is, if I am not mistaken, a key concept in the historiographers' over-all view of the literati: they are imperfect because they fail to achieve the dual Confucian ideal of self-cultivation and distinguished public service. Had they been equally successful in both pursuits, they would not have been relegated to the "Garden of Letters."

In one of the biographies, this view is neatly summed up by P'ei

Hsing-chien, who is credited, like Ts'ui Hsin-ming's neighbor, with "a knack for appraising character." Speaking of the four famous literati Wang P'o, Yang Chiung, Lu Chao-lin, and Lo Pin-wang (they flourished in the second half of the seventh century), P'ei said: "Whether a gentleman goes far depends primarily on his ability and knowledge, and only secondarily on his literary skill. Although P'o and the other three possess literary talent, they are unsteady and shallow. Surely they are not made of the stuff required for achieving high rank. . . . "[59]

In epitome, what is the composite picture of the T'ang literary man emerging from these one hundred and one biographies? He was usually a bureaucrat, but rarely rose to the top. He entered his career through the civil service examination system, or through the recommendation of a patron, or both. Much of his life and work was influenced by his associations with relatives, friends, colleagues, superiors, and subordinates. His fate was closely linked to the rise and fall of his present or former patrons. His innate talent as a writer became manifest early in his life. He was precocious, bookish, learned, and endowed with a prodigious memory. He could produce poetry and prose at fantastic speed when the occasion demanded it. He was inordinately proud of his literary achievements. He tended to seek inspiration for his work in wine, music, horses, singing girls, and other pursuits unworthy of a Confucian gentleman. He was often indiscreet in divulging confidential information. Nevertheless, imperial and princely courts, high officials, and military commanders sought his company and found his services indispensable.

This was fortunate for posterity, for it made possible the creation of literary masterpieces that have endured to this day.

Robert Ruhlmann

TRADITIONAL HEROES
IN CHINESE POPULAR FICTION

Heroes in literature and art express more than the personal opinions and dreams of particular authors. They also embody current values and ideals, and convey a powerful image of the conflicting forces at work in the society of their time. Superhuman yet human, these prestigious personalities inspire and encourage imitation, initiate or revive patterns of behavior, and thus play a significant role in shaping history.

Some are created by writers and artists in a definite time and place; others are passed on from ages immemorial by continuous or intermittent traditions. Some are myths which in the course of time were given a historical character; others are figures from history transformed into myths.[1] Stable eras tend to mirror themselves in a "classical" type of hero, a healthy and reasonably happy man who is successfully adapted to his circumstances; dynamic tensions and crises of an age of change, in contrast, are usually embodied in a "romantic" hero, a younger man, often the victim of tragedy—a misfit, a rebel, a defender of the old order or founder of a new one. Study of heroes, of their genesis and mutations, has much to contribute to the understanding of social and intellectual history.

For this purpose fictional literature is of exceptional interest; the novel, the drama, and some forms of narrative poetry all have a broader appeal and offer more direct and explicit means of expression than nonfiction, music, and visual arts. Indeed, students of European and American literature have for some time been mining fiction for historical data relating to the economic, the religious, and other aspects of the past. Leo Lowenthal, in his brilliant book *Literature and the Image of Man,*[2] extracts from texts of European dramas and novels—from Vega and Cervantes to Ibsen and Hamsun—elements for a picture of three centuries of social change.

Scholarly studies of Chinese fiction for the history of Chinese thought and institutions are relatively few and recent,[3] primarily because the novel and the drama have until this century traditionally been disdained by Chinese literocrats[4] as inferior genres and, when written in the colloquial language, as altogether unworthy of the name of literature. It is becoming clear that Chinese fiction may well be the only available source for the study of certain values and attitudes that have influenced the course of Chinese history. Chinese fiction offers an indirect but fruitful approach precisely where direct research into motivations is difficult—among the illiterate and semiliterate common people of China.

In Chinese fiction there are popular heroes, scholarly heroes, and also those resulting from the interaction between the first two types. This paper seeks to analyze some of the specific attributes of these heroes, some of the political, moral, and sentimental values they stand for, some of the reasons for their appeal to men's hearts, and some of their effects on human behavior at particular periods.

POPULAR FICTION AND CONFUCIAN SCHOLARS

Mencius distinguishes, in a famous formula, between "those who labor with their minds" and "those who labor with their physical strength," adding that the former govern the latter and are supported by them.[5] This formula could hardly ever have applied literally to China, but it is reflected to some extent in the more or less permanent division of Chinese society into two distinct strata—the peasantry and a small and proud elite based on land, office, and literacy. It was the elite that produced for its own consumption the bulk of Chinese literature and Chinese historiography. All formal works, such as commentaries on the Classics, poems, technical treatises, and documents of an ideological or administrative character were written by scholar-officials for other scholar-officials, and remained inaccessible to the illiterate masses. The same is true of the anecdotes and parables, the "tales of the marvelous" (*ch'uan ch'i*), the "occasional notes" (*pi chi*), the short stories, and the other kinds of fiction composed by scholars in the classical language across a span of more than two thousand years. Ming and Ch'ing novels, though written in colloquial language and patterned in form after popular fiction, were obviously intended to be read only by the educated.[6] One should no more assume that these scholar-writings accurately expressed the beliefs and feelings of the masses than that the thoughts of the two communities coincided at any given time.

These genres, however, are only a part of Chinese fiction. The remainder is basically oral and addressed to a motley audience—mostly peasants, artisans, shopkeepers, and merchants, and often their womenfolk too, who throng the marketplace or the teahouses to listen to storytellers, puppeteers, and singing girls, crowd around stone stages of temples at festival times, or gather before crude wooden platforms of open-air theaters to watch the actors. Singing girls are seldom found outside big cities. But storytellers and theatrical troupes are everywhere, and often wander from place to place, even into out-of-the-way villages[7] and the secluded women's quarters of large mansions.[8] Then, those who have heard stories and plays retell them for those who have not.

Chinese oral literature also includes innumerable songs, proverbs, children's rhymes, work chanties, and dialogues of all sorts. Different degrees of elaboration can be found among them, from pure folklore, if such a thing exists, to the most sophisticated prose and poetry. And, while many of these forms are peculiar to their own province or district (the number of local schools of theater runs into hundreds), there is a constant exchange of themes and techniques among them.

These forms of entertainment have proved to be very enduring. From a comparison of contemporary observations with T'ang and Sung documents,[9] it is clear that most of them have been thriving for more than a thousand years with few changes in form. Their regular audiences in today's Peking and those of Ch'ang-an during the T'ang, of Kaifeng and Hangchow during the Sung, seem to be, *mutatis mutandis*, of closely comparable social level and occupation. The language they use is the colloquial speech of their time, with only a few passages in formal style. The subjects of Sung storytellers fall into six traditional categories: ghosts and supernatural manifestations; Buddhist miracles and reincarnations; love and aspects of daily life; crimes and their detection; feats of strength and courage; and historical tales commemorating exploits of great men or the founding and collapse of dynasties. Each of these themes was handled by a specialized guild, among which the guild of *chiang-shih*—"raconteurs of history"—enjoyed the most dignity. As a result of this specialization, each group of stories long retained its distinctive character while apparently losing nothing of its popularity and vitality.

Many texts have been preserved to this day, some only recently rediscovered and lately published. Among these are dozens of pre-T'ang and T'ang "popularizations" or *chantefables* (*pien-wen*), three Sung plays of the Southern tradition (*hsi-wen*), several Sung dramas in narrative form (*chu-kung-tiao*), and more than two hundred Yüan plays (*tsa-chü*). From Yüan times on, there are a number of "ballads" which were partly recited and partly sung (*ku-tz'u, t'an-tz'u*), novels (*yen-yi, ts'ai-tzu-shu*), hundreds of short stories (*p'ing-hua, hsiao-shuo*), and thousands of plays (*hsi, ch'ü*).[10] These are, however, only a small fraction of the total.[11] Some performers used promptbooks, but most could not read or write: the transmission of the repertory from fathers to sons or from masters to apprentices was more often than not entirely oral. Of the extant texts, many are anonymous or of collective authorship, and some, products of cumulative authorship spread over several centuries, were long passed on in oral form before being transcribed.

Texts available for research, though only a portion of the rich oral repertory, are a valuable means of access to the thought of the illiterate population whom narrators and actors not only entertained but also educated. For centuries, Chinese with little or no formal schooling have derived from theatergoing an amazing knowledge of, and concern for, the history of their country. More important still, storytelling and the theater provided channels of expression for feelings that had little or nothing to do with elite influence; they describe not only the life and routine circumstances of the common people, but also "heterodox" beliefs, immoral conduct, and political activities directed toward subversion or revolt.

Actually, the very existence of a fiction of this sort has always been a challenge to Confucians. Some authors of fiction were literati who refused to take official posts, or who retired under the influence of "heterodox" (Taoist or Buddhist) ideas or out of personal frustration and disenchantment. Others had successful careers as Confucian administrators while writing fiction surreptitiously; they regarded their penchant for these despised genres as a weakness and tried to hide it behind pseudonyms and outward conformity.

The outward conformity, of course, was to the code of the Confucian elite. For the best part of twenty centuries, most Confucians were agreed on certain basic attitudes about the issues of life and on every man's duty to cultivate corresponding inner values and to organize society accordingly. Literature's function and *raison d'être* in this perspective were to teach truth and virtue: it must contribute to uplifting men by attracting them emotionally toward approved ideals.

Storytelling and drama fell far from these standards. Primarily interested in entertaining, not in improving morals, free to improvise as the occasion might dictate, performers were often indecorous and sometimes indulged in irreverent or even subversive satire. Some of their heroes conform to established social and ethical standards; others, however, belong to mythologies which Sung Confucianism wanted to suppress, or exemplify chivalric values altogether foreign to Confucian orthodoxy. Many tales and plays take pains to caution the public explicitly against violating the Confucian codes, and illustrate their point by punishing evil and rewarding good. But this moralizing appears often as superficial and superimposed, a mere sop to would-be censors. The picture of sin, represented vividly and with warm human understanding, engraves itself more deeply upon the consciousness than the moral exhortations.

It is essentially fiction's indifference to conventional morality that explains the Confucian attitude toward it and the efforts of Confucian bureaucrats to restrict its influence. During the Ming and Ch'ing dynasties, the government repeatedly tried to ban "seditious plays,"[12] and "novels and licentious works" (*hsiao-shuo yin tz'u*), calling them "frivolous, vulgar and untrue."[13] Even so unconventional and nonconformist a man of letters as Chin Sheng-t'an (*ca.* 1610–61) saw fit to alter and truncate the text of the *Water Margin* in order to discourage banditry: in his 1644 edition, no honorable surrender is possible for the outlaws; they must all be executed.[14] Further evidence of the effort to keep the theater under control is found in the low legal status given to actors; all law codes denied them the designation of "normal commoners" (*liang-min*). They were classified with slaves, prostitutes, and yamen-runners in the lowest class of the population, as "vile subjects" (*chien-jen*). This discrimination worked hardship, since offenses committed by *chien-jen* were more severely punished than those committed against them.[15] Again, local magistrates, responsible for maintaining public morals, checked theatrical performances in town and countryside, and insisted that every time romantic stories like *Hsi Hsiang Chi* were staged, actors should also perform plays stressing fidelity, filial piety, chastity, and charity. This way of injecting moral elements into the repertory (and so have the Devil spread a Confucian gospel) is comparable to the technique the Buddhists had used for centuries, that of making their doctrine palatable by coating it in colorful adventures of rebirths. Why not present to the "inferior men" and "selfish and money-motivated" tradespeople, through the best mass medium available, examples of pious sons, devoted subjects, and other virtuous heroes?

Study of popular fiction, as it was appreciated by common folk and manipulated by officialdom, can help us to a variety of understandings: of the ambivalent attitude of the literati toward popular media; of their own differences of view on Confucian principles; of the attitudes of the common people—always drawn to and always resistant to the culture of their betters. We shall here explore these problems through one of the many possible approaches: a consideration of the heroes of popular literature.

FACT AND FANCY

Historiography purports to describe events as they really happened; it takes pains to ensure unbiased, impersonal observation. Fiction, on the other hand, connotes the invention of characters and situations by a creative mind for audiences seeking entertainment or escape. To absorb and move is the storyteller's and the playwright's aim; their livelihood is at stake, and they cannot afford the dry matter-of-fact tone of police files or official statistics. They can and do "falsify" history for dramatic effect. Yet the very nature of dramatic effect usually limits the extent to which such falsification is possible, bound as it is by the mental habits of authors and audiences alike.

Paradoxically, the Chinese official histories may be less reliable than pure fiction. They

report everything as seen from the imperial court, generally neglecting the viewpoint of the provinces. . . . And they are naturally prejudiced in favor of the established institutions and beliefs—the Chinese type of monarchy, the Confucian code of ethics, etc. Also, the historiographers as a body are generally hostile to certain groups of people, such as eunuchs, merchants, monks, foreigners, and soldiers.[16]

The historiographer had often to use a "crooked brush" (*ch'ü pi*) in favor of family or clique, of the reigning house, and of powerful individuals. The reader can never be sure that statements of "historical fact" were not in reality calculated moves in some literary or political dispute, or selections of particulars meant to drive home a moral lesson, to encourage the good and warn the evil.[17]

Chinese novelists and playwrights, by contrast, are not tied by all these intentions, conventions, pressures, and prejudices. They bring the common people and the local interests into the picture, and throw a colorful light on minor events omitted by histories. They deal with techniques, tools, food, and dress, with institutions, customs, and psychology. Largely free from didactic and missionary purpose, they show man as he is or would like to be, not as the rules say he should be. They offer a candid and intimate view of the society of their time:

Without resorting to abstract discussion, they let us understand the conscious and unconscious assumptions of a society. . . . They indicate what has happened to religious and ethical ideals after they have been popularized and perhaps diluted, or as they are reflected through the novelist's individual mind; they reveal the imperfect ways in which social institutions operate in ambiguous and refractory human situations. The novel stands at the point where social history and the human soul intersect.[18]

Love stories, ghost stories, and Buddhist tales seek the moving and the sensational, but their narrations and dialogues are commonly realistic: the motions may be unnatural but the furniture is real. Detective stories give us a welcome view from below of the administrative process and help us visualize the lives of lesser officials and their aides.

As for specifically historical tales, romances, and plays, their method is what an expressive Chinese phrase calls *ch'i shih san hsü,* "70 per cent truth and 30 per cent falsehood," which might here be paraphrased as "70 per cent unreliable history and 30 per cent revealing fiction"; they add to the historical record a wealth of pithy anecdotes and appealing details, suggest motivations, reconstruct conversations, and accomplish "the infusion of the spirit of life into figures of the past, and the re-creation of the circumstances which surrounded them."[19] For this imaginative 30 per cent, authors rely on their own knowledge and experience, and all falsifications, adornments, and rationalizations, whether spontaneous or due to official pressure, all shifts of emphasis and of sympathy detectable in their writings, throw precious light on ideas and beliefs current in their time.

The writer of fiction seldom alters the broad outline of past events as represented in the histories; his fictional touches are limited to well-defined episodes. Nor does fictitious embroidery often affect the spirit of the sources. For example, stories and plays about the agrarian reformer Chia Ssu-tao (d. 1275) unquestioningly adopt the prejudiced views of the *History of the Sung,* which was written by Chia's political opponents. According to this official account, Chia rises to high office on the recommendation of his sister, a favorite of the emperor, becomes notorious for his luxury and many iniquities, and finally betrays the country to the Mongols. Fiction adds some highlights to this portrait of a typical "bad last minister," in particular a description of Chia's ordering one of his concubines beheaded for a minor offense: she had watched two young men boating and whispered, "How handsome they are!"[20]

In other cases, there are interesting differences of outlook between history and fiction. In moral standards and political legitimacy, there was no great disparity among rival protagonists of the Three Kingdoms (A.D. 220–80). Their first historiographer, Ch'en Shou (233–97) handles them impartially. But the later novels *San-kuo chih P'ing-hua* and *San-kuo chih Yen-i,* as well as numerous ballads and plays, strongly favor one kingdom over the other two: Shu is right and good, Wu wrong and bad, Wei very wrong and very bad. This emotional preference expresses a popular prejudice already current in Sung times,[21] and an opinion of political theorists, including the illustrious Chu Hsi, who eventually determined that Shu-Han was the legitimate dynasty.

One consequence of this is that the great Ts'ao Ts'ao (A.D. 155–220), founder of Wei, appears in fiction as an unregenerate and sometimes slow-witted villain, probably because he had been the most powerful opponent of the "right side" in the civil war. The horror felt by audiences for him and his machinations was matched by their sympathy for his adversaries.

Clearly fictional literature, while a help in correcting biases of histories, has biases and distortions of its own. Sophisticated novels like *Chin P'ing Mei* and *Hung Lou Meng*, as well as related stories and plays, are best suited to describe subtle nuances and to suggest more elusive aspects of a complex society. But the peculiar optics of historical and heroic storytelling and drama require, as medieval theatricals and modern television bear out, that, in a way, all must be good in one camp and bad in the other, and most characters must be either 100 per cent black or 100 per cent white.

Some specifically Chinese factors may have accentuated this Manichean pattern; one is the high degree of formalization in Chinese behavior. Despite the sweeping alternations of peace and war, order and anarchy, and the deep but slow changes effected by urbanization, technical progress, and the evolution of juridical and political structures, society remained for centuries "embedded in the cake of custom."[22] Education relied mostly on imitation of one's elders, and moral excellence was thought to lie rather in the proper fulfillment of established *social* roles in family and community living than in individual accomplishments (as in Western civilization). The concept of "roles" was more stereotyped than in other societies, and the *right* and *wrong* ways to play these roles were more sharply defined.

This is confirmed and reiterated in Chinese biographical writing, which classifies its subjects not only by status or role, but also by ethical judgment of performance; hence such categories of biographies as "principled officials" (*hsün li*), "oppressive officials" (*k'u li*),[23] "filial sons and faithful friends" (*hsiao yu*), "traitors" (*chien ch'en*), and "virtuous women" (*lieh nü*).[24]

Popular fiction does not speak of nondescript fathers and sons, but of "good" and "bad" fathers and "filial" and "ungrateful" sons. Good characters say and do exactly what is expected of them, invariably with identical phrases and attitudes; evil ways inspire a somewhat freer invention and more colorful details, but their depiction remains very stereotyped. To give a few examples: the typical bad stepmother has her stepsons dressed in light clothes during the winter, and the father discovers it by accident. Ruthless ambition is portrayed in an everrecurring cliché: a young married man passes his examinations, is thereupon offered an official post and a rich marriage to a minister's daughter, claims to be a bachelor in order to be free for the flattering alliance, and forgets his wife back home or drowns her.[25] There seem to be only two kinds of courtesans: the heartless one who squanders all a man's money and then has him thrown out into the cold a beggar;

and the tender, generous one who helps her penniless lover through his studies.[26]

Critics have classified the subject matter of Yüan opera into a small number of stock characters and situations;[27] the rich variety of human experiences in the rest of fictional literature may be similarly classified.

There is the myth of the wicked prime minister, as conventional and stereotyped as the bad last ruler. From Chao Kao of the Ch'in to Yen Sung of the Ming, there are many representatives of this type, all carbon copies of each other, villains appearing on stage with face conventionally whitened, wearing the regulation jade belt and long-winged court hat, each with his contemptible offspring—typically a daughter in the imperial harem who spies for her father, and an idle and lustful son who roams around the capital with his bodyguards, on the lookout for young women to seize. These wicked prime ministers promote worthless men, dismiss good officials or have them put to death, and often plot for the throne. They double-cross hard-pressed generals on the frontiers, deprive them of supplies and reinforcements, then accuse them of losing battles deliberately. Sometimes they even conduct treacherous negotiations with the enemy.

The hero's role in all these cases is to unmask the villain, to awaken the emperor ot his duties, and, if not heeded, to face death resolutely. Variations occur in details,[28] but the over-all treatment of the theme is a cliché.[29]

Names of great men readily turn into common names, synonymous with specific attributes or virtues. An incorruptible judge will be called "a Pao Kung"; "a Chang Fei" will mean a man of impetuous and reckless courage. Ch'ü Yüan becomes the symbol of the loyal minister misunderstood by an unworthy prince, Kuan Yü the symbol of unwavering fidelity to his lord. On these prototypes are molded a whole series of characters who display the same qualities and resemble each other physically.[30]

Skillful use of the stereotyped technique is made in the play *Hsiao Yao Chin*, in which Ts'ao Ts'ao puts to death the Empress Fu and the two sons of Hsien-ti, the last Han emperor, almost before his eyes. The villain does not know that the dynasty he is about to found will end in a similar way; that his own great-grandson Ts'ao Fang, Emperor Fei of Wei, is going to suffer the same fate at the hands of his prime minister, Ssu-ma Shih (this is the subject of another play, *Ssu-ma Pi Kung*). Nor does he dream that the grandfather of this future agent of divine retribution is Ssu-ma I, his silent lieutenant, who stands right now by his side. History repeats itself: the familiar irony of a theme that has become a staple of the literary craft here ushers in a masterpiece of pathos.[31]

Despite intriguing literary effects of this kind, individualization is generally sacrificed to the emphasis on heroic traits. The hero emerges as a rather ingenuous, obvious, and single-minded fellow who makes his decisions without qualms or hesitations and demonstrates little psychological growth. Yet once this literary convention is accepted, each reader or theater-goer fills in the stereotypes with his own emotions.

In China as elsewhere, in fiction as well as in historiography, yesterday's hero may become tomorrow's villain when he represents the ideals or interests of specific groups in society. Witness the Taipings and their adversary Tseng Kuo-fan (1811–72), or the Yellow Turbans, the robbers of Mount Liang, Li Tzu-ch'eng (1605?–45) and Chang Hsien-chung (ca. 1605–47), the Boxers.[32] Hero worship is a touchstone for the social historian: "Tell me who your hero is, and I'll know who you are."

Moral teaching around the world has traditionally emphasized temperance and moderation; a distrust of excess and a cult of perfection understood as a golden mean were ideals of both Hellenic and Confucian thought, and of many other cultures as well. On the other hand, poetry and fiction everywhere traditionally glorify extreme virtues and accomplishments. Ordinary people behave with circumspection, avoid head-on clashes whenever possible, fear men in power, accept and propose all kinds of compromises. Heroes are made of sterner stuff; scorning vulgar formulas for success and looking beyond the dilemmas and vacillations that defeat more scrupulous and fearful souls, they satisfy our yearning for an existence that is self-transcending and meaningful in the deepest reaches of the imagination.

The Chinese equivalents for "hero" include *ying-hsiung* ("male," "outstanding man"), the archaic phrase *ta-chang-fu* ("great man"), and the plebian *hao-han* ("good fellow"); also widely used in fiction texts are the term *fei-ch'ang jen* ("extraordinary man") and the epithet *ch'i* ("remarkable," "strange"). These words most often connote unusual physical or moral strength, energy and purposefulness, devotion to a great cause—good or bad—unconventional behavior, and sometimes striking traits of physiognomy and stature.

Liu Pei, Kuan Yü, and Chang Fei, meeting for the first time and by coincidence, are mutually attracted by each other's size and distinctive features: Liu Pei "is eight feet tall, the lobes of his ears touch his shoulders, his hands hang down below his knees; his eyes are set so that he is able to see his ears." Chang Fei is also eight feet tall; "he has the head of a leopard, round eyes, the chin shaped as the tail of a swallow, the whiskers of a tiger, a voice like thunder and the strength of a horse." Kuan Yü is even taller, nine feet, with a two-foot-long beard.

"His face is as brown as dates, his lips as red as seal-ink; he has the eyes of the phoenix and his eyebrows resemble sleeping silkworms." "Clearly," each remarks of the others, "this is no ordinary man!"[33]

Physical details are all signs;[34] they signify and reveal inner greatness even before words and deeds prove it. Passionate and sensitive, the heroes possess "outstanding gifts of personality and talent, and the resolution to behave on a level higher than that of the sages and the wise."[35] They are kind, generous, and refuse rewards; for duty and ideal, they sacrifice their dearest and closest attachments. This is "supramoral."[36] A general orders his son beheaded for a breach of discipline, even though he realizes that his son had to do what he did, and served the country best by doing so.[37]

Here appears the fundamental difference between the heroic and the "sublunary"[38] genres in popular fiction. Tales of love and crime, novels of manners, and other stories, ballads, and plays belonging to the sublunary genre describe the world as it is, with little or no idealizing. Protagonists of their comic or tragic plots are often evil people, who enjoy money, sex, and power, even if this means early death, or they are common cowards, weaklings, or no-nonsense realists. Sometimes the leading role is played by virtuous men cast from the Confucian mold, men who walk with cautious prudence mostly along paths of compromise chosen as lesser evils. These characters, while being true to ordinary life, are petty and weak when seen from the "supramoral" level of heroic fiction. True heroes are "more than life-size."[39]

And heroic actions are exceptional and extraordinary. Critics continuously debate their credibility in literature.[40] But is heroism unnatural? Every man secretly cherishes the ambitions of his youth, and ascribes to conflict and compromise the failure of his high aspirations. He sees in heroes strong persons able to do what he hoped to do, overcome all obstacles and handicaps, withstand all compromise. Thus, heroic behavior expresses human nature and its desires more truly than nonheroic behavior.

In China, as elsewhere, the hero and the ordeal he experiences and surmounts are often viewed as a symbol of man's spiritual ordeal. There are several classic types of ordeal. Hercules, Chu-ko Liang, and Wu Sung perform superhuman labors assigned to them. Su Wu, Pao Ch'eng, and Joan of Arc remain faithful to voices heard in their youth. Hector and Achilles, Kuan Yü, Chang Fei, and Yüeh Fei sacrifice their lives in service to their king, their country, their cause. Theseus and Jason, Ulysses and Alexander, Mu-lien, Hsüan-tsang, and San-pao confront the mysterious dangers of the other world, or of distant countries; not all come back alive, but all win everlasting glory.

Along this lonely path, so high above his fellow men and utterly isolated from them by his own greatness and the uniqueness of his trials, the hero often experiences the tragic despair of Vigny's Moses:

> O Seigneur! j'ai vécu puissant et solitaire,
> Laissez-moi m'endormir du sommeil de la terre![41]

But this anguish does not stop him any more than other obstacles or conditions do: driven by passion and faith, he gives himself entirely to his goal, resolved to persevere against all odds. Death itself does not deter him. Thus he knows no failure: his venture succeeds on a moral plane, for all of us; we re-experience it and gain new dimensions. The hero thrills the imagination because he proves what so many respectable citizens secretly doubt—that virtue ultimately triumphs over vice.

The popularity of military heroes and of the upright judge Pao Ch'eng during the Sung and Yüan dynasties, an era when people were distressed by centuries of misery, military defeat, and wounded pride, is to be understood in these terms. The poor and downtrodden could find little to console and uplift them in the traditional advice of those in power, that they should reconcile themselves peaceably to their lot (an fen). More appealing was the image of a savior who would come to relieve their suffering, and to rescue them from invasion, natural catastrophes, and abuses of authority. Such hopes were nourished not only in meetings of secret societies but in the relaxed and escapist atmosphere of theatrical performances. Playgoers could watch Pao Ch'eng redressing wrongs, regardless of the wrongdoer's eminence, and ordering the execution of a murderous brother-in-law of the Emperor despite the pleas and threats of Princess and Empress Dowager.[42] They were even afforded in Hung Tsung Lieh Ma ("Lady Precious Stream") the spectacle of a beggar marrying the prime minister's daughter, winning battles and becoming emperor, after which he sentences the villains who conspired against him and rewards the deserving.[43]

If love for fictional heroes were in proportion to their visible triumphs or to their power of inspiring optimistic dreams, the most popular tales would be those of the marvelous, which draw upon the heterogenous body of popular religious beliefs and weave elaborate plots that revolve around the workings of Heaven and Hell and feats of divination and magic. Chains of reincarnations lead virtuous men upward through successive rebirths—for example, from official to monk, and finally to emperor—while the wicked are gradually degraded to the status of animals.[44] Worthy youths receive from venerable immortals heavenly books containing secrets of warfare that enable them to win battles and establish empires.[45] Ghosts hound their murderers, and by dreams and miracles engineer their conviction and punishment.[46] Snakes and vixens appear in the shape of comely maidens to bewitch scholars and drain them of their vital substance.[47] The well-known novels *Feng Shen Yen-i* and *Hsi Yu Chi* are rich in supernatural episodes.

Though protagonists of these tales are heroes in a sense, the sphere of their activities is as naïve in conception as a child's fairy story. The marvelous seems to be exploited for its own sake, catering to popular delight in the mischievous, quaint, and comical antics of demons and gods in whose world laws of gravity and rules of common sense are suspended. The victor in these tales is not the most virtuous man, or the strongest, or the most courageous, but the one with the showiest bag of tricks; and this is hardly a valid criterion of heroism.

By contrast, historical romances and plays[48] tell mostly of actions that really took place in the past, or still happen regularly, or at least belong in the sphere of the plausibly human. Here the notion of heroism is more genuine; reduced to their own resources and facing critical situations, men show what they are really worth. Psychological evaluations reappear; heroes emerge against a credible background.

This is not always true, however, and the line dividing the heroic and the magical is hard to draw. There is no single and clear-cut answer to whether popular imagination conceived its heroes as gods, genii, or just superior men. The use of the word "divine" (*shen*) in fiction is suggestive: Wu Sung lightly tosses about a stone pedestal, and enthusiastic onlookers cheer, "This is no common man! Truly he is a god!" (or, "divine man!" *T'ien shen, shen-jen*). But obviously this record-smashing champion is considered part of the human race.[49]

If it remains possible to distinguish between the heroic and supernatural classes of fiction, the difference lies in the relative number of marvels and other-world events. Kuan Yü has been worshipped for centuries as the warriors' God of Loyalty, but most of his deeds, even in fiction, are those of an exemplary man, not of a deity. Heroes display human or suprahuman rather than supernatural strength and energy: this is true of the famous captains, knights-errant, outlaws, statesmen, and diplomats of the Warring States, and of their emulators in all periods of Chinese history; of the Lady Mi who kills herself to save her son, and of Mu-lan, so devoted she joins the army to free her aged father from conscription.[50]

Most characteristic of heroic fiction are the unyielding patriots, Su Wu and Yüeh Fei. Sent by the Han Emperor Wu as ambassador to the Hsiung-nu, Su Wu was held prisoner by them for nineteen years. First thrown into a pit to die of hunger, he managed to keep himself alive by eating snow; after a few days the Hsiung-nu relented and sent him to the frontiers of their land, near the "Northern Sea" (probably Lake Baikal), where he lived as a shepherd. Several times the Hsiung-nu offered him honorable posts, but he always refused, to the discomfiture of his countryman Li Ling, who had been captured in battle by the Hsiung-nu and had accepted high office at their court. Su Wu, set off against the traitor Li Ling, becomes the symbol of refusal to collaborate with the enemy.[51]

Psychologically similar to Su Wu is Yüeh Fei, leader of the twelfth-century resistance war against the Chin. Whatever may have been the facts of the long strife between the War and Peace parties at the Sung court and at Yüeh Fei's camp—and the circumstances are far from clear —his motto, "Give us back our rivers and mountains!" (*huan wo ho shan*), has remained a battlecry of Chinese patriots through the centuries. (It was often chalked on walls in areas occupied by the Japanese during World War II.) One play shows Yüeh with his mother before he leaves for a critical campaign; he is asking her to tattoo on his back the vow "A perfect fidelity to repay our Country!" (*ching chung pao Kuo*). Yüeh Fei's tragic death is the subject of another play. It begins with the treacherous intrigues of Ch'in Kuei and the recall of Yüeh Fei from his front-line camp to the capital. On his way, the hero stops at the Chin-shan monastery, where the abbot warns him not to proceed to the court and to retire at once from public life. Yüeh ignores this advice, moves on, and is arrested and put to death, along with his two sons, in the Dungeon of Wind and Waves. The execution takes place in the middle of the night, two days before the New Year (1142); outside a monotonous drizzle falls, "as though Heaven were shedding bitter tears at the injustice."[52]

The preceding pages make clear that the division of popular fiction into realistic, supernatural, and heroic genres cannot be clear-cut. Few novels, stories, ballads, or plays lend themselves to tidy classification; "sublunary" tales, for instance, often include some heroic or supernatural episodes. But even so, heroic fiction may be seen to exist by itself, between the two other genres, and to embody values and ideals in a way which is both exalted and attractive: this explains the influence it exerts on human behavior. Su Wu and Yüeh Fei are dedicated to aspirations untarnished by concern for gross, mundane hindrances. Yet, their achievements do not discourage imitation because they appear humanly possible, not divinely miraculous.

To teach by imitation has long been the practice in China, where, traditionally, education has relied on models and precedent more than on rules. When youngsters studied the *San Tzu Ching* and the *Erh-shih-ssu Hsiao*, they did not memorize a precept, "Honor thy father and mother." Rather, they read of (Huang) Hsiang, who "aged nine, knew how to warm the bed of his parents."[53] A well-known passage of the *Li Chi* makes its point simply by describing in everyday detail the filial piety of King Wen as a young crown prince.[54]

Buddhist preachers used the same technique very early, proposing Buddhas and Bodhisattvas as models of altruistic self-denial. Even the Taoist free ideal of conformity to nature and noninvolvement is illustrated by exemplary drunkards, poets and hermits—oblivion-bent heroes whose heroism is tested against the blandishments and threats of temporal powers that seek to enlist their services.

Some heroes of popular fiction conform closely to Confucian, Buddhist, or Taoist patterns; others demonstrate original ways of playing human roles, ways that reveal the impact of the "little traditions" of thought alive within the common people and sometimes indigenous to a particular province or district.

Chinese of all classes are accustomed from childhood to seeing the hero as exemplar, to persuading each other when necessary by references to historical or legendary precedents.[55] This fact gives an added dimension of interest to our consideration of three heroic types: the prince, the scholar, and the swordsman.

PRINCES

Kings and emperors of fiction reveal much about popular sentiment toward Chinese monarchy and toward individual rulers of the past. The popular imagination was fascinated by their prestige, their apparently arbitrary exercise of power for good or evil, and their leisurely and luxurious life in palaces "of gold and jade."

Analyzing in this volume the life of Sui Yang-ti in history and in fiction, Arthur Wright describes the wide possibilities offered to popular fiction by the stereotype of the "bad last ruler," a political formula exploited by incipient dynasties for almost two thousand years.[56]

Another popular stereotype, predominant from the T'ang onward, was the bad last minister, upon whom the fall of the Sung and of the Ming was blamed, as the fall of the Han had been for centuries. Hsien-ti, the last Han emperor, is helpless. In the play *Hsiao Yao Chin*, those he loves most have just been massacred by Ts'ao Ts'ao; foreseeing his own abdication and years of captivity, he sings the poignant lament well known to opera lovers, in which the words, "How he humiliates Us!" (*ch'i kua-jen . . .*) are fifteen times repeated, each time with a comparison: ". . . like a mouse in a cat's paws," ". . . like a bird in a cage," ". . . like a little boat on the Yangtse." Victim and no real hero, placed on the Dragon Throne when a child, Hsien-ti remains in his last years what he has always been, a pawn in the hands of his crafty ministers: first Tung Cho, and later Ts'ao Ts'ao. Aware of their crimes, he has been incapable of curbing them. Still, in this play, his rank as legitimate holder of the Mandate gives him the audience's sympathy.[57]

One degree higher is the last Ming emperor: his suicide lends him the aura of a tragic hero. In the play *Mei Shan Hen*,[58] his armies having been defeated, he is abandoned by all except a faithful eunuch, and hangs himself from a tree in the imperial park after having first killed his wife and his daughter. He leaves the rebel leader a letter, written in his own blood, asking protection for his subjects: "My life I give up without regret, but do spare my people." A palace maidservant, moved by this cruel spectacle, disguises herself as the princess, hoping to attract the rebel and then murder him. Her plan almost works: she slays his lieutenant, the Tiger General Li Hu. This play pictures the rebels as odious and idealizes loyalist devotion to the fallen dynasty.

Other rulers are dismissed with some condescension as "muddle-headed" (*hun chün*). A typical example is the spineless Liu Ch'an, second and last ruler of Shu in the time of the Three Kingdoms, who leads an indolent life in his harem while his men defend hard-pressed frontiers, and who thinks only of surrender when the enemy approaches.[59] The remonstrances and noble suicide of his fifth son are not enough to open his eyes.[60] Later, a captive at Wei, he "listens to music and forgets his country."[61]

Popular fiction also considers as muddle-headed T'ang Hsüan-tsung and Sung Hui-tsung, two "rather bad" rulers who did not lead their dynasty to final ruin but weakened it significantly. Romantic figures, remarkable for their artistic tastes and talents, they lack moral integrity. They exhibit primarily the *passive* features of the Wright characterology: neglect of upright officials, favoritism toward corrupt officials, drunkenness, sloth, lack of personal virtue, addiction to sorcery and "heretical" religious practices, etc. They do not show the *violent* characteristics: abuse of officials, exactions, harsh punishments, cruelty, sadism. Their self-indulgence and licentiousness escape condemnation by most authors.

Hsüan-tsung appears in *Ch'ang-sheng Tien*[62] as a patron of the arts, the Maecenas to the poet Li Po and to the musician Li Kuei-nien, and the founder of the Pear Garden, the first theater school in Chinese history; but driven to exile by rebellious forces, he cannot save his beloved Yang Kuei-fei from the cruel fate he himself has brought on her by entrusting to her brother the powers of state. The *Water Margin* describes Sung Hui-tsung's passion for rare stones and art objects, his skill in painting and calligraphy, and his love of football. But, blind in his choice of ministers, the aesthete is unable to keep peace and order in the empire and to secure its frontiers: the corrupt administration which causes Sung Chiang's and Fang La's revolts and invites the encroachments of the Chin is a consequence of the artistic ruler's ineptitude.

Average emperors, not being endowed with any such gifts and tastes, reveal better what seems a fundamental outlook of popular fiction since Sung times: the concept of a transcendent but outwardly passive ruler. He has the Mandate of Heaven, but takes no direct part in government and lets his ministers and generals act for him. He lives in secrecy, surrounded only by women and eunuchs; men in his government are admitted to his presence once a day at most, unless a crisis necessitates an extraordinary audience. On the stage, he appears preceded by a retinue of young court ladies. His behavior suggests that he is far above the cares and hurly-burly of the world and administrative routine. This concept of monarchy is related to the Taoist ideal of *wu-wei*, "no intervention against Nature," and to the Confucian theory that the ruler ensures order and harmony merely by the emanation of his Virtue, without stepping out of his palace, or even taking his hands out of his sleeves. The dramatic possibilities of such a role are obviously limited.

Founders of dynasties are more spectacular figures, closer to the type of the European hero-king. The rise of an outsider, from a farm or a bandit's lair, through constant challenges and dangers up the ladder to imperial majesty, will cover, of course, a wider range of events and provide the setting for a more colorful show than the flat career of a spoiled porphyrogenite. Here are bold spirits, men who at one point decided to burn their bridges and to plunge into the great adventure of outlawry and rebellion. They measured the stakes: success meant the glorious inauguration of a new dynasty; failure, a cruel and ignominious death, and the name (perhaps forever accursed) of rebel and usurper. They gambled.

Such are Liu Pang, Liu Pei, Li Shih-min, Ch'ien Liu, Chao K'uang-yin, Chu Yüan-chang, and a few others. While drawing the individual features of such a man, the novel and the drama commonly give a stereotyped account of the principal stages of his climb to power: he starts out as a strong man charged with the protection of a local community in a period of anarchy and disorder; his tiny band of followers snowballs into an army, and he eventually takes over provinces and perhaps the whole country, in part by battles and negotiations, but also in part by a mysterious charisma which wins him the spontaneous support of all who meet him.

The crimes and the amoral opportunism of these dynasty-founders are sometimes glossed over in fiction, but they are not concealed. Liu Pang ungratefully permits the execution of Han Hsin, to whom, above all others, he owes his throne.[63] Four centuries later, he will be punished by the disintegration of his empire into the Three Kingdoms.[64] In the play *Ta Tao*,[65] young Chao K'uang-yin, a reckless bully, is shown killing the two smiths who forged his sword; later, when on the throne, in a fit of drunkenness, he orders the beheading of Cheng En, his loyal friend and supporter, because of a well-meant remonstrance.[66] These examples, and many more, illustrate the concept of the corrupting influence of supreme power. But more than crimes and corruption, popular fiction emphasizes the fundamental passivity, if not weakness, of the rulers. The founding of a dynasty is credited to Heaven's protection of the challenger, but is directly brought about by the exploits and sacrifices of his men. Liu Pang's army is besieged in a fortress by Hsiang Yü and on the verge of surrender because of lack of food; Liu Pang sends a double disguised as himself to Hsiang Yü's camp, ostensibly to negotiate a surrender, while he himself escapes in humble attire through another gate when the ruse makes the enemy less vigilant. By the time Hsiang Yü discovers his mistake, Liu Pang is already far away and safe. His double is put to a cruel death. The idea that saved Liu Pang on this occasion was not even his, but an adviser's.[67] Another play shows him as Han Kao-tsu a few years later, with his "Three Heroes," Han Hsin, Chang Liang, and Hsiao Ho, shortly after his enthronement. To their congratulations he replies: "Without you I would never have succeeded." And he is right.[68]

His descendant Liu Pei does not love books or serious learning, but dogs, horses, and fine clothes. He lacks initiative and his chief resource when faced with danger is tears. For some time he has been prudently devoting himself to gardening in order to appear harmless; Ts'ao Ts'ao suspects him, nevertheless, and one stormy day, to search out his character and intentions, starts a discussion about heroes. Presently he states: "The only heroes in our time are you and I!" Shocked, Liu Pei lets his chopsticks drop to the floor. He is saved by luck: at that very moment there is a clap of thunder and he pretends to have been frightened by it, not by Ts'ao's words.[69] He would never dream of challenging Ts'ao to his face.

In battles, he lets his men plan and fight for him; he is critically defeated in an expedition undertaken after the death of his old companions and against the advice of his strategists.[70] Not his own wits, but those of his adviser Chu-ko Liang, allow him to escape from the Yellow Crane Tower in which Chou Yü thought he had safely impris-

oned him, and from the Sweet Dew Temple, where soldiers were lying
in ambush to kill him. The play *Huang Ho Lou* emphasizes his pusil-
lanimity almost to the point of farce: he foresees danger and refuses
repeatedly to leave; prodigies of eloquence from Chu-ko Liang are
needed to convince him; then, he learns that he is supposed to proceed
alone with only one bodyguard, and he refuses again.[71] When his adviser's prophetic resourcefulness has turned the ambush at the temple
into a fortunate and satisfying marriage, Liu Pei forgets all his duties
to his country and stays with his bride for months on end, wholly intoxicated by her charms, never leaving her apartments, and barely listening
to his good captain Chao Yün's admonitions. Escaping finally, he owes
the success of his flight to the ingenuity of his bride, who deceives the
pursuers: he is too frightened to think.[72]

Dynastic founders seldom take the decisive step of claiming the
throne; they are usually pushed by their followers and refuse several
times before finally accepting. Moreover, refusal is not a pure formality.[73] Chao K'uang-yin's men dress him in yellow robes and cap during
his drunken sleep; terrified, when he wakes up, by the *lèse-majesté*
situation he finds himself in, he has but one way open: to accept.

Yet these seemingly weak men climb to and stay in power. They
attract and keep devoted followers. The inhabitants of Ching-chou
follow Liu Pei in his retreat when Ts'ao's army attacks; a pitiful column
of refugees, they have voluntarily abandoned homes and possessions to
cast their lot with the humane ruler.[74] In this episode we see three elements: the Mencian image of people flocking to a sage king, an echo
of the terror and mass flight induced by the Mongol conquest, and the
power of attraction exercised by a ruler's passivity.

This power is partly explained when the passivity is viewed not as
a weakness, but as wily scheming. "Cry-baby Liu Pei" ("*K'u Liu Pei*"
is a Chinese proverb), and Sung Chiang, the "uncrowned king" of
Mount Liang, rely constantly on subtle diplomacy to keep balance
among their men, to play one against another, and to check strong
personalities indirectly rather than openly opposing them. Liu Pang
is a monument of hypocrisy compared with his straightforward, noble,
artless rival Hsiang Yü. Liu Pei, on his deathbed, slyly tests his loyal
Chu-ko Liang, saying, "My son is a weakling. . . . You are a genius.
. . . If he proves incapable, then take the throne yourself." He does
this only to elicit Chu-ko's public and formal protest.[75]

A rational explanation does not suffice, however. In popular fiction,
a supernatural atmosphere surrounds the founders. At the time of their
birth, their mothers have prophetic dreams. The prince's high destiny
is announced by omens and portents: balls of fire or dragons appear in

the air above him, or a red snake crawls in and out of his mouth, ears, and nostrils while he sleeps.[76] As a boy he already shows promise of leadership: the round tree near which the young Liu Pei plays soldiers with his peasant playmates resembles the canopy of a nobleman's carriage and is taken by neighbors for a sign that a great man will some day come forth from that house.[77] Later the prince is miraculously protected in danger and war: Liu Pei's horse leaps across a torrent impassable to his pursuers; Chao Yün rescues an infant prince from a pit while a flash of light frightens the enemy;[78] a goddess hides Sung Chiang from the police who search for him, gives him a heavenly book on strategy, and later appears in a dream to advise him.[79]

Apparently writers and actors of fiction represent the typical ruler as helpless in order to underline his transcendent character, to demonstrate that human ability needs supplementing by a mysterious charisma. This suggests a comparison between the princely hero and the conventional romantic hero of love tales. The lover, too, shows an almost morbid lack of initiative, and depends on others for the success of his suit. If villains or ill luck separate him from his beloved, he will languish for months without stirring to fight for his happiness, and he depends on a savior for release from his troubles:

[He] is generally a quite unheroic person, . . . a scholar, with all a Chinese scholar's disdain of physical prowess, who naturally leaves to his inferiors such matters as the rescue of fair maidens. . . . Well-educated, handsome, lacking experience of the world, often weak in character, and endowed with sensibility to a high degree, he is seldom capable of thinking or acting for himself and for the protection of his lady. . . . In place of the knight of western story and legend, whose life was spent in rescuing maidens in distress, there is in many Chinese tales a secondary hero whose business it is to solve the problems and difficulties of the situation and make everything easy for the hero and his lady.[80]

A hero's ability to attract devotion without apparent effort or spectacular action is the best measure of his merit and prestige. When Wu Tzu-hsü flees, pursued by an evil king's horsemen, a boatman and a girl who have helped him on his way commit suicide before his eyes to assure him that his secret will not be betrayed.[81] True lovers do not need to take active steps toward each other, because they are marked by predestination (*yüan*). Similarly, the true prince does not need to act: he and his people are also destined for each other, and the success of the men in his service is proof enough he holds the Mandate. His essential gift is the ability to choose and administer men well, to distribute responsibilities appropriately. He must also show his men proper respect, treating his adviser as a teacher (*hsien-sheng*) and his swordsman as a friend. These test his will and character before tying their destiny to his.[82]

To sum up, popular fiction often represents its typical prince as fundamentally a weak personality, dissolute and hypocritical, and something of a figurehead. Sometimes exaggerated, this picture is probably well meant, drawn thus to enhance the prestige of ministers and fighters, and also to suggest the necessarily mysterious charisma which flows from a prince. On the stage, the prince has a noble countenance, a low-pitched voice, and the discreet gesture that traditionally belong to the kingly way.

To many princely heroes of Chinese fiction, Donald Keene's description of Genji would apply:

Genji has no need of his fists to prove his status as a hero. . . . He is a superman who breathes no fire. . . . His capacity to love, his beauty, wit and talent mark him as a hero, though he performs no heroic deeds.[83]

SCHOLARS

The apparent passivity of the ruler leaves the front of the stage to his men. In the imperial courts, literature finds not only some of its greatest heroes and worst villains, but also a mirror for the psychology of ordinary mankind. There the fevers of ambition, jealousy, and hatred run highest, intensified by constant proximity to fortune and ruin.

An important distinction immediately appears among the rulers' men, between the advisers and musclemen: the brains that conceive, and the arms that execute. In Chinese opera performances, these two functions have been developed into a pair of dramatically contrasted psychological types.

The difference is definitely not a generic one between the man of peace and the man of war, the "soft" intellectual and the "violent" man of action. Both are men of action and of violence, normally involved in strife. They are fighters who use different weapons: the one would kill his enemy with the point of his sword, the other with the tip of his tongue or, better, of his brush. Both are equally daring and courageous, the swordsman on the battlefield, the scholar usually in court and council.

Both also play indispensable and complementary parts in the great civilian enterprise of organizing society and ensuring its survival, while bringing or restoring peace and order in the world (*chih kuo, p'ing t'ien-hsia*). The adviser assesses situations, maps out plans, advises the ruler; his formalized behavior embodies norms of an orderly state and society. The muscleman is called upon when brute force has to be applied, when normal patterns must momentarily be discarded under pressure of some emergency; once "unleashed" by the ruler into his natural element, the free-for-all of a battlefield, he rushes forth with his troops and kills untiringly.

To their different vocations correspond different psychologies and attitudes: the impetuous, rash, outspoken, and candid ways of the one set off the suave, inscrutable, and considered manner of the other. The swordsman speaks his mind, without concern for the "face" of people around him, who appreciate, and sometimes resent, his frankness. The scholar manages to use men smoothly for his own ends while diplomatically letting them think they are deciding matters for themselves. Before committing himself, the scholar takes time for reflection; the swordsman's nature is to "kill first and talk later."

The scholar-heroes are the Chinese equivalent of our "polytropos Odysseus." Classical anecdotes, often rewritten into popular tales or plays, revolve around the ingenuity of these heroes and the ruses they invent to extricate themselves from dangerous predicaments and turn defeat into victory: Lin Hsiang-ju "returns to Chao with the jade disc unbroken" and "gets the king of Ch'in to beat the drum";[84] Su Ch'in, an itinerant politician of the fourth century B.C., cleverly intrigues for the "international" alliance of the Six States against Ch'in;[85] Yen-tzu the Dwarf enters the capital of Ch'u through the main gate, shames into silence a rude king, and "with two peaches kills three giants."[86]

One of the most important characters in the *Water Margin* is another scholar, the strategist Wu Yung, nicknamed "the star of much wisdom." Never dismayed by difficult situations, he always has a plan—simple, elegant, efficient, and, if need be, treacherous. He traps enemies in snow-covered pits, tricks all kinds of useful people into joining his band, and is a master in tactics and the use of spies and fifth columnists.[87] One of his lesser triumphs is maneuvering a caravan of pseudo-merchants, ostensibly laden with dates but actually with drugged wine, through a mountain pass to meet escorted wheelbarrows en route to the capital with the prime minister's birthday presents. The day is hot and the escorters happily drink themselves senseless; when they awake, the presents are gone.[88]

"Young people should not read the *Water Margin*, old people should not read the *Three Kingdoms*"; thus runs a Chinese proverb, meaning that the young are disposed enough to rash behavior, and the old to intrigues. The *Three Kingdoms* is a mine of all tricks and stratagems (*chi ts'e*) needed in war and politics. By using a pretty girl—this is the *mei-jen chi* ruse ("ruse de la Belle") that worked so well for Hsi Shih[89]— Wang Yün arouses jealousy and hatred between the dictator Tung Cho and Lü Pu, Tung's adopted son and devoted henchman, in order to secure Lü's support in murdering Tung.[90] Ts'ao Ts'ao rashly beheads his able admirals after his enemy, young Chou Yü, has cunningly encouraged a spy to steal a forged letter that fraudulently implicates the admirals in an imaginary plot.[91]

Without doubt, the keenest and most clever is Chu-ko Liang, whose name is still used proverbially as a synonym for intelligence. His career begins when, at the age of twenty-seven, he conceives a tripartition of China by exploiting the rivalry between Wei and Wu which would allow Szechwan to exist as an independent "third force" and later, hopefully, to restore the Han dynasty a second time. He goes to ask the advisers of Wu to commit their ruler's strength against Ts'ao Ts'ao. In a "battle of tongues" with twelve experienced and self-confident politicians, in the presence of twenty others, all hostile, the young debater, alternately moralistic, provocative, disdainful, persuasive, and ironic, always superbly aware of each opponent's background and character, refutes all objections and shatters the opposition.[92]

Chu-ko is a master of all the old tricks of war and diplomacy, and ingenious at inventing new ones. He fails in his major enterprise—to reunify China—but through no fault of his own. For he anticipates his enemies' every move, and by flattery and provocation gets the best from his warriors. He founds military farms, invents "the wooden oxen and the rolling horses,"[93] uses doubles and, when necessary, blackmail. In a campaign against the aborigines in the fever-ridden mountains of the Southwest, he captures their chieftain seven times. Six times the chief claims that he has been cheated or caught by surprise; each time Chu-ko releases the chief. The seventh time, the chief surrenders, overcome more by Chu-ko's "psychological warfare" than by his battalions.[94]

Most spectacular and full of suspense are the episodes in which Chu-ko faces opponents as subtle as himself. His resentful young ally, the jealous Chou Yü, cannot be happy as long as Chu-ko is alive, but Chu-ko escapes his repeated snares. Chu-ko promises to bring 100,000 arrows within three days; Chou Yü, believing that Chu-ko is merely boasting and will never be able to deliver the arrows, makes him pledge his head, and goes to bed charmed by the prospect of Chu-ko's impending death. But, at dawn of the third day, a thick fog covers the Yangtze River, and Chu-ko launches twenty boats covered with straw mats toward the opposite bank where their common enemy Ts'ao Ts'ao is encamped. Ts'ao, fearful that he is being attacked, orders his archers to shoot at these boats which are vaguely outlined in the fog. The arrows stick in the straw, and Chu-ko returns to camp triumphant.[95]

Years later, because of a subordinate's defeat, Chu-ko finds himself trapped in an almost defenseless fortress, with only a few old and wounded soldiers to face a huge enemy army. He quickly sees that his only hope of salvation, at least until the expected arrival of reinforcements, lies in making the enemy believe that the fortress is full of troops. He orders the four gates opened wide and the ground in front of each swept clean as if to welcome the enemy. Standing himself on the wall, he drinks wine and plays on his lute with apparent unconcern. When Ssu-ma I appears at the head of his thousands, Chu-ko invites him to enter, and states repeatedly that the fortress is empty. The trick works: Ssu-ma suspects a snare and refuses to take the risk. Chu-ko's masterly lute playing impresses and misleads Ssu-ma because it seems to imply perfect self-control and ease of mind: "I know music! These notes would not ring so pure if he had a single care!"[96]

The scholar-hero has no nerves. Neither good news nor bad news affects his composure; he displays neither hatreds nor affections. He has infinite patience. He can prepare and wait twenty years to take revenge, and, in the meantime, he smiles and talks courteously to the man on whom he intends to wreak vengeance. Knowingly, he watches and interprets others' actions, but he seldom reveals his own feelings. Lifelong concentration helps him to hide his quick and intense sensitivity under a mask of relaxed self-confidence. The impassivity which he exemplifies is a virtue traditionally ascribed to fathers, judges, and administrators in this country where uncontrolled emotional outbursts even within the family are exceptional and considered childish and uncivilized.

Scholar-heroes, however, have more than intellectual strength and self-control; they are also endowed with supernatural powers. They interpret dreams, deal with the other world, and master the forces of nature. The Pao Ch'eng of fiction is in daytime a judge of the Sung court; at night, he may have to sit in Hades to decide a difficult case for King Yen, the Chinese Yama.[97] In his black robe embroidered with eight Trigrams in white, waving a white feather fan, Chu-ko Liang appears on the stage with some features of a Taoist magician, almost like an Immortal (*shen-hsien*): by performing a mysterious ceremony in front of a black altar, he is able to conjure an east wind that will propel his incendiary boats against the enemy fleet;[98] he reads in the stars the day set for his death and, through another black mass, almost succeeds in averting Fate.[99] Although he may not have manufactured the providential, life-saving fog on the river,[100] his ability to forecast weather accurately appears supernatural.

Some scholar-heroes encourage belief in vulgar superstitions, even though they themselves are unbelieving: Chu-ko Liang orders his old soldiers to open the gates of the empty fortress, notices their fright, and reassures them: "I have twenty thousand 'celestial troops' (*shen ping*) hidden inside."[101] The first Ming emperor also exploits the credulity of simple souls, telling the two princes who planned to poison him that he knows of their plot because Heaven has warned him in a dream. In reality, he was informed by a spy.[102] These statements are readily believed since the supernatural powers of both heroes are taken for granted.

Imperfect heroes such as Chou Yü and Shen Lien, and villains such as Wang Lun and Ts'ao Ts'ao, set off the perfection of a Chu-ko Liang.[103] Chou and Shen are nervous and impulsive. Wang is neurotic, unsure of himself, overly suspicious. Ts'ao Ts'ao has been built up into a monster of evil: he murders people in cold blood, terrorizes court and state by periodical mass killings, plots for the throne, torments and humiliates the emperor.[104] With blatant partiality, traditional fiction charges him with "low cunning" and "treacherous perfidy," while his rival Liu Pei is credited with "skillful dissimulation"; theatrical audiences roar with delight at the "clever stratagem" of Huang Chung who, in order to provoke the enemy to battle, shoots a poisonous arrow into the back of a newly released prisoner.[105]

The Ts'ao of fiction lacks intelligence as well as virtue. Although his army is larger than the combined armies of the other two kingdoms, time and again he is defeated by the smaller forces, and falls into his enemies' traps.[106] Here can be seen a distinctive idea often found in Chinese tradition: moral superiority is more important and essential for success, in war as well as in other endeavors, than technical skill; that is, skills cannot be acquired until one earns them through moral cultivation.

It must be observed, however, that novels and plays which condemn Ts'ao also find in him a certain greatness. The first few chapters of the *Romance* describe him as a clear-sighted and responsible young statesman who acts while the intellectuals only speak.[107] And it is interesting to note that on stage Ts'ao is played by a large-framed actor of imposing presence, whose face is chalk white except for two long black slits indicating half-closed eyes, who speaks in a low and powerful voice and suggests boundless energy and vitality. This "perverted hero" (*chien hsiung*)[108] might be said to be "perverted, but a hero."

The seventeenth-century commentator Mao Tsung-kang recognizes the ethical value of his open defiance of convention:

The killing [by Ts'ao] of [Lü] Po-she's family resulted from a mistake and is excusable. But his killing of Po-she is a crime odious to the extreme, and his statement, "Rather hurt others than allow anyone to hurt me!" is even worse. All readers at this point hate him, swear at him, even wish to kill him. They do not realize that here resides [Ts'ao's] superiority [*kuo jen*]. I wonder who on earth does not feel as he does; but who dares to voice it? Our moralizing worthies turn this sentence the other way around and say: "Rather have others hurt me than to have me ever hurt others." This sounds nice indeed, but check their behavior: every step is a covert imitation of [Ts'ao's] motto. He is despicable, but at least his heart and mouth are in accord. The hypocrisy of that bunch is worse than his carefree directness.[109]

Scholarly heroes and villains, of which the Chu-ko Liang and the Ts'ao Ts'ao of fiction represent two extremes, are at home in both the literary and the popular literatures of China. Their superior mental capacities and, once in a while, their supernatural talents satisfy both the sophisticated tastes and the primitive needs which coexist in illiterate as well as in learned minds. They express some of the ideals and dreams of the authors who are usually scholars themselves; they also reveal the common people's imaginings about life in court and government, and their mixed feelings toward the "father-and-mother officials." Sometimes honest, like Pao Ch'eng, more often elegantly rapacious, like magistrate T'eng,[110] frighteningly impassive as they sit in their yamen tribunal and decree beatings and torture, always skilled in the noble art of speech and clever at arranging compromises, these representatives of law and power, who know the books so well, appear to the humble as a different human species, refined and formidable.

SWORDSMEN

The swordsman-hero's primary attribute is great bodily strength. There are times of crisis which require the use of force, and in a war the most astute planning will lead nowhere if officers and men are unable to fight better than the enemy. But the swordsmen are not merely useful auxiliaries of the princely and scholarly heroes. Their powerful muscles immediately attract attention and command respect. Kuan Yü, Chang Fei, and the heroes of the *Water Margin* and of more modern novels of adventure, such as *Ch'i Hsia Wu I* and *Erh Nü Ying-hsiung Chuan*, are able to lift stones weighing several hundred pounds. They are not flushed or out of breath after these exertions, and their hearts do not beat faster. Little Hsüeh Chiao is only twelve but he can hoist the stone lions standing outside his house, each weighing half a ton.[111] Wu Sung, when his stick breaks in two, kills a tiger with his bare hands after a fierce struggle; it takes sixty or seventy punches on the head to knock the beast out.[112]

Good fighters have trained for years in "military arts" (*wu-shu*), i.e., boxing and wrestling, fencing and the use of various weapons. These arts remain their favorite pastime. They also jump and climb high walls, walk on roofs, and so on, with exceptional agility. Some know how to walk under water.[113]

Novels abound in detailed descriptions of fights, calling the various blows by all their technical names. The theater stages long and spectacular battles and displays great skill in changing weapons from one scene to another in order to avoid any possible monotony. And the audiences' enthusiasm for a good "military" actor (*wu-sheng* or *wu-ch'ou*) has some of the features of authentic hero worship.

Not content to fight well and bravely, the true swordsmen-heroes add to their prowess the spice of an often humorous bravura, crowning serious action with an aura of playful art. Kuan Yü in a war volunteers to kill the enemy general, rushes out and decapitates him, then brings the head back to camp, all in such a short time that the cup of wine he left there is still warm.[114] Chang Fei with twenty scouts patrols a walled city occupied by the Yellow Turbans, intent on provoking them into battle; when he grows tired of waiting under the hot sun for them to come out, he takes a bath in the moat with his men under a barrage of arrows falling like rain.[115] Another time, left behind with a rear guard to cover the retreat of Liu Pei, he destroys a bridge and stands alone, fiercely defiant, facing Ts'ao's troops. His dark face shines, his bulging eyes blaze, his hair and bushy beard stand on end as he shouts, "Here is Chang I-te! Who wants a fight to the death? Come on! Come on!" At this the enemy flees in terror.[116] Chang's twelfth-century counterpart Li K'uei, to save the life of his chieftain Sung Chiang, on the very day set for his public beheading in Chiang-chou city, gives the signal to his companions hidden in the crowds by leaping, stark naked, from a roof into the execution square, brandishing two battle axes.[117]

These heroes show the same courage in resisting pain as in fighting battles. Suffering from an old wound, Kuan Yü accepts his surgeon's decision to cut open his arm and scrape the bone: the bloody operation is performed during a drinking feast and Kuan Yü continues talking and playing chess as if nothing were happening.[118] And Wu Sung, when he is to receive the "customary" hundred blows on entering prison, refuses to be held down during the punishment and boasts that he will not utter one cry. He even challenges the jailers to strike harder.[119]

Outspoken bluntness and a volcanic temper characterize most swordsmen-heroes in popular fiction. They are obtuse, guileless, childish, belligerent, tempestuous, irascible, devoid of manners, and completely uninhibited. They boast and quarrel as a pastime, and occasionally kill by mistake. Chang Fei stubbornly refuses to open the city gate to his sworn brother coming back from years of captivity because he suspects him of treason, and he will let the poor man perish under the arrows of his pursuers without giving him a chance to explain his innocence.[120] Li K'uei too readily believes slanderous reports against his chieftain Sung Chiang and rushes to kill him forthwith.[121] An ever-present menace to the neighborhood, the swordsman indulges in a kind of behavior that is frowned upon among ordinary men. He eats and drinks to excess, threatening to break everything in the house if more wine is not forthcoming. Once intoxicated, he brawls like a thug, often on the silliest pretexts. Lu Ta bullies monks into eating meat against their vows.[122] Drunk one winter night, Wu Sung takes a dislike to a dog and pursues it, knife in hand, along a brook, stumbling and falling twice into the icy water, where he is caught by some men he has pre-viously insulted and beaten.[123]

Why are these raving bullies still so loved by their companions and by the devotees of fiction? First, because they are honest and straight-forward in a world in which persons officially vested with authority prefer the devious approach. With them one knows where one stands. Their friendships, born in the street, in wineshops, or in other humble places, are disinterested, spontaneous alliances of congenial souls. They are totally indifferent to money and will not take a penny of what is not theirs. They do not fawn and flatter, and nothing can make them shift their loyalty. All deserve the nickname "Do-or-die," bestowed on Shih Hsiu, one of their number. They are resolute men, always ready to lay down their lives for their friends, never willing to surrender or to let themselves be curbed or humiliated. Muscle play brings them a natural exhilaration, their strength and courage lead to a careless self-confi-dence, their crude jokes reveal a robust sense of humor, and their whole manner exudes *joie de vivre*. They have all the companionable qualities that are subsumed in the phrase *hao-han*, "good fellow."

Impulsive generosity is their most likable trait. One day Chang Fei, with angry curses, orders a prisoner beheaded. "All right! Have me put to death," says the prisoner calmly, "but why get nervous about it?" Delighted by this *sang-froid*, Chang Fei sets the man free and asks him to join his staff.[124] Often a crafty scholar takes advantage of a swordsman's big-heartedness. Spectators look up to the former, but give their sympathy to the latter. They love Chang Fei and Li K'uei as one loves children, admiring their open defiance of authority and regretting that real life gives adults so few opportunities to act as they do.

As might be expected, the *hao-han* are little interested in women. "They waste no time in amorous dalliance, but conserve their energies for feats of valor."[125] Following traditional theories on *yin-yang* and on cultivating one's vitality (*yang-sheng*),[126] they believe their training in boxing to be incompatible with other claims on their energy. One of the unfaithful wives in the *Water Margin* starts an affair with a monk because her husband, too interested in gymnastics, spends his nights at the yamen barracks and leaves her alone.[127]

Outlaws and rebels are potential heroes in all literatures: even without a just cause, they have a glamour of their own when they are daring and true to themselves; and if they are victims of official injustice, or represent the right against oppressive government, the prestige of ethical justification is added to their glamour. Their controversial situation and the immediate danger in which they involve those who help them (or who merely fail to report them to the authorities) force the common people to take sides: no neutrality or indifference remains possible. Everybody is concerned; outlaw and rebel become consummate heroes *or* villains. This division of public opinion into two camps may separate friends or members of the same family—a splendid source of dramatic interest for poetry, novels, and the theater.

Chinese fiction has no inherent predisposition against the government and in favor of rebels, or vice versa. The "three musketeers" and the "five rats"[128] who help put down the revolt of the Prince of Hsiang-yang, as well as Huang T'ien-pa, who catches bandits for his detective master Shih Kung,[129] are well-loved heroes of law and order; but no less admired are the 108 robbers whose case the *Water Margin* presents so convincingly:

Unscrupulous, defiant, stern as the fates, but true in covenant and brave in conflict, these men and women are not of the smiling, temperate, human sort; they are terrible: beings of the cave and the mountain den. Their implacable demand . . . for a justice which the law is too feeble and too corrupt to give underlines the cruelties and oppressions of an age when right is defenseless and authority takes the side of the wrong-doer.[130]

The *Water Margin* is a classic text for motivational research into Chinese revolutionary movements. Its heroes are not asocial or maladjusted psychopaths. They had no desire to rebel in the first place, and would have been happy members of a normal community. Some of them are the innocent victims of frame-ups; others have run to the defense of the weak without reflecting how heavy their fists could be; most go spontaneously to face trial at the official yamen. They only repair to the "greenwood," to the "rivers and lakes" (Chinese terms corresponding to the Corsican "maquis"), when a bitter experience convinces them that there is no other way to survive. Many rebels in Chinese history, successful and unsuccessful alike, claimed the right, implicitly asserted by Mencius, to revolt against an evil ruler. It may seem timid of the *Water Margin* to hold the administration, not the emperor, responsible for the prevalence of corruption, but the novel is truly radical in its assumption that the society of the outlaws is more authentically Confucian than orthodox society[131]—indeed, that in the sorry circumstances of the time the mountain lair of the robbers is the *only* place men can behave like Confucian gentlemen (*chün-tzu*). In this light their motto, "Accomplish the Way for Heaven!" (*T'i t'ien hsing tao*), a typical rebel slogan, is a proud challenge to imperial authority and a claim to interpret the will of Heaven—in short, to act on absolute standards. Against a system that is looked upon as betraying the fundamental "Confucian" values, the outlaws of Mount Liang have recourse to an inner truth and a higher allegiance.

Their common purpose is symbolized by the oath of brotherhood they all take. The day after they first meet, the three heroes of the *Three Kingdoms* take a similar oath: "We were not born the same year, the same month, the same day, but we swear to die the same year, the same month, the same day."[132] Instead of the normal types of loyalties between prince and subject, lord and vassal, father and son, which can be called *vertical*, the oath of brotherhood, found in all secret societies, establishes between swordsmen a bond of *horizontal* loyalties. These brotherhoods of swordsmen have always, as have the "parties" and "cliques" (*tang, p'eng*) among scholars, been resented by the monarchy as an intolerable threat to itself.[133] Liu Pei, Kuan Yü, and Chang Fei themselves were standing on the side of the law at the time of their oath, and their common will was to fight the Yellow Turbans, a rebel movement; yet their oath as recorded in fiction has made them patrons of illegal societies for centuries. It would be farfetched to regard the *Three Kingdoms* as a novel of rebellion, cleverly camouflaged by its Yellow Turbans episode into a tale of devotion to the Han throne. But the fact remains that the very formulation of the heroes' solemn vow indicates its priority over other loyalties, including those professed at the same time, and therefore contains the germ of rebellion. The novel is from the beginning spun around the founding of a new dynasty.

The *hsia*, or "adventurer," does not openly challenge the government as the rebel does. His calling is to break laws, not to question their validity. By killing or other unconventional means, he acts where legal action is bound to fail, for example in cases when his adversaries have won immunity by bribery or intimidation. He puts loyalty to his friends above all, to the extent of ignoring his natural duties toward state and ruler as well as toward his parents: he is a virtual rebel against the established order. Bold and self-reliant, he is prepared to sacrifice his peace and happiness and, if necessary, his very life. He can also, thanks to his extraordinary strength and agility, escape capture repeatedly and live for years in the wilderness with the wind and rain as his companions.

Traditional fiction, however, requires somewhat more of him before his lawbreaking can be idealized into chivalric heroism. The wicked acrobats who break into people's houses at night to steal their valuables or seduce their daughters[134] do not seem to qualify as genuine *hsia*, nor do the perverted prizefighters who impose their unwanted "protection" on tradespeople[135] or who rob travelers on deserted highways, sometimes killing them, slicing them up, and selling their flesh in the form of what might be called "manburgers" (*jen-jou pao-tzu*).[136] Directing one's skill toward criminal ends can be an overpowering temptation, but victimizing the helpless is all too easy a job. The "good" swordsman is tested through tougher trials and fights adversaries whose strength at least matches his. Moreover, he is not hired or paid for his prowess, and does not expect personal profit or advantages out of it. The typical *hsia* is depicted as a savior of the weak, a man who embraces their cause when they cannot or dare not defend themselves, and does it gratuitously, solely for the sake of justice (*cheng-tang*). The people he saves are not his relatives, and they may well be total strangers; he thus deserves the appellation "chivalric" (*i*), which signifies behavior beyond the limits of strict duty. Playful thefts, robberies committed against the rich and the mighty, flogging of corrupt officials,[137] and other such deeds are winked at by fiction in direct proportion to the selflessness of the perpetrator's motive; murder itself is judged by the same standard. Storytellers and playwrights reserve their full blessing for violence on behalf of unknown victims,[138] and for disinterested vengeance pursued for the benefit of others, such as the assassination of Wang Liao, "tyrant" of Wu, by Chuan Chu,[139] and the unsuccessful attempt of Ching K'o against the life of the First Emperor, then King of Ch'in. In each of these two instances, the *hsia* has been noticed by a prince in distress who has treated him as an equal and convinced him of the justice of his cause: these are further examples of "horizontal" loyalty.

The themes underlying their stories in fiction of recent centuries have their roots in very ancient times. In his chapter on "wandering adventurers" (*yu-hsia*, often translated "knights-errant") and in other chapters of his history, Ssu-ma Ch'ien[140] describes the peculiar status of political assassins and the armies of "guests" kept by certain feudal lords of the Warring States period. He notes that the true *hsia* cannot be bought for money, but that one meets them on a footing of equality and must convince them of the importance, patriotic or other, of the crime expected of them.

While pointing out how much the *hsia's* achievements shocked Confucians and Legalists alike, Ssu-ma underlines the honorable side of the "have sword, will travel" specialists of ancient China: "The words are reliable, their deeds effective; once they have given their word, they stick to it."[141] Scholars, it is implied, are more skilled at diplomatic compromises and at cautious evasions.

No society leaves its members wholly free to question its basic rules and to act according to their own judgment. Yet folklore all over the world glorifies noble-hearted outlaws such as Robin Hood, Rozsa Sandor, the "bandits corses," or the Chinese *hsia*. The place of rebels and *hsia* in Chinese fiction is to be understood in relation to a recurrent, if unofficial, institution, that of the private guards hired by merchants and village notables for escorting goods and for help in other businesses requiring *manu militari* handling. Called "guests" and enjoying a status above that of servants or employees, these boxers and fighters rise, with their "hosts," to positions of local importance each time that insecurity of any kind threatens the peace in the vicinity: wars, foreign invasions, natural catastrophes, or economic and social collapse cause the common people to turn toward local strong men for protection against bandits, plundering troops, and rapacious officials. Holders of these incipient lordships and their "guests" thus constitute power nuclei with which the authorities have to reckon, and which may grow to august proportions: some dynasties have begun with far fewer than 108 men! The *Romance of the Three Kingdoms* realistically shows Chang Fei, a well-to-do farmer (a butcher in some plays) offering a feast to the young men of his village in order to enroll them into his sworn brothers' band. The band is then given horses, gold, and iron by traveling merchants.[142] A bid for the empire begins in this way!

A private guard turned into a soldier of the government by accidents of disorder and war found himself feared by the average peasant at the beginning and at the end of his typical career, but experienced in between, when greater dangers made him appear as a protector instead of a menace, a time of popularity. The *hsia* of fiction, nonprofit champion of the underdog, is, I suggest, an idealized image of this intermediate-stage swordsman.

After Ssu-ma Ch'ien, no official history contains a chapter on the *hsia*. Since the virtues of the *hsia* are seen as appropriate for times of disorder and aberrant in times of peace and good government, it is in direct proportion to national disunity and public unrest that the *hsia's* prestige grows in literature and that his distance from the common robber widens. Government pressure, as reflected in the banning or edulcorating of subversive books and plays, is also most effective in periods of maximum law and order. Typical instances in Ch'ing dynasty works concern the tamed swordsmen who serve on the side of the law.[143]

Here the sympathies of fiction and of its consumers go rather to the cops than to the robbers: that was not the case with the *Water Margin*.

KUAN YÜ, A COMPOSITE HERO

The fact that the *hsia* and the rebels in literature are so easily admired sets up a critical moral dilemma. On the one hand, heroic stories and hero worship make virtue attractive; on the other hand, stories that exalt heroism encourage strong personalities to ignore the laws, to seek the autonomy of the hero, and to espouse his unorthodox ways. Confucians in particular felt strongly that the heroic code of honor was detrimental to respect for family ties and for authority. As administrators and judges, they were bound to resent stories such as those of Hsiao En taking justice into his own hands by killing the local squire, of the Mount Liang robbers banding together against the government. Of course they recognized the deep-rooted popularity these stories enjoyed and knew from experience that suppressing them was an impossible task. Besides, there was an advantage in letting dissatisfied souls discharge their aggressive energies in the imaginary arena of the heroes' misfortunes and revenges. But as men responsible for raising and refining the people's ethical standards, the Confucians at the same time recognized some of the basic values which inspired this kind of fiction, and sympathized to a large extent with the aspirations it expressed. After all, the Confucians themselves were not immune to conflicts of loyalty; they often sought guidance on such questions as what to do when duty to father and ruler came into conflict.

Moreover, the most enlightened Confucians probably realized that, despite appearances, the *hsia* of fiction contributed more to social stability than to subversion. *Hsia* commonly flourished in troubled times, when the normal, vertical relationships were upset in any case, and their moral transgressions amounted to no more than a daring readiness to cope with issues beyond the immediate power of the established hierarchies. Finally, they set in motion new political constellations which organized local peasantry for work and taxation along more or less traditional lines, and which could ultimately be brought back into a lawful framework through the legitimation process which novels call *chao-an* ("calling to peace"), i.e., letting rebels rally to the side of the government and admitting them into the regular army.[144]

It was easier, of course, for Confucians to accept the "good" heroes—men explicitly committed to values such as *i* ("selflessness," "generous behavior beyond duty") and *chung* ("loyalty")—than to accept wild, uninhibited bandits whose example could exercise a dangerous influence on public mores. Loyalty of almost any description could be interpreted as exemplifying the virtue of loyalty to the emperor and the proper authorities. This explains the evolution of the official worship of Kuan Yü, a hero of popular tradition, and his build-up into a universally accepted paragon of virtue.

The biography and the character of the historic Kuan Yü emerge clearly in the *History of the Three Kingdoms,* written about fifty years after his death,[145] and in the fifth-century commentary to this history. First an outlaw, then a bodyguard of Liu Pei, he became a general and governor of a province, and died in battle after an eventful career of adventure and war. He was haughty, extremely brave, unshakably faithful to his lord. Ts'ao Ts'ao once captured him in a battle and tried vainly to win him over with lavish presents. Beginning in T'ang times, poetry and fiction magnify the historic facts into mythical proportions, and add many hues to an already colorful picture: a story of righteous homicide rationalizes his outlaw origins, and vivid details enrich various moments of his life, especially his now naïve, now ingenious resistance to the temptations engineered by Ts'ao,[146] his "lone sword" meeting with the men of Wu,[147] and his tragic death.[148]

As Kuan Yü's stature grows in storytelling and drama, he assumes an increasing importance both in popular religion and in the official cult. Miracles and apparitions mark his high rank in the Other World. He becomes the most potent aide in evoking spirits and exorcizing devils, and becomes the god protector of actors, who call him, with a respectful familiarity, *Lao-yeh* ("our old Lord") and honor him with a backstage shrine. His role is played with unique and spectacular solemnity, as a god and not as a man. Meanwhile, he has been awarded posthumous titles—ducal, princely, and imperial—by Sung and Ming edicts, and, from Yüan times on, he has replaced Chiang T'ai-kung as the official god of warriors. Ch'ing emperors order him worshiped in thousands of temples (*Kuan Ti Miao*) and, in the midst of their struggle against the Taipings (1856), decree him the equal of Confucius. From the K'ang-hsi reign onward, official committees of scholars compile successive editions of his hagiography.[149] They hold him up as the incarnation of loyalty (*chung*) and stress his undeviating devotion to his lord in a period of anarchy when it would have been easy for him to set up a kingdom for himself as others did.

The obvious political intent of these efforts was to indoctrinate the populace in loyalty and submission to authority, even as the "Twenty-four Filial Sons"[150] were used to inculcate submission to the head of the family. Kuan Yü literature reveals many of the ways in which Neo-Confucians sought to couple "loyalty" (*chung*) and "filial submission" (*hsiao*). Yet it also exemplifies the conflicts which arise between the two moral imperatives. In times of crisis loyalty to one's prince may conflict with loyalty to principle or to country as well as with one's obligations to one's parents. Kuan Yü's example could encourage hesitating officials and soldiers to serve an apparently doomed dynasty against attractive challengers. But perplexing tensions also emerge from his hagiography. The hero once spares a fallen enemy who defects to his side and thereafter remains loyal.[151] Is this sort of generosity in war always to be approved by those responsible for the state? Another time, Kuan Yü captures Ts'ao Ts'ao and releases him unmolested.[152] Does this not mean that by settling a personal debt in this way, he has allowed the archenemy of his prince to fight on and continue to menace the state which Kuan Yü serves? The resourceful panegyrists of Kuan Yü do not deny this episode: they find involved explanations and excuses to justify it.

The story of the warrior hero Kuan Yü—part swordsman, part scholar, with princely characteristics[153]—illustrates the interaction of folklore and institutionalized religion. It demonstrates how fiction was affected by the state worship of one of its heroes and, conversely, how the popularity of a hero of fiction encouraged his officially managed apotheosis as a model of exemplary behavior.

But the primary virtue—loyalty—that Kuan Yü is supposed to exemplify soon appears as a knot of multiple loyalties, a knot that easily becomes an impossible tangle. Kuan Yü's story shows how difficult it is to serve simultaneously parents, friends, prince, country, and justice. Despite the efforts of official hagiographers, this heroic figure has all the complexity of life.

The heroes we have considered seem reducible to three types: the impetuous, uninhibited, and generous Swordsman, a lovable and explosive "good fellow"; the Scholar, of outstanding intelligence, resourcefulness, eloquence, and self-control, "knowing all knowable things and some others," whose powers of reading minds, of seeing into the future, of influencing the forces of nature have a supernatural cast; and the Prince, holder of Heaven's mandate, who does nothing spectacular himself, but is skilled in judging men and in choosing the Scholars and Swordsmen who will enable him to fulfill his destiny.

To what extent are they Confucian? Some of them behave like saints in the Books, and exemplify the correct Confucian ways of playing various roles in society; others carry to extremes the selfish ways of ordinary men, subtle or brutal, with an instinctive disdain for the weakling "give-in" (*jang*) morality of the herd, with a passion for avenging offenses despite the law. One will find, among the first group, sage rulers and loyal subjects, loving parents and filial children, devoted friends, who promote the Confucian ideals of an enlightened humanism and of the general welfare of society. One also finds, on the other hand, tyrannical emperors whose rule reeks of Legalism and self-indulgence. Among the scholars there are cynics and hypocrites who use their cleverness to flaunt common morals. There are gangs of robbers in the woods, rebellious masses, and men whose passions lead them into orgies of indiscriminate killing and destruction.

We have noted the officially managed apotheosis of one hero, and we can see the effects of Confucian indoctrination in countless situations and characters. We have mentioned the pressure of censorship on writers, publishers, and actors, particularly in the later dynasties. It is not surprising, therefore, that no novel or play directly challenges the privileged position of the "gentry" or ventures to idealize the merchant, the immemorial object of Confucian scorn and discrimination. But factors were at work which limited the effort to make fiction an instrument of social control, a servant of an official orthodoxy. One was simply the demand of audiences and readers for verisimilitude — for believable human situations and conflicts. Such a demand meant that fiction had to be peopled with recognizable characters and not simply with positive and negative exemplars. The second factor is more complex. The Confucian tradition itself sanctioned behavior in periods of crisis that it would heavily censure in an age of peace. The swordsman-hero in particular had the moral right to lead others in revolt against corrupt government. His behavior suggested that wisdom and goodness is present in all people and that the difference between a Confucian gentleman (*chün-tzu*) and a common person (*hsiao-jen*) was a moral, not a social one. Once his moral *raison d'être* is established, the swordsman, in the hands of novelists, storytellers, and playwrights, takes on characteristics which make him the object of delighted admiration on the part of the common folk, and disdain or alarm on the part of staid conformist Confucians.

Thus all efforts to "Confucianize" fiction remained only partly successful. It is this relative freedom that keeps fiction close to the common life of China through many centuries, thus providing us with vivid insights into the hopes, the desires, the hates and affections of innumerable generations. The scholarly use of fiction for the purposes of social history will help us penetrate the veil of myth perpetuated in the vast corpus of official historical writing.

4 Men and Power

Arthur F. Wright

SUI YANG-TI:
PERSONALITY AND STEREOTYPE

Yang Kuang (569–618), who ruled as Yang-ti of the Sui, is of interest to the student of Chinese history and civilization in a number of ways. First of all, he is an interesting historical figure in his own right. He was the second and last ruler of a dynasty which successfully brought to an end China's longest period of disunity and laid many of the institutional foundations of the empires that followed; a gifted and brilliant man whose fate it was to bring himself and his empire to spectacular ruin. Second, he has his place in the history of Chinese political thought, as the "bad last" ruler *par excellence,* one in a long sequence of negative exemplars reaching back to Chou Hsin, the last ruler of Shang, and Chieh, the last king of Hsia. In this role he has been stereotyped by the conventions of moralistic history; his personality and behavior have been reduced to a collection of attributes and qualities which later monarchs would do well to study and abjure. Third and last, he figures as a perennial stock villain in folk myth and popular literature—a wretch whose spectacular vices long titillated the readers of fiction and sent thrills of horrified delight through peasant audiences gathered round storytellers and rural dramatic troupes.

These three roles suggest the principal divisions of this paper. First, I shall attempt to sift the evidence and present an interpretation of the historical personality of Yang-ti; a more detailed study will appear at a later date. Second, I shall analyze Yang-ti as the political stereotype of the depraved last ruler. Third, I shall attempt to describe the stock villain, the Yang-ti of popular myth and story.

An undertaking of this kind is beset by many problems. It is not easy to discern historical reality behind the moralistic ornament and evaluative verbiage of Confucian historical writing. To come up (in this instance) with something resembling a human being of the sixth and early seventh century, we must read between the lines, sensing the orthodox historian's subtle suppressions of evidence, some of them conscious, some probably unconscious. Buddhist writings and fragments of unofficial literature help us. So do some of the insights of modern psychology. But the fact remains that the basic source for this period, the *Sui-shu*, was written under the succeeding dynasty of T'ang, which specifically ordered its official historians to record the history of the Sui in such a way as to explain its dramatic fall from the heights of power and unequivocably justify the T'ang succession.. The closeness of these historians to the events they recorded made a fair appraisal of the Sui not only difficult but politically dangerous. Yet we should not regard these men as time-serving fabricators of evidence. Two principles of Chinese historiography operated to make their writing of history something far more complex than an opportunistic response to political pressure. One was the historian's obligation to write an accurate account, for only from such an account could posterity learn the lessons of history. The other was the assumption that historical truth, when told, would automatically carry a moral message; when a historian rejected an item that did not support his moral convictions, he felt that he was merely sifting out an item of untruth. It is in histories written from this point of view that we seek the historical personality of Yang-ti.

The political stereotype is easier to discern than the historical personality. The stereotype emerges in the final judgments which the T'ang historians pass on this ruler; it is reiterated in political essays and discussions, in memorials to the throne, in all writings which generalize about the rise and fall of dynasties and about the sorts of men who bring dynasties to ruin. It is fully intelligible only when placed within the traditional characterology of the bad last ruler. We shall attempt to see the stereotype within that context.

The popular figure can be built up out of the tales and stories which have been read and drawn on from the early T'ang until yesterday. Here too some attention must be paid to the literary conventions which governed the formation of the type. What did a popular audience expect of its villains, especially of its imperial villains? Was the purpose in presenting Yang-ti as villain wholly to entertain or partly for moral instruction? Further, we must recognize that the purpose in various literary presentations varied with the changing times and the shifting outlook of various writers.

When we have seen something of these three avatars of Yang-ti, we may ask what the relations among them were. What can we say about the relation of political stereotype to historical personality? Did the political stereotype—the particular property of the literate elite—

pass over unchanged to become the stock villain of popular tales? Or did the popular figure—or the sources for its portrayal—influence the work of the historians and moralists? These questions bear on the fundamental question of the relations between elite and peasant cultures within Chinese civilization. Perhaps this study may at least help in the exploration of this broader problem.

THE PERSONALITY OF SUI YANG-TI

Yang Kuang, the future Yang-ti, was born in 569, the second son of a twenty-eight-year-old Northern Chou official and his non-Chinese wife. The unexpected and meteoric rise of his father, who proclaimed himself emperor of a new dynasty in 581, need not be described here,[1] except in terms of its probable effects on the formation of the child's character. In the first place the Yang family came suddenly to imperial power in a time of great tension and uncertainty, emerging through a nightmare sequence of murder, treachery, and intrigue. They were uneasy of their imperial honors, fearful lest a sudden turn of fortune's wheel should displace them, suspicious of old friends and trusted advisers, avid of supernatural reassurances from all sources: Buddhist monks, Taoist adepts, sycophantic courtiers. Perhaps more important, their rise to power immediately made their children key political pawns in the predatory struggle for power and wealth which went on around the throne.

Their father, burdened by the herculean tasks of reuniting a China that had been culturally and politically divided for nearly three centuries, was wracked by insecurity. On more than one occasion he flew into a rage and beat an official senseless in the throne hall. He regularly sought spiritual solace from Buddhist monks, and was relentless in his demand for favorable portents. He was intensely parsimonious; he would not permit himself or his family to enjoy the luxuries of supreme power lest the gods who had raised them up should jealously strike them down.[2] He threw himself into state affairs, great and small—drudgery which was an anodyne to his fears and his sense of hubris. Further, his dependence on his strong-minded wife—which makes him the most notoriously henpecked emperor in Chinese history—also suggests his basic insecurity. All these traits made him a suspicious, tyrannical, and fickle parent; and none of his defects were offset by the character of his consort.

The Empress Tu-ku was the daughter of a Toba noble who had served the Northern Chou, fallen into disfavor, and been obliged to commit suicide.[3] The future empress saw at first hand the horrors of the Northern Chou court under the mad ruler Yü-wen Pin (among other things, his savagery at one point threatened the life of her daughter). From that time on she was close to her husband at each hazardous stage of his rise to power, and she remained his close confidante until her death in 602. She was in some respects a typical northern woman of the period: harsh, puritanical, a fanatical monogamist, a sharp and economical household manager;[4] she was also meddlesome, vindictive, and insanely jealous. Chao I considers her the most jealous of the palace women of Chinese history.[5] She meddled constantly in her children's affairs, spying upon their private lives, criticizing their extravagance, censuring their habits, intervening whenever she detected any deviation from her rigid standards. Her second son, Yang Kuang, was her darling, the special object of her cloying solicitude, the beneficiary of her jealous intrigues.

These two neurotic parents dominated the youth of the future Yang-ti and of his brothers and sisters. Both parents were devout Buddhists; their children were given Buddhist childhood names (*hsiao-tzu*).[6] Sutra readings took place daily at the palace; the princes all had their clerical mentors, and became patrons of temples or of pious works.[7] The young Yang Kuang, it is said, was handsome, perceptive, impulsively generous to his attendants, fond of study, and good at literary composition.[8] Although this description smacks of the biographical cliché, Yang Kuang did indeed display an impressive literary virtuosity in later life, and something of the other qualities as well. We know nothing of his early reading or intellectual interests, but we may infer from his later writings that he developed a wide acquaintance with Chinese literature and Buddhist scriptures.

His political apprenticeship began early in 581 when, at the age of twelve, he was made Prince of Chin and governor of Ping-chou—a post with general responsibility for the defense of the northern frontier.[9] His father appointed trusted older men to guide the young prince. In the same year the emperor sought a bride for him among the royal princesses of the small southern satellite state of Liang.[10] The oracles dictated the choice, but the young prince was married to a woman he came to love and respect. She is said to have been studious, literary, and of compliant disposition, and to have been esteemed by her father-in-law the emperor.

This marriage to a southern princess was perhaps Yang Kuang's first introduction to the culture of South China. Nature and history had combined, by the last quarter of the sixth century, to produce a culture south of the Yangtse which was strikingly different from that of the north. The land was green and beautiful, the climate benign; living was easier than it was in the dry plains of the north. The Chinese who had settled there in the centuries of disunion had developed a way of life which was more leisurely, more elegant, and more sensuous than the life of the north under its succession of barbarian overlords.[11] And despite centuries of political weakness and ineptitude, the southern dynasties claimed "legitimate" descent from the great Empire of Han and proprietorship of all the orthodox traditions in literature, music, and the arts. The culture of the south proved irresistibly attractive to Yang Kuang—the son of parents whose values and manners epitomized the harsh uncouth culture of the north. Yang Kuang's fondness for southerners and southern ways later became almost an obsession, very like the perennial Northern European infatuation with the culture of the Mediterranean world.[12]

Like some of the Germanic rulers he resembled, he participated in the conquest of the region he had come to love. In 589 he moved in a command position with the Sui forces toward the long-planned conquest of the Ch'en, the last of the "legitimate" dynasties of the south. So far as we know, this was the prince's first trip into the Yangtse valley and below; it may well have had a strong influence on the development of his character and his policies. When the Ch'en empire fell to the northern invaders, the tasks to be faced were formidable: first, military occupation and pacification; second, the integration of the southern areas and populations into the new ecumenical empire of Sui. In 591 the young prince succeeded his brother Chün as viceroy of the south, with his capital at Yang-chou.[13] There he began the work of mollifying southern opinion, of governmental reorganization—of, in short, making the rich areas of the south an integral part of the Sui empire—an enterprise which was to occupy him for the next nine years.

One of his first acts as viceroy was to summon to his capital Chih-i, the founder of the T'ien-t'ai sect and the outstanding southern Buddhist leader of the time. There, on December 14, 591, in the midst of a splendid assembly of monks, the young prince knelt to receive from the great monk the "Bodhisattva vows" for lay Buddhists, and the religious name of Ts'ung-chih p'u-sa, "Bodhisattva of Absolute Control."[14] In Yang Kuang's continuing relations with Chih-i and the clerical communities of the south, strands of personal and political interest on both sides are interwoven with religious feelings and aspirations. The prince, as the representative of Sui power, was interested in reassuring southern Buddhists, both lay and clerical, who had recently been loyal subjects of the old Ch'en dynasty. As I have shown elsewhere, it was Sui policy to use Buddhism to knit together the long divergent polities and societies of north and south; the viceroy's acts were consistent with that policy. The southern clerics, for their part, saw in the prince a powerful patron and a rising political figure whose favor might be of long-term importance for their faith.

Yang Kuang became the donor and patron of temples and shrines, the sponsor of innumerable pious projects. His discipleship to Chih-i and his successors at T'ien-t'ai is fully recorded in the pages of the *Kuo-ch'ing Pai-lu*. Through the ornate rhetoric of these documents glimmers something of Yang Kuang's Buddhist faith. He appears to have been widely read in Buddhist literature, and particularly versed in the Lotus sutra; he was committed to the Mahayana vision of salvation and to the T'ien-t'ai interpretation of it. He recognized the deep conflict between Buddhist religious ideals and the exercise of power in a worldly kingdom. At the same time he could visualize himself as a Buddhist ruler, commanding the reverence and loyalty of all the Buddhists of the realm. When his master presented him with a Bodhisattva chaplet, he wrote in his letter of thanks:

As to the making of the present chaplet, its conception appears to be de-rived from divine will, and its design is comparable to a work of Maudgāl-yayāna. The wonder of its workmanship excels the artistry of the mason of Ying. . . . A chaplet does honor to the wearer. With formal solemnity, I fitted it to my head; kneeling to receive it, I wore it upon my head. As I looked in a hand mirror, and walked back and forth, it seemed to flatter my homely face; adding grace, it changed my appearance. . . .[15]

He goes on in this letter and elsewhere in these documents to pledge himself to uphold and spread the teachings of Buddha both in private life and in the exercise of power. In all these expressions, there is a mixture of sentiment and calculation: sincere religious feelings linked to a deep self-love; a genuine regard for the great cleric who was his master compounded with a desire to win over southern Buddhists and demonstrate his religious zeal for the benefit of his pious parents.

His tenure as viceroy was thus a period of deepening association with Buddhism. But he by no means neglected the southern traditions of Confucianism and Taoism. He drew to his southern capital repre-sentatives of both and displayed himself as an impartial patron of all the best in the culture of the south.[16] These years as viceroy undoubt-edly strengthened his ties with the south and with southerners; many of the palace confidants of his viceregal days accompanied him to Ch'ang-an when he became crown prince and then emperor, and the official appointments of his reign—as well as his later preference for southern generals—may be explained in part by the alliances that he formed in these years.

While he must have given close attention to the immense work of reconstruction and reorganization which ultimately transformed the south into a productive and loyal part of the Sui empire, he did not neglect his relations with his parents in Ch'ang-an. It is said that when he went to take leave of his mother just before starting for his new post in 591, he found her in a rage at the extra-marital activities of the crown prince, whom she suspected of poisoning his consort; and that she became maudlin over her favorite son's departure for a distant post. This interview, say the chroniclers, left Yang Kuang with the impression that it would be possible to eliminate his elder brother and replace him as crown prince.[17] In the distant south he could live as he pleased, far from his parents' suspicious prying. And, in his frequent visits back to report to the emperor, he was a model of pious and proper deportment. His earnest patronage of Buddhism in the south, his devotion to the noted cleric Chih-i, his many public wishes for the well-being of his parents, his frugal and decorous behavior in Ch'ang-an, all served to ingratiate him further with the emperor and empress.

It is hard to say just what touched off Yang Kuang's imperial ambitions. The environment in which he grew up, the adulation of his mother, the self-serving flattery of his courtiers whose fortunes were tied to their master's, all were calculated to induce an inflated view of himself and his destiny. From his success as a viceroy he may have concluded that no one could be better qualified to carry on the dynasty his father had founded. His ambition was certainly fed by the flattery and prognostications of the learned and pious men who graced his viceregal court; after all, the testament of the great Chih-i had placed in him the hope of a vast, peaceful Buddhist state; had he not seen himself in a mirror wearing the divine chaplet of a Bodhisattva sent him by his master?[18] Moreover, his actual prospects were grim; an able and popular imperial prince had a very limited life expectancy once an elder brother succeeded to the throne, and the alternative to liquidation-through-intrigue was civil war.

It seems clear that he saw himself as a man endowed with unusual gifts, a man with proven military and administrative abilities, a man of culture who could knit together with understanding the north from which he came and the south which he had come to love; and above all as a man of imagination and vision—not a prudent bureaucratic drone like his father—who could expand and glorify the Sui until the imperial name echoed throughout the known world. It is a measure of his ambitions that he likened himself to the great and ruthless Han Wu-ti (ruled 140–87 B.C.), who brought his dynasty to the zenith of power in eastern Asia. Such a self-image explains many of the steps and stratagems in Yang Kuang's pursuit of power. His artistic sensibility and imagination are clues to both the strengths and the weaknesses of his imperial poli-

cies. Lasswell, in discussing *homo politicus*, says, "Indeed, self-deception is perhaps the rule, for the political personality with a strong
artistic component possesses a florid imagination which dramatizes his
personal history and subordinates all reality to ambitious plans."[19]
Yang Kuang's self-image was the product of this sort of imagination,
of flattery, and of cumulative successes. It dissolved disastrously under
the impact of adversity.

To return to our narrative, the year 600 was a critical one in the life
of Yang Kuang's father, the reigning emperor. In July he completed
a full sexagenary cycle of life—to his own surprise and that of most of
his subjects.[20] But he did survive, and a week after his birthday, his
third son Chün was poisoned—an event which caused the father little
remorse and possible relief at the disappearance of a potential rival.
Late in the year Yang Kuang's long intrigues against Yung, the crown
prince, finally bore fruit; Yung was degraded, and he and his family
were reduced to the rank of commoners. On December 13 Yang Kuang
was proclaimed crown prince, and with the new year, a new era was
proclaimed—Jen-shou, "Benevolent Longevity," symbolizing the end of
the crisis and the beginning of long years of benevolent rule by the
aging emperor.

The new crown prince moved to the capital with his southern wife
and entourage. There he built a mansion near the beautiful lake in
the southeast corner of the city. Nearby he built the Jih-yen temple
and invited there many of the leading southern clerics who had graced
the viceregally supported temple in Yang-chou.[21] In his new temple
he sponsored sutra readings, Buddhist scholarship, and religious observances. In these years the emperor and empress became ever more
deeply involved in Buddhist activities, and it was necessary for the
crown prince to make seemly displays of piety. The vow he made about
this time to give a maigre feast for one thousand monks at Mount T'ien-
t'ai contains passages which are blatant flattery of his parents:

Your disciple has happily been able to rely on a most fortunate destiny . . .
I was born in a Buddhist family. The Emperor and Empress instructed me
in the womb with kindness and benevolence. They are possessed of the love
which Candrākadīpa showed to his eight royal sons, of the stimulating power
for goodness which Mahābhijñā Jñānābhibhu manifested to his sixteen
śrāmanera sons. . . .[22]

After Yang Kuang became crown prince, his father increasingly
depended on him for the conduct of state affairs. The chronicles say
that whenever the old man went to his summer palace to escape the
heat, he ordered the crown prince to take charge.[23] In September of
602, the empress died; Yang Kuang had lost his most consistent partisan

supporter, the emperor his lifelong confidante. The filial and dutiful
crown prince ordered the monks of his Jih-yen temple to hold special
services in her memory.[24] A late source says that the prince publicly
showed unbearable grief at his mother's death but privately ate, drank,
and joked as usual.[25] Here is the hypocritical, unfilial ingrate painted
by the moralistic historians of later times (see below), a picture to be
viewed with skepticism.

On January 27, 603, the emperor degraded his fourth son on evidence of black magic manufactured by Yang Kuang's henchmen. Another potential rival was out of the way, and Yang Kuang was drawing
nearer to the imperial position. In the summer of 604 the emperor fell
ill, and Yang Kuang's moment was at hand. The "Annals" of the *Sui-shu*
baldly state that the emperor died and the prince succeeded to the
imperial position in the Jen-shou palace,[26] but several biographies hint
at dark intrigues.[27] The emperor's favorite, the lady Hsüan-hua of the
defunct Ch'en ruling house, reported to the dying emperor that the
crown prince had improperly accosted her. The old man rallied, it is
said, and sent an order summoning the deposed crown prince Yung,
presumably with the idea of reinstating him; but Yang Kuang and his
henchman Yang Su intercepted the message. At that point another of
Yang Kuang's men, Chang Heng, entered the sickroom and ordered
the lady Hsüan-hua and the other attendants to leave the room. Shortly
thereafter they heard that the emperor had died. The palace attendants
were suspicious of foul play and feared for their lives. Yang Kuang
continued his pursuit of the lady Hsüan-hua and used the collective
fears of the palace attendants to force her to submit to him. That night
he had his way with her.

We can never know the truth; we can only judge the extent to which
these alleged acts fit in with our other information on Yang Kuang's
behavior. Clearly this behavior suggests the belated resolution of an
Oedipus complex. Do we find other symptoms of such a complex in
other known behavior of Yang Kuang? Again, is the forcing of a daughter of the defunct "legitimate" dynasty of Ch'en to be interpreted, as
Balazs has suggested, as supercompensation for the northern prince's
feeling of social and cultural inferiority?[28] To take the second question
first, I think not. I have suggested that Yang Kuang's emotional identification with the south sprang in part from his disgust with the uncouth and overbearing ways of his parents. If this is correct, there is
something to be said for the oedipal interpretation. Moreover, it seems
more than likely that Yang Kuang resented his father. He was his
mother's adored favorite. He clandestinely and later openly cultivated
habits of the sort his father despised: sensuous indulgence, high living,

aesthetic pleasures. And in many of his policies he reversed his father's altogether: for example, his tolerance of Confucianism, his political favoring of southerners over northerners, his development of imaginative and often extravagant plans for the glorification of the dynasty at home and abroad. Our evidence is incomplete, but what we do know suggests the possibility of an oedipal drive.

Yang Kuang ascended the throne as Yang-ti of the Sui on August 21, 604. In discussing the events of his reign, we shall be concerned only with those which shed light on the development and disintegration of Yang-ti's personality. Immediately on his accession he took steps to rehabilitate Confucian education and to set up an examination system.[29] In doing this he reversed his father's harsh anti-Confucian measures of the year 601, but spiting his father was far from being his main motive. He had, rather, two political purposes, both designed to broaden and strengthen the basis of imperial power. One was to curb the power of the great entrenched northern—particularly northwestern—families on whom his father had almost exclusively depended. The other was a corollary: to enfranchise the southern gentry and the gentry of the northeast, whose scholarly traditions would favor them in an examination system.[30] The total effect would be to redress the balance of power between northerners and southerners—also between those of non-Chinese and those of Chinese stock—and assure the emperor of a wider and more diversified pool of competent officials. There is preliminary evidence that there was a trend toward this diversification during Yang-ti's reign.[31] With Yang-ti Buddhism continued to contribute to both the miranda and the credenda of state and dynasty, but Confucianism was revived as the body of knowledge whose acquisition gave access to power.

Another measure early in the new reign was the building of an eastern capital at Loyang. The city had been a Han capital, later became one of the capitals of the Western Chin, and was to be the eastern capital of the T'ang; it was culturally important and a significant center of trade; and it had been, as recently as the period 494–577, the political and military hub of the rich and populous east China area. Moreover, it was distant from the estates of the northwestern gentry whose power Yang-ti was seeking to curb, and more accessible than Ch'ang-an to the east China gentry and the southerners whom Yang-ti favored. There were, therefore, sound reasons for Yang-ti's desire to build here a new and magnificent capital which would be a symbol and a center of Sui power.[32] He proceeded to recruit corvée labor—even as his father had done for the construction of his new capital at Ch'ang-an, and the building of the city, the palaces, and the imperial parks was completed at high speed. The *Sui-shu* tells us that four or five laborers out of ten died under the intense pressure of the work,[33] a result of the emperor's impatience to occupy his new and impressive capital.

The greatest of the new emperor's building projects was the improvement and extension of the canal system which his father had begun to link together the new empire. The southward extension from the new eastern capital at Loyang to a point near the head of Hang-chow bay was the most ambitious part of the project, though much of the route utilized natural watercourses. Again masses of corvée labor were used, and by 605 the emperor was able to make a progress by barge to Chiang-tu (Yang-chou), his "Yangtse capital," where he had long served as viceroy. The spectacular luxury of the imperial flotilla is roundly denounced by the moralists and lovingly embroidered by the storytellers, but this and subsequent progresses were, as Balazs has pointed out, sound political acts. They were demonstrations of Sui power and wealth along a waterway which served to link together the long disunited areas of north and south;[34] they were tangible evidence of the ruler's concern for the recently incorporated southern areas whose culture and people he found so appealing. And, as the T'ang use of these canals was to show, they were vital links between the economically expanding south and the seats of political power in the north. In building them Yang-ti displayed what appears to us to be remarkable political and economic vision. But Confucian historians of later years—interested only in a stable, balanced agrarian economy—saw all Yang-ti's building projects as acts of vainglorious profligacy, a reckless and pointless ravaging of the full treasury and the bulging granaries left by his father. Here, as in so many other cases in Chinese history, policies necessary to the vigorous and expansive exercise of imperial power are condemned by gentry officialdom as violations of their principles and their interests.

In 607 Yang-ti turned to another of the classic concerns of vigorous Chinese rulers: the western and northern frontiers. He began to open up contact with the peoples of Central Asia, and followed up his first overtures by sending out military expeditions, establishing military colonies, and asserting political power among the leaders of steppe tribes. Thus was developed a costly "full forward" policy along the steppe frontiers, designed to free the empire of the barbarian incursions which had plagued the preceding reign. Another frontier measure was the reconstruction of the Great Wall, a common move in the early years of a new dynasty. The chroniclers of Yang-ti's reign dolefully report that of the million laborers conscripted for this work, more than half died.[35] Despite the appalling human costs of all these programs of building and expansion, each one was well calculated to assert and solidify the power of the dynasty.

The attempt to bring the kingdom of Koguryō (northern Manchuria and northern Korea) to full submission was, of course, the beginning of Yang-ti's downfall. Yet it was not an altogether foolish project: a dynasty bent on expansion clearly could not tolerate a threatened subversive alliance between the king of Koguryō and the Eastern Turks—an alliance which would have menaced all the northern marches and routes of trade. Yang-ti planned his expedition against Koguryō with great care and led his armies to initial victories in the valley of the Liao River. It was no doubt in the hopeful summer months of 612 that Yang-ti composed this poem celebrating the campaign:

East of the Liao, north of the Sea, we will kill the monstrous beast,
And the wind-driven clouds are clearing for ten thousand *li*.
Now we should smelt down our weapons, disperse our horses and cattle,
And return in triumph to feast in the ancient capital.
Those in front will sing, those behind will dance, rousing our martial ardor,
And with libations in the ancestral hall we shall doff our warrior's garb.
Would anyone judge that we have vainly marched ten thousand *li* away
Or returned empty-handed to the five plains?[36]

Yet the autumn came without success, and the unhappy ruler returned to his capital, not for a triumph, but to deal with serious economic and political difficulties. Perhaps at this point he should have given up the effort to chastise Koguryō and concentrated wholly on relieving the mounting distress within the empire, but such a move would have been out of character for this ambitious, imaginative, and supremely egotistical monarch. He now needed success to rehabilitate his reputation and his self-esteem. Twice more he imposed special tax levies, raised conscripts, commandeered supplies, and marched to the northeast. In the course of the third campaign, which ended in the autumn of 614, rebellions broke out all over the empire, and Yang-ti's regime was in dire straits.[37]

Under the impact of these disasters and of a narrow escape from capture by the Eastern Turks in the autumn of 615 the emperor's personality disintegrated. His judgment and decisiveness deserted him. He expressed his frustration in murderous rages against his advisers, in orgies of self-pity, in sensuous indulgence, and finally in a last burst of extravagant display: the ordering of a new imperial flotilla in 616. He turned his back on problems he now found too great to solve, left Ch'ang-an for Loyang, and shortly thereafter sailed in splendor down the canal to his beloved Yang-chou.

Through the year 617 the emperor watched the country sink into civil war, as rival claimants to the succession arose throughout the land. He was haunted by dreams, wracked by fears of impending doom, and filled with the bitterness of defeat. There is no evidence that his Buddhist faith helped reconcile him to the loss of his worldly kingdom or caused him to question his lifelong pursuit of power and glory. Even the soft beauty of spring in his lovely Yangtse capital no longer had its old power to please and comfort him. Everything spoke with the voice of doom. In the spring of 618, he wrote this poem:

> I seek to return but cannot get away.
> When, in sober fact, I face such a spring as this,
> The songs of the birds spur on our toasting,
> But the plum blossoms make mock of our company.[38]

In this same tragic spring the poet-emperor was murdered and his empire passed to the rising house of T'ang. Yet, as we shall see in the following sections, the death of this man was but the beginning of the two other lives he was to have: as a political stereotype and as a figure in popular mythology.

SUI YANG-TI AS A POLITICAL STEREOTYPE

The transmutation of the historical personality of Yang-ti into a political stereotype may be considered under several aspects. First, it is the work of historians, moralists, political thinkers, and officials motivated by various conscious and unconscious drives. They viewed the past as a rich repository of experience, as a collection of situations whose causes, configurations, and effects would serve the living as a guide to action; they viewed the past also as a continuum within which certain moral principles operated, permanent and universal principles laid down by the sages. The past could only teach its lessons if the moral dynamics of history were pointed out, abstracted from the manifold of events, hammered home by argument and illustration. One of the most persuasive ways to present such lessons was to exemplify in certain historical figures the virtues or vices which governed the course of human events.

In doing this the tendency was to paint in black and white, to strip the subject of all characteristics that blurred the positive or negative image, to portray events as a simple continuum in which the subject's basic personal qualities were decisive.

Other factors also helped shape the image, notably literary and historiographical conventions and existing historical stereotypes. By Yang-ti's time, Chinese history numbered half a dozen or more rulers—

from the remote last ruler of the Hsia to the last emperor of the Ch'en—dead but a decade or so—whose fatefully evil behavior had already been abstracted from the record and related to simplified versions of the path to political disaster. These figures were described in metaphor and allusions which linked the earlier and later figures together in a single literary nexus. When the historians of the early T'ang set to work on Yang-ti, the fall of the Ch'en and the character of its last ruler had been shaped to the established pattern in the memory of living men.

Finally, as we have seen, there were specific political pressures upon the early T'ang historians that affected the ultimate stereotyping of Yang-ti. At the inception of most new dynasties there is an urgent need to find sanctions, to formulate an ideology in support of the regime. And one of the time-honored ways of sanctioning a new dynasty is to write a history of the defunct regime, showing it to be corrupt, ineffectual, and tyrannical, a rule whose disruptions of the interrelated natural and human orders has produced signs of Heaven's displeasure, of Heaven's wish to see the political mandate pass to another house.

Early T'ang historians shared with their imperial masters a deep interest in explaining the fall of the Sui in such a way as to justify its displacement by the T'ang. Discussions between the Emperor T'ai-tsung and Wei Cheng, the head of the commission for the compilation of the Sui history, reveal this common interest and suggest the political atmosphere in which the historian worked. In a memorial of 636 Wei Cheng presented a rousing indictment of the iniquities of Yang-ti and sounded many of the notes that we shall find reiterated in the histories; he followed the indictment with a strikingly contrasted picture of the wise beneficence of the new dynasty.[39] On another occasion Wei Cheng gave a still more impassioned denunciation of Yang-ti, and the emperor reminded his official that some of the blame for the Sui's iniquities devolved upon its ministers who failed in their duty to remonstrate.[40] This interchange again suggests the tension that existed in the historian's task: paint the last ruler in darkest hues, for a last ruler must have been immoral, and his immorality sanctions the new dynasty; but do not go so far as to distort history and destroy its didactic value.

In sum, the stereotyping process was constrained by a historical tradition which approved a stress on the moral dynamic in human affairs but disapproved the fabrication and distortion of evidence. It was molded by a millenial political myth which stressed the quintessential virtue or vice of a ruler as a prime historical force. It was stimulated by the immediate demands of a regime which required both historical and moral justification.

Perhaps before turning to an analysis of the growth of the Yang-ti stereotype, we should ask what sort of a class bias influenced those who developed it. Clearly the power and material interests of the gentry-literati had been favored by many of Yang-ti's policies: the reinstitution of the examination system, the revival of the Confucian curriculum,[41] the building of a new capital that was geographically more accessible to the sons of educated families. Thus he was negatively judged and ultimately stereotyped by those whose class interests he had favored. In seeking to explain this apparent anomaly, we would refer to a theme that has become increasingly clear in recent studies: the endemic tension between monarchy and bureaucracy. The gentry-literati needed the monarchy, and the monarchy was dependent on skills which the gentry-literati alone possessed. Yet in ethos the two were perenially at odds. The prudential economic thought of the gentry clashed with the more expansive ideas of a vigorous monarch; the gentry were bitterly critical of the pomp and display by which the monarchy asserted the power and greatness of the dynasty; the court always seemed to gentry families flamboyant and improvident, always tainted with immorality, always at odds with the gentry's ideal of a frugal, wise, judicious and self-denying exercise of kingly power. These and related attitudes constitute the class bias of the interpretations we shall consider.

Traditional Characterology of a Bad Ruler

It may help us to understand the force of traditional models in the stereotyping of Yang-ti if we consider some earlier representatives of the type. One of the earliest and most important of these was Chou Hsin, the last ruler of the Shang, which was traditionally brought down by the virtuous house of Chou in the twelfth century B.C.[42] In most respects the stereotype finds its complete expression in this early exemplar. The accompanying paradigm of the behavioral attributes of Chou Hsin can serve as a basis for the analysis of later figures in the same sequence, including Yang-ti.

The vices presented in this outline have, of course, ramifying relationships to other Chinese values and attitudes. These vices are also interrelated, sometimes in an obvious fashion, sometimes more subtly. For example, the ruler's desire for conspicuous consumption and extravagant construction works is often stimulated by his favorite and opposed by an "upright minister" who gives a lecture on the frugality and prudence of ancient sage kings, the suffering of the people and its probable consequences, etc. The upright minister is promptly and cruelly executed for his pains, and a vicious sycophant replaces him. In such a sequence the characteristics we have numbered A,1,2,3, B,2,3, and C,5 are all closely linked in something like a causal nexus whose

STEREOTYPE OF THE BAD-LAST RULER

Shu-ching and *Shih-chi* references for the stereotype of Chou Hsin*

	Shu-ching	Shih-chi
A. Tyranny (the abuse of supreme political power)		
1. Neglect or abuse of upright officials	284, 285 291, 295 303	201–2
2. Favoritism toward sycophants and corrupt officials	303, 468 513	203
3. Callousness toward the suffering of the masses	468	200–201
(a) Unreasonable and unseasonable exactions of taxes and labor		
(b) Harsh laws and cruel punishments	284	201
(c) The flouting of good laws	295	
B. Self-indulgence (unrestrained use of supreme power and wealth for self-gratification)		
1. Drunkenness	471	199
2. Passion for rare and expensive goods: clothing, food, etc.		200
3. Elaborate and extravagant construction: palaces, pleasure pavilions, gardens, carriages, boats, etc.	284	
4. Pleasure before work, sloth	468, 513	199
C. Licentiousness (sex-linked behavior of disapproved kinds)		
1. Lust, sexual overindulgence	284	199
2. Orgies, "unnatural" sex acts		200
3. Sadism	285	
4. Promotion of lascivious music		200
5. Blind infatuation with a favorite	295	199
D. Lack of personal virtue (i.e., flouting of established norms of interpersonal relations and of relations with supernatural powers)		
1. Unfilial behavior	294	
2. Unbrotherly behavior	294	
3. Improper conduct toward wife	294	
4. Improper treatment of paternal and maternal relatives	303	
5. Lack of ceremonial respect to Heaven, the spirits, and ancestors	286, 295 303	204–5
6. Addiction to sorcery and "heretical" religious practices		

* The page numbers in the right-hand columns are first to James Legge, *The Chinese Classics*, Vol. II, and second to Edouard Chavannes, *Les Mémoires historiques de Se-ma Ts'ien*, Vol. I. A few subheadings have been added for vices that are not specified but implied.

starting point is a sort of undifferentiated "badness" of character in the ruler. To take another example, licentiousness (C) leads to absorption in pleasure and neglect of duty (B,4) and also to the trespasses numbered D,1–4; sometimes the upright remonstrator protests the licentious conduct of his master and is killed (A,1).

The weight given to licentiousness as a dynamic in the process of personal and dynastic ruin might seem to the historian of the West—or of the Middle East—to be somewhat excessive. Fully to explain this weighting would take us far afield, but the traditional Chinese view of sex helps us to understand it. Sexual intercourse is approved for procreation only. The sexually demanding woman is believed to sap the vitality of the male. Male energy, whether physical or intellectual, is dissipated by sexual indulgence; the male becomes depleted and unfit to play his role in life.[43] Thus, in the case of a ruler, sexual overindulgence undermines his moral stamina, his judgment in state affairs, his ability to perform all the complex ritual and practical duties of his exalted office. His position entitles him to take his pleasure with the most attractive women of the empire, but in the stereotype, he is usually the victim of a *femme fatale*—an unprincipled and demanding favorite who lures and seduces him to the utter depletion of his energies. She is in many ways the analogue of the "fox women" of the popular stories who lure men to their ruin. It is the duty of the righteous succeeding regime to execute her, and this is usually a part of the story.

It will be noted in our outline that nearly all the evil characteristics of Chou Hsin which appear in the *Shu-ching* are found in Ssu-ma Ch'ien's account of the fall of the Shang. There is a sharp contrast, however, in the tone of the two characterizations. The *Shu-ching* documents, whatever their varying dates may be, reflect in their colorful rhetoric the urgent need of the Chou to justify itself; Ssu-ma Ch'ien is far enough from the events to adopt the sober circumstantial moralizing tone which dominates the standard histories which were to follow.

The historians of the Han were not agreed on how to interpret the fall of the unifying empire of Ch'in, to whose drastic measures of centralization and reorganization the Han owed so much. They were somewhat awed by Ch'in Shih Huang-ti's accomplishments, though they found his cruelty, ruthlessness, and anti-traditionalism abhorrent.[44] Ssu-ma Ch'ien and Chia I placed much of the blame for bringing the empire to ruin on literally the *last* ruler, Prince Tzu-ying, who held the shadow of power against a host of enemies for a mere three months. This view was attacked by Pan Ku, at the invitation of the Emperor Hsiaoming (reigned A.D. 58–75). Pan Ku accepts what he says is a widespread tradition that Ch'in Shih Huang-ti was the instigator of all the evils, but that Erh-shih Huang-ti carried them to extremes. For all this lack of agreement, the picture of the second—and last effective ruler—of the Ch'in which emerges from the *Shih-chi* is presented within the conventions of the traditional characterology of the bad-last ruler. It is his misdeeds that reduce the Ch'in empire to ruin. Erh-shih Huang-ti is explicitly credited with all the defects under heading A in our outline, and with all the ones under B except drunkenness and sloth. Derelictions under C are implied but not specified, and the absence of the favorite, the *femme fatale*, is notable. Category D is represented by unbrotherly behavior and by failure to respect the ancestral altars.[45]

Perhaps the most striking thing about this characterization is that the regimes of two totalitarian monarchs—new in Chinese history—added no new categories to the characterology in the *Shu-ching*. This suggests that the relative effectiveness of institutional means for the realization of evil designs is of little weight in the allocation of blame.

We now pass over some seven hundred years and consider a ruler who was transmuted into a bad-last stereotype by the Sui dynasty itself: the last emperor of the Ch'en, whose dynasty was extinguished by the Sui in its conquest of the south in 589. In the spring of 588, the Sui emperor issued an edict specifying twenty crimes committed by the Ch'en ruler. Then, as part of his "psychwar" preparation for the attack on the south, he ordered 300,000 copies made and broadcast throughout the area south of the Yangtse.[46] Three aspects of this move are of interest to us here. First, despite the extensive use which the early Sui made of Buddhism to provide sanctions for their regime, the content of this communication is wholly within the Confucian tradition; this suggests that this tradition continued to provide the ideology of political transition even in a dominantly Buddhist age. Second, it is important to note that the northerners, despite their mixed culture and the thinness of their Confucian learning, recognized the usefulness of this segment of the Confucian tradition for accomplishing their ends. Third, the mass propaganda use of the edict indicates that the Sui leadership believed that the traditional arguments would be accepted by large elements of the southern population—not proof, perhaps, but surely presumptive evidence that the tradition was widely accepted. Finally, we note with interest that the characterology of bad-last rulers was not wholly the work of historians working after the fact but played a role in actual political-ideological struggle.

The Sui denunciation gives the Ch'en ruler nearly all the characteristics specified in our outline. He executes the worthy and those who speak truthfully (A,1). The worthies fly into hiding while the mean get their way (A,1,2). Soldiers are forced to manual labor in hunger and cold; his levies of all kinds are unceasing and even fall on women and children (A,3a). He extinguishes blameless families; he uses the punishment of slicing and cruelly exterminates the good and the talented (A,3b). His flouting of all good laws and established mores (A,3c) is clearly implied throughout. There is drunkenness in the women's apartments, and drinking which turns the day into night, i.e., the days are spent sleeping off the excesses of the night (B,1). There is limitless indulgence in jeweled clothing and costly foods (B,2). He ruthlessly uses forced levies to build his pálaces, and work never stops (B,3). He pursues his pleasures night and day; from dawn to dusk he attends to no business of state (B,4). His concubines are numbered in the tens of thousands (C,1). He cuts out men's livers and drains off their blood (C,3). His drinking bouts are accompanied by lascivious music (C,4). His blind infatuation with a single favorite does not figure in this document, but the *femme fatale* is identified in the course of the Sui conquest, and despite Yang Kuang's wish to have her for his harem, the stern Kao Chiung has her executed, citing the precedent that King Wu of the Chou executed the favorite of the last Shang king.[47] We find no specific details on the Ch'en emperor's lack of familial virtues, but he outrages heaven with his evil deeds and worships demons to seek their help (D,5,6), and the graves of the dead are violated (D,5). In heaven and earth, in the world of beasts and of men, there are monstrous occurrences which testify to his neglect of the proper observances; he is wildly contumacious toward the five elements and insolently ignores the three principles of heaven, earth, and man.[48]

The attribution to the last ruler of the Ch'en of most of the elements of the traditional characterology of the "bad last" ruler demonstrates its continuing vitality in the Sui period. Yet it is interesting to note that the Sui were not so carried away by their rhetoric as to execute this "monster," who was comfortably pensioned off. Nor did this portrait long survive the ideological demands that had given rise to it. By the time the Ch'en history was in final form, the T'ang had succeeded the Sui, and its historians were not interested in blackening the character of a ruler who had been overwhelmed by the Sui conquest.[49]

Yang-ti as Stereotype

These examples may have suggested the conventions within which the historical Yang-ti was transmuted into a stereotype. It remains for us to consider how this was done. The first and authoritative transmutation was accomplished by the authors of the *Sui-shu* writing, as we have seen, under the pressure of the new T'ang ruling house. Let us first see how the complexity of Yang-ti's character and the momentous events of his reign were simplified and moralized in the three summations of these events in the *Sui-shu* (here referred to as texts I, II, and III).[50] The letter and number combinations below once again refer to our outline of the stereotype.

Category A is amply filled out by the authors of the *Sui-shu*. A,1: "He dismissed remonstrating officials in order to conceal his faults"; "He slaughtered the loyal and the good" (I). "He became estranged from his brave officers in the field and was suspicious of the loyal and the good at court" (II). Category A,2 is mentioned or implied in many passages: "Cunning officials exploited the people so that they could find no way to live" (I). A,3,a: "The army standards stretched out for ten thousand *li*; the tax levies became ever more numerous"; "The disgruntled soldiery was urged on again and again, and construction work never ceased" (I). A,3,b and A,3,c: "Those who received gifts from him were not aware of their merit; those who were killed by him did not know what their crime was" (I). "Then he took harsh measures to harass the people; he made punishments more severe therewith to threaten the people; he used troops and brute force to control them" (I).

The general theme of self-indulgence (B) is presented as a corollary of an immense vanity, an insatiable lust for self-glorification. Describing the last doomed court at Yang-chou, the historians say, "No one gave a thought to the uprisings; they flapped their silly wings and played out their long night revelries" (I). Elsewhere in the *Sui-shu* we are given a picture of Yang-ti at the end as a maudlin drunk,[51] but in the appraisals we are considering, drunkenness (B,1) is relatively unstressed. The passion for rare and expensive goods (B,2) is only hinted at. Naturally, Yang-ti's elaborate construction work, B,3, is fully stressed. "Construction work was unceasing" (I). "Thus he ordered canals dug and roads built; the former were shaded by willow trees and the latter decorated with gilded arms . . . Mountains were cut open and valleys filled up. Boats sailed on the canals to the sea. The people's resources were exhausted, and there was no limit to the corvée and frontier military service" (II). The theme of "pleasure before work," Category B,4, is brought in only in connection with the last years of the dynasty: the accusation is not that Yang-ti was slothful but that his vanity produced a frenetic energy which drove him and his regime to undertakings which were beyond their resources.

Category C, "Licentiousness," is rather understressed. "He wantonly indulged in licentiousness," and did so clandestinely so as to keep his mother's favor (I). But we find no reference to orgies, unnatural sex acts, sadism, or lascivious music (C,2,3,4), and no *femme fatale*.

Category D, the flouting of established norms of relations with men and gods, is far less elaborated for Yang-ti than for earlier stereotypes. "He slaughtered his blood relatives" (I) serves to suggest defects D,1,2,4, but given the strong suspicion of patricide and connivance in fratricide in the historical accounts themselves, this range of vices is rather strikingly understressed. On the other hand, text III achieves the ultimate simplification of the Sui collapse by attributing it to Yang-ti's loss of virtue: "One man lost virtue, and the world collapsed into ruin." It is also said that "his teaching violated the four cardinal virtues [propriety, righteousness, integrity, morality]," but there is no mention whatever of D,5 or D,6. (The record shows that he maintained in fact a full ceremonial calendar.) Again he is not accused of addiction to sorcery or "heretical" religious practices (D,6).

Thus the T'ang historians lay particular stress on Yang-ti's tyranny and self-indulgence as factors in the downfall of the Sui and only touch on the other two principal categories of our outline. In fact, their appraisal, in deviating significantly from the traditional stereotype, is occasionally close to the conclusions which a modern rationalistic historian might reach; certainly this appraisal is far more "rational" than the historical estimates of earlier bad-last rulers.

Nonetheless, the writers of the *Sui-shu* explicitly fit Yang-ti into the tradition of bad-last rulers. Note in the following passage from text II the favorable estimates of the two fathers which serve to emphasize the vice and folly of the two sons:

As to the Sui dynasty's achievements and shortcomings, its preservation and destruction, these are generally analogous to those of the Ch'in. Shih-huang [of the Ch'in] unified the country; so did Kao-tsu [Sui Wen-ti]. Erh-shih [of the Ch'in] tyrannically used force and harsh punishments. Yang-ti wantonly indulged in malevolent cruelty. In both cases their ruin began with the uprisings of rebels, and they lost their lives at the hands of commoners. From beginning to end, they are as alike as the two halves of a tally.

This is an excellent example of the way all the variations and differences, all the special features of a given regime, can be disregarded in the interests of making a didactic moral point. Clearly, throughout all these estimates, we see a tension—a conflict—between the urge toward moralistic simplification within the traditional characterology and the demands of specific historical data. The conflict is not resolved in these estimates, and they are thus made up of two distinguishable strata— one produced by the first urge and the other molded by historical knowledge.

In another respect the authors of the *Sui-shu* come very close to one important point made in our analysis of the historical personality of

Yang-ti; they identify the crisis point in his life and his regime and stress the rapid disintegration of both after that point. At one point text II suggests that it was only after his narrow escape from capture by the Turks in 615 that his spirit broke. Elsewhere the same text sees his abandonment of his two northern capitals as the crisis point. "Yang-ti's spirit was stripped and his courage gone." And then they suggest that his flight southward was following the pattern of the Chin, which abandoned the north and fled to the Yangtse valley in 317. The general tendency throughout is to begin the full development of the bad-last ruler characterology from the northeastern campaigns or from one of the other two points in time mentioned above. In some cases, to be sure, the "good" policies of the earlier part of his reign are forgotten and the "badness" is projected back over the whole period— notably in the matter of legal enactments, which were unusually mild in the early years and became increasingly draconian as the crisis deepened.[52] Nonetheless, the identification of a turning point in Yang-ti's career brings the T'ang estimate close to what a sifting of the evidence reveals.

At still another point the estimates agree with what a critical sifting of the evidence has shown: in their emphasis on Yang-ti's enormous vanity, what we might call his delusively inflated self-image. Text II puts it this way:

He considered that owing to his mighty deeds all creation would instantly obey him, that he was the great prince whose merit was higher than that of the ancient exemplars. He needed no "outside" relatives to win the succession, nor help from subordinates to gain power. In stature he compared favorably with Chou and Han rulers. Ten thousand generations hence there would be none to equal him. From high antiquity onward there had been only one such prince.[53]

In later historical writings Yang-ti appears again and again. My impression is that the stereotype survives almost as a cliché and that the variations suggested in the Sui-shu estimates tend to drop away. In Chao I's discussion of the Prince of Hai-ling (ruler of the Chin, 1149–61) Yang-ti is used as a kind of crude standard of "badness." Chao I remarks that although Yang-ti killed his father and his brothers (assertions not to be found in the Sui-shu), the Prince of Hai-ling killed several hundred members of his own house. Yang-ti was not this bad! Again, the massive conscriptions of the Prince of Hai-ling for his campaign against the Sung equaled the exactions of Yang-ti for his expeditions against Koguryŏ; here they are equally "bad." Finally, both were murdered by their own subordinates. Chao I adds that Shih Hu of the Later Chao (ruled 334–49) was the most immoral (wu-tao) ruler prior to Yang-ti and the Prince of Hai-ling.[54] Chao I is writing "notes" and not organized essays, but it is odd that he should not have mentioned the long line of depraved rulers prior to the fourth century A.D., some of whom we have considered. For him the criterion of "badness" is Yang-ti, and it is as this bald stereotype that Yang-ti appears in the literati's essays and memorials of the 1,300 years from his fall to the end of the Chinese empire.

SUI YANG-TI AS A STOCK VILLAIN

If the moralized political image just described was the particular property of the elite, Yang-ti as a stock villain had a broader clientele: readers of short stories and tales of the remarkable, town and village storytellers, rural dramatic troupes, and, eventually, the novel-reading audiences of the eighteenth and nineteenth centuries. Our knowledge of the historical sociology of Chinese fiction is so imperfect that we cannot say with certainty when, or in what form, the popular image began to take shape. But since palace gossip, retailed and embroidered as it spread through the empire, lies behind the fictionalized accounts of more recent emperors, we may reasonably suppose that the earliest tales of Yang-ti's character and activities were based on just such gossip, possibly supplemented by eyewitness accounts from those who had returned from the wars or from the capitals. The basic elements of a good story were all there: a high-born and handsome leading man who climbed the heights of power and descended dramatically to a tragic end; family intrigue which linked the lowliest Chinese family to the highest; the splendor of great deeds which linked the listener through wish-fulfillment fantasy with the protagonist; scenes of luxury and sensuality. And behind this high drama were the presiding fates, who lent a touch of solemnity and pointed the moral lesson without which many of the audience might have felt unsatisfied. The fates in this case were heaven—that amorphous deity which yet sent disaster to the tyrannical and the unrighteous—and the prevailing moral norms of Chinese society: not deities, not divine laws, yet somehow working for those who adhered to them and against those who did not.

The storytellers' tales, for a number of reasons, went unrecorded for centuries.[55] For the early years, we have only the ch'uan-ch'i tales, written down in a rather loose-jointed classical style for the entertainment of the literate. No canons of historiography restrained the authors; their purpose was solely to entertain. The ch'uan-ch'i stories dealing with Yang-ti's reign seem to me to be relevant materials for the early popular image in two respects. First, it appears to be from these stories that later storytellers and novelists drew much of their material for vernacular fiction dealing with Yang-ti; it is in these stories that the stereotyped "bad ruler" mentioned in much of later fiction begins to take shape. It seems likely, therefore, that there was a considerable overlap in content between the *ch'uan-ch'i* stories and the lost tales of the oral tradition, since both presumably derived from recent memories of great events. The Sui lived on in the palaces, the canals, the cities which dotted the landscape; it lived on in collective memories in which the differences between elite and folk levels may well have been slight.

The editors of the imperially commissioned "Catalogue of the Four Treasuries Collection" comment disparagingly on three of the collections of anecdotes we shall consider. They point out anachronisms and errors, and they say disdainfully, "They are close to vulgar *ch'uan-ch'i* tales and, it goes without saying, are utterly unreliable."[56] Since it is the "vulgar" image of Yang-ti that we seek in these stories, this comment is reassuring.

Reverting once again to the outline on p. 62, we shall summarize the content of four works by T'ang and Sung writers: *Mi-lou Chi* (MLC), *Hai-shan Chi* (HSC), *K'ai-ho Chi* (KHC), and *Ta-yeh Shih-i Chi* (TYC).[57] Many of the stories in these collections describe how good and evil omens were borne out by events. In some stories Yang-ti is a rather incidental figure; in a good many others, the prognostications have to do with his own fall, and he emerges as superstitious, volatile, and subject to black moods. Another large category of anecdotes is concerned with the misdeeds of Yang-ti's officials, particularly Yang Su (HSC) and Ma Shu-mou, who was in charge of the building of the Pien section of the Grand Canal (KHC). These men are represented as corrupt, rapacious, and fiendishly cruel—even worse, it would seem, than their imperial master.

Our Category A, "Tyranny," is filled, and with florid detail. Officials who protested the fiendish exactions of Ma Shu-mou were flogged (KHC). Ho-jo Pi, advising against the plan to rebuild the Great Wall, cites the ills that befell the Ch'in regime in their work on it. The emperor becomes angry with the remonstrator; Ho-jo is put under house arrest and commits suicide (KHC). Category A,3, "Callousness toward the suffering of the masses," is still more fully developed: perhaps one-fourth of the stories describe the people's ills under Yang-ti's tyranny. The lament of a veteran of the Koguryō campaign disturbs the emperor's repose aboard his barge; his song tells of near-starvation in the northern campaigns; now the man is forced to pull the imperial barge. Everyone in the country is hungry; he has not a grain of his daily ration; the canal towpath stretches out 3,000 *li* ahead; surely he will die alone far from home (HSC). The emperor exacts a flotilla of five hundred large canal boats from people in the Huai and Yangtse valleys; families assigned a quota of one boat are bankrupted, family members are pilloried and flogged and finally sell their children to meet the demands (KHC). Yang-ti is enraged at the discovery of shallow stretches in the Grand Canal; he orders that the people living opposite the shallows be tied up and buried alive, head first, in the banks of the canal. Fifty thousand are buried alive (KHC).

All the headings of category B, "Self-indulgence," are represented with stories, stories replete with vivid, sometimes titillating, detail. A reference to Yang-ti's visiting his harem when drunk (TYC) is the sole mention of drunkenness in these texts, although elsewhere we read of his physician's warning him against excessive drinking (MLC). But the emperor's passion for rare and expensive goods is recounted in detail. For example, the sun-shades over the bows of the imperial barges were woven in Central Asia of the eyelashes of a rare animal and the threads of young lotus root; the sails were embroidered, and the tow ropes were made of silk (TYC). To please the emperor's fancy, his women daily received a huge quantity of costly eyebrow paint imported from Persia (TYC).

Yang-ti's extravagant building projects are given full treatment. The building of the canal is presented as a personal whim, to give him easy and luxurious transport to the place he found most pleasurable, Yang-chou (KHC). The *K'ai-ho Chi*, as the name suggests, deals largely with the cost of this project in lives and treasure. (According to this text, Yang-ti had trees planted along the watercourse to keep the sun off the beautiful girls who were recruited to pull the barges.) The building of the Western Plaisance (Hsi-yüan) is described in detail: a million conscripted laborers were at work at one time fashioning its artificial lakes, its four artificial seas, its artificial mountains, and its sixteen courtyards, and stocking it with birds, animals, plants, and flowers (HSC). The *Mi-lou Chi* is rich in detail on extravagant construction and on the lascivious conduct of Yang-ti. For the Mi-lou was the "Maze Pavilion," so named because of its intricate labyrinth of secret rooms and secret passages, designed to ensure the emperor privacy for his carnal pleasures. It was built of precious materials on a magnificent scale—"a thousand doors and ten thousand windows." Several tens of thousands of laborers managed to complete it in a year, and the treasury was totally depleted.

The licentiousness (C) of the emperor in this sumptuous setting is described in loving detail. He stocked the pavilion with several thousand girls of good family and sometimes stayed there a month at a time. One of his ministers designed a "virgin car" which apparently held the victims' hands and feet while they were deflowered by the lustful Yang-ti. The walls of the palace were hung with pornographic pictures, but these were replaced with polished bronze screens which mirrored what went on in the imperial bed. Yang-ti resorted to aphrodisiacs, and was able to take "several tens" of women each day. All these passages of the *Mi-lou Chi* conjure up scenes of vast luxury and sensuous indulgence. Singing and music are mentioned, but the use of "lascivious music"—perennial object of the Confucian moralist's disapproval—is scarcely mentioned. The storyteller was not interested in the moral effects of music.

In these four texts no *femme fatale* appears to hasten Yang-ti's doom. He has a succession of favorites, but his historical empress appears in many scenes as an object of his indulgence or sometimes as a jealous wife. It appears to be only in later stories that the empress takes on the attributes of the *femme fatale*—sapping Yang-ti's vitality, spurring him to folly, leading him to final disaster.[58]

Turning to category D, "Lack of personal virtue," we find that these texts are virtually silent. The one account of the death of Wen-ti (HSC) does not accuse Yang Kuang of patricide. There is no mention of his role in the liquidation of his brothers, nor are there references—good or bad—to his religious and ceremonial observances.

The storytellers are not really concerned with moral dynamics in the historical process. At the end of the *Mi-lou Chi*, T'ang T'ai-tsung appears on the scene, comments that the Maze Pavilion has been built of the flesh and blood of the people, and orders it burnt down. This, says the text, bears out the prophetic lines in a popular song and a poem of Yang-ti's which had been previously recounted. "Hence one knows that the rise and fall of dynasties is never accidental." This is far different from the laboring of the moral dynamic in the historical accounts; it really says no more than that coming events cast their shadows before them, or that a person with a sharp eye for signs and portents can know what is to come.

This shift of emphasis—the relative underplaying of the moral dynamic and the relative neglect of Yang-ti's defects of "personal virtue"—is understandable enough: it is hard to make an entertaining story out of unfilial or unbrotherly behavior, or out of the neglect of proper ceremonial conduct. Moreover, the moral dynamic may have been far less persuasive with the lower classes, or the lower levels of the elite, than it was with officials, historians, and political thinkers.

Common sense also explains the great emphasis on Yang-ti's tyranny.

The tyranny stories are what we would call "tear-jerkers"; they are designed to evoke a quick response from those who share the experience of living under an autocratic bureaucracy. The waste, the corruption, the oppressive officials, the fads and follies of the supreme autocrat—all these are part of the real-life experience of the people who read these stories, and this serves to make them both interesting and believable.

The emphasis on self-indulgence and licentiousness is a different matter. The ordinary Chinese who heard the storytellers' versions of these stories, or who in later times became literate enough to read vernacular versions of them, led hard-working, impoverished, self-denying lives; they were constrained by the state, by the straitjacket of convention, by the pressure of the family. What better escape than into the perfumed halls of Yang-ti's sumptuous palaces to consort for an hour with beautiful and compliant damsels? This combination of verisimilitude and wish-fulfillment fantasy often occurs in Chinese fiction. As a tyrant—whether operating directly or through his minions—Yang-ti was eminently believable. As a cultivated debauchee, he provided vicarious satisfaction for many suppressed desires.

It should be clear by now that the stereotyped "bad last" ruler of the historians was not by any means reproduced in the early popular writings about Yang-ti.

In the seventeenth century and after, the early fictional accounts were drawn upon, elaborated, and collected in books which reached a far broader literate audience than ever before. One of these books is the *Sui Yang-ti Yen-shih* ("A Colorful History of Sui Yang-ti").[59] It is written in a style close to the vernacular, and its colorful dialogues are far more intelligible to a popular audience than the semi-classical speeches in the earlier stories. Its forty dramatic incidents were admirably suited for serialized storytelling or for use as the basis of popular dramatic skits. In content the *Sui Yang-ti Yen-shih* is an elaborated compendium of all the themes of the earlier fictionized accounts, with particular development of the sex interest. One writer on Chinese fiction says that the "Colorful History" sold very widely, and that thanks to its incorporation of the lurid stories of the *Mi-lou Chi*, Yang-ti became, among the common people, the most familiar example of an extravagant and corrupt monarch.[60] The "Colorful History" contains the poetical introductions that are so familiar in modern popular fiction, and these occasionally make a feeble effort to point the moral lesson of the incidents they introduce. But the purpose of the work was to entertain a popular audience, and in doing this it spread a stereotype in which spectacular extravagance and sexual license are far more emphasized than violations of ritual, moral, and political norms.

A somewhat more sober account of Yang-ti appears in the *Sui T'ang Yen-i*, which dates from the late seventeenth century.[61] Its author tells us that he drew on earlier tales but also on the accounts in the histories. He made extensive use of the *Sui Yang-ti Yen-shih*,[62] but he omitted much of its titillating detail and replaced the more lurid descriptions with euphemisms. Moreover, his introductory passages and asides are more explicitly moral in intent. In short, the *Sui T'ang Yen-i* is clearly more "respectable" than the "Colorful History." Nevertheless, its utterly black image of Yang-ti is clearly derived from the popular tradition. The "toning down" of the Yang-ti story in the *Sui T'ang Yen-i* was in part, perhaps, a reflection of the increasingly puritanical mores encouraged by official neo-Confucianism or perhaps also a reaction against the vogue of pornographic fiction that had produced the *Chin-p'ing Mei* and the "Colorful History." Its more respectable tone may also have served to protect authors and readers from the government censors and book-burners of the late seventeenth and eighteenth centuries. The *Sui T'ang Yen-i* certainly carried the popular image of Yang-ti into many a gentry and city household where the *Sui Yang-ti Yen-shih* would have been regarded as too salacious for family reading.

In another novel of the sixteenth or the seventeenth century—a novel which may have been influenced by the revival of popular Taoism—Yang-ti is shown as having a cosmically evil influence:

The next day he [the Venerable Teacher] takes possession of his Sun Palace where he gives audience to his subjects. Suddenly from the north an atmosphere of dissatisfaction reaches the heavens. The Venerable Teacher discusses it with his followers. The cause is the misrule of Emperor Yang of Sui. The evil influence of the cosmos fills heaven and the subjects of the Supreme Ruler start a rebellion.[63]

There can be little doubt that the *ch'uan-ch'i* accounts and their successors influenced the elite image just as the historical records influenced the popular image. It is worth noting that Ssu-ma Kuang, in the compilation of the *Tzu-chih T'ung-chien*, specifically instructed his staff not to be afraid to draw upon such anecdotes and tales as were consistent with an accepted historical version of a given event.[64] In the *T'ung-chien*'s account of Yang-ti's reign a number of these works were consulted; in some cases their versions were rejected, but in others they unquestionably colored the final narrative.[65] Moreover, despite their moral strictures against fiction, the literati read it avidly; and one might speculate that when, from the eighteenth century on, they referred to the misrule of Yang-ti in a memorial to the throne, the image presented in the *Sui Yang-ti Yen-shih* and the *Sui T'ang Yen-i* was as likely to be in their minds as the image found in the *Sui-shu*. It would be too much to say that the elite and popular images of Yang-ti fused into a single myth, but it is certain that the two images, influencing each other, have drawn closer together during the thirteen centuries since the death of Yang-ti.

The myth of Yang-ti persists in the People's China today, and there it has been further embroidered with the demonology of vulgar Marxism. In a small popular volume called "Talks on Chinese History," the chapter concerning Yang-ti is headed: "Yang-ti Builds the Canal to View the Hortensia Flowers."[66] Here are the familiar stories, partly from the histories, more from the stories and novels. Extravagance, licentiousness, and oppression of the people are laid out in well-worn clichés, and the new Marxist terms of opprobrium are added. Yang-ti becomes a "feudal autocrat," and a particularly oppressive representative of this reprehensible type.

A work with some scholarly pretensions is Han Kuo-ch'ing's *Sui Yang-ti*, published by the Hupeh People's Publishing House in 1957. The treatment is an incredible mishmash of Communist clichés and uncritical retailing of accounts from popular stories and the "feudal ruling class" histories. The author's Marxism has apparently failed to liberate him from the old mythology of bad-last rulers or from the stereotyped image of Yang-ti that was the joint product of the interests of the elite and the popular imagination. Here is his final judgment:

Yang-ti had the animal courage and the ambition of Ch'in Shih-huang-ti and Han Wu-ti, but his abilities were not the equal of theirs; he was as cruelly tyrannical as Chieh [the last ruler] of Hsia and Chou [the last ruler] of Shang, but in treachery and coldbloodedness he exceeded them. He had all the extravagance and fantastic licentiousness of Tung-hun Hou of the Ch'i and Hou-chu of the Ch'en [last rulers of the Southern Ch'i and Ch'en respectively], but their extravagant palaces [named] did not approach the grand scale of Yang-ti's Western Plaisance and Maze Pavilion. Yang-ti was truly a grand composite of ancient Chinese rulers. But he had few of their good points, while their treachery and cruelty, their licentiousness and extravagance, were all embodied in him. Therefore we say that his achievement was slight and his guilt was heavy; his goodness little, his evil great. He constituted a barrier to social development [!] He was *the* tyrannical ruler [*pao-chün*] of Chinese history, *the* criminal oppressor of the people.[67]

Of the three problems discussed in this essay—Yang-ti the personality, Yang-ti the political stereotype, and Yang-ti the villain of story and drama—the first must be the object of more intensive research, of study that proceeds in close relation with a deepening scholarly understanding of Chinese psychology and historiography. The third, which has been largely exploratory in this paper, could only be fully developed if other figures from Chinese history and folklore were subjected to similar study and if the techniques of such study were perfected through testing and progressive refinement. The second, the genesis and evolution of a political stereotype, likewise deserves far fuller treatment than has been attempted here. For example we can now only speculate as to when and how the authority of such politically motivated stereotyping began to wane; there is evidence that those who analyzed the fall of dynasties from the Sung onward tended to do so in somewhat more "rational" terms and, when moralizing, to point the finger of blame toward the bad last minister or servitor and not to the monarch himself.[68] Did this reflect the increasingly despotic character of the Chinese throne and its consequent immunity from moralistic criticism? Yet those who have observed the Chinese Communist demonography of Chiang Kai-shek might wonder whether the authority of the "bad last ruler" image has been altogether dissipated. Rather it would appear to be one of those elements in the Confucian tradition that lingers on with a semblance of vitality long after the system which gave it point has been fragmented and dispersed.

Gung-wu Wang

FENG TAO:
AN ESSAY ON CONFUCIAN LOYALTY

During the eighteenth century, the editors of the *Hsü T'ung-chih* classified disloyal ministers and officers into ten groups. In the category reserved for the worst examples were only two men, the soldier Hou I (886–965) and the minister Feng Tao (882–954), both of the period of the Five Dynasties (907–59) and both accused of having "confounded the great relationships and not known shame."[1]

The *Hsü T'ung-chih*, which consists largely of biographies of the T'ang, Five Dynasties, Sung, and Yüan periods, was compiled by imperial order in the years 1767–85, during the Ch'ing dynasty. Under the circumstances,[2] the Chinese editors, as one would expect, placed a great deal of emphasis on the question of dynastic loyalty and expressed themselves strongly about those who had disgraced the profession of "official." It is not surprising that they should consider Feng Tao reprehensible, for no other man had served as a chief minister to five different imperial houses and ten emperors. Hou I could be taken less seriously as he was by origin a mere soldier and, unlike Feng Tao, a devout Buddhist who had never pretended to be a Confucian.[3] But the editors were, in a sense, not responsible for heaping so much odium on Feng Tao. They were merely carrying to a logical conclusion the judgment of two famous Sung historians, Ou-yang Hsiu (1007–72) and Ssu-ma Kuang (1019–89), who had in the eleventh century made a new and vigorous Confucianism the basis of their historiography.

Ou-yang Hsiu, rewriting the history of the Five Dynasties, singled out Feng Tao as the symbol of the period's degeneracy. It was in his preface to Feng Tao's biography that he made his pronouncements on honor and loyalty and bemoaned the fact that the prominent Confucians of the time lacked both.[4] Ssu-ma Kuang enlarged upon this in the *Tzu-chih t'ung-chien* and argued that whatever good Feng Tao might have done by remaining in office was as nothing since he had lived without honor. "The Superior Man [*ta-jen*] will achieve humanity through sacrifice but not prolong his life if it would destroy that humanity."[5]

These were very strong words to use about a man who had been respected in his lifetime. Feng Tao was highly regarded among many of his contemporaries as a conscientious Confucian, a temperate man, and even a model Chief Minister. For nearly a hundred years after his death this reputation survived in some circles, although it was acknowledged that he had done little to justify the faith placed in him by the various emperors. Among those who thought well of him were Fan Chih (911–64), the first historian of the Five Dynasties,[6] Hsüeh Chü-cheng (912–81) and the other compilers of the *Chiu wu-tai shih*,[7] and later, Wu Ch'u-hou (fl. 1060–86), a contemporary of Ou-yang Hsiu and Ssu-ma Kuang.[8] But the adverse judgment of the two great Sung historians prevailed, and from then onward Feng Tao was the example of how not to serve a dynasty and the butt of many jokes about loyalty. His name even went into the Chinese idiom in somewhat the same way as "the Vicar of Bray" went into the English.

What was Feng Tao really like? Was he really unworthy of the respect his contemporaries had for him? Or did his contemporaries really regard him as highly as has been made out? Also, did he deserve to be "revalued" in the annals of China or was he merely a victim of a great change in social, political, and philosophical values? This paper proposes to consider some of the possible answers to these questions.

The period in which Feng Tao lived has been given little attention by Western historians. Even among Chinese historians the Five Dynasties have always been treated either as an extension of the T'ang or as the prelude to the Sung. Only recently has a more systematic approach begun to reveal the significance of the period as a time of great social and political change,[9] lending a new dimension to its usual characterization as a time of anarchy and confusion. So unstable were the conditions that the T'ang empire was divided intermittently among six to eight "kingdoms," and North China saw a succession of five dynasties, the longest of which lasted sixteen years and the shortest only four.

North China was especially unstable. The rebellion of An Lu-shan in the middle of the eighth century resulted in the loss to central control of much of North China, and throughout the ninth century the region of Ho-pei (roughly the present province of Hopei) proceeded to develop independently of the rest of the empire. The descendants of An Lu-shan's officers, including many non-Chinese (Khitan, Hsi, Koreans, and Uighur Turks), commanded the three major armies that came to dominate the affairs of the area, and in the third decade of the ninth century, after a series of abortive attempts to appoint its own governors, the imperial court gave up trying to control internal affairs there. In line with its policy of tolerance, the imperial government resigned itself to accepting tribute in lieu of regular taxes from the arrogant military governors of the three "provinces" of Lu-lung, Ch'eng-te, and Wei-po in the Ho-pei region.[10]

Feng Tao was a man of Ho-pei. According to him, his family was originally from Chi-chou in Ch'eng-te province, but, as far as we know, his immediate ancestors had lived for a long while in Ying-chou.[11] Although not far from Chi-chou, Ying-chou came eventually under the jurisdiction of the military governor of Lu-lung (capital at Yu-chou, the modern Peking). Ying-chou was one of the frontier prefectures of this extensive province and one that was often fought over by rival governors from the east, west, and south. The situation there was especially unstable during the last decade of the ninth century, and if Feng Tao did spend his early years in his home town, it is possible to imagine him growing up under conditions that would have well prepared him for the troubled era of the Five Dynasties. The province of Lu-lung was notorious for its powerful army, whose organization of guards chose the governor or unseated him virtually at will. From 821 to 894, for example, the province had nineteen governors, one of whom governed for twenty-two years. The eighteen remaining governors averaged less than three years each. In fact, of the nineteen governors, only four died in office (two of them within a year of taking office) and one retired (also within a year). Of the rest, six were killed and eight were driven out, in most cases by the very guards organization that had put them in.[12]

This frequent change of governors would have made administration virtually impossible had it not been for officials recruited locally from the gentry families of the province. These families provided the literate assistants to the governor and to his aides and some of the accountants and clerks who handled the routine business of provincial government. This local "civil service" was not entirely independent of the central government at Ch'ang-an. It was possible for the senior officials to acquire honorific titles and to have a minor court rank while holding a local provincial office. Eventually, if some of them decided that it was to their advantage to leave for the capital, their titles and qualifications would give them a fair chance of getting a regular official appointment. If, on the other hand, their intention was to follow their careers within Lu-lung province, they had to develop a high degree of resilience. In order to survive the quick succession of governors, the wise official avoided too close an identification with any particular governor and cultivated a reputation for discretion and trustworthiness. By contrast, young men of gentry families elsewhere in the empire, being without an autonomous provincial service in which to build their careers, were dependent ultimately on the favor of the central government for advancement. Feng Tao, having grown up on the border of the province, would have been well aware that in Lu-lung he could rise to high provincial office with only local competition. There is no evidence that he ever left the province in his youth, nor is there evidence that experience elsewhere would have qualified him better for his local career.

Regionalism had by this time so undermined the T'ang empire that all that was needed to destroy the empire altogether was another sizable rebellion, and this Wang Hsien-chih and Huang Ch'ao provided from 875 on. The rebellion burned its way through most of China, leaving in its trail a greatly intensified regional growth. What land remained in the hands of the T'ang imperial court was then bitterly fought over until Chu Wen, one of Huang Ch'ao's generals who had surrendered to the T'ang, thought himself ready to found a new dynasty. Without waiting to crush the regional governments which had partitioned the old T'ang empire, he established himself as emperor of Liang. The problem of regionalism persisted and troubled the empire for the years that formed the period of the Five Dynasties. The dynasties were:

LIANG (907–23)

T'ai-tsu (Chu Wen), 907–12
Prince of Ying (Chu Yu-kuei), 912–13
Prince of Chün (Chu Yu-chen),
  913–23

T'ANG (923–36)

Chuang-tsung (Prince of Chin, Li
  Ts'un-hsü), 923–26
Ming-tsung (Li Ssu-yüan), 926–33
Prince of Sung (Li Ts'ung-hou),
  933–34
Prince of Lu (Li Ts'ung-k'o), 934–36

CHIN (936–46)

Kao-tsu (Shih Ching-t'ang), 936–42
Shao-ti (Shih Ch'ung-kuei), 942–46

Interlude 947

Liao (Khitan) emperor T'ai-tsung
  (Yeh-lü Te-kuang), 927–47

HAN (947–50)

Kao-tsu (Liu Chih-yüan), 947–48
Yin-ti (Liu Ch'eng-yu), 948–50

CHOU (951–59)

T'ai-tsu (Kuo Wei), 951–54
Shih-tsung (Ch'ai Jung), 954–59
Prince of Liang (Ch'ai Tsung-hsün),
  959

These dynasties, when not fighting for survival, were struggling against the deep-rooted regionalism that had grown up during the ninth century.

Feng Tao was born just after the peak of the Huang Ch'ao rebellion in 882 in the county of Ching-ch'eng in Ying prefecture. Feng Tao's family had at this time every reason to be grateful for the regionalism that was to destroy the T'ang dynasty, for it was this very regionalism that protected the Ho-pei region from the Huang Ch'ao rebels, the only region, except Szechwan, to enjoy this freedom. After the rebellion, the region became one of the major battlegrounds in the long struggle for supremacy among the military governors of North China. Before Feng Tao was ten, there had been a mutiny of the prefectural garrison, which the county magistrate had been able to put down only by rounding up some thousand citizens in the area. This magistrate, Liu Jen-kung (d. 914), later governor of Lu-lung province, was the father of the man who gave Feng Tao his first provincial post.[13]

Feng Tao's autobiography claims that his family was descended from the aristocratic Feng clan of the old commandery of Ch'ang-lo (also called Hsin-tu, later Chi-chou, the present Chi-hsien).[14] His immediate ancestors, however, appear to have been content to be gentleman farmers professing themselves Confucians. None of them was known to have held any office, and Feng Tao seems to have been proud of his humble but once eminent family. Liu Jen-kung must have known the Feng family, a prominent one in his county, and possibly it was through Liu Jen-kung that Feng Tao was able to get a post at the provincial capital.

We first find him mentioned in our records only after he was twenty-five, that is, after 907. A great mystery surrounds his youth. He himself says nothing about it except that he had lost his parents during the troubled times when he was young and thus did not know the exact date of his birth.[15] In the eulogistic biography preserved in the *Chiu wu-tai shih,* based probably on his Account of Conduct (*hsing-chuang*),[16] it is said that "when he was young, he was sincere, fond of learning, and talented in writing. He was not ashamed to have poor clothes and poor food. Apart from carrying rice to offer to his parents, he worked only on his reading and reciting. Although his house might be covered by a heavy fall of snow or his whole mat by thick dust, he remained undisturbed."[17]

It is difficult to determine how much truth there is in these stock phrases about the filial son and earnest scholar. They do, however, match the account of the deep effect on him of his father's death and they agree with his later frugality and stoicism. Although the greater part of what we know of Feng Tao seems to have come from Feng Tao himself or from his sons and friends, there is no reason to doubt that this general picture of him as a simple man with the conventional virtues is a correct one.

Certainly his youth was filled with vivid experiences. In 894, when he was twelve, the governor of his province was driven out of the capital and, while passing through the county of Ching-ch'eng, was murdered by the neighboring governor from the province to the east.[18] Six years later, Ching-ch'eng was the battleground between Chu Wen, fighting in the name of the T'ang emperor, and the new governor of Lu-lung province. The prefecture was captured by Chu Wen's forces and Feng Tao probably experienced a little of Chu Wen's administration.[19] Feng Tao was eighteen at the time, old enough to have been conscious of the military and political struggles taking place.

His early career at Yu-chou, the provincial capital, was precarious, and it is claimed in his biography that he counseled the brash young governor Liu Shou-kuang (d. 914) to be cautious and was jailed for his pains. After his release in 911 he escaped to T'ai-yüan to join the leader of the Sha-t'o Turks, at that time the main opponent of Chu Wen's Liang dynasty and the professed leaders of the movement to "restore the T'ang." There Feng Tao, who was then twenty-nine, entered the service of the old eunuch Chang Ch'eng-yeh (846–922) in the Office of Army Supervision,[20] serving in this office for eight years. His service was without distinction and there is no record of what he did. As he was known only for his literary talents, it is supposed that he acted as one of the eunuch's secretaries. He was no longer young at the time (twenty-nine to thirty-seven years old) and had no special skill to justify rapid promotion. What he learned, however, must have been very important to him and may even explain many features of his later life. Chang had served off and on for more than forty years at the T'ang court and could have taught his aide many things about court practice, the role of a civilian in a military organization, and the pitfalls awaiting an official in such unstable times. Feng Tao apparently absorbed much useful information from the successful eunuch, for soon after the Sha-t'o leader, the Prince of Chin, had lost his chief secretary during a battle in 918, Feng Tao was promoted to this post over the head of an ex-T'ang official from a distinguished family.[21] As chief secretary to the prince most likely to succeed to the throne at a time when most of the Prince's earlier supporters were either dead or very old, Feng Tao was virtually assured of a successful career.

Almost immediately after his appointment, he made a show of courage by standing up to the Prince during one of the Prince's childish bursts of anger.[22] It is important to note the prominence given the accounts of Feng Tao's courage in front of Liu Shou-kuang in 911 and before the Prince of Chin in 919 in Feng Tao's biography. Never again until the last year of his life did he disagree with his emperor. His sons and his friends must have been conscious of this and after his death carefully inserted the accounts of these incidents in his biography. The fact is that when Feng Tao admonished the Prince of Chin, he was still under the patronage of Chang Ch'eng-yeh and was to remain under his influence until Chang's death at the end of 922. His so-called act of courage before the Prince in 919 was thus made while still a protégé of Chang's and reflected not the moralistic protests of a Confucian literatus but the tactful advice of an intimate counselor.

The theme of intimacy and highly personal relationship between ruler and minister which derived from the old provincial organization runs through the Five Dynasties. Such relationships were evident at the very first court Feng Tao served, the court of the Prince of Chin himself, better known as the Emperor Chuang-tsung (923–26). This was the court of the T'ang "restoration," and Chuang-tsung set about restoring the T'ang court organization with the eunuchs and their entourage as well as filling most of the posts in the imperial central government. But at the same time, like the Liang emperors before him, he retained most of his provincial officers by giving them posts as commissioners around him, and made his commanders generals in the imperial army. Chuang-tsung was, moreover, unusually fond of acting and kept his own troupe of actors and musicians, who were allowed to advise him on affairs of state. In the ensuing struggle for power among the various groups, the bureaucrats and the generals who were remote from the emperor lost. Of the remaining three groups—eunuchs, actors, and ex-provincial officers—the most influential was the favored acting troupe, which came from the lowest class of society. Against the actors, even Kuo Ch'ung-t'ao (d. 926), Chuang-tsung's most intimate adviser, who had served since 917 in his provincial government, was powerless. And in 926, the actors and the eunuchs were to cause the death of Kuo, thus touching off the mutiny that brought Chuang-tsung to his death and the "restoration" to an end.[23]

This was the last time the eunuchs played a prominent part in politics for many centuries and the last time actors had a chance to do so. The period 923–26 was not a time for the bureaucrats, and it was just as well that Feng Tao was in mourning for about half that time. But he could not have missed the significance of the power struggle in Chuang-tsung's court. It was not between the eunuchs and the bureaucrats as in the past but between imperial favorites, including eunuchs, and the new class of former provincial officers. The bureaucrats, utterly discredited by their weak leadership in the last years of the T'ang,[24] could not regain their power and authority without aligning themselves with one side or the other. Feng Tao and his colleagues were forced to act as old members of the provincial organization rather than simply as traditionally aloof Confucian bureaucrats.

Feng Tao played no part in any of the maneuvers for power. Under Chuang-tsung's successor, Ming-tsung (926–33), his literary ability was further recognized and he rose quickly to the post of Chief Minister. Just before this appointment, there was more evidence that the bureaucrat was at a disadvantage against the officer from the provincial cadre. While Jen Huan, the Chief Minister, tried to appoint a literatus of known ability to assist him, An Ch'ung-hui and his supporters of the provincial cadre supported a man who was pliant and nearly illiterate. Emperor Ming-tsung suggested, as a compromise, Feng Tao, who was acceptable largely because "he had no quarrel with any living thing" (*yü-wu wu-ching*).[25] Soon after his appointment, he became a trusted friend of Ming-tsung. He knew how to flatter, he had a good sense of humor, and at the same time he had an air of earnestness and a readiness to quote the Confucian classics to support any advice he gave.

This was the key to his success with the nine other emperors he served in the twenty years after Ming-tsung's death. With the tolerant Ming-tsung, he first perfected the art of good-natured advice and gentle flattery and was recognized by his contemporaries as a man skilled in the intimate and personal approach to emperors. The emperors liked him, above all, because "he had no quarrel with any living thing" and never failed to have pleasing, comforting words.

From 927 to his death in 954, there were only two breaks in Feng Tao's career as prime minister and fond intimate of emperors. In the middle of 934 he was sent out to be governor of a minor province for more than a year. This was directly connected with his failure to act with propriety when Ming-tsung's adopted son, the Prince of Lu, claimed the throne from Ming-tsung's young son, the Prince of Sung. The act of usurpation early in 934, just four months after Ming-tsung's death, had taken Feng Tao by surprise. Feng became unduly agitated and, while waiting for the Prince of Lu's entry into the capital of Lo-yang, Feng ordered his secretary to call upon the Prince to ascend the throne. When the secretary refused, Feng himself exhorted the Prince to do so.[26] His efforts did not save him entirely and soon afterward he was asked to leave for the provincial appointment. On his return from the provinces in the middle of 935, he was unemployed for about six months, the only time he was unemployed in his whole career. But he seems to have been indispensable, and by early 936 he was back at the court as *Ssu-k'ung*, one of the highest offices of the empire.[27]

The incident of Feng Tao's intervention at the gates of Lo-yang is omitted in his official biography. In fact, while Feng Tao was alive, no attempt was made to compile the Veritable Records (*Shih-lu*) of the two brief reigns of the Prince of Sung and the Prince of Lu, and it was not until 957, three years after Feng Tao's death, that the first official record of his part in the accession of the Prince of Lu appeared. Before that, his part was probably well known among his contemporaries, but no one, except possibly the compilers of the Account of Conduct of Lu Tao (866–941), the secretary who refused to comply with his orders, placed it on record.[28] It is also an interesting reflection on Chinese biographical compilations that a dishonorable incident like this should not appear in Feng Tao's own biography in the *Chiu wu-tai shih* but only as a story in the career of Lu Tao.

Feng Tao's loss of court office in 934–35 was short and his discomfiture virtually ignored by his friends. But his loss of office in the middle of 944, during the reign of Shao-ti (942–46) of Chin, was more serious. Once again Feng Tao was sent out to a minor province for a year and a half, and after that to another until the Khitan conquest of North China in early 947. This time he was away for two and a half years, very important years in Chinese history. The Khitan victory, which finally cut off the sixteen northern prefectures from Chinese control for 420 years,[29] could not in any way be attributed to Feng Tao. In fact, he was probably appointed to the provinces because he opposed the war policy of the emperor's chief advisers. Whether or not this was so, it is clear that he was of little use to the Chin court. It was apparently the consensus that "Tao is a good prime minister only for normal times, for he can do nothing to rescue the empire in a period of difficulties, rather like a Ch'an priest with no skill in falconry."[30]

Loss of court office in this case proved no embarrassment to Feng Tao. When the Khitans entered the Chin capital, K'ai-feng, Feng Tao left his province to pay his respects to their emperor and found himself welcomed as someone who did not have the taint of having defied them. He promptly exercised his tact on the emperor and, by fortuitous circumstances, soon afterward found himself in a position to save many Chin officials' lives.[31]

Feng Tao's long career also had its more positive side. In 932, under the Emperor Ming-tsung, he and two of his colleagues ordered the editing and first printing of the Nine Classics, one of the best-known events of the Five Dynasties period and one that was to revolutionize education and civil service recruitment in the centuries following.[32] Under Chin Kao-tsu (936–42), Feng Tao was the head of the important mission to the Khitans in 938, which preceded the official handing-over of the sixteen northern prefectures of the Ho-pei and Ho-tung regions (present northern Hopei and Shansi provinces). Feng Tao was present when all the prefectural and county records, including those of his own prefecture of Ying-chou and county of Ching-ch'eng, were delivered to the Khitans. At this memorable ceremony, Feng Tao saw his county being made into the southernmost county of the Khitan empire. He handled the mission so well that on his return Kao-tsu entrusted him with the difficult task of maintaining the peace. At Kao-tsu's deathbed, he was asked to see that Kao-tsu's baby son succeeded to the throne. But Feng Tao did not think this was wise and, after Kao-tsu's death, helped in making his nephew, aged twenty-eight, the new emperor (Shao-ti, 942–46).[33]

Under the Han dynasty (947–50), he lived very quietly and wrote the unusual autobiography, the *Ch'ang-lo lao tzu-hsü,* that was to turn the weight of historical opinion against him during the Sung (see discussion below of Feng Tao's biographers). But his active career really came to an end in the first weeks of 951, when Kuo Wei (Chou T'ai-tsu, 951–54) sent him as emissary to welcome a member of the Liu clan who aspired to the Han throne. Feng Tao's reputation as a sincere and honest man was the reason for his choice, and he may have suspected that he was being used as a decoy to bring a claimant to the throne into Kuo Wei's hands. Feng Tao was entirely successful: Kuo Wei killed the prince and seized the empire. For his part in Kuo Wei's smooth accession, Feng Tao was further rewarded with the highest court titles. He was already an old man of sixty-nine, old enough to be Kuo Wei's father, and so respected that Kuo Wei never called him by name.[34]

It has been noted that Feng Tao never openly opposed the wishes of the emperors he served. He criticized the Lu-lung governor Liu Shou-kuang in 911, and stood up to the Prince of Chin in 919, but thereafter always accepted his emperor's decisions, right or wrong, without question or protest. In his last year of life, almost as if he had suddenly become conscious of this defect in his record, Feng Tao reversed himself and made a spirited protest against Emperor Shih-tsung's (954–59) proposal personally to lead his armies into battle. The protest angered Shih-tsung and was ignored. Two weeks later Shih-tsung won a great victory, and less than a month after that Feng Tao was dead following a very short illness. In his third and final venture into criticizing an emperor Feng Tao had blundered dramatically.[35]

There is no doubt that Feng Tao himself and most of his contemporaries thought that he lived a Confucian life and acted as a Confucian in his public career. Few men of his distinction in the T'ang and the Five Dynasties periods could claim comparable aloofness from Taoism and Buddhism. The insistently Confucian and conventional tone that permeates all his writings and reported conversations was so obvious that his contemporaries delighted in telling stories attributing to him some of the Confucian absurdities of the time. These stories, though probably apocryphal, convey a vivid impression of prevailing attitudes.

Feng Tao's punctiliousness regarding the taboo on personal names in conversation produced this story using a pun on his own name. Feng Tao, commenting on a young scholar, Li Tao, pointed out that the young man's name sounded like his own, but added, in an unlikely joke at his own expense, that Li Tao's *tao* had the character for "inch" under the phonogram that was Feng Tao's personal name. In the Chinese idiom, a man without "inch" was one without a proper sense of values.[36]

Another story concerns Feng Tao's failure while governor of a province in Honan to repair a temple to Confucius after a dozen or so "liquor households" had petitioned to be allowed to do so. Someone then appended a poem to the petition mocking Confucian scholars who reached high office but waited for such lowly people to repair Confucian temples.[37]

These stories reflect an age renowned neither for its Confucians nor for the prevailing view of Confucianism, and it is important, I think, to see Feng Tao clearly in this context. The cultural history of the Five Dynasties period has been notable for its anarchy and for hermits and great poets in the *tz'u* form. The prose of the time was later regarded as exceptionally bad and the thought and the thinkers undistinguished. It was under such circumstances that Feng Tao became famous in his time as a prose writer and Confucian. Among the emperors he served, two could be said to have been ardent believers in the supernatural (the Prince of Lu and Chin Kao-tsu). All the rest were also practicing Taoists and Buddhists.[38] Feng Tao was an intimate friend to at least eight of the eleven emperors and had opportunity enough to increase that intimacy by sharing in their religious practices if not in their faith. But he seems to have been able to remain on intimate terms without reference to religion. In all the literature there is on Feng Tao's relations with his emperors, he is only once said to have been consulted on anything not pertaining to the Confucian state. This was when the Emperor Chin Kao-tsu asked him about the value of the *Tao-te ching* and invited him to attend the classes given by a prominent Taoist at the palace. It is not known whether Feng Tao ever went, but his answer to the emperor was entirely consistent with his way of mixing flattery and a ponderous earnestness. He gave the tolerant but equivocal reply that neither the Taoist lecturing on Lao Tzu nor the Buddhist receiving his vows should be taken lightly.[39]

In fact, Feng Tao's firm adherence to Confucianism was unusual for his time. Most of his successful contemporaries were inconsistent in their beliefs: for example, the two men Chao Feng (885–935) and Liu

Hsü (888–947), both of whom were also from Lu-lung province in Ho-pei and had served as Chief Ministers together with him. Chao Feng became violently anti-Buddhist in later life but had been a Buddhist priest as a youth. Liu Hsü (who was related to Feng Tao by marriage) was closely associated with both Buddhist priests and Taoist hermits. Again, Ma Yin-sun (d. 953), Chief Minister in 936 when Feng Tao was out of favor, had started life as a great admirer of Han Yü (786–824) and then turned to Buddhism with enthusiasm.[40]

Perhaps it would be more accurate to say that the majority of men at the court were either indifferent or lukewarm toward religion and Confucianism. This was in keeping with the traditions of the ninth-century T'ang court—traditions of artistic virtuosity and sophistication which, from the Confucian point of view, were very superficial. Feng Tao seems to have scorned these traditions and is known to have played his part in suppressing "the frivolous and unstable" (fou-tsao) men descended from distinguished T'ang families while helping impoverished scholars of promise.[41] In the well-known anecdote of Feng Tao's encounter with two snobbish court officials who laughed at his use of a popular reference book of Confucian quotations—the T'u-yüan ts'e (a sort of "selections from the classics")—Feng Tao is said to have retorted that the old quotations were surely more worthy of reading than the pretty phrases of the examination hall plagiarized from the successful candidates.[42]

Yet it is clear that Feng Tao was not an impressive Confucian in any way. His professed Confucianism was supported by a limited knowledge of the classics, and even his understanding of the Confucian state seems to have been vague. It is, of course, easy to be unfair to him since his collected works have not survived. Apart from a few congratulatory messages and a number of formal addresses to the throne which had little to do with either Confucian institutions or state policy, we cannot identify any surviving state papers as having been written by Feng Tao.[43]

Feng Tao undeniably had a part in the memorials from the Imperial Secretariat (chung-shu) and the Chancellery (men-hsia), particularly during the reigns of T'ang Ming-tsung and Chin Kao-tsu when he was the senior minister. But we have evidence that he avoided all difficult policy decisions, especially if they involved finance or the army. These were the two realms where there was always potential conflict with more ambitious and specialized officers, and he was probably prudent to stay away from them and leave them to the military secretaries and finance commissioners. On the other hand, he was not active in the strictly Confucian spheres of government either. There is no evidence that he contributed anything to the fields of rites, law, music and ceremonies, examination, and recruitment. Here again, he preferred to leave the work to specialists. If this is taken together with the anecdote about Feng Tao's dependence on a Confucian phrase book, it sustains the picture of Feng Tao as a very superficial Confucian.

There remains the historic printing of the Nine Classics in 932, which nearly every history ascribes to Feng Tao. But it is by no means clear that Feng Tao himself initiated the project. The other Chief Minister in 932, Li Yü (d. 935), who was a great admirer of Han Yü, is also named, and since the knowledge of the advantages of printing had come from Szechwan after the conquest of the kingdom of Shu in 926 and Li Yü had been the senior executive secretary in the Szechwan campaign, it is more likely that he or one of his colleagues during the campaign was responsible for proposing the official enterprise.[44] The work of re-editing the classics for printing was left largely in the hands of T'ien Min (880–971) and his assistants, and Feng Tao is not known to have contributed any scholarship. His Sung biographer Ou-yang Hsiu went so far as to give him no credit at all for the printing of the classics. Feng Tao's main connection with the publication seems to have been that he was the senior Chief Minister in 932 and still the highest official in the empire when the completed work was presented to the throne in 953.[45]

What then have we left to help us to define, if possible, Feng Tao's Confucianism? We have extracts from a few memorials, we have his many reported conversations, and finally we have two informal but important documents written in 950 when he was sixty-eight.

The extracts from memorials do not reveal much. Several of them exhorted the Emperor Ming-tsung (926–33) to be careful and to learn the lessons of his predecessor's downfall. Others assured Ming-tsung that the empire, primarily because of the emperor's sagacity, was at peace.[46] We also have one that dealt with the order of precedence at the audiences of the Emperor Chin Kao-tsu (936–42).[47] Perhaps the best example of Feng Tao's Confucianism can be found in his memorial of the second month of 933 concerning the education of Ming-tsung's heir apparent. Here he argued that the empire's foundations lay with having virtuous men around the throne and showed how Chuang-tsung's (923–26) failure to rule by virtue (te) was the main reason for his downfall. He then argued,

The strength of the empire is found in its men. The men at present important to the empire are just the military governors, the prefects, the magistrates, and the county secretaries. If the men are rightly chosen, there is good government. If the men are poorly selected, there will be confusion. One cannot but choose carefully. As the *Book of History* says, "It is like treading on a tiger's tail or walking on spring ice." Each day there is need for greater caution. I merely ask Your Imperial Majesty not to forget dangers in times of peace and not to forget anarchy in periods of good government.[48]

His reported conversations are more interesting. He was the only man in the Five Dynasties period to have snatches of his conversation preserved in the official records. The *Chiu wu-tai shih* quotes these conversations both in the Basic Annals and in his biography, while scattered throughout the *Ts'e-fu yüan-kuei* are several more not preserved in the official History. Since these two compilations are known to have followed closely the Veritable Records (*shih-lu*), there is no reason to doubt that the conversations were taken from those sources. The Veritable Records were themselves compiled from the Imperial Diary (*ch'i-chü chu*), the Court Diary (*shih-cheng chi*), the Daily Record (*jih-li*), and the Account of Conduct (*hsing-chuang*) of each prominent official. At each stage of compilation, the Chief Minister had a great deal to say about what was to be included. This was particularly true with regard to the Court Diary, which was compiled by one of the Chief Ministers himself. It is, of course, often noted that Confucians dominated the business of history writing in all dynasties and there is nothing unusual in the inclusion of Feng Tao's Confucian sayings for their own sake.[49]

But it is interesting to note that almost all of Feng Tao's sayings (as well as most of his memorials) were recorded for the reigns of T'ang Ming-tsung and Chin Kao-tsu. These are two of the longer reigns in the period (seven and six years respectively), and Feng Tao got on very well with both emperors. But a problem does arise when it is noted that their Veritable Records are only two of the four compiled in Feng Tao's lifetime, the other two being those of Chin Shao-ti (942–46) and Han Kao-tsu (947–48).[50] Excluding the Khitan emperor in 947 and T'ang Chuang-tsung, whom Feng Tao did not serve as Chief Minister, there were five other emperors whose Records were not compiled until three to six years after their death. For the Records of Chin Shao-ti compiled in 950–51 the various Diaries were probably incomplete because of the Khitan wars. Feng Tao, who was away from the court during the later half of the reign, might not in any case have cared to be associated with an emperor who had failed disastrously. As for the Records of Han Kao-tsu compiled in 949, although the reign was so short, we have a full account of Feng Tao's role in saving the Chinese from the Khitans by the way he spoke to the Khitan emperor. There is, I believe, sufficient evidence to suspect that Feng Tao had a prominent part, if not in the compilation of the Veritable Records, at least in preparing the Imperial and Court Diaries. This does not necessarily mean that Feng Tao tampered with the archives. Feng Tao did have the right to include or exclude material, and it would be in keeping with his concept of Confucian duty to include as much Confucian wisdom as possible, even his own. I have already shown that the one great embarrassment in his career, occurring when the Prince of Lu usurped the throne in 934, was never recorded in his lifetime. When the Records of the two Chin emperors were being compiled in 950–51, it would not have been out of place to consider filling the gap in the official records between 934 and 936, but this was not done. Feng Tao could not have prevented this gap from being filled, but if he was as embarrassed as he appears to have been, he might easily have discouraged it.[51]

Feng Tao's reported conversations must therefore be examined in the light of his own involvement in history compilation. Considering how some of his admirers, who noted that he died at the same age as Confucius,[52] were ready to compare him to Confucius himself, these conversations take on the coloration of the "sayings of a sage." He himself was not averse to making the same comparison, and in a conversation with a colleague about his supporters and detractors, he said, "All men who agree with you will approve of you, all who do not will defame you and nine out of ten perhaps defame me [at the court]. In ancient times, Confucius was a sage and yet he was slandered by Shu-sun Wu-shu. How much more would people slander someone as empty and mean as me!"[53] This smacks of false modesty; it mentions Confucius and himself in the same passage while following the convention of comparing oneself unfavorably with the ancient sages.

In fact, the most striking thing about the many sayings of this articulate sage is their conventionality and their complete lack of originality. A typical conversation ran as follows:

The Emperor Ming-tsung asked, "How are the affairs of state?" Feng Tao replied, "The crop seasons are regular and the people at peace." The emperor asked again, "Apart from this, what is there to note?" Tao replied, "Your Majesty is pure and virtuous and truly in accord with the wishes of heaven. I have heard that rulers like Yao and Shun have been admired by all and masters like Chieh and Chou have been hated by all. This is the difference between those with principles and those without. Now Your Majesty carefully observes self-restraint and pays full attention to the art of government. The people are not weighed down by taxes and services and tell one another that this is like the years of Yao and the days of Shun. This is merely because the people are satisfied and everyday things are abundant. After the tenth year of Chen-kuan [636], the Minister Wei Cheng memorialized T'ang T'ai-tsung, asking that all should be like the beginning of the Chen-kuan period. Now I also wish Your Majesty to think of the good things you did at the beginning of your reign. If Your Majesty would do so, then the empire would be fortunate indeed."[54]

Even the pattern of the conversations changed but little. There was the profound Baconian theme followed by the exposition and then the admonition. This was the formula of the sages and, no doubt, Feng

Tao's pretensions stem from the noblest of motives—to reaffirm tradition and order in an age of troubles. The consistent, almost dreary, reiteration of Confucian tenets that characterized his conversations reflected a deep conviction that a return to traditional ways, rather than startling innovation, was the solution to the problems besetting the state and the people. Young Confucians of the time, used to the widespread neglect of their creed, must have been heartened by the sight of so successful an official espousing Confucianism. The mediocrity of his life and thought, if noted at all by his young admirers, would have detracted little from his singular importance as proof of the flexibility possible in applying the old Confucian principles.

There are, finally, the preface to his poems for a deceased friend and his famous autobiography, the *Ch'ang-lo lao tzu-hsü*, both written in 950 when he was an old man. The preface, completed in the second month of 950 soon after the death of his fellow provincial and early associate, Liu Shen-chiao (877–950), revealed an intense, in some ways romantic belief in the superiority of Confucian duty. After eulogizing Liu Shen-chiao as a good man who had done harm to no one, Feng Tao took note of his undistinguished public record but asked: Why then was he so loved by the people in the prefecture he administered?

It is really because he did not use whippings and beatings and was not oppressive. He did not take advantage of his office for private ends nor did he harm others to profit himself. He certainly worked in a way becoming a high official. He lightened punishment and forgave wrong; he was careful in his conduct and economical in his expenditure. It was enough for him to be content with his emoluments and live with decorum.

Of all those who served in this capacity, who could not achieve what he did? But the prefects before him were not like that. That is why the people sigh with admiration for him. In these days when the empire has suffered from war and everywhere there can still be seen the consequences of banditry, when the looms are empty while the taxes are burdensome, when the people are scattered and the granaries depleted, it is not easy to say that there is well-being and peace. If the nobles and provincial officials felt concern for this situation, they would not amass private fortunes, or kill the innocent. If they had realized that people form the base of the country and good government is the life of the people and all acted with benevolence and moderation, what then would there be to praise in the work of Mr. Liu? And why need they fear they will not reach great fame?[55]

Feng Tao used the occasion to make a general comment on the prevailing standards of public office. He was obviously aware that when rapacious officials were everywhere, the selfless official, even an undistinguished one, gained stature. Whether he realized it or not, his comments could have been applied to himself. He stood out in his generation not because of his own excellence, but because he withheld himself from the decadence around him. It is hard to believe that he was insensitive to his own inadequacies. More likely he was gratified by his own incorruptibility.

The death of his friend moved him deeply, and I think it was reflection upon his friend's life and small achievements that brought him to think of his own and, about two months afterward, to write his autobiography.[56] This was a curious piece of writing, quite unprecedented in its form, and more like a skeleton of an autobiography. It carried all his ranks and titles and all the formal information about his family. Only at the end did he set forth what he thought were the minimum requirements of a Confucian life.

I quietly think of what is important and what is not and what blessings extend to life and death. Through imperial favors and by strictly following our clan traditions, I have received the great teachings and opened them to others. I have observed filial piety in the home and shown loyalty to the state. Also, my mouth has not spoken what is improper and my gates have not been open to things I should not have. All that I have wished is that I should not deceive earth that is below, man that is with us, and heaven that is above, and have regarded these "three no-deceptions" as a rule of behavior. I have been thus when I was lowly, when I was in high office, when I grew to manhood, and when I was old. In the service of my relatives, my emperor, and my elders, and in my relations with my fellow men, I have been favored by the mercy of heaven. Several times when I encountered trouble and escaped with fortune and when I was in the hands of the barbarians and returned safely to the Central Plain [China], it was not due to the devices of man but to the protection of heaven.[57]

He was a great believer in the good man being protected by heaven and never failed to say so in both prose and poetry on appropriate occasions. As this was obviously an article of faith with him, he must have been sincere in the modesty of the following passage:

Thus in the world there is one who is fortunate, one who will have a decent grave when he dies. As he is inferior to the ancients, he does not deserve to be buried with jade or pearl in his mouth, but should have his body prepared in his ordinary clothes and buried simply on a coarse bamboo mat at a place selected because it did not yield crops. There should not be the sacrifice of male goats, for one should abstain from taking life. There should instead only be the sacrifice of things without life.[58] As there have not been inscriptions for the graves of three generations of his ancestors, there should also not be an inscription. And as he has no virtue to speak of, there should not be a request for posthumous titles.[59]

It was probably the death of Liu Shen-chiao that turned Feng Tao's mind to thoughts of death. And having written about the inconsequential life of his friend, he must have wondered how posterity would consider him. He knew well the power of history in Chinese civilization.

Was his conscience disturbed by the thought of his negative virtues? Or did he believe that he should present his life for the betterment of all the Confucians to come? From all that we know of him, I feel that the latter belief would be consistent with his idea of Confucian duty.

Feng Tao was certainly no scholar of the classics, nor did he give unbending loyalty to any emperor, but in his adherence to the prevailing brand of Confucianism he was honest and firm. Few of his contemporaries would have denied that he was a genuine Confucian. Yet in the age of Confucian revival which followed a century later, he was denounced as despicable, and the new biography written from that vantage point soon became the accepted story of his life.

The first to condemn Feng Tao was Ou-yang Hsiu, followed soon after by Ssu-ma Kuang. Both contrasted Feng Tao's Confucian pretensions with his disloyalty and self-satisfaction. Ssu-ma Kuang carefully reinforced his predecessor's argument to meet the objections to their judgment that had been raised by other historians of the time. Men like Wu Ch'u-hou had pointed to Feng Tao's many good acts.[60] Others had expressed the opinion that Feng Tao was being made the scapegoat for all the ills of the Five Dynasties period. The defense of Feng Tao ran thus: Thousands of officials had been disloyal. Why pick on Feng Tao? And even if he did act disloyally at least five times, was it so much more hateful to be disloyal more than once? Wasn't once enough?

Ssu-ma Kuang angrily answered,

Feng Tao was Chief Minister to five dynasties and eight surnames, like an inn to many travelers. Enemies at the break of dawn would become emperor and minister by evening. He changed his face and transformed his words and never once was he ashamed. Such having been his attitude toward loyalty, what is there to praise if he did do a little good? . . . While the emperors followed one another closely in their rise and fall, Feng Tao prospered as before. He is the worst of treacherous officials. How can he deserve to be compared with other men?[61]

This has been the main theme of all of Feng Tao's later critics—the number of times he had been disloyal. It must have appeared absurd to have a man serve eleven emperors in a row. There was no emperor Feng Tao could have served whom he did not serve. This was unprecedented. And even more extraordinary was that he should have held the highest ranks in all but one of these reigns. Certainly no civilian official in the whole history of China had ever had a comparable career. How was he to be classified? How could he be classified? The majority opinion was that he was the worst of the worst and a little ridiculous as well.

But there were a few who spoke up in Feng Tao's favor. For example, Wu Ch'u-hou in defending him quoted the famous minister Fu Pi (1004–83), who had compared him to Mencius' Superior Man (*ta-jen*). And Wu Tseng (fl. 1150–60) said that Feng Tao was highly regarded by Su Shih (1036–1101) and Wang An-shih (1021–86) and argued that Ou-yang Hsiu was probably very young when he condemned Feng Tao. But Wu Ch'u-hou and Wu Tseng were associated with Ts'ai Ching (1046–1125) and Ch'in Kuei (1090–1155) respectively, both condemned in Chinese history as "evil officials" (*chien-ch'en*). Their opinions were therefore not taken very seriously.[62]

After the twelfth century, when Ou-yang Hsiu's and Ssu-ma Kuang's views prevailed, there were very few voices raised in Feng Tao's defense. There were Wang Shih-chen (1528–93) and Li Chih (1527–1602), but both were regarded as literary men trying to be "different." On the other hand, the praise of the Ming martyr Wen Huang (1585–1645) was more difficult to dismiss. His main argument was that Feng Tao was a good man with honest intentions who had been cruelly dealt with by historians. It is indeed true that the only historian of distinction to try to understand Feng Tao was Chao I (1727–1814), who argued that loyalty was simply not a problem during that period; but even he maintained that Feng Tao was without shame. On the whole, the few voices raised on behalf of Feng Tao have been regarded as either eccentricity or special pleading.[63]

The fact is that the Five Dynasties period was an extraordinary one. The conditions at the end of the T'ang and throughout those dynasties were unprecedented and the actions of a whole generation were peculiar to the times. Never before had the empire been divided into seven or eight states, and there was no way to fit the scheme of things into the orthodox view of imperial succession (*cheng-t'ung*). Was there in fact an empire? After all, none of the so-called emperors controlled more than a third of the T'ang empire at any one time. And there was no reason why the *cheng-t'ung* should have remained in the north. In Szechwan to the west, in the Yangtze provinces, even in Kwangtung and later in Fukien, claims to be the only true emperor were made by various people from time to time. The claims of the rulers of Nan T'ang on the Yangtze were no less valid than those of the northern dynasties.

Then after fifty-three years of uncertainty the Sung dynasty succeeded the last of the Five Dynasties and, eighteen years later, conquered all the other states. It was this that the Confucian historians seized upon to help explain what could not be reconciled within the orthodox framework. The Sung emperors inherited the empire, and that could only be so because the emperors of the Five Dynasties had each inherited the empire before them. Therefore, those Five Dynasties were obviously bearers of the Mandate of Heaven and all the standards of the Confucian state could fairly be applied to them.[64] By these standards, it was clear that the emperors were inferior, the regimes consequently short-lived, the ministers un-Confucian, and, most of all, men like Feng Tao appallingly disloyal.

I think it is necessary to see the period as it was and to see how it differs from the Confucian distortion so essential to justify the Sung empire. If we return to the beginning of the struggle to replace the T'ang, that is, to the years after 884, we see the struggle developing until Chu Wen, who held the whole stretch of the Yellow and the Wei rivers, was pitted against the northern alliance of the Sha-t'o Turks and the Ho-pei armies. As neither side could win decisively, Chu Wen was rushed into killing the last T'ang emperor and founding his dynasty of the Liang. The struggle continued for sixteen years into the next generation. Then in 923 the other side won and, under the dynastic names of (later) T'ang, Chin, Han, Chou, and Sung, the Sha-t'o and Ho-pei alliance controlled North China. And, conforming to the traditions of the Turks and the unstable pattern of gubernatorial succession in the Ho-pei provinces, twelve emperors succeeded one another between 926 and 960. All twelve were from the original alliance, whose continuity was remarkable and which through the years had become identified as one progression (hsi-t'ung), even one organization. Of the twelve, three were sons, two were adopted sons, one was a nephew, and one a son-in-law of emperors.[65] Of the remaining five, the first Emperor Chuang-tsung was the son of the original leader of the alliance and the other four were either previous commanders in chief or chiefs of staff who usurped power in the best traditions of the Ho-pei provinces.[66]

Since all the successions had taken place within the same allied grouping, it is obvious that the concept of loyalty in the eyes of Feng Tao and his contemporaries was different from that of the Sung historians a hundred years later. Feng Tao served ten of these emperors, the first Emperor Chuang-tsung, two sons, two adopted sons, one nephew, and one son-in-law of emperors in addition to three others. Of the three others, Ming-tsung in 926 was an able and popular general who had not set out to usurp the throne, Han Kao-tsu in 947 had merely recovered Chin territory from the Khitans, and Chou T'ai-tsu in 951 was a victim of court intrigue who became emperor in order to save his own life.[67] All three men had been friends and colleagues of Feng Tao and respected him for his sagacity. In fact, had Feng Tao lived another six years, he would have seen the foundation of the Sung by yet another Ho-pei Chinese who was born into the organization, and no doubt

Sung T'ai-tsu (960–76) would also have employed him.[68] Thus ten of the eleven emperors whom Feng Tao served were members of the same Sha-t'o and Ho-pei organization. The question of disloyalty did not occur to him, or to his contemporaries, or even to the emperors, who were happy to employ him.

The only emperor who came from outside the group was the emperor of the Khitans, whom Feng Tao served for four months in 947 till the Khitan's death. Yet even in this relationship, there were the links of the Sha-t'o tradition. The Khitan emperor had been Chin Kao-tsu's "Imperial Father" (*fu huang-ti*) since 938, and Feng Tao had led one of the missions sent to arrange for this.[69] And if the links are traced further back, the Khitan founder, A-pao-chi (872–926), and the founder of the Sha-t'o and Ho-pei alliance, Li K'o-yung (856–908), were sworn brothers in 905.[70] Anyway, the wars of 944–46, which ended in Khitan victory, had arisen partly because Chin Shao-ti was only willing to be a "grandson" (*sun*) but not a "minister" or "subject" (*ch'en*) of the Khitan ruler.[71] The Khitans themselves regarded the war as partly a war to chastise a disrespectful member of the family. Since to Feng Tao the Khitan emperor did have a claim to North China, it would not have been disloyal to serve him.[72]

It is easy to see how such a series of imperial successions in North China baffled Confucian historians and how the problem of Feng Tao's loyalty defied classification. But, once it was decided to treat the self-professed dynasties in the orthodox way, Feng Tao naturally came to be judged by the orthodox definition of loyalty to emperor or at least loyalty to dynasty. By this definition, he was undoubtedly disloyal. But when the Confucian distortion is removed and Feng Tao and his contemporaries are seen as the officials of a rather unstable organization that had seized control of a part of China, then the concept of loyalty in a Confucian state would not apply. Such a concept should have been limited to those T'ang officials who had abetted Chu Wen in the downfall of the T'ang or to those Liang officials who were glad to serve Chuang-tsung after 923. These were clear examples of disloyalty by any definition, and Ou-yang Hsiu's collection of "six T'ang ministers" who turned from the T'ang to the Liang certainly represents the most culpable kind of disloyalty of the whole period.[73] At worst, Feng Tao could have been regarded as a man who kept himself aloof from the internal intrigues and quarrels of his leaders and who saw no reason to abandon high office at every change in their fortunes.

The Sung biographers of Feng Tao applied *their* Confucian dynastic view to the history of the Five Dynasties. His exceptional career could not be taken lightly. It had to be evaluated and classified, and in the context of the new Confucianism of Sung it was obviously unforgivable, even disgusting. Thereafter, this remained the only possible view of Feng Tao.

Yet his biographers were not entirely to blame for judging him by eleventh-century standards. After all, Feng Tao claimed to have lived a Confucian life and followed a Confucian career. He was even compared with Confucius, and his "sayings" were prominent in the official records. Not only that; he wrote an account of his own life which showed clearly how pleased he was with his Confucian achievements. This was the crucial point. In every discussion of Feng Tao, there is reference to this unusual piece of writing, his autobiography. In a sense, Feng Tao had invited comparison with the best, and this to men like Ou-yang Hsiu and Ssu-ma Kuang was intolerable conceit.

Autobiography has tended to be self-justification and Chinese autobiographies are no exceptions. But most of the examples we still have from before the Sung were written in order to explain a lack of interest in high office. Beginning with the poet Yang Hsiung's (53 B.C.–A.D. 18) Chieh-ch'ao and the historian Pan Ku's (A.D. 32–92) Pin-hsi chu-jen, autobiographical writing gradually evolved toward essays justifying the life of a recluse, such as those written by Huang-fu Mi (215–82, Hsüan-shou lun), T'ao Ch'ien (365–427, Wu-liu hsien-sheng chuan), and Liu Chün (462–521, Tzu-hsü).[74] A slightly different tradition was that of the Han humorist Tung-fang So (b. 160 B.C.), who wrote his Ta-k'o nan to show his political views.[75] Somewhat similar to this tradition was the Tzu-hsü of Yüan Chen (779–831), the T'ang poet, but Yüan Chen's was much more of an autobiography with short comments on his own career.[76] Another example of autobiographical writing, Wang Ch'ung's (A.D. 27–97) account of his philosophical development, stood alone until the Sung dynasty.[77] Except for Yüan Chen's Tzu-hsü, there was nothing in Chinese tradition to justify a proud account of one's official career. But Yüan Chen had been content merely to mention some of the problems he had dealt with. There was certainly no precedent for Feng Tao's detailed list of all the emperors he had served, all his ranks, offices, and titles, and all the honors conferred upon his ancestors as well as all the ranks and offices held by his sons. The tradition in autobiography had clearly been to disparage high office, but Feng Tao did not follow this tendency toward what might be described as inverted snobbery. Instead, he preferred to record his connection with an eminent family and give a full account of how he had done his Confucian duty to his ancestors (the posthumous honors), to his family (his children's achievements), and to his sovereign (his own titles as evidence of his emperors' gratitude). As he said,

I have been a son, a brother, a minister of the emperor, a teacher, a husband, and a father, and I have sons, nephews, and grandchildren. What I have given to my times has been inadequate. Where I have been inadequate is that I have not helped my emperor to unify the empire and bring order to the country. I am truly ashamed to have held all my various offices and ranks without success and wonder how I can repay the gifts of heaven and earth.[78]

He had clearly broken with tradition, and this Ou-yang Hsiu and Ssu-ma Kuang must have noted with disapproval. Even his modesty in the passage quoted above could not have absolved him from the terrible heresy of pride in high office. And to have done it with reference to Confucian principles was in very bad taste indeed. Furthermore, Feng Tao had spoken of his loyalty to the state and of the "three no-deceptions" and, even worse, attributed to heaven's protection his success in outliving all his emperors (as quoted above). He mentioned the possibility of official burial, of eulogistic inscriptions, of ritual sacrifice and posthumous titles for himself. Although he had asked all this to be denied to him, it was vulgar conceit to have even thought about these subjects. Finally, he was contented and self-satisfied. With obvious complacence he wrote, "I sometimes open a book and sometimes drink a cup of wine. Is there not food to be tasted, music to be heard, and colors to wear till I grow old and contented in these times? When one is happy with oneself when old, what happiness can compare with that?"[79]

Feng Tao could not have known that a higher Confucianism was to develop a century after his death. He could not have known that he was living in an age of transition and that important changes in social, political, and philosophical values were about to take place. He asked to be considered as a Confucian, not realizing that the Confucianism of his time would prove ineffectual and shallow and be replaced by a more severe and vigorous creed. He saw himself as loyal and true and did not anticipate the judgment of a later orthodoxy. His contribution to his times was too slight to matter in later ages. Men of the eleventh century, bent on revitalizing the Confucian tradition, showed little tolerance for the rather flaccid Confucianism of Feng Tao. Generally overlooked was his contribution as a "Confucian" in his own time who had helped keep alive in adversity the rudiments of the tradition, giving those who followed a foundation on which to build the vigorous new Confucian system.

Hellmut Wilhelm

FROM MYTH TO MYTH:
THE CASE OF YÜEH FEI'S BIOGRAPHY

There is no dearth in Chinese history of personalities whose lives have become the object of mythologization. Emperors and commoners, poets and bandits, officials and warriors—all have had their words and deeds transfigured. Few, however, have been so intensively mythologized as the heroic warrior, patriot, and tragically frustrated savior of his country, Yüeh Fei (1103–41), who became the first warrior to have his mythologized life exhaustively and exclusively treated in a great Chinese novel.[1] Even in the generation after his death the number of temples dedicated to him seems to have been considerable. Only one other warrior shares with Yüeh Fei the honor of a place in the official pantheon.[2]

Taken together, the "historical" facts of Yüeh's life quickly yield the germination point of this process. To be sure, for reasons to be discussed later, biographical data on Yüeh Fei are scanty and unusually unreliable. But even those facts definitely or at least very probably historical produce a picture of Yüeh Fei's life rich in the substance of myth. His life story resembles strangely the myths of St. George, Siegfried, or other sun-heroes in a Chinese variation: the forceful youth of almost unknown family background, as proud as he is naïve, who overnight gains entrance into his chosen vocation; the loyal attachment to those who guide him in his activities; his somewhat ostentatious display of all the shining virtues the tradition demands; his always successful battles against the enemy which is devastating his country; his sudden retreat at the peak of his success; and his end at the hands of a villain of blackest hue, Ch'in Kuei. We even find the evil woman who urges the villain on to commit the fatal deed. These and other elements of the Yüeh Fei biography were highly conducive to the creation of the Yüeh Fei image of later popular and official lore, but I shall resist the temptation to analyze more closely this superb example of the myth-making process. To keep these elements in mind might, however, contribute to an understanding of Yüeh Fei's attitudes, words, and deeds. As will be shown, he constantly and consciously worked toward producing an image of himself as a hero of mythological proportions, rigidly patterning himself after the myths of the past. This "impersonation" of a myth was to dictate the events of his life and, finally, his fate.

We are singularly unfortunate with regard to the sources on Yüeh Fei's life. The circumstances of his death precluded the tomb inscription or other obituary matter on which biographies in the *Sung shih* to a large extent depend. Instead, his official biography is based on a rewritten version of a biography by his grandson Yüeh K'o, written sixty years after Yüeh Fei's death.[3] This biography was incorporated by Yüeh K'o into a collection compiled with the avowed purposes of reestablishing the prestige and stature of his grandfather.[4] In addition to the natural bias of filial piety, and the promotion of family interests which it shares with the biographies based on obituaries, it is open to doubt on account of this propagandistic purpose. Furthermore, in sixty years, knowledge about the facts of Yüeh Fei's life had already become blurred. This is reflected in a number of verifiable errors.[5] How many other, unverified errors it contains will probably remain forever unknown.[6]

We are not much better off with regard to the official documentation of Yüeh Fei's public activities. The contemporary official records, of course, do not survive. They were used, however, at the time of the compilation of some sections of the *Sung shih* pertinent to Yüeh Fei's life, particularly the Annals of Emperor Kao. They were also available to Sung historians like Hsiung K'o,[7] Liu Cheng,[8] and Li Hsin-ch'uan.[9] From the indirect quotation of the official records concerning Yüeh Fei in these compilations it becomes abundantly clear—and this seems to be the present consensus—that these records were doctored during the decade and a half Ch'in Kuei remained in power after Yüeh Fei's death. We have thus to cope not only with the poor quality of the *Sung shih* in general but also with the fact that Yüeh Fei's official record has been falsified.[10]

Parts of these records have survived outside the official archives. Yüeh K'o incorporated in his compilations a number of memorials and reports addressed to the throne by Yüeh Fei as well as various imperial rescripts and decrees addressed to Yüeh Fei. This appears to be the most reliable body of documentary material available, as there is no reason to suspect tampering. It is, however, highly improbable that this collection of documents is complete. The tenor of the imperial rescripts is almost uniformly appreciative of Yüeh Fei's character and his actions, with next to nothing in the way of criticism or reprimand.[11]

It is inconceivable that an emperor who constantly expressed this degree of indebtedness and even tender personal care would have condoned the course of action that led to Yüeh Fei's death. Either Yüeh Fei himself failed to keep those documents critical of him and his actions or Yüeh K'o's compilation was highly selective.

Yüeh Fei's own writings have come down to us in very sad condition.[12] Except for memorials and official reports (seven out of eight *chüan*), there are only a few stray items. There is evidence that Ch'in Kuei had Yüeh Fei's home raided and his writings destroyed.[13] Equally scanty are references to Yüeh Fei in the writings of his contemporaries and independent biographical sources.[14] It is from this brittle material, then, that we have to build our image of Yüeh Fei, the man.

I do not propose to present here an integrated biography of Yüeh.[15] I would like, rather, to discuss Yüeh Fei as a historic figure seen in the context of his time and, second, to see how the historic character is related to the heroic tradition of which he was self-consciously a part.[16]

Yüeh Fei's family background is not well explored. It is not only recent Communist descriptions which stress that he came from a farming family. His father, Yüeh Ho, appears to have been a man of modest affluence, in a position at least to earmark some of his income for welfare projects. He is specifically reported to have drawn income from a field of rushes, although this was swept away, and his financial status in consequence seriously curtailed, by a flood that occurred when Yüeh Fei was still a baby. Yüeh Fei's miraculous escape from this flood together with his mother (née Yao) in a big water jar was an event that contributed to the myth of his life. A similarly prophetic incident was the flight of a large bird over the house at the time of his birth. This was responsible for his name Fei as well as his *tzu* P'eng-chü, without doubt a reference to the roc, which had been made famous by Chuang-tzu and remained the symbol of a superior and imaginative personality.

That Yüeh Ho chose this *tzu* for his son indicates the sophisticated level of his education, especially for a man of his rural surroundings. He is reported to have tutored his son personally, and some of the Confucian virtues Yüeh Fei exhibited with such consistent devotion must have been instilled in him by his father. There is no evidence, however, that Yüeh Ho ever endeavored to pursue an examination career.

Without question, the extent of Yüeh Fei's own learning and his general love of scholarship were very considerable. In his youth he was particularly attracted by the *Tso-chuan* and the military classics of Chou. A sustained effort was, however, necessary to achieve the intensity of historical knowledge and the subtlety of historical interpretation that Yüeh Fei displayed in his surviving writings. Moreover, he wrote a smooth, almost elegant style and his calligraphy has become a model for later artists in this field.[17] But, like his father, he never pursued an examination career.

Yüeh Fei seems to have been a serious-minded and taciturn child, at the same time endowed with unusual physical strength. In addition to his literary studies he took up archery, swordsmanship, and lance-play, apparently under the tutelage of a certain Chou T'ung. When Chou T'ung died, Yüeh Fei paid him unusual posthumous honors. This overdramatized behavior testifies to an important trait in Yüeh Fei's character: a penchant for giving symbolic expression to genuinely felt emotions. There are too many incidents in Yüeh Fei's biography to leave any doubt that his reverence for his tutors and guides was genuine, representing more than mere compliance with a Confucian imperative. This is shown by his relationship to Chang So, who had launched him on his military career.[18] When about a decade later Yüeh Fei received by imperial grace the privilege of promoting his own son, he substituted Chang So's son. The closeness of Yüeh Fei's relationship in later life to his colleagues and more particularly to his subordinates is universally attested to. His paternal care for them and his liberal rewards have become almost proverbial. But always dramatic expression was given to a genuinely felt and also consciously cultivated human emotion. His somewhat ostentatious sacrifice at the tomb of Chou T'ung sets the pattern for this kind of attitude: the reticent youth makes a considered display of himself, and the pattern of the hero he knows he is and wants to be is established in the public eye.

The sacrifice at the tomb of Chou T'ung was the occasion for one of those anticipatory remarks that are part and parcel of almost every biography, the remark that presages the future fate of the hero. His father took him to task for his action, saying: "When you are employed to cope with the affairs of the time, will you then not have to sacrifice yourself for the empire and die for your duty?" The only logical mean-ing of this remark is that once Yüeh Fei had aimed for a high public position, he would have to live up to the image he had created of him-self, even to the point of sacrificing his life. Yüeh Fei did live up to this image and eventually paid the ultimate price. The remark also made it possible for posterity to interpret his death as a sacrifice to the empire and to his duty and to brand the one who had brought about this death as an enemy of the empire and a villain. Myth in the making!

To play the role he had assumed for himself, however, Yüeh Fei had to find an appropriate route to prominence. His family was apparently not well enough established or affluent enough to permit his rise "the easy way" through inheritance or sponsorship. One incident in his life might indicate that for a time he strove to establish relations with influential persons who might sponsor his entry into officialdom. He became a tenant-retainer of the Han family, a gentry-official family of high standing in the neighboring district of An-yang. His functions there included the exercise of strong-arm methods to prevent the depredations of marauding bands on the Han property.[19] But he soon abandoned this approach.

This left only two ways open to him, development of his literary skills and development of his martial skills. He chose the second. This fateful choice seems strange. There is no doubt that Yüeh Fei would have qualified for a literary career. The literary career undoubtedly offered much more security and, particularly at the time when Yüeh Fei's decision was taken, much higher prestige. This was the year 1122, the last period of Hui-tsung's reign. The power of the Chin was already in the ascendant; it was the year in which they conquered the Southern capital of the Liao, Peking. Their future onslaught against the Sung was, however, by no means anticipated. Thus there was not yet an urgent need to strengthen the military in order to save the country.

Furthermore, military prestige at the end of Northern Sung was particularly low, considerably lower than could be explained by the traditional ideological precedence of the civilian over the military. All through Northern Sung times, the performance of the military had been mediocre. There had not been any glorious campaigns or any feats of personal military prowess like those for which earlier dynasties had been justly famous. This was at least in part due to conscious government policy. The founder of Sung, even though, or possibly because, he had come to power through the military, was particularly aware of the double-edgedness of his own profession; and ever since then it had remained an unshaken principle of the government to keep the military in check rather than to make positive use of it. To be sure, in the later part of Northern Sung the military had proliferated again, but even then the military career was despised. Why should an ambitious youth planning his career have thrown in his lot with a profession that counted for so little?

One reason might be that government civil service had not been a tradition in the Yüeh family; what was a compelling reason for some youngsters to go through the examination drudgery—to maintain and raise the family position by emulating or surpassing their elders—was of no account for Yüeh Fei. It might also be noted that the high degree of centralization of civilian government in Northern Sung times left very little beyond routine activities for even the high official, with the consequence that excess energy found an outlet in clique struggles, which were ideologically and personally repulsive and reduced individual security to a very low level. The same degree of control over the military had not yet been achieved. Although the government had succeeded in keeping the military conspicuously inactive, there remained, within the military establishment, appreciably greater opportunity for the exercise of personal initiative.

Finally, we must remember that Yüeh Fei was not yet twenty when he made this decision. A youth of his age and temperament might well have been acting under the inspiration of great heroes of the past, but Yüeh Fei's decision is likely to have stemmed also from a conviction that this was in accord with his appointed destiny. He felt within himself the potential of the submerged dragon.

Having made his decision, Yüeh Fei now had to establish a reputation for military skills and define a personal goal. The occasion offered itself in 1122, when Liu Chia, staff officer of T'ung Kuan, recruited daredevils (kan chan shih).[20] Yüeh Fei enlisted and participated in the attempt by the Sung army to capture Peking from the Liao. History records the tumultuous retreat of T'ung Kuan's army, Peking was left to the Chin, but Yüeh Fei had glimpsed with his own eyes the awesome walls of this great and long-lost northern metropolis, in his myth-oriented terminology the City of the Yellow Dragon, which from that time on figured so largely in his strategic reasoning.

When T'ung Kuan returned to Kaifeng, Yüeh stayed with Liu Chia, then stationed at Chen-ting. Liu employed him mainly in the suppression of "local bandits." Colorful descriptions exist of his first military encounters. He was portrayed not only as a powerful wielder of the sword and bow, endowed with an almost superhuman courage, but also —his study of the military classics had not been in vain—as a sharp strategist and clever tactician who knew how to use tricks and ruses.

This first experience of organized military life lasted less than a year. Toward the end of that year his father died, and Yüeh Fei, true to the imperatives of an established behavior pattern, immediately returned home. This unquestioning self-denial was genuine but at the same time exemplary. Although it meant reverting to obscurity for four long years, the young dragon had made his appearance in the field.

By the time Yüeh Fei returned to military life, in response to a recruitment drive late in 1126, the political situation had changed considerably: the Northern Sung dynasty was at an end. In the ensuing turmoil circumstances had arisen whose configuration suggested a potential "restoration" of the dynasty.[21] To bring this potential to fruition required among other things: an image of the empire which was persuasive enough to command not just routine loyalty but personal commitment to the cause of restoration; a head of government who would in his person symbolize the common cause and be ingenious enough to marshal and coordinate the necessary forces; a number of imaginative restoration leaders who would have the drive as well as the freedom of action to gather up, organize, and lead the shattered parts of the empire; and finally an entirely new pre-eminence of the military. Yüeh Fei saw his opportunity.

On rejoining the military Yüeh had at first enjoyed the sponsorship of Chang So. Following Chang's dismissal, Yüeh joined an at best semi-independent commander, Wang Yen. Incompatibility of personal ambitions led Yüeh to leave Wang, and for a time Yüeh became the entirely independent commander of an independent army unit, officially speaking a "bandit" or at best a petty warlord. Then he rejoined the official army under the command of Tsung Tse,[22] whom he highly respected, and after Tsung's death he served under his successor, Tu Ch'ung,[23] who eventually surrendered to the Chin. In this period Yüeh fought his colleagues rather than the common enemy, gradually assembling an army of great potential striking power and immaculate prestige, his own army, the Yüeh-chia-chün.

Episodes abound that show how Yüeh forged this tool for action and maintained its sharp edge ever after. Very strict discipline prevailed in his army, and heavy punishment was meted out even for inadvertent mistakes. Recognition, rewards, and grants of responsibility and initiative came to those who lived up to Yüeh's expectations. And as Yüeh's military genius guaranteed that no military action undertaken ever ended in defeat, he succeeded in creating unique cohesion and spirit in his army.

The prestige of his army was also increased by its irreproachable behavior. Again episodes abound to illustrate this point. Its repute, and that of its commander, surpassed all others. Wise rehabilitation measures, by which reconquered territory was restored to productivity and the roaming population resettled in a new kind of security, contributed to this effect. His army was made to carry out these rehabilitation measures in addition to performing its martial functions.

His grandson Yüeh K'o summarized his technique for welding an army together as follows:

Among the methods by which Yüeh Fei managed his army, there were six great ones. The first was: careful selection. He stressed quality and did not stress quantity. From those selected, one counted as much as a hundred. Once the emperor had transferred to his army the troops of Han Ching and Wu Hsi; not all of them were used to battle, and many of them were old and weak. After he had selected those who could be used, he had not got even a thousand men; the rest were all dismissed and sent home. After a few months of training he had in consequence an army unit of high quality. The second was: careful training. When the troops were stationed at garrison quarters, he had them instructed in all the pertinent arts. This instruction became increasingly strict until they would not enter for a visit when they passed their own gate, and until they would regard days of leave like days of action. For instance, they had to crawl through moats and jump over walls, and all that in full armor. When they had completed their training, people would regard them as saints.

The third was: justice in rewards and punishments. He treated all his people alike. A private named Kuo Chin from the unit of Chang Hsien had earned merits at Mo-yeh-kuan.[24] Yüeh unhooked his golden belt and gave it to him as a reward together with silverware for his personal use, and in addition he promoted him. His son Yüeh Yün once was practicing jumping a moat in heavy armor when his horse stumbled and fell. Yüeh Fei, angry on account of his lack of training, said: "Would you also act this way when facing the great enemy?" And then he ordered him to be decapitated. All his generals knelt before him and begged that his son be spared. Thereupon he had him bastinadoed a hundred times and let him go. Other examples are Fu Ch'ing, who was executed because he had boasted of his merits; Hsin T'ai, who was dismissed because he had not followed orders; and Jen Shih-an, who was bastinadoed because he had followed an order too slowly. All failures, irrespective of their seriousness, were heavily punished. When Chang Chün[25] once asked him about the art of using soldiers, he replied: "Humaneness, reliability, wisdom, courage, and strictness [jen, hsin, chih, yung, yen]; of these five not one may be missing." And when Chang asked about strictness, he replied: "Those who have merits are heavily rewarded; those who have no merits are stiffly punished."

The fourth was: clear orders. He gave his soldiers clear delineations and his commissions were always clear and simple, so that they could be easily followed. Whoever went against them was invariably punished.

The fifth was: strict discipline. Even when his army was on the march, there was never the slightest misdemeanor such as the trampling of the people's fields, damaging of agricultural labor, or inadequate payment for purchases. This he would never condone. A soldier once had taken a hempen rope from a man in order to tie his hay. He questioned him as to where he had got it and had him immediately decapitated.

The sixth was: community of pleasure and toil. He treated his men with grace [en]. He always ate the same things as the lowest of his soldiers. When there was wine or meat he shared it equally with all his subordinates. When there was not enough wine to go around, he had it diluted with water until everybody got a mouthful. When the army was on the march, he camped in the open together with his officers and soldiers; even when quarters had been prepared for him, he would not enter them alone.

To be sure, these rules and episodes have been compiled by a pious grandson. There is no reason, however, to doubt their authenticity. They all fit into the character of a man who genuinely endeavored to live up to his ideal of a warrior-hero.

The prestige of Yüeh Fei's army and the stature of his personality soon attracted a large number of civilian hangers-on. In this respect, Yüeh Fei's army was not unique; the great armies of Liu Kuang-shih,[26]

Han Shih-chung,[27] and others also welcomed and employed civilian degree-holders, who were used for administrative tasks or just kept around to lend color to the camp and wit to the feasts. They were called "serving personnel" (*hsiao-yung shih-ch'en*). Their exact functions have to my knowledge not yet been properly explored, but they seem to have been the forerunners of the *mu-yu* of later times.[28] Scholars were welcome at Yüeh Fei's camp at all periods of his career. Yüeh Fei had genuine respect for scholarship, and he also used the scholars to enliven the spirit of his soldiery by having them recount the great deeds of the heroic warriors of the past. These deeds were no doubt told in the legendarized versions already current in Yüeh Fei's time. Thus Yüeh kept before his soldiers the models on which his own life was patterned. He did not even hide his desire to go down in history as the peer of these past heroes and may have hoped that among the scholars were some who would help to establish his future position as a mythological hero. He specifically mentioned that he wanted to be likened to the great men of the period of the Three Kingdoms, Kuan Yü in particular. Later official mythology has actually put him on a par with his great model.[29]

Yüeh Fei's respect for scholars is referred to repeatedly and it is also recorded that he discussed current affairs with them and listened to their advice. It was in one of these conversations that Yüeh Fei, who was always quick to coin a winged phrase, was asked when the empire would have peace again and replied: "When the civilian officials do not love money, and when the military officials are not afraid to die, the world will get peace all by itself."[30] How could he help growing into a myth when he could answer the burning human question of his time with such a highly quotable phrase? He also said, however, that his great care always to exhibit "virtuous" conduct was motivated by the fear that the Confucianists in his camp might otherwise record personal behavior for which later generations would condemn him. Thus he built up an image of his personality not only for his time but for posterity.

Parenthetically, his relationship to women might be mentioned here, as it brings out the contours of his character. His extreme filial piety toward his mother is of course widely praised. However, when his position in the north became untenable and he had to retreat southward with his army, he left her behind in the care of his wife. Circumstances dictated this rather unfilial behavior, unfilial in particular because he must have known that his wife was not one to endure adversity. Actually his wife left him (and his mother) and remarried. His mother subsequently experienced some real hardships. Eventually rescuing his mother, he settled her adequately but not luxuriously in the Lushan Mountains near Kiukiang. At her death in 1136, Yüeh Fei immediately left camp for the prescribed mourning, even though the military situation made his personal conduct of affairs imperative. A number of imperial messages to recall him to active duty went unheeded; and only repeated pressure from his officers "to substitute loyalty for piety" brought him back to the front.

His relationship to his second wife was more intimate. He even discussed affairs with her. But she always had to take second place to his mother, whose care, under pain of severe reprimands, was her responsibility. He did not tolerate her interference with his plans, even if this concerned her own safety and that of his mother.

He did not permit his sons to have concubines. Once a colleague, who had been entertained at his camp and apparently found his hospitality somewhat dull because of the absence of girls, sent him a girl as a present. Before he had set eyes on her he asked her through a screen whether she would be willing to share the hardships of camp life. When she giggled in reply, he took this as a sign that she was frivolous and sent her back. Had she possessed the presence of mind to give him a heroic reply, he would have kept her. One is reminded of the role the girl plays in the life of the hero in Western films.[31]

He did drink rather heavily during his earlier career, apparently believing this fitted the image of a martial hero. Only the emperor's personal intervention, after Yüeh had almost killed a colleague in drunken anger, exacted from him a promise not to touch wine again until the Chin had been defeated.

Yüeh Fei's conception of the empire was far from petty. What he wanted restored was not only the original frontier of Northern Sung, but all Chinese lands north of it, including Peking and Tatung, and beyond that the territory up to the passes. Early in his career, when he was still serving under Chang So, he argued this conception in a colorful and symbol-ridden exposition, which reveals the strength of his emotional commitment to his goal as well as the soundness of his strategic reasoning. The conception remained his own, however, and not the court's.

When he discussed restoration in his memorials to the emperor, the great Han model loomed large in his argument. The element he took from this model was the inspired leadership of the Kuang-wu emperor. But the role of the general Kuo Tzu-i, who had restored the tottering T'ang empire, also figures conspicuously in his reasoning. The task of restoration had been carried out by a great military leader and Yüeh Fei was seeking the analogous role.

But again it has to be stressed that Yüeh Fei's commitment to this empire—his patriotism—was as much an emotional commitment as a reflection of conscious or even studied attitudes. This is revealed in the few remaining fragments of his nonofficial prose, a handful of poems and three songs. No one who was not genuinely committed to the point of obsession would have been able to produce as powerful a patriotic song as his *Man-chiang-hung*. It needed a Yüeh Fei to garb this emotion with words that have remained symbols of patriotism ever since:[32]

> My hair bristles in my helmet
> I lean against the railing, the pattering rain has ceased.
> I raise my eyes, and toward the sky I utter a long-drawn shout.
> My breast is filled with violence.
> At the age of thirty fame and merits are but earth and dust,
> Eight thousand miles of land are like the moon covered with clouds.
> Do not tarry! The hair of youth grows white.
> Oh, vain sorrows.
> The shame of the year Ching-k'ang [1126] not yet wiped away,
> When will the hate of the subject come to an end?
> Oh, let us drive endless chariots through the Ho-lan Pass.
> My fierce ambition is to feed upon the flesh of the Huns,
> And, laughing, I thirst for the blood of the Barbarians.
> Oh, let everything begin afresh.
> Let all the rivers and mountains be recovered,
> Before we pay our respect once more to the Emperor.

The last two verses of this song speak his dream of recovering the north, the old mountains and rivers, and his dream of entering the palace gate for his final and triumphant audience. His conception of and commitment to the empire included its symbolic actual head, the emperor. The special flavor of Yüeh Fei's loyalty and subservience reveals his character structure more clearly than anything else. Again there is no doubt that Yüeh Fei felt genuinely loyal to the emperor and that he genuinely felt himself to be a servant in the cause of which the emperor was the highest exponent. But again his image of the emperor was idealized. What he revered was the model emperor, composite image of all the model emperors of the past, the saint of immaculate virtues—an image that had been built up by successive generations of Chinese political philosophers. This emperor image coincided with the actual Emperor Kao only accidentally. In the case of Yüeh Fei this incongruity meant, however, more than the implicit tension between the ideal and its actual representative. He himself strove to be a model and exemplar, and his loyalty was attached to the emperor only in so far as he was, in the eyes of Yüeh Fei, a model and exemplar. To those manifestations of the emperor's character and the emperor's will that could not be thus designated he owed nothing. Loyal to his own ideals and goals, and confident of the power of his army, Yüeh in his responses to imperial commands frequently came close to insubordination. It is little wonder that an autocratic emperor like Kao-tsung had little use for Yüeh Fei's kind of loyalty.

There are accounts of Yüeh Fei's efforts to persuade the emperor to act more in accord with the ideal. Yüeh had been received in audience by the future Emperor Kao-tsung, at that time still the Prince of K'ang, in 1127, and apparently made a brilliant impression. But immediately after Kao-tsung had ascended the throne, Yüeh Fei, then barely in his mid-twenties, submitted with touching naïveté—or was it naïveté?—a memorial urging the emperor to provide the inspired leadership Yüeh Fei felt was needed. Yüeh could hardly have been surprised that his newly gained first official title was taken away from him for this presumption. On another occasion Yüeh Fei attempted to influence an imperial decision regarding the heir apparent. Again he was rebuffed with the rebuke that a military official should not interfere in civilian affairs.[33]

This does not mean that Yüeh did not show satisfaction and pride whenever imperial grace came his way. When he was made Regional Commandant (*chieh-tu-shih*) in 1134, that is, in his early thirties, he had even the *hybris* to liken himself to the founder of the dynasty, the only person coming readily to his mind who at an equally early age had achieved such a high position. He responded to imperial grace always with the utmost formality. Going beyond the dictates of propriety, he declined the honor of the *chieh-tu-shih* four times; his appointment to the position of a Lesser Protector (*shao-pao*) he even declined five times. Such excesses of modesty were interpreted as arrogance.

In the foregoing discussion the information on Yüeh Fei's character has been telescoped. Incidents and reactions from different parts of his life have been used to illustrate a certain trait or a certain attitude. It is not by chance that our sources induce this kind of treatment. They already present a highly typified Yüeh Fei, a man who from cradle to grave was consistent and uniform. A closer scrutiny of the verifiable and datable material reveals, however, that there was an unusual consistency in his character structure. There is very little evidence of a developing and maturing process. He appears to have entered the stage with a set of ready-made attitudes to which he stuck unflinchingly until his final hours. It is the force of the Chinese tradition, more specifically the Confucian tradition—generalized to be sure and congealed into a myth—that imposed this consistency on him and that makes him look like a bronze monument rather than a living human being, more immovable than a mountain, as the Chin said of him. It was natural for Chu Hsi to praise Yüeh Fei as the unsurpassed hero of his time.

What did change, however, were the circumstances of his life, which led him with clocklike precision to penultimate triumph and ultimate disaster. The main stations along this fatal road are quickly recounted. When, after the capitulation of Tu Ch'ing in 1129, the position of Yüeh's army in the north became untenable, he withdrew, as did the other army leaders, to the south of the Yangtze. He stationed his army at I-hsing, immediately west of the T'ai-hu lake. This was not an assigned garrison but a place of his own choice, and again for a time he and his army led an almost entirely independent existence. In the general military debacle, his army was, however, too strong a force for the court to neglect. Thus he was gradually raised in rank and responded to imperial calls for assistance. Several skirmishes with Chin troops are recorded after they had crossed the Yangtze, and in 1130 Yüeh was mainly responsible for raising the siege of Chien-k'ang (Nangking). He was then stationed at T'ai-chou (north of the Yangtze, east of Yangchow) to guard the frontier, then shifted to Hung-chou (west of Lake Poyang), Chiang-chou (present-day Kiukiang), and eventually in 1132 to O-chou (present-day Wuchang).

During this period he was mainly active in suppressing "bandits." The banditry he had to cope with was of two entirely different types. The first was represented by military leaders who, like Yüeh himself, had succeeded in extricating themselves and their armies from the military debacle in the north and had attempted to carve out for themselves independent spheres of activity south of the river. Formally, their position differed very little from Yüeh's during his I-hsing period. Unlike Yüeh, however, they had failed to recognize and acknowledge the gradual reassertion of imperial power and organized government.

The second type of banditry was local uprisings, unconnected with the development in the north. One of these was the revolt led by Li Tun-jen in Kiangsi, in which gentry influence seems to have been strong. The most interesting among these movements is the one founded by Chung Hsiang and later led by Yang Yao (original name T'ai). This rebellion seems to have had a secret-society type of ideology with certain egalitarian slogans. What Chung vowed to eradicate by his movement were: officials, scholars, monks, shamanistic medicine men, and sorcerers. The power of his organization must have been quite formidable, as he could boast of a navy that included paddle-wheel ships "swift like birds."[34] Contemporaries pointed out that this movement was an expression of genuine popular feelings, quite different in nature from the roaming army bandits, and that it should be utilized rather than suppressed. As it stood in the way of his cause, Yüeh Fei suppressed it as swiftly and as skillfully as he had suppressed the others.

It is interesting to note that later in his career Yüeh Fei did not hesitate to recognize, and cooperate with, local independent movements. His successes during his northern campaigns are at least in part explained by the fact that he could rely on these "rebellions." They paved the way for his army and acted as his intelligence. ·

Beginning in 1134, Yüeh Fei's army was active in a number of major campaigns against "the great enemy," the Chin and the puppet state of Ch'i, which the Chin had established as a buffer between themselves and the Sung. These campaigns were conceived within the framework of an empire-wide strategic plan and had to be coordinated with the movements of other major bodies of troops. Several of these campaigns were designed to secure the Huai-hsi region, others led deep into central and western North China. In 1134 his army went up to Kuo-chou and Ch'ang-shui on the one hand and to Ts'ai-chou on the other; and in his final and most penetrating campaign of 1140, Yüeh proceeded up to Ying-ch'ang and from there sent pincers to Lo-yang and Ch'en-chou.[35] In these campaigns Yüeh scored major successes against the army of Ch'i and finally also against the armies of Chin. It might be true that the Chin felt so hard pressed that they contemplated withdrawing beyond the Yellow River, as Yüeh stated in one of his memorials.

This last major campaign of Yüeh's army coincided, however, with the endeavors of the Sung court to come to an understanding with the Chin by surrendering Sung claims to the territory north of the Huai and submitting to a series of other conditions made by the Chin. In the last phase of this campaign, the understanding had actually been concluded. The Sung court had therefore a vital interest in having the advance armies withdrawn in accordance with the conditions of the treaty. This included Yüeh Fei's army. The emperor is reported (possibly spuriously) to have sent twelve urgent messages within one day ordering Yüeh Fei to withdraw. Yüeh did withdraw, not simply in obedience to an imperial command, but in response to the pressure of his officers, who pointed out that after the other armies had withdrawn, their position was strategically untenable. He had to withdraw or lose his army. Yüeh was aware that this was the end of his dreams. He is reported to have said: "The merits of ten years are wiped out in one morning; all the recovered territory is completely lost in one day. The altars of the empire, its rivers and mountains, will hardly be restored again. The universal world [*ch'ien-k'un shih-chieh*] can no longer be recovered."

What had happened here? Why is it that the Sung court conceded defeat in the face of a very real chance of victory?

After the debacle of 1126, the Sung court had a choice of two policies—restoration or retrenchment. A restoration policy would, as mentioned, have involved a pre-eminence of the military and a great amount of freedom of action for the military leaders. As long as the Chin or Ch'i were on the attack, the court could not but give the military free play. As soon as the Chin showed signs that they wanted to come to terms, the Sung court chose the second way, that of retrenchment. The military leaders could not be left under the impression that they were indispensable. Strict civilian control was more important than lost territory.

In the late thirties, Ch'in Kuei was responsible for the implementation of this policy. He therefore was made the villain in the piece, and was actually the one primarily responsible for the dirty work involved. It was, however, Emperor Kao-tsung's policy, and many besides Ch'in Kuei had argued for it. To break the license of the generals was a task of greater importance than to beat the Chin. This is most dramatically expressed in a remark of Emperor Kao-tsung, after one of the attacks of Ch'i had been turned back: "What makes me happy is not that Ch'i has been defeated, but that the generals have obeyed orders." In the end there was no such thing as a Sung restoration.

After Yüeh Fei had withdrawn his army, he was used once more in a minor campaign designed to ward off a supposed threat to the region south of the Huai; then he was called to the capital for an audience. On this occasion the policy of retrenchment was finally consummated: the three principal generals, Han Shih-chung, Chang Chün, and Yüeh Fei—Liu Kuang-shih had already been eliminated—were stripped of their commands, given high civilian titles, and appointed to a vaguely defined supervisory committee. Central control over the army was thus established; despotism had triumphed.

Deprived of their leaders, the armies were, however, not yet deprived of their spirit. This called for more drastic action. The first army to experience this was Han Shih-chung's. Next was Yüeh Fei's. One of the chief subcommanders of the Yüeh army, Chang Hsien, and Yüeh's son were accused of plotting to revolt, and Yüeh Fei himself was said to have been involved in this plot and imprisoned. The court could with impunity publicly execute Chang Hsien and Yüeh Yün on the strength of this trumped-up charge and have Yüeh Fei himself murdered in prison.

It is inconsequential whether or not the death of Yüeh Fei was one of the secret conditions laid down by the Chin in treaty negotiations. It is also inconsequential whether Ch'in Kuei had Yüeh Fei murdered on his own initiative or in collusion with the emperor. How the emperor felt about Yüeh Fei's death is indicated by the fact that Ch'in's position was in no way impaired by this deed.

Thus ended Yüeh Fei's life, but not his role in Chinese history and in the Chinese tradition. By creating a myth of himself, his army, and his cause, he was not able to save himself or his country, but he was able to establish a persuasive symbol for later generations. Being the hero in a dawning new age, he shared, to borrow a phrase from Campbell, "the supreme ordeal, not in the bright moments of his tribe's great victories, but in the silences of his personal despair."[36]

5 Protest and Dissent

David S. Nivison

PROTEST AGAINST CONVENTIONS AND CONVENTIONS OF PROTEST

Students have often been found to complain about what they are required to learn and how they are held accountable for their lessons. Often their complaints follow a time-worn pattern. But if we look behind the pattern and if the students are serious, we may find that their complaints are both penetrating and important. This has been true even in China, that land of exemplary students, where teachers were respected as nowhere else, and where the emperor himself was the chief examiner.

Let me begin by telling some stories.

I

Shortly before 1060, Ou-yang Hsiu, the early Sung historian, official and man of letters, wrote a short essay, as was often done by Chinese literary men, in the back of a particularly treasured old book from his personal library. The book was an early print, from Ssu-ch'uan, of the collected prose of the ninth-century writer Han Yü. In this essay, Ou-yang Hsiu relates that as a young man, being of a poor family, he had had no books; but, finding this book discarded in the house of a friend, he begged for it and read it with fascination, not fully understanding it but nonetheless aware of its worth. In his own time, regular, so-called "modern" prose (*shih wen*) was preferred over the free style or "ancient" prose (*ku wen*) of Han Yü. "People who were skilled in it," writes Ou-yang Hsiu, "passed the examinations and were the only persons who had any reputation; no one ever talked about the writings of Han Yü." Just at this time, Ou-yang Hsiu himself had attempted the examinations unsuccessfully, and this failure had strengthened his dissatisfaction with the literary standards of his age. "I took my copy of Han Yü," he continues, "and, rereading it, I sighed and said, 'Scholars ought to go no farther than this!' And I marveled that people of the present day were so misguided." Admitting to himself that he must study for the examinations now, to obtain an official position and so be able to support his parents, he nevertheless had resolved that after he had succeeded he would turn back to what he really valued. "Later," Ou-yang Hsiu continues, "learned men throughout the world all turned their attention gradually to the past, and Han Yü's writings eventually became well known. Thirty-odd years have passed since that time, and people now study nothing but Han Yü."[1]

Ou-yang Hsiu clearly feels that his values as a young student were right and the officially sanctioned and conventionally approved ones wrong, and that he has been vindicated, inevitably, by time. Furthermore, he is able to assure himself, his pursuit of learning has been motivated only by the purest interest in learning itself—"It was simply that I was devoted to the past," he says—and not by hope of fame or material advantage. In him, as in other Confucians of his time, conservatism, a love of antiquity, is actually a protest against an ignoble conventionality. But did not Ou-yang Hsiu capitulate? He did study for the examinations, and with conspicuous success. Further, he did this, as he admits, precisely in order to qualify for a salaried official post. The intensity of this conflict, between devotion to higher ideals and the practical necessity of coming to terms with the world, can be seen in the fact that the ultimate Confucian social duty, that of filial piety, had to be invoked to set matters right.

Yet the reasonableness of the appeal can hardly be gainsaid. It is indeed the duty of a Confucian to provide for his parents; and so here is another conflict, now between two values, both of which were Confucian: one social, one intellectual; on the one hand family duty, on the other one's own personal development.

It will be instructive to turn, for a slightly different sort of case, to the early part of the T'ang period, when the modern examination system first became important. The historian Liu Chih-chi in the early eighth century wrote, in an autobiographical essay in his *Shih T'ung* ("General Principles of History"), that when he was a child it had been determined that he should specialize in the third of the Confucian Classics, the *Shang Shu*. But, he writes, "I was always bothered by the difficulty of its language, and . . . although I was frequently beaten, I got nowhere in my study. But when I happened to hear my father teaching my elder brothers the *Spring and Autumn Annals* and the *Commentary of Tso*, I always put aside my books and listened . . . and sighing to myself, I said, 'If only all books were like this, I would no longer be lazy!'" Liu's father was surprised at his son's independence of inclination, and, surprisingly, relented; Liu was allowed to read the *Tso Chuan*, and finished his study of it rather quickly. But now, his father would have him specialize in the *Tso Chuan* alone, going on to read all the existing commentaries to that text. To understand the father's point of view, we need to be aware that an intense study of one or two Classics served a man well in the T'ang examinations: the *chin-shih* and *ming-ching* examinations were probably the two most frequently taken even in Liu's time; and in offering for the first of these, one had to prepare one Classic, and be prepared further to find the questions dealing with commentaries rather than with the text itself. For the latter, one had to prepare somewhat less intensively in two or three Classics.[2]

But although his father's wishes in view of this situation may have been sensible, Liu fought free again. He had wanted to read the *Tso*, not because it was an examination text but because it was history; he now wanted to read more history—not because it would get him somewhere but because it was interesting, and because he thought he had insights into it worth having. Eventually he turned aside from his interests for a few years to learn to write in the poetry and essay forms required in the examinations. He does not indicate that he was bitter about this interruption, but he makes it perfectly plain that it was an interruption in his work.[3]

Both Liu Chih-chi and Ou-yang Hsiu, it is evident, found themselves as young men pursuing conflicting goals. The interest of Ou-yang's and Liu's experience and of their attitudes toward it would be slight, if this experience and these attitudes were unique; but we shall see that, far from being unique, they are so common among Chinese writers of the past thousand years as to seem stereotyped. This surely makes the matter of great interest; for people worry about conflicts, in whatever mode of life they are in; and when people worry, they think.

There exist, I suggest, recognizable conventions of protest against the educational mold into which a student felt himself forced. (1) There is the tendency, perhaps found in any aristocratic social order, to suspect values which are popular and modish of being shallow. Consider the curious feeling often encountered that only a very few people are likely to appreciate a really good painting or book. Surely we see something of this in Ou-yang Hsiu's conviction as a youth that only he saw matters rightly, and that generally accepted literary standards were "misguided." There is much more of this, offered with delicious frankness, in Han Yü himself. And whenever the relative merits of "ancient" and "contemporary" prose come up, no matter how *de rigueur* it may be for a critic to come down on the side of *ku wen*, or in favor of a "devotion to the past," he will usually in doing so manage to think of himself as alone in a Philistine wilderness (for Ou-yang Hsiu's conviction that only he appreciated Han Yü is surely nonsense). (2) But there is another motif which is simply the uncomplicated rebelliousness of a man of original temper when forced to do something distasteful, a motif likely to be found wherever such pressure exists. This was the sort of reaction we found in Liu Chih-chi. Yet, if these two modes of protest are not peculiar to Chinese culture, they certainly arise very naturally in a culture like China's which has been authoritarian—for Liu's independence was a reaction against a strict parental authority—and which has always had the persuasion that there are "superior" men, capable of perceiving values to which ordinary men are obtuse.

These two styles of self-assertion and protest may be seen in the lives and recollections of other writers, even very recent ones; and often we have the impression that specific literary models are playing a role. To cite two modern examples, the contemporary historian Ku Chieh-kang, like Liu Chih-chi, says he wanted, as a boy, to study the *Tso chuan* despite the objections of his parents and his teacher (his *bête noire* was the *Book of Odes*, not the *Shang Shu*), and surprised his mentors with his ability when finally allowed to study it.[4] Hu Shih writes in his autobiography that he happened, while in a neighbor's house, to discover a dilapidated copy of *Shui Hu Chuan*, which he was allowed to keep. This was the beginning of Hu's interest in popular literature, which he championed successfully against the established values of *his* day.[5] I assume that this incident happened; and it may even have had the importance ascribed to it. But the fact that it was worth relating surely owes something to Ou-yang Hsiu.

Wang Yang-ming, in the year 1518, wrote a letter of advice to two young men who were preparing for the examinations:

Since your home is poverty-stricken and your parents are old, what else can you do but seek emolument and official position? If you seek emolument and official position without studying for the examinations, you will not be able to carry out your duties as men, and will pointlessly find fault with fate. This is hardly right. But if you can firmly fix your aim, in all your pursuits fully express the Tao, and be influenced in thought neither by desire for success nor by fear of failure, then, though you study for the degree, this will be no real hindrance to your learning to become virtuous men.[6]

Wang, like Ou-yang Hsiu, here justifies the pursuit of worldly ends by appeal to the obligation of *filial duty*. There is more, of course, to Wang's attitude than this. He reveals himself highly suspicious of the influence the examinations had on a young man's mind. It may be possible, he reluctantly concedes, for a man to study for the degree of *chü-jen* or *chin-shih* without detriment to his self-development; all too many, however, through "lack of a fixed aim," as Wang puts it, "have come to think exclusively of honor, gain and literary style"; and as a result "they cannot avoid cherishing the desire for small advantages and quick results."

A young man must always resist this temptation the examinations present to him to succumb to vulgar values and to let his desires be involved in what he is doing.

One of the most intriguing cases of the use of these conventions of protest and self-assertion in a man's appraisal of himself is to be found in Chang Hsüeh-ch'eng (1738–1801). Chang, like Liu Chih-chi (and Ku Chieh-kang) was interested in the *Tso Chuan* when he was a boy, to the point of starting a project of rewriting it in standard history form, a project which he carried on in secret and which was sniffed at by his teacher when discovered—for it was in fact a rebellion against his routine study of examination essays and Classics. Chang's dislike of this training was expressed forcefully in early letters, in which we find him complaining that the examination form of essay (*shih wen*) is a worthless waste of time; yet he must study it in order to pass and get a position, "for my family is poor and my parents are old."[7]

One specific youthful episode about which Chang wrote is especially curious. In his seventeenth year, he recalls, he bought a copy of Han Yü; but his teachers had forbidden all extracurricular reading—lest Chang acquire literary habits which would injure his chances in the examination halls—and as a consequence Chang read his new purchase in secret, not fully understanding it, he confesses, yet with such great delight that he could not bear to let the book out of his hands. It is interesting to find here again that a young man would normally have his access to books and his choice of studies rigidly controlled. But more interesting, it looks very much as if Chang had been reading Ou-yang Hsiu; and indeed he had. Ou-yang Hsiu's reflections were set down in an essay on an old edition of Han Yü, and as in Chang's case, they deal with events in his seventeenth year. Chang's remarks are made in an essay on another old edition of Han Yü, Chu Hsi's *Han Wen K'ao-i*. Ou-yang Hsiu had remarked that he was writing of happenings thirty years past. Chang's own essay concludes, "As I fondle this book, the scenes of thirty years ago come back as though I were living them again."[8] Apparently Chang wrote because he had reached the appropriate time of life to express sentiments in just this way.

A few examples cannot establish the point that the individual writer's subjective protests against the examinations and the sort of training they required follow a fascinating pattern of stereotyped detail. But they may lend this point a plausibility which ensuing discussion will strengthen.

II

We have not been dealing merely with a curious but meaningless set of literary conventions. The civil service examinations have been called the hallmark of the "Confucian state." Preparing for them in order to seek an official career was a basic duty to family and to the world. Their existence as an institution more than anything else signalized the ascendancy of the man of learning and culture in society. Yet, almost from the beginnings of this institution in the later empire, the examinations, and the educational standards they produced, were resented and criticized. Students resented being fettered and constrained. Statesmen found the institution wanting as a means of "nurturing talent" and recruiting the best men for public service. Literary critics and moral philosophers bewailed its influence on the quality of letters and on the state of public and private virtue. This polyphony of protest may be found in every generation. And the surprising fact is that throughout all this we find the examination-education complex, the function and effect of which was to ensure the dominance of the Confucian classical tradition, criticized precisely by appeal to *Confucian* moral, aesthetic, and political values.

This is not a situation we would have expected. Its oddity may help to explain the fact that, for all of the attention scholars have given to the imperial examination system and its ramifications, the long tradition of protest against this system has been almost completely ignored. In what follows I shall attempt to open the matter up. My attempt will of necessity be extremely superficial, for the volume of relevant literature is enormous: in this literature we must include innumerable personal letters and essays, novels (such as *Ju-lin Wai-shih* by Wu Ching-tzu, 1701–54) on the life of the literati, as well as many official and unofficial treatises on public policy. Simply to relate the history of reforms and proposed changes in the system would require volumes. But an analysis of some of the ideals and motivations which perpetually generated this criticism may be more feasible.

The motive of Liu Chih-chi's self-assertion was his wish to pursue an easily comprehended interest—namely, in history and in the traditions of historical writing; and for this interest he has little compulsion to offer any further justification (though there is ample Confucian justification for it). With Ou-yang Hsiu the case is different. He admired the writing of Han Yü, yes; but this was not all. He was also "devoted to the past," and he scorned present-day styles, mastery in which served others in the mere pursuit of gain. We are inclined to ask, On behalf of just what ideals is this disinterestedness urged? Ou-yang Hsiu does not say, but it is fair to note that this very disinterestedness, the claim that the quest for gain and fame for oneself is unworthy of a writer, is itself an ideal of a higher order. Why should it seem appropriate to Ou-yang Hsiu to link this attitude with an esteem for Han Yü?

The reason may be that Han Yü has given this ideal for the literary man in China perhaps its most beautiful and intensely moving expression. In a letter "In Reply to Li I," Han, for the benefit of his correspondent (who apparently had asked questions about literary art, and perhaps had sent some writings), describes his own earlier efforts to learn to write. First, Han Yü says, he buried himself in the writings of the Han and of pre-Han antiquity, uncritically admiring all that he found. He was oblivious to the world around him and quite unaware of the criticism or amusement of others. At this stage, he says, in what he wrote he tried to keep out "hackneyed phrases," but the going was very difficult; the words that came to him just didn't fit. At a later stage in his progress, he began to be more critical of ancient writers, seeing the good and the bad in their writings distinguished "as clearly as black and white." When he tried to write himself, words now came much more freely; and he tested the results by observing reactions of others to his literary efforts: "If people were amused at my work, then I was happy; if they praised it, then I was worried, since then I knew that other people's ways of talking must still infect it." Now, words came in a flood; but this imposed a severe task of self-examination on him. He must hold up the flow of language, make sure that it was all "pure," by "cultivating" it, "guiding it into the path of goodness and right, reinvigorating it in the springs of the *Shih* (*Book of Poetry*) and the *Shu* (*Book of History*)."

The task of learning to write is not at all one of learning verbal tricks and forms; it is a task of self-cultivation, a *moral* exercise, a matter of nourishing one's *ch'i* or spirit; *ch'i* is like water, words the mere objects that "float" in it; if *ch'i* is adequate, there will be no trouble with words. This literary ideal is found everywhere in Chinese critical thought since T'ang (it is surely related to the ideal of the "gentleman painter" described by Mr. Cahill elsewhere in this volume) and has had the effect of making literary criticism in China a variety of moral philosophy. "If you hope to grasp the ancient ideal of writing," Han tells his reader, "then do not hope for quick success, do not be tempted by power and advantage; nourish your roots and wait for the fruit; add the oil and wait for the light . . ."

A person who does this will come close to perfection. But, Han stresses, he will be largely unappreciated; he will "seldom be used by others," i.e., employed by those in power. Setting out to be a good writer is not to be advertised as a good way to get a position. Han closes by saying that it is just because he realizes his friend is not interested in "gain" that he is willing to speak to him frankly. "If you wait to be employed by others, you will be like a mere utensil; your being used or neglected will depend on others. The superior man is not like this. In ordering his mind, he has the Tao. In conducting himself, he is upright." Rank and position mean nothing to him. "When he is employed, he ap-

plies his Tao to others. When he is unemployed, he transmits it to his
disciples, commits it to writing and creates a model for later generations."⁹

For anyone taking Han's view of writing really seriously, it is difficult to see how studying for the literary examinations—deliberately
seeking the road to "gain" and preferment—could be anything but a
stumbling block on the path of self-cultivation. And we should notice
in particular how Han Yü associates not only writing, but also teaching,
with indifference to mundane success or failure. The good man does not
seek office. If it comes his way, he does his best. If it does not, he writes
and teaches. In both modes of life he serves and is devoted to the Tao.

But was the literary and moral ideal expressed in the letter to Li I
actually related in this way to the problem of the examinations in Han
Yü's mind? Han has answered this question explicitly in a letter to another friend named Ts'ui Li-chih.

At the time of writing, Han had for the second time failed to obtain
office through the placing examinations offered under the Board of Civil
Office, and Ts'ui had written to urge him not to lose heart. Han replied
with a long *apologia*:

> When I was sixteen or seventeen, I had no knowledge of the realities of
> the world. I read the books of the sages, and thought to myself that when a
> man enters official service, he is acting only for others with no advantage for
> himself. When I reached twenty, I was distressed by the poverty of my house-
> hold; I consulted with members of my family and came to understand that
> official service is not just to the advantage of persons other than oneself.

Han went to the capital, noted that men who became *chin-shih* were
highly honored, and set out eagerly to acquire the skill to become one of
them. He was shown examples of questions that had been used in the
examinations administered by the Board of Ceremonies—calling for
pieces of rhymed prose, poetry, and essays, and considered that he could
write these things without studying, so he tried at the examinations; but
the examiners' standards were purely subjective: Han tried four times
before succeeding, and even then was not given a post. Following this
he tried twice at the placing examination, excited by the idea of the
fame he would gain by passing—though he noticed with surprise when
he looked at successful essays that they were of just the kind required
by the Board of Ceremonies. He set to work, like an actor learning his
lines, for several months; again, however, he was disappointed in his
quest for office.

Then, Han says, he took stock of himself, and realized that the standards he was following and those of the examiners were utterly different.
If Ch'ü Yüan, Mencius, and Ssu-ma Ch'ien were to find themselves com-

peting for these honors they would be ashamed; they simply would not push themselves forward in this way;

but if they did take part in this abysmal competition, they would surely fail. Yet, if these men were living today, though their Tao were not recognized by the world, would this shake their confidence? Would they be willing to have their worth decided in competition with mere time-servers by the rating of one dunce of an examiner, and be pleased or distressed at his decision?

Han then realized that the most he could hope to gain from success in the examinations would be advantages of a paltry material sort.

He concluded by assuring Ts'ui (and himself) that he was not (as Ts'ui had suggested) to be compared to Pien Ho in Han Fei-tzu's story, who had twice tendered his "uncut jade" to the King of Ch'u only to have a foot cut off on each attempt. He has offered no "jade" to his ruler—yet. But he can. The times are troubled; the world has fallen short of ancient ideals; the dynasty is militarily insecure; the emperor and his ministers are worried; Han can analyze these difficulties and offer his views. Perhaps he will be recognized and rewarded with a high post; but if not, Han said, he can tend his sequestered plot in quietness, and search out the details of the history of the dynasty, the lives of its great men, and write a "classic" on the T'ang, which will condemn villains and sycophants and praise examples of concealed virtue. This he will pass on to posterity forever.[10]

A really good man, apparently, is above playing the ordinary game, and will refuse to accept the judgment meted out to the many. If the court has the wisdom to use him, good; if not, he is not hindered in his devotion to the Tao. His position approaches that of the recluse described by Professor Mote in this volume, and the writing of history— traditionally a critical exercise—appears as a peculiarly suitable occupation for the man who withdraws.

Han's concern with the examinations in relation to his own literary ideals suggests that in his time the examination system was an active political issue. This seems indeed to have been the case. In the later T'ang empire, as Mr. Pulleyblank's study in this volume indicates, profound (and as yet inadequately understood) social changes were taking place. The great aristocratic families of the north, which had been powerful in an earlier era, were declining or breaking up, and "new men" from outside this closed elite were coming on the scene. The availability of office to members of different social or regional groups was therefore a matter of intense interest, and the question was raised whether the examinations brought into office men who truly deserved it.

A prominent criticism was that the examinations rewarded the man who merely happened to have a good memory, though he might have no grasp of the "essential meaning" of the Classics—their relevance to current moral and political issues. Another persistent issue was the propriety of requiring of the candidate a facility in highly artificial literary forms such as the *fu* ("rhymed prose") and *p'an* ("decision") which could have nothing to do with his performance in office. Yüan Chen in 806, for example, in an essay submitted at the Palace Examination, made a revolutionary proposal that chief emphasis in the examinations be placed on knowledge of contemporary law and history, and that the competition be opened to all ranks of society (he would have abolished the examination on which Han Yü foundered, the placing examination, which required a candidate to prove that his father was neither an artisan, nor a merchant, nor a criminal).[11]

But such criticisms do not question the value of the examination system in principle. One important kind of criticism did do just this. Curiously, we find this criticism brought out with special clarity in a somewhat backhanded justification of the literary requirements. This appears in the "Monograph on Examinations" of the *Hsin T'ang Shu*. The authors observe that although in the *chin-shih* examination "the choice is made on the basis of literary compositions written in a vague style and on subjects of little practical value," still the successful candidates do perform well in office. They continue:

In later ages (i.e., after classical antiquity), customs became more and more corrupted, and superiors and inferiors came to suspect each other. Hence it came to be thought that the correctness of a candidate's use of rimes would allow examiners to judge his merits objectively. Whenever this procedure was abandoned, . . . no stable standard could be established. And consequently, it has never been possible to change anything. Alas, it is clear therefore that the method used in the Three Dynasties of antiquity, whereby local districts presented men to the sovereign because of their virtuous conduct, is one which cannot obtain except under a perfect government.[12]

Here eleventh-century historians are picking up ideas from a proposal made in 763 to "restore" certain features of a system for the direct recommendation of "virtuous" men to the court. Nonetheless, they are editorializing; and we might bear in mind that the editor who directed the compilation of this part of the *Hsin T'ang Shu*—in all probability writing parts of it himself—was Ou-yang Hsiu.

The idea of doing away with the examinations entirely, and of filling the ranks of government servants by recommendation of "virtuous" men from below, was resurrected again and again.[13] It bears witness to an almost incredible extreme of political idealism in Sung and Ming China. The vision was of a perfect society supposed to have existed in antiquity, a government of perfect virtue, in which there would be complete mutual trust and harmony between men of high and low estate. Inferiors would know their station and have no desire to rise beyond their merits, while those above would be motivated only by the purest love of virtue itself. In such a world order, the best man would always be chosen (and those not chosen would have no resentment), for it would always be the best who would come to the attention of the rulers, and the rulers would always be able to recognize the best. Examinations would not only be superfluous in such a state of affairs, they would be incompatible with it, for they would excite a spirit of striving and of selfish competition among the people. This is just what the examinations do; and for many Sung and Ming philosophers this corrupting and disturbing influence exercised upon the mind, preventing men from "fixing their aim" on ultimate moral values instead of short-term gains, is the greatest fault of the system.

The utopian picture of an ancient, prebureaucratic, perfect Confucian society was a basic element underlying and shaping opinion about educational policy and examination practices in the factional politics of the Sung; indeed this utopian conception seems to be central in all reformist and counterreformist thought in that period. Here I cannot take up the details of these policy struggles, save to note that these questions were always important. Examination requirements were changed constantly, and this must have resulted in much anxiety, leading in turn to an intensification of concern over these problems.[14] Basically, the call for ending the examinations and turning back to some earlier and presumably better method of bringing good men into government—easily combined with a Mencius-inspired concern for the reform of local schools—was of a piece with Mencian "well-field" utopianism in economics and land policy. Essentially it was part of an idealistic regret that the "Confucian" bureaucratic state, with its contamination of Legalism and its (real or fancied) attendant moral corruption in official life, had come into existence at all.[15]

Two illustrations will bear this out, both from Sung philosophers of first rank. Ch'eng I (1033–1107), in a long discussion of examinations as conducted in the "three colleges" of the Sung Imperial Academy, expressed the usual regrets: the formal, detailed, legally prescribed literary requirements were not of use in evaluating the moral worth of the students, while the atmosphere of competition turned their minds to a love of "profit," and made them actually forget their parents. The trouble is that the government relies on "detailed regulations" for appraising candidates for the civil service, rather than on whatever ability those in high places may have to recognize "virtue." But are "detailed regulations" really dispensable?

Someone may say, "If the right men are obtained for the highest positions, then all is well. But if not, it is better to have many detailed regulations to guard against wrongdoing, so that there will be a clear course to follow." Such a person fails entirely to realize that the ancient rulers devised laws in the expectation that there would be suitable men to carry them out. I have never heard that they made laws for the case in which capable men could not be found. If the high officials are not good men, and do not understand the principle of education, but merely adhere to the empty letter and the minute details of the law, surely they will not be able by these means to lead men to perfect their talents.[16]

Ch'eng's reply is a standard Confucian rejoinder to quasi-Legalist recipes: the law cannot effect its own implementation; at best it is a guide for the judgment of good men.

But Ch'eng did not proceed very far with these anti-bureaucratic regrets. Another philosopher, Chang Tsai (1020–77), however, was so repelled by the spectacle of vulgar competition for positions that he praised, in contrast, the giving and holding of hereditary offices, which had persisted in the later bureaucratic empire as a not very significant and rather artificial continuation of ancient feudal forms.

The distinction of hereditary office is the way a ruler gives recognition to those who achieve great things and honors the virtuous, cherishing them and being generous to them, displaying his boundless grace. Their heirs therefore ought to be happy with their duties and be encouraged to achievement . . . excelling in purity and abstaining from the pursuit of profit.

But in these times, Chang complained, "descendants of high dignitaries like to compete with ordinary people, working at the craft of verse-making and selling their wares to the authorities," i.e., sitting for the examinations in the hope of getting appointments, "not realizing that actively seeking for office is wrong."[17]

Chang Tsai's feeling that it is unseemly for a man of quality to engage in the common scramble for advantage is here perhaps reinforced by another persuasion: that the gentleman will not push himself forward. This is the conduct one expects of a social climber; the true "superior man" waits until his prince calls him. But this is not for excess of humility; on the contrary, he may be deeply offended if it be thought that his merits are open to question. An amusing story told of "the philosopher Ch'eng" (either Ch'eng I or his brother Ch'eng Hao, 1032–85) shows how ingrained these attitudes were.

Hsieh Chi passed through Loyang on his way from Shu to the capital and saw Ch'eng-tzu. The master asked him, "Why have you undertaken this trip?" He answered, "I am about to take the examination for a post in the Bureau of Education." The master did not reply. Chi said, "What do you think of it?" The master said, "Once when I was buying a servant-girl I wanted to test her. Her mother became angry and would not permit it, saying, 'My daughter is not one who may first be tried out.' Today you want to become a teacher of men and want to undergo a test for this purpose! You would certainly be laughed at by that old woman." Chi subsequently did not go.[18]

Dignity is a precious thing indeed! Clearly, a dignified and lofty refusal to compete, a high-minded protest that one is not interested in advancement and will leave this matter to fate, and the cherishing of a picture of society in which the poisonous craving for "profit" is absent, are all attitudes which fit closely together.

In considering the bearing of Neo-Confucian ethical thought upon the examination problem, we cannot neglect the most famous of Sung philosopher-statesmen, Chu Hsi (1130–1200). Chu, describing the idealized ancient practice of recruiting officials by direct recommendation without examinations, says that as a result of it "men's minds were composed and they had no distracting desires. Night and day they were diligent, fearing only lest they be wanting in virtue, and not caring whether rank and salary came their way." Clearly he too shared the common Neo-Confucian nostalgic utopian ideal.[19]

Chu Hsi made the foregoing statement in an essay which in its day was famous—a "Private Opinion on Schools and Examinations," which, the "Monograph on Examinations" in the *Sung Shih* tells us, "was read by the whole world."[20] In it he was bitterly critical of examination standards and practices in his day. He proposed at least a limited use of direct recommendation, and an end to practices of favoritism; in particular he called for fairer geographical distribution when allocating quotas of candidates to be passed. The main part of his proposal, however, would have had the effect of making the examinations very different in content and tone: he would change the subject matter of the examinations through a twelve-year cycle, guaranteeing that the state would have at its disposal men with a wide variety of specialized backgrounds. Examinations in poetry and *fu* would be suppressed. Chu wanted his candidates to think, and to know how to think for themselves; in studying the Classics, they should study not only the classical texts but also the commentaries of different schools of interpreters, and in answering a question should be prepared to cite different opinions, concluding with their own judgment. Chu went on actually to list commentaries he would have examinees required to read; somewhat surprisingly, commentaries by Wang An-shih are included for all the most important Classics, although Chu was in general opposed to Wang's policies. Chu expected much if his proposals were acted upon. If they were adopted, "men's minds would be composed and there would be no spirit of hustling and striving; there would be actual virtuous conduct and none of the corruption of empty words; there would be solid learning and no unusable talent."[21]

Chu in this essay was flailing away at the system, and doing so, at least in part, in terms of his ideal of a perfect social and political order. But this ideal of a perfectly virtuous world was ambiguous. It could be used, not to criticize the edifice of requirements, standards, pressures, or unfair practices which confronted the student, but rather to upbraid the student himself. For one can say that in a perfectly virtuous society the government would not make the mistakes the examination system embodied; but, by the same argument, students would not exhibit the qualities of restless self-seeking and anxiety that these mistakes induced. Chu has a rather often-quoted remark that "it is not that the examinations are a vexation to men, but simply that men vex themselves about the examinations." And he continues,

A scholar of lofty vision and broad understanding, when he reads the books of the sages, will produce writing which reflects what he grasps, and all considerations of gain and loss, advantage and disadvantage, are set aside. Even though he constantly works at preparing for the examinations, he is undisturbed. If Confucius were to come back to life now, he would not avoid the examinations; but surely they would not disturb him.[22]

Chu goes on to admit that as a young man he himself had a certain disdain for the examinations, but this feeling was not, he argues, based on any understanding of the matter. The situation could be compared to that of one who has a natural dislike for the taste of wine or for a certain color, this natural and unreasoned reaction being of no importance.

The foregoing remarks, along with much more of the same sort, are preserved in a systematic anthology of Chu's sayings and writings on various subjects compiled by the Ch'ing government in the early eighteenth century, the *Chu Tzu Ch'üan Shu*, edited by Li Kuang-ti. The *Ch'üan Shu* was intended as an orthodox presentation of Chu's philosophy from the official point of view; and in the section presenting Chu's opinions on the examination problem, remarks by Chu are culled out of his writings and put together so as to justify the system against typical complaints made by students. Needless to say, in these pages the editors do not even hint at the existence of Chu's "Private Opinion." We do not need to regard the *Ch'üan Shu* as purely a Ch'ing document, however. It illustrates not only the way in which Neo-Confucian idealism could be turned about to justify the status quo, for the student complaints which Chu is shown to have answered in the *Ch'üan Shu* must after all have been complaints actually brought to him by his contemporaries. They are quite possibly as typical of student dissatisfaction in the twelfth century as in the seventeenth.

Let us see how some of the complaints and answers go. Notice that in the remarks just reproduced Chu preaches that a really worthy scholar would "set aside" considerations of "gain and loss." This sounds like Han Yü. But there is an important difference; namely, in the one case we have a defiant scholar bravely telling himself and the world that he will not be moved by the temptations to "fame and profit" that the state and the pressures of society create; whereas here we have a teacher pontifically telling students that they ought not to be so moved, and adding that if they are not, they can have no reason to complain of what is expected of them.

In this same passage there is another element worth noting. Chu says that he himself as a young man found examination studies naturally distasteful to him, but argues that this natural disinclination was of no significance. The plain implication in this is that Chu was approached by unhappy students who also found their examination studies distasteful, who felt that the guidance of their own inclinations was valuable, and who found themselves, like Ou-yang Hsiu and Liu Chih-chi, inclined to spend their time on other lines of study and self-improvement. Chu is shown by the *Ch'üan Shu* editors to have dealt with this plaint in various ways. Sometimes he simply pooh-poohs all the fuss about the matter:

Concerning study for the examinations, there is really nothing very important to be said. When a man of worth devotes himself to it, he will presumably have some energy to spare. If he has understood the true philosophy, then in the course of his daily activities, whatever their degree of importance, he will not need to divide his attention: if he always first understands "this," he will succeed at "that."[23]

In other words, see that you cultivate yourself properly and study the right point of view, and there will be no conflict—you will automatically do well in the examinations. As Han Yü had said, a good man will naturally write well. Chu's friend and rival philosopher Lu Chiu-yüan picked up the same idea when, in 1181, he was guest lecturer at Chu's White Deer Grotto Academy. Cultivate yourself circumspectly, says Lu, instill in yourself a devotion to right, and learn to have no impulses toward selfish expediency. "When one who conducts himself in this way approaches the examination halls, his writing will always express the learning and self-cultivation in which he is constantly engaged and the richness stored up within himself, and he will not offend against the sages."[24]

What if a young man self-importantly and loftily says that he has better things to do with himself than study examination essays? Chu offers the following dash of cold water:

Not taking the examinations is really only a small matter. But nowadays when someone says he is not going to take the examinations it is treated as something surprising and extraordinary. As I see it, as soon as one devotes one's thought to understanding the Tao, one takes a bit of respite from this sort of thing (i.e., the examinations), and there is obviously nothing of importance in this fact. I don't know why, but [when people begin to understand the Tao] they automatically look down on all sorts of wealth, honor, and attainment . . .[25]

This is less interesting as an example of Chu's attitude than it is as a negative image of a point of view which must have been prevalent among students.

Chu recognizes the common rationalization of students that they must study for the examinations in order to support their parents, and he condemns it. Such an attitude merely indicates that the student's mind is not composed—that he still feels a conflict between studying for the examinations and "real learning."[26] Sometimes, however, Chu admits by implication that there can be such a conflict, and attempts to deal with it or resolve it by some argument or stratagem. On one occasion, a disciple named Huang Ch'ien was ordered by his father to go to the prefectural school and study for the examinations, a course the young student was much disinclined to take. Huang laid his situation before Chu, who replied, "You can study for the examinations in the daytime and read the books you want to at night!" and added that if Huang refused to follow his father's wishes, father and son would become estranged, a situation which, he implies, would be as detrimental to Huang's program of "study" (i.e., self-cultivation) as the examinations course could ever be.[27]

As we might expect, Wang Yang-ming shared the Neo-Confucian vision of a perfect, strife-free society. Writing in 1525, he gives this idyllic picture of antiquity:

The man at the village well or in the rural district, the farmer, the artisan, the merchant, everybody had this (the true) learning . . . and looked only to the perfecting of character as important. How is this to be accounted for? They were not subject to the confusion inherent in much hearing and seeing, nor to the annoyance of remembering and reciting, nor to extravagance of speech and composition, nor to the striving and gaining of honor and advantage. The result was that they were filial toward their parents, respectful to their elders, and faithful toward their friends.

In this remote age, "the government schools were devoted to perfecting virtue, . . ." and "the people of the empire, with clear, resplendent virtue, all viewed one another as relatives of one home. . . . They did not strive for exalted position," each being content with his station. People at this time were not envious of others' accomplishments: "They did not distinguish between themselves and others. . . . They can be compared with the body of a single person . . ." and as one's eyes are not ashamed because they cannot hear, likewise no man was ashamed or was thought ill of for lack of the intellectual attainments found in the great.[28]

If this is noteworthy, it is chiefly as an intense (if dreamy) re-expression of a common Neo-Confucian political ideal. It is obvious, at least, that the addition of an examination system would seriously mar Wang's pretty scene. If there is a novel emphasis in what he says, it is found in his almost Taoist feeling that the purity of men's minds will be injured by too much "seeing and hearing," "remembering and reciting," or by "extravagance of speech and composition." For it is typical of Wang that he has a rather wholesale distrust of the verbal, conceptual side of man's mental existence. His distrust of mere "words" fits into a growing intellectual trend which became very important in the Ch'ing.

This attitude can be more easily understood if we examine the character of the district and metropolitan examinations during the Ming (to a large extent the description will fit the Ch'ing also). The Ming examinations followed, with some modification, the form of the Sung examinations as revised in 1071 when, as a result of one of the reforms of Wang An-shih, the *ming-ching* examination was abolished and certain features of it incorporated into the *chin-shih* examination. As it ultimately took shape, the Ming examination scheme (for both *chin-shih* and *chü-jen* degrees) consisted of three sittings or tests several days apart. The first test consisted of "essays on the meaning of the Classics" (*ching-i*)—three on the Four Books, and four on texts from other Classics. The second test was given over to *lun* ("essays") and *p'an* ("decisions," a T'ang examination form) and to questions on imperial "instructions"; the third, to *ts'e* ("dissertations") on history and current problems.[29] As far as this description goes, such an examination might be quite comprehensive. Actually, as Ku Yen-wu points out, the only test given any careful attention by the examiners was the first, on the meaning of the Classics and the Four Books.[30] Further, although all candidates had to answer questions on the Four Books, it was possible to get by with specialization on just one other Classic. This was certainly very far from what Chu Hsi had wanted in his "Private Opinion."

But this was not all. Where Chu had wanted candidates to have a knowledge of many different schools of criticism, the Ming system required candidates to prepare themselves in the views of just one school, ironically the school of Chu Hsi himself. After the official publication, in the Yung-lo reign, of the compendium of the opinions of this school, the *Ssu-shu Wu-ching Ta-ch'üan*, even the standard T'ang commentaries were dispensed with. In consequence, less and less came to depend on wide learning or genuine understanding, even of the Classics themselves; more and more it came to be crucially important for the candidate to excel in the style of his essays on the meaning of classical texts in the first test.[31]

What of the form of these essays? A form for the *ching-i* essay had been fixed by the Board of Ceremonies shortly after Wang An-shih's reform; and as such official forms will, it evolved over successive reigns and dynasties. By the Ming, it had come to be fixed in eight sections (hence its popular name, *pa-ku,* "eight legs"). The number of words to be used in the essay was also fixed from time to time. A typical specimen takes the announced topic—a passage from one of the Classics—and analyzes it into two subthemes. The essay then moves into a more and more elaborate treatment of these two themes. In the main body of the essay, an extended sentence or group of sentences will be put forward on one of the themes; these are in loose, "ancient prose" style, but they are at once followed by an exactly similar sentence or set of sentences on the other theme, which mirror the earlier ones character for character. This game will be played several times before the essay reaches its close. In tone, the entire piece can effectively be compared with a sermon on a text from sacred scripture.[32]

The total effect is not at all displeasing, if one is merely browsing through a few of these curios, and surely some value must be acknowledged in any literary form which required the Chinese literati to write well-constructed and systematically organized pieces of prose. But if one had to read and imitate such essays as if one's life depended upon it for the years needed to acquire sufficient skill to satisfy the examiners, one can readily imagine that ennui would soon give way to intense distaste. The necessity of finding antitheses in the theme in order to carry the essay through was particularly galling, since it was a purely formal requirement which took precedence over whatever meaning the classical passage might contain. Candidates had to be prepared to distort, or even invent, meaning in the assigned text, and had by long practice to learn this art thoroughly.[33]

Worse, the examiners over the centuries not unnaturally developed a little tradition of playing a game with the candidates, by choosing texts which would be difficult to handle in the required way, or which were chopped out of context in the most misleading fashion possible, with the natural phrasing and breaks in meaning of the original text largely ignored. An example, given by Chu Hsi (who excoriated the practice in his "Private Opinion") is a Sung examination question consisting of three lines from the *Shih ching,* viz.,

> Shang t'ien chih tsai
> Wu sheng wu ch'ou
> I hsing Wen Wang[34]

Legge's translation is as follows:

> The doings of high heaven
> have neither sound nor smell.
> Take your pattern from King Wen, . . .[35]

The second half of the second pair of lines, which is dropped, is approximately "and all countries will give you their confidence." But of course much more context even than this would be required if one were to make sense out of the passage. Still, Chu Hsi's example is tame compared to what sometimes happened. Imagine yourself writing an essay on the following five words:

> Kou wei wu pen ch'i[36]

These words correspond approximately to the italic words in the following passage from *Mencius*:

The disciple Hsü said, "Chung-ni often praised water, saying, 'O water, O water.' What did he find in water to praise?" Mencius replied, "There is a spring of water; how it gushes out! It rests not day nor night. It fills up every hole, and then advances, flowing on to the four seas. Such is water having a spring! It was this which he found in it to praise.

"*But suppose that* the water *has no spring.—In the seventh* and eighth months when the rain falls abundantly, the channels in the fields are all filled, but their being dried up again may be expected in a short time. So a superior man is ashamed of a reputation beyond his merits."[37]

In the *pa-ku* as part of the examinations, clearly, we have a prime example of violation of the classical principle that "one must not let words injure meaning." The term *pa-ku* came widely to connote an exercise in mere verbal cleverness with utter disregard for content. Reflect that every schoolboy had to struggle with this form, and that often all possible social, family, and pedagogical pressure was put upon him to master it. And consider that in order to master it he had to develop by long practice at least a hypothetical sort of taste for it, and thus condition himself in a device for which he was likely to have both philosophical and aesthetic disgust. The bitter complaints about *shih wen* (this term now had come to mean *pa-ku*) in the letters and reminiscences of seventeenth- and eighteenth-century writers are not hard to understand.

Ku Yen-wu, in the seventeenth century, was one of several now famous men who meditated and wrote on the reasons for the decline and fall of the Ming Dynasty. Much of his *Jih-chih Lu* has this sort of point, and in particular the parts of that book dealing with examinations and schools, though treating these subjects in great historical depth, are pointed up into a criticism, often extremely biting, of the character and operation of the Ming examination system. In many of these critical sections, however, he writes as though he were talking of contemporary conditions, and we probably must assume that at the time he wrote conditions had not greatly changed.

Ku insists that writing, to be worth anything, must say something, and the writer must be unencumbered by formal restrictions in the saying of it:

Writing can have no fixed form. When a form is set for people to follow in their writing, the writing will not be worth talking about. The T'ang selected its officials on their skill in writing *fu*, and the *fu* became utterly decadent. The Sung selected men on their skill in composing essays and dissertations (*lun ts'e*) and these genres likewise decayed. The Ming selected men on the basis of their essays on the meaning of the Classics (*ching-i*, i.e., *pa-ku*), and this form of writing became worse than anything that had been seen before. The reason in each case was that writing was required to follow a fixed form, and as a result the writing continually became worse. The reason the examination replies of Ch'ao Ts'o, Tung Chung-shu, and Kung-sun Hung are outstanding in history is that in their day there was no fixed form for writing. If we wish to invigorate the writing of the present day we must not fetter it with forms, and then outstanding talent will make its appearance.[38]

In Sung, Yüan, and Ming, the characteristic objection to the examination system had been its tendency to induce a fever of competition. Ku's indictment of *pa-ku* suggests that the characteristic objection was now to the examinations' bad influence on writing and thinking. By stressing purely formal, merely verbal inducements to stagnation, the examinations actually deprived the state of a supply of good men. The situation has become so bad, Ku thinks, that the only remedy is to suspend the examinations altogether for a time, and teach people anew how to study. Ku also attacks the brainless orthodoxy which he feels the examinations propagate, and recommends that examination questions on the Four Books deal with "doubtful" matters, questions which will probe into embarrassing contradictions. Ku cites the *p'an* genre on the T'ang examinations as exemplifying what he intends, but it is likely that some of the examination questions prepared by Wang An-shih would have served him even better. Ku, however, had a rather low opinion of the Sung reformer.[39]

Ku reserves his strongest language for a somewhat different matter, however. Just because the examinations place so much emphasis on formally correct essay writing, they do nothing to recognize or encourage really solid scholarship. Instead, the examinations are so contrived as to allow mere know-nothings to pass. Ku's exposé of the abuses by which this can occur is one of the bitterest and most interesting parts of his treatise. The trick consists of a practice Ku calls *ni t'i*, or "making up questions." There is, he says, no evil greater than this in the whole system. It works as follows: In the crucial first test, when a candidate has to write essays on the Classics he has chosen as a specialty, there will usually be only a few dozen questions likely to be asked.

Rich families and powerful clans engage well-known scholars and install them in their family schools. The scholar then takes these few dozen themes and writes an essay for each, receiving pay according to the number of essays he writes. The sons and younger brothers in the family, and servant boys who are especially clever, are then made to memorize and study thoroughly these essays. When they go to the examination halls, eight or nine out of every ten themes announced will correspond to the themes they have studied, and they need only copy down the writings they have memorized.[40]

This procedure, Ku observes, is incomparably easier than the examinations as they are traditionally pictured; for plainly, the son of a rich family might in this way pass without having read through the text of even one Classic. "The same procedure," Ku writes, "is used for the Four Books. And when the grades are announced, these fellows turn out to be at the top. Many who are mere pretty-faced youths are selected for official appointments."

Ku then adds that from time to time parts of the Classics have ceased to be drawn upon for examination themes, so that what a young man has to contend with in his preparation has become less and less, and the trick of "making up likely themes" becomes that much easier. As a result,

What men in former times needed ten years to accomplish can now be finished in one; what once required a year to learn can now be finished in a month. . . . But if by chance you ask someone about a Classic he has not read, there are those who will be so confused they will not know what book you are talking about. Therefore, I say that the injurious effects of *pa-ku* are as great as the effects of the Burning of the Books, and the ruination of talent that it brings about is worse than the result of the Burial of the Scholars. . . .

Ku then recommends, citing Chu Hsi's "Private Opinion," that candidates be examined on passages in the Classics that would call for some original thinking, and that in studying one Classic they be required to gain a general acquaintance with the rest; that they be required to become familiar with conflicting interpretations, and that in their answers they be required to render their own judgment. Further, themes used in the examinations should not be so standard that they can be guessed at in advance. "Then their essays will have to be written in the examination halls, and it can really be determined whether a scholar understands the Classics or not, and his ability to write can really be tested."[41]

Not the least interesting part of what Ku says is his conviction that it is characteristically the rich who are most easily able to get away with murder. But the substance of his plea is that solid scholarship should be demanded of a candidate at the examinations and should be the criterion of his worth. In this plea Ku perhaps had real influence, for his prestige as a classical scholar mounted enormously in the next century. Successive generations of scholars grew up who looked back to him with reverence, and many such men, of course, served frequently as examining officials. One can well imagine that one of Ku's "pretty-faced youths" would have scant chance of passing under such an examiner as, say, Juan Yüan.[42]

But this same prestige of Ku as a classical scholar, and the philological *zeitgeist* which developed in the eighteenth century, had eventually another and very different effect on examination standards. For although the tendency occasionally improved the caliber of examining officials, still, in any given case, the chances were that an examiner would find himself in the situation of passing judgment on a candidate or candidates who knew more philology than he did. Examiners caught in this sort of situation tend to look for a simple and foolproof line of defense into which to retreat. The examiner's recourse in the present case was to limit his inspection once again to mere questions of form: not, now, to the formal correctness of the candidate's essays, but to the form of the individual characters he wrote—to his calligraphy. By the second and third decades of the nineteenth century, it was a ritual perfection in the handling of the brush which was the mark of the candidate most likely to succeed.

Needless to say, this new situation provoked protests appropriate to it. Such an expression of protest is to be found in a bitterly sarcastic essay by Kung Tzu-chen, an intense, brilliant, and erratic scholar-official, philologist, poet, and friend of Wei Yüan and Lin Tse-hsü, who attempted the examinations repeatedly before attaining the *chin-shih* degree in 1829, failing, however—as he believed, because of poor handwriting—to pass the palace examination which a successful *chin-shih* normally took. Kung's essay pretends to be a preface to a book he has written on calligraphy. He describes first, with mock reverence, the ritual of the palace examination in which he failed.- The examining officers, "in court robes, face the throne and kneel thrice, touching their heads to the floor nine times. All the candidates do likewise, respectfully taking their positions. When the examination is over, the eight examiners then respectfully make a selection of ten papers in which the elevation of characters is according to form and in which even and deflected tones have been properly used, and which exhibit a formal calligraphic style which is especially sparkling and delicate, presenting these for the emperor's perusal. . . ."

Kung describes more examinations—the preliminary examination before the palace examination, and the examination following it, both, again, turning on the candidate's skill in calligraphy. He misses no chance to dwell on the grave and weighty importance of success which turns on so trivial a matter. "Those who place high in all three examinations are appointed to the Han-lin Academy. In our dynasty, the highest officials invariably arise from among members of the Han-lin, and more than half of the assistant ministers at court and of the governors of provinces are chosen in the same way." To be chosen for a clerkship in the Grand Council is likewise a great honor; for "in time of war the function of the Grand Council is to assist the throne in making plans by which victory is decided, while in time of peace it provides advice based on the records of earlier emperors in the issuance of edicts affecting the imperial household." But, "when one is recommended to the Grand Council there is an examination, in which selection is made as before on the basis of calligraphic skill." Kung goes on to explain to us how other important posts are filled, and always with the same final twist.

Finally Kung tips his hand:

I, Kung Tzu-chen, passed the examination in the Board of Ceremonies; three times I went up for the palace examination and three times I failed. I was not assigned to the Han-lin Academy. I was examined for the Grand Council but was not given a post there. . . . So I have withdrawn to my home and have reproached myself, and have written a book in self-criticism. Its contents consist of twelve sections discussing the principles of selecting a fine brush-tip, five sections on the proper method of grinding the ink and impregnating the brush, . . . one hundred and twenty sections on fine points in the drawing of the dot and in the execution of the sweeping down-stroke, twenty-two sections on the framing of characters, twenty-four sections on the spacing of characters in column, three sections on quality of spirit; and seven sections on natural temper. Having finished the work, I have entitled it *A New Treatise on Gaining Office*, and am entrusting it to my descendants.

Kung dates his "preface" the fourteenth year of Tao-kuang (1834).[43]

Needless to say, Kung's *Treatise* was never written or even seriously contemplated. Kung's bitterness about calligraphy, it should be stressed, was provoked by a situation peculiar to his time. We find a very different attitude in Ku Yen-wu. Ku would have his candidates know how to write characters well, and no nonsense. He cites in this connection, and with evident approval, a practice in court examinations in the Northern Ch'i Dynasty. In those high and far-off times, it seems, if a candidate's writing was sloppy, he was required as a penalty to drink a pint of ink.[44]

The Chinese civil service examinations were not discontinued until 1905. The remainder of the story, however, would be a study in itself, and I lack both the space and the knowledge to enter upon it. But it does seem plain that it would be hasty to ascribe the Chinese state's rejection of the examination system simply to a Westernizing fever, or to say that the Chinese did away with that system merely in order to be rid of a conservative institutional force. Perhaps it will turn out that what the "impact of the West" accomplished was to tip the balance in favor of persuasions which were centuries old, but which had not been strong enough radically to alter the set institutions of a bureaucratic state. The complaint that the examinations failed to nourish talents of practical use to the state was not a new and radical idea in the nineteenth century; on the contrary, it was a familiar criticism in the ninth. The complaint of Ku Yen-wu (and Chu Hsi) that the examinations fostered a cult of "empty words" and dead forms was an argument repeated with force in memorials preceding the system's abolition. The idea of a Confucian utopia, in which Neo-Confucian philosophers lodged their moral objections to the system, was an idea which was by no means dead in the late nineteenth century. Perhaps it is not dead yet.

The examination system must certainly be called Confucian. It gave form to the ideal that the ruler should select the best men as his officials, and it provided in most periods a fixed if narrow and difficult avenue to prestige and position for that social group who had a special interest in reading and cherishing the Confucian classical texts. And yet the bitter regrets the Chinese have had about the system must also be called Confucian. The Neo-Confucian utopian ideal, and the "anti-formalist" and moral criteria of literary value enunciated by Han Yü in the ninth century and by Ku Yen-wu in the seventeenth are essential parts of the idealistic side of the Confucian tradition which has its roots in Mencius.

When we consider the position of the individual student or candidate, we see that he was pushed in two directions at once. He must do the right thing for his parents and family; the *ipsissima verba* of the Master could be cited in abundance to assure him of this; also it was the duty of a Confucian to take office and "put his Tao into practice" if he could. In the later empire, the only apparent way to perform these duties was to prepare for the examinations and seek official position thereby.

Yet the Confucian also had a duty to cultivate himself and to respect his own dignity. Entry into the competition for office obliged him, it seemed, to place "profit" ahead of "right" in his own personal ordering of values, and at least to seem to be seeking the approbation of persons, whether gossiping townspeople or examining officials, whom he might regard as vulgar or petty-minded. If we read reflectively a novel such as *Ju-lin Wai-shih*, we suspect that the scorn measured out to examiners and examination writing is, so to speak, but the exposed part of an iceberg whose bulk is the pervasive revulsion of independent-minded men against social pressures to conform, to accept the vulgar conventions and values, to chase after the pretty tags of so-called success, to court favor with the "best" families in town. Beneath this disposition was always the conception of the Superior Man, who cannot be moved by mere things.

A Chinese who thought seriously about himself and his society did not live in a placid intellectual world in which all his questions had ready answers. He lived in a world of tensions, both social and intellectual—tensions such as those I have been describing; and if we are to understand his politics, his literature, his philosophy, we must measure these tensions and their effect upon him. We must see him as he was.

Frederick W. Mote

CONFUCIAN EREMITISM
IN THE YÜAN PERIOD

The Mongols conquered North China in the early 1230's, and completed their conquest of the rest of the country in the years 1275–79. The North already had been held for a century by the Chin Tatars, another alien and (in Chinese eyes) barbarian conquering people from beyond China's northern frontiers. The wounds caused by this long division between alien-ruled North China and Chinese-ruled South China were further aggravated by the attitudes and policies of the Yüan dynasty, as the Mongol government of the newly reunited Chinese world was called.

The Mongols themselves faced a difficult adjustment when, as nomadic tribesmen, they suddenly became the rulers, or at least the holders of power within the ruling group, of a vast sedentary population. Moreover, with each of the first few generations of their rule the role they assigned to China in their world empire shifted and changed. Only gradually did these Mongol rulers come to see themselves as the successors to earlier Chinese dynasties, and as Chinese emperors. The Chinese, on their part, often were moved to fierce resentment of the Mongols, not so much by the fact of alien rule itself as by the lack of regard in which these barbarian rulers, beyond all others in their history, held their ancient and revered way of life. Those things which the Chinese held to be the essentials of civilization—their Confucian ethical and social principles; their theories and forms of civilian-administered, bureaucratic government; their humanistic culture—suffered serious decline, and seemed to many to face the danger of extinction. An incipient racism made brief appearance, contradicting in its spirit the traditional patronizing Chinese attitude toward "barbarian" neighbors.

Of all the rulers in China's history, the Mongols were perhaps the least well-equipped to deal with Chinese problems and the least concerned about dealing with them. Moreover, the Yüan period was a period of instability, in which many kinds of new forces were at work. In some respects this was beneficial, but in many respects it was not, and in almost all respects it alarmed and grieved the educated, thinking Chinese of the time. The magnificent achievements of the Mongols in such matters as military organization and technique scarcely impressed their Chinese subjects, who saw only the low quality of Mongol government and the deterioration of social order. By the same token, the developments in literature and painting for which we now value the Yüan period offered little solace to the Chinese literatus of the time. The times were hard; as the Yüan dynasty wore on, they became harder, and China sank deeper into pessimism, frustration, and apathy. The intellectual climate and moral tone of the Mongol era in China cannot be described in greater detail here,[1] but must be kept in mind; they are essential to an understanding of what follows.

VARIETIES OF EREMITISM

Even in the Yüan period some persons remained zealously devoted to Confucian ideals—to an active life in the service of the Yüan, and to heroism as Confucianism defined it. Far more of the literate turned in despair to the other extreme: to various forms of escapism, and *fin de siècle* frivolity. There is a third group which renounced both state service and extreme self-indulgence and chose instead some variety of withdrawal.

Recluses, or hermits, are often called *yin-i* in historical writings, and usually referred to themselves as *ch'u-shih* or *chü-shih*. All these terms are customarily translated "recluse" or "hermit"; in Chinese society they signified withdrawal from the active public life in the service of society that Confucian ethics prescribed as the most suitable course for all whose abilities, cultivation, and learning qualified them for it. To bar one's gates and earn one's own living without reliance on the emolument of office, to display a lack of regard for the social status which could be attained only by entering officialdom, and to devote one's life to self-cultivation, scholarship or artistic pursuits made one a recluse. By the mores of Confucian society, this was a step which set one apart, which justified the special appellation.

The distance to which one withdrew, the firmness with which one barred the gate, and the seriousness with which one cultivated oneself all admitted of wide variations, even among those whose motivations in withdrawing were sincere. (We are not concerned here with the many who became recluses when it suited their purpose to do so, and returned to public life at their convenience.) The variations, however, were of only secondary importance; the degree of a man's commitment to withdrawal had no effect on his status. It was the renunciation of office-holding—either at the outset or after a period of public life—that defined the recluse.

Nemoto Makoto's recent book, "The Spirit of Resistance in Authoritarian Society: A Study of Chinese Eremitism," is the first full-scale study of the recluse in Chinese civilization, and more particularly in the "middle period" of imperial history.[2] Nemoto sees eremitism, especially the kind suggested by the title of his book, as a reflection of some of the deepest problems afflicting authoritarian society. He is at his best in describing the special character of Chinese eremitism, its contrast with Indian and Christian European eremitism, and the relation of the Chinese recluse to the rest of Chinese society. He describes well the significance of the renunciation of the official life, which as we have seen is the keystone of Chinese eremitism, and which distinguishes it from the connotations of the word in other civilizations (e.g., religion, solitude, eccentricity) and also from the really unrelated general problem of Buddhist monasticism in China.

This is not to imply that Buddhist eremitism is altogether foreign to our subject. Actually, some potential scholar-officials did become Buddhist or Taoist, rather than Confucian, recluses. The three types of eremitism, although distinct in character, are all more or less congenial to each other. The Buddhist, for example, may have become a monk, or may merely have become a lay-associate (*chü-shih* also has the specific meaning of a Buddhist lay-associate who has taken certain vows; both this meaning and that of a non-Buddhist recluse were and still are current for the term). The Buddhist recluse might continue to live with his family in normal conjugal life, or he might withdraw to celibacy and seclusion. In most cases we may assume that Buddhist thought had an intellectual appeal, and that the Buddhist literatus-recluse retained the respect and the acquaintance of his non-Buddhist friends. Such learned Buddhists, both monks and lay-associates, some of them as famous as their more worldly friends in the fields of poetry, painting, literature, and scholarship, are known in all ages, and were particularly numerous in the Yüan period.

The Taoist recluse likewise may have taken up the dress and hairdo of the professed Taoist adept, or may have maintained a looser connection with religious and popular Taoism. In either case he typically withdrew to a rural place, had a small following of apprentices, and practiced some more-or-less obscure Taoist art such as medicine or alchemy. He was likely to be at least slightly eccentric, if not awesomely unfathomable, but usually not to the point of losing the respect of the conventional intellectual community on whose fringes he lived.

It is the Confucian recluse, however, who interests us the most.

Usually he was less cut off from the normal pattern of life in society than the Buddhist or the Taoist. He cultivated nothing as metaphysically profound as Buddhism, or as mysteriously incommunicable as Taoism. If, beyond literature and the arts, he cultivated anything in the realm of the spirit, it was Confucian thought, which—unless one becomes wrapped up in the study of the *I-ching*—cannot take one far from the everyday world of man. He might indeed be somewhat eccentric, or he might be simply what we would call a retired gentleman of leisure, perhaps even one of great means living in elegant fashion. More often he was a man of modest means, living by teaching or working his own land, or a scholar living in poverty. The Confucian recluse might double as a devotee of the poetry-and-wine type of escapism; the serious life is not demanded of him, although it is more common. These various types of recluse, including the Buddhist and Taoist, had only one thing in common: they had withdrawn voluntarily from active participation in public life.

Although the pattern of the recluse has existed for millennia in China, it became an alternative way of life of particular importance in times of disorder and impending doom, when thoughtful pessimism seemed more attractive to educated men than the normal pattern of life. The Yüan period was preeminently such an age.

Many of the Yüan literati, we must presume, wanted office. Some would have accepted it but lacked ambition or energy; some did accept it and served the dynasty, even loyally. For the many who did not obtain office, the pose of a righteous indifference may have been an easy solace. But there can be little doubt that, for an important and influential number, withdrawal was genuine—an honest expression of protest prompted by their Confucian ideals.

But were there no literati who were neither recluses, nor scholar-officials loyal to the Yüan, nor passive idlers—no group, however small, who saw the inevitability of the Yüan dynasty's downfall and actively sought to hasten it? In the last generation of Yüan rule it is possible to discern the outlines of such a group. Dissociation with Mongol interests usually was their first step. Some merely became recluses, or scholars in retirement, who thought and sometimes wrote about social and political problems of their age, awaiting opportunities to become active. Some participated in the creation of local or regional forces which assumed some governmental responsibilities, but which made no open break with Yüan rule. Others lived by choice in territories under rebel rule, waiting to evaluate the rebellion's chances of success before openly joining it, but in their own minds condoning rebellion. Still others (few until the very end) openly served rebellious movements, movements which originated with and represented non-literati social forces but which could not begin to function on the level of government without the technical assistance of the literati. It must be emphasized, however, that activists and potential activists of this sort were few, scattered, and without much influence. The vast majority of the literate remained passively loyal to Yüan rule, and most of the educated members of society hoped for nothing more than improvement in the effectiveness of the legitimate government and a restoration of social order.

THE ORIGINS OF CONFUCIAN EREMITISM

Confucianism is normally and properly associated with the ideology of participation, of public service. In fact, however, there is an equally valid aspect of Confucianism, apparent in the thought of Confucius and Mencius, which justifies withdrawal from public life and official service under some conditions. Withdrawal is not to be preferred to the active life: it is not to be regarded (as by Taoism) as intrinsically valuable; but in some circumstances it is necessary and laudable. To Confucius and Mencius it was clear that a man should serve when he could maintain and actively promote his principles, and that he should withdraw when the conditions of public service were degrading, or when his principles were threatened. A man's personal ethical standards were to determine the decision.

It is a commonplace that this early Confucian thought is often at variance, in matters of specific detail and in tone and emphasis, with the "imperial Confucianism" of the Han and subsequent ages. The reasons for this are clear: the political and social realities of an authoritarian state could scarcely have been fully anticipated by Confucius and Mencius, two unemployed thinkers reflecting on an age of decaying feudalism. There are significant differences even between Confucius and Mencius, and still greater ones between Mencius and Hsün-tzu, reflecting both the development of Confucian thought and the changing conditions of successive ages. If early Confucian thought had not centered so heavily on the ethics of political and social situations, the ever-changing conditions of the political and social worlds would have borne less relevance to it, and the discrepancies between earlier and later Confucianism might have figured less importantly in the history of Chinese thought. If, for example, Confucius had been concerned primarily with religious or metaphysical concepts, his followers in later ages would have had less trouble adjusting to changing times, for they would have felt less compelled to become involved in government and practical affairs. But Confucianism, by its nature, demands action, or at least commitment. Moreover, there exists within it the roots of possible tension between the individual's observance of his ethical standards and the demands of society and state. To Confucius and Mencius, it was comparatively easy to draw the line between when a man should serve and when he should not, although in fact both were criticized by some of their own followers for apparent inconsistencies in such decisions. But, Confucius and Mencius discussed the motives of men who did or did not serve, and fixed their evaluations of them accordingly. Often those who did not serve received high praise.

Hsün-tzu, as might be expected, was harder on the recluse. Although a Confucian and a believer in the ethical foundations of society, in his insistence on the importance of ruler and state, he left little room for a man to maintain any private and personal moral standards that might under any circumstances conflict with the primary duty of serving the ruler. The later Legalists, among them especially Hsün-tzu's pupil Han Fei-tzu, were still more severe. Legalist writers pronounced the hermit guilty of a crime meriting death; in his eremitism he was "ungovernable" and "disloyal," and his existence could not be tolerated by the authoritarian state.

Legalist principles and practices exerted a significant influence on the character of imperial Confucianism. In fact, during the formative Han period Legalist and Confucian principles were in some measure mixed and blended together; the resulting amalgam, though it continued to be called Confucianism, was not the Confucianism of old. Fung Yu-lan, adopting the terminology of William James, refers to the materialistic, realistic Hsüntzian trend in Confucianism as the "tough-minded" side of it, as opposed to the "tender-minded" idealism of the Mencian tradition, and he sees the dominant Ch'eng-Chu school of Neo-Confucianism as the heir to the tough-minded tradition.[3]

Eremitism fared better with the tender-minded. It is clear that eremitism of all kinds was tolerated to a much greater degree in earlier history, and in particular that the nobly motivated eremitism of the uncompromising man of principle was highly praised.[4] Gradually, in the early imperial period, it lost favor, perhaps in part because it was associated with the religious eremitism of Taoism and Buddhism, but primarily, it would seem, because of the increasingly authoritarian character of the state.

Devaluing eremitism meant reinterpreting the words of Confucius and Mencius, and a perhaps unconscious acceptance of the attitudes of Hsün-tzu. Even the Neo-Confucianists, who ostensibly ranked Mencius highest among the followers of the Sage, bowed to this necessity. As Hsiao Kung-ch'üan has pointed out, the Sung Neo-Confucianists held the very un-Mencian idea that the servitor had the duty of absolute and unswerving loyalty to the ruler and his dynasty, even at the price of death or forced retirement. Moreover, they held this principle to be based on the teachings of Confucius himself, despite certain explicitly contradictory teachings of Confucius and Mencius.[5] Living in an age when the need to strengthen the state was apparent, they came to look upon even the most idealistically motivated refusal to serve the state as morally suspect. Ultimately they demanded absolute loyalty to the ruler and his dynasty, and looked upon one man's successive service to two ruling houses as being incompatible with morality. On the one hand, refusal to serve in ordinary times came almost to imply sedition; on the other, willingness to serve a new dynasty after serving the old implied moral degeneracy.

From various kinds of evidence, but in particular from that found in the dynastic histories, it becomes clear that the concept of Confucian-sanctioned eremitism underwent a remarkable transformation, the results of which can be seen most clearly with the emergence of Neo-Confucianism in the Sung period. Two kinds of Confucian eremitism, distinct in character and very differently evaluated, had come into being.

One of these I will call "compulsory" eremitism. It was imposed as a moral duty in the name of *chung*, or loyalty, and theoretically it was binding on all servitors of a fallen dynasty. Its usefulness to the holders of power was so great that even newly founded dynasties, which suffered from it during the first years of their rule, nonetheless promoted and praised it. They even honored those who practiced it against them, and have been known to censure those who did not.[6] The roots of this kind of eremitism do not go deeply into the thought of Confucius and Mencius, where in fact its ideological foundations are at least implicitly denied, but stems from Hsün-tzu and the Legalists. And it did not assume its later significance until Neo-Confucian thought promoted a new concept of loyalty consonant with its exaltation of the ruler and the state.

The second I shall call "voluntary" eremitism. It has valid roots in the thought of early Confucianism. However, by Sung and Yüan times it was slightly stressed if at all, and where mentioned in the official histories, greatly de-emphasized.

No work of the time known to me contains an explicit statement of the two aspects of eremitism, the one compulsory and approved of, and the other voluntary and of doubtful worth. Only the *Hsin Yüan Shih*, a product of the early twentieth century, views the eremitism of the Yüan period with this division in mind, albeit without reference to its philosophical and historical implications.[7] Yet both the division and its implications are clearly reflected in the writings of the men of the time, especially those who practiced some form of eremitism, as we shall see in the following pages.

Refusal to serve on moral grounds is clearly an expression of protest against impossible conditions of service, and more or less directly a protest against the ruler and his government. Eremitism so motivated is essentially voluntary, for although a person may feel morally compelled to refuse to serve, the problem of recognizing the evil conditions is his individual problem; his decision is a matter of his own conscience and is made on his own initiative, commonly in the teeth of personal and social pressures. A decision to withdraw usually led to hardship, and sometimes, when it was irritating to a jealous tyrant, to danger. To most of the recluse's contemporaries, even to his own family, it might well appear foolish, impractical, eccentric. Nemoto notes that honor and praise were accorded such hermits, because their eremitism was vaguely felt to be an expression of the otherwise unarticulated feelings of protest and of resistance that authoritarianism engendered in society. This to a certain extent must have been true, and personal satisfaction was an additional compensation. But to most recluses, these compensations must have appeared less than adequate for the sacrifice of the official career, the career their society valued above all others.

On the one hand, Confucian ethics put the highest possible premium on the maintenance of ethical standards; on the other, they demanded that a man serve society, not only for social but also for family reasons. A man should achieve prominence for the sake of the family name and fame, to win respect and honor (in some instances, posthumous ranks and titles) for his ancestors, and for the material benefit of his living parents and family members. To many persons these noble-sounding reasons may have carried less weight than baser motives, such as the lust for power and wealth, but that is inconsequential. The important thing is that such Confucian principles existed, and strengthened the demands on men to serve. In this conflict of values, with Confucian principles seemingly supporting either decision, the factors favoring office-holding were real, positive, practical, and immediate. Those favoring withdrawal were abstract, negative, difficult to maintain and to defend. Thus a kind of open choice remained. It is for this reason that I call this kind of eremitism "voluntary" and Nemoto refers to it as "subjectively determined."[8]

Evidence of the Neo-Confucian impatience with dissent can be traced in historiography, and particularly in the historical writings of

Ou-yang Hsiu, who did more to form the intellectual and ethical standards of the Sung period than any other figure of his time. Ou-yang used history as Confucius had used it in editing the *Spring and Autumn Annals*, to promote morality by praising the good and blaming the unworthy. The influence of his historiography on the writing of history in the Yüan and Ming periods (particularly the official dynastic histories) was enormous.

In his *Wu-tai Shih Chi* ("Historian's Record of the Five Dynasties"), Ou-yang departs from several precedents of historiography, among them the precedent of including a chapter devoted to biographies of recluses. He confines himself to commenting on certain aspects of eremitism of which he approved, thereby avoiding any all-inclusive approval of the concept of withdrawal, and particularly of the eremitism of protest. He mentions noble scholars who withdrew from public service in the chaotic and degenerate times of the Five Dynasties, to be sure, but he discusses them in his introduction to the chapter of biographies of persons of "singular conduct" ("I-hsing Lieh-chuan," ch. 34)—his version of the "Tu-hsing" ("unique conduct") or "Cho-hsing" ("extraordinary conduct") chapters of earlier historiography whose subjects were men of heroic virtue, and characteristically martyrs, often in the public service. The implication is that voluntary eremitism is commendable only when it becomes extraordinary, and that even at its most commendable it is merely one kind of extraordinary devotion to moral principles. Ou-yang's recluses, moreover, are by no means typical of the Confucian literati patterns. Two are Taoist adepts, one is a military man who sacrificed his life in blind loyalty to an unworthy ruler, and one is presented as an extraordinary example of filial piety. Only one is a Confucian scholar-official who refused to continue to serve under humiliating conditions.

The pattern is fairly clear. Ou-yang wished to devalue the behavior of the recluse. In his mind it was possible to justify voluntary eremitism only as one of the varieties of extraordinary conduct, and even then as something possible only in the most degenerate of ages. By merging it with extreme acts of devotion to other specific moral principles, such as filial piety, he sought to gloss over its political significance. By grouping true recluses with Taoist adepts, he sought to dim the luster of eremitism for the Confucian literati. His introduction to *chüan* 34 reads in part as follows:

Alas! The Five Dynasties period reached the extreme limits of chaos. It was a period like that referred to in the [*I-ching, Wen-yen*] *chuan*, where it states: "Heaven and Earth are closed; the worthy man withdraws." It was an age when servitors murdered their rulers, sons killed their fathers, and scholar-officials of high rank and position placidly accepted their emolument and took their places at court, unabashed and with no appearance of integrity or shame. All were thus!

I have always said that, since antiquity, loyal servitors and righteous scholars have appeared in large numbers in times of disorder, yet I am surprised that, in that age, those who merit mention are so few. It cannot be that there really were no such persons. Even when we grant that warfare had arisen and schools had been destroyed, so that propriety and righteousness were in decline and the people's practices had degenerated accordingly, yet never in history has there been a time when in all the world there were no worthy men. I mean that there must have been upright and uncompromising scholars who resented their world and kept themselves far distant from it, and thereby became lost to our view. Since antiquity there always have been able and worthy men who have cherished their noble principles within and not made them visible without, living in poverty in lowly lanes or hiding themselves in the wilds. Even such a man as Yen Hui would not have become known if he had not met Confucius. How much more likely it is that such a man should remain unknown in an age of decline and disorder, when the *tao* of the superior man was on the wane. Therefore I maintain that there must have been able and upright persons who simply sank out of sight, disappearing so completely that we can know nothing of them. When we seek for them in the records and annals, we find that the written records of that age of chaos and collapse are scanty and incomplete, and such persons are not recoverable. Thus I have have been able to find only four or five such persons . . .

Here the "loyal servitor" and the "righteous scholar" are discussed together. To be sure, "worthy men who withdraw into seclusion" are praised, and unworthy men who serve in office, condoning if not committing crimes of regicide and parricide, are scorned. But the outlines of the concept of voluntary Confucian eremitism are somewhat blurred by subsuming it under the more general rubric of "singular conduct"; and the scope of its application has been greatly narrowed to times that merit total condemnation.

The decision to withdraw, as praised by Ou-yang Hsiu, is less a personal one, less a matter of individual choice; it is one that objective conditions make necessary, without reference to a man's private ethical standards. Significantly, the recluse is warned that probable obscurity will be his only reward for withdrawing from the world. In all ways the value of the independent act of protest is deemphasized, and its clear definition is obscured.

Nonetheless, Ou-yang preserved a certain indestructible basis for withdrawal to which the voluntary recluse of the Yüan dynasty could still appeal. He could not proclaim himself a righteous recluse without taking a stand openly inimical to the authority of the state and the person of the ruler, but he was fairly safe if he limited his protest to veiled sentiment and indirect expression. In the Yüan dynasty the recluse was actually safer than in the following two dynasties, because of the wall that separated the Chinese people from the alien court, and the lack of close communication and real concern from the one side of that wall to the other. People could say with impunity in the Yüan period things that it would have cost them their lives merely to hint at under Ming T'ai-tsu. But even so, after the passage of seven centuries, the rediscovery of the true feelings of a recluse of the time is no simple, straightforward matter.

With this background in mind, we shall now consider a representative recluse of the Yüan period, Liu Yin.

LIU YIN AND EREMITISM

Liu Yin (1249–93) was one of the most eminent scholars and teachers of the age of Kubilai Khan. His biography in the *Yüan Shih*[9] tells us that he was a native of Jung-ch'eng in Pao-ting prefecture, in what would be modern Hopei, and that his forebears for generations had been scholars. His father, Liu Shu, is described as a scholarly, unambitious man who refused an appointment to a magistracy in a nearby prefecture on the excuse of illness. According to the *Yüan Shih*:

> At the age of forty, he still had no son. He sighed: "If Heaven indeed causes me to have no son, so be it. But should I have a son, I would surely make him a scholar." On the evening when Yin was born, Shu had a dream in which a divine being came riding a horse and bearing a child to his house, saying to him: "Rear him well!" When Shu awoke, Yin was born.

Such circumstances surrounding the birth of talented persons are common enough, as are the descriptions of Liu Yin's youthful precosity. Perhaps we cannot take too literally the statement that at the age of two or three

> . . . he could recognize characters, and each day could memorize passages of a hundred or a thousand characters. He need pass his eyes over something but once to memorize it. At the age of five he could write poetry and at six prose. Whenever he set his pen to paper he amazed people by what he produced. By the time he reached the age of twenty his genius had fully flowered.

Liu Yin, beyond doubt, was a brilliant young scholar of whom great things were expected. His father was a student of the Neo-Confucian theories of human nature, and Liu Yin also studied near his own home under Yen Mi-chien (ca. 1204–ca. 1281), a southern scholar who had been brought to the North during the conquest of the South. Liu Yin is said to have been impatient with mere lexical and philological studies of the exegetical works, wanting to know the "true essence of the Sages' teachings." The *Sung-yüan Hsüeh-an*, both in the biography of Liu Yin and in that of Yao Shu, makes it clear that Liu felt he had really encountered the new Sung learning only when he went to Mount Su-men in Honan to study under Yao Shu.[10] This is what his biography in the *Yüan Shih* is referring to when it states:

Subsequently, when he encountered the writings of Chou Tun-i, Ch'eng I, Chang Tsai, Shao Yung, Chu Hsi, and Lü Tsu-ch'ien, he was able to expound their subtleties on first reading. "Ah!" he exclaimed, "I always said that this must exist!" Commenting on the best points of each, he said: "Shao is the most comprehensive, Chou the most intensive, and Ch'eng the most correct. Master Chu achieved the limit in comprehensiveness, exhausted intensiveness, and made it all concrete with correctness." His insight and profound perception were customarily of this order.

Struck with admiration for Chu-ko Liang's (A.D. 181–234) phrase "Quiescence wherewith to cultivate the self," he adopted the name Chinghsiu or "Quiescent Cultivation" for his studio. This well suits the description of his personality given in his biography:

By nature Liu Yin was not gregarious; he did not enter lightly into association with other people. Although his family was very poor, he would accept nothing if it did not accord with his principles. He lived at home and taught there, maintaining rigid observance of the teacher's role. Students who came to him were taught in accordance with their native abilities, and all showed progress. High officials in great number passed through Pao-ting and hearing of Liu Yin's fame, often went to call on him. Yin usually hid himself and would not come forth to meet them. People who did not know him took this for arrogance . . .

Liu Yin had no son and heir. He died at the early age of 45 *sui* in the summer of 1293, probably at home and of some illness.

These scanty biographical data include very little that contributes to our understanding of Liu Yin as a recluse. For this we must turn to his own writings. A preface by the late sixteenth century writer Shao Pao to a reprinting of Liu's works[11] states that in Liu's essay " 'Hsi Sheng' chieh" ("An Explanation of 'Aspiring to Become a Sage' "), written when he was only eighteen, "his purpose in life is already more or less apparent." A partial translation of it follows:

It was the year *ting-mao* [1267], at the end of the . . . month. The autumn scene was as if freshly bathed. The Milky Way was bright and sparkling white. Heaven was high and the air clear. All life was at rest. At that time I, Liu Yin of I-ch'uan, was sitting in my central court. I had a goblet of wine, but on drinking it, I found it tasteless. I had a lute, but when I strummed it, no music came forth. I had a book, from the hand of Master Chou Tun-i. Called the *I-t'ung*, it is subtle of meaning and difficult to grasp. Looking aloft seeking its meaning, I found it as lofty as the blue Heavens. Taking it up again to pursue its ideas, I found it as deep as the Yellow Springs.

So I took it up and read it under the stars and moon, until I came to the sentence: "The scholar aspires to become a Worthy, the Worthy aspires to become a Sage, the Sage aspires to become Heaven." This I could not comprehend, and I said with a sigh: "What vacuous words! How vast and all-enfolding is Heaven, that lofty intelligence, that divine wisdom. Who can aspire to that? Does this not deceive us who belong to later ages? How vacuous are these words!" Then I hummed a poem to the pure wind, and enjoyed the bright moonlight. I grasped at Existence, and drank of the Great Harmony. I chanted the words of the song "T'ai Ku Ts'ang Lang" ["How Vast and Empty the Primordial Beginnings"]. I raised my head to Heaven and whistled; I sighed as I sang: "How pure is the Great Void, wherein life dwells! How brilliant is the Great Source, wherein the power of creation is lodged! The Emperor Fu-hsi is remote; whom shall I acknowledge my sovereign? The age of Confucius is far away; whom shall I take as my guide and companion?" So I hummed and chanted unceasingly. I sat and dozed, and only after a long time again arose, when suddenly my courtyard was overwhelmed with an auspicious air; I seemed to hear the sound of feet on the steps, and when I looked about, saw three old men. . . . [In his dream Liu converses with the three old men, who identify themselves metaphorically as the forces governing the universe. They discuss philosophical concepts, and one of the three asks Liu why he doubted the validity of the sentence of Chou's *I-t'ung*, claiming it as his own words. This dialogue follows; Liu speaks:] I replied to him, asking, "Can Sagehood then be aspired to?" He answered, "It can." "Is there some important prerequisite for attaining it?" He replied, "There is." I asked him what this was, and he replied, "The important thing is singleness." "What is singleness?" He said, "It is the absence of desire." When I asked who can be without desire, he replied, "All the people in the world can be without desire." Then I asked if all the people in the world could not become Sages, and he replied. "They can." "In that case, this student's confusion of mind is great indeed, and I do not understand you."

The master said: "Sit down. I shall discuss it with you. You have heard that in all of Heaven and Earth, there is but one Principle [*li*] and nothing else, and through interactions it dispersed to become all things. In the end, it again comes together, again becoming one principle. Heaven and Earth are man, man is Heaven and Earth. Sages and Worthies are I, I am the Sages and Worthies. That of *li* which is present in man is perfect and penetrable. That of *li* which material things receive is imperfect and nonpenetrable. Being imperfect and nonpenetrable, there is no way by which it can be transformed. But in the case of man, the perfect and the all-penetrable can indeed be penetrated. Then what can it not achieve?

"The Sage aspires to be as Heaven. When he succeeds, he becomes one with Heaven; when he does not succeed, he is a Great Sage. The Worthy aspires to be a Sage. Surpassing that, he becomes one with Heaven; not achieving it, he is a Great Worthy. The Scholar aspires to become a Worthy. Surpassing that, he becomes a Sage; not achieving it, he still does not fail to become a man of renown. This is what makes a Sage a Sage, and what makes a Worthy a Worthy. You have been given a nature midway between Heaven and Earth, and are endowed with a physical nature that is blemish-free and submissive to the Five Constants. Your nature is the same substance of which the Sage is made; the teachings you study are the same as that which constitute the Sage's achievement. You are the same as the Sages; the Sages are the same as you. You would challenge this, at the same time thinking my words vacuous. Are you vacuous? Or is your teacher vacuous? If you pursue self-cultivation to achieve quiescence, exert yourself to achieve tranquillity, satisfy the design of your bodily organization, and fulfill your nature, from the level of mere thought you will proceed to that of divine wisdom. Being enlightened, you will possess sincerity. Do you aspire to be a Sage, or do the Sages aspire to be you? You would cast this truth aside, thinking I have cheated you! Do you cheat your teacher? Or does your teacher cheat you?" . . . [At this, Liu confesses his stupidity and his stubborn foolishness, and humbly thanks the divine visitor for his instruction. As the three take leave of him, they pat his shoulder and say encouragingly:] "Apply yourself diligently. There will come a day when we shall hear of a man of purity in the world; and that man will be you."[12]

Dominant in this interesting essay is the idea, stressed by Mencius, that anyone who works hard enough at perfecting his basically good nature can become a Sage or a Worthy. More immediately, Liu takes his language and concepts from Chou Tun-i's (1017–73) *I-t'ung* (also known as the *T'ung-shu*), or "Explanatory Text on the *Book of Changes*."[13] Liu's presentation of these concepts is somewhat naïve and impressionistic, evidence of his youth and also perhaps of the primitive state of philosophic and scholarly studies in the Mongol-ruled North China of that time. Of greatest interest to us, however, is the three sages' encouraging prediction that Liu will become known as a man of purity (*ch'ing-ts'ai*), and that he applies to himself here this term that Confucius reserved for two praiseworthy recluses: "It may be said of Yü-chung and Li-i that while they hid themselves in their seclusion, they gave a license to their words; *but in their persons they succeeded in preserving their purity, and in their retirement they acted according to the exigency of the times*."[14]

At this age Liu did not regard purity and the official career as necessarily incompatible. In fact, many of his poems show that his devotion to purity complemented his natural desire to seek fame as a scholar and a writer and to win high position in recognition of his undoubted talents. An example is an undated poem called "Overcome with Thoughts on an Autumn Evening,"[15] the second half of which reads:

> In this life, the years of youth
> Are so fleeting. How sad it is!
> Beside the humble scholar's window, when one is old—
> How petty that life; what good comes of it?
> Learn swordsmanship, and win with it a princedom!
> With martial valor face every enemy.
> If man's ambition is to serve men,
> What use has this devotion to book and sword?
> My mind is bright and clear,
> It holds within it ways to rule the world in peace.

> If someday I encounter recognition and opportunity,
> And on all sides worthy routes open,
> I shall mount to the highest power and rank,
> Soaring aloft, borne up by strong wings.[16]
> I shall bring all the universe to order,
> Thereby establishing my name for a thousand years.

Many of these sentiments are rather conventional clichés, but the message is clear and forceful. The sword and the book, representing ability in war and peace, symbolized the ambitious young Confucian scholar's equipment and aspirations. But Liu has a mind of a higher order, enough so that sword and book are no longer needed. He feels he can "conquer the world" without sword and book, and speaks of his great ambition. He implies, however, that the times are not auspicious, and says that he must wait for "worthy routes" to open to him.

His attitude toward eremitism is set forth rather explicitly in his brief essay "An Explanation of the Sui-ch'u ["Following the Original"] Pavilion":[17]

The original mind of the superior man is to do good, and not to do evil; it is to be a superior man, and not to be a petty man. This is all there is to the matter. If a person acts in a way that is good, and does what the superior man does, then his original mind has been followed [i.e., fulfilled]. For *tao* is everlasting and omnipresent.

Hence if one wants to do what is good and be a superior man, there is no time or place in which one cannot do so. Hence there is no time and no place in which our original natures cannot be followed.

Suppose that one were to say: "My original mind-nature is to go forth and devote myself to the affairs of the world. If the times do not permit this to me, then throughout my life I shall not succeed in following my original mind-nature." That would be to say that *tao* is all on the side of coming forth to serve, and that withdrawal is in no sense ethically permissible.

Suppose that one were to say: "My original mind-nature demands that I withdraw and follow my own interests. If the times do not give me freedom for this, then throughout my life I shall not succeed in following my original mind-nature." That would be to say that *tao* is all on the side of withdrawal, and that there is nothing to be said for the life of active service.

Is *tao* in truth like that?

The *chan-shih*,[18] Mr. Chang Tzu-yu, is a man whose mind I know most intimately. He is a man who takes delight in doing what is good, and whose only fear is that he will not act as a superior man should. Recently he has built a pavilion to which he has given the name "Following the Original." His inclination is to enjoy ease and to pursue his own interests. Yet the gentlemen who have composed poems and essays about his pavilion have all stressed that since he is a man of whom great things can be expected, and since he is greatly endowed with talent and learning, he should devote himself to assisting the state and succoring humanity.

Both are wrong. His ideal principles lead him to leisurely pursuit of his interests, yet the times demand assistance and succor. Both are things of which we can approve. Yet, of his original nature, we cannot say that it has predetermined him to either of these before it can be said to have been followed. If his nature is thus—and nothing is beyond the scope of man's nature—then it is because he has sequestered himself in a sheltered corner. For *tao* is by nature omnipresent, and when it is forcibly confined to one small area, the harmful consequences can be great. If Chang Tzu-yu will think about my words, he will eventually understand my meaning.

Written in the year *jen-ch'en* of the reign period *chih-yüan* (1292), by Liu Yin.

Liu's friend Chang not only refuses to serve, but evidently refuses to take a broad interest in life and current problems as well. He has returned to his villa and built his Sui-ch'u pavilion to proclaim to the world that it is in keeping with his original nature to withdraw. Liu writes this essay not to urge him to come forth and serve, but to correct his thinking. Chang's attitude smacks of Taoism; Liu provides a Confucian corrective. He says, in essence, what Confucius meant when he stated that there was nothing for which he is predetermined and nothing against which he is predetermined. Liu wrote this in 1292, shortly before his death, and after repeatedly refusing calls to office. Clearly, then, Liu himself does not regard withdrawal as intrinsically superior to active service. There is another reason.

The same attitude toward office-holding is presented, though from a slightly different angle, in a very brief essay called "An Explanation of the Tao-kuei ["Tao-noble"] Hall." The circumstances are similar: a friend has named a hall in his home and has asked Liu for an essay explaining the name. The name comes from a poem by Shao Yung (1011–77), an outstanding Neo-Confucian of the Northern Sung who never held any office, who lived an idyllic if austerely simple life, and who was a fine poet. Liu evidently admired Shao Yung and felt close in spirit to him; his works contain frequent references to Shao's writings. In this brief essay he is as concerned about representing Shao's idea correctly as he is about gratifying his friend. He writes:

> In Shao K'ang-chieh's poetry we find:
> "Though lacking office, he is of himself lofty;
> But how could one lack *tao*, and be of himself noble!"

This is not intended to relate *tao* to office, but rather is to say that the presence of *tao* is not to be decided in terms of whether or not one holds office.

If one were to understand *tao* and office as correlative, then the meaning of the two lines would be shallow and narrow, forced and strained. Not only would this interpretation display lack of knowledge of what it is that makes *tao* the *tao*, it also would display envy for superficial externals, and would be too full of errors for me to name them all. Mr. Li of Ho-chien has taken words from Shao's poetry as a name for his study, calling it Tao-kuei and has asked me to write an explanation of it, hence this.[19]

Tao here, as in the last essay quoted, means ethical principles. There are two ideas here: first, that there is no necessary correlation between the ethical evaluation of a man and the kind of a career he follows; second, that a man who lacks ethical principles is not a laudable person regardless of his career and status.

Office-holding, then, can be a good thing, but it is not the greatest good thing in the world, and it confers no glory on a man with moral deficiencies. Liu was not of course admitting moral deficiencies in himself. On the contrary, as he saw it, the chief threat to ethical principles in his time lay precisely in office-holding; hence his consistent refusal to hold office. This was undoubtedly his reasoning when he chided his contemporary, Hsü Heng, for his alacrity in accepting appointment to office.[20] When Hsü replied that unless one were eager to serve the state one could not serve the *tao*, Liu remarked that to serve the state was to fail to show proper respect for the *tao*.

Liu could have held any kind of office he might have wanted. He was offered very high and honorable positions in the Confucian Academy and the Chi-hsien Yüan (roughly equivalent to the Han-lin), and educational posts. His letter to the government official who recommended him for office the last time, in 1291, is included in his biography in the *Yüan Shih* presumably as being a work representative of his character. It reads, in part:

I have since my early youth been engaged in study, and thus have acquired some knowledge of the discourses of great persons and superior men. Though I may have learned nothing else, I can say that at least I have a very clear and thorough conception of what is meant by the moral principle of "the duties that should be observed between ruler and minister."[21] Nor need the general meaning of this be discussed; let me rather talk only in terms of its daily application in actual affairs. For by whose power do all of us of the people have the opportunity to live in peace and plenty, and thus to multiply and prosper in happiness? This is all bestowed by our ruler. And accordingly all of us who live must give either of our strength or our knowledge and abilities, but in any event each must contribute something in order to discharge his responsibility. The truth of this principle is obvious: from the most ancient times it has been unvaryingly so. This is what Chuang Chou meant when he said that "There is no escaping [the duties that should be observed between sovereign and minister] anywhere in the whole wide world."[22] I have lived forty-three years, and have not yet contributed the least bit of my strength toward repaying the nation's beneficence to me in nurturing and sustaining me. Moreover, the imperial grace has repeatedly favored me with appointments to office. Could I dare to secrete myself and not come forth to serve, to court a reputation for lofty nobility as a form of self-indulgence, thereby repudiating my nation's gracious favor in recognizing me, and still have received the most excellent and righteous teaching of the Sage? On the contrary, from my early youth onward, in my mind I have never for even one day dared to be in any way aloof and superior, eccentric or deviant from the usual course. All my friends, if they know me at all, know that this is the true state of my mind. However, it may be that rumors exist about me which fail to represent the truth of the case. Seeing only what my actions might seem to indicate, some have labeled me a proud and lofty recluse. However, you, sir, know that I have never so considered myself. Please permit me to explain the circumstances of my repeated refusals to serve item by item . . . [There follows a detailed résumé of his illnesses, the illness and death of his mother, and the like.] I am in truth a most remote and humble servitor. My case is different from that of the many gentlemen who hold office, for their coming to accept office and retirement from it seems to present no difficult problems for them. I am always dependent on your excellency's assistance to me.[23]

This letter was addressed to an unnamed chief minister who had been responsible for recommending Liu's appointment. It was not a simple matter to decline such an appointment; the government of Kubilai Khan had been known to bring persons forcibly to the capital, and it might not accept mere disinclination to serve without satisfactory reasons. Liu's closing sentence is an appeal for assistance in prevailing upon the court to accept his refusal. The court did not subject Liu to further pressure to serve, and the Emperor Kubilai Khan on hearing of the matter is said to have remarked: "In antiquity there were the so-called 'servitors who could not be summoned.' They must have been of the same type as this person!"

The remark about servitors who cannot be summoned, of course, is a reference to Mencius. Liu was forced to counter rumors that he was arrogant and critical of the government; his illness at the time was probably real, but it was not the real reason for his refusal. The real reason was known to Kubilai Khan, for in using Mencius' phrase he must have been conscious of the context in which Mencius used it. The passage reads:

Mencius said: ". . . The philosopher Tseng-tzu said, 'The wealth of Ch'in and Ch'u cannot be equaled. Let their rulers have their wealth—I have my benevolence. Let them have their nobility—I have my righteousness. Wherein should I be dissatisfied as inferior to them?' Now shall we say that these sentiments are not right? Seeing that the philosopher Tseng-tzu said them, there is in them, I apprehend, a real principle. In the Empire there are three things universally acknowledged to be honorable. Nobility [i.e., noble or royal rank] is one of them; age is one of them; virtue is one of them. At the court, nobility holds the first place of the three; in villages, age holds the first place; and for helping one's generation and presiding over the people, the other two are not equal to virtue. How can one who possesses only one of these presume to despise one who possesses the other two? Therefore a prince who is to accomplish great deeds will certainly have *ministers whom he cannot summon.* When he wishes to consult with them, he goes to them. The prince who does not honor the virtuous, and delight in their ways of doing, to this extent, is not worth having to do with."[24]

Mencius here establishes the ideal of the proud and independent scholar, the man of ability and virtue, who sets his own standards for service and who need not consider himself in any way inferior to the ruler himself. It is to the credit of Kubilai Khan's intelligence that he labeled Liu Yin correctly, and to the credit of his magnanimity that he let the matter rest with an amused remark, which incidentally contained a gracious compliment to Liu.

It should be pointed out that Liu's refusal to serve did not spring from any sense of loyalty to another dynasty. Liu was born under Yüan rule. Moreover, he evidently felt no sense of attachment to the Sung as a dynasty, to judge from his poems, which include a *fu* "On the Crossing of the Yangtze" celebrating the progress of the Mongol forces against the collapsing Southern Sung in 1275.[25] Much less was he attached to the Chin dynasty, which fell in 1234, fifteen years before his birth.[26] On the other hand, that he strongly endorsed the virtue of absolute loyalty to one dynasty is clear from his poem ridiculing Feng Tao, who served four dynasties in succession in the Five Dynasties period. Ou-yang Hsiu's history of the period, in discussing Feng, served to make him a symbol of the unrighteous servitor wanting in every virtue, but particularly in the virtue of loyalty.[27] Liu concurred completely with this judgment; his four short lines on Feng are even more devastating than Ou-yang's long and vehement discourse.[28] Elsewhere, too, Liu shows himself to be completely in harmony with the Neo-Confucian concept of loyalty, notably in his admiration for the recluse T'ao Yüan-ming (also known as T'ao Ch'ien, A.D. 372–427), whose eremitism Liu considered to have been motivated by loyalty to the Eastern Chin dynasty (317–419).[29]

LIU YIN AND TAOISM

We have seen that Liu Yin was devoted to the principle of loyalty and all of the Neo-Confucian connotations of the word and that he felt no sense of attachment to any dynasty other than the Yüan. Accordingly, we must look further for a clear expression of his reasons for refusing to serve the Yüan government.

It should be clear by now that Liu felt himself to be completely within the Confucian fold, and that Taoism, with its self-centered lack of concern for the world of affairs, could not have appreciably influenced his decision to withdraw. To be sure, there was, and there continued to be, a natural tendency to associate eremitism with Taoism; and later writers, seeing Taoist terms used in Liu's poetry, have accused him of promoting Taoist concepts.[30] But if any doubt remains, it is easily dispelled by Liu's specific and emphatic statements of his attitude toward Taoism.

Liu was not bigoted toward Taoism, but he was convinced that it was unreasonable, in some ways fundamentally unethical, and in many ways inferior to the Confucian teachings. In a long essay outlining what a man should study and why it merited study, Liu mentions the Taoists first under the "various schools of philosophy":

After studying history, one can go on to read the various schools of philosophy. *Lao-tzu, Chuang-tzu, Lieh-tzu,* and the *Yin-fu Ching*[31]—these four works are all of one kind. Although they are classified as Taoist writings, within them are contained some things which are quite in accord with principle. One does well to take from them merely those things which accord with principle, and ignore their [misleading] metaphors . . .[32]

Perhaps Liu's attitude toward Taoism is best seen in his essay on a painting of Chuang-tzu dreaming that he was a butterfly, portions of which follow:

Chuang Chou's theories are a development from those of the Diplomatists.[33] They represent the thought of persons whose ambitions have been frustrated by the conditions of their age, and who seek only safety in a world of chaos. Nonetheless his genius was great, and his concepts are very broad. There are persons who cannot be self-sustaining. They see how vast the world is, and how great the span of time from the past to the present. They observe how comprehensive and how abundant are the achievements of the Sages and Worthies, and how tiny and insignificant they themselves are, how they are as if adrift among all the innumerable and motley things of this world for but a brief moment of time. Thus they say "right" and "wrong," "permissible" and "not permissible," are things which should be left beyond our concern, while they concern themselves with matters of gain and loss, long life or short. They do not admit the relevance of righteousness to their problems. They fall back on adopting the manners and attitudes of the unlettered common people, seeking to achieve by this means a kind of temporary security, but they do not achieve it. It is all vague fancy and specious ramblings. They take some real object or event and transfer it to the realm of fantasy, and having achieved a simile, they enlarge on it in the most unrestrained and unwarranted fashion. Blindly they proclaim themselves to be beyond the present realities of Heaven and earth and all creation. Seen in this light, even though they themselves speak of fantasy, they do not perhaps see wherein the fantasy really lies. It is a fantasy which they do not recognize as fantasy.

Hence they can scarcely apprehend what I mean when I speak of "equalizing"; they can hardly be expected to fathom what I mean when I speak of "no end that cannot be reached." What I refer to when I speak of "equalizing," when I speak of "no end that cannot be reached," are things which are subject to *tao* [i.e., ethical principle], and therefore one can lead the most active of public lives without increase of it, and one can live in the extremity of withdrawal without loss of it. It accommodates itself to times and situations, it fits its form to the reality about it. Where does one go that there is not equalization? Where would one go that one cannot? This is what I mean by "equalizing" and "the possible." For [in philosophy] it is necessary to follow step by step and to exhaust the limits of reason; only in that way can one talk about a thing.

But Chuang Chou does not proceed in that fashion. He starts by recounting some tale in the realm of fantasy, and insists that somewhere in the dark and vague confusion of it all there lies what he calls *tao*. What careless person with no patience for details is not delighted by such simplicity, and anxious to adopt it? And as for persons who find themselves rebuked by the strict principles of morality and propriety, or whose ambitions have been frustrated by the conditions of their time, how many of them feel benefited by such theories and drawn to them! Of course it is unnecessary to mention those who felt this way among the *Cheng-shih* and *Hsi-ning* factions.[84] But even among men known in the world as leading Confucians there are frequently encountered those who, on suffering setbacks, fall back on such ideas, seeking solace and diversion. In short, it can only be said that none of them know the meaning of righteousness . . .[85]

Liu's argument here is entirely directed against the central ideas of the chapter "Ch'i-wu lun" in *Chuang-tzu*, which closes with the anecdote illustrated in the painting on which he wrote this essay. Chuang-tzu, awaking after dreaming he was a butterfly, asks: "Am I Chuang Chou who dreamed I was a butterfly, or am I really a butterfly dreaming I am Chuang Chou?" This chapter sums up the Taoist concept of the relativity of truth and falsehood, right and wrong, and all the other distinctions which Confucianism meticulously maintained. To Chuang-tzu, such distinctions are essentially inconsequential. Liu states in the beginning of his essay that he simply does not know what Chuang-tzu meant by the butterfly metaphor. If Chuang-tzu chooses to speculate that there are no distinctions or restrictions in the realm of fantasy, he has the right to do so, but fantasy after all is not reality. Real equalization and power can come only through recognizing the omnipresence of an *ethical Tao*.

Throughout this essay we see Taoism rejected on several grounds. First, it is irrational; it relies on "dark and vague confusion." Second, it ignores the fundamental ethical questions. The repudiation of true and false, of right and wrong, is self-deception that has evil social consequences. Selfish concern solely with one's own immediate good is both evil and impractical to Liu. Taoists fall back on primitive ways, rejecting civilization, but the security they seek is not to be had in that way. Liu's faith is in a Confucian concept of security to be gained through the application of human intelligence in ordering society and maintaining standards of morality.

Third, and of most interest here, Taoists in Liu's mind are weak defeatists; they are frustrated persons seeking easy solutions. Taoism is to them a respectable-sounding cover for their inability to meet the problems of life, to maintain their integrity and to do what society expects of them. This aspect of Taoism he rejects most positively. He rejects it for himself, and he warns others to avoid confusion which may result from careless use of terms that are capable of a Taoist interpretation. Note in this connection his "Explanation of 'The Studio of Stupidity'":

Scholars and gentlemen in recent ages have often selected words meaning ignorance and stupidity and lack of refinement—things in themselves not at all laudable—as their studio names. Such persons are not necessarily really like that, nor are they intentionally making a mere gesture of humility. There is, to be sure, some reason in it; their intent can be of two kinds.

It may be that they are distressed by the great departure from ethical standards as evidenced in the lack of integrity and the low public morality. In this case their intent is to cling to fundamental values as a kind of self-corrective. Thus they adopt such names with the feeling that it is necessary to do so, and their intent is as if to say: "Rather than err in that direction, I would prefer to err in this one." Having this kind of attitude, they are guilty of no moral fault.

Or it may be that some are expressing the ideas of Lao-tzu and Chuang-tzu, in which case it is quite a different matter. They feel that the whole world, past and present, must inevitably revert to such a state [of ignorance and lack of refinement] in order to approach the *Tao* with no expenditure of effort. They retain all their resources in order to keep themselves whole. They adopt such names as a matter of preference, and not because they feel compelled to do so. Their purpose is to benefit themselves, and nothing more.

Should the former theory be generally practiced, it would cause everybody to uphold the basic values, and would not be without benefit to the world at large. But if the latter should come to be widely accepted, then all the people in the world would take to crude rusticity and would flee from the world; how far its harmful effects would spread! Alas! Even in so small a matter the subtleties of intent and method and the distinction between righteousness and selfishness can be so great as this! One cannot be careless in such things . . .[36]

In another essay written on a similar theme and with a similar purpose in mind, Liu again states this idea very forcefully. He grants that Lao-tzu's concept of the *Tao* has certain admissible features, but condemns its practical manifestations as self-centered individualism, as incompatible with ethics, and as potentially disastrous to the nation and the people. This is in an essay explaining the name of "The Studio of Withdrawal." The use of such a Taoist-sounding name is permissible, Liu feels, if it is used in the self-corrective sense, but not if it is used in the Taoist sense. "I am delighted," he says of his friend, "about Chung-li's withdrawal, but at the same time I want him to be most careful about his own reasons for having chosen to withdraw."[37]

To sum up, Liu Yin evidently was very clear-minded about Taoist thought and its implications. That is not to say that he was conscious of Neo-Confucian borrowings from Taoism, i.e., that he would have explained them as such, or that he wished to rout them from the canon. But he was very conscious of a gulf between his own Confucian orthodoxy and what he and like-minded Confucians called Taoist heterodoxy. He was particularly sensitive to the fact that withdrawal seemed to imply the acceptance of Taoist principles and emphatically denied the implication. Thus we must look beyond Taoism for the explanation of Liu's withdrawal.

LIU YIN AS A VOICE OF PROTEST

The real reason for Liu's eremitism is by now clear. "To serve under such conditions would be to show lack of respect for *tao*." Times were hard. Liu's teacher Yao Shu withdrew to a life of seclusion and teaching at Mount Su-men in protest against the corruption of government and the sense of defilement he felt on participating in it. Liu's fellow scholar at Su-men, Hsü Heng, whose sense of responsibility led him repeatedly to serve in high positions at court, nonetheless was frequently overcome with despair, and frequently resigned out of a sense of frustration and protest. Throughout the Yüan period it became increasingly difficult for men of integrity to remain in office. Liu had no less desire than others to achieve fame and honor, but he had a clearer perception of the extent of the compromise that office-holding would demand of him. Moreover, having early fixed for himself an ideal of purity, he was more than usually sensitive in ethical matters, with the result that his personal bent reinforced his objective conclusions. Only one decision was possible. He stubbornly refused to serve, devoted himself to teaching others the same moral standards by which he lived (most of his students refused appointments), and by implication rebuked those who did serve, especially those who served dishonorably. In addition, as we have seen, he occasionally gave vent to his feelings in his writings, above all in his poetry.

If one reads Liu's poetry with care, one finds in it much that can be taken as the expression of his resentment. There is nothing explicit or dramatic; nothing of the ringing accents of a Tom Paine or the incisive satire of a Voltaire. No precedent for either existed in the China of Liu Yin, and nothing in Liu Yin's life is without precedent. Yet the protest is there. Its influence can only be estimated, but it must have been significant.

Consider the following stanza:

When one is born in a degenerate and disorderly age
And there is no one worthy of being called a ruler, who would want
    to serve?
If one must drift and float like a cross-current in a measureless ocean,
Is it because one would have chosen to do so?

This stanza is quoted out of context. Does it really mean what it seems here to mean, or is there perhaps some less subversive explanation? As it happens, the above stanza is the first four lines in a poem of fourteen lines; the remaining lines speak of the pleasures of peaceful rural existence, and the poem ends with an expression of the people's cause for rejoicing in the good fortune of having an emperor whose might assures their peace and happiness. Moreover, the poem is one of a collection written to the rhyme patterns and poetic forms of T'ao Yüan-ming.[38] It is usually possible to construe these poems as poetic extensions of the mood of T'ao's originals, thereby making them Liu's conception of the voice of T'ao, rather than the voice of Liu himself. In their poetic ambiguity, it is also often possible to see them as philosophic reflections on theoretical rather than on actual conditions. It is precisely this poetic ambiguity that Liu relied on as a veil for his true intent, a veil that could protect him without obscuring his meaning from those readers by whom he wanted to be understood. Ch'ien Mu, the modern scholar and historian of Chinese thought, has quoted the above stanza as an expression of Liu Yin's true feelings about his own environment and his own fate;[39] I wholly concur with this interpretation. However, in bald translation and out of context, the poem's essential ambiguity is lost, and no problem of interpretation seems to exist. The degree to which translation represents interpretation and eliminates the ambiguity which is a consciously-employed element in the original must be kept in mind.

If I am right about Liu Yin's intentions, it is in this collection of poems written on the model of T'ao Yüan-ming's poetry that we find the most profound expression of Liu's protest. Liu's seven poems written matching the form and rhyme of T'ao's "Ho Yung P'in Shih ("In Praise of Poor Scholars") are of interest here, because Liu has adopted T'ao's subject as well as his form. The fourth is as follows:

Sticks and stones can bear being spit upon,
Minister Lou Shih-te is not alone in that.
And if spitting were as rain,
Not even the most intemperate man would react to it.
To be without preconceptions is the "upright way."
To suppress one's natural feelings is in truth the way of Chuang Chou.
"What is beyond my own self is of no concern to me."

> "What does it matter to me if one stands by my side with breast and
>   arms bare!"
> Po I looked upon the whole world
> And wished that all men might stand with him.
> I say that it was Liu-hsia Hui who was narrow-minded;
> Let the reader himself find my reasons for saying so.

The allusions in this poem are to a historical figure of the T'ang dynasty, and to two officials-turned-recluse who are discussed and compared both in the *Analects* and in *Mencius*. Lou Shih-te (630–99) of the T'ang was a man whose forbearance was so great that he did not approve of a man's so much as flickering an eyelid if someone spat in his face. When someone asked him, "Do you mean you would just wipe it off and nothing more?" he replied that he would not even bother to wipe it off; he would be so unmoved that he would let the spittle dry by itself.[40] This, says Liu, is unnatural in humans, but comes naturally to sticks and stones, if there is any virtue in men's adopting the standards of sticks and stones! Liu extends this idea, and applies it to his comparison of the two figures of antiquity. To be without preconceptions is bad; it implies being without ethical standards, since ethical standards must be fixed in advance so that they can be adhered to under all conditions. The "upright way" is the way in which Confucius described the conduct of Liu-hsia Hui, and it is not unqualified praise; it implies a kind of straightforward integrity without any sensitivity to higher moral principles. Lou Shih-te and Liu-hsia Hui, Liu feels, were alike in unnaturally suppressing their feelings, in insensitivity to feelings of defilement. This is Taoistic (line 6); the Taoist has his whole world within himself, hence cannot be defiled or revolted by his surroundings or by what people do to him (line 7).

The poet's real intent is seen in his comparison of Liu-hsia Hui and Po I in the last lines. Line 8 quotes Liu-hsia Hui in the anecdote told in Mencius, from which the poem takes its text. Mencius says of Po I that he

"would not serve a prince whom he did not approve, nor associate with a friend whom he did not esteem . . . He thought it necessary, if he happened to be standing with a villager whose cap was not rightly adjusted, to leave him with a high air, as if he were going to be defiled."

Liu-hsia Hui, on the other hand,

. . . was not ashamed to serve an impure prince, nor did he think it low to be an inferior officer. When advanced to employment, he did not conceal his virtue, but made it a point to carry out his principles. When neglected and left without office, he did not murmur. When straitened by poverty, he did not grieve. Accordingly, he had a saying, "You are you, and I am I. Although you stand by my side with breast and arms bare, or with your body naked, how can you defile me?" Therefore self-possessed, he companied with men indifferently, at the same time not losing himself. When he wished to leave, if pressed to remain in office, he would remain. He would remain in office, when pressed to do so, not counting it required by his purity to go away. Mencius said, "Po I was narrow-minded, and Liu-hsia Hui was wanting in self-respect. The superior man will not follow either narrow-mindedness, or the want of self-respect."[41]

Liu wished to present Po I in a better light. He sees Po I as identifying himself with the will of the people, and hence insistent on standards of ethics which benefited all of the people. Thus he would not serve, and thus no doubt Liu saw himself, for to serve a ruler who commanded no respect, or to serve side by side with persons of whom one could not approve, would require that one unnaturally curb one's spontaneous reactions to them, and this to Liu would have been Taoistic.

We can well imagine that Liu saw Hsü Heng as the very type of a contemporary Liu-hsia Hui. Hsü responded eagerly to calls to serve at the Yüan court under what to Liu must have seemed most defiling conditions, yet undeniably served with uprightness. It is pertinent to recall that Liu criticized Hsü as being superficially Confucian, but Taoistic at heart. Confucius gives qualified praise to Liu-hsia Hui for being upright (*Analects*, XVIII/2), but elsewhere criticizes him for having "surrendered his will and submitted to taint his person" (*Analects*, XCIII/8/3). This is Liu Yin's criticism of Liu-hsia Hui, and by implication he extends it to all men who serve, however honestly and uprightly, in evil times like his own. Mencius intended to point out a middle course of action, between Po I's extreme insistence on personal purity and Liu-hsia Hui's utter lack of self-respect. Liu Yin feels that the Mencian judgment fails to do justice to Po I, and he makes a strong defense of his ideal of purity.

In another poem in the same collection, Liu says:

Those who uphold *tao* (i.e., ethics) frequently are led to follow a solitary course.
This practice has existed since Chou and Ch'in times.
The solitary course of the recluse moreover merits approval;
What kind of person would weakly submit to defiling himself?

.   .   .   .

In a degenerate final age,
Is it not meaningless to possess Confucian rank and office?[42]

And in another:

Is not this life of man a life of toil?
Through all antiquity it has been so declared.
Who can be idle and unproductive?

Rise early, and only at dusk return and sleep.
To live such a life is not what I most honor,
But neither is having to till my own land what I sigh about.
However, if I can but attain my desire,
How gladly I'll surrender the glories and comforts of high station.

There follow allusions to worthy recluses of history who suffered want
and discomfort in maintaining their high principles, and Liu ends by
invoking their decisions as a justification for his own.[43] Praise of the
recluses of antiquity is frequently seen in Liu's poetry; in particular, he
refers several times to the "four white-haired ones" (*ssu hao*), and wrote
two poems in praise of them. They were four old men who, having fled
the terrors of Ch'in, ignored repeated calls to come forth and serve the
founder of the Han dynasty. At last Han Kao-tsu's chief minister Chang
Liang (d. 192 B.C.) used a ruse to get them to appear at court in the
retinue of the heir-apparent. The emperor, astonished at their appearance, reproached them: "I have sought you for many years, and you have
always fled from me and concealed yourselves. How is it that you are
now in the service of my son?" They replied: "You, sire, despise scholars
and are given to reviling them. It is contrary to our principles to submit
to insult, and we accordingly fled and concealed ourselves. But we have
heard that the crown prince is benevolent and filial, respectful and reverent, and venerates scholars. All the world would strain to die in the
crown prince's service, hence we too have come forth."[44] Liu's praise of
these four inevitably calls to mind this famous conversation, recorded in
the *Shih Chi*. The implications are obvious.

Many other passages from Liu's poetry could be cited to the same
effect, but it is perhaps best to spare the reader further translations,
which (in my hands, at least) do far less than justice to the originals.

It remains to consider the extent to which Liu Yin spoke for the
literati of his time, and the extent of his influence. The more one reads
in the writings of the period, the clearer it becomes that Liu in his
eremitism represents a large and growing segment of the Yüan literati.
Read the biographies of recluses, of persons in residence away from
their native places, and of local worthies and literary figures in the local
gazetteers of the Yüan, or in the sections devoted to the Yüan in the
much more numerous extant gazetteers of the Ming. Particularly in the
less troubled areas of the South, where such persons tended to gather,
you will find a disproportionately large number of persons who are presented as recluses, or as former officials who had been forced to retire
from the official career, and were living in seclusion or eking out a living
by teaching. Or look through Ku Ssu-li's comprehensive anthology, the
Yüan Shih Hsüan, and note the large number of pessimistic poems writ-

ten by persons to whose names is added the comment "lived as a recluse, and would not serve in office."

Many other sources could be cited. All that can be learned of the period reinforces the belief that it was one in which ambitious Confucian scholars found official appointments both hard to come by and unattractive on ethical grounds. Both those who like Liu refused to serve, and those who tried to serve only to become disillusioned, suffered feelings of resentment and frustration. Their Confucian training led them to hold the ruler and his government responsible for their own and the country's sorry plight. Most, like Liu, expressed some resentment, but generally accepted the situation as a matter of fate. Few indeed were spurred to rebellion. This passivity, this inclination to blame fate and wait for a better day, is yet another problem, and one whose explanation goes beyond the scope of this study. But can it not be said that this low potential for defiant political action was in part the result of the Neo-Confucian stress on loyalty, and its acceptance in principle of extreme authoritarianism exercised by an unapproachable and unreproachable emperor?

COMPULSORY EREMITISM

As we have seen, the Neo-Confucian concept of loyalty demanded that the loyal official of a fallen dynasty withdraw into lifelong retirement on the fall of the dynasty under which he first took service. This concept of loyalty, which one looks for in vain in the thought of Confucius and Mencius, gradually took form in the imperial period, and in fact assumed its later importance only in the Northern Sung period, when the concept of unlimited despotism was reaching its theoretical heights. Unlimited despotism demanded theoretical adjustments. The position of the ruler had to be elevated, and the gulf between ruler and servitor had to be deepened. Ssu-ma Kuang (1019–86), an influential spokesman and theoretician for this position, went so far as to repudiate the Mencian theory that the virtuous servitor was entitled to oppose the wishes of the tyrannical ruler. Mencius had said that of the three most honored things—age, noble rank, and virtue—virtue is by far the most valuable to state and society, thereby giving the virtuous servitor a kind of equality with the ruler. Ssu-ma Kuang found this wholly unacceptable.[45]

In the spurious "Classic of Loyalty" (*Chung-ching*), a work whose text and commentary are falsely attributed to Ma Jung and Cheng Hsüan, respectively (both of the Han period), there exists a most interesting expression of this new extreme in Confucian authoritarian thinking. This work is now regarded as a forgery of the period from the late T'ang to the early Sung, but was widely accepted as genuine in the Sung and later periods.[46] Similar in form and style to the *Hsiao-ching*, or "Classic of Filial Piety," it develops at length the theme that *hsiao* (filial submission) and *chung* (loyalty) are parallel virtues, different only in the area of their application and equally fundamental to all morality. However, *chung* here is not the ancient reciprocal loyalty of Confucius and Mencius, but is redefined as a one-way, utterly blind devotion to the sacrosanct ruler by all of his servitors. To be sure, the servitors of an erring ruler are required to censure and guide him in a humble and respectful manner, but they must remain obedient and loyal whether or not he heeds their censure. They must look upon death as a small matter as compared to compromise of virtue. The concept of loyalty embodied in this work became general among Neo-Confucianists of the rationalist school; hence it is not surprising to find it echoed by Chu Hsi, who wrote: "Father and son, ruler and servitor—herein lies the fixed principle of the universe. There is no escaping it anywhere in the whole wide world."[47] The second sentence is straight from the *Chuang-tzu*, where it is used to disparage what the Taoists considered to be the Confucian error of overstressing the duty of loyalty. In applying it to both *hsiao* and *chung*, Chu Hsi not only reflects the attitudes of the "Classic of Loyalty," but accepts as correct Confucianism a statement about loyalty that originated not in Confucianism, but in Taoist ridicule of Confucianism.

The unity of the Ch'eng-Chu or orthodox school of Neo-Confucianism on the subject of compulsory loyalty can be further illustrated by referring again to the case of Feng Tao (d. A.D. 954), the high official of the Five Dynasties period who served four dynasties in succession. Feng Tao by objective standards was anything but an evil man. Originally the historians dealt favorably with him, reporting factually that in his youth he had displayed unusual filial piety, that as a high official he had served ably and energetically, and that as a man he was cultivated, humane, and possessed of literary talent, albeit a trifle conceited. Ou-yang Hsiu was the first to reverse this judgment. In his vehement comments on Feng's biography in the *Wu-tai Shih-chi*, Ou-yang makes Feng the very symbol of the immoral servitor; for all his virtues, his incredible readiness to transfer his allegiance convicts him of an utter lack of integrity and of the sense of shame. Ssu-ma Kuang, in his *Tzu-chih T'ung-chien* (ch. 291), repeats Ou-yang's condemnation:

Heaven and Earth have their fixed positions; the Sage takes them as his models in determining the social norms [*li*] and establishing laws [*fa*]. Within, there is the relationship of husband and wife; without, that of ruler and servitor. The wife follows her husband, and to the end of her days will not remarry.

The servitor serves his ruler, and will die in preference to serving another. This is the great standard of human ethics. Should it be abandoned, no greater chaos could be imagined. . . . If a servitor is not loyal, even though he be possessed of abundant ability and intelligence and have an excellent record in administration, he is not to be highly valued. Why is this? It is because he lacks the most fundamental aspect of integrity. . . . Rulers rose and fell in succession; Feng Tao continued to hold wealth and high position as if nothing had happened. This is indeed the extreme example of the treacherous official. I believe that the servitor can lose his life thereby preserving his virtue complete, but cannot seek to preserve his life thereby destroying his virtue; how then can we call a man worthy who specializes only in preserving his life and fending off dangers to himself? . . . Moreover, this is not solely the crime of Feng Tao; the rulers of the time must also assume some of the responsibility.

Chu Hsi takes the same line. The *T'ung-chien Kang-mu*, while only in small part directly from Chu Hsi's pen, was produced under his supervision and can be considered as expressing his sentiments. In its comments on the death of Feng Tao (ch. 59), the criticisms originating with Ou-yang Hsiu and developed by Ssu-ma Kuang are further extended. Feng's objective virtues and abilities are again recorded (as they are throughout this period, to the credit of Chinese historiography), but they are explicitly said to have been completely negated by his one great failing, and he is once again presented as the most sinister kind of moral leper. By this time his symbolic value had come completely to overshadow the objective truth about him. Even Chu Hsi, astute critic of history that he elsewhere showed himself to be, had no thought of setting this matter straight. For him it was "straight" as Ou-yang Hsiu presented it. For him, too, the symbolic value outweighed the objective facts.

In contrast with earlier moral thinking, Neo-Confucianism laid greater stress on formalized patterns of behavior; moral principles now came to require rigid observance of strict rules. The virtues of chastity and filial piety and the observance of mourning all became increasingly rigid and severe; and the same was true of "loyalty."

For example, the concept of chastity, prior to the Sung Neo-Confucian redefinition of it, had little of the harsh and unnatural character it subsequently acquired. Relations between the sexes were relatively free in T'ang and earlier times, and the re-marriage of widows was commonplace, even in the highest levels of literati society. Subsequently, however, upper-class women were ever more rigorously confined, and the re-marriage of a widow, or even of an affianced girl who had never seen her husband-to-be, became a shameless and even a legally punishable act. And there was a similar transformation in many of the other virtues of earlier Confucianism. Filial piety came to mean the utter subservience of younger to elder. A strict and unreasoning observance of mourning became obligatory, at times to the complete extinction of its humane content. These extremes, which were witnessed and commented on by nineteenth and twentieth century Westerners in China so much that we have come to think of them as typical expressions of the spirit of Chinese civilization, are in fact late developments quite out of keeping with the entire atmosphere of earlier China.

A forced and unnatural withdrawal from life, in the name of morality, was demanded of widows. Filial submission, when extreme, intruded unnaturally into both family and public life. At least a temporary withdrawal was demanded of persons in mourning for their parents, overriding the duty of the official to the state, and disrupting unnaturally the life of the family. Thus both family and state, the twin foci of Confucian emphasis, suffered from the dehumanizing effects of Neo-Confucian morality, a morality which in fact strove to strengthen the authoritarian character of both family and state. Ultimately, this morality was detrimental to both; in a word, it was irrational.

Demanding absolute loyalty to a fallen dynasty of its servitors was equally irrational. In theory, it imposed a lifetime of uselessness on countless proven and experienced statesmen, and denied a career to many young men who had only just launched their careers under the old dynasty, men who were in no sense personally responsible for their misfortune. Of course this moral prohibition was never fully effective; some found ways to evade it, and some flouted it. But by and large it was precisely those persons who could not bring themselves to evade or flout moral prohibitions who were potentially the most valuable servants of state and society, and whose services successor dynasties were denied.

EXAMPLES AMONG SUNG LOYALISTS

The active career of the famous Sung loyalist Hsieh Fang-te[48] (d. 1289) began in the 1250's, some twenty-five years before the fall of the Sung. From the very beginning of his career he was noted for his penetrating criticism of Sung government and officials. He courageously disputed with powerful ministers, and repeatedly got into trouble. He was deprived of his official posts for several years, was demoted, rebuked, and punished. A participant in the military disaster at the time of the Mongol conquest, when Sung armies would not fight, he saw at first hand the incompetence of the Sung forces and the inevitability of the Sung collapse. Hsieh knew Sung government from the inside, saw its faults and weaknesses, and was sternly critical of it. After the fall of Hangchow in 1276 he returned to his home in Fukien, where he lived in retirement as a teacher.

The Yüan court thought such a man might be willing to serve, and offered him a number of attractive posts. He refused every one, not because he considered the Yüan government inferior to the Sung (though he doubtless did), not because he had any expectation that the Sung might rally and return to power, not primarily because of his distaste for the crude and cruel Mongol conquerors, but from his emotional devotion to the principle of loyalty itself. As far as can be seen, Hsieh was a clear-headed and practical-minded man up to the year of the disaster, 1276; his irrational behavior commenced in that year. When the Yangtze Valley bastions were falling rapidly to the Mongol forces in the winter of 1275-76, many of them without a fight, Hsieh (in disguise and wearing mourning robes) went into the newly occupied areas and wept in the market places, making a display of his grief on the passing of the dynasty as a rebuke to those who had surrendered. Throughout the remainder of his life—until he finally starved himself on being taken to the Mongol capital in the hope he could be made to accept office—he displayed unwavering loyalty to the fallen Sung, refusing to use the new Yüan calendar, referring to the former emperor as if he were still reigning, reproaching Chinese who had accepted the Mongols as their legitimate rulers, and doing his best to incite resistance to the new dynasty (albeit without any real program or organization). Moreover, for this irrational behavior he was so generally praised that even the Mongol court was obliged to recognize a kind of moral correctness in his defiance. As for the Chinese literati class, Mongol-servers and Mongol-haters alike made a hero of him.

Very similar was the case of Hsieh's most famous fellow Sung loyalist, Wen T'ien-hsiang. Wen was a brilliant scholar turned military leader, a heroic and upright man, and an entirely sympathetic character. The comments appended to his biography in the *Sung Shih* (ch. 418) praise him above all for working tirelessly at his military effort to turn back the Mongols after the fall of Hangchow when he and everyone else could see that it was doomed to failure. A Ming writer, in a colophon to Wen's collected works, praises him on the same grounds:

At the fall of the Sung those righteous and unyielding servitors who died in the service of their dynasty were very numerous. But of all of those who died maintaining their moral principles, there were none whose heroic qualities equaled Wen's. . . . The Sung dynasty, by the *Te-yu reign* [1276], was ended; the Mandate of Heaven had left it. It was a situation that no one scholar could save. Nor was Wen unaware of this . . .[49]

Wen T'ien-hsiang earned the praise of eight hundred years of Chinese writers, not for showing stubborn faith in victory which would have to be earned against great odds, but for remaining loyal to the principle of loyalty when he knew his cause was hopeless, even lacking the sanction of Heaven.

Perhaps the extreme of such irrational behavior in a national hero is seen in the case of a third Sung loyalist, Cheng Ssu-hsiao. Cheng was in his twenties at the time of the fall of Hangchow. He had passed the first examinations, but had had no career as an official in the Sung government. He nonetheless spent the rest of his life expressing his implacable hatred of the Mongols and his intense devotion to the fallen Sung. In his writings, which may have circulated in manuscript during the Yüan period (they were not published until they were rediscovered late in the Ming),[50] he calls the Mongols inhuman beasts and uncivilized trespassers on China's soil. But his devotion to the Sung cause was far less a matter of racial antagonism than of attachment to what he regarded as the tenets of Confucian morality, among them the oneness of the virtues of filial subservience, of the faithfulness of wives to one husband, and of loyalty to one dynasty. He wrote:

I have heard my father say: "To live or to die is a small matter, but a moral lapse is a great matter. The servitor of one ruler will die in preference to serving another." Moreover, he told me: "The family teaching that I received from my father and grandfather, and that sustained the family, has consisted purely of filial piety and loyalty. I pass it on to you. Do not forget your father's words!" Often I have sat through the night, alone and forlorn, overcome with grief and choking with sobs, turning over and over in my mind these thoughts of country and of family. Ruler and teacher alike have instructed and nourished me with these same principles. My father and mother have taught me and reared me the same way. Yet today I am forced to be otherwise. How can I bear it![51]

His idealization of Sung rule, a constant theme of his writings, is seen in his poem "Thinking about the Men of the Past Generation":

In the past, in the age of the former emperor,
Who faced the sun for forty years,[52]
The bright light of learning and refinement flooded the world,
And superior and heroic men stood before their ruler.
But once the barbarian soldiers invaded,
With sudden shock, Han rule was toppled.
To this day the proper ways of men are in chaos.
To lonely mountain valleys have fled all the worthies of the former age.
In that age of peace, the ways of the superior man flourished,
Men of talent appeared who were models of human achievement.

With open hearts they looked on the sun and moon,
From their mouths flowed words of lofty and noble import.
The auspicious atmosphere was almost that of the Three Dynasties of
    antiquity,
Literary standards were taken directly from the Six Classics.
Today the likes of it are not to be seen.
As I look about there is darkness on all sides.[53]

Cheng himself was faced with the necessity of reconciling conflicting demands of the Confucian morality which he so venerated. In his "Song Written on Falling into Captivity," written in the winter of 1275–76 after the fall of Soochow, where Cheng was living, he first describes the treachery by which Soochow was surrendered and his chagrin at seeing others associating with the conquerors, and then reflects:

As I remember my father's teachings
Day and night I shed tears of blood, and am nearly mad with grief.
There is my old mother, ill with her old illness,
Dependent on me to keep her alive a bit longer.
I want to die, but cannot die and be a filial son.
I must live, but cannot live and be a loyal servitor.[54]

Because of his duty to his mother, Cheng did not commit suicide on coming under Mongol rule, but he spent the remainder of his life regretting his decision, hating the new dynasty, praising fellow loyalists like Wen T'ien-hsiang, and heaping scorn on Chinese who served the Mongols. The bitter intensity of his feelings can only be appreciated by reading his poetry and essays.

Why did the Mongols tolerate such a trouble-maker? There were several reasons. First, the Mongols were relatively insensitive to the attitudes of the Chinese. Second, Cheng was not a threat, not the leader of any organized rebellious movement. Third, his actions were an extreme expression of a moral principle that all Chinese acknowledged. And finally, his agitation was more or less clandestine—noticeable, perhaps, but in the circumstances not obtrusive enough to disturb an unconcerned government.

Cheng Ssu-hsiao, to be sure, is an extreme example. But a definite element of the irrational is obvious in the actions of all the Sung Loyalists, and they were a large group. They refused to make any formal acknowledgment of the fact of Mongol rule, and some even went so far as to avoid standing, sitting, or lying facing the north, the position assumed by the servitor acknowledging his prince. They avoided the use of the Yüan reign-period titles. They developed a secret language of complex allusions to the Sung, and gathered together to write poetry in this language.[55] There could be no question of rebellion: they were a large group, but they were not an army, and no army could be rallied to a cause so plainly lost. Their political influence was greatest as a restraining force on others who would have been willing to serve the Mongol government but for the fear of being labeled shameless and immoral traitors. Some who braved this scorn suffered greatly from it.

THE CASE OF CHAO MENG-FU

Chao Meng-fu (1254–1322) was one who suffered. His defection to the Mongols was a double enormity, for not only had he held office under the Sung, but he was a lineal descendant of one of the Sung emperors, a member of the imperial clan, and an official under the Sung. When his move became known, many of his friends refused to speak to him, and some members of his own clan refused to recognize him as a clan member and wrote strong criticism of him. Remarkably enough, however, Chao's ability was so impressive that he largely succeeded in rising above this criticism, and he became in many ways the great figure of his age.[56] His biographers, unable to deny his accomplishments, can only observe sadly that it was Chao's unfortunate fate to have been a man of one dynasty whose great talents could only be employed in the succeeding dynasty.

Chao did not rush to seek office under the Mongols. In his twenties at the time of the conquest, he retired to intense study and self-cultivation for some years, and only accepted office ten years later in 1286. He immediately attracted the attention of the aging Kubilai Khan, and held positions of high trust under Kubilai's successors. He made many constructive contributions to government. He was a competent scholar, but is best known as a poet, artist, and calligrapher (he has been called the last of the "eight princes of calligraphy"). He was a man of facile genius, akin to Li Po of the T'ang and Su Shih of the Sung, to whom he was compared by the Mongol Emperor Jen-tsung (1312–20). An imaginative and romantic figure and a forceful personality, he gives the Yüan period much of its color and interest.

Nonetheless, later writers found it hard to forgive his "treason." He himself was uneasy about his position, as we can see from his poem on a painting depicting T'ao Yüan-ming's return to his recluse home after resigning his official position (T'ao, it will be recalled, was thought of as a man forced into the recluse life by loyalty to a fallen dynasty):

> Each person lives his life in this world according to his own times;
> Whether to come forth and serve, or to retire in withdrawal, is not a
>   fortuitous decision.
> Consider T'ao Yüan-ming's poem "On Returning";

The excellence of his course is not easily explained.
Subsequent ages have much admired him,
Closely imitating him, sometimes well and sometimes crudely.
And in the end, themselves unable to withdraw,
They remain, irresolute, in this dusty world.
But this man T'ao truly possessed *tao*.
His name hangs aloft like the sun and moon.
He followed his lofty way, noble as the green pines.
He was like a chrysanthemum, touched by the frost and still bright.
How readily he gave up his official position.
And bore poverty, dozing contentedly by his north window.
Rolling up this painting, I sigh repeatedly;
How long since the world has known the likes of this Worthy!

T'ao was a difficult subject for Chao to write about. He acknowledges the correctness of Tao's motives and admires his noble character as seen in his withdrawal and his uncomplaining acceptance of the humble life which that imposed on him. Yet he suggests that this is a matter in which each person must make his own decision, according to his own times.

This his contemporaries and writers of subsequent ages would not grant. A Ming writer, discussing the poem, wrote: "From this poem we can see that Tzu-ang [Chao] had the greatest admiration for T'ao Yüan-ming. Yet he himself served the barbarian court, inviting the derision of later ages. In truth he was one who knew how to speak but whose own actions did not measure up to his words."[57] Thus Chao Meng-fu, who could not be brushed aside so easily as a man like Feng Tao, has remained not an evil villain in Chinese history, but a guilty man, a great man upon whom there is an ineradicable blemish that later ages must not be permitted to overlook.

It has been noted above that the concept of loyalty was so generally accepted, and potentially so useful to a new dynasty, that the new ruler had to seek a course between two possible dangers. By promoting the concept too zealously, he might lose the service of valuable officials and conceivably strengthen the potential forces of rebellion; by condemning it, he might antagonize equally valuable officials and weaken a useful buttress of his own authoritarian power. The Yüan government, and particularly the Emperor Kubilai Khan, who reigned at the time of the conquest of Sung, played this game skillfully. On several occasions he publicly rebuked prominent persons who had too readily abandoned the Sung, but he did not do so until the conquest was assured. He praised certain hold-out Sung loyalists, particularly after the immediate period of the conquest had passed. He and his successors knew the value of the concept of loyalty, and if they failed to promote it as well as the Sung, it was only because of the general inefficiency of their administration.

The forces making for involuntary eremitism in the name of loyalty never again functioned so effectively as they had on the fall of the Sung, except, perhaps, on the fall of the Ming in 1644, when an intensely felt, emotional kind of loyalty to the fallen dynasty served to create a serious problem for its successor. The Manchus were neither as confident in their military superiority, as willing to try and rule without integrating the Chinese into their administration, nor as insensitive to the feelings of their Chinese subjects, as were the Mongols. Hence the disaffection of a large portion of the leading class in the society of the newly conquered country created a much greater problem in 1644 and the generation thereafter than it had in 1276.

The comparison is instructive. The Sung was a revered dynasty; the Ming, although fallen on evil days, still offered the ambitious scholar-official the possibility of a satisfying career in its service. Both were succeeded by fierce and barbaric aliens. It seems almost certain in the circumstances that in both instances the literati's resentment and fear of the conquerors reinforced their righteous feelings of loyalty to the old dynasty, and to the old world which threatened to pass with it.

The fall of the Mongol dynasty bears out the hypothesis that the workings of the loyalty concept varied with varying circumstances. In 1368 an unloved government, which for nearly a century had frustrated and alienated the literati class, and which for a generation had failed to maintain order and command obedience, at last was expelled and replaced. The new government had exceptional credentials: not only had it brought peace and order to the realm, but it was a Chinese government and it had just succeeded in expelling the first alien conquest dynasty ever to rule all of China. Rules or no rules, it could scarcely be considered shocking for a person to transfer his loyalty from the Mongols to the Ming. In any event, the fall of the Yüan was accompanied by no such wave of loyalty as had attended the fall of the Sung. Chao I, the Ch'ing period historian, in an item entitled "Many Literary Figures of the Early Ming Refused to Hold Office,"[58] discusses a long list of men who refused to come forth and serve because of the uncertainties and dangers of service under the vicious and unpredictable Ming tyrant, but notes that only two of those on his list refused out of loyalty to the old dynasty. Certainly no figures comparable to Wen T'ien-hsiang, Hsieh Fang-te, and Cheng Ssu-hsiao appeared, to be made national heroes for their spirit of resistance to the successor dynasty.

Other names can be found to add to the list of Yüan loyalists (many others, of course, had resisted the rebel movements prior to 1368, when they still had the character of local or regional bandit operations); they were respected for their principles, but attained no prominence either in their own time or later.[59]

Disloyalty to the Yüan, however damnable in theory, was in practice at worst a minor offense. Sung Lien (1310–81), Liu Chi (1311–75), and many others among the leading officials of the court of the Ming founder all had held office under the Yüan, yet suffered no scorn from their contemporaries and but little and mild criticism from historians. The *Ming Shu* argues their case as follows:[60]

. . . Moreover, the rightness of Ming T'ai-tsu's assumption of rule over the nation surpasses that of any other ruler's since antiquity. That all of the servitors of the Yüan followed and served him was in accord with Heaven and in response to mankind. Neither did they thereby violate the righteous principle set forth in the *Spring and Autumn Annals*. They are not to be put in the category of P'ei Chü, who transferred his loyalty to the T'ang, or Chao Meng-fu, who was a traitor to the Sung. How can they be criticized?

Nevertheless, when the news of victory over the Yüan was received, Ming T'ai-tsu forbade all servitors who had previously served the Yüan to submit congratulatory memorials. Moreover, he had memorial shrines constructed to honor the memory of Yü Ch'üeh and Li Fu,[61] bestowed a posthumous title on Fu Shou,[62] each year despatched officials to conduct sacrifices in his honor, and appointed Fu Shou's son Ch'en-kung, who was but a minor prefectural military official, to the high post of *T'ai-p'u-ch'ing*. And when [Fu Ch'en-kung was] later implicated in the Hu Wei-yung faction treason case, [the emperor] specially excused his guilt. When T'ai-tsu heard the shuffling sound of the old servitor's shoes, he rebuked him by reminding him of Wen T'ien-hsiang, and he went away and died.[63] His practice of instructing [his court in the virtue of loyalty] was indeed profound and far-reaching.

Therefore, I am taking as my model Ou-yang Hsiu's "History of the Five Dynasties" in setting up here the category of Miscellaneous Biographies, selecting those who had previously served the Yüan specially for inclusion here, arranging them in sequence according to the rank of their official position held under the Yüan. . . .

Here we see Ming T'ai-tsu following the same practices as Sung T'ai-tsu and Yüan Shih-tsu before him. Of greater interest, however, is the historian's attitude: he is not very critical of officials disloyal to the Yüan cause, and argues that they are not to be compared with the likes of Chao Meng-fu, who was, in his eyes, really guilty of treason. He is prepared to honor T'ai-tsu's technical distinction to the extent of relegating all officials who had served the Yüan to a special category of biographies, but he makes it clear that he regards them as being morally without fault. A similar defense of the same figures can be found wherever the problem of their breach of loyalty is discussed.

It seems evident that the concept of loyalty itself underwent no change between 1276 and 1368, and that its importance remained undiminished. Rather, other elements, which the Chinese historian would describe as the "rightness" or the "justice" of the rise to power of a new dynasty, but which we might call the natural consideration given to other factors, operated to affect its workings. Even the most rigidly upheld standards of Neo-Confucian morality were not absolute; even its most central tenets could not command assent when they conflicted with the overwhelming sentiment of the times.

6   A Tradition's End

Joseph R. Levenson

THE SUGGESTIVENESS OF
VESTIGES: CONFUCIANISM
AND MONARCHY AT THE LAST

Hommes de l'avenir souvenez-vous de moi
Je vivais à l'époque où finissaient les rois . . .
                              Apollinaire, *Alcools*

THE HUNG-HSIEN EMPEROR AS A COMIC TYPE

In 1914 Yüan Shih-k'ai, trying to be the strong man not by
muscle alone, but by mystique, contrived a bit of ceremonial. He still
called his state the *min-kuo,* the Republic, and he still called himself a
president, not an emperor, but he meant to be a president with a quite
remarkable staying power, and he looked for some awe to reinforce his
political arrangements. Accordingly, he embellished his presidential
election law (which was frankly designed as a guarantee that Yüan
would succeed himself and succeed himself) with a ritualistic rig-
marole to add a touch of suspense—three names, the president's private
and secret choices, put in a gold box kept in a stone house in the presidential palace enclosure, the president with the one key to the gold box,
the president and two of his appointees with the three keys to the stone
house, the dramatic disclosure to a safe electoral college of the three
names three days before the election, the thoughtful addition of the
president's name to his roster of tame candidates, etc.[1] It was a cunning
plan.

However, he never used it. His real aim was to invoke a sanctity,
not to create one, and the comical complexity of his "republican" devices—his mummery for presidents and his plethora of schemes for
treadmill rounds of provisional parliaments and provisional constitutions
—were better made to mock the Republic than to make it seem legitimate. Total discredit of the Republic was the preamble; then, the body
of the tale might be a new dynastic history.

Yet, when Yüan finally inaugurated the Hung-hsien reign on January 1, 1916, the parody of a republic yielded to only a parody of the
empire. And this was perhaps inevitable, the result not of some failure
of dignity in Yüan himself, but of a condition of modern Chinese history
in the large: the vitiation of old conventions, an invincible staleness

which not all the evident futilities of the republican alternative could dispel. Goethe's Faust had seen his emperor's court as a world of masks for emptiness, and court and carnival as one.[2] And the question that needs to be asked about Yüan's imperial masquerade, about all the vestigial monarchism in the Chinese Republican era, is the question that Mann's Faust-as-the-artist put to himself: "Why does almost everything seem to me like its own parody? Why must I think that almost all, no, all the methods and conventions of art today are good for parody only?"[3]

The imperial office in 1916 could not be taken seriously because the Republic, while a failure, was not a mistake. Its failure lay in its social meaninglessness; the revolution seemed to have had no substance. But the Republic, however insubstantial, did have meaning as a symbol: by its mere existence after thousands of years of monarchy, it offered license to new thought, the solvent of Chinese pieties. When Yüan Shih-k'ai, by trying to make himself stick as emperor, asserted in effect that no political revolution had occurred in 1911 and 1912—only at most a traditional rebellion intervening between dynastic periods—his monarchism, in defiance of this interpretation, was fatally compromised by the revolution which *had* occurred, the intellectual revolution. When the Republic, devoid of social achievement though it may have been, shameless political fake though it may have seemed, nevertheless stood for something—iconoclasm—its rival, monarchy, had to stand for something (and something, in the circumstances, equivocal), traditionalism.

In Yüan's gentle demurrers at the offer of the throne in early December, 1915 ("Our sage-master emerged with destiny . . . the people submit to your virtue, the whole country of one mind," pronounced his Council of State, humbly petitioning that he "graciously indulge the feelings of the people"),[4] and in his discreet extraction of a formal blessing from the Ch'ing ex-emperor ("In accordance with the command of the Ch'ing emperor: with regard to changing the form of state and raising the president to imperial honors, the Ch'ing royal house deeply approves"),[5] he conformed to the pattern of *shan-jang*, cession and seemly initial rejection, which derived from the *Shu-ching* lore of Yao and Shun. When modesty ceased to forbid him, Yüan accepted the offer ("For the empire's rises and falls the very commoner has responsibility; shall my love of country lag behind others?")[6] in Chinese phrases of classical cadence and in part, at least, in direct echo of the seventeenth century's Ku Yen-wu.[7] The republican bureaucracy's *ch'eng* ("submit" [a document]) gave way to the grand old *tsou* ("memorialize"); the ancient monarchical *ch'en*, for "official" (the Ch'ing mark of Confucian distinction between the Chinese official and the Manchu *nu*, or "slave"), supplanted the current *kuan* in the bureaucratic nomenclature.[8] And on the last day of 1915, when the next year was proclaimed as Hung-hsien I, Yüan gave to the *Yen-sheng kung*, the "Holy Duke," K'ung Ling-i, direct descendant of Confucius, the brevet rank of *chün-wang*, a feudal title of Han devising and long in imperial use.[9] In these and a hundred other ways old legitimacies were solicited for Yüan Shih-k'ai. But when the Emperor Yüan was traditionalistic, as he had to be, he ran through an emperor's lines, he followed the ancient stage directions, but he was not (nor could anyone else then be) an authentic, traditional emperor.

LATE CH'ING: CONFUCIANISM REDEFINED AS THE COUNTER TO MODERN THOUGHT

Actually, monarchy was lost when the Ch'ing were forced to improvise after the Boxer debacle of 1900, and the untraditionally traditionalistic monarchy was preordained for Yüan Shih-k'ai by his Ch'ing dynastic predecessors. For the Ch'ing were in a hopeless dilemma in their last decade. Modernization was necessary if they were to avoid being held responsible for continued Chinese disasters. But their sponsorship of modernization, the abandonment of traditional Chinese ways, would end their only claim, as an ethnically foreign people, to legitimacy as Chinese rulers, a legitimacy which prenationalistic culturalism had once accorded them, but which Chinese nationalism, necessarily spreading as Chinese culture changed, found inadmissible. In short, in their last decade the Ch'ing had a discouraging choice between going down in a traditional way, out of simple cyclical weakness in a world of outer pressures and inner strains, or going down as moderns, aspiring, at least, to strengthen China and strengthen their hold and thereby extend their title to the traditional mandate, but running afoul of the nationalism which modern, foreign strengthening methods entailed. Quite naturally, no clear-cut choice was made. Given a situation in which the best of both worlds in another light was the worst, they tried to be modern enough to defend their traditional status and traditional enough to take the curse off modernism.

And so one finds the anomalies of a 1906 decree about the new educational system—a sharp departure from the examination system, which was centuries old and of incalculable significance for the traditional social order and cultural values. The new education was to have military spirit, industrial spirit, and public spirit generally among its main objectives—so much for the leanings to modernism—and loyalty to the emperor and reverence for Confucius as vital bequests from the past. At the same time, as if to reinforce the latter strain, the Ch'ing decreed that sacrifices to Confucius were raised to the grade of *ta-ssu*, "great sacrifices," the highest grade of three.[10] But this Confucian zeal of the Manchus (always apparent in Ch'ing history as a means of their growing into China on a principle other than ethnic, and heightened, if anything, at the last) only intensified Confucianism to the point of its exhaustion. For Confucianism, when "worked at" for a social purpose—as something to spoil the potentialities, anti-Manchu, of implicitly nationalistic modern thought—was deprived of almost its last intellectual substance and left as mainly a symbol of resistance to revolution. And when revolution came, and the Republic, justified by Sun Yat-sen as the "latest thing" politically in a universal progressive evolution (and thus implying, if not compensating for, denial to China of her long-assumed Confucian autonomy), opened the lid on the latest things in every other sphere, people with vested interests in the old regime, or simply nostalgia, clung fiercely and particularly to Confucianism, which was, after all, an early thing itself, and a glorifier of early things.

THE REPUBLIC: CONFUCIANISM AND MONARCHISM NARROWED AND INTERWOVEN

It was an attenuated Confucianism, then, more a sentiment than a teaching, which confronted republican skepticism about the value of the past and which gravitated unerringly to any monarchical movement that seemed to have a chance. Prominent among the petitioners for monarchy in 1915 were the *K'ung she*, Confucian societies, of Chihli and Honan.[11] Yen Fu, one of Yüan Shih-k'ai's "six *chün-tzu*" (to quote a contemporary sardonic analogy between Yüan's monarchical inner circle and the "six martyrs" of 1898, whom Yüan Shih-k'ai was alleged to have sold to the Empress Dowager),[12] made a clear and characteristically untraditional statement of the new traditionalism's associations: "Chinese honor the prince and venerate the ancient; Westerners honor the people and venerate the modern."[13]

What is untraditional here is the identification of Chinese monarchism with intellectual traditionalism pure and simple. This was a change from the live imperial days, when the monarchy, or its centralizing agents, often strained against the conservatism of the bureaucratic intelligentsia; from their very beginnings the traditional Chinese bureaucratic and monarchical institutions had existed in a state of mutual and ambivalent attraction-repulsion (of which more below). What is characteristic here, in the contemporary context of Yen's untraditional assumption, is the air of conscious response to a serious foreign challenge, that of democratic thought and other intellectual novelty. The intellectually subversive revolutionary nationalists had injected the *min*, "the people," into modern political consciousness, and the *min* (or their self-styled representatives) not only had ousted the old monarchy, but had forced their way into the new monarchical thinking—indeed, had made it new.

Wu T'ing-fang (1844–1922), Sun's representative in conversations with the Ch'ing camp in late 1911, made a statement on December 20 to the effect that the new republican government would be based on *jen-min i-chih*, the people's "will."[14] On February 1, 1912, the dynasty itself ordered Yüan, its last agent, to come to terms with the revolutionary *min-chün*, "people's army": "The people's will has become clear . . ." And in the first edict of abdication, on February 12, came the sad renunciation: "By the indications of men's minds the mandate of Heaven is known."[15] Here was the contradiction of the principle of heavenly selection, to which popular control and ratification were essentially irrelevant. In the ensuing contradiction of republicanism, "the people" could not be exorcised from the monarchists' apologies. Sometimes "the people's will" was retained, in the Bonapartist sense, as in Yüan's amusingly hyper-successful plebiscite for monarchy in the fall of 1915; more often the Chinese people's "spirit," not their will, was emphasized as the guarantor of the imperial institution. The famous Goodnow memorandum along these lines inspired or released a flood of Chinese writings on *kuo-t'i* and *kuo-ts'ui* and *kuo-ch'ing*, the people's proper form of state, the national "spirit" or temperament, which implied not that this Chinese republic was puerile but that no Chinese republic was possible, that monarchism was inexpungeable from the Chinese people's spirit.

Why must the idea of "the people" as the source of political authority be seen as essentially modern in China, and therefore appropriate enough to an untraditional republic, but not to a monarchy needing to trade on authentic traditional lineage? After all, it has been a familiar enough suggestion in the last half-century or so that Western democratic theory was anticipated in ancient China, where the imperial idea (as it is alleged) demanded the people's happiness as the test of fulfillment of the will of Heaven by the Son of Heaven.[16] But such suggestions confuse the priorities in classical Chinese thought. A modern appeal to "the people" for validation denies, not derives from, the old imperial sanctions.

To say that *vox populi* is *vox dei* is not to define the latter but to displace it; the "voice of God" is metaphorized out of current acceptance, and now no more than lends emphasis through historical tone to the acknowledgment of a new supreme authority. In imperial China the *t'ien-tzu* held the *t'ien-ming* as long as he expressed the *t'ien-i*.[17] Heaven's son, mandate, and will were unequivocally the classical founts of supremacy, and the people's will, when it was worked at all by Confucian thinkers into political theory, was purely symbolic, not effective, in establishing legitimacy. Heaven's hand could not be forced.[18]

In traditional monarchical theory, that is, popular discontent did not itself invalidate an emperor's claims—nor, by the same token, did popular approbation legitimize him. Popular discontent was a *portent,* as a flood might be a portent, of the loss of the mandate; it was a sign, perhaps, of the loss of the imperial virtue. But a flood was not to be greeted with fatalistic acceptance. While an emperor should read the signs aright, he still should try to check the flood. And just so, the outbreak of a popular rebellion was no guarantee of its success or of its Confucian acceptability (far from it). It might be a portent, but it, too, should be and legitimately might be resisted. For the famous "right to rebel" was a contradiction in terms. People rebelled not because they had any legal right, but because actually existing legal arrangements left little scope to their lives. Until they succeeded, rebels had no right, and the people's will, if they claimed to express it, had to wait on Heaven's choosing.

If he had the name, the "rectified name," of Son of Heaven, the ruler had the *te* which the Ju (Confucian) school thought intrinsic to him—a *te* which was power on the outside and virtue, the *tao i hsing,* in his inner nature, a *te* which would bring no harm to the people's lives.[19] But popular satisfaction was one thing only in the classical political ideal: a sign of some higher ratification of the emperor's legitimacy. It was another thing in the modern aura of secular democracy: the legitimizer itself.

And just as vestigial monarchy derived, allegedly, from the people's will, instead of simply according with it while reflecting Heaven's, so vestigial Confucianism took the people's will as its novel justification. "If our parliamentarians really want to represent the people's will, then they cannot but establish Confucianism as the national religion," wrote a petitioner in 1917, the year after "Hung-hsien" and unpropitious for Confucian special pleaders. "Catholics oppose the idea of a state religion," he went on, "but some three million Catholics are not the people's will."[20] Mass identification with Confucianism, then, established by the evidence of history, was the ground of Confucian authority for this thinker and many others. It was the same sort of ground Yüan had sought as the basis of his dynasty.

But post-Ch'ing monarchism and Confucianism were linked more directly than by their merely invoking in common an identification with the people's will. The writer of this memorial for Confucianism (*not* a Confucian memorial), coming after Yüan's fiasco, had an embarrassed recognition of general opinion, which held Confucianism implicated in the discredited monarchical effort. It was hard to reconcile Confucianism with the symbolically modern Republic, but he did as well as he could. He admitted the charge of the Yüan affinity, dismissed it as a foible of Confucianists rather than a necessity of Confucianism, and suggested an act of oblivion. Christian churches, too, he pointed out, had launched prayers for Yüan's success. Christians, he alleged, were Yüan's loudest extollers, and took part in his government. Buddhists and Mohammedans repeatedly cheered him on. Yüan, he acknowledged, had fabricated a "people's will" for his own monarchical purposes. But the genuine people's will was with Confucianism, and Confucianism, if established as the national religion of the Republic, would be the indispensable institution for the state's consolidation.[21]

In short, quite plausibly under the circumstances, this Confucian partisan was really trying to make Confucianism independent of polity. Republics or monarchies were uncertain but Confucianism was permanent while a Chinese people lived, for it was particularly (historically) a part of the Chinese people, its very essence. "Every country has a form which is natural to it and it alone. Our country ought to establish Confucianism as the national religion . . . especially to protect the national essence."[22] When Norway split off from Sweden in 1905 (ran another expression of opinion), many changes were made in the constitution, but Lutheranism, long the state religion, remained so, as the link with the people's past. Moral: "As the physical body without the spirit must die, so must the nation without a national religion."[23] "Other countries, in some numbers, have established national religions. Is there not still more reason for us to do likewise? For Confucianism is our religion by nature."[24]

It is true that rationalistic as well as romantic apologia were still put forward, like the commendation of Confucianism above religions of the outside, Confucianism being termed a *jen-tao chiao,* a humanistic creed, and thus allegedly an advance over the *shen-tao chiao,* theologies, "superstitions," of the non-Chinese world.[25] Yet, in the context of Republican iconoclasm, such statements of rational conviction may represent romantic particularism in a special form—one which emphasized not that foreign bodies would die if grafted onto the Chinese organism (hence, for example, the hopelessness of the Republic) but that the Chinese organism might die of the intrusion, an intrusion which could indeed take place. Consequently, rational argument, depending on appeals to universal criteria, may rather derive from a feeling for the national essence than challenge it, so that a special concern for "our" religion would drive one to establish it as generally "better."

"Our religion": Chinese, that is, characteristically and exclusively

so, as long as any people could be called Chinese. This allegation of permanence—an unshakable attribute of essence, and safer as an approach to "the people's will" than any electoral soundings of what was, after all, a manipulable public—was the real trump (and the last card) of Confucianists under the Republic. And whatever their ultimate tactical wish to disengage from Yüan, it had been monarchy's card, too. The particular spirit of the Chinese people, not the universal reason of the way of Heaven, became an emperor's justification.

By this doctrine of romantic determinism, then, free choice among values of whatever historical origin, the premise of republicans' detachment from tradition, was ruled out. Chinese traditionalism became a relative, not an absolute, principle, a charge upon China, not upon man; compulsion to preserve the gifts of the Chinese past was psychological now, from a feeling of individuality threatened—not philosophical, as of old, from the mind's conviction of the general value of Chinese classic experience. Conservatism and monarchy were welded together, but when novelty was repelled on grounds of the limitations of the Chinese genius rather than on grounds of its fullness or universality, this conservatism was novelty itself, and—equally paradoxically—this monarchy, trading on the symbols of the past, was itself, no less than the Chinese Republic, a symbol of revolution.

For truly traditional, not merely traditionalistic, Chinese monarchy was ideally monarchy for the world, though centered in one intellectually self-sufficient society. Now, when republican nationalistic iconoclasts defined the world as larger than China, and Chinese society as very far from intellectually self-sufficient, monarchist traditionalists, finding it simply impossible in modern times to sustain Chinese cultural pretensions to universality (a Lutheran Norway as justification for a Confucian China!), could preserve the ideal of Chinese monarchy only as monarchy for China alone, and the ideal of intellectual self-sufficiency (i.e., renewal of Confucian dominance) only as (something new to Confucianism) "spirit-of-the-people" imperviousness to new ideas. Yüan Shih-k'ai could not be the "son of Heaven"; he could only, possibly, be king of China. And Yüan at the winter solstice, miming in the Temple of Heaven (and contemplating plowing in the spring) was a parody—and not just because he pulled up to the Temple in an armored car.

THE CONFUCIANISM-MONARCHISM COMPLEX BEFORE ITS
MIN-KUO TRANSFORMATION

Yüan ends, then, supported by a Confucianism turned inside out, a Confucianism, that is, which for the most part no longer initiated a philosopical commitment to tradition, but which itself derived from a psychological commitment to tradition: when the people's Chinese identity seemed threatened by Republican Westernization, the "Chineseness" of Confucianism, more than its own traditionalist message, made it an object of traditionalists' reverence and a pillar of the throne. Thus, as suggested already, the cement of the "national spirit" joined the new monarchism and the new Confucianism in a new sort of partnership, new in its rather simple, uncomplicated character in contrast with the devious, uncertain partnership of pre-Western days. For the classical imperial system, for which Confucianism became the philosophy *par excellence*, was founded by Ch'in (221 B.C.) on anti-Confucianist Legalist principles, and this paradox, right from the start, remained at the core of Chinese history; a bureaucratic intelligentsia, while it cherished the social stability attending imperial centralization, yet was recurrently centrifugal, hence dangerous to a dynasty, by reason of acquisitive tendencies. The ancient imperial paradox, whose existence distinguishes true Confucian monarchy from its parody, deserves to be examined.

Over the long span of imperial Chinese history, there developed a Confucian literati-type; the figure of the emperor failed to conform to it. In many of his cultural and institutional affinities, he offended literati taste. The literati were eclectic enough philosophically, of course, and for any period from the Warring States (403–221 B.C.) on, Confucian texts may be shredded into all sorts of ingredients—Taoist, Buddhist, and what-not—but Chinese history does know intellectual confrontations, not just a happy melange, and relatively pure distillations of non-Confucian ideas had tendencies to seem at least in part imperial. Nonphilosophical Taoism, for example, jarred on fundamentally rationalistic Confucianists not only in its form of popular "enthusiasm" but in its connection with the elixir lore often strongly associated with emperors. Buddhism, too, had not only popular backing (often, from late T'ang on, as an anti-gentry, i.e., anti-Confucian, symbol) but imperial patronage as well, in times when its standing was extremely low or at best equivocal among the literati.[26] What could cause more revulsion in Confucianists, with their code of ethical relationships, than the patricidal or fratricidal episodes that disfigured so many imperial family histories? Eunuchs, whom Confucianists scorned and often hated and coupled with monks as "bad elements," were characteristic members of imperial retinues. Trade, which Confucianists affected to scorn (while Buddhism gave it impetus),[27] was a matter of imperial interest—given a court society's demands for luxury, not Confucian-approved—an interest manifest in such various phenomena as the eunuch Cheng Ho's voyages (1403–33), which Confucian historians buried;[28] eunuchs' prominence, protested by officials, in trading-ship control organs;[29] and the Canton system of trade

(1759–1839), in which the superintendent, the "Hoppo," was a specifically imperial appointee and outside the regular bureaucratic chain of command.[30] And the history of aesthetics in China records the distinction, Sung and later, between the "officials' style" (*shih-ta-fu hua*) and the style of the court academy (*yüan-hua*), a distinction which may be blurred by artistic eclecticism but is nonetheless significant, for it speaks of the self-detachment of the literati critic, his sensing of a dissonance of gentry and palace tones.[31]

Now, cultural rifts like these were far from extreme, for, after all, the social roles of bureaucracy and monarchy were only clashing, not incompatible, and were complementary even as they clashed. To put it another way: at least from the reign of Han Wu-ti (140–87 B.C.), monarch and civil official had a common stake in anti-feudalism (and in this their interests were complementary), while at the same time each had leanings (and here they clashed) to just that side of feudalism which was poison to the other. The ambivalence of bureaucracy toward monarchy and of monarchy toward bureaucracy was comprehended in the ambivalence of each toward feudalism: bureaucracy had some, at least, of the dynamics of feudalism without the statics; monarchy had the reverse.[32]

The imperial state was the proper milieu for bureaucracy (emperor and official, that is, were to this extent drawn together) in the following sense: a pre-Ch'in feudal nobility exploited land withdrawn from the reach of the public power, the state, which thus became a nullity; but the instability attendant on China's fragmentation reduced the private feudal power itself, and in the post-Ch'in empire the feudal nobility was superseded by a bureaucracy, which exploited the power of an anti-feudal state. The centralized state, as the universal tax-gatherer, inhibiting instability, had a basic though ambiguous value to a power-seeking bureaucracy—it provided something rich and real that could be eaten away in the feeding of private power. And it was eaten away recurrently. The process began anew each time the imperial state was reconstituted, after such attrition had brought it toward an impossible (because self-dissolving) feudal dissolution. Bureaucracy, then, perennially suspicious of imperially-backed suspect-radical strong men, with their various ideas for checking private aggrandizement in land (the *hsien-t'ien,* or "limit-the-fields," central-government policies), was, though abortively, a "feudalizing" force.

But it was never feudal. Needing the centralized state as it did, after its fashion, the Confucian corps had very serious anti-feudal commitments. As a type, Confucian intellectuality runs counter to the feudal admiration of martial vigor. War is mainly for the young, and Confucian opposition to a chivalric code of heroes was a turn to the elders, to learning over courage, and to a system of examinations of learning as the ideal road to power and prestige, circumventing those juridical guarantees of status which feudalism accorded to birth. And the examinations stressed a *traditional* learning, not original thought, because age over youth means not only counselor over warrior but old over new— the rule of precedent, the rule of example. Such reverence for precedent may sound close to feudalism, but feudal spokesmen for the most part dwell extensively on tradition only when feudalism is coming to be obsolete and under fire.

However, this Confucian hostility to the "static" attributes of feudalism implied tension, too, with monarchy. It was a tension explainable socially by the monarch's resistance to that erosion of public power which bureaucracy furthered dynamically, in its own gesture toward feudalism; and it was explainable intellectually by monarchy's leaning to just those feudal attributes that Confucianism countered. For in a feudal system, after all, monarchy had its familiar place at the pinnacle, and, with the marked exception of the feudal propensity for draining the central power (the Confucian bureaucracy's side of feudalism), many feudal associations were Chinese-imperial as well. Dynasties were not Confucian-pacifist but military like the feudalists, always trying to keep a grip on the Confucian-suspect military organs.[33] The Confucian ideal, embodied in the examination system and the model-emperor lore, of uninherited qualification for political standing, was inapplicable to hereditary monarchy, as it was to a feudal system in the round[34]—and to the simulated feudal systems which dynasties successively created and literati continually condemned.[35]

From the monarchy's side, too, the priority of family might be deplored: the Confucian *hsiao,* filial piety, was potentially irreconcilable with *chung,* political loyalty, an imperial requirement as well as originally a feudal conception;[36] while on their side Confucianists (especially of the Sung variety), at least in their ideals, tended to moralize *chung* as they had moralized other originally feudal concepts. They accepted loyalty as an obligation, but they meant to impose their definition of loyalty upon the emperor, not simply to have a blind requirement imposed upon themselves. As the Neo-Confucianist Ch'eng Hao (1032–85) put it, the emperor must distinguish between those who are loyal and those who are disloyal.[37] This imperative distinction implies a Confucian sense of discrimination. The onus is on the emperor. Loyalty may not be defined as unquestioned obedience to his (perhaps improper) wishes. Rather, the advice or example (the same thing) of a true Confucianist expresses it, and the emperor should recognize that those who agree with such sage advice are the loyal ones.

And when it came to the rule of law (more acceptable in feudal than in Confucian political theory), Ch'in Shih Huang-ti (reigned 246–210 B.C.) was the Legalist and truly the First Emperor, the prototype, for the codes were imperial and their very existence an implied rebuke to emperors, whose virtue, thought Confucianists, was evidently not enough to make for a flawless (law-less) social order.[38] A Stoic parallel in the Greek and Roman world (the Stoics, like the Confucianists, stressed harmony rather than action) corroborates the logic of this anti-legalist deprecation of actual monarchical power. Like the Confucianists again, the Stoics were far from admitting the unqualified legitimacy of contemporary absolute monarchy. Only the Sage, they felt, is capable of absolute royal rule, and he rules by calling others to imitation of himself (see Cicero, *De Legibus* and *De Republica*). Possessing reason in himself, he can dispense with written laws; he is the living law.[39] In China, when the Sung scholar Ch'en Liang (1143–1194) professed to discern sage-king patterns not merely in classical high antiquity but in the prosaically historical Han and T'ang dynasties, Chu Hsi (1130–1200), incomparably more influential, denounced him, and with appropriate emphasis stressed *hsiu-chi*, self-cultivation—the "inner" pole of a famous Confucian dichotomy—over the "outer" pole, *chih-jen*, ruling men.[40] Morality, the inner test which non-ideal, actual monarchs do not pass, transcends the legally constituted externals.

The over-all distinction between the necessary partners, Confucian literati and monarchy, and the basic condition of the tension between them, lay in their respective attitudes toward tradition. Here Ch'in Shih Huang-ti again, at the beginning, and the *T'ien-wang* of the Tai-pings (1850–64) near the end, seem the purest representatives of anti-literati, anti-traditional, undiluted monarchy. They were too pure to survive, too unequivocally unrestricted, without that blurring of the timeless monarchical abstraction which could make them historically viable; dynasties in general had to make the adjustments these disdained with traditionalist Confucianism. But the adjustments came from practical necessity, not from the genius of the institution of Chinese monarchy itself. One who contemplates the relation of monarchy to bureaucracy from this standpoint may reverse a familiar emphasis: perhaps the real issue is not the degree to which alien dynasties proved acceptable to Chinese literati, but the degree to which native dynasties proved alien to the same. In the total complex of Chinese political society, foreign dynasties may well have been nothing peculiar, only native dynasties to a higher power; and ethnic distinction no bureaucratic-dynastic problem in itself, only an exacerbation of the endemic problem of the division of powers. A foreign conquest-people and its chiefs might well in their hearts be culturally out of touch with the ideals of the literati. But so, to some extent, would any Chinese court. What Manchu prerogatives represented to Ch'ing Confucianists, the prerogatives of eunuchs may have represented to their predecessors under the Ming. And eunuchs or no, Manchus or no, Ming and Ch'ing were dynasties that Confucianists could live with. The Taipings' anti-Manchuism—symbolic, perhaps, of a proto-nationalistic revulsion from gentry culture—was a sham as an anti-Ch'ing weapon; for the gentry-literati-Confucianists, who were ostensibly more likely than any other Chinese to respond to the anti-Manchu call (since they suffered from the unfair proportion of Manchus to Chinese in high governing circles, while nineteenth-century peasants could barely have known Manchus as such), were loyal. They felt no special ethnic revulsion from the Manchus, but simply an expected strain between monarchical and bureaucratic bodies, a strain far less traumatic than the Taiping break appeared.

By this token, the familiar statement that prenationalistic culturalism legitimized any patrons of Confucianism, whatever their ethnic background, can be stated more precisely as follows: Any dynastic establishment, whatever its ethnic background, had the same need to patronize *but also the same need to qualify* Confucianism. It was not that foreign dynasties met a minimum of expected cultural conformity; it was rather that foreign dynasties practiced no more nonconformity than the maximum expected of rulers in general and grudgingly allowed them. It is because this was the state of affairs that we find Confucianism, for its part, always needing monarchy and always assuming its existence, but always implying restraints on its innate waywardness.

For what monarch could be justified in his pride of place when Confucius, the sage, had not been king? Kingship was not despised by Confucianists, but what the world saw as the king's "position," the outer trappings (and that meant kings in history, not the ideal conception), was hardly precious when the true king in his own day was the uncrowned Confucius, a *su-wang,* a "monarch unadorned."[41] "*Su-wang*" implied a possible separation between *wang-tao,* the Confucian ideal of the hidden royal "way," and *wang-i,* the monarchy's statement of visible royal rank. It was the impulse to restrain this natural tendency of monarchy to be *visible* that gave point to some of Confucianism's most vital conceptions.

Inescapably, everywhere, splendor and spectacle attach themselves to monarchy. As the ultimate leader of society, and as one not to be scrutinized for human frailties (for in that case, he might not pass), a monarch requires acceptance as something more than man, something related to divinity; majesty is the visible reflection in society of a divine splendor.

But it is a special conception of divinity—the transcendental—which spectacle connotes. Just as it sets the monarch apart, so it speaks of a divine power that is truly "other," and truly power, the combination that spells Creator. A creator, however, is alien to Confucian thought as the literati came to profess it. However much a transcendental sentiment may be recognized in popular Chinese religion or suspected in the Classics, in a perhaps irrecoverable stratum of meaning, buried far beneath the commentaries, the literati's Confucianism — certainly by Sung, the civil bureaucracy's time of fulfillment—was committed unequivocally to immanence. Scholars have recently suggested that in the period of the Warring States, in the time and region of Confucianism's first emergence, the *Huang* of *Huang* [*t'ien shang*] *ti* (sovereign heavenly emperor) had passed over into its homonym, in *Huang-ti*, the "Yellow Emperor."[42] What had been heavenly became a supposedly historical monarch, and the first one, thereafter, in the Confucian list of the five model sage-kings. This would represent etymologically the Confucian transfer of emphasis from the celestial to the earthly-political sphere—a shift from a vision of transcendental power to one of the monarch as exemplar.

Philosophically, no Creator meant no "in the beginning," hence no progressive concept of time threatening the Confucian ideal of equilibrium and the non-"time-ridden" historical theory (more paradigmatic than process-oriented) that accorded with it. The corollary in political theory was a Confucian ideal of an emperor radiating virtue, magically reflecting harmony to society, not logically interfering with it to move it; he should be sympathetically stabilizing an eternal cosmos, which had never been once created and should never be freshly tampered with by some mock-transcendental earthly ruler, acting, creating anew.

In the *Shuo-wen*, where the *Tso-chuan* is given as *locus classicus* (*cheng i cheng min*), *cheng*, "to govern," is a cognate of *cheng*, "to adjust." The emperor's role is government, its definition "adjustment" of the people's transgressions and errors.[43] The assumption here is of an eternal pattern; *cheng* is the process of restoring conformity to it. The Sung Neo-Confucianist Ch'eng Hao, memorializing his emperor, saw the "way" of Yao and Shun as the perfecting of the five social relationships, achieving adjustment to heavenly reason.[44] This is essentially the task of a silent one, a sage in concealment (the immanent is always hidden, never spectacular). The very idea of it clashed with a real emperor's natural place as a focal point for spectacle, and with his natural penchant for wielding power to change the world, not for emanating perpetuation of a changeless pattern.

In the most completely austere of transcendentalisms, with idolatry under an absolute ban, the monarchical idea is fundamentally discouraged: if God is King, there ought to be no king to play at God (see I Samuel 8: 4–7, before the enthronement of Saul in Israel). For that is surely what kingship carries with it. To the Byzantine philosopher Themistus (fourth century A.D.), the ruler's primary attribute, the divine *philanthropia* (love of man), made the emperor God-like, with God's prerogative of mercy being the emperor's prerogative, too, marking for both transcendence over what they give the world—the legal codes of justice.[45] For dominant Christianity in the Byzantine Empire, this was the ground for submission to imperial authority; for dominant but very different Confucianism in China, this imperial link with formulated law, with its transcendental implications, was, we saw, a ground of conflict. From the standpoint of Samuel's terrible warning of what a king would really mean in exercise of power (I Samuel 8: 11–18), the Byzantine's active *philanthropia* was a myth to gloss over the true potential of monarchy. From the same standpoint, the Confucian ideal of sage-like non-activity was a myth, too: the king does not stay hidden. The difference between the myths is that the Byzantine coincided with an emperor's naturally transcendental pretensions, and strengthened his hold; while the Confucian was at odds with the character of the throne, and stood as a reproach. Byzantines conceived of imperial government as a terrestrial copy of the rule of God in Heaven.[46] Confucianists had no God in Heaven, no autonomous Voice that spoke from the outer and above; and in so far as monarchy inevitably approached that model, the Confucianists strained against it—not condemning it (in the Hebraic fashion, out of an utter transcendentalism unvitiated by the Greek idea of incarnation), but correcting it, as far as they could, toward silence.

Perhaps the nearest approach a Chinese emperor made to this quasi-Taoist non-activity[47] which Confucianists commended to the throne was in the imperial ineffectualness which often accompanied social breakdown. But in that case, one may be assured, there was no Confucian accolade. Instead, the emperor's virtue was disparaged (usually from the safe vantage point of a later dynasty), since he had evidently not fulfilled his symbolic responsibilities as holder of Heaven's mandate. Clearly, the Chinese emperor was subject to checks: material noncooperation in his own day and at least posthumous moral reproach.

I have already suggested (in discussing "the people's will"), and Wittfogel has also emphasized, that these moral reproaches, for whatever they were worth, were no testimony to "the innate democracy of Chinese political thinking."[48] But what still needs to be emphasized—and Wittfogel, preoccupied with a model of absolute despotic power, neglects to dwell on it—is that the immanentist *t'ien-ming* (mandate) doctrine really was an expression of conflict with the emperor (Byzantine Christian officials, much more than Chinese Confucianists, were a despot's faceless men), though a bureaucratic, not democratic, expression. Bureaucratic historians, in their Confucian moralism, charged up to the emperor symptoms of social decay which were actually effects of the normal functioning of the bureaucracy itself.

Confucianists had to have an emperor as a reflector of morality (in social terms: officials needed a state), but by the system of morality he capped, the emperor could be indicted to cover the part which officials played in wasting the state they needed. "Mandate" theory was no defense of the people, mitigating absolutism, but it was a defense of gentry-literati in their conflict-collaboration with the emperor in manipulating the state.

I have no wish to imply here any organized cynicism, or conscious cabals to fool the people and bind the emperor. This is a statement of the logic of a world, not an assumption of cool detachment and logical calculation on the part of the world's leaders. What we see in the Confucian political order is an inner consistency—something not depending on the exercise of rational cunning or on any other melodrama—a consistency of intellectual theory and the intellectuals' social concerns. A conservative social group, opposed above all else to revolution while it contributes provocation to that end, favors an almost exquisitely appropriate doctrine: by making an explanation of the workings of the social system moral, inner, rather than social, outer, it makes the system sacrosanct, untouchable intellectually. Dynasties, the Confucianists' lightning rods to draw off the fury of social storms, go through *ko-ming,* exchanges of the mandate, but bureaucracy goes on and on, not subject to revolution.

Finally there was a revolution in China, establishing the Republic, and its participants called it *ko-ming.* But was it the same old term? It seems rather a translation back into Chinese, as it were, of the modern Japanese *kakumei,* which had used the "mandate" characters metaphorically to convey the idea of revolution. It could have been nothing but metaphor in Japan, where a monarchist theory, stressing descent, not heavenly election, genealogical qualifications, not moral ones, had never been Confucian.

For the primordial heroes in Confucian myth are men, not gods or descendants of gods; but the Japanese myth begins with the sun-goddess and her Japanese warrior-offspring. Thus a Chinese monarch is legitimate when he repeats the example of sage-kings of independent lineages, while a Japanese monarch is legitimate when he descends from divinity, which bequeaths his line eternity; *his* mandate is irrevocable. Only revolution, which explicitly denies the old legitimacy, can bring it to an end, and "change of mandate," which a Chinese Confucianist could contemplate with equanimity, as a perpetuation of legitimacy, could not be reconciled with the Japanese monarchical system. One of the most highly esteemed of Ming writings published in Japan (Hsieh Chao-chi [*chin-shih* 1593], *Wu Tsa Tsu* ["The Five Assorted Vessels," there being five sections, on heaven, earth, man, objects, and events]) had its passages from Mencius deleted; as a modern scholar explains it, the *ko-ming* conception was thought inappropriate to the Japanese form of state.[49]

Ko-ming, then, had no natural place in the Japanese vocabulary as long as its literal Confucian sense, which was nonsense in Japan, was the only sense it had. But when modern Japan, moving from Chinese traditions to Western for foreign influences, enlarged her vocabulary to encompass Western ideas, the *ko-ming* compound had enough flavor of sharp political break to be assigned the meaning of revolution. Modern Chinese, enlarging their vocabulary in their turn, and finding in the Japanese language a repository of modern terms in characters, reached for "revolution" and made the same transformation, from literal to figurative, in *ko-ming* (Sun Yat-sen accepted himself as leader of a *ko-ming tang* only when [1895], in a flash of revelation of new meaning in the old term, he read in a Kobe newspaper that that was what he was.)[50] The phrase was not stripped of its old associations; its historical depth was recognized. But this very recognition reduced an ancient Confucian concept to something quaint and "period." For a modern, to say that Hsüan-t'ung lost the mandate in 1911 was to strive with conscious anachronism for allusive effect. Once-serious Confucian content was turned into rhetoric. And Yüan Shih-k'ai, the Hung-hsien Emperor, buckling on his virtue where the Ch'ing had dropped it and implicitly denying the anti-traditional purport of the republicans' *ko-ming* (as his followers explicitly countered anti-traditionalism in general), was an anachronism, a farceur, a period piece come to life.

It was a starved life and it had to be. The royal latecomer was forced to look back to a sacred past, in which his brand of traditionalism and his Confucian supporters', unfortunately, was not prefigured, and in which Confucian support for monarchy, anyway, was not so straightforward. How could "the spirit of the people," the basis of traditionalism for modern monarchists and modern Confucianists, have any place in the earlier Chinese complex, in which a foreign dynasty, patently unassimilable to the "spirit" of the Chinese people, was always, nevertheless, an orthodox possibility? And where was the old tension between essentially Legalist, anti-traditionalist dynastic monarchy, whether Chinese or foreign in ethnic and cultural origin, and literati-Confucian traditionalism?

In the great imperial ages some Confucian ideals, sacrificed in practice to the need for accommodation with the throne, had remained in force implicitly as restraints on imperial power, while, *mutatis mutandis,* the same may be said on the other side. But now, when revolutionaries were occasionally helping themselves to some of the old Confucian-bureaucratic specifics against the pretensions of the throne (Yao and Shun as "democrats," for example, since they were anti-dynastic),[51] such checks had to be dropped by Confucian-traditionalist anti-republicans (though not by Confucianists who were defeatist about monarchy and tried to make a go of the Republic).[52] Now the old tension was released. Yet it was a release that brought only the rest of death, as a wraith-like monarchy and a wraith-like Confucianism faded into a final association, untroubled at last by each other, but untroubled, also, by very much of life.

FORM AND CONTENT

Thus, the apparent emptiness of the Chinese Republic did nothing for monarchy. The monarchical symbols were just as thoroughly drained, and this in itself reminds us that the new form of republican China was not only form but content; the Republic was really new, and *sui generis* in Chinese history. If literal monarchy was a hollow shell, then the supposition that figurative monarchy has been the setting of post-Ch'ing history is hollow, too. The early republican period should not be viewed as just one more warlord pendant to an imperial era, with the Nanking government of Chiang K'ai-shek as the Ch'in or Sui type of abortive dynasty, unifying and preparing the way for a longer-lived bureaucratic centralized regime. If the Hung-hsien movement was monarchical in form only (because its justifications and associations had to be new), the Republic could not have been monarchical in all but form.

For radical depreciation of the significance of "form" in comparison with "content" (a depreciation involved in suggestions that things are "really" the same as ever in what is merely formally the Republican era in Chinese history) is both trite and misleading. If form has any "mereness," it is not in its unimportance when it changes; it is in its failure to hold a specific content when it, form, remains the same. The forces revising monarchy's content likewise made the Republic more than superficially new: if Yüan Shih-k'ai was a parodist as Emperor, he was not in essence Emperor as President.

What was really involved in Yüan's effort to reinstate *ch'en* as the word for "official" in his reign? There was the simple fact of its monarchical affinities, of course: there were the classic pairs of *chün* and *ch'en,* prince and minister, a relationship found in such famous catalogues as the *Tso-chuan's* "six *shun*" and "ten *li*," the *Li-chi's* "ten *i*" and "seven *chiao*";[53] and *wang* and *ch'en*, monarch and minister, bound together as firmly as the *Ch'un-ch'iu* and *Tso-chuan*, for of the two reputed authors, when Confucius was called a *su-wang*, Tso Ch'iu-ming was a *su-ch'en*.[54] But there was something more deeply significant about *ch'en* than any merely verbal associations. It was something relating not just to monarchy but to the cultural air of Confucian, imperial China, so that its banishment from the Republic (and consequently, Yüan's effort to restore it) symbolized a genuine change of social and intellectual climate.

Kuan, the Republic's term for official which Yüan wished to displace, was a very old one, too, but in the pre-republican, Confucian bureaucratic world it had a sense quite distinguishable from *ch'en's*. *Kuan* denoted the bureaucrat in his technical, functional, impersonal capacity. It had no connection with personal cultural dignity and individuality. For example, *kuan-t'ien*, set apart from *min-t'ien* in the Ming tax system,[55] was not "officials' land," the land of officials as persons; it was "official land," i.e., public land as opposed to private. *Kuan* suggests the state apparatus and *min*, here, the private sector. If "people" and "official" were being counterposed as human types, "official" would be *ch'en*.

For the outstanding attribute of *ch'en* (and this made it a "grander" word) was personal status, free of technical, professional connotations. Not the task but the personal tie defined him: "The loyal *ch'en* does not serve two princes."[56] An official was *kuan* in his job, something akin to being a tool, a means—and *ch'en* in his position, an end.

One of the outstanding, all-pervasive values of Confucian culture was its anti-professionalism. The Confucian ideal of personal cultivation was a humanistic amateurism, and Confucian education, perhaps supreme in the world for anti-vocational classicism, produced an imperial bureaucracy, accordingly, in which human relations counted for more than the network of abstract assignments (just as in Confucian society generally, human relations counted for more than legal relations). In these respects—not by accident—it differed from bureaucracies of the modern industrial West and, at least in conception, from that of the Chinese Republic.[57] A comparison of the Ch'ing dynasty's *mu-liao* or *mu-yu* and the Republic's *k'o-chang mi-shu* may be illustrative. All these designations, on both sides of the great divide, applied to the private secretary-advisers of administrative heads. There was nothing fundamentally dissimilar in their roles, but there was a great difference in their relationships with their respective seniors and in their legal status: the Republic's secretary-adviser was formally an official (*kuan-li*); his Ch'ing counterpart was the official's friend and technically not attached to the *pu*, the office, or paid from the public granaries.[58] As Chang Chien, a modern-minded industrialist (and later one of Yüan's supporters, though out of "strong man" sympathies, not out of archaism), caustically observed, all Ch'ing officials, provincial and local, could appoint their own assistants, as in the Han and T'ang *mu-chih*, government by staffs of intimates.[59]

The Republican emphasis on *kuan*, then, to the exclusion of *ch'en*, was the mark of a specifically modern commitment, to a professionalized, anti-literati world in which science, industry, and the idea of progress (all of them having impersonal, hence un-Confucian, implications) claimed first attention. This was not just the preference of a faction. It was really the world which for some time had been making over and taking over China, not only manfacturing iconoclasts but transforming traditionalists, in ways we have seen. The *ch'en*, the nonspecialized free man of high culture as the master-creation of civilization, who relegated to the *kuan* category the "jobs," the "business" of government (necessary even in the old regime, of course, but faintly unsavory, more the price paid than the prize won with prestige), was a figure of the unredeemable past. The Republic of *kuan* meant a genuine change from the Empire of *kuan* and *ch'en*.

The Empire dissolved in *ko-ming*. *Ko-ming*, itself drained of its traditional literal meaning and metaphorized into modern "revolution," freed men's minds and made them aware of the changing content of Chinese civilization. Chinese imperial forms became anachronisms. And *ch'en*, one of them, had its meaning changed like the *ko-ming* that had destroyed its proper world.

For *ch'en*, as we early suggested, had been paired not only with *kuan*, but in the Ch'ing dynasty with *nu*, "slave." *Nu* was the term for Manchu officials, relating them to the Ch'ing as Manchu monarchs, while the Ch'ing as Chinese emperors left Chinese officials the Confucian status of *ch'en*, in the classically noble relationship of minister to throne. Revolutionary republicanism, however, extended the application of the term "slave," and in this way, also, marked the obliteration of the world of *ch'en*. By doctrinaire republicans, "slave" was stripped of its literal, technical significance (which it had had for the Manchu officials, who were *nu* in a juridical sense for all that their use of the term may seem to be simple etiquette) and made expressive, metaphorically, of all subjects of supreme monarchs. As the republican minister, Wu T'ing-fang, put it in 1912, in a placatory cable to anti-republican Mongol princes, all had suffered the bitterness of slaves under the Ch'ing crown—Chinese, Manchus, Mongols, Moslems, Tibetans—and all would be brothers in the one great republic.[60] From the republican standpoint, then, to have been *ch'en* was not to have distinguished oneself from slaves but precisely to have been a slave. For there was no *ch'en* without his *wang* or *chün*, no Confucian gentleman outside a realm—at least an ideal one, however much the actual may have strained against Confucianism (Confucianists *had* required the Empire, even if they execrated Ch'in Shih Huang). *Ko-ming* as change of mandate would have struck off *nu* and left *ch'en* in a continuing imperial bureaucracy. But the *ko-ming* revolution, anti-imperial and in more than form, retroactively confounded *ch'en* and *nu*, struck them off together, and in this alone set a seal on the end of the Empire.

Nevertheless, just as for Mao Tse-tung and his regime today, so for Yüan Shih-k'ai in his lifetime (and the same theoretical issue is at stake: changing content behind changing form, or not?), some contemporaries saw analogies with patterns of the old monarchical past. A Japanese observer in 1914, Sakamaki Teiichirō, fixed Yüan as the Wang Mang in a late version of the fall of the former Han. Yüan, as rumor had it, was implicated in the death of the Emperor Kuang-hsü (1908), just as Wang Mang was involved in the murder of the Emperor P'ing (A.D. 5). Subsequently, Yüan's engineering the transfer of power to himself from Kuang-hsü's young successor was precisely the story of Wang Mang and the Emperor P'ing's successor. Yüan's *Chung-hua min-kuo*, to sum up, stood in the same relation to regular dynastic history as the *Hsin-kuo* of Wang Mang.[61]

Two of Yüan's puppets (one of them his "sworn brother" Hsü Shih-ch'ang, who had been brought up by Yüan's father, Yüan Chia-san) became "Grand Guardians of the Emperor" in November 1911, after the Prince Regent retired.[62] Sakamaki was not the only one to feel that Yüan, in imperial fashion, was easing out the Ch'ing. There is a note of innuendo in some of Sun Yat-sen's expressions in late January, 1912, when Yüan was proceeding, in sweet independence of the Nanking Kuomintang, to set up a government in Peking, a city Sun feared for its imperial associations.[63] "No one knows whether this provisional government is to be monarchical or republican," said Sun on January 20. "Yüan not only specifically injures the Republic, but is in fact an enemy of the Ch'ing emperor," said Wu T'ing-fang, at Sun's direction, on January 28.[64] By 1913, though Yüan had crowned the occasion of the Ch'ing abdication in February 1912 with a statement that monarchy would never again function in China,[65] Sun was sure that Yüan was imperial as well as imperious. The very term "Second Revolution" for the Kiangsi rising in the summer of that year had anti-monarchical overtones, and Sun's provocative public cable to a variety of addressees, on July 18, read

Yüan out of the Republic, right back to the ranks of Chinese absolute monarchs. Public servants, said Sun, should be subject to the people's appraisal. This was the case even in constitutional monarchies—how much more should it be so in a republic![66]

Yet, despite the pedantic or polemical impulses of the moment which moved men to interpret Yüan's republic as a monarchical regime, Yüan himself knew that his republic was not his empire—knew it emotionally, at the level of desire for an emperor's baubles and trappings, and knew it intellectually, at the level of tactics, in his grasp of the need to shift his base of support. Nationalism, with its iconoclastic implications, was the Republic's grain of novelty. As at least the ostensible exponent of the nation's cause against Japan in the 1915 crisis of the "Twenty-one Demands," Yüan, the president, had the most solid public support of his life. But immediately thereafter Yüan was a would-be emperor, and he tried to feel his way to Japanese support, tried this reversal quite plausibly, in a search for something to replace the nationalists' backing, which had been available to him as a nationalistic president, but would necessarily be withdrawn from a traditionalistic emperor.

Yüan succeeded only imperfectly in gaining useful Japanese support. He was too old a foe of Japanese diplomacy to be rehabilitated in that quarter overnight, and his monarchical chances, it was soon apparent, seemed too dim to proclaim him at the last a likely protégé. Given the Japanese aims in China, and Yüan's billing, for so many years, as China's strong man, Japanese leaders quite naturally found their habit of hostility to Yüan hard to break.

Yet Yüan as emperor, by his forfeiting of the support of modern-minded nationalists, actually had potentialities as China's weak man, potentialities for exploitation by expansionist Japan, since he needed aid to make himself strong enough to survive, and, once surviving, to recognize his debt. Japanese support of Chinese monarchy would bring Japan at least a minority Chinese backing, minor enough to need Japan to protect its cause in China, not major enough to threaten Japan with Chinese independence. Japanese who looked on China as empty of vitality and devoid of national feeling (as many did in 1916, more than were able to later) might think this solicitude for Chinese monarchism unnecessary, and resent Yüan as an ambitious flouter of these anti-nationalist Chinese virtues. But when Chinese nationalism was invoked against Yüan as emperor, invoked in its aspect of anti-traditionalism, its sanction for the free thought and open prospects which the latter-day monarchists' historicism denied, some few Japanese recognized at last the impending maturity of Chinese nationalism (which must ultimately work against Japan, though Japan had helped tremendously to bring it to birth), and turned pro-Yüan in the end.

The balance was still against him, in Japan as in China. But the Hung-hsien movement was the turning point for Japan in China and Japanese influence on Chinese culture. From being the school of Chinese radicals and nationalists, Japan became the temple of the deepest Chinese traditionalism. And Chinese monarchy was ultimately relegated to foreign sponsorship, foreshadowed in the ambiguous Japanese attitude toward Yüan in 1915, and culminating in the Japanese revival of the Ch'ing dynasty in Manchuria. When nationalism implied both iconoclasm culturally and anti-Japanism politically, the cause of Chinese monarchy quite plausibly qualified for Japanese backing; for with its imprisonment in cultural traditionalism, latter-day Chinese monarchy committed itself to anti-nationalism, and to a political ambience, accordingly, at least passively pro-Japanese.

THE JAPANESE AND CHINESE MONARCHICAL MYSTIQUES

Ironically enough, Chinese monarchism not only ended as bankrupt with Japanese receivers, but had marked its panic long before with a desperate reaching out for Japanese procedures. The Ch'ing and their supporters, back in the days of the post-Boxer "Manchu Reform Movement" and right down to 1911, had taken to insisting on Ch'ing eternity in the midst of the myriad changes that the Ch'ing were forced to bless, and they did it by reiterating "Wan-shih i-hsi," the *Bansei ikkei*, "One line throughout ten thousand ages," that celebrated Japan's imperial house. It hardly belonged in China, with the latter's long centuries of nonfeudal imperium, in which the mandate was not necessarily inheritable.

It is this difference between the premodern societies, Chinese bureaucratic and Japanese feudal, that accounts for the different fates of the Chinese and Japanese monarchies. In modern Japan, monarchy has been no parody; the mystique of the throne has been strengthened, not dispelled (the repercussions of the recent war are not considered here). For in Japan, unlike China, a postfeudal regime could cite prefeudal precedents against the feudal intermission. The Japanese revolution, that is, could strike against the *de facto* Tokugawa feudal shogunate in the name of Nara, and Meiji, *de jure* imperial control: modernization could be combined with myth-making about antiquity. But in China the modern breach with things as they were was a breach precisely with a *de jure* situation, a dynastic and bureaucratic regime which was, in general terms, as tradition had accepted it, and modernization required myth-breaking. Compare only the early-modern contemporaries, the Chinese "Han Learning," with its probing for forgeries and its ultimately revolutionary and republican implications, and the Japanese "Pure Shintō," with its writing of forgeries and its ultimately revolutionary but monarchist implications. The Japanese could combine a prefeudal form with postfeudal content; the strengthening of Japanese monarchy was compatible with modernization. But the strengthening —or the mere reestablishing—of Chinese monarchy was incompatible with modernization. Indeed, as we have seen, Yüan Shih-k'ai's effort to reestablish monarchy was undertaken deliberately as an anti-modernist counterthrust.

Kokutai, or "national form," intimately individual polity, was an ancient Japanese term with tremendous modern and nationalist-monarchist currency. But its Chinese counterpart, with the same characters, *kuo-t'i,* was just another of those terms proper to Japan, exotic in China, which were rushed to the aid of a Chinese monarchism having none of the favorable circumstances of monarchy in the modern age in Japan. Liang Ch'i-ch'ao (1873–1929), rebuffing Yüan's son's *kuo-t'i* monarchical blandishments in 1915, with their invitation to see the *kuo-ch'ing* or "national spirit" in just this form of state, preferred to speak, he said, of *cheng-t'i,* of the practical question of the workings of government rather than the more metaphysical, "essential" question of the location of national authority[67]—this distinction having first been made as a Japanese distinction, between *kokutai* and *seitai,* in the *Kokutai Shinron* of Katō Hiroyuki in 1874.[68] *Kokutai* was a living word; *kuo-t'i* was a contrivance.[69] To speak a living language, one must say that the Hunghsien reign was supposed to be the revival of Chinese *kokutai.* But how could a Chinese *revive* in China a new and foreign importation? What was this traditional national form which tradition had never named and nationalists could hardly accept? It was paradox which made of Yüan a parodist.

For the kings were truly finished — *wang* and *su-wang* both, the merely royal and the Confucian sage-ideal. Monarchism and Confucianism, which had belonged together in their own way and run dry together, were garbled together in a new way now that failed to elicit the old responses. When republican "men of the future" set the pace, they not only abandoned traditionalism on their own account but transformed the traditionalism of those who never joined them, turning it into nostalgia—which is thirst for the past, not a life-giving fluid itself.

NOTES

NOTES TO AN ANALYSIS OF CHINESE CLAN RULES

1. Hui-chen Wang Liu, "An Analysis of the Chinese Clan Rules: A Study of Social Control" (Ph.D. thesis, University of Pittsburgh, 1956; University Microfilms, Ann Arbor, Michigan, Publication No. 18,242) (hereafter cited as Liu, *Analysis*). This is now revised and will be published shortly by the Monograph Series, The Association for Asian Studies, under the title *The Traditional Chinese Clan Rules*.

2. *Ibid.*, pp. 36–72.

3. Chang Tsai, *Ching-hsüeh Li K'u*, cited in the encyclopedia, *Ku Chin T'u shu Chi-ch'eng* (1884 ed.), section on *Tsung-tsu* ("clans"), "Tsung-lun" (general discussion), part 2, p. 2.

4. Chu Hsi, *Chin-ssu Lu*, cited *ibid.*, p. 8.

5. Mano Senryū, "Mindai no Kaki ni tsuite" ("Family Rules during the Ming Dynasty"), *Tōhōgaku*, VIII (1954), 83–93; Makino Tatsumi, "Sōshi to Sono Hattatsu" ("On the Ancestral Hall and Its Historical Development in China"), *Tōhōgakuhō*, IX (1939), 173–250; and Makino Tatsumi, "Peipin Toshokanzō Mindai Zempon Zokufu" ("On Various Family Monographs Belonging to the Ming Period Found in the Catalog of the Rare Books in the National Library of Peiping"), *ibid.*, VI (1936) [extra number], 169–202.

6. *Hung-tung Chin Shih Tsu-p'u* (1735), Vol. II; *Jen-ch'iu Pien Shih Tsu-p'u* (1772), Vol. II; *Huai-ning Ma Shih Tsung-p'u* (1876), Vol. I; *Ching-k'ou Shun-chiang-chou Wang Shih Chia-ch'eng* (1893), Vol. I. Generally, I have cited in these notes only the clan rules printed during the Ch'ing period, since those printed in 1912–36 are covered in my dissertation (see note 1).

7. *Wu-shan Hsi-chin-ts'un Wu Shih Shih-tsu-p'u* (1682), Vol. II; *Pan-yang Kao Shih Chia-mu Hui-pien* (1738); *Pi-ling Shih Shih Tsung-p'u* (1880), Vol. I; *Hsiao-shan Ch'ang-hsiang Shen Shih Tsung-p'u* (1893), Vol. VI; and *Hsiao-shan Wu Shih Tsung-p'u* (1904), Vol. I.

8. *Ku-jun Ching-k'ou Chu Shih Tsung-p'u* (1903).

9. Liu, *Analysis*, pp. 291–304.

10. "Family Instructions," in *Wan Huai Tsou Shih Tsung-p'u* (1796).

11. "Family Rules," in *Hung-tung Chin Shih Tsu-p'u* (1735), Vol. II.

12. "Rules by Common Decision," in *Lu-chiang Ho Shih Chia-ch'eng* (1848), Vol. I; "Ancestral Hall Rules" in *Pi-ling Hsieh Shih Tsung-p'u* (1921), Vol. I.

13. "Instructions of Ancestor Madame Wu," in *Hai-ning Chu Shih Tsung-p'u* (1879), Vol. IV.

14. "Clan Regulations," in *Yun-yang T'u Shih Tsu-p'u* (1930), Vol. II.

15. "Family Rituals," in *Hsiao-shan Tao-yuan T'ien Shih Tsung-p'u* (1837).

16. "Family Regulations," in *Ch'eng-chiang Hsiang-shan Hu Shih*

316

Tsung-p'u (1872), Vol. I.

17. Wada Kiyoshi, "Min no Taiso no Kyōiku Chokugo ni tsuite" ("On the Educational Edict of Ming T'ai-tsu"), *Shiratori Hakushi Kanreki Kinen Tōyōshi Ronsō* ("Essays in Oriental History in Honor of Dr. Shiratori") (1925), pp. 885–904.

18. The Han period: Pan Chao (Ts'ao Ta-ku). The Northern Ch'i period: Yen Chih-t'ui. The T'ang period: Liu P'in. The Sung period: Chang Tsai, Chang Shih, Chang Hsiao-hsiang, Chang Chih-pai, Chen Te-hsiu, Ch'eng Hao, Ch'eng I, Chou Tun-i, Chu Hsi, Fan Ch'un-jen, Fan Chung-yen, Hu An-kuo, Hu Yüan, Lin Ho-ching, Liu An-shih, Liu K'ai, Lu Yu, Lu Chiu-shao, Lü Kung-chu, Lü Ta-lin, Lü Tsu-ch'ien, Ou-yang Hsiu, P'eng Chung-kang, Shao Yung, Ssu-ma Kuang, Su Shih, Wang Ke, Ying Chün, and Yüan Ts'ai. The Yüan period: Hsü Heng. The Ming period: Chan Jo-shui, Ch'en Chi-ju, Ch'en Hsien-chang, Fang Hsiao-ju, Hsia Yin, Hsü San-chung, Hsüeh Hsüan, Kao P'an-lung, Lu Shih-i, Lü K'un, Lü Wei-ch'i, Wang Yang-ming, Yang Chi-sheng, and Yen Mao-yu. The Ch'ing period: Chang Lü-hsiang, Chang Ying, Ch'en Hung-mou, Chiang I, Chu Yung-ch'un, Ch'ü Ch'eng-lin, Ku Yen-wu, Lu Lung-ch'i, T'ang Pin, Ts'ai Shih-yüan, Tseng Kuo-fan, Wang Chih-fu, and Yü Ch'eng-lung.

19. "The Ten Rules for Clan Harmony," in *Ning-chin Chang Shih Tsu-p'u* (1757), Vol. I.

20. *Ku Chin T'u-shu Chi-ch'eng* (1884 ed.), "Chia-fan-tien," ch. 1–116.

21. Ch'en Hung-mou, *Wu Chung I-kuei* ("The Five Collections of Rules") (1828 ed.).

22. "Clan Regulations," in *Lu Shih Feng-men Chih P'u* (1888), Vol. II.

23. "Ancestors' Instructions," in *Pan-yang Kao Shih Chia-mu Hui-pien* (1738).

24. "Instructions of Ancestor Yeh-kung" in *Wu-hsing Yao Shih Chia-ch'eng* (1911), Vol. IV.

25. "Family Instructions," *ibid.*

26. Obata Tatsuo, "Mindai Gōson no Kyōka to Saiban" ("Public Instructions and Village Elders' Instructions in the Ming Period"), *Tōyōshi Kenkyū*, XI (1952), 423–43; E. Chavannes, "Les Saintes Instructions de l'empereur Hong-wo, 1368–1398," *Bulletin de l'Ecole Française d'Extrême-Orient*, III (1903), 549–63; Wada Kiyoshi, "Min no Taiso no Kyōiku Chokugo ni tsuite," *loc. cit.* (note 17); and Sogabe Shizuo, "Min Taiso Rokuyu no Denshō ni tsuite" ("The Tradition of the 'Six Instructions' of T'ai-tsu of Ming"), *Tōyōshi Kenkyū*, XII (1953), 323–32.

27. Higashionna Hiroatsu, "Rokuyu Engi ni tsuite" ("On the Commentaries on the Six Instructions"), *Shigaku Zasshi*, XXXV (1924), 758–67.

28. Li Lai-chang comp., *Sheng-yü T'u-hsiang Yen-i*, in Li Li-shan, *Li-shan-yüan Ch'üan-chi*; Wu Yün-sun, comp., *Sheng-yü Kuang-hsün Chi-cheng* (1901); and Liang Yen-nien comp., *Sheng-yü Hsiang-chieh* (1681 comp., 1903 ed.).

29. See a memorial dated 1737 in *Huang-ch'ao Ching-shih Wen-pien* (1898), ch. 23, pp. 5–6.

30. *Ta Ch'ing Sheng-tsu Jen-huang-ti Sheng-hsün* ("The Imperial Edicts of the K'ang-hsi Emperor") (hereafter cited as *Sheng-tsu*), ch. 6, pp. 7b–8a; *Ta Ch'ing Shih-tsung Hsien-huang-ti Sheng-hsün* ("The Imperial Edicts of the Yung-cheng Emperor") (hereafter cited as *Shih-tsung*), ch. 26, p. 11;

Ta Ch'ing Kao-tsung Shun-huang-ti Sheng-hsün ("The Imperial Edicts of the Ch'ien-lung Emperor") (hereafter cited as *Kao-tsung*), ch. 263, p. 5a.

31. *Shih-tsung*, ch. 26, pp. 1b–2a; *Kao-tsung*, ch. 261, pp. 3a, 5a.

32. *Shih-tsung*, ch. 26, pp. 14b–15a; *Kao-tsung*, ch. 261, pp. 13a–14a and ch. 264, pp. 4b–5a; and *Huang Ch'ing Tsou-i* ("Memorials of the Ch'ing Dynasty") (hereafter cited as *Tsou-i*), ch. 60, p. 15.

33. *Kao-tsung*, ch. 261, pp. 3a, 5; ch. 262, p. 5a; ch. 263, p. 5a.

34. *Ibid.*, ch. 264, p. 2a.

35. *Ibid.*, ch. 261, p. 9b.

36. *Ibid.*, ch. 262, p. 5b.

37. *Tsou-i*, ch. 25, pp. 8b–9b.

38. *Ibid.*, ch. 33, p. 34b.

39. *Ibid.*, ch. 55, pp. 1a–9a; Makino, "Sōshi to Sono Hattatsu," *Tōhō-gakuhō* (Tokyo), IX (1939), 197–201.

40. *Kao-tsung*, ch. 264, p. 6a.

41. "Instructions," in *Jen-ch'iu Pien Shih Tsu-p'u* (1772), Vol. II.

42. Liu, *Analysis*, pp. 249–52.

43. *Ibid.*, pp. 252–57.

44. *Ibid.*, pp. 16–17.

45. Ch'u Ch'eng-lin, *Hsi Shih Pien*, quoted in "Mottoes" of Hsia-p'u Hsu Shih Tsung-p'u* (1921), Vol. I.

46. Yen Mao-yu, *Ti Chi Lu*, quoted in "Collection of Family Instructions" of *Shang-hai Ke Shih Chia-p'u* (1928).

47. Liu, *Analysis*, pp. 45–55; Niida Noboru, *Chūgoku no Nōson Kazoku* ("The Chinese Rural Family"), 2d ed. (1954) (hereafter cited as Niida, *Kazoku*), pp. 75–76.

48. "Charitable Land," in *K'uai-chi Chung-wang Shen Shih Chia-p'u* (1879), Vol. I.

49. "Charitable Estate Regulations," in *Chi-yang Chang-ch'ing Chao Shih Tsung-p'u* (1883), Vol. V.

50. "Ritual Land Regulations," in *Huai-an Yang-ch'iao Tu Shih Tsu-p'u* (1870), *chüan* 1, pp. 18a–18b.

51. "On the Restoration of the Ancestral Hall Property," in *Pi-ling Shen Shih Tsung-p'u* (1904), Vol. I.

52. Manchukuo, Ministry of Justice, *Manshū Kazoku Seido Shūkan Chosa* ("Customs of the Manchurian Family System") (1944), pp. 50–53, 511–13; and Ōyama Hikoichi, *Chūgoku-jin no Kazoku Seido no Kenkyū* ("A Study of the Chinese Family System") (1952) (hereafter cited as Ōyama, *Kazoku*), pp. 30–34.

53. Liu, *Analysis*, p. 155.

54. *Ibid.*, p. 263; "Family Instructions," in *Wu-hsi Ch'ien K'un Li Shih Chia-p'u* (1888).

55. Liu, *Analysis*, p. 264.

56. *Ibid.*, pp. 263–64; "Clan Standard," in *Chiang-yin Ming-wei Kuo Shih Tsung-p'u* (1879); also "Family Instructions," in *Pi-ling An-shang-ch'iao Shao Shih Tsung-p'u* (1889).

57. Liu, *Analysis*, pp. 203–8.

58. "Charitable Granary Regulations," in *Shan-yin An-ch'ang Hsü Shih Tsung-p'u* (1884).

318

59. Liu, *Analysis*, pp. 204–6.
60. *Ibid.*, pp. 197–202.
61. *Ibid.*, pp. 178–79.
62. "Ancestral Hall Rules," in *Chieh-hsiu Chang-lan Ma Shih Tsu-p'u* (1843); "Record of the Management of the Common Land," in *Hai-ning Chu Shih Tsung-p'u* (1879), Vol. IV; "Clan Agreement," in *Pi-ling Sun Shih Chia-ch'eng* (1873), Vol. I; and "Ancestral Hall Regulations" in *Ching-chiang Tai Shih Chia-ch'eng* (1885).
63. *Ibid.*
64. Liu, *Analysis*, p. 175; cf. Niida Noboru, "Chūgoku Nōson Shakai to Ka-fu-cho Ken-i" ("Chinese Rural Society and Parental Authority") in *Kindai Chūgoku no Shakai to Keizai* ("Modern Chinese Society and Economy") (1951), pp. 259–60.
65. Record of the Ching-yin Charitable Estate," in *Wu-ch'ü Wang Shih Chih-p'u* (1910), Vol. I.
66. "Record of the Charitable Estate," in *Wu-chung Yeh Shih Tsu-p'u* (1911), Vol. I; "Regulations of the Charitable Estate" (1876), in *Wu-men P'eng Shih Tsung-p'u* (1923), Vol. III; "Clan Relief Association," in *Ssu-ming Ts'ang-chi Ch'en Shih Chia-p'u* (1934), Vol. II; cf. Liu, *Analysis*, pp. 176–77.
67. *Tsou-i*, ch. 33, pp. 32b–33a.
68. Liu, *Analysis*, pp. 209–13.
69. *Ibid.*, pp. 145–47, 193–94, 218–19.
70. Robert Redfield, *Peasant Society and Culture* (1956), pp. 75–76.
71. Liu, *Analysis*, pp. 172–73.
72. "Family Rules," in *Lo-p'ing Kao Shih Tsung-p'u* (1692), Vol. I; "Ancestors' Instructions on Self-cultivation," in *Hai-yü Tz'u-ts'un Chin Shih Chia-ch'eng* (1824); "Ancestral Hall Regulations" in *P'u-li Hsü Shih Chia-ch'eng* (1837), Vol. I; "Injunctions," in *Hsiao-shan Hsiang-feng-ts'un Chu Shih Tsung-p'u* (1870), Vol. I; and Liu, *Analysis*, pp. 113–15.
73. "Injunctions," in *Ti-hsi Tzu-yang Chu Shih Chia-ch'eng Hsu-hsiu* (1838), Vol. I; "Family Instructions," in *Yün-yang P'ei Shih Tsung-p'u* (1874), Vol. I; and Liu, *Analysis*, p. 237.
74. "Clan Injunctions on Sixteen Vices," in *Ching-chiang Liu Shih Tsung-p'u* (1891), Vol. I; and Liu, *Analysis*, pp. 283–85.
75. "Family Instructions," in *Yen-ling Ching-chiang Wu Shih Tsu-p'u* (1900); "Family Instructions," in *Chin-ling Cha-t'ou Liu Shih Tsu-p'u* (1905); Vol. I; and Liu, *Analysis*, pp. 285, 303.
76. "Ancestral Hall Regulations," in *Yen-ling Ching-ts'un Wu Shih Tsung-p'u* (1865), Vol. I; Liu, *Analysis*, pp. 226–29.
77. "Clan Agreement," in *Yü-yao Chiang Shih Chia-ch'eng* (1854), Vol. I.
78. "Clan Instructions," in *Ch'ien-yüan Hsi-li T'ang Shih Tsung-p'u* (1906), Vol. I.
79. Liu, *Analysis*, pp. 81–82.
80. "Three Types of Behavior Prohibited and Three Punished," in *Wan T'ung Hsi-hsiang Mao Shih Tsung-p'u* (1865), Vol. I.
81. "Family Instructions," in *Hsiang-yin Fu Shih Chih-p'u* (1845); "Clan Agreement," in *Yü-yao Chiang Shih Chia-ch'eng* (1854), Vol. I; and

Liu, *Analysis*, pp. 81–88.
82. Niida, *Kazoku*, pp. 121–27, 136–43.
83. Liu, *Analysis*, pp. 91–95.
84. Martin C. Yang, *A Chinese Village* (1946), p. 129; Niida Noboru, "Chūgoku Nōson Shakai to Ka-fu-cho Ken'i" in *Kindai Chūgoku no Shakai to Keizai* (1951), p. 282.
85. Ōyama, *Kazoku*, pp. 93–94.
86. "The Six Articles Appended," in *P'u-li Hsü Shih Chia-ch'eng* (1837), Vol. I; "Family Instructions," in *Huang-kang Lü-yang-ts'un Hsieh Shih Tsung-p'u* (1865), Vol. I.
87. "The Sixteen Family Instructions," in *Shan-yin Niang-ch'uan Wang Shih Tsu-p'u* (1784), Vol. I.
88. Liu, *Analysis*, pp. 98–100.
89. "The Eight Items Added to Family Instructions," in *Shan-yin Chou-shan Wu Shih Tsu-p'u* (1840), Vol. I.
90. "Clan Agreement," in *Yü-yao Chiang Shih Chia-ch'eng* (1854), Vol. I.
91. Liu, *Analysis*, pp. 100–104; Manchukuo, *op. cit.* (note 52), pp. 40–41, 500–501; Niida, *Kazoku*, pp. 19–20, 104–16; and Niida Noboru, ed., *Chūgoku Nōson Kankō Chōsa* ("Chinese Rural Customs and Practices") (1952–55) (hereafter cited as *Kankō Chōsa*), IV, 70–93.
92. "Clan Agreement," in *Chao Shih Tsung-p'u* (1883), Vol. I.
93. Liu, *Analysis*, pp. 105–6.
94. Manchukuo, *op. cit.*, pp. 31, 492; and Ōyama, *Kazoku*, pp. 18–19, 20–21.
95. Liu, *Analysis*, pp. 126–30.
96. *Ibid.*, pp. 135–54.
97. *Ibid.*, p. 139.
98. *Ibid.*, pp. 137–40.
99. Niida, *Kazoku*, pp. 45–50, 243–310.
100. "Family Rules," in *Lo-p'ing Kao Shih Tsung-p'u* (1629), Vol. I.
101. "Regulations for Ancestral Hall and Ancestral Graveyard," in *Pi-ling Shih Shih Tsu-p'u* (1915), Vol. I.
102. Liu, *Analysis*, pp. 161–66.
103. *Kankō Chōsa*, III, 111, 149.
104. "On Aiding Clan Members," in *I-feng Ch'ü Shih Tsu-p'u* (1908).
105. Liu, *Analysis*, pp. 225–26.
106. *Ibid.*, pp. 244–46.
107. "Instructions of Ancestor Madame Wu," in *Hai-ning Chu Shih Tsung-p'u* (1879), Vol. IV.
108. "On Clan Harmony," in *Pi-ling Hsi-t'an Ch'en Shih Tsung-p'u* (1882), Vol. I.
109. Liu, *Analysis*, pp. 246–48.
110. *Ibid.*, pp. 237–41.
111. "Instructions of Ancestor Madame Wu," in *Hai-ning Chu Shih Tsung-p'u* (1879), Vol. IV; "Family Instructions," in *Wu-hsing Yao Shih Chia-ch'eng* (1911), Vol. IV.
112. Liu, *Analysis*, p. 289.

113. *Ibid.*, pp. 56–60.
114. *Ibid.*, pp. 273–75.
115. "Family Standard," in *Ch'i-i K'u-chu Wang Shih Tsung-p'u* (1696), Vol. I.
116. "Clan Regulations," in *Hsin-t'ien Shih Shih Tsung-p'u* (1877), Vol. I; "Ancestral Hall Regulations," in *Yün-yang Chang Shih Tsung-p'u* (1887), Vol. I.
117. "Family Instructions," in *Yen-ling Ching-chiang Wu Shih Tsu-p'u* (1900).
118. "Family Standard," in *Ch'i-i K'u-chu Wang Shih Tsung-p'u* (1696), Vol. I; "Family Instructions," in *Ts'ung-ch'uan Ch'ien Shih Shih-p'u* (1866), Vol. I.
119. "Clan Agreement," in *Yü-yao Chiang Shih Chia-ch'eng* (1854), Vol. I; "The Original Clan Regulations," in *Pi-ling Ch'en Shih Hsü-hsiu Tsung-p'u* (1876), Vol. I.
120. "Family Teachings," in *Shan-yin Ch'ing-hsi Hsü Shih Tsung-p'u* (1883), Vol. I; "Clan Regulations," in *Hsin-t'ien Shih Shih Tsung-p'u* (1877), Vol. I.
121. "The Original Clan Regulations," in *Pi-ling Ch'en Shih Hsü-hsiu Tsung-p'u* (1876), Vol. I; "Instructions in the Genealogy" in *Chiang-yin Kao Shih Tsung-p'u* (1881), Vol. I .
122. *Tsou-i*, ch. 9, p. 5a.
123. *Kao-tsung*, ch. 261, p. 5; ch. 262, p. 5a; ch. 263, p. 5; ch. 264, p. 2a.
124. *Ibid.*, ch. 264, p. 2b.
125. Liu, *Analysis*, pp. 272–76.
126. Uchida Tomoo, *Chūgoku Nōson no Kazoku to Shinkō* ("Chinese Rural Family and Beliefs") (1948), pp. 176 ff.
127. Liu, *Analysis*, pp. 276–77.
128. *Kao-tsung*, ch. 261, p. 3a.
129. *Shih-tsung*, ch. 16, p. 8b; ch. 26, pp. 1, 3; cf. Nieh Ch'ung-ch'i, "Nü-tzu Tsai-chia Wen-t'i ti Li-shih Yen-pien" ("The Historical Development of the Problem of Remarriage of Women"), *Ta-chung Yüeh-k'an* ("Ta-chung Monthly"), I, No. 4 (1942), 31–38.
130. "Family Regulations," in *Chin Shih Hsü-hsiu Tsu-p'u* (1884); and Liu, *Analysis*, p. 133.
131. "Family Regulations," in *Wan T'ung Hsi-hsiang Mao Shih Tsung-p'u* (1865), Vol. I; "Family Regulations," in *Pi-ling Ch'en Shih Hsü-hsiu Tsung-p'u* (1876), Vol. I; "Family Discipline," in *Hsin-t'ien Shih Shih Tsung-p'u* (1877), Vol. I; and "Family Regulations," in *Chin-sha Lu-chuang Shih Shih Tsung-p'u* (1877).
132. "Instructions of Ancestor Mien-wu-kung," in *Chin-ling Kao Shih Shih-p'u* (1915); and "Instructions in the Genealogy," in *Chiang-yin Kao Shih Tsung-p'u* (1881), Vol. I.
133. Liu, *Analysis*, pp. 147–48.
134. *Kankō Chōsa*, III, 111.
135. Liu, *Analysis*, pp. 145–47, 203–5.
136. Redfield, *op. cit.*, pp. 68–71, 91–96, 151.
137. *Ibid.*, pp. 124–25.
138. Niida, *Kazoku*, 122, 415–16.

NOTES TO CONFUCIANISM AND THE CHINESE CENSORIAL SYSTEM

Besides being indebted to the participants of the Fourth Conference on Chinese Thought at which the original draft of this paper was discussed, I am grateful to Professor F. W. Mote for many additional suggestions.

1. Etienne Balazs, *Le Traité juridique du "Souei-Chou"* (Leiden, 1954), p. 11.

2. Cf. A. F. P. Hulsewé, *Remnants of Han Law* (Leiden, 1955), p. 297; J. J. L. Duyvendak, *The Book of Lord Shang* (London, 1928), p. 129.

3. Hulsewé, p. 298.

4. Cf. C. O. Hucker, "The Traditional Chinese Censorate and the New Peking Regime," *The American Political Science Review,* XLV (1951), 1041–57; C. O. Hucker, "Governmental Organization of the Ming Dynasty," *Harvard Journal of Asiatic Studies,* XXI (1958), no. 1/2.

5. Cf. Kao I-han, *Chung-kuo Yü-shih Chih-tu ti Yen-ko* ("The Evolution of the Chinese Censorial System") (Shanghai, 1933). I disagree with several of the interpretations relating to censorial history given in Richard L. Walker, "The Control System of the Chinese Government," *The Far Eastern Quarterly,* VII (1947), 2–21.

6. Cf. Burton Watson, *Ssu-ma Ch'ien, Grand Historian of China* (New York, 1958), pp. 70 ff.

7. Cf. pp. 147 ff. of Wang Yü-ch'üan, "An Outline of the Central Government of the Former Han Dynasty," *Harvard Journal of Asiatic Studies,* XII (1949), 134–87; Sah Mong-wu, "The Impact of Hanfeism on the Earlier Han Censorial System," *Chinese Culture,* I (1957), 96.

8. Cf. Robert des Rotours, *Traité des fonctionnaires et traité de l'armée* (2 vols.; Leiden, 1947), I, 143–51.

9. Cf. E. A. Kracke, Jr., *Civil Service in Early Sung China, 960–1067* (Cambridge, Mass., 1953), p. 28; Sun Ch'eng-tse, *Ch'un-ming Meng-yü Lu* ("Memories from a Dream of the Capital") (Ku-hsiang Chai pocket ed.), ch. 48, pp. 21b–22a; *Sung Hui-yao Kao* ("Draft Institutes of the Sung") (photolithographic ed., 1936), *chih-kuan* section, ch. 17, pp. 16a–b.

10. *Yüan Shih* ("History of the Yüan") (Po-na ed., 1936), ch. 6, pp. 15b.

11. *Lun-yü,* 13.6; trans. by Arthur Waley, *The Analects of Confucius* (London, 1938), p. 173.

12. Esson M. Gale and others, "Discourses on Salt and Iron (*Yen T'ieh Lun*: Chaps. XX–XXVIII)," *Journal of the North China Branch of the Royal Asiatic Society,* LXV (1934), 85–86. This is a supplement to, and should be used in conjunction with, Esson M. Gale, *Discourses on Salt and Iron* (Leiden, 1931).

13. *Lun-yü,* 17.24, 12.16; trans. Waley, pp. 216, 167. *Mencius,* 4.2.9; trans. James Legge, *The Chinese Classics,* 2d ed. (7 vols.; Oxford, 1893–95), II, 321.

14. Duyvendak, p. 300. Cf. Duyvendak, pp. 121, 279; W. K. Liao, *The Complete Works of Han Fei Tzu,* I (London, 1939), 122–23; Derk Bodde, "Authority and Law in Ancient China," in *Authority and Law in the Ancient Orient* (*Supplement* to the *Journal of the American Oriental Society,* No. 17, July–September, 1954), p. 53.

15. Kao I-han, p. 43.

16. Cf. *Ta Ming hui-tien* ("Collected Institutes of the Ming"), chs. 209–11, 213.

17. Cf. Lung Wen-pin, *Ming hui-yao* ("Ming Precedents") (Kuang-hsü blockprint ed.), ch. 33, p. 9b; *Ming Shih* ("History of the Ming") (Po-na ed., 1937), ch. 158, pp. 2b–4b; and H. A. Giles, *A Chinese Biographical Dictionary* (London, 1898), item 997.

18. *Hsüan-tsung Shih-lu* ("True Records of the Hsüan-te Emperor") (photolithographic ed., 1940), ch. 112, p. 4a.

19. Lung Wen-pin, ch. 37, p. 2b.

20. Cf. C. O. Hucker, "The Tung-lin Movement of the Late Ming Period," in J. K. Fairbank, ed., *Chinese Thought and Institutions* (Chicago, 1957), p. 140.

21. Cf. Chu Tung-jun, *Chang Chü-cheng Ta-chuan* ("Biography of Chang Chü-cheng") (Shanghai, 1947), pp. 217–22.

22. Chu Tung-jun, p. 219. The italics are mine.

23. *Lun-yü*, 12.18; trans. Waley, p. 167.

24. For examples, cf. *Mencius*, 1.1.4; 1.2.6; 5.2.9; trans. Legge, *The Chinese Classics*, II, 133, 164–65, 392–93.

25. *Lun-yü*, 3.19, 12.23; trans. Waley, pp. 98–99, 170.

26. *Lun-yü*, 14.23, 13.15; translation and paraphrase from H. G. Creel, *Confucius the Man and the Myth* (New York, 1949), p. 160. Comma added.

27. *Li-chi* ("Record of Ceremonial") (Sung-pen Shih-san-ching Chu-shu ed., 1887), ch. 54, p. 6a; trans. James Legge in *Sacred Books of the East*, ed. Max Müller, XXVIII (Oxford, 1895), 345.

28. *Mencius*, 4.2.3; trans. Legge, *The Chinese Classics*, II, 319.

29. *Lun-yü*, 14.8; trans. Waley, p. 181.

30. *Mencius*, 1.2.4; 2.2.2; 4.1.1; trans. Legge, *The Chinese Classics*, II, 161, 212, 292.

31. *Li-chi*, ch. 51, p. 16b; ch. 48, p. 23a; trans. Legge, *Sacred Books of the East*, XXVIII, 290, 228.

32. *Hsiao-ching* ("Classic of Filial Piety"), chs. 17, 15.

33. Gale, Supplement (see n. 12), p. 106. Commas and semicolon added.

34. Kracke, p. 22.

35. Cf. Liao, pp. 69 ff., 78–85, 87–88, 88–89, 89–92, 216–17, 228–58.

36. *Han Fei Tzu* (Han Fei Tzu Chi-chieh ed.; Shanghai, 1897), ch. 5, pp. 3a, 1a; trans. Liao, pp. 142, 135.

37. *Han Fei Tzu*, ch. 8, p. 7b; trans. Liao, pp. 262–63. The italics are mine.

38. *Lun-yü*, 8.13, 2.24; trans. Waley, pp. 135, 93.

39. *Han Fei Tzu*, ch. 4, p. 7a; trans. Liao, p. 112.

40. *Han Fei Tzu*, ch. 4, pp. 4a–7b; cf. Liao, pp. 106–12 and Arthur Waley, *Three Ways of Thought in Ancient China* (New York, 1956), pp. 183–88. The translations quoted are from Liao, p. 108, and Waley, p. 188.

41. Cf. *Mencius*, 2.2.5 and 5.2.9; *Li-chi*, ch. 5, p. 30b and ch. 35, p. 15a. I am not concerned here with the problem of whether statements in *Li-chi* attributed to Confucius are genuinely his, since traditional Chinese bureaucrat-scholars accepted them as being his.

42. F. W. Mote has clarified the Imperial Confucian rationalization of such withdrawal in his "Confucian Eremitism in the Yüan Period," *supra* pp. 252–90.

43. Cf. Wu Han, *Chu Yüan-chang Chuan* ("Biography of Chu Yüan-chang") (Shanghai, 1949), pp. 148–49.

44. Stated by the seventeenth-century grand secretary Yeh Hsiang-kao. *Hsi-tsung Shih-lu* ("True Records of the T'ien-ch'i Emperor") (photolithographic ed., 1940), ch. 17, p. 16b.

45. Lung Wen-pin, ch. 33, pp. 2a–b.

46. *Hsi-tsung Shih-lu*, ch. 5, p. 6a. Cf. *Kuang-tsung Shih-lu* ("True Records of the T'ai-ch'ang Emperor") (photolithographic ed., 1940), ch. 1, p. 22a.

47. Cf. Sun Ch'eng-tse, ch. 48, pp. 19b–21b.

48. *Ming Nan-ching Tu Ch'a-yüan T'iao-yüeh* ("Regulations of the Ming Nanking Censorate"), cited in Yü Teng, "Ming-tai Chien-ch'a Chih-tu Kai-shu" ("Survey of the Ming Dynasty Surveillance System"), *Chin-ling Hsüeh-pao*, VI (1936), 225.

49. Cf. *Ming Shih*, ch. 163, pp. 1a–4a; *Ming-ch'en Tsou-i* ("Memorials of Ming Officials") (Ts'ung-shu Chi-ch'eng ed.), ch. 2, pp. 20–22; Ku Chieh-kang, "A Study of Literary Persecution during the Ming," trans. L. C. Goodrich, *Harvard Journal of Asiatic Studies*, III (1938), 270–72.

50. Cf. *Ming Shih*, ch. 188, pp. 27a–29a; Wolfgang Seuberlich, "Kaiser-true oder auflehnung? Eine Episode aus der Ming-zeit," *Zeitschrift der Deutschen Morgenländischen Gesellschaft*, CII (1952), 304–14.

51. Cf. *Ming Shih*, ch. 16, p. 11a.

52. Cf. *Ming Shih*, ch. 17, p. 4b; Ku Ying-t'ai, *Ming-shih Chi-shih Pen-mo* ("Topical Analysis of Ming History") (Wan-yu Wen-k'u ed.), ch. 50.

53. Cf. Ku Ying-t'ai, ch. 67; Hucker, "The Tung-lin Movement," especially pp. 140–41; Lin Yutang, *A History of the Press and Public Opinion in China* (Chicago, 1936), p. 65.

54. Cf. Ku Ying-t'ai, ch. 71; Hucker, "The Tung-lin Movement," pp. 153 ff.; Lin Yutang, pp. 70–73.

55. *Tung-lin T'ung-chih Lu* ("Record of the Tung-lin Comrades"), in *Cho-chung Chih-yü* ("Supplementary Treatise on Palace Life") (Cheng-chüeh-lou Ts'ung-k'e ed.), ch. 1, pp. 24–29.

56. For example, cf. *Hsi-tsung Shih-lu*, ch. 8, p. 12a.

57. *Ming Shih*, ch. 164, pp. 6b–7b.

58. For example, see the censor Yang Lien's famous denunciation of Wei's "24 great crimes" in *Yang Ta-hung Chi* ("Collected Works of Yang Lien") (Ts'ung-shu Chi-ch'eng ed.), pp. 1–7.

59. For example, cf. *Hsüan-tsung Shih-lu*, ch. 14, pp. 2b–3a.

60. For examples, cf. *Hsi-tsung Shih-lu*, ch. 21, p. 20b; ch. 24, pp. 15a–b; ch. 19, pp. 30a–b; ch. 21, pp. 20a–b; ch. 26, pp. 11a–b; ch. 32, pp. 9a–b.

61. For example, cf. *Hsi-tsung Shih-lu*, ch. 42, pp. 4a, 5a; *Hsüan-tsung Shih-lu*, ch. 47, pp. 12b–13a; ch. 51, pp. 7a–b; ch. 65, p. 9a.

62. Cf. *Hsi-tsung Shih-lu*, ch. 21, pp. 14b–15a.

63. *Hsüan-tsung Shih-lu*, ch. 36, p. 10a.

64. Cf. *Hsi-tsung Shih-lu*, ch. 50, p. 12b, for one example: a proposal that strict time limits be established within which newly appointed or transferred officials must arrive at their duty posts.

65. Hua Yün-ch'eng, *Kao Chung-hsien-kung Nien-p'u* ("Chronological Biography of Kao P'an-lung") (Kao-tzu I-shu ed.), pp. 24b–25b.

66. *Ming Shih*, ch. 188, p. 2a, in the biography of Liu Ch'ih.

67. Tso Tsai, *Tso Kuang-tou Nien-p'u* ("Chronological Biography of Tso Kuang-tou") (Pi-ts'e Ts'ung-shuo ed.), ch. 2, pp. 14a–b, 15b, 15b–16a.

NOTES TO CONFUCIAN ELEMENTS IN THE THEORY OF PAINTING

I am indebted to a number of people for corrections and suggestions, especially to Professor Kai-yu Hsü of San Francisco State College and Professor David S. Nivison of Stanford University.

Citations from the early treatises on painting, unless otherwise noted, are from the Wang-shih Hua-yüan edition.

1. W. Theodore de Bary, "A Reappraisal of Neo-Confucianism," in Arthur Wright, ed., *Studies in Chinese Thought* (Chicago, 1953), p. 82. This is not, of course, de Bary's own opinion.

2. Ernest Fenollosa, *Epochs of Chinese and Japanese Art* (London, 1912), I, 29.

3. Arthur Waley, *Zen Buddhism and Its Relation to Art* (London, 1922), p. 22.

4. Joseph R. Levenson, "The Amateur Ideal in Ming and Early Ch'ing Society: Evidence from Painting," in John K. Fairbank, ed., *Chinese Thought and Institutions* (Chicago, 1957), p. 326.

5. The same parallel has been drawn in the Sung period between two tendencies in poetry and the schools of Ch'an; see Yen Yü, *Ts'ang-lang Shih-hua* (Ts'ung-shu Chi-ch'eng ed.), pp. 1a ff. Since Yen Yü was referring to poetry produced before the rise of Ch'an in China, there is certainly no suggestion of a Ch'an aesthetic being involved. The author, in fact, ends his discussion with the statement that in determining the schools of poetry, he has merely "borrowed Ch'an as an analogy." Tung Ch'i-ch'ang only applied the same analogy to painting.

6. Alexander Soper, "Standards of Quality in Northern Sung Painting," *Archives of the Chinese Art Society of America*, XI (1957), 13.

7. Victoria Contag, *Die Beiden Steine* (Braunschweig, 1950), pp. 13–51: "Versuch einer Erklärung des Begriffs Ch'i Yün Sheng Tung"; also "The Unique Characteristics of Chinese Landscape Painting," *Archives*, VI (1952), 45–63. Two other exceptions to my generalization about the failure of recent writers on Chinese art to take sufficient note of Confucianism may be cited: Osvald Sirén's discussion of the Six Laws of Hsieh Ho (*A History of Early Chinese Painting* [London, 1933], I, 31–36); and Laurence Sickman's excellent short presentation of the Confucian and Taoist poles of Chinese thought and their effect upon art, in Sickman and Soper, *The Art and Architecture of China* (London, 1956), pp. 22–24.

8. Alfred Forke, trans., *Lun-Heng*. Part II. "Miscellaneous Essays of Wang Ch'ung" (Berlin, 1911), pp. 250, 352; adapted from Forke's translations.

9. Chang Yen-yüan, *Li-tai Ming-hua Chi*, ch. 1. See William Acker, *Some T'ang and Pre-T'ang Texts on Chinese Painting* (Leiden, 1954), pp. 72–75. Acker's translation. For the parts of *Li-tai Ming-hua Chi* not included in Acker's book, I have used the Chi-ku-ko edition of Mao Chin. See also F. S. Drake, "Sculptured Stones of the Han Dynasty," *Monumenta Serica*, VIII

there were none that were omitted; the evil to warn the world, the good to teach posterity."

10. Acker, *Texts*, p. 151. Acker's translation. Quoted also in many other books. The same observation is attributed to the painter Ku K'ai-chih, among others.

11. De Bary, "Reappraisal," p. 84.

12. Chow Yih-ching, *La Philosophie morale dans le néo-confucianisme (Tcheou Touen-yi)* (Paris, 1954), pp. 32–33 and 181; Chinese text on pp. 196–97. The Chinese text of Chou Tun-i's works is included in this book, which I cite hereafter as *Chou Tun-i*. The translations are my own.

13. The fragmentary essay by Wang Wei (not to be confused with the T'ang dynasty poet-painter) is included in ch. 6 of *Li-tai Ming-hua Chi*.

14. Tsung Ping, "Hua Shan-shui Hsü"; contained, along with the Wang Wei essay, in ch. 6 of *Li-tai Ming-hua Chi*. I have translated these and other passages from these essays, and discussed them at greater length, in the introduction to an unpublished study, "The Theory of Literati Painting in China." In that study I treat more fully some of the questions dealt with in the present paper, and provide more thorough documentation than I can introduce here.

15. See Fung Yu-lan, *A History of Chinese Philosophy*, trans. Derk Bodde (Princeton, 1952), Vol. II, chap. 5; also Arthur Wright's review of A. A. Petrov, *Wang Pi (226–249): His Place in the History of Chinese Philosophy*, in *HJAS*, X (1947), p. 86, for Wang Pi's concept of "images."

16. Fung Yu-lan, *A Short History of Chinese Philosophy*, chap. 20, "Neo-Taoism: the Sentimentalists."

17. Liu Hsieh, *Wen-hsin Tiao-lung* (Kuang Han Wei Ts'ung-shu ed.), section 46: ch. 10, p. 1a.

18. Acker, *Texts*, p. 61. Acker's translation, except that I have altered the opening phrase and removed the parentheses enclosing explanatory matter introduced by the translator. I have removed parentheses and brackets, in the interest of smooth reading, in some other quotations as well.

19. Acker, *Texts*, Introduction, p. li.

20. *Li-tai Ming-hua Chi*, ch. 8, p. 4a.

21. Acker, *Texts*, p. 153. Acker's translation.

22. *Li-tai Ming-hua Chi*, ch. 10, p. 4b.

23. Quoted from the "Yüeh-chi" ("Record of Music") section of the *Li-chi*, part III, par. 5; see Legge's translation (*Sacred Books of the East*, Vols. XXVII–XXVIII, *The Li Ki*), II, 116.

24. Quoted from the *Lun-yü*, Part VII, par. 6. Cf. Alexander Soper, *Kuo Jo-hsü's Experiences in Painting* (Washington, D.C., 1951), p. 15 and note 181. Adapted from Soper's translation.

25. *Li-tai Ming-hua Chi*, ch. 8, p. 1b.

26. Acker, *Texts*, p. li.

27. Forke, *Lun-Heng*, p. 229. Adapted from Forke's translations.

28. Chung Jung, *Shih P'in* (Kuang Han Wei Ts'ung-shu ed.), ch. 2, p. 4b.

29. *Wen-hsin Tiao-lung*, section 48: ch. 10, p. 8b.

30. *Chou I*, "Hsi-tz'u" part I, section xii; Legge's translation (*Sacred Books of the East*, Vol. XVI, *The Yi King*), pp. 376–77. The words are ascribed to Confucius.

31. From his preface to the *Lun-yü*; see *Sung Yüan Hsüeh-an* (Kuo-hsüeh Chi-pen Ts'ung-shu ed.), ch. 24, p. 11a.

32. Legge, *The Shih King* (*The Chinese Classics*, vol. IV), p. 34.

33. Legge, *The Li Ki*, II, 131.

34. "Shih Chi-chuan Hsü," in *Min-an Hsien-sheng Chu Wen-kung Wen-chi* (Ssu-pu Ts'ung-k'an ed.), ch. 76, p. 3a. Chu Hsi is speaking of the *Shih-ching* poems in particular, but surely intends his words to have a more general application to other poetry.

35. See the "Yüeh-chi," section 2; pp. 105–14 in Legge's translation. The pertinent statements are too long to be quoted in full. See also Chou Tun-i's statement of the moralizing power of music (*Chou Tun-i*, p. 176; Chinese text, p. 198).

36. Chu Hsi, "Shih Chi-chuan Hsü"; see note 34 above.

37. *Mencius*, Book V, Part 2, ch. 8. Translation adapted from that of Legge, *The Chinese Classics*, II, 391–92.

38. Forke, *Lun-heng*, p. 102. Forke's translation.

39. Acker, *Texts*, p. lvi. Acker's translation.

40. Wei Heng, "Ssu-t'i Shu-shih," in *P'ei-wen-chai Shu-hua P'u*, ch. 1, p. 4b.

41. The essay is included in *Fa-shu Yao-lu* (comp. by Chang Yen-yüan), ch. 4.

42. Fung, *History of Chinese Philosophy*, I, 342. Bodde's translation.

43. Quoted in *Pei-wen-chai Shu-hua P'u*, ch. 6, p. 5b.

44. The practice never seems to have gone so far as the theory; subject matter was never entirely neglected, however close the paintings' approach to abstraction. This question of the role of subject matter is a complex one, which we cannot take up fully here.

45. Carsun Chang, *The Development of Neo-Confucian Thought* (New York, 1957), pp. 75, 236.

46. *Chou Tun-i*, pp. 25–26.

47. *Sheng-hua Chi*, comp. by Sun Shao-yüan, ch. 2, p. 1a. The *Sheng-hua Chi* is a twelfth-century compilation of poems written as inscriptions for paintings.

48. See note 24.

49. *T'u-hua Chien-wen Chih*, ch. 1, p. 12a. Adapted from Soper's translation (see note 24).

50. There is a possibility that it is not *shuo*, "discourse," but the other reading of the character, *yüeh*, "pleasure," which is intended here. Painting is sometimes spoken of, in the literati school, simply as an enjoyable occupation. In the present context, however, *shuo* seems more likely.

51. *Shan-hu Mu-nan*, comp. by Chu Ts'un-li (1444–1513), ch. 3, p. 24b. An inscription on a landscape.

52. *Fa-yen* (Kuang Han Wei Ts'ung-shu ed.), ch. 4, p. 3a.

53. *T'u-hua Chien-wen Chih*, ch. 1, p. 12b.

54. *Hsüan-ho Hua-p'u* ("Imperial Catalog of the Collection of the Emperor Hui-tsung"), ch. 20, p. 8b.

55. *Hua-chi*, ch. 3, p. 15a, on Fan Cheng-fu.

56. Quoted in *P'ei-wen-chai Shu-hua P'u*, ch. 6, p. 14b.

57. *Chung-yung*, ch. I, sec. 4. Legge's translation (*Classics*, I, 384).

58. Fung, *History*, I, 374.

59. *Kuang-ch'uan Hua-pa*, ch. 1, p. 11a.

60. *Tung-p'o Wen-chi Shih-lüeh* (Ssu-pu Ts'ung-k'an ed.), ch. 53, p. 3a.

I have abbreviated the passage.

61. *Kuang-ch'uan Hua-pa,* ch. 1, p. 12a–b.

62. Cf. Li Ao: "When the mind is calm and not in action, the corrupted thoughts will stop naturally. As long as one's nature is enlightened, no corruption can be produced." (Carsun Chang, *Development,* p. 110.)

63. *Chou Tun-i,* Chinese text, p. 204. Beginning of section 2, of his "T'ung Shu."

64. In the Addenda to Wen T'ung's collected literary works, *Tan-yüan Chi,* p. 32a.

65. *Hai-yüeh T'i-pa,* ch. 1, p. 1a.

66. From his essay "Ting Hsing"; see *Sung Yüan Hsüeh-an,* ch. 13, pp. 11–12.

67. *Chung-yung,* ch. 20, sec. 18. Legge's translation (*Classics,* I, 413).

68. Huang T'ing-chien, *Shan-ku T'i-pa,* ch. 3, p. 18a.

69. *Kuang-ch'uan Hua-pa,* ch. 6. Tung is referring, perhaps more as a loyal subject than as a candid critic, to the painting of the Emperor Hui-tsung, who "transformed" less than most, being a relatively realistic painter.

70. *Chung-yung,* chs. 22, 23. Translations adapted from Legge, *Classics,* I, 415-17, and Derk Bodde, "Harmony and Conflict in Chinese Philosophy," in Wright, ed., *Studies in Chinese Thought,* p. 55.

71. Fung, *History,* II, 523.

72. *Tung-p'o Wen-chi,* ch. 54, p. 9a.

73. *Kuang-ch'uan Hua-pa,* ch. 2.

74. *Hua Shan-shui Chüeh,* section 29.

75. *Chung-yung,* ch. 33, sec. 1; adapted from Legge's translation (*Classics,* I, 430-31).

76. *Jen-wu chih* (in *Kuang Han Wei Ts'ung-shu*), beginning of ch. 1.

77. *Chou Tun-i,* p. 23; Chinese text, p. 191.

78. *Kuang-ch'uan Hua-pa,* ch. 3.

79. Quoted in *P'ei-wen-chai Shu-hua P'u,* ch. 50, p. 58a.

80. See note 24. I have used Waley's translation (*The Analects of Confucius* [London, 1938], p. 123) for the first half, but prefer Soper's "seek delight in the arts" to Waley's "seek distraction in the arts" for *yu yü i.*

81. *Hsüan-ho Hua-p'u,* ch. 1, p. 1a.

82. "Chu-tzu Lun Wen," in *Chu-tzu Ch'üan-shu,* ch. 65, p. 6a.

83. "Hui-an T'i-pa" (in *Chin-tai Pi-shu*), ch. 2, p. 7a. Chu Hsi was probably alluding to a famous story (related by Kuo Jo-hsü, among others; see Soper, *Kuo Jo-hsü's Experiences in Painting,* p. 96) about a rustic who was caught laughing at a famous painting of fighting oxen. Asked to explain himself, he said: "I know nothing about paintings; I only know what cattle are really like when they are fighting."

84. *Ibid.,* ch. 3, p. 5a; ch. 3, p. 27b; ch. 3, p. 37a.

NOTES TO T'ANG LITERATI

1. *Chiu T'ang-shu* (*CTS*), ch. 190. The biographies can be counted in more than one way. My figure 101 takes in all those, including "attached" biographies, that give information beyond the man's name and his relation-

ship to the person to whose biography he is attached, but I have excluded those "attached" biographies that do not mention literary achievements.

2. See Hans H. Frankel, "The K'ung Family of Shan-yin," *Tsing Hua Journal of Chinese Studies*, N.S., II, No. 2 (1961), pp. 303–4.

3. *CTS* (Po-na ed.), ch. 190A, p. 2a.

4. *Ibid.*, ch. 190C, p. 1b. The very title of the *fu*, "Felling Cherry Trees," is perhaps a jab at Li Lin-fu, whose surname means "plum tree." But the full significance of this episode escapes me. Does it reflect the conflict between the northwestern aristocrats, headed by Li Lin-fu, and the literati, represented here by Hsiao Ying-shih? On the other hand, Li in this story and elsewhere appears anxious to draw the literati to his side. The T'ang historiographers, strongly biased against Li, are ever ready to include material that tends to discredit him. See E. G. Pulleyblank, *The Background of the Rebellion of An Lu-shan* (London, 1955), p. 55.

5. *CTS*, ch. 190C, p. 20a.

6. *Ibid.*, ch. 190A, p. 3a.

7. *Ibid.*, ch. 190B, p. 11a.

8. *Ibid.*, pp. 10b–11a.

9. *Ibid.*, pp. 2a–b.

10. *Ibid.*, p. 3b.

11. *Ibid.*, pp. 14b–15b.

12. *Ibid.*, ch. 190C, pp. 1a–3a.

13. *Ibid.*, ch. 190B, p. 13b.

14. *Ibid.*, p. 1b.

15. *Ibid.*, ch. 190A, p. 8a.

16. See Hans Bielenstein, *The Restoration of the Han Dynasty* (Stockholm, 1953), pp. 73–74.

17. *CTS*, ch. 190A, p. 7a.

18. *Ibid.*, ch. 190C, pp. 1b–2a.

19. *Ibid.*, ch. 190A, p. 5a.

20. Stephen Spender, "The Making of a Poem," in Brewster Ghiselin (ed.), *The Creative Process* (New York, Mentor Books, 1959), pp. 122–23.

21. Malcolm Cowley, "Remembering Hart Crane," in *The Creative Process*, pp. 145–46.

22. *CTS*, ch. 190B, p. 2b.

23. Ho Chih-chang, *CTS*, ch. 190B, p. 15a; Li Po, ch. 190C, pp. 4a–b; Tu Fu, ch. 190C, p. 5a; Ts'ui Hsien, ch. 190C, p. 8a.

24. See Wang Yao, *Chung-ku wen-hsüeh shih lun chi* (Shanghai, 1956), pp. 28–48.

25. *CTS*, ch. 190C, p. 8a.

26. *Ibid.*, p. 2a.

27. *Chen-kuan cheng-yao* (Ssu-pu ts'ung-k'an ed.), ch. 7, pp. 8a–b.

28. *CTS*, ch. 190B, p. 5a.

29. *Ibid.*, pp. 11b–12a.

30. *Ibid.*, pp. 14b–15a.

31. *Ibid.*, ch. 190A, pp. 11b–12b.

32. *Ibid.*, ch. 190B, pp. 5b–7b.

33. *Ibid.*, pp. 13b–14a.

34. *Ibid.*, p. 20b.

35. *Ibid.*, ch. 190A, p. 10a.

36. *Ibid.*, ch. 190C, pp. 11a–18b.
37. *Ibid.*, ch. 190B, pp. 1b–2a.
38. *Ibid.*, ch. 190C, pp. 22b–23a.
39. *Ibid.*, ch. 190B, p. 3b.
40. Nagasawa Kikuya and Eugen Feifel, *Geschichte der chinesischen Literatur*, 2d ed. (Darmstadt, 1959), p. 202.
41. *CTS*, ch. 190C, p. 19b. Ling-hu Ch'u compiled a small anthology of recent T'ang poetry (Li Shang-yin is not included) for the emperor's perusal; see *T'ang-jen hsüan T'ang-shih* (Shanghai, 1958), pp. 191–255.
42. *CTS*, ch. 190B, p. 10b.
43. *Ibid.*, ch. 190C, p. 19a.
44. *Ibid.*, ch. 190B, p. 20a.
45. *Ibid.*, p. 2a; *Tzu chih t'ung-chien,* Ch'ien-feng second year, ninth month.
46. *CTS*, ch. 190B, p. 2a; *Tzu chih t'ung-chien,* Ch'ien-feng second year, ninth month.
47. *CTS*, ch. 190A, p. 14a.
48. *Ibid.*, ch. 190C, pp. 21a–b.
49. *Ibid.*, ch. 190B, pp. 9b, 10a.
50. *Ibid.*, ch. 190A, p. 6b.
51. *Ibid.*, p. 11a; ch. 190C, p. 6b. I am proud to point out that my own son has learned to recognize more than 1,500 Chinese characters before reaching the age of four (five *sui*).
52. *Ibid.*, ch. 190C, p. 2b.
53. *Ibid.*, p. 7a.
54. *Ibid.*, ch. 190B, p. 17b.
55. *Ibid.*, ch. 190C, p. 9b.
56. *Ibid.*, ch. 190B, pp.16a–17b.
57. *Ibid.*, ch. 190C, p. 2a.
58. *Ibid.*, ch. 190B, pp. 18a–20a.
59. *Ibid.*, ch. 190A, pp. 14a–b.

NOTES TO TRADITIONAL HEROES IN CHINESE POPULAR FICTION

1. See Joseph Bédier, *Les Légendes épiques* (Paris, 1914), 4 vols.; Marcel Granet, *Danses et légendes de la Chine ancienne* (Paris, 1926), 2 vols.; H. M. Chadwick and N. K. Chadwick, *The Growth of Literature* (Cambridge, England, 1932), 3 vols., especially III, 697–772; F. R. S. Raglan, *The Hero* (London, 1936); Max Kaltenmark, "Le Dompteur des Flots," *Han Hiue*, III (Peking, 1948), 1–113; R. A. Stein, *L'Epopée tibétaine de Gesar* (Paris, 1956); Rufus Mathewson, *The Positive Hero in Russian Literature* (New York, 1958), especially pp. 5–6, 265.
2. Published in Boston, 1957. See the neat synthesis on pp. 4–5 of the Introduction ("Social Meanings in Literature").
3. Abbreviations:

CKCK: *Chin Ku Ch'i Kuan,* a Ming collection of 40 short stories (Shanghai, 1888), 6 *ts'e.*

CPC: *Chui Po Ch'iu,* collection of libretti of K'un-ch'ü operas (preface,

1770, re-ed., Shanghai, 1955), 12 vols.

KCHS: *Ku Chin Hsiao Shuo,* a Ming collection of 40 short stories (Peking, 1958 ed.), 642 pp.

KP: *Ku Pen Yüan Ming Tsa Chü* ("Yüan and Ming Dramas in Rare Editions") (Peking, 1957), 4 vols.

KTH: Chao Ching-shen, *Ku Tz'u Hsüan* ("Anthology of Drum Ballads") (Shanghai, 1957), 164 pp.

SH: *Shui Hu Chuan* ("Water Margin") (Peking, 1954 ed.), 1,834 pp.

SKPH: *San Kuo Chih P'ing Hua* ("Narration of the Three Kingdoms"), a Yüan novel (Shanghai, 1955 ed.), 145 pp.

SKYI: *San Kuo Chih Yen I* ("Romance of the Three Kingdoms"), a Ming novel (Peking, 1953 ed.), 990 pp.

YCH: *Yüan Ch'ü Hsüan* ("Anthology of Yüan Operas"), Wan Yu Wen K'u ed. (Shanghai, 1930), 48 vols.

Collections of libretti of Peking operas:

CCHP: *Ching Chü Hui Pien* (Peking, 1957), 27 vols.

CCTK: *Ching Chü Ts'ung K'an* (Shanghai, 1958), 958 pp.

HC: *Hsi Chien* (Shanghai, 1948), 4 vols.

HK: *Hsi K'ao* (Shanghai, 1918), 30 vols.

The Histories are cited in the Po-na-pen edition (Shanghai, 1930–36).

4. This word has been aptly coined by C. C. Wang: see "Chinese Literature," *Chambers' Encyclopaedia,* III (New York, 1950), 491.

5. *Meng-tzu Chu-shu* (Ssu-pu Pei-yao ed.), ch. 5B, pp. 1b–2a. See Ch'ü T'ung-tsu, "Chinese Class Structure and Its Ideology," in J. K. Fairbank, ed., *Chinese Thought and Institutions* (Chicago, 1957), pp. 235–50.

6. See Wang, "Chinese Literature," pp. 492–96, and the outlines and bibliographies in J. R. Hightower, *Topics in Chinese Literature* (Cambridge, Mass., 1950), pp. 14–21, 72–79, 95–102. See also W. Eberhard, *Die chinesische Novelle* (Ascona, 1948).

7. See Lu Hsün, "She-hsi" ("Village Opera"), *Na-han* (Shanghai, 1926), pp. 235–53.

8. See *Hung Lou Meng,* chaps. 18–19, 22–23, 43, 53–54.

9. Especially detailed are, for the Northern Sung, Meng Yüan-lao, *Tung-ching Meng Hua Lu* (twelfth century), and for the Southern Sung, three works of the thirteenth century: Nai Te-weng, *Tu-ch'eng Chi Sheng;* Wu Tzu-mu, *Meng Liang Lu;* Chou Mi, *Wu Lin Chiu Shih.* See J. Prusek, "Researches into the Beginnings of the Chinese Popular Novel," *Archiv Orientalni,* XI (1939), 91–132; J. L. Bishop, *The Colloquial Short Story in China* (Cambridge, Mass., 1956), pp. 7–12; and J. Gernet, *La Vie quotidienne à l'époque des Song* (Paris, 1959), pp. 240–45.

10. See Wang, pp. 494–97, and the outlines and bibliographies in Hightower, pp. 84–102, and in R. G. Irwin, *The Evolution of a Chinese Novel* (Cambridge, Mass., 1953), pp. 1–8, 213–23. See also *YCH, KP, CPC, KTH, HK, HC, CCTK, CCHP.*

11. For instance, 737 Yüan dramas are mentioned in lists, but the texts of only 217 have been preserved.

12. See L. C. Goodrich, *The Literary Inquisition of Ch'ien-lung* (Baltimore, 1935), pp. 194–97.

13. See Yao Chin-kuang, *Ch'ing-tai Chin-hui Shu-mu Ssu Chung* ("Four Lists of Books Banned under the Ch'ing Dynasty"), Wan Yu Wen K'u ed. (Shanghai, 1937); and A-ying, "Kuan-yü Ch'ing-tai ti Ch'a-chin Hsiao-shuo" ("On Novels Banned under the Ch'ing Dynasty"), in *Hsiao-shuo Erh T'an* ("More Talks about Novels") (Shanghai, 1958), pp. 136–42. See also Goodrich, p. 261; W. Fuchs, *Monumenta Serica*, III (1937–38), 305; and Cheng T'ien-t'ing and Sun Yüeh, eds., *Ming-mo Nung-min Ch'i-i Shih-liao* (Shanghai, 1952), pp. 355–56.

14. See Irwin, *Evolution of a Chinese Novel*, pp. 87–90.

15. See Ch'ü, in *Chinese Thought and Institutions*, p. 249.

16. H. H. Frankel, "Objektivität und Parteilichkeit in der offiziellen chinesischen Geschichtsschreibung vom 3. bis 11. J." ("Objectivity and Bias in Chinese Official Historiography from the Third to the Eleventh Century"), *Oriens Extremus*, V (1958), No. 2, p. 134.

17. *Ibid.*, pp. 133–44; see also Frankel's authorities, from the *Ch'un-ch'iu* on.

18. Y. T. M. Feuerwerker, "The Chinese Novel," in Wm. Theodore de Bary, ed., *Approaches to the Oriental Classics* (New York, 1959), p. 172.

19. C. Birch, "*Ku-chin Hsiao-shuo*, A Critical Examination," manuscript thesis (London, 1954; hereafter Birch, Thesis), p. 295.

20. *KCHS*, ch. 22, pp. 333–54, esp. 335, 339. See Uchida Michio, " 'Kokon-shōsetsu' no Seikaku ni Tsuite" ("On the Nature of the *KCHS*"), *Bunka*, XVII, No. 6 (1953), pp. 26–45, and H. Franke, "Die Agrarreformen des Chia Ssu-tao," *Saeculum*, IX, No. 3/4 (1959), pp. 345–69. See also the play *Hung Mei Ko*, in *HK*, XIV, ch. 20. On the term "bad last minister," see above, pp. 155–56.

21. Found in the well-known text of Wang P'eng quoted by Su Shih, *Tung-p'o Chih-lin*, ch. 1, p. 7b, trans. Prusek, in *Archiv Orientalni*, p. 111, and Irwin, *Evolution of a Chinese Novel*, p. 23.

22. J. I. Crump, "The Elements of Yüan Opera," *Journal of Asian Studies*, XVII (1958), 419.

23. See J. T. C. Liu, "Some Classifications of Bureaucrats in Chinese Historiography," in David S. Nivison and Arthur F. Wright, eds., *Confucianism in Action* (Stanford, 1959), pp. 170–72.

24. See *Shih Chi*, chs. 119–20, 122; *Han Shu*, chs. 89, 90; *Hou Han Shu*, chs. 106, 107, 114; *Chiu T'ang Shu*, chs. 185, 186, 188, 193; *Hsin T'ang Shu*, chs. 195, 197, 205, 209, 223–25; *Sung Shih*, chs. 426, 460, 471–77; *Ming Shih*, chs. 281, 301–3, 308.

25. *KCHS*, ch. 27, trans. C. Birch, "The Lady Who Was a Beggar," in *Stories from a Ming Collection* (London, 1958), pp. 17–36; *CKCK*, ch. 32; *Hung Luan Hsi, HK*, II, ch. 19.

26. *Ch'ing Lou Meng: HK*, XX, ch. 10. *Ching Shih T'ung Yen*, ch. 32; *CKCK*, ch. 5; *HK*, VIII, ch. 8. *Yü T'ang Ch'un: HC*, I, 316–17; *CCTK*, p. 97; L. C. Arlington and H. Acton, *Famous Chinese Plays* (Peiping, 1937), p. 414.

27. See this traditional list in Crump, in *Journal of Asian Studies*, XVII, 420.

28. As when the loyal censor Sun An brings nineteen coffins with him to memorialize to the Wan-li emperor, in *Chia Chin P'ai, HK*, XVII, ch. 3.

29. Chao Kao: in *Yü-chou Feng, HK*, II, ch. 14, *CCTK*, pp. 279–83. Ts'ao Ts'ao: see p. 165. Ssu-ma Shih: see p. 149. On Kao Ch'iu, one of the arch-villains in *Water Margin*, see also *Pao Chien Chi*, by Li K'ai-hsien (1501–68), and *Yen Yang Lou, HK*, XI, ch. 9. Ch'in Hui: in *Feng Seng Pao Ch'in, CCTK*, pp. 928–34. Chia Ssu-tao: see p. 147. Li Liang: in *Ta Pao Kuo, HK*, IV, ch. 8, and *Erh Chin Kung, HK*, V, ch. 7. Yen Sung: in *KCHS*, ch. 40, and *Ta Yen Sung, HK*, III, ch. 9, *HC*, I, 280–99, *CCTK*, pp. 700–714.

30. One can draw the following equations between heroes of the *Three Kingdoms* and of the *Water Margin*:

$$\text{Kuan Yü} = \text{Kuan Sheng} = \text{Chu T'ung}$$
$$\text{Chang Fei} = \text{Li K'uei}$$
$$\text{Chu-ko Liang} = \text{Wu Yung} + \text{Kung-sun Sheng}.$$

31. *Hsiao-yao Chin, HK*, IV, ch. 1; *HC*, I, 564–83. *Ssu-ma Pi Kung, HK*, XIII, ch. 1. Compare *SKYI*, chs. 66, 119. The play *Li Ling Pei* (*KP*, 93; *HK*, XI, ch. 1; *HC*, I, 352–58) builds up another dramatic parallelism.

32. The rebels Li Tzu-ch'eng and Chang Hsien-chung, now glorified by the Communists as revolutionary leaders, were the villains of two traditional plays, *Tz'u Hu* and *Feng Huo Mei* (see above, p. 156), which were focusing sympathy on the two "Judiths" who attempt to kill them. On the Kuomintang's switch of feelings, in the late twenties, from the Taipings to Tseng Kuo-fan, see Mary C. Wright, *The Last Stand of Chinese Conservatism* (Stanford, 1957), pp. 304–5. Similarly the respect for Confucius in the twentieth century is a barometer of change in the Chinese intellectual climate.

33. *SKPH*, pp. 10–11; *SKYI*, ch. 1, pp. 3–4. The Han foot was shorter than ours.

34. Fortune-tellers read Ts'ao Ts'ao's destiny and evil genius from the bones of his face: *SKYI*, ch. 1, p. 6.

35. Thus is Thirteenth Sister judged by her father-in-law: *Erh-nü Ying-hsiung Chuan*, quoted by Fung Yu-lan, *Hsin Shih-lun* (1940), p. 78, trans. Yang Lien-sheng, "The Concept of Pao," in *Chinese Thought and Institutions*, p. 296.

36. Fung, *Hsin Shih-lun*, p. 78.

37. *Yüan Men Chan Tzu: HK*, III, ch. 6. *Chen T'an-chou: HK*, XIX, ch. 12.

38. This word, used by Bishop (*The Colloquial Short Story in China*, p. 15), characterizes this kind of fiction more aptly than the word "realistic."

39. Birch, Thesis, p. 272.

40. See a polemic against Hu Shih about a novel of Maupassant and Chinese heroic fiction: Jen Fang-ch'iu, "Stereotyping and Humor in Classical Literature," in *Ku-tien Wen-hsüeh Yen-chiu Chi* ("Studies on Classical Literature") (Wuhan, 1956), pp. 109–11.

41. Alfred de Vigny (1797–1863), "Moïse," *Poèmes antiques et modernes* (Paris, 1822).

42. In the play *Cha Mei An, HK*, VII, ch. 3, pp. 7–8, *HC*, II, 759, *CCTK*, p. 753.

43. *HK*, V. ch. 1, VIII, ch. 5, and XI, ch. 3; *HC*, I, 416–28, 521–32, II,

234–40; *CCTK,* pp. 256–71; *CCHP,* XXI, 1–119; trans. S. I. Hsiung (London, 1936).

44. *KCHS,* chs. 31, 37.

45. Chang Liang, for example, in *I Ch'iao Chin Lü, KP,* 12.

46. *Wu P'en Chi, HK,* XIII, ch. 6, *HC,* I, 583–600.

47. *Pai She Chuan, HK,* X, ch. 11, XXIII, ch. 10; *CCTK,* pp. 688–700; *KTH,* pp. 155–59. *Ch'ing Shih Shan, HK,* IX, ch. 12. Eberhard, *Die chinesische Novelle,* pp. 94–98.

48. Both stem from the *chiang-shih* storytelling (see p. 143). The best known of the romances are the *Tung Chou Lieh Kuo Chih,* 108 ch., the *Tung Hsi Han Yen I,* 18 ch., the *San Kuo Chih Yen I,* 120 ch., the *Ying Lieh Chuan,* 34 ch., whose titles speak for themselves, then the *Shuo Yüeh Ching Chung Chuan,* 80 ch., which deals with Yüeh Fei and the founding of Ming. The *Shui-hu Chuan,* 120 ch., the *Ch'i Hsia Wu I,* 120 ch., the *Hsiao Wu I,* 120 ch., the *Erh Nü Ying-hsiung Chuan,* 54 ch., and the various *kung an,* very popular detective novels, can be classified with the romances.

49. *SH,* ch. 28, p. 443.

50. Lady Mi: *SKPH,* pp. 73–74; *SKYI,* ch. 41, p. 346, and *Ch'ang Pan P'o, HK,* IX, ch. 6, pp. 6–7, *CCTK,* pp. 74–77, trans. Acton, *Famous Chinese Plays,* pp. 31–32. Mu-lan: *HK,* XXIX, ch. 3, *HC,* II, 37–71.

51. *CPC,* I, 1–25, VII, 66–80, XII, 180–88; *HC,* III, 289–312. See E. Chavannes, *Mémoires historiques* (Paris, 1895), I, xxxvii–xxxix, and K. P. K. Whitaker, "Some Notes on the Authenticity of the Lii Ling Su Wuu Letters," *Bulletin of the School of Oriental and African Studies,* 1953, pp. 113–37, 566–87, especially "The Story of Su Wuu and Lii Ling," pp. 113–16.

52. *Yüeh Mu Tz'u Tzu: CPC,* VI, 65–71; *CCTK,* pp. 243–47. *Feng Po T'ing: HK,* XVII, ch. 1; *HC,* IV, 70–99.

53. See *San Tzu Ching,* attributed to Wang Ying-lin, 1223–96 (Chang Ping-lin ed., pp. 2b–3a), and Baba Harukichi, *Wa-Kan Nijushikō Zusetsu* ("The Japanese and Chinese 24 Examples of Filial Piety, with Illustrations and Commentaries") (Tokyo, 1941).

54. *Li Chi* (Ssu-pu Ts'ung-k'an ed.), ch. 6, pp. 12a–b: trans. J. Legge, *Li Ki,* I (Oxford, 1926), pp. 343–44.

55. That is how Shen Lien seeks to imitate Chu-ko Liang (in *KCHS,* ch. 40; *CKCK,* ch. 13), how the emperor Hsien abdicates (in *SKYI,* ch. 80, pp. 653, 655–56; *HK,* XXVI, ch. 2), how Meng Ta justifies his desertion (in *SKYI,* ch. 79, pp. 648–49).

56. See pp. 47, 58; see also *Chao-ko Hen, HK,* XVIII, ch. 1, and Granet, *Danses,* pp. 394–97.

57. *HK, IV,* ch. 1, p. 13; *HC,* I, 580–81.

58. *HK,* XVIII, ch. 6; XXII, ch. 4.

59. *SKPH,* pp. 135, 143–44; *SKYI,* ch. 115, pp. 945–46; ch. 116, pp. 952–53; ch. 118, pp. 967–69.

60. *SKYI,* ch. 118, pp. 967–68; *HK,* XXII, ch. 2.

61. *SKYI,* ch. 119, pp. 976–77.

62. The famous play by Hung Sheng (1645–1704), and its modern popularizations such as *Ma Wei P'o* (*HK,* XV, ch. 1).

63. *Wei Yang Kung, HK,* XVI, ch. 5. See also *Chuan K'uai T'ung, YCH,* III, and *Chang Liang Tz'u Ch'ao, HK,* XVII, ch. 10.

64. *SKPH,* pp. 3–6; *KCHS,* ch. 31.

65. *HK*, XXII, ch. 9; *CCHP*, II, 77–106.

66. *Chan Huang P'ao, HK*, III, ch. 11; *HC*, IV, 267–87.

67. *Ch'ü Jung-yang, HK*, IV, ch. 7.

68. *CCHP*, X, 2–3.

69. *SKYI*, ch. 21, pp. 178–79.

70. *SKYI*, ch. 81, pp. 661–63; ch. 84, pp. 686–90; *Fa Tung-Wu, HK*, XIII, ch. 11; *Lien Ying Chai, HK*, VI, ch. 1; *HC*, I, 615–33; *CCTK*, pp. 951–58.

71. *KP*, ch. 22; *HK*, I, ch. 12; *HC*, II, 282–301. Acton, *Famous Chinese Plays*, pp. 230–51.

72. *SKYI*, chs. 54–55; *HK*, XVIII, ch. 9; V, ch. 11; *CCTK*, pp. 438–58.

73. Ts'ao P'ei and Liu Pei in *SKYI*, ch. 80, pp. 655–56, 657–59. See Granet, *Danses*, p. 79, n.2, and pp. 86–87: "modération rituelle."

74. *SKYI*, ch. 41, pp. 340–41.

75. *SKYI*, ch. 85, pp. 695–96.

76. *KCHS*, ch. 21, pp. 298, 307; ch. 37, p. 557. *HK*, XVIII, ch. 7, p. 2; XXV, ch. 8; *CCHP*, XXI, 4. *Mo Fang Ch'an Tzu, HK*, XXVIII, ch. 5. Writers of historical romances found much material of this kind in the standard Histories. See *Shih Chi*, ch. 3, p. 1a; ch. 4, p. 1a; ch. 8, pp. 2a–b, 4b, 6a; *Han Shu*, ch. 1, pp. 1a–2b.

77. *SKPH*, p. 12; *SKYI*, ch. 1, p. 3. From *San Kuo Chih*, ch. 2, pp. 1a–b.

78. *SKYI*, ch. 34, p. 290; ch. 41, p. 347. Chao's horse changes suddenly into a dragon in the play *Ch'ang-pan P'o, HK*, IX, ch. 6, pp. 7–8, trans. Acton, *Famous Chinese Plays*, pp. 34–35.

79. *SH*, ch. 42, pp. 677–80; ch. 88, pp. 1,445–47.

80. E. D. Edwards, *Chinese Prose Literature of the Tang Period*, II, 22, 26. See also Birch, Thesis, pp. 176a, 185. The story of *Hsi Hsiang Chi* illustrates the point well.

81. *Wan Sha Chi: YCH*, XX, 27–40; *Tung Chou Lieh Kuo Chih*, chs. 72–73; *CCTK*, pp. 152–56.

82. On Chu-ko Liang testing Liu Pei, see *SKPH*, pp. 65–68; *SKYI*, chs. 37–38; *HK*, XIX, ch. 3; *CCTK*, pp. 55–67; see also *San Kuo Chih*, ch. 5, p. 9b.

83. Donald Keene, "The Tale of Genji," in de Bary, ed., *Approaches*, p. 194.

84. *Wan Pi Kuei Chao, HK*, XI, ch. 1. *Sheng-ch'ih Hui, KP*, ch. 8.

85. *YCH*, XIV. See H. Maspero, "Le Roman historique dans la littérature chinoise de l'Antiquité," in *Mélanges posthumes*, III (Paris, 1950), 53–62.

86. *KCHS*, ch. 24, pp. 384–90. *Tung Chou Lieh Kuo Chih*, ch. 69, p. 633.

87. *SH*, chs. 14–16, 39–40, 48–50, 61, 77, and others.

88. *SH*, ch. 16, pp. 225–26, 232–36.

89. *HC*, II, 1–37.

90. *SKPH*, pp. 33–34; *SKYI*, chs. 8–9, pp. 62–72. *Lien Huan Chi, YCH*, XLIII; *CPC*, X, 204–13; *HK*, XVII, ch. 12; *HC*, II, 560–90; *CCTK*, pp. 407–23; Acton, *Famous Chinese Plays*, pp. 353–59.

91. *SKYI*, ch. 45, pp. 378–80; *HK*, III, ch. 2, pp. 7–8; *HC*, II, 440–47; *CCTK*, pp. 167–73.

92. *SKYI*, chs. 43–44, pp. 356–68, trans. J. Steele, *The Logomachy* (Shanghai, 1907); *HK*, XIX, ch. 4.

93. *SKPH*, pp. 134, 138–39; *SKYI*, ch. 102, pp. 849–53.

94. *SKYI*, chs. 87–90.

95. *SKYI*, ch. 46, pp. 383–86; *HK*, III, ch. 2, p. 14; *HC*, II, 450–51, 453–56; *CCTK*, pp. 175–81; Acton, *Famous Chinese Plays*, pp. 202–6; *KTH*, pp. 148–51.

96. *HK*, I, ch. 1; *HC*, I, 401–16; *CCTK*, pp. 1–11; *SKYI*, ch. 95, p. 787 (less detailed).

97. *T'an Yin Shan*, *HK*, II, ch. 6. *Cha P'an-kuan*, *CCHP*, Vols. XXIV and XXV.

98. *SKPH*, pp. 84–85; *SKYI*, ch. 49, pp. 404–5; *HK*, XV, ch. 7; Acton, *Famous Chinese Plays*, pp. 208–9.

99. *SKPH*, p. 142; *SKYI*, ch. 103, pp. 860–61.

100. See p. 163.

101. *HK*, I, ch. 1, p. 4; *HC*, I, 411; *CCTK*, p. 7.

102. *Ying Lieh Chuan* (Shanghai, 1955), ch. 24, pp. 127–28.

103. Shen Lien, whose biography is in *Ming Shih*, ch. 209, is the hero of a patriotic story in *KCHS*, ch. 40 (*CKCK*, ch. 13). He models his behavior on Chu-ko Liang; see above, n. 55. Wang Lun is the first leader of the Mount Liang lair; see *SH*, chs. 11–19.

104. Eloquent lists of Ts'ao's crimes are the climaxes of the plays *Chi Ku Ma Ts'ao* (*HK*, I, ch. 5; *HC*, I, 254–66; Acton, *Famous Chinese Plays*, pp. 39–52), and *Hsü Mu Ma Ts'ao* (*HC*, II, 178–86). See similar lists in *SKYI*, chs. 23–24, 36. On the real Ts'ao, see E. Balazs, "Ts'ao Ts'ao, Zwei Lieder," *Monumenta Serica*, II (1936–37), 410–20.

105. *SKYI*, ch. 71, p. 588; *Ting Chün Shan*, *HK*, VI, ch. 7, p. 10.

106. See pp. 161, 164.

107. *SKYI*, chs. 4, 5.

108. "In a time of peace and order, you are to be an able subject [or minister: *ch'en*]; in a time of disorder, you are to be a perverted hero," a physiognomist tells him: *SKYI*, ch. 1, p. 6.

109. *Ti-i Ts'ai-tzu-shu* (other name of *SKYI*) with the commentaries of Mao Tsung-kang, published by Chin Sheng-t'an, 20 *te'e* ch. 1, 27b. Mao comments here on Ts'ao's first alleged crime, as told in *SKYI*, ch. 4, pp. 32–33, and staged in the play *Cho Fang Ts'ao*, *HK*, I, ch. 6, pp. 8–10; *HC*, I, 600–615.

110. *KCHS*, ch. 10.

111. *Shuang Shih T'u*, *HK*, XXIII, ch. 2.

112. *SH*, ch. 23, pp. 345–47; *HK*, XVII, ch. 11; *CCTK*, pp. 659–60. Favorite episode of storytellers.

113. Chiang P'ing, one of the Five Rats of *Ch'i Hsia Wu I*, can remain days in the water: *T'ung Wang Chen*, *HK*, XVII, ch. 5.

114. *SKYI*, ch. 5, p. 40.

115. *SKPH*, p. 18.

116. *SKPH*, p. 75, *SKYI*, ch. 42, pp. 349–50; *HK*, IX, ch. 6, pp. 9–10; Acton, *Famous Chinese Plays*, p. 25.

117. *SH*, ch. 40, p. 646.

118. *SKPH*, p. 116; *SKYI*, ch. 75, pp. 615–16; from *San Kuo Chih*, ch. 6, pp. 2b–3a.

119. *SH*, ch. 28, p. 448.

120. *Ku Ch'eng Hui*, *HK*, XV, ch. 2. See *SKYI*, ch. 28, pp. 236–38.

121. *Li K'uei Fu Ching*, *YCH*, XLIII, 14–30. *SH*, ch. 73.

122. *SH*, ch. 4, p. 73.

123. *SH*, ch. 32, pp. 495–96.

124. *SKPH*, p. 111; *SKYI*, ch. 63, p. 526; from *San Kuo Chih*, ch. 6, p. 5a.

125. Birch, Thesis, p. 294.

126. See H. Maspero, "Les Procédés de nourrir le principe vital," *Journal Asiatique*, CCXXIX (1937), 380–81.

127. *SH*, ch. 45. *Ts'ui-p'ing Shan: HK*, III, ch. 7, pp. 1–2; *HC*, II, 538–39. Acton, *Famous Chinese Plays*, pp. 364–66.

128. In the novels *Ch'i Hsia Wu I* and *Hsiao Wu I*.

129. *Shih Kung An, passim*, and *HK*, VI, chs. 9–10 and XX, ch. 5.

130. G. T. Candlin, *Chinese Fiction* (Chicago, 1898).

131. See the eloquent sentences in Li Chih's preface to *SH*, translated by Irwin, *Evolution of a Chinese Novel*, p. 86; also the remarks in Y. Muramatsu, "Some Themes in Chinese Rebel Ideologies," *The Confucian Persuasion*, pp. 264–65.

132. *SKPH*, p. 12; *SKYI*, ch. 1; *KP*, ch. 65; *HK*, XXVI, ch. 8.

133. See the imperial dissertations about cliques in D. Nivison, "Ho Shen and His Accusers," *Confucianism in Action*, pp. 222–32.

134. Such as Hua Yün-lung in *Chao Chia Lou, HK*, XV, ch. 13, and Hsieh Hu in *Yi Chih T'ao, HK*, XVII, ch. 14.

135. Such as Chiang "the Gate-God": *SH*, ch. 29; *CCTK*, pp. 672–73.

136. Such as Chang Ch'ing and his wife Sun Erh-niang: *SH*, chs. 27–28, pp. 426–37, and ch. 31, pp. 478–84. *CCTK*, pp. 667–72.

137. See Chang Fei flogging Tu Yu: *SKYI*, ch. 2, pp. 12–13.

138. Kuan Yü: *SKYI*, ch. 1, p. 4. Lu Ta: *SH*, ch. 3, pp. 50–51.

139. *YCH*, XX, 46–52. *Tung Chou Lieh Kuo Chih*, ch. 73. *Yü Ch'ang Chien, HK*, II, ch. 9, pp. 2–4; *CCTK*, pp. 157–58.

140. *Shih Chi*, ch. 124 (Yu-hsia Chuan), ch. 75 (Meng-ch'ang Chün Chuan), chs. 76–78, and others. See an analysis of the *hsia* institution and of the *"jen hsia* temperament" in Tatsuo Masubuchi, "The Yu Hsia and the Social Order in the Han Period," *Annals of the Hitotsubashi Academy*, III, No. 1 (1952), pp. 84–101. On the *hsia*, see also Lao Kan, in *T'ai-ta Wen-shih-che Hsüeh-pao*, I, 1–16, and Yang Lien-sheng in *Chinese Thought and Institutions*, pp. 294–96, 305–8.

141. *Shih Chi*, ch. 124, p. 1b.

142. *SKYI*, ch. 1, p. 4; *San Chieh I, HK*, XXVI, ch. 8.

143. For instance, Huang T'ien-pa: see above, n. 129.

144. See Chang Fei calling the Yellow Turbans to rally in *SKPH*, pp. 15–20, and the campaigns of the *Water Margin* robbers against the Liao and the rebels T'ien Hu and Fang La in *SH*, chs. 83–119.

145. *San Kuo Chih*, ch. 6, pp. 1a–4a. See above, p. 167.

146. *SKPH*, pp. 51–62; *SKYI*, chs. 25–28; *Ch'ien Li Tu Hsing, KP*, ch. 27; *HK*, XL, ch. 13, XXI, ch. 3, XIII, ch. 3 and XIX, ch. 2; *CCTK*, pp. 350–72.

147. Kuan Han-ch'ing, *Tan Tao Hui, KP*, ch. 2; *SKPH*, pp. 116–17; *SKYI*, ch. 66, pp. 546–49; *HK*, XVI, ch. 3; *CCTK*, pp. 464–71.

148. *SKYI*, chs. 76–77. *Tsou Mai-ch'eng, HK*, XX, ch. 1. *Hsien Sheng, HK*, XXII, ch. 3.

149. See, for instance, the *Kuan Sheng-ti-chün Sheng-chi T'u-chih Ch'üan-chi* ("Complete Collection of Writings and Illustrations Concerning the Holy Deeds of the Saintly Sovereign Kuan"), 5 *ts'e*, published in 1693, and its successive re-editions in 1756, 1824, 1899, 1921 (all in the Harvard-Yenching Library).

150. See n. 53.
151. *SKYI*, ch. 53; *Chan Ch'ang-sha*, *HK*, VI, ch. 2.
152. At Hua-jung Tao: *SKYI*, ch. 50; *HK*, XI, ch. 13.
153. His appearance on the stage is more prestigious than any emperor's.

NOTES TO SUI YANG-TI

1. I have dealt in some detail with this in "The Formation of Sui Ideology," in John K. Fairbank, ed., *Chinese Thought and Institutions* (Chicago, 1957), pp. 71–104. Peter A. Boodberg's study of the house of Yang in "Marginalia to the Histories of the Northern Dynasties," *HJAS*, IV (1939), 253–70, is of prime importance for any study of the Sui ruling house.

In the notes that follow, editions cited are Ssu-pu Ts'ung-k'an unless otherwise noted. The histories are cited in the edition of the T'ung-wen Shu-chü, 1884. In the writing of this paper I have benefited greatly from talks with my colleague Dr. K'ai-yu Hsü and, on Yang-ti's poetry, with Professor Jinichi Konishi. The comments of participants in the Third Conference on Chinese Thought have also proved enormously helpful.

2. Cf. Boodberg, *op. cit.*, p. 266. Boodberg was the first to point to the various symptoms of a sense of hubris in the behavior of Wen-ti and to relate that sense to the speed with which the Sui rose to power—a speed which precluded the usual ritual-symbolic preparations for usurpation which Chinese political ideology demanded.

3. Her biography from *Sui-shu*, ch. 36, pp. 4–6, exists in the pioneer translation of August Pfizmaier, *Darlegungen aus der Geschichte des Hauses Sui* (Vienna, 1881), pp. 25–29.

4. For characterizations of northern women of the period in contrast to southern, see *Yen-shih Chia-hsün*, ch. 1, p. 18, and Moriya Mitsuo, "Nanjin to Hokujin" ("Northerners and Southerners"), *Tōa Ronsō*, VI (1948), 36–60.

5. Cf. Chao I, *Nien-erh Shih Cha-chi* (photolithographic ed. of the Wen-jui Lou, Shanghai, n.d.), ch. 15, p. 13b.

6. Yang Kuang's childhood name was A-mo, a transliteration of the Sanskrit *ambā* ("mother"), often used as a title of respect. The feminine overtones of such a name suggest that it might have been chosen to confuse the evil spirits which prey on male children.

7. The Buddhist activities of the Sui princes are discussed in Yamazaki Hiroshi, *Shina Chūsei Bukkyō no Tenkai* ("The Development of Medieval Chinese Buddhism") (Tokyo, 1942), pp. 291–94.

8. *Sui-shu* (hereafter SS), ch. 3, pp. 1a–1b.

9. *Tzu-chih T'ung-chien* (hereafter TC), ch. 176, p. 6, commentary. The edition cited, including Hu San-hsing's commentary, is that of Yamana Zenjō (Tokyo, 1882).

10. For the biography of Yang Kuang's wife, née Hsiao, see SS, ch. 36, pp. 7–9. TC, ch. 175, p. 14b, places the marriage in 582. The bride's father was the Emperor Ming of the Later Liang—a small state in Hupeh which was successively a satellite of the Western Wei, the Northern Chou, and the Sui. It was abolished by the Sui in 587. The girl, in her upbringing, had been

the victim of a southern superstition that children born in the second moon are a threat to their parents and must be adopted out. The SS text may here have the character for "two" as a mistake for "five," since other sources specify fifth-month children as the unlucky ones. Cf. *Feng-su T'ung-i* (ed. of the Centre Franco-chinois, Peking, 1943), ch. 2, p. 20.

11. For a detailed study of the differences in human relations, manners, festivals, ceremonies, food, and customs in general, see Moriya Mitsuo, *op. cit.*

12. Among monarchs of northern origin Frederick II, Hohenstaufen and Christina of Sweden are among those who "took up" Mediterranean culture with full-blooded zeal. The tradition of sentimental lyricizing about the dulcet ways of the south begins in China at this time, and there are many Chinese analogues to Goethe's

> Kennst du das Land, wo die Zitronen blühn,
> Im dunkeln Laub die Gold-Orangen glühn, . . .

13. SS, ch. 3, pp. 1b–2.

14. Cf. Tsukamoto Zenryū, "Zui no Kōnan Seifuku to Bukkyō" ("The Sui Conquest of the South and Buddhism"), *Bukkyō Bunka Kenkyū*, III (1953), 8–9. Tsukamoto makes extensive use of the valuable documents on the relations between Yang Kuang and Chih-i to be found in the *Kuo-ch'ing Pai-lu* by the monk Kuan-ting (561–632). Cf. *Taisho*, XLVI, 793–823. Mr. Leon Hurvitz is making an exhaustive study of this text. Yang Kuang's Buddhist name was drawn from Seng-chao's commentary to the *Vimalakīrtinirdeśa*. It signifies absolute control, the embodiment of thought, meditation, and wisdom.

15. *Kuo-ch'ing Pai-lu*, ch. 3, p. 807b.

16. Cf. Tsukamoto, *op. cit.*, pp. 16–17.

17. SS, ch. 45, p. 4.

18. For the testament, see *Kuo-ch'ing Pai-lu*, ch. 3, pp. 809–10.

19. See Harold D. Lasswell, *Psychopathology and Politics* (Chicago, 1930), p. 50.

20. Boodberg, *op. cit.*, p. 267, was the first to stress the importance of the completion of the sixty-year cycle.

21. Yamazaki Hiroshi, "Yōtei no Shi Dōjō" ("Yang Ti's Four Temples"), *Tōyō Gakuhō*, XXXIV (1952), 22–35, includes a study of the new Jih-yen Ssu. Yamazaki observes that of the total complement of monks in the temple, nearly one-third came from Yang-chou, and all but three came from either the Huai or Yangtse valley areas. This is one of the ways in which southern Buddhism was brought north to dominate the religious life of the capital.

22. *Kuo-ch'ing Pai-lu*, ch. 3, p. 813c. All the allusions are to the Lotus sutra, which was, of course, the supreme scripture of the T'ien-t'ai. Candrākadīpa is the title of the 20,000 Buddhas who succeeded each other preaching the Lotus. The eight are the mortal sons of the last of this series; all became Buddhas. The second Buddha is the fabulous begetter of sixteen sons, including Sakyamuni, all of whom became Buddhas after hearing their father preach the Lotus. For a similar pious salute to his parents, see ch. 2, p. 803b.

23. SS, ch. 3, p. 2.

24. *Hsü Kao-seng Chuan*, ch. 11, in *Taishō*, L, 110b.

25. *TC*, ch. 179, p. 13.

26. SS, ch. 3, p. 2.

27. See particularly the biography of the lady Hsüan-hua, SS, ch. 36, pp. 6–7, and the collection of accounts discussed in Hu San-hsing's commentary to TC, ch. 180, pp. 2–2b. A full analysis of all accounts must await a later study.

28. See Etienne Balazs, Le Traité économique du 'Souei-chou' (Leiden, 1953), p. 10, note 1.

29. See SS, ch. 75, pp. 2b–3, introduction to the biographies of Confucians (ju-lin). The account of the revival of Confucian learning by Yang-ti is in marked contrast to the remarks on the Confucians' sad fate in the latter years of Wen-ti's reign. The authors of the Sui-shu sense a conflict in historical interpretation here: Wen-ti was indifferent or hostile to Confucianism, yet left the empire strong and prosperous; Yang-ti favored Confucianism, yet brought the empire to ruin. Two explanations of this are offered: (1) the disintegrating effect of struggles against the barbarians; (2) the theory that Yang-ti's Confucian revival was more apparent than real. "There was the empty name of organizing Confucian studies, but there was no reality of spreading Confucian teachings."

30. Yang-ti was furious with official compilers of a new gazetteer who had referred to the inhabitants of the Wu area in the lower Yangtse valley as "eastern barbarians (tung-i) who trespass against the rites and the principle of righteousness." Yang-ti chastised them and expatiated on the brilliant culture of the area as far back as the Han, its prime importance as the very center of Chinese culture during the period of disunion, and its incomparable contribution of Confucian scholars, literary figures, and men of talent since the incorporation of the area into the Sui empire. Cf. Sui-shu Ching-chi-chih K'ao-cheng, ch. 21, in Supplements to the Twenty-five Histories, IV, 5413.

31. Yamazaki, Chūsei, pp. 278–79, estimates that only 26 per cent of all top-ranking Sui officials were of non-Chinese origin, as against 65 per cent under the Northern Chou. He also notes that non-Chinese officials under the Sui tended to be concentrated in the Board of Works and the Board of War. Yamazaki's recent and detailed study "Zuichō Kanryō no Seikaku" ("The Character of Sui Officialdom") in The Bulletin of the Tokyo Kyōiku University Literature Department, VI (1956), suggests at several points the trend toward a greater share of power for southerners during the reign of Yang-ti. "The Treatise on Geography," SS, ch. 31, p. 14, remarks that the worthy people of the Kiangsu-Chekiang area subsisted on their official stipends. Cf. Balazs, op. cit., p. 317.

32. I am inclined to reject the account in TC, ch. 180, p. 8, which sees the move to a new capital simply as a reaction to advice from oracle-takers.

33. Cf. SS, ch. 24, pp. 17–17b, and Balazs, op. cit., pp. 165–66.

34. Cf. Balazs, op. cit., p. 226, note 182.

35. Cf. SS, ch. 24, p. 18, and Balazs, op. cit., p. 168.

36. One of two poems commemorating the Liao-tung campaign. Cf. Yüeh-fu Shih-hsüan, ch. 79, p. 54. The term translated "monstrous beast" is literally "great whale," a metaphor for evil men, here the emperor's enemies; "ancient capital" is literally Hao-ching, said to have been the capital of the Chou conqueror Wu-wang. The term wu yüan, "the five plains," refers to the area of Ch'ang-an.

37. For useful materials on the increase of domestic rebellion during and after the Koguryō campaigns, see Woodbridge Bingham, The Founding of

the T'ang Dynasty (Baltimore, 1941), pp. 37–58, 130–41, and Maps IIa and IIb.

38. For the text, see SS, ch. 22, p. 24.

39. *Chen-kuan Cheng-yao* ("Essentials of Government of the Chen-kuan Period"), compiled by Wu Ching (670–749), ch. 1, pp. 17b–18a. Contains the political views of the great T'ang T'ai-tsung and his ministers, arranged topically. Much of the material is thought to have been drawn from the *shih-lu*, the "veritable record" of T'ai-tsung's reign, a contemporary source that no longer exists. The *Chen-kuan Cheng-yao* was read in both China and Japan for many centuries, and its judgments of Yang-ti were widely influential.

40. *Ibid.*, ch. 3, pp. 1b–2a.

41. Franke, *Geschichte des chinesischen Reiches*, II (Berlin, 1936), 328–29, attributes Yang-ti's patronage of Confucian learning and revival of the examination system to vanity and love of ostentation. The historical reasons for these activities are likely to be found on the level of interpretation I have suggested.

42. I do not consider the *Shu-ching* accounts of the bad-last ruler of the Hsia dynasty; these seem to me to be Chou fabrications designed to lend the persuasion of "historical precedent" to their own ideological interpretation of the supplanting of the evil Shang by the virtuous Chou.

43. Cf. John Weakland and Ruth Bunzel, "An Anthropological Approach to Chinese Culture" (dittographed, Columbia University, 1950), and Warren Muensterberger, "Orality and Dependence: Characteristics of Southern Chinese," *Psychoanalysis and the Social Sciences*, III (1951), 37–69.

44. Cf. Chavannes, *Les Mémoires historiques de Se-ma Ts'ien*, II, 242.

45. Cf. *ibid.*, pp. 235–36, 243; also the speech in his own defense by Li Ssu from *Shih-chi*, ch. 87, as translated by Derk Bodde in *China's First Unifier* (Leiden, 1938), p. 49.

46. Cf. SS, ch. 2, pp. 1–3, and TC, ch. 176, pp. 12b–13.

47. Cf. SS, ch. 41, p. 3.

48. This accusation is drawn verbatim from the *Shu-ching*, "The speech of Kan." Cf. Legge's translation, p. 153. The translation of *san-cheng* is in doubt. I can only guess how contumely toward the five elements may have manifested itself in the Ch'en emperor's behavior.

49. Cf. *Ch'en-shu*, ch. 6, pp. 15b–16.

50. Text I is SS, ch. 4, pp. 16b–18. Text II is SS, ch. 70 (comment on the biographies of rebels against the Sui). Text III is SS, ch. 5, p. 4 (comment on the reign of the shadow emperor K'ung-ti, Yang-ti's grandson, who "ruled" as a pawn in the struggle for dynastic succession from June 24, 618, to May 25, 619). Cf. Balazs, *Traité économique*, p. 231, note 208. Estimates in the *Pei-shih* differ only in detail, giving further evidence that, in respect to the Sui, this "private history" deviated only slightly from the *Sui-shu*.

51. Cf. SS, ch. 22, p. 24.

52. Cf. Etienne Balazs, *Le Traité juridique du 'Souei-chou'* (Leiden, 1954), pp. 89–90.

53. Text II offers a point-by-point comparison between Yang-ti and his father designed to highlight the folly and vice of the son. This exaltation of Wen-ti is strikingly at variance with the historians' judgments on many sepa-

rate aspects of his reign and his character.

54. *Nien-erh Shih Cha-chi*, ch. 28, pp. 13b–15a. Chao I has a quantitative approach to the judgment of evil which he shares with other Chinese political moralists. This attitude deserves a separate study.

55. Cf. J. R. Hightower, *Topics in Chinese Literature* (Cambridge, Mass., 1950), pp. 92–93. In this whole section I find myself on unfamiliar ground, and answers to many of the questions raised must await intensive research.

56. *Ssu-k'u Ch'üan-shu Tsung-mu* (photolithographic ed. of the Ta-tung Shu-chü, Shanghai, 1930), ch. 143, p. 2a.

57. The first three works are discussed in *ibid*. They are usually listed as anonymous and of T'ang date, but they show signs of later reworking, probably in Sung times. The *Ta-yeh Shih-i Chi* is often attributed to Yen Shih-ku (581–645), but this seems to me doubtful. For the first three texts I have used the editions of the Wu-ch'ao Hsiao-shuo Ta-kuan (Shanghai, 1926). For the fourth I have used *Shuo-fu*, ch. 110.

58. This characterization is never fully developed, but Empress Hsiao as the *femme fatale* appears in the moral-pointing introduction to a story, probably of Ming date, entitled "Hsin-ch'iao-shih Han-wu Mai Ch'un-ch'ing," in *Ku-chin Hsiao-shuo* (Peking ed., 1955), Vol. I, ch. 3, p. 1b. There the author cites two historical examples of women who brought men to ruin: Empress Hsiao and Yang Kuei-fei, favorite of Emperor Hsüan-tsung of the T'ang. Since Yang Kuei-fei is the most famous of all the *femmes fatales* of Chinese history, the stereotyping of Empress Hsiao in this context is complete.

59. The *Sui Yang-ti Yen-shih* was written under the pseudonym of "Ch'i-tung Yeh-jen," and is in eight *chüan* and forty incidents (*hui*). The copy consulted was from the East Asiatic Library of the University of California, and this appears to be a late run-off—minus illustrations—of the plates used for the 1631 edition described in Sun K'ai-ti, *Chung-kuo T'ung-su Hsiao-shuo Shu-mu* ("Bibliography of Chinese Popular Fiction") (Peking, 1932), p. 46. [Stanford University has acquired what appears to be a complete copy of the 1631 edition. I shall publish a note on this in the near future.] There is a 1946 edition by the Chung-yang Shu-chü, Shanghai.

60. Cf. Li Hua-ch'ing, *Sung-jen Hsiao-shuo* ("Fiction of the Sung") (Taipei, 1956), ch. 2, p. 26.

61. I use the 1956 edition of the Ku-tien Wen-hsueh Ch'u-pan She, Shanghai. The author, Ch'u Jen-hu, is said to have flourished ca. 1681. The publishers' preface cites the author's acknowledgment of his indebtedness to the standard histories and to informal writings concerning the Sui and T'ang, but it goes on to say that the author's own area of invention was very wide and that the novel is to be regarded as a work of creative fiction.

62. Kuo Chen-i in his *Chung-kuo Hsiao-shuo Shih* ("History of Chinese Fiction"), II (Ch'ang-sha, 1939), 262, suggests that the *Sui Yang-ti Yen-shih* was written under the influence of the famous *Chin-p'ing Mei*, and that the *Yen-shih* was one of the principal sources drawn upon by Ch'u Jen-hu in writing the *Sui T'ang Yen-i*. A limited comparison of the two texts suggests that whole sections were taken from the earlier novel with certain deletions and rearrangements.

63. This novel, a biography of the god Chen-wu which is of Ming date, is known under seven different titles. The quotation is from Willem A.

Grootaers, "The Hagiography of the Chinese God Chen-wu," *Folklore Studies*, XI (1953), 157.

64. Cf. Ssu-ma Kuang's *T'ung-chien K'ao-i*, ch. 8, pp. 56–59.

65. Cf. Edwin G. Pulleyblank, "Chinese Historical Criticism" (mimeographed, London, 1956), p. 15. This important paper will shortly appear in a symposium volume on Far Eastern historiography edited by Professor William Beasely.

66. Hsü Li-ch'un, *Chung-kuo Shih-hua*, pp. 76–78. The work was first published in Yenan in 1942 and appeared in a revised (!) edition in Peking, 1950.

67. Han Kuo-ch'ing, *Sui Yang-ti* (Changsha, 1957), p. 92. We are indebted to the same author for *Sui-ch'ao Shih-lüeh* ("Brief History of the Sui Dynasty") (Shanghai, 1954). This work is similar in composition to his life of Yang-ti: uncritical acceptance of all data from the standard histories plus random and meaningless injections of Marxist liturgical phrases.

68. The *Yüan-shih Chi-shih* ("Record of Yüan Dynasty Poetry"), compiled under the Republic by Ch'en Heng, remarks: "When a dynasty falls, there must be 'a person who was negligent in state affairs' whom people can point to and look at, one who will appear in songs. . . . For the fall of the Sung, Chia Ssu-tao [d. 1276] was this person." Cf. Commercial Press edition, p. 76. I am indebted to Professor Mote for this reference. An exception to the more recent treatment of last rulers might be Shun-ti of the Yüan, who was given many of the qualities suggested in our paradigm of the "bad last" ruler. Cf. Herbert Franke, "Some Remarks on the Interpretation of Chinese Dynastic Histories," *Oriens*, 3 (1950), 117–20.

NOTES TO FENG TAO

Most of the material on Feng Tao is to be found in the *Chiu wu-tai shih* (hereafter *CWTS*) and the *Ts'e-fu yüan-kuei* (hereafter *TFYK*), both of which were based on official records, notably, the Veritable Records of the Five Dynasties. Supplementary material has been found scattered in miscellaneous works of the early Sung period, for example, the *Wu-tai shih pu* and the *Wu-tai shih ch'üeh-wen*. Background material is largely from the well-known sources, the old and new versions of the *Wu-tai shih* (the *CWTS* and the *HWTS*) and *T'ang shu* (the *CTS* and the *HTS*) and the *Tzu-chih t'ung-chien* (hereafter *TCTC*). In cases where this material has been discussed fully in my study *The Structure of Power in North China during the Five Dynasties* (University of Malaya Press, 1962) detailed references have not been attempted here.

All quotations from the twenty-four histories are from the Po-na-pen edition. For the *TCTC*, I have used the Ku-chi ch'u-pan she edition (ten vols., 1956), and for the *TFYK*, the edition with colophon dated 1672.

1. *Hsü T'ung-chih* (Wan-yu wen-k'u ed.), ch. 607, p. 6609. This opinion was so harsh that, soon afterward, Chao I (1727–1814) tried to explain why Feng Tao was respected by his own contemporaries; *Nien-erh-shih cha-chi* (Shih-chieh shu-chü ed., 1958), ch. 22, II, 302.

2. On the circumstances of Ch'ien-lung's reign (1736–95), see David S. Nivison, "Ho-shen and His Accusers: Ideology and Political Behavior in the

Eighteenth Century," in *Confucianism in Action*, ed. David S. Nivison and Arthur F. Wright (Stanford, Calif., 1959), pp. 218–32. Also L. Carrington Goodrich, *The Literary Inquisition of Ch'ien-lung* (Baltimore, 1935), pp. 30–36, 44–53.

3. *Sung shih*, ch. 254, pp. 1a–4b; *TFYK*, ch. 52, pp. 16a–b.

4. *HWTS*, ch. 54, pp. 1a–2a.

5. *TCTC*, ch. 291, p. 9512.

6. Fan Chih was the author of *Wu-tai t'ung-lu* in 65 chuan, *Sung shih*, ch. 249, p. 4b. Ssu-ma Kuang quotes him on Feng Tao in *TCTC*, ch. 291, p. 9511. According to Hung Mai, *Jung-chai san-pi* (Wan-yu wen-k'u ed.), ch. 9, p. 7b, it was Fan Chih who preserved admiringly Feng Tao's notorious autobiography, the *Ch'ang-lo lao tzu-hsü*.

7. *CWTS*, ch. 126, p. 12a. The historians' comment on Feng Tao had reservations about his loyalty, but the biography (pp. 1a–11b) was flattering to him. On Hsüeh Chü-cheng and the other compilers, see Gung-wu Wang, "The *Chiu wu-tai shih* and History-Writing during the Five Dynasties," *Asia Major*, IV (1956), 4–6.

8. Wu Ch'u-hou, *Ch'ing-hsiang tsa-chi* (Pei-hai ed.), ch. 2, pp. 4b–5b.

9. Professors Y. Sudō, K. Hinō, and their students have followed some of the suggestions of Professor T. Naito and investigated some of the economic and political problems, and we now have a much better understanding of the main changes during the ninth and tenth centuries.

10. For want of more accurate and convenient terms to represent *chieh-tu shih* and the territories they controlled, I have used here the general names "military governors" and "provinces," respectively. The material on these "provinces" has been briefly summed up in the *HTS*, chs. 210–12. See Wu T'ing-hsieh, "T'ang fang-chen nien-piao," *Erh-shih-wu shih pu-pien* (K'ai-ming ed.), VI, 7382–93.

11. *CWTS*, ch. 126, pp. 1a, 7a. Ying-chou was in Wei-po province, 763–75, and in Lu-lung province, 775–900, with a short break of a few months in 822. In 763–75 it bordered Lu-lung and Ch'eng-te provinces and in 775–900 it bordered Ch'eng-te and Ts'ang-ching provinces and was not far from the Wei-po provincial frontier; *HTS*, ch. 66, pp. 5a–14a.

12. *HTS*, chs. 210–12; Wu T'ing-hsieh, VI, 7385–87.

13. *CWTS*, ch. 135, pp. 1a–b; father of Liu Shou-kuang (ch. 135, pp. 4b–8a).

14. *CWTS*, ch. 126, p. 7a. This would mean that he was a descendant of the family of Feng Pa (d. 430), the founder of the Northern Yen dynasty, 409–36 (*Chin shu*, ch. 125, pp. 9b–14b), and Feng Hsi (fl. 450–65), the brother of an empress dowager and the father of two empresses of the Toba Wei dynasty, 386–534 (*Wei shu*, ch. 83A, pp. 9b–17a); and also of Feng Tzu-tsung (d. 571), a relative by marriage of the imperial house of Northern Ch'i, 550–77 (*Pei Ch'i shu*, ch. 40, pp. 2a–4a). This aristocratic family lost eminence in the early years of the T'ang dynasty and could only boast of two "good officials" (*liang-li*) who found a place in the *CTS* (ch. 185A, pp. 11a–b; also in *HTS*, ch. 112, pp. 11b–12a). Both these men, the cousins of Feng Yüan-ch'ang (fl. 680–705) and Feng Yüan-shu (fl. 684–710), had their homes at An-yang, nearly two hundred miles southwest of their ancestral home, and it is possible that the family dispersed during the seventh century and that Feng Tao's ancestors went about a hundred miles northeast to Ching-ch'eng.

15. *TFYK*, ch. 331, p. 27a; Hung Mai, *Jung-chai*, III, 77. Feng Tao said this soon after 942, when he was about sixty years old. It is, however, on record that his father died in late 923 or early 924, when he was already forty-one, hardly "young."

16. Denis Twitchett, "Chinese Biographical Writing," in W. G. Beasley and E. G. Pulleyblank, eds., *Historians of China and Japan* (London, 1961), pp. 85–114; also Wang, *Asia Major*, p. 6.

17. *CWTS*, ch. 126, p. 1a.

18. *CTS*, ch. 20A, p. 11a; *TCTC*, ch. 259, p. 8459; *TFYK*, ch. 7, p. 19a.

19. *CTS*, ch. 20A, p. 21a; *CWTS*, ch. 2, pp. 3a–b, and ch. 135, p. 12b; *TCTC*, ch. 262, p. 8535.

20. *CWTS*, ch. 72, p. 2a, and ch. 126, p. 1a; *TCTC*, ch. 268, p. 8747. It is possible that Feng Tao had joined Liu Jen-kung before 907 (that is, before Liu Shou-kuang seized power from his father), if we are to believe the biography of Han Yen-hui in *Liao shih*, ch. 74, p. 2a.

It is interesting to note that Feng Tao's service with Chang Ch'eng-yeh is recorded in detail in Chang's biography (*CWTS*, ch. 72, p. 2a). This either suggests that Feng Tao had a hand in Chang's Account of Conduct (see note 16) or in the collection of biographies compiled in 934 (Wang, *Asia Major*, p. 11) and wanted to show his gratitude to the old eunuch, or shows that the compilers of the *Chiu wu-tai shih* thought so highly of Feng Tao that they thought it to Chang's credit to have recognized Feng Tao's merits so early.

21. *CWTS*, ch. 67, pp. 4a–5a, and ch. 93, p. 1b. Feng Tao was supported by both Chang Ch'eng-yeh and Lu Chih (867–942), the Chief Administrator (*chieh-tu p'an-kuan*) at the time. They had both defended Feng Tao against the opposition of the expert in physiognomy, Chou Hsüan-pao (fl. 900–927). Chou's opposition to him was probably the result of Feng Tao's skepticism of anything non-Confucian. The art of physiognomy based on the writings of Yüan T'ien-kang (fl. 605–34) and Hsü Chen-chün (fl. 320–74) had always been associated with Taoists, while Chou himself had started life as a Buddhist priest. *TFYK*, ch. 843, pp. 27a–b, and ch. 929, pp. 5a–b; Chou's biography, *CWTS*, ch. 71, pp. 8a–9a; Yüan's biography, *CTS*, ch. 191, pp. 3b–5a; Hsü's biography in Chao Tao-i, *Li-shih chen-hsien t'i-tao t'ung-chien* (Tao Ts'ang ed. 1923), *ts'e* 143, ch. 26, pp. 1a–20b.

22. *CWTS*, ch. 126, pp. 1b–2a; *TCTC*, ch. 270, p. 8848.

23. I examine this question of intimacy in the provincial organization and the Wu-tai courts in my study *The Structure of Power in North China*. For the events of Chuang-tsung's reign, see *CWTS*, chs. 30–34, and *TCTC*, chs. 272–74.

24. *TCTC*, chs. 256–66.

25. *TFYK*, ch. 337, pp. 31a–32a; *CWTS*, ch. 58, p. 6a; *TCTC*, ch. 275, p. 8999.

26. *TFYK*, ch. 551, pp. 20b–21a; *CWTS*, ch. 92, p. 7b; *TCTC*, ch. 279, pp. 9112–13, 9115.

27. *CWTS*, ch. 47, pp. 12a–b.

28. *CWTS*, ch. 92, pp. 7a–8a; *HWTS*, ch. 54, pp. 14b–15a.

29. "The sixteen prefectures of Yen and Yün" were offered to the Khitans by Shih Ching-t'ang in 936 as the price for their help in putting him on the throne. They were formally handed over in 938 and were a definite part of

enemy country after 947. The Jurchens inherited them in 1124 and the Mongols after that in 1234. It was not until 1368, under the Ming dynasty, that a Chinese emperor ruled over the area again.

30. *CWTS*, ch. 126, p. 5b. The reference to a Ch'an priest and falconry was an idiom of the T'ang and Sung periods; see *Yüan-chien lei-han* (Tungwen shu-chü ed., 1926), ch. 317, p. 8b, and *P'ei-wen yün-fu* (Wan-yu wen-k'u ed., 1937), ch. 25, p. 1265/3.

31. *CWTS*, ch. 126, pp. 5b–6a; *HWTS*, ch. 54, pp. 4a–b; *TFYK*, ch. 864, p. 7a.

32. *TFYK*, ch. 608, pp. 29b–31a. See T. F. Carter, *The Invention of Printing in China and Its Spread Westward* (New York, 1925), pp. 47–54.

33. *CWTS*, ch. 88, p. 1b; *Ch'i-tan kuo-chih* (Wan-yu wen-k'u ed.), ch. 2, p. 17. On Feng Tao's mission to the Khitans, *CWTS*, ch. 126, pp. 4a–b; *TFYK*, ch. 329, p. 19b, and ch. 654, pp. 13a–b; *Liao shih*, ch. 4b, pp. 1b–3a; *TCTC*, ch. 281, pp. 9188–89. On Ying-chou being given to the Khitans and its recovery in 959 (*TCTC*, ch. 294, p. 9897), the clearest analysis on this very controversial subject is Chang Ting-i's in *Hsien-hsien chih* (1925), ch. 2, pp. 4a–b. This is an improvement on *Ch'ien-lung Ho-chien-fu chih* (1760), ch. 1, pp. 26a–b, and certainly superior to the garbled versions in *Ch'ien-lung Hsien-hsien chih* (1761), ch. 1, p. 11b, and *K'ang-hsi Ho-chien-fu chih* (1678), ch. 2, pp. 12b–13a. See also *T'ai-p'ing huan-yü chi* (Chin-ling shu-chü ed., 1882), ch. 66, pp. 1b–2a, and *Tu-shih fang-yü chi-yao* (Chung-hua shu-chü ed., six vols., 1955), ch. 13, I, 573.

34. Wang Yü-ch'eng, *Wu-tai shih ch'üeh-wen* (Ch'ien-hua-an ts'ung-shu ed.), pp. 9b–10b. T'ao Yüeh, *Wu-tai shih pu* (Ch'ien-hua-an ts'ung-shu ed.), ch. 5, pp. 10a–b. Briefly summarized in *CWTS*, ch. 126, p. 10b.

35. *CWTS*, ch. 114, p. 3a, and ch. 126, p. 11a; *TFYK*, ch. 57, pp. 17a–b; *TCTC*, ch. 291, pp. 9502–3.

36. *T'ao yüeh*, ch. 5, p. 10b.

37. *T'ao yüeh*, ch. 3, p. 6b. Also *Ku-chin shih-hua*, quoted in *Ch'ien-lung Hsien-hsien chih*, ch. 19, pp. 23b–24a. Cf. a similar story about Li Ku (903–60) in *T'ao yüeh*, ch. 5, p. 11a. The "liquor households" (*chiu-hu*) were lowly families licensed to manufacture liquor.

38. *TFYK*, ch. 52, pp. 13a–17b, and ch. 54, pp. 23a–25b. Chou Shih-tsung (954–59) was very severe to some of the rich Buddhist temples but also paid his respects to the faith. In any case, Feng Tao served him for less than three months before his death.

39. *TFYK*, ch. 54, pp. 24b–25b.

40. Chao Feng, *CWTS*, ch. 67, pp. 6b–7b; Liu Hsü, *TFYK*, ch. 865, p. 21b; Ma Yin-sun, *TFYK*, ch. 821, p. 24b.

41. *CWTS*, ch. 126, p. 2b; *TFYK*, ch. 320, p. 17b. Examples of Feng Tao's help, *CWTS*, ch. 108, p. 1b; *TFYK*, ch. 955, pp. 4b–5a.

42. Sun Kuang-hsien, *Pei-meng so-yen* (Pei-hai ed.), ch. 19, pp. 5b–6a; *TFYK*, ch. 337, p. 23b; *CWTS*, ch. 126, p. 2b. The *T'u-yüan ts'e* in thirty *chüan* by Tu Ssu-hsien (c. 634–74) was lost during the Southern Sung dynasty. Four T'ang ms. fragments have been recovered from Tun-huang. The three of the Stein collection at the British Museum (S.614, S.1086, and S.1722) show that the work was presented in the form of "question and answer." The fragment S.1086 includes numerous quotations from philosophical and historical works extending from the *I Ching* to the history of the

Liu Sung dynasty (A.D. 420–79). The fourth fragment in Paris (no. 2573) I have not seen.

Opinion on the *T'u-yüan ts'e* has varied considerably. Sun Kuang-hsien says it was well done in the style of Hsü Ling (507–83) and Yü Hsin (513–81); Ou-yang Hsiu held the work in contempt (*HWTS*, ch. 55, p. 8b); while Wu Lan-t'ing considered Ou-yang Hsiu to have been too harsh (*Wu-tai shih-chi chuan-wu pu* [Chih-pu-tsu chai ed.], ch. 4, pp. 5a–b). Also, Wang Ying-lin (1223–96) described the author as a minor follower of the T'ang Prince of Chiang (d. 674); *K'un-hsüeh chi-wen* (Wan-yu wen-k'u ed.), ch. 14, p. 1174; while Chao Kung-wu (fl. 1150–64) attributed the work to the famous scholar Yü Shih-nan (558–638) and might have confused the work with the *Pei-t'ang shu-ch'ao; Chün-chai tu-shu chi* (1884 ed.), ch. 14, pp. 16b–17a.

43. Feng Tao's three collected works were his *Ho-chien chi* in five *chuan*; a *Chi* in six *chuan* and a *Shih-chi* in ten *chuan*; *Sung shih*, ch. 208, pp. 10a–b. They were probably seen by Sung historians like Ou-yang Hsiu and his contemporaries and do not seem to have impressed them in any way. Nor perhaps did the works help the historians determine which of the official memorials were drafted by Feng Tao.

44. *CWTS*, ch. 67, pp. 8a–11b; *TFYK*, ch. 841, p. 9a. See Carter, *op. cit.*, pp. 47–54, where Feng Tao is described as a man of great power and ability. Anonymous, *Ai-jih chai ts'ung-ch'ao* (Shou-shan ko ts'ung-shu ed.), ch. 1, pp. 2a–3b.

45. *Wu-tai hui-yao* (Wan-yu wen-k'u ed.), ch. 8, p. 96; *TFYK*, ch. 608, pp. 29b–31a; *Sung shih*, ch. 431, pp. 27b–29a.

46. *TFYK*, ch. 37, pp. 24b–25a, and ch. 314, pp. 14b–16a.

47. *TFYK*, ch. 108, pp. 17b–18b. *Wu-tai hui-yao*, ch. 6, p. 76.

48. *TFYK*, ch. 314, pp. 15b–16a. The quotation from the *Book of History* comes from the Chün-ya section; *Shih-san ching chu-su* (Taipei, 1955), vol. 2, ch. 19, p. 11a.

49. Twitchett, "Chinese Biographical Writing," *loc. cit.* (n. 16); Wang, *Asia Major*, pp. 6–7.

50. Wang, *Asia Major*, Table I, p. 8.

51. See notes 26 and 28; Wang, *Asia Major*, pp. 13–14.

52. *HWTS*, ch. 54, p. 6a.

53. *CWTS*, ch. 126, pp. 5a–b.

54. *TFYK*, ch. 314, p. 14b.

55. *TFYK*, ch. 792, pp. 19a–20a.

56. *CWTS*, ch. 106, p. 4a, says Liu Shen-chiao died in the spring of 949, while *CWTS*, ch. 103, p. 1b, says he died in the second month of 950. Feng Tao's autobiography was dated the *chu-ming* month (that is, the fourth month) of 950; *CWTS*, ch. 126, p. 10b.

57. *CWTS*, ch. 126, p. 9b; *TFYK*, ch. 770, p. 27b. The *TFYK* text is corrupt.

58. I am grateful to Professor D. C. Twitchett for pointing out the latent Buddhism in Feng Tao's attitude to sacrifices. There is no evidence that Feng Tao was ever consciously Buddhist. His specific request here, I feel, reflects clearly how deeply Buddhist notions had penetrated into the Chinese mind, to the extent that they could even modify the oldest ideas of Confucian ritual.

59. *CWTS*, ch. 126, pp. 9b–10a; *TFYK*, ch. 770, p. 28a. Both texts omit the word *wu* before the remark on the sacrifice of male goats. The sentence does not make sense, however, except in the negative.

60. *Ch'ing-hsiang tsa-chi*, ch. 2, pp. 4b–5b.

61. *TCTC*, ch. 291, p. 9512.

62. *Ch'ing-hsiang tsa-chi*, ch. 2, p. 5b; *Neng-kai chai man-lu* (Shou-shan ko ts'ung-shu ed.), ch. 10, pp. 21b–22a.

63. For summaries of the main views on Feng Tao, see *Ch'ien-lung Ho-chien-fu chih*, ch. 17, pp. 38a–39b, and *Hsien-hsien chih*, ch. 11B, pp. 24a–27b. For Chao I's views, cf. *Nien-erh shih cha-chi*, ch. 22, p. 302.

64. Ou-yang Hsiu's famous essay "Cheng-t'ung-lun" ("Essay on the Orthodox Succession") and Su Shih's essay with the same title bring out the main argument of Sung historians; *Ou-yang wen-chung kung chi* (Wan-yu wen-k'u ed.), ch. 21, pp. 5–9.

The question of the Five Dynasties had been debated for a century before Ou-yang Hsiu. The problem was whether the Liang dynasty was orthodox or not and whether there were in fact only *four* rather than five dynasties. The issue was not resolved even after the term *wu-tai* had come into common usage early in the Sung, and the *TFYK* relegates the Liang dynasty to the section on dynasties not in direct line of succession (*jun-wei*).

65. Prince of Sung, Han Yin-ti, and Prince of Liang were sons; Prince of Lu and Chou Shih-tsung were adopted sons; Chin Shao-ti was a nephew and Chin Kao-tsu was the son-in-law of Ming-tsung.

66. On the traditions of the Ho-pei provinces, see note 12. The four were Ming-tsung, Han Kao-tsu, and Chou T'ai-tsu (see following note), and Sung T'ai-tsu in 960.

67. Ming-tsung, *TCTC*, ch. 274, X, pp. 8965–76; Han Kao-tsu, ch. 286, X, pp. 9335–66; Chou T'ai-tsu, ch. 289, X, pp. 9429–50.

68. Sung T'ai-tsu, Chao K'uang-yin, was a native of Cho-chou in Lu-lung province and descended from three generations of officials in the province. His own father then joined the service of the governor of Ch'eng-te province, also in Hopei, before joining the Sha-t'o leader Chuang-tsung. Chao K'uang-yin himself was born in the barracks of Ming-tsung's imperial army at Lo-yang; *Sung shih*, ch. 1, pp. 1a–2a. And Sung T'ai-tsu retained as his most senior minister Fan Chih, the great admirer of Feng Tao (see note 6); ch. 1, pp. 4a–b.

69. See note 33; *CWTS*, ch. 137, pp. 8a–b.

70. *Liao shih*, ch. 1, p. 2a; *CWTS*, ch. 137, p. 2a (the date is wrongly given here as 907) and pp. 8a–b; K. A. Wittfogel and Feng Chia-sheng, *History of Chinese Society: Liao* (Transactions of the American Philosophical Society, 1948), pp. 239, 573.

71. *CWTS*, ch. 137, pp. 8b–9a; Yang Lien-sheng, "A 'Posthumous Letter' from the Chin Emperor to the Khitan Emperor in 942," *Harvard Journal of Asiatic Studies*, X (1947), 424–28.

72. *HWTS*, ch. 54, pp. 4a–b; *CWTS*, ch. 126, p. 5b; *Liao shih*, ch. 4, pp. 14b–15a; *TCTC*, ch. 286, X, p. 9330.

73. *HWTS*, ch. 35, pp. 1a–2a and 7b–9b. This is clear in Ou-yang Hsiu's comments on the six men. The irony is that they were so obviously disloyal that no one argued about them afterward, whereas Feng Tao's case was fought over in the eleventh century and thus had special attention drawn to it.

74. *Han shu,* ch. 87B, pp. 6a–14a, and ch. 100A, pp. 18b–23b; *Chin-shu,* ch. 51, pp. 1a–b, and ch. 94, pp. 19b–20a; *Liang shu,* ch. 50, pp. 9b–10a.
There are several more examples, like Chang Heng's (78–139) *Ying-wen* (*Hou Han shu,* ch. 89, pp. 2a–12a), Ts'ai Yung's (131–92) *Shih-hui* (*Hou Han shu,* ch. 90B, pp. 2a–11a), and Shu Hsi's (fl. 280–300) *Hsuan-chü shih* (*Chin shu,* ch. 51, pp. 13a–14b).
75. *Shih chi,* ch. 126, pp. 8a–9a, and *Han shu,* ch. 65, pp. 15b–18b.
76. *CTS,* ch. 166, pp. 7a–8a.
77. Wang Ch'ung, *Lun-heng chi-chieh* (Ku-chi ch'u-pan she ed.), ch. 30, pp. 579–92. Alfred Forke, *Lun-heng: Philosophical Essays of Wang Ch'ung* (Leipzig, 1907), pp. 64–82.
78. *CWTS,* ch. 126, p. 10a; *TFYK,* ch. 770, p. 28a.
79. *CWTS,* ch. 126, p. 10a, *TFYK,* ch. 770, p. 28b.

NOTES TO FROM MYTH TO MYTH

1. *Shuo-Yüeh ch'üan chuan.* For earlier versions see Sun K'ai-ti, *Jih-pen Tung-ching so chien Chung-kuo hsiao-shuo shu-mu* (Shanghai, 1953), pp. 50–52. A wide collection of popular lore of Yüeh Fei is found in *Yüeh Fei ku-shih hsi-ch'ü shuo-ch'ang chi* (Tu Ying-t'ao ed.) (Shanghai: Ku-tien wenh-süeh, 1957). See also Robert Ruhlmann, "Traditional Heroes in Chinese Popular Fiction," *supra* p. 135 and its note 52. The latest literary treatments of Yüeh Fei's life are the dramas *Yüeh Fei* by Ku I-chiao (Commercial Press, 1940) and Cheng Lieh's *Ching-chung po shih-chü,* 4 vols. (Nanking, 1948).
2. See L. C. Arlington and William Lewinsohn, *In Search of Old Peking* (Peking, 1935), pp. 231–32.
3. By Chang Ying (*Sung shih,* ch. 404), a historiographer who wanted in this way to rid Yüeh K'o's (1183–?) compilation of the odium of private bias. Chang finished his rewrite only three years after Yüeh K'o had finished his biography, and incorporated it into his book *Nan-tu ssu chiang chuan,* which also contains biographies of three other generals of the time. His version is contained in the *Chin-t'o hsü-pien,* ch. 17. See Teng Kuang-ming, *Yüeh Fei chuan* (Peking, 1955), pp. 284–85.
4. *O-wang hsing-shih pien-nien,* incorporated in the *Chin-t'o ts'ui-pien.* The *Chin-t'o ts'ui-pien* and the *Chin-t'o hsü pien* have been used in the Che-chiang shu-chü edition of 1883.
5. One of them has been pointed out by Ichimura Sanjirō, Chinese translation by Ch'en Yü-ch'ing in *Shih-hsüeh tsa-chih,* I (1929), and by Teng, *op. cit.,* pp. 282–83; others by Teng, *op. cit.,* pp. 281–82 and 289–303.
6. After all this has been said, it must be stated that in face of these handicaps Yüeh K'o worked with a remarkable degree of integrity. The *Ssu-k'u t'i-yao* authors are full of praise for his reliability. Cf. Wan-yu wen-k'u edition, II, 1959.
7. Hsiung K'o's biography is in *Sung shih,* ch. 445. The *Kuang-ya ts'ung-shu* contains a reprint of the *Yung-lo ta-tien* version of his *Chung-hsing hsiao-li.* See *Ssu-k'u t'i-yao,* I, 1035.
8. 1129–1206. His compilation is entitled *Chung-hsing liang ch'ao sheng-cheng.*
9. 1166-1243. His *Chien-yen i-lai hsi-nien yao-lu* is also contained in the

Kuang-ya ts'ung-shu. On his book, see *Ssu-k'u t'i-yao,* I, 1041.

10. See Otto Franke, *Geschichte des chinesischen Reiches,* IV (Berlin, 1948), 4–5, following the *Ssu-k'u t'i-yao.*

11. On this point see Liang Yüan-tung, "Yüeh Fei Ch'in Kuei chiu an," in *Jen-wen Yüeh-k'an,* VIII, No. 5 (June 15, 1937).

12. *Sung Yüeh chung-wu-wang chi* (Pan-mou-yüan ed., 1865). A handy annotated selection is contained in *Wu chung chi,* Hu huai-shen ed. Cheng-chung wen-k'u, XXXI (Taipei, 1954).

13. See *Nien-erh-shih cha-chi* (Ts'ung-shu chi-ch'eng ed.), ch. 25, pp. 514–16; *Ssu-k'u t'i-yao,* III, 3312.

14. Most of what remained at that time was compiled by Yüeh K'o in the section "Po shih chao-chung lu" of his *Chin-t'o hsü-pien* and by Hsü Meng-hsin in his *San-ch'ao pei-meng hui-pien* (various editions: Hsü's dates are 1124–1204; on his book, see *Ssu-k'u t'i-yao,* II, 1070). Hsü's work also contains an anonymous, apparently independent, but not entirely reliable biography of Yüeh Fei. The Pan-mou-yüan edition of Yüeh Fei's collected works has appended a collection of episodical material, drawn from a variety of private sources.

15. Two *nien-p'u* have been helpful, the one by Ch'ien Ju-wen, *Sung Yüeh O-wang nien-p'u,* 6 *ts'e,* preface dated 1924 (a careful edition of Yüeh's works is appended), and the one by Li Han-hun, *Yüeh Wu-mu nien-p'u,* 2 vols. (Shanghai: Commercial Press, 1948). Of recent biographies the one by Teng Kuang-ming, mentioned in note 4, seems to be the most critical. The first edition of this was published by Sheng-li in 1945. Wilfrid Allan, *Makers of Cathay* (Shanghai, 1938), pp. 144–52, contains a short biographical sketch. As far as a critical compilation of the dates of his life goes, Teng Kuang-ming's recent book appears to exhaust almost all the possibilities our sources offer.

16. My exposition is based on the sources mentioned above unless otherwise indicated.

17. The collection *Yüeh Chung-wu-wang wen-chi* (prefaces by Ts'ao K'un and Wu P'ei-fu, dated 1921) contains some specimens of his calligraphy. Most famous is his calligraphy of the two *Ch'u-shih-piao* by Chu-ko Liang, which have been carved in stone. See *Yüeh Wu-mu shu ch'u-shih-piao* (Ta-chung ed.) (Shanghai, n.d.).

18. Biography in *Sung shih,* ch. 363.

19. His biography puts this incident only into the period after his first term of military activity.

20. T'ung Kuan, together with Ts'ai Yu, pursued at that time the make-believe war of Sung against the crumbling Liao.

21. See Mary Clabaugh Wright, *The Last Stand of Chinese Conservatism* (Stanford, 1957), chap. iv.

22. 1057–1128. Biography in *Sung shih,* ch. 360.

23. Biography in *Sung shih,* ch. 475.

24. Chang Hsien was one of the main commanders of the Yüeh-chia-chün and was executed with Yüeh Fei's son.

25. Died 1154. Biography in *Sung shih,* ch. 369. He was one of the four great field commanders of the time.

26. Died 1142. Biography in *Sung shih,* ch. 369.

27. 1089–1151. Biography in *Sung shih,* ch. 364.

28. Ho Fu (Sung) states in his *Chung-hsing kuei-chien* that Yüeh Fei himself started his military career as a *hsiao-yung*.

29. See Ruhlmann, *supra* pp. 154–56, for a description of Kuan's personality in popular fiction.

30. There are slight variations in the tradition of this phrase.

31. On this trait see Ruhlmann, *supra* p. 149.

32. Adapted from the translation by Wang Sheng-chih found in Robert Payne, ed., *The White Pony* (New York, 1947), p. 359. The one given in Wong Man, *Poems from China* (Hongkong, 1950), p. 108, is another song to the same tune.

33. The way this incident is recorded leaves doubtful how and when Yüeh Fei voiced his displeasure. There is reason to believe that the sources have been manipulated here in Yüeh's disfavor. There is enough evidence, however, to show that Yüeh Fei felt grave concern about this matter, and there is no reason to dismiss the entire incident as fictitious.

34. See Jung-pang Lo, "China's Paddle-Wheel Boats," *Tsing-hua Journal*, New Series, II, No. 1 (May 1960), 195–97.

35. Why the myth has added Chu-hsien-chen as a final point of this campaign is a riddle to me. Chu-hsien-chen would have brought him somewhat closer to the old capital, K'ai-feng, but not near enough to make an issue out of it. Color symbolism is the only explanation that comes to mind.

36. Joseph Campbell, *The Hero with a Thousand Faces* (New York, 1956), p. 391.

NOTES TO PROTEST AGAINST CONVENTIONS AND CONVENTIONS OF PROTEST

I wish especially to thank Mr. Fang Chao-ying of the East Asiatic Library, Berkeley, and Mr. Conrad Schirokauer of Swarthmore College, for the many helpful suggestions with which they have assisted my work on this paper.

1. Ou-yang Hsiu, "Chi Chiu Pen Han Wen Hou" ("An Essay Attached to an Old Edition of Han Yü"), *T'ang Sung Pa Chia Wen*, Vol. I (in *Kokuyaku Kambun Taisei*, Ser. 2, Vol. 7), ch. 12, pp. 135–36.

2. Robert des Rotours, *Le Traité des Examens, traduit de la Nouvelle Histoire des T'ang*, Bibliothèque de l'Institut des Hautes Etudes Chinoises (Paris, 1932), II, 147.

3. P'u Ch'i-lung, *Shih T'ung T'ung Shih* (Wang Family reprint, published by Han-mo-yüan, no date), ch. 10, p. 11b.

4. Ku Chieh-kang (A. W. Hummel, trans.), *The Autobiography of a Chinese Historian*, Sinica Leidensia Vol. I (Leiden, 1931), pp. 8–10.

5. Hu Shih, *Ssu-shih Tzu-shu* ("Autobiography at Forty") (Shanghai, 1940), pp. 46 ff.

6. F. G. Henke, *The Philosophy of Wang Yang-ming* (Chicago, 1916), p. 453 (my translation differs slightly from Henke's).

7. Hu Shih, Yao Ming-ta, *Chang Shih-chai Nien-p'u* (Shanghai, 1931), pp. 7, 18.

8. *Chang Shih I-shu* (Chia-yeh-t'ang edition, 1922), Vol. 2, ch. 13, pp. 19a–b.

9. *Chu Wen-kung Chiao Ch'ang-li Hsien-sheng Chi* (Ssu-pu Ts'ung-k'an edition), ch. 13, pp. 9a–10a.

10. *Ibid.*, pp. 7a–9a.

11. Arthur Waley, *The Life and Times of Po Chü-i, 772–846* (London, 1949), pp. 27, 40–41.

12. Rotours, *Traité*, pp. 185–86.

13. This idea, basically a piece of Confucian feudal utopianism, should not be confused with the system of promotion by recommendation actually in use in the Sung period. The Sung recommendation device, as Kracke makes clear (E. A. Kracke, Jr., *Civil Service in Early Sung China, 960–1067*, Cambridge, Mass., 1953, pp. 58, 75–76, 119, 190) was essentially a means of promoting and assigning officials rather than a means of recruitment into the civil service. It was a practice which evolved gradually in the early Northern Sung period. For recommendation practices prior to the T'ang, cf. Donald Holzman, "Les Débuts du système médiéval de choix et de classement des fonctionnaires: les neuf catégories et l'impartial et juste," en l'Institut des Hautes Etudes Chinoises, *Mélanges*, tome premier (Paris, 1957), pp. 387–414.

14. Ch'en Tung-yüan, *Chung-kuo Chiao-yü Shih* ("History of Chinese Education") (1934), pp. 271–72.

15. For further description of this attitude, see my introduction to *Confucianism in Action* (Stanford, 1959), especially pp. 4–9.

16. Chu Hsi, *Chin-ssu Lu*, Ts'ung-shu Chi-ch'eng edition, p. 250; Olaf Graf, *Dschu Hsi, Djin-si Lu, Die Sung konfuzianische Summa* (Tokyo, 1953), II, p. 564. I am indebted to Mr. Conrad Schirokauer for bringing this and the following two items from *Chin-ssu Lu to* my attention.

17. *Chin-ssu Lu*, p. 220; Graf II, pp. 497–98.

18. *Chin-ssu Lu*, p. 216; Graf II, p. 491. The translation is Mr. Schirokauer's.

19. *Chu Tzu Wen-chi* (Commercial Press, Kuo-hsüeh Chi-pen Ts'ung-shu edition), p. 471.

20. *Sung Shih* ("History of the Sung"), ch. 156, K'ai-ming edition 4851.1–2.

21. *Chu Tzu Wen-chi*, pp. 473–75, 472.

22. *Chu Tzu Ch'üan Shu* (compiled by imperial order under the editorship of Li Kuang-ti, in 66 *chüan;* memorial of submission dated 1714), ch. 65, p. 26, a, b. The "disturbance" which for Chu is to be avoided here is concern about worldly success and failure, emotional involvement in events affecting oneself; his attitude (he seems to assume anyone would have it) is perhaps a Neo-Confucian transformation of the Buddhist ethic of nonattachment. For a similar point of view in Ch'eng I, see *Chin-ssu Lu*, p. 219; Graf II, pp. 495–96. Li Kuang-ti's essays in *pa-ku* form were highly recommended as models to students preparing for the examinations. For his political views, see my "The Problem of 'Knowledge' and 'Action' in Chinese Thought since Wang Yang-ming," in A. F. Wright, ed., *Studies in Chinese Thought* (Chicago, 1953), p. 133.

23. Chu Hsi, "Reply to Sung Shen-chih," in *Chu Tzu Ch'üan Shu*, ch. 65, p. 28b.

24. *Chu Tzu Ch'üan Shu*, ch. 65, pp. 30b–32b.

25. *Ibid.*, ch. 75, p. 27b.

26. *Ibid.*, ch. 65, p. 25b.

27. *Ibid.* The Ch'ien-lung Emperor of the Ch'ing Dynasty made skillful

use of the side of Chu's thought represented in the *Chu Tzu Ch'üan Shu* when he addressed an edict of moral instruction to the students in the Imperial Academy in 1740, urging them to avoid being too much concerned with passing the examinations and to make it their primary aim to become better men. See my "Ho-shen and His Accusers: Ideology and Political Behavior in the Eighteenth Century," in *Confucianism in Action*, p. 223.

28. Henke, pp. 328–30.

29. *Ming Shih* (Palace edition), ch. 70, pp. 1b–2a.

30. Ku Yen-wu, *Jih-Chih Lu* (Kuo-hsüeh Chi-pen Ts'ung-shu edition, 1933 [1935]), Vol. 1, Bk. 6, p. 46.

31. *Ming Shih*, ch. 70, p. 2a.

32. Liu Lin-sheng, *Chung-kuo P'ien-wen Shih* (*Chung-kuo Wen-hua-shih Ts'ung-shu*, Ser. I, Commercial Press, Shanghai, 1936 [1937]), pp. 117–18. Many Ming prose writers, notably Kuei Yu-kuang (1506–71), are recognized as masters of this form. Cf. *Chang-shih I-shu*, ch. 2, p. 36a.

33. This feature of the *pa-ku* was also characteristic of the *ching-i* of Chu Hsi's day, and he complained about it strongly: "Not only does it not result in classical scholarship; it does not even result in acceptable writing." (*Chu Tzu Wen-chi*, p. 476.)

34. *Chu Tzu Wen-chi*, p. 476.

35. James Legge, *The Chinese Classics* (1895 edition), Vol. VI, p. 431.

36. Liu Lin-sheng, p. 120.

37. Legge, II, 324–25.

38. Ku, *Jih-chih Lu*, Vol. 1, Bk 6, p. 52.

39. *Ibid.*, pp. 45, 49; Williamson, I, 333–35.

40. *Ibid.*, p. 47.

41. *Ibid.*, pp. 47–48.

42. In this and the following paragraph, I am indebted to Mr. Fang Chao-ying for some useful suggestions.

43. Kung Tzu-chen, "Kan Lu Hsin Shu Tzu Hsü," *Ting-an Wen-chi* (Kuo-hsüeh Chi-pen Ts'ung-shu edition, 1936), pp. 138–39.

44. Ku, p. 54.

NOTES TO CONFUCIAN EREMITISM IN THE YÜAN PERIOD

1. As originally presented to the Committee on Chinese Thought in the conference held at Stockbridge, Massachusetts, in September 1957, this paper included a long introductory chapter entitled "The Intellectual Climate of the Yüan Period," in which the character of the age was discussed in detail. It has been deleted here in order to reduce this paper to a more suitable length. In revised form it will be published elsewhere as an essay on the intellectual history of the Yüan period.

2. Nemoto Makoto, *Sensei Shakai ni okeru Teikō Seishin* (Tokyo, 1952).

3. Cf. Fung Yu-lan, *A History of Chinese Philosophy* (tr. D. Bodde), I, 281.

4. As originally presented at the Stockbridge conference, this paper also contained a lengthy digression into the ideological foundations of Confucian eremitism, in which this point was explored in considerable detail. A revised

and expanded treatment of this subject will be published as a separate study.

5. Hsiao Kung-ch'üan, *Chung-kuo Cheng-chih Ssu-hsiang Shih* ("History of Chinese Political Thought") (reprint, Taipei, 1954), esp. pp. 66, 102. This modern classic contains, in passing, the most useful remarks on Chinese eremitism in relation to Chinese thought that have come to my attention, and in many places the present study draws directly or indirectly on Professor Hsiao's work.

6. A striking example of the censure of officials who displayed insufficient loyalty to the fallen dynasty by the ruler of the succession dynasty is referred to in the prefatory remarks to the chapters of biographies of loyal officials in the *Hsin Yüan Shih*, K'ai-ming ed., ch. 230, p. 7038.

7. *Ibid.*, p. 7056.

8. Nemoto Makoto, *Sensei Shakai ni okeru Teikō Seishin*, pp. 51–54.

9. *Yüan Shih*, ch. 171. The *Hsin Yüan Shih* biography in ch. 170 is roughly the same, slightly shorter through the omission of some details. The information about Liu in Giles, *Bio. Dict.* (No. 1370), is inaccurate and misleading, as is that in Giles, *A History of Chinese Literature*, Book the Sixth, Part I.

10. Yao Shu (1203–80), a very young man serving in the secretariat of a high Chinese official in the Mongol expeditionary forces at the time of the Mongol conquest of Chin North China in the early 1230's, saved the life of the famed Southern Sung scholar Chao Fu, who had been taken prisoner. Chao was taken to the North, and Yao became his pupil. In this first scholarly contact between North and South China in over a century, the Neo-Confucian synthesis of Chu Hsi was spread to the North and propagated there chiefly by men like Yao and other pupils of Chao Fu. See also p. 224.

11. I.e., Liu-TSCC. Liu's works are quoted here in two standard editions: (1) The *Ching-hsiu Hsien-sheng Wen-chi* (poetry and prose), in the Ssu-pu-ts'ung-k'an 1st series, quoted here as "Liu-SPTK"; this is the 22-*chüan* edition of 1330. (2) The Chi-fu Ts'ung-shu edition, reprinted in the *Ts'ung-shu Chi-ch'eng* (Vols. 2076, 2077, and 2078) in 12 *chüan*; this will be quoted here as "Liu-TSCC." The government-sponsored edition of 1350 in 30 *chüan* referred to in ch. 166 of SKTY may be no longer in existence. A large selection of Liu's poetry and prose also is included in the *Yüan Wen Lei* ("Classified Anthology of Yüan Literature") compiled by Su T'ien-chüeh (1294–1352); this is referred to hereafter as YWL. A brief selection of Liu's poetry with biographical data and comment of later writers appears in *chüan* 5 of the *Yüan-shih Chi-shih* by the late Ch'ing scholar Ch'en Yen; this will be referred to hereafter as YSCS.

12. Translated from Liu-TSCC, ch. 1; not included in Liu-SPTK.

13. Cf. Fung Yu-lan, *History*, II, 443–51, and bibliographic note, p. 731. I have drawn on Professor Bodde's work, adopting his translations of many philosophic terms, here and elsewhere.

14. *The Analects* (Legge), XVIII/8/4, italics mine.

15. "Ch'iu-hsi Kan Huai," Liu-TSCC, ch. 6, p. 116. Expressions of this mood and attitude are numerous in Liu's poetry. Much of his poetry is more personal and more revealing than his prose, if at the same time more easily misinterpreted. I have not translated more of it for inclusion here because its highly allusive nature demands that it be burdened with bulky footnotes and explanations in order to be intelligible in translation. Hence the reader is re-

ferred directly to Liu's poetry for a more accurate presentation of his thought and feelings.

16. The translation of this line is tentative. The reference seems to be to the *Chou Li* ("The Ritual of the Chou Dynasty"), *incipit* "yü jen" in ch. 4, "Ti-kuan," p. 37b of the SPTK edition. The term appears also in the "Song of Ch'u" which Han Kao-tsu recited, as quoted in the *Shih Chi*, ch. 55, in roughly the meaning in which it is translated here.

17. Liu-SPTK, ch. 20, p. 3a; Liu-TSCC, ch. 1, p. 21.

18. Chang Tzu-yu has not been identified. He apparently had at one time held the office of *chan-shih*, an office in the retinue of imperial princes frequently given to persons of learning and exemplary conduct and carrying little or no official responsibility.

19. "Tao Kuei T'ang Shuo," Liu-SPTK, ch. 20, p. 3b; Liu-TSCC, ch. 1, p. 20.

20. Hsü Heng (1209–1281), the outstanding Confucian of the Mongol-ruled North China in the time of Liu Yin, is more important as an upright and conscientious official who sought to promote a Confucian revival in the North than as a scholar or thinker. His name is often coupled with that of Liu Yin, although Liu disapproved of him. See also pp. 224 and 227.

21. Cf. *The Analects* (Legge), XVIII/7/5.

22. *Chuang-tzu*, ch. 4, "Jen Chien Shih," where it is attributed to the Confucians and quoted disapprovingly. Cf. also Hsiao Kuang-ch'üan, *Chung-kuo Cheng-chih Ssu-hsiang Shih*, p. 66.

23. The text of this letter is to be found in both the *Yüan Shih* and the *Hsin Yüan Shih* biographies, as well as in Liu-SPTK, ch. 21, p. 1a; Liu-TSCC, ch. 3, p. 52; and YWL, ch. 37.

24. *Mencius*, "Kung-sun Ch'ou," part II, II/6–7. This translation is altered but slightly from Legge; the italics are mine.

25. I.e., the "Tu-chiang fu," Liu-TSCC, ch. 5, p. 94.

26. Note, for example, the critical tone of his comments on the Chin, as in his preface to "Chai Chieh-fu Shih," Liu-SPTK, ch. 1, p. 8b; Liu-TSCC, ch. 6, p. 105; and YWL, ch. 3.

27. Ou-yang Hsiu, *Wu-tai Shih-chi* ("Historian's Record of the Five Dynasties"), a preface to ch. 54, and comments in the biography of Feng Tao in the same *chüan*. Cf. Giles, *Bio. Dict.* No. 573.

28. This poem is quoted with interesting comment in YSCS, ch. 5.

29. Note in this connection particularly the poems "Ts'ai-chü T'u" and "Kuei-ch'ü-lai T'u" in Liu-SPTK, ch. 4, p. 3b; Liu-TSCC, ch. 7, p. 122; and YWL, ch. 5. The legend that loyalty prevented T'ao from serving or even from acknowledging the new Liu Sung dynasty (420–78) is one that came to be widely accepted in the later imperial age, reflecting the mores of that age (and one that has been disproved by modern scholarship).

30. See the comments appended to the poem "Yung Tseng Tien" in YSCS, Commercial Press Kuo-hsüeh Chi-pen Ts'ung-shu edition, ch. 5, pp. 49–50. The comments refer to the use of the term *tso wang* ("sitting and forgetting"), although in the version of the poem printed there the parallel (Taoistic) term *hsin chai* is used in place of *tso wang*. Other editions, such as Liu-SPTK, ch. 13, pp. 3a–b, have *tso wang* for *hsin chai*. These comments show but a shallow understanding of Liu's thought.

31. For the *Yin-fu Ching*, see SKTY, ch. 146, first and second entries; also

Liu's preface, dated 1271, to a new edition of the work, in Liu-TSCC, ch. 2, p. 26. This is a Taoistic work forged in the T'ang period. Liu's interest in this work is one he shared with Chu Hsi and many other Neo-Confucian scholars.

32. This long essay, "Hsü Hsüeh," Liu-TSCC, ch. 1, pp. 3–8, merits study as a document expressing attitudes toward all fields of thought and learning.

33. I.e., *tsung-heng chia*—this translation of the term is Bodde's, as used in his translation of Fung Yu-lan.

34. Cheng-shih (A.D. 240–48) and Hsi-ning (A.D. 1068–77) were reign-periods which from the strict Confucian point of view represented the triumph of heterodoxy: the former is associated with the Taoist-inspired *ch'ing-t'an* episode in intellectual history; the latter is the period when the arch-villain in Neo-Confucian history, the reformer Wang An-shih, was in power.

35. "Chuang Chou Meng Tieh T'u hsü"; see Liu-SPTK, ch. 19, pp. 5a–b; Liu-TSCC, ch. 2, p. 27; and YWL, ch. 33.

36. "Ch'un-chai Shuo," Liu-SPTK, ch. 20, p. 2a; Liu-TSCC, ch. 1, p. 21.

37. "T'ui-chai Chi," dated 1276; see Liu-SPTK, ch. 18, p. 7a; Liu-TSCC, ch. 1, p. 42; YWL, ch. 28.

38. I.e., "Ho T'ao Chi," Liu-SPTK, ch. 3; Liu-TSCC, ch. 12.

39. Ch'ien Mu, *Sung-Ming Li-hsüeh Kai-shu* ("A General Account of Sung and Ming Neo-Confucianism") (Taipei, 1953), p. 180.

40. Lou Shih-te's biography appears in the *Chiu T'ang Shu*, ch. 93, and in the *Hsin T'ang Shu*, ch 108. This anecdote appears only in the latter. This became a famous anecdote, and it was much discussed by writers of the Yüan period, some of whom praised Lou, and some of whom like Liu found nothing praiseworthy in such conduct.

41. *Mencius* (Legge), "Kung-sun Chou," Part I, IX/2–3.

42. Lines from the poem "Jen Chün T'ien-hsia Shih," in the *Ho T'ao Chi*, No. 20 of the "Ho 'Yin Chiu' " poems.

43. This poem is not in the *Ho T'ao Chi*, but is composed of lines taken from T'ao Yüan-ming's poetry and reassembled by Liu to make a new poem. It therefore bears the title "Chi T'ao Chü" ("Assembled Lines from T'ao"), and appears in Liu-SPTK, ch. 1, p. 4b, and Liu-TSCC, ch. 6, p. 100.

44. This famous anecdote appears in Ssu-ma Ch'ien's *Shih Chi*, ch. 55, " Liu Hou Shih Chia."

45. Hsiao Kung-ch'üan, *Chung-kuo Cheng-chih Ssu-hsiang Shih*, pp. 482–84.

46. This work is discussed by Hsiao, *ibid.*, pp. 506–7. References to the work here are to the edition of the late Ming scholar Mao Chin, in his collectanea, the *Chin-tai Pi-shu*.

47. Chu Hsi, *Chin-ssu Lu*, ch. 2, pp. 19a–b, in the photolithographic reprint of the Commercial Press in the collectanea *Ssu-k'u Ch'üan-shu Chen-pen Ts'ung-shu*; here the work bears the title *Chin-ssu Lu Chi-chu*. Cf. also the translation of this passage in Olaf Graf, *Djin Sï Lu* (Tokyo, 1953), II (Part I), 151. The discussion of the remonstrating but loyal servitor in the *Chin-ssu Lu*, esp. ch. 10, p. 6b, seems to reflect both the wording and the general meaning of the passage in the *Chung Ching*, section 15, pp. 10a–b. Otherwise also there seems to be *no* evidence that Chu Hsi, in summing up the Neo-Confucian rationalist position that was to become the orthodox one, differed with what have been described here as the Neo-Confucian connotations of the

concept of loyalty, or with the intensified authoritarianism in political philosophy in general. It should be noted that in his reply to Ssu-ma Kuang's essay "I Meng" ("Doubts about Mencius"), Chu Hsi does not defend Mencian liberalism against Ssu-ma Kuang's authoritarian-minded attack on it. Rather, he tries to harmonize what he considers to be Mencius' real intent with Ssu-ma Kuang's philosophic position. Thus he sums up one of his arguments by saying, "Seen in this way, Ssu-ma's argument really reinforces Mencius' position"; and in several other places he says, "If Ssu-ma Kuang had only understood that this is what Mencius really meant, he would have had no reason to doubt him." However, the whole subject of the relation of Neo-Confucian rationalism to Mencius is a complex one, and one that merits fuller study. Cf. also Hsiao Kung-ch'üan, *Chung-kuo Cheng-chih Ssu-hsiang Shih*, pp. 482–83, discussing Ssu-ma Kuang's rejection of Mencius.

48. Hsieh's biography is in *Sung Shih*, ch. 425.

49. A portion of the colophon by P'an K'an, dated 1575, appended at the end of the SPTK edition of Wen T'ien-hsiang's collected literary works, the *Wen Wen-shan Ch'üan-chi*.

50. Some doubt has existed about the authenticity of the collection known as *Hsin-shih*, or *T'ieh-han Hsin-shih*, recovered in 1638 in an iron box (i.e., *t'ieh-han*) in a well in Soochow where Cheng is purported to have concealed it 350 years earlier. It appeared at a time when its racist sentiments and its appeal to loyalty were of potential use in stiffening Ming resistance to the Manchu threat. However, these doubts have been dealt with by several modern scholars, and I am inclined to accept the authenticity of the work. See the various prefaces and colophons to the recent edition of the work published in the *Min-tsu Cheng-ch'i Ts'ung-shu*, one of the several portions of a new collectanea being published by the World Book Company under the title *Ssu-pu K'an-yao*, Series I, Taipei, 1955. This edition is cited here.

51. "Hou Ch'en-tzu Meng hsi," *Hsin-shih*, pp. 76a–b.

52. I.e., tang yang, to face the sun, or the south, in the position of the ruler. The reference is to the Emperor Li-tsung, who reigned 1225–64.

53. "I Ch'ien-pei," *Hsin-shih*, p. 44b.

54. "Hsien Lu Ko," *Hsin-shih*, pp. 25a–b.

55. One such society of Sung loyalists was the famous Yüeh-ch'üan She, prominent throughout the last quarter of the thirteenth century. For some idea of its size and importance, note the number of poets listed as its members in YSCS, especially ch. 6, pp. 96–105, and pp. 596 ff. (in the edition of this work cited in note 11 above).

56. Chao Meng-fu is the subject of a study by Herbert Franke entitled "Dschau Mong-fu," in *Sinica* (Frankfort), XV, 25 ff.

57. YSCS, ch. 8, p. 125, quotes this poem, entitled "T'i T'ao Ch'ien Kuei-ch'ü-lai T'u," with comment, portions of which are translated here. Note in the same work, p. 124, the comment of later writers on the poem which Kubilai Khan commanded Chao to write ridiculing Liu Meng-yen, a high Sung official who quickly transferred his allegiance to the Yüan and took service under the Mongols. A later writer, expressing a common opinion, states that even the Mongol emperor, although an alien to Chinese civilization, knew enough to despise Liu Meng-yen's character, and the poem he commanded Chao to write ridiculing Liu actually becomes self-ridicule of Chao as well.

58. Chao I, *Nien-erh Shih Cha-chi*, ch. 32, "Ming-ch'u Wen-jen To Pu Shih."

59. K'o Shao-min in his *Hsin Yüan Shih,* ch. 230, prefatory remarks to the biographies of loyal officials, says that the number of Yüan loyalists at the end of the dynasty was very great, but his comparison is with the end of the Liao and the Chin, and not with the Sung loyalists of ninety years earlier. Moreover, in this place he is moralizing about the virtue of loyalty and the beneficial effects of Kubilai Khan's maintenance of it. The facts do not bear out his statement that the literati were enthusiastically and devotedly loyal to the doomed Yüan cause and anxious to die for it.

60. Fu Wei-lin (died 1667), *Ming Shu,* introductory remarks to ch. 143. Here again the influence of Ou-yang Hsiu's historiography is attested to, for the *Ming Shu* follows the example of his *Wu-tai Shih-chi,* which had created the classification of *tsa chuan,* "miscellaneous biographies," for persons who had served more than one dynasty and thus were more or less tainted with immorality. Despite the tone of the remarks translated here, Fu was not a Ming loyalist.

61. Yü and Li were famous Yüan period figures who died in the bandit movements of the late Yüan, loyally defending the Yüan cause.

62. Fu Shou was a Tangut, a military leader under the Mongols defending Nanking when Ming T'ai-tsu led his small bandit army to capture it in 1356. Fu alone among the Yüan officials on the scene died defending the city. See his biography in *Yüan Shih,* ch. 144, and *Hsin Yüan Shih,* ch. 217.

63. The "old servitor" whose shuffling shoes aroused T'ai-tsu, and prompted the conversation between them referred to here, was Wei Su (1295–1372). The *Ming Shu's* indirect reference to the anecdote here uses the same words with which it is told in Wei's biography in the same work, ch. 144.

NOTES TO CONFUCIANISM AND MONARCHY AT THE LAST

1. *North-China Herald,* CXIV (Jan. 9, 1915), 87.

2. *Faust,* Part II, Act 1, Scene 3.

3. Thomas Mann, *Doctor Faustus* (New York, 1948), p. 134.

4. Kao Lao, *Ti-chih Yün-tung Shih-mo Chi* ("An Account of the Monarchical Movement") (Shanghai, 1923), p. 17.

5. *Ibid.,* p. 19.

6. *Ibid.,* p. 18.

7. Ku Yen-wu, *Jih-chih Lu* ("Record of Knowledge Day by Day"), ed. Huang Ju-ch'eng (1834), ch. 13, pp. 5b–6.

8. Kao, pp. 20–21.

9. *Ibid.,* p. 22.

10. Imazeki Hisamaro, *Sung Yüan Ming Ch'ing Ju-chia Hsüeh Nien-piao* ("Chronological Tables of Sung, Yüan, Ming, and Ch'ing Confucianism") (Tokyo, 1920), p. 216 (in Chinese). The other Ch'ing *ta-ssu* were the rites for Heaven and Earth, the Celestial Emperor (Shang-ti), the imperial ancestral temple, and the gods of the land and grain.

11. Kao, p. 7.

12. T'ao Chü-yin, *Liu Chün-tzu Chuan* ("Biographies of the 'Six Martyrs'") (Shanghai, 1946), p. 2.

13. Chou Chen-fu, "Yen Fu Ssu-hsiang Chuan-pien chih P'ou-hsi" ("A Close Analysis of the Changes in Yen Fu's Thought"), *Hsüeh-lin,* No. 3 (1941), p. 117.

358

14. Sakamaki Teiichirō, *Shina Bunkatsu Ron: Tsuki, "Gen Seikai"* ("The Decomposition of China: Supplement, Yüan Shih-k'ai") (Tokyo, 1914), p. 183.

15. *Ibid.*, pp. 228, 229.

16. E.g., "Rinji Taiwan Kyūkan Chōsakai Dai-ichi-bu Hōkoku" ("Temporary Commission of the Taiwan Government-General for the Study of Old Chinese Customs, Report of the First Section"), *Shinkoku gyōseihō* ("Administrative Laws of the Ch'ing Dynasty"), kan 1, revised (Tokyo, 1914), I, p. 46.

17. Cf. Tung Chung-shu, *Ch'un-ch'iu Fan-lu*, "Shen-ch'a ming-hao," ch. 10, pp. 1–4: "The monarch who has received the mandate is given the mandate by the will of Heaven; therefore he is called the son of Heaven . . ." (This reference comes from Vincent Shih, "The Ideology of the T'ai-p'ing T'ien-kuo," ms.)

18. A proper corrective to the authority cited in note 16 is Hara Tomio, *Chūka Shisō no Kontai to Jugaku no Yūi* ("The Roots of Chinese Thought and the Preeminence of Confucianism") (Tokyo, 1947), p. 183, which emphasizes that in classical Chinese thought *t'ien-i* was independent and self-existent. That is, it was not derived from *min-i* and was certainly not reduced, in the modern metaphorical fashion, to being simply a rhetorical equivalent of the latter term.

19. Sagara Yoshiaki, "Toku no Go no Igi to Sono Hensen" ("The Meaning of the Word *te* and Its Evolution"), in Tsuda Sokichi, *Tōyō Shisō Kenkyū* ("Studies in Asian Thought"), No. 1 (Tokyo, 1937), pp. 290–91.

20. Wang Hsieh-chia, "Chung-hua Min-kuo Hsien-fa hsüan ch'uan chang ting K'ung-chiao wei kuo-chiao ping hsü jen-min hsiu chiao tzu-yu hsiu-cheng an" ("Proposal that the constitution of the Republic of China promulgate a special clause establishing Confucianism as the state religion and permitting modification of the freedom of religion"), pp. 1, 4–5, in Tsung-sheng hsüeh-pao (publ.), *K'ung-chiao Wen-t'i* ("The Problem of Confucianism") (Taiyuan, 1917). (Hereafter, KCWT).

21. *Ibid.*, pp. 1–3.

22. *Ibid.*, p. 10.

23. "Hu-pei kung-min Liu Ta-chün shang ts'an chung liang yüan ching ting kuo-chiao shu" (Letter from Liu Ta-chün of Hupeh to the parliament requesting establishment of a state religion), in KCWT, pp. 4–5.

24. Wang Hsieh-chia, in KCWT, p. 1.

25. Li Wen-chih, "Ching ting K'ung-chiao wei kuo-chiao ti erh-tz'u i-chien shu" ("Second communication of views favoring establishment of Confucianism as the state religion"), in KCWT, pp. 2–3.

26. For example, cf. Jacques Gernet, *Les Aspects économiques du Bouddhisme dans la société chinoise du Ve au Xe siècle* (Saigon, 1956), pp. 293–94 et seq., for the exploitation of Buddhism to support the imperial power. To cite a later period: Ming imperial indulgence toward Buddhism was marked. Even while Confucian scholars biased in favor of their master, the Yung-lo emperor (reigned 1403–24), taxed his predecessor (whose throne he had usurped) with favor to Buddhists, Yung-lo himself retained his ties with the monks who had helped him to power; see David Chan, "The Usurpation of the Prince of Yen, 1398–1402," unpublished Ph.D. dissertation, University of California, 1957.

27. For the Buddhist contribution to trade and capital formation, see Gernet, esp. pp. 138–90.

28. J. J. L. Duyvendak, *China's Discovery of Africa* (London, 1949), pp. 27–28.

29. For Ming, see Charles Whitman MacSherry, "Impairment of the Ming Tributary System as Exhibited in Trade Involving Fukien," unpublished Ph.D. dissertation, University of California, 1957.

30. For the Hoppo's appointment by the "inner court" (imperial) rather than the "outer court" (general bureaucratic), see William Frederick Mayers, *The Chinese Government* (Shanghai, 1886), p. 40; and for his practice of sending memorials directly to the emperor, not through normal channels, see *Shinkoku Gyōseihō*, kan 5 (Tokyo, 1911), pp. 311–12.

31. See the chapter, "The Amateur Ideal in Ming and Early Ch'ing Society: Evidence from Painting," in Joseph R. Levenson, *Confucian China and Its Modern Fate* (Berkeley and Los Angeles, 1958), pp. 15–43. It is interesting to note that a Chinese Communist critic, in the interests of isolating the literati tradition as "the enemy," has set the "academic" style apart (the Sung Emperor Hui-tsung is specifically praised) as the anti-Confucian precedent for the Communist-sponsored "realism" in art; see Chang Jen-hsia, "Flower-and-Bird Painting," *China Reconstructs*, III (1953), 51.

32. As an interesting analysis of how a monarchy may naturally strain against an association which is nevertheless essential to it and inseparable from it, see, for comparison with China, Alexis de Tocqueville, *The Old Regime and the French Revolution* (New York, 1955), p. 8: he cites Mirabeau's letter to Louis XVI in 1790, pointing out the elements in the developing Revolution which should be reassuring to monarchy because of their centralizing, rationalizing contributions to the liquidation of feudal institutions, including those against which the crown had historically struggled. Yet, as Joseph Schumpeter shows in "The Sociology of Imperialism," in *"Imperialism" and "Social Classes"* (New York, 1955), pp. 57–58, the French monarchy's struggle against the feudal aristocracy had been such as to bind the former to the now modified feudal system. Thus, it is not surprising that the Revolution, which may be seen as completing the work of the monarchy against feudalism, should have marked the two together for destruction.

Although French historical issues are by no means the same as Chinese, this French example may encourage one to recognize, and not simply be mystified by, paradox and ambivalence in Chinese institutional relationships.

33. As Pow-key Sohn has pointed out in "The Theory and Practice of Land-systems in Korea in Comparison with China" (ms., University of California, 1956), the Koryö victory of military over civil interests played a large part in defeating the trend in Korea toward a private-property system; it encouraged, rather, a return to a strict system of state ownership and state allocation—a system, be it noted, which T'ang and other rulers in China favored at times, but which civil-official recalcitrance broke down.

34. It is probably in this connection that the Confucian sage-emperor lore (of which more below, in text) has its greatest significance. The Yao-Shun period preceding the Hsia is sometimes referred to as the "Yao Shun *shan-jang* era"; and the *shan-jang* convention for solemnizing an imperial abdication and succession was a convention for transmission of the throne to one of a different surname (see Tezuka Ryōdō, *Jukyō Dōtoku ni Okeru Kun-*

360

shin Shisō ("The Sovereign-minister Idea in Confucian Ethics") (Tokyo, 1925), p. 112; and Miyakawa Hisayuki, "Zenjō ni Yoru Ōchō Kakumei no Tokushitsu" ("The Special Quality of Dynastic Overturns Depending on *shan-jang*"), *Tōhōgaku*, No. 11 (1955), p. 50.

What was the *shan-jang* idea (projected into the past by Confucianists) but an expression of Confucian anti-dynastic feeling? It is after Yao and Shun, who chose their successors by the Confucian criterion of virtue, not the feudal criterion of hereditary right, that dynasties begin: a falling-off.

35. See Shih ms. (*op. cit.* note 17) for this literati opinion. *Ming-shih*, Shih-huo chih, ch. 77, pp. 11a–11b: "Nothing did more harm to the people than the *huang-chuang* and *chuang-t'ien* (villas) of the princes and princesses, eunuchs and nobles." Note the emphasis on eunuchs and aristocrats, both nonbureaucratic types, and both having corporate existence only as imperial affiliates. We may assume that post-Ch'in enfeoffment did not represent any genuine monarchical sentiment for retrogression to a stage of feudal fragmentation of the state power. Rather, the monarch permitted what was after all a shadow feudal structure—never with a weight of power to threaten the bureaucracy's—to exist because the state was bureaucratically centralized enough to survive it; and the monarchy willed this feudal structure to exist because bureaucratic centralization had its inner seed of impermanence. The imperially patronized nominal feudal system—mainly an extended imperial family affair—was of such a character as to be safe for the emperor as long as gentry-literati-officials were with him, while it symbolized his awareness of their potential defection.

36. As Shih points out, the Taiping state stressed the motto *i hsiao tso chung*, "transform filial piety into loyalty." The Taipings seem to me to represent in Chinese history (among other things) the assertion of a pure monarchical spirit, i.e., a spirit of unqualified autocracy, a refusal to compromise with bureaucratic ideals. A regime which understandably alienated the Confucian literati unequivocally, the Taiping state was trying to rule out the possibility of the traditional intrabureaucratic conflict between private and public impulses.

37. Carsun Chang, *The Development of Neo-Confucian Thought* (New York, 1957), p. 203.

38. See R. H. van Gulik, tr., *T'ang-Yun-Pi-Shih*, "*Parallel Cases from under the Pear-Tree*" (Leiden, 1956), p. vii, for the oft-quoted statement applying to the scholar-official, "One does not read the Code," and its bearing on theories of the ideal state and ideal ruler.

39. Louis Delatte, *Les Traités de la royauté d'Ecphante, Diotegène, et Sthénidas* (Liège and Paris, 1942), pp. 140–42.

40. Shōji Sōichi, "Chin Ryō no Gaku" (The Thought of Ch'en Liang), *Tōyō no Bunka to Shakai*, V (1954), 98–100.

41. According to Tung Chung-shu (second century B.C.), Confucius received the "imperial mandate" in principle; see Fung Yu-lan, *A History of Chinese Philosophy* (Princeton, 1955), II, 63, 71, 129. For Confucius as *su-wang* see Tu Yü (222–84), *Ch'un-ch'iu Tso-chuan Hsü* (Preface to *Ch'un-ch'iu*, with *Tso-chuan*): cf. *Tz'u-hai*, II, 61.

42. Toda Toyosaburō, "Gogyō Setsu Seiritsu no Ichi Kōsatsu" (Reflection on the Formation of Five-Element Theory"), *Shinagaku Kenkyū*, XII (1956), 44.

43. Hara (*op. cit.* note 18), p. 233.

44. Ch'eng Hao, "Lun Wang Pa Cha-Tzu" (Memorial on *wang* and *pa*), *Erh Ch'eng wen-chi* ("Collection of Writings of the Two Ch'engs") (Changsha, 1941), p. 4.

45. Norman H. Baynes, "The Byzantine State," in *Byzantine Studies and Other Essays* (London, 1955), pp. 55–57.

46. Baynes, "Eusebius and the Christian Empire," *ibid.*, p. 168.

47. The *su-wang* as the true sage and implied rebuke to the politically visible royal incumbent figures in the Taoist *Chuang-tzu* (T'ien-tao section); see *Tz'u-hai*, II, 61; also Inoue Gengo, "Juka to Haku I Tō Seki Setsuwa" ("Confucianism and the Tales of Po I and Tao Chih"), *Shinagaku Kenkyū*, No. 13 (1955), p. 21, where *Kung-yang* Confucian influence on Chuang-tzu is seen in the *su-wang* concept. In so far as we speak of Taoism as politically anarchistic, we identify it with an *essential* Confucianism which affects Confucianism-in-action but is not coterminous with it. The Confucianism which is implemented, visible in history, is the credo of officials, who are naturally no anarchists. But the Taoist boycott of the world of affairs (as by hermits, who flout the values of Confucianism-in-action, i.e., Confucianism-cum-Legalism, but confirm them, too, by abandoning the world to Confucianists—and dynasts—alone) dramatizes the theoretical principle which Confucianists invoke, in their Confucianism-cum-Taoism, to rebuke emperors.

48. Karl A. Wittfogel, *Oriental Despotism: A Comparative Study of Total Power* (New Haven, 1957), p. 103.

49. Ojima Sukema, "Shina Shisō: Shakai Keizai Shisō" ("Chinese Thought: Social and Economic Thought"), in *Tōyō Shichō* ("Far Eastern Thought-Tides") (Tokyo, 1936), pp. 23–24.

50. Ch'en Shao-pai, "Hsing Chung Hui Ko-ming Shih Yao" ("Essentials of the Hsing Chung Hui's Revolutionary History"), in *Hsin-hai Ko-ming* (Documents on the 1911 Revolution) (Shanghai, 1957), I, 32: "We saw the characters 'Chung-kuo ko-ming tang Sun Yat-sen.' . . . Hitherto our cast of mind had been such as to consider *ko-ming* something applying to the will to act as emperor, with our movement only to be considered as rebelling against this. From the time we saw this newspaper, we had the picture of the three characters *ko-ming tang* imprinted on our minds."

51. E.g., Sun Yat-sen on Yao and Shun ("The name was monarchy, the fact was the rule of democracy"), and on Confucius and Mencius as "pro-people's-rights" on the strength of their praises of Yao and Shun; cf. Kuo Chan-po (Kōya Masao, tr.), *Gendai Shina shisō shi* ("History of Modern Chinese Thought") (Tokyo, 1940), p. 108.

52. E.g., Wang Hsieh-chia, in KCWT, p. 2, for the admission that Confucianism uses a heavily monarchical language—but—"What is the origin of *ko-ming*?" A "people's rights" version of Confucianism had, of course, been worked up by K'ang Yu-wei and his Reform group, and was frequently refurbished by men like Wang, here adapting himself to the republican environment and quoting, without referring to K'ang, some of the latter's old proof-texts in the Li-yün section of *Li-chi*. Liu Ta-chün (see note 23, above) does the same (KCWT, pp. 1–2). The thinness of Confucianism in this "republican" version is apparent, not only from its highly special selectivity but from the fact that authority has clearly been stripped from it; Confucianism, instead of dictating the polity, must be interpreted by its defenders

so that it conforms to a polity established on other authority. The rhetorical question "What is the origin of *ko-ming?*" suggests, at bottom, not that the Republic is Confucian, but that Western standards have invaded even Confucianism: *ko-ming* as revolution was from the Western political vocabulary, out of Japan.

53. Tezuka (*op. cit.* note 34), pp. 17–19.

54. Tu Yü: see note 41.

55. *Ming-shih*, ch. 77, p. 4a, cited in Sohn ms. (see note 33).

56. Tezuka, p. 130. Note that the connection between *chün* and *ch'en* (and *ch'en* is located only in this or an equivalent connection) is always denoted by *lun*, human relationship; see *Li-chi*, Mencius, etc., *passim*.

57. I have explored this subject more fully in "The Amateur Ideal . . ." (see note 31).

58. Chang Ch'un-ming, "Ch'ing-tai ti Mu-chih" ("The Private-Secretary System of the Ch'ing Dynasty"), *Lingnan hsüeh-pao*, IX (1950), 33–37.

59. *Ibid.*, p. 47.

60. Sakamaki, (*op. cit.* note 14), p. 210.

61. *Ibid.*, pp. 54–55.

62. *Ibid.*, p. 139.

63. Kuo Pin-chia, "Min-kuo Erh-tz'u Ko-ming Shih" ("History of the Republic's 'Second Revolution'"), part 2, *Wuhan Quarterly*, IV (1935), 843.

64. Sakamaki, pp. 214–15. Sun's friend Huang Hsing, trying to win over the Ch'ing loyalist, General Chang Hsün, to the anti-Yüan cause in the summer of 1913, declared: "Not only is Yüan Shih-k'ai abhorrent to the Republic, he was a robber of the Ch'ing house." Cf. Kuo, part 1, *Wuhan Quarterly*, IV, 650.

65. Li Ting-shen, *Chung-kuo Chin-tai Shih* ("Recent History of China") (Shanghai, 1933), p. 312.

66. Kuo, part 2, *Wuhan Quarterly*, IV, 642.

67. T'ao Chü-yin, *Chin-tai I-wen* ("Anecdotes of the Recent Era") (Shanghai, 1930), p. 2.

68. Heibonsha: *Seijigaku jiten* ("Dictionary of Political Science") (Tokyo, 1957), p. 449.

69. *Kuo-t'i* had some vague ancient usage, as in the *Ku-liang chuan*, irrelevant to modern monarchists, and a colorless existence in occasional documents thereafter. The monarchists' *kuo-t'i* had as much novelty infused in it from Japan as the republicans' *ko-ming*.

Contributors

JAMES FRANCIS CAHILL received his B.A. degree in Oriental languages from the University of California at Berkeley, and his M.A. and Ph.D. degrees (1953 and 1957) in Fine Arts from the University of Michigan, with a thesis on the Yüan Dynasty painter Wu Chen. He has also studied at Kyoto University. In 1957 Dr. Cahill was appointed to the staff of the Freer Gallery of Art in Washington, D.C., where he is presently Curator of Chinese Art. His major publication is *Chinese Painting*, published by Skira in 1960. Other books are *Chinese Painting, XI to XIV Centuries* (1960), and *Chinese Album Leaves in the Freer Gallery of Art* (1962).

HANS H. FRANKEL was educated at the Gymnasium of Göttingen, Stanford University, and the University of California, Berkeley, where he received his Ph.D. in 1942. For several years he edited the Chinese Dynastic Histories Translations series at the University of California. He is now Associate Professor of Chinese Literature at Yale, having previously taught at the University of California, National Peking University, and Stanford. His field of interest is Chinese literature, particularly from the second century B.C. to the thirteenth century A.D.

CHARLES O. HUCKER, Chairman of the Department of History and the Committee on Asian Studies at Oakland University (Michigan), is a specialist in China's early modern history and traditional political institutions. He was formerly on the faculties of the University of Chicago and the University of Arizona. In 1952-54 he was a postdoctoral research fellow of Academia Sinica in Taiwan and at Kyoto University in Japan. His writings include monographs on Ming Dynasty government and on political and intellectual movements of the late Ming period, as well as bibliographical compilations on Chinese history in general.

JOSEPH R. LEVENSON received his B.A. (1941) and Ph.D. degrees from Harvard, where he was a member of the Society of Fellows. He is now Professor of History at the University of California, Berkeley, where he has taught since 1951. He is the author of *Liang Ch'i-ch'ao and the Mind of Modern China* and *Confucian China and Its Modern Fate*.

HUI-CHEN WANG LIU *(Mrs. James T.C. Liu)* was trained in sociology at Yenching University in Peking and later joined its staff. After two years of service in Japan as a research member of the Chinese Mission after World War II, she resumed her graduate work at the University of Washington, Columbia University, and finally the University of Pittsburgh where she took her Ph.D. Her thesis appeared under the title *The Traditional Chinese Clan Rules* (Monographs of the Association for Asian Studies, No. VII, 1959). As Assistant Professor, she started the Chinese Language program at the University of Pittsburgh and remained responsible till 1960. At present, she lives in Palo Alto, California.

FREDERICK W. MOTE took his B.A. in Chinese history at the University of Nanking in 1948 and received his Ph.D. from the University of Washington in 1954. He taught Chinese at Leiden on a Fulbright exchange lectureship in 1955-56. He is now Professor of Oriental Studies at Princeton University. His research interests are in late Yüan and early Ming history. His study of the intellectual history of the fourteenth century entitled *The Poet Kao Ch'i* has recently been published by the Princeton University Press.

DAVID S. NIVISON obtained his professional training in Far Eastern languages at Harvard, receiving the doctorate there in 1953. For a number of years he has been teaching at Stanford, where he is now Associate Professor of Philosophy and Chinese. He is the author of several articles dealing with Chinese intellectual history and of a forthcoming volume on the eighteenth-century philosopher of history Chang Hsüeh-ch'eng.

ROBERT RUHLMANN was trained in classical and medieval humanities at Paris, in Chinese at Paris and Peking. He spent the years 1946 to 1953 in Peking. Since 1954 he has been teaching Chinese at the Ecole Nationale des Langues Orientales Vivantes in Paris, and Chinese literature at the Chinese Institute of the Sorbonne. In 1962-63 he taught at the University of Michigan. His major interest is the history of Chinese fiction, drama, and folklore as materials for the study of Chinese thought. He has published translations from the *Kuo Yü*, and the *San Kuo Chih*, and a study on the Saga of the Wu Sang in the Yangchou tradition of storytelling.

BENJAMIN SCHWARTZ, following wartime service in the Pacific, took his Ph.D. at Harvard, where he is now Professor of History and Government. He is best known for his two books on the development of the Communist movement in China, *Chinese Communism and the Rise of Mao* and *A Documentary History of Chinese Communism* (with C. Brandt and J. K. Fairbank). His new book, entitled *In Search of Wealth and Power: Yen Fu and the West*, was published by the Harvard University Press in 1964. His primary interest, however, is in the whole range of intellectual history in China and Japan, and his current research is in this broad field.

GUNG-WU WANG received most of his education in Malaya and also studied at the Central University, Nanking. He obtained his doctorate from London in 1957 and is now Senior Lecturer in history and Dean, Faculty of Arts, at the University of Malaya in Kuala Lumpur. He has published *The Nanhai Trade, a Study of Early Chinese Trade in the South China Sea,* and *The Structure of Power in North China during the Five Dynasties.*

HELLMUT WILHELM received his Ph.D. in Chinese Studies from the University of Berlin in 1932. He served as Lecturer and Professor at Peking National University and is now Professor of Chinese Studies at the University of Washington, Seattle. His publications include numerous books and articles concerning the intellectual and literary history of China; he is currently at work on a study of intellectual trends in nineteenth-century China.

ARTHUR F. WRIGHT was trained at Stanford, Oxford, and Harvard Universities and studied in Japan and China 1940-47 and 1953-54. He was Chairman of The Committee on Chinese Thought from 1951 to 1962 and contributed, as author and editor, to the Committee's five symposium volumes. His publications include *Buddhism in Chinese History* (1959) and articles on Chinese Buddhism and intellectual history, especially of the period 200-750 A.D. He is now Charles Seymour Professor of History at Yale University.

Committee on Chinese Thought

STUDIES IN CHINESE THOUGHT *(Chicago, 1953)*

Arthur F. Wright, Introduction.
Derk Bodde, *Harmony and Conflict in Chinese Philosophy.*
W. Theodore de Bary, *A Reappraisal of Neo-Confucianism.*
David S. Nivison, *The Problem of "Knowledge" and "Action" in Chinese Thought since Wang Yang-ming.*
J. R. Levenson, *"History" and "Value": The Tensions of Intellectual Choice in Modern China.*
Schuyler Cammann, *Types of Symbols in Chinese Art.*
Arnold Isenberg, *Some Problems of Interpretation.*
I. A. Richards, *Toward a Theory of Translating.*
Achilles Fang, *Some Reflections on the Difficulty of Translation.*
Arthur F. Wright, *The Chinese Language and Foreign Ideas.*

CHINESE THOUGHT AND INSTITUTIONS *(Chicago, 1957)*

John K. Fairbank, Introduction.
Benjamin Schwartz, *The Intellectual History of China: Preliminary Reflections.*
Wolfram Eberhard, *The Political Function of Astronomy and Astronomers in Han China.*
Arthur F. Wright, *The Formation of Sui Ideology, 581-604.*
James T. C. Liu, *An Early Sung Reformer: Fan Chung-yen.*
Charles O. Hucker, *The Tung-lin Movement of the Late Ming Period.*
W. Theodore de Bary, *Chinese Despotism and the Confucian Ideal: A Seventeenth-Century View.*
John K. Fairbank, *Synarchy under the Treaties.*
T'ung-tsu Ch'ü, *Chinese Class Structure and Its Ideology.*
E. A. Kracke, Jr., *Region, Family, and Individual in the Chinese Examination System.*
C. K. Yang, *The Functional Relationship between Confucian Thought and Chinese Religion.*
Lien-sheng Yang, *The Concept of "Pao" as a Basis for Social Relations in China.*
Hellmut Wilhelm, *The Scholar's Frustration: Notes on a Type of "Fu."*
Joseph R. Levenson, *The Amateur Ideal in Ming and Early Ch'ing Society: Evidence from Painting.*

CONFUCIANISM IN ACTION *(Stanford, 1959)*

David S. Nivison, Introduction.
Wm. Theodore de Bary, *Some Common Tendencies in Neo-Confucianism.*
Benjamin Schwartz, *Some Polarities in Confucian Thought.*
Hui-chen Wang Liu, *An Analysis of Chinese Clan Rules: Confucian Theories in Action.*
Denis Twitchett, *The Fan Clan's Charitable Estate, 1050-1760.*
C. K. Yang, *Some Characteristics of Chinese Bureaucratic Behavior.*

James T. C. Liu, *Some Classifications of Bureaucrats in Chinese Historiography.*
Charles O. Hucker, *Confucianism and the Chinese Censorial System.*
David S. Nivison, *Ho-shen and His Accusers: Ideology and Political Behavior in the Eighteenth Century.*
Joseph R. Levenson, *The Suggestiveness of Vestiges: Confucianism and Monarchy at the Last.*
John Whitney Hall, *The Confucian Teacher in Tokugawa Japan.*
Donald H. Shively, *Motoda Eifu: Confucian Lecturer to the Meiji Emperor.*

THE CONFUCIAN PERSUASION *(Stanford, 1960)*

Arthur F. Wright, Introduction.
Hisayuki Miyakawa, *The Confucianization of South China.*
Arthur F. Wright, *Sui Yang-Ti: Personality and Stereotype.*
Edwin G. Pulleyblank, *Neo-Confucianism and Neo-Legalism in T'ang Intellectual Life, 755-806.*
James F. Cahill, *Confucian Elements in the Theory of Painting.*
Robert Ruhlmann, *Traditional Heroes in Chinese Popular Fiction.*
David S. Nivison, *Protest Against Conventions and Conventions of Protest.*
Frederick W. Mote, *Confucian Eremitism in the Yüan Period.*
Yuji Muramatsu, *Some Themes in Chinese Rebel Ideologies.*
Joseph R. Levenson, *Ill Wind in the Well-Field: The Erosion of the Confucian Ground of Controversy.*
Tse-tsung Chow, *The Anti-Confucian Movement in Early Republican China.*

CONFUCIAN PERSONALITIES *(Stanford, 1962)*

Arthur F. Wright, *Values, Roles, and Personalities.*
Denis Twitchett, *Problems of Chinese Biography.*
Albert E. Dien, *Yen Chih-t'ui (531-591 +): A Buddho-Confucian.*
Hans H. Frankel, *T'ang Literati: A Composite Biography.*
Denis Twitchett, *Lu Chih (754-805): Imperial Adviser and Court Official.*
Gung-wu Wang, *Feng Tao: An Essay on Confucian Loyalty.*
Hellmut Wilhelm, *From Myth to Myth: The Case of Yüeh Fei's Biography.*
Conrad M. Schirokauer, *Chu Hsi's Political Career: A Study in Ambivalence.*
Igor de Rachewiltz, *Yeh-lü Ch'u-ts'ai (1189-1243): Buddhist Idealist and Confucian Statesman.*
Herbert Franke, *Chia Ssu-tao (1213-1275): A "Bad Last Minister"?*
Frederick W. Mote, *A Fourteenth-Century Poet: Kao Ch'i.*
Nelson I. Wu, *Tung Ch'i-ch'ang (1555-1636): Apathy in Government and Fervor in Art.*
Richard C. Howard, *K'ang Yu-wei (1858-1927): His Intellectual Background and Early Thought.*
Joseph R. Levenson, *Liao P'ing and the Confucian Departure from History.*

Atheneum Paperbacks

Atheneum Paperbacks